THE VISUAL GUIDE TO
VISUAL C++™

THE VISUAL GUIDE TO
VISUAL C++™

The Pictorial Encyclopedia
of the Windows
Programming Language

Nancy Nicolaisen

VENTANA
PRESS

The Ventana Press Visual Guide™ Series

The Visual Guide to Visual C++: The Pictorial Encyclopedia of the Windows Programming Language

Copyright © 1994 Nancy Nicolaisen
The Ventana Press Visual Guide™ Series

Library of Congress Cataloging-in-Publication Data

Nicolaisen, Nancy.
      The visual guide to Visual C++ : the pictorial encyclopedia of the Windows programming language / Nancy Nicolaisen. -- 1st ed.
            p. cm.
      Includes index.
      ISBN 1-56604-079-5
      1. C++ (Computer program language) 2. Microsoft Visual C++. I. Title.
   QA76.73.C153N53 1994
   005.265--dc20   94-14294
                                                      CIP

Book design: Marcia Webb
Cover design: John Nedwidek, emDesign
Index service: Richard T. Evans, Infodex
Technical review: Steve Ross
Editorial staff: Angela Anderson, Walter R. Bruce III, Eric Edstam, Tracye Giles, Pam Richardson, Becky Whitney
Production staff: Patrick Berry, Cheri Collins, John Cotterman, Dan Koeller, Ron Jackson, Jaimie Livingston, Midgard Computing, Dawne Sherman, Marcia Webb
Proofreader: Martin Minner

First Edition 9 8 7 6 5 4 3 2 1
Printed in the United States of America

Ventana Press, Inc.
P.O. Box 2468
Chapel Hill, NC 27515
919/942-0220
FAX 919/942-1140

Limits of Liability and Disclaimer of Warranty

Trademarks

About the Author

Nancy Nicolaisen is an experienced programmer, author and teacher. As a software architect and project manager, she has been recognized for her work on scientific data exchange and has been appointed to several federal management committees. A graduate of Western State College of Colorado, she edits and contributes to numerous consumer and trade publications, including *Windows Sources, Dr. Dobbs Journal, McGraw Hill/Data Pro, Object Magazine, Computer Shopper, C++ Journal* and *BYTE.*

CONTENTS

SECTION III   A Cookbook Approach to Creating Windows Applications

SECTION IV   Alphabetical Reference to the Microsoft Foundation Classes C++ Library

O

P

SECTION I

· · · · · · · · · · · · ·

USING

APPWIZARD

· · · · · · · · · · · · ·

SECTION ONE   Using APPWIZARD

Why a wizard? Microsoft seems to have them everywhere. In the *Microsoft Press Computer Dictionary,* a wizard is defined as someone who is particularly adept at performing computer magic. And I'm sure this is how Microsoft wants you to think of its wizards. Each one has its own field of expertise, and within that field it sweats the details so you can focus on the results. This is, after all, what any good software should do—and why not let good software help you write good software?

As you work, the wizards almost effortlessly impose a standardization of structure in the code and the user interface. This becomes increasingly important as system environments and the applications that use them become more complex. AppWizard's standardization makes programs better. This is a bonus for the programmer, just as a presentation that conforms to expectations is a bonus for the user. This automated approach to creating software is not restrictive, however. As we shall see, the wizards and application frameworks in Visual C++ offer all the flexibility needed to modify programs as you wish.

What AppWizard Does for You

"Well begun is half done." The saying may be hackneyed, but it's true. AppWizard initializes and creates the core of your programming project—the classes, objects and programming you need in the proper files. It will even provide comments in the skeleton code that it generates, showing you where to place your own code.

The trickiest thing about AppWizard is finding it, since it doesn't appear in any of the menus or toolbars. In fact, you don't find it so much as it finds you. Open a new file, select Project from the file type list and it appears. (In the movie *The Hobbit*, a dwarf tells Bilbo, the hobbit, that wizards come and go as they please. Fortunately, they do seem to show up at all the right times in Visual C++.)

Some of us prefer to try out a new application without the manual and refer back to it when we get stuck. Others prefer to be more methodical. In this section, we have tried to accommodate both types. AppWizard exposes itself as a series of four to six dialog boxes, depending on the complexity of your project. These amount to a guided interview. Once it knows what you want, it creates the initial code and supporting files for you.

On the following pages, we step through each dialog box field by field. If it all seems familiar or obvious, just skim this section and then begin. If you get stuck, the linear approach to AppWizard dialog boxes should make it easy to find the answer you need.

Starting the AppWizard

Start with a new project:

1. From the File Menu, select New.

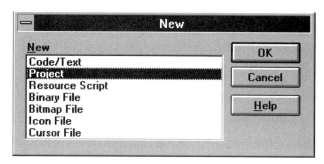

Figure 1-1: The New dialog box.

2. From the New dialog box, shown in Figure 1-1, select Project. The AppWizard displays the New Project dialog box, as shown in Figure 1-2.

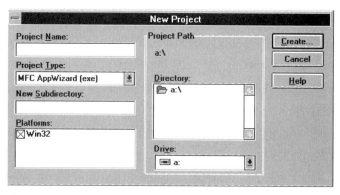

Figure 1-2: The New Project dialog box.

3. Type a name in the Project Name text box. This name will serve as the basis for all the AppWizard-generated files and classes that are specific to your project. Naming conventions depend on which disk file system you set up on your hard drive: FAT, NTFS or HPFS.

. . . .

File Systems

FAT (File Allocation Table): This is the MS-DOS system and follows the classic DOS restrictions for file names:

○ Names can be up to eight letters long with an optional three-letter extension, which is separated from the name by a period.

○ Letters are not case sensitive.

○ You may use A through Z, 0 through 9, and the following special characters:

 _ ^ $ ~ ! # % & - ( ) { } @ '(apostrophe) '(single quote)

NTFS (New Technology File System): You had the option of switching to NTFS when you installed Windows NT. It gives you much greater flexibility:

○ Names can be up to 255 letters long.

○ Periods and spaces can be inserted as you see fit, as long as you stay under the 255-character limit.

○ Names are not case sensitive, although upper- and lower-case are preserved on the screen. (But be warned, *filename.txt* will overwrite *FILENAME.TXT*.)

○ You may use the characters A through Z, 0 through 9.

○ You may use any special characters *except* the following:

 ? \ * " < > | / :

NTFS also creates a FAT file name so that its files will work in an MS-DOS system. These names are created by removing all spaces and periods (except the last period with at least one character following it), converting disallowed characters to underscores (_), truncating the name to six characters and adding a ~ and a number, and finally, truncating the extension to three letters.

HPFS (High Performance File System): This is the OS/2 file system. It follows the same rules as NTFS.

. . . .

4. Click the drop-down arrow in the Project Type drop-down list box and select from among the following choices, as shown in Figure 1-3. (***Note:*** This is the spot where you decide whether to use AppWizard. If you select one of the first two choices, MFC AppWizard (exe) or MFC AppWizard (dll), AppWizard kicks in, just as the names suggest. The other four choices allow you to build projects without AppWizard. We list them here for completeness, but we won't discuss them further.)

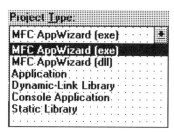

Figure 1-3: The Project Type drop-down list box.

○ *MFC AppWizard (exe).* This is a stand-alone application. AppWizard queries you about what features you would like to include. It then generates the code for features you want included and places it in the files appropriate for compilation and linkage. You end up with a skeletal form of a Windows application that has minimally working windows, menus, toolbars and so on. Much of the standard functionality of the application is in place at this point. Menus drop down, the common file dialogs appear in response to the File.New command and so on. This complete and functional framework allows you to start work directly on the parts of your application that are unique. If you like, AppWizard will include comments in the code to show where you need to code your application's activity.

○ *MFC AppWizard (dll).* In this case, AppWizard gets you started on a dynamic-linked library. This is a library of classes that is not linked until runtime. The advantage is that several applications that use the dll's classes can share a single copy of memory-resident code, saving space if classes are used by more than one application or more than one instance of an application.

○ *Application.* Select this for a stand-alone application. The assumption is that you have your own class libraries and won't be using Microsoft Foundation Class (MFC) libraries.

○ *Dynamic-Link Library*. This is a shared library, but one that doesn't rely on the MFC libraries.

○ *Console Application.* A console application is a character-mode application that runs under MS-DOS or in the DOS window of Windows.

○ *Static Library*. A static library is not dynamically linked. It is linked at build time, and as a result every application that uses it must have its own copy.

5. When you entered a project name, a subdirectory based on the name was also created. This name is automatically entered in the New Subdirectory text box (see Figure 1-4). You will probably change the name only if you already have a sub-directory with source code files you want to use. To specify a different subdirectory, either type the name and path in the New Subdirectory text box or use the Directory and Drive boxes to traverse the disk's directory structure.

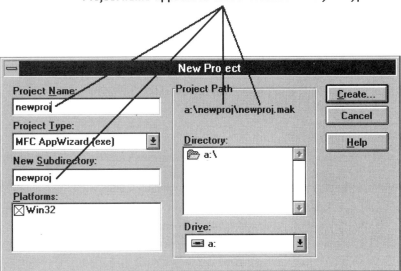

Figure 1-4: The New Project dialog box, showing the project name in four locations.

6. Next, choose your weapon. In the Platforms check box, choose the machine and operating system environment for which your project is intended. Win32 is, of course, for 32-bit windows environment. To build for other platforms, such as the Macintosh, you will need a cross-platform development kit.

7. Finally, click the Create button to start AppWizard.

There are two possibilities at this point. One is that you are building the MFC AppWizard executable application. The second is that you are building the MFC AppWizard dynamic-linked library. Let's consider the second option first, since it is by far the simpler.

Building an MFC AppWizard dll

When you are using AppWizard to build a dynamic link libarary (dll), follow these steps. Here, as elsewhere, selected options are reflected in the sample application on the side of the dialog box.

1. The AppWizard asks whether to include comments to show where your own code should be inserted. Click the Yes, please button. In addition to the comments, AppWizard generates a README.TXT file that describes the files produced.

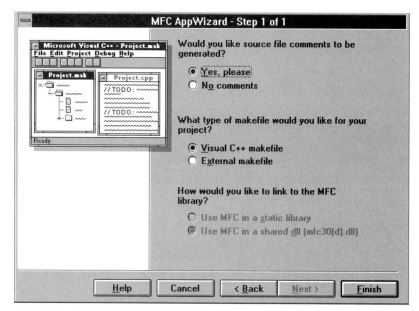

Figure 1-5: Select options in this dialog box to generate an MFC AppWizard dll.

2. Select a button to indicate whether you want to generate a Visual C++ makefile or an external makefile.

That is all there is to the MFC AppWizard dll. From here you progress to a box that shows what files you will get.

Building an MFC AppWizard exe

Before it can build an executable file (exe), AppWizard needs some idea of what you want. To that end, it presents several dialog boxes to ask about your application. It works its way down from the general to the specific, which is just good top-down thinking. Follow these steps:

Step 1: Selecting Application Type & Language Support

AppWizard first asks what type of application you would like to create. You have your choice of three radio buttons (see Figure 1-6): *Single document*, *Multiple documents* or *Dialog-based*. As you choose, the Application window on the left side of box reflects each selection.

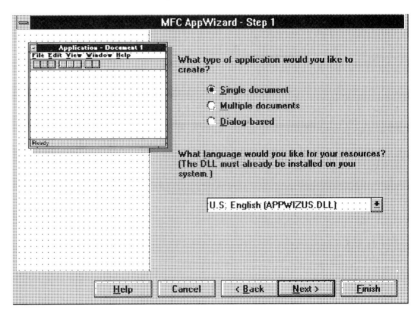

Figure 1-6: The Step 1 dialog box.

Documents

In the world of MFC, a central organizing principle is the concept of the Document/View architecture. A document object stores an application's data. The data may encapsulate a particular type of data source, such as a spreadsheet or bitmap, or it may hold data that reflects the state of the application at runtime. The important thing about a document is that it is a distinct object. Though it provides its data to other objects through its public data member and public functions, it is separate from the part of the application responsible for displaying the data to the user.

The *View* is the part of the application that actually presents (draws) the data on the screen or the printed page. It interacts with the document to get data to display. A document may have several views. For example, a spreadsheet document might have views attached that display its data as a table of numbers, a line graph and a pie chart. By contrast, a view can be attached to only one document at a time.

○ *Single document*. A single document application can have only one active document at a time. An SDI application may alternate among multiple documents by disconnecting from one and attaching another, but to reiterate, no more than one can be in use at a time. An individual document can have many views active simultaneously.

○ *Multiple documents*. A multiple document application can have multiple active documents at a time. For example, it could have a document to encapsulate word processing text and one to encapsulate a live television feed. As in the case of a single document application, each document can have many views, and the views can be active simultaneously.

○ *Dialog-based*. Dialog-based applications are usually oriented toward collecting formatted keyboard data from the end user. Choosing this option automates the setup of Dialog Data Exchange and Dialog Data Validation (DDX/DDV) support code in your application.

The Step 1 dialog box also asks what language you would like for your resources. If your application is intended for foreign markets, here is where you can select resources for another language. Your standard choices are U.S. English, French or German. The dll files are present for all three. For other languages, you will have to get the proper dll support file form Microsoft.

Step 2: Choosing Database Support

In Step 2, AppWizard displays the Step 2 of 6 dialog box and asks what type of database support you would like (see Figure 1-7).

The MFC framework provides Open DataBase Connectivity (ODBC) classes that encapsulate access to a variety of data management systems. ODBC establishes a standard interface for connecting to a database management system (DBMS) for accessing and manipulating data and for passing SQL syntax to supported database management systems. In a nutshell, a Visual C++-generated database application can access data in any ODBC-compliant database management system, using a single consistent, portable API. The options in this box let you decide to what degree your application will use the ODBC mechanism.

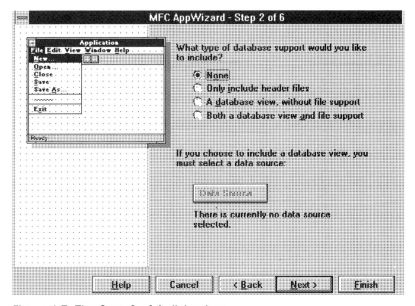

Figure 1-7: The Step 2 of 6 dialog box.

○ *None.* Obviously, if you aren't using a database, you won't need the support and don't want the extra code that would be generated.

○ *Only include header files.* AppWizard will provide the header files and link libraries for you to build your own database classes. It does not provide the classes themselves needed for data entry, record organization, viewing or storage.

9

❍ *A database view, without file support.* This option provides the classes for data entry, record organization, and viewing data, but does not provide for storing data in permanent files on disk. If you wanted a viewer for examining but not updating someone else's DBMS—for example, stock price information—this option would be suitable.

❍ *Both database view and file support.* This option provides full support for data entry, record organization, viewing and file storage on disk.

If you choose either of the last two options—the ones that include database views—the Data Source button is no longer dimmed. You must go to the SQL Data Source and Data Table dialog boxes before continuing.

Step 3: Adding Support for Object Linking & Embedding (OLE)

Step 3 enables support for Object Linking and Embedding (see Figure 1-8). You won't see this box if you are building a dialog-based application.

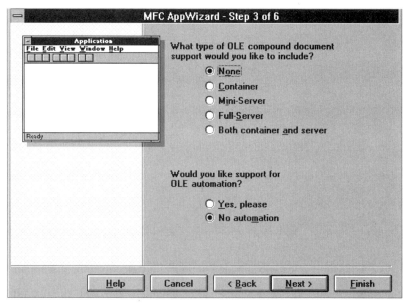

Figure 1-8: The Step 3 of 6 dialog box.

Object Linking and Embedding (OLE) is the most exciting but most complex area of Windows programming today. AppWizard and the MFC classes make it possible to create a powerful, reliable OLE application in a fraction of the time it would take to code from scratch using the C language API.

Because OLE is a complicated technology, AppWizard's generation of OLE class support is structured to let developers work toward full implementation of the technology in their code incrementally. You can start out by implementing the least complicated OLE behaviors, such as drag and drop support, and incorporate more powerful OLE support as your understanding grows. Choose one of the following options:

○ *None.* AppWizard writes no code for implementing OLE interfaces.

○ *Container.* AppWizard enables your application to receive embedded data and become a compound document. In other words, it will be able to access the standardized data objects created by an OLE server. There is no support for sending data, so the application cannot be a server.

○ *Mini-Server.* A mini-server can create an object for embedding, but it cannot save it as a file. This, of course, precludes any linking. This sort of server can be launched from within the container that will hold the object, such as a tool for building a graph or table for embedding in a spreadsheet.

○ *Full-Server.* A full-server supports the creation of embeddable data and, because of its file support, can support linking as well. This is a stand-alone application that can also be activated by a container to edit an embedded object.

○ *Both container and server.* The title says it all. This application can create and access embeddable data, and it supports linking.

Would you like support for OLE automation? Answer "yes" to this question if you wish to make objects and their member functions accessible to other applications. This goes beyond access to data and entails access to the workings of the other application itself. Automation attempts to make all objects available across applications, across programming languages, and even, ultimately, across machines in a network. Supporting automation may yield some payoffs in terms of sharing resources and interacting with other applications.

Step 4: Selecting Application Features

In Step 4 you can select application features. The Step 4 of 6 dialog box, shown in Figure 1-9, will have fewer features if you are building a dialog-based application.

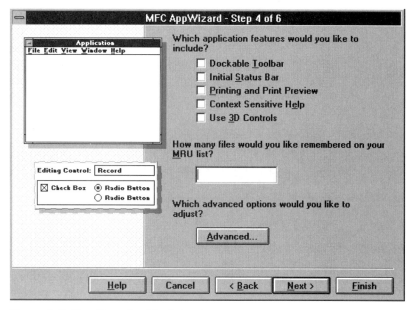

Figure 1-9: The Step 4 of 6 dialog box.

Choose from among the following features. As you click each option, the miniature window in the dialog box reflects your choice (see Figures 1-10 and 1-11):

○ *Dockable Toolbar.* The dockable toolbar can attach to any side of a window, have its own window, or float. AppWizard performs the three steps to create a dockable toolbar:

1. Prepares the window by enabling docking in the frame window.

2. Prepares the toolbar by enabling docking for the toolbar.

3. Brings the two together and docks the toolbar to the window.

The option of docking to a side, to float, or to have a separate window can be initialized by the application or decided by the end user. AppWizard stops short of creating a toolbar that is customizable or that can be dynamically reconfigured. This doesn't mean it can't be done; it just means AppWizard won't do it for you.

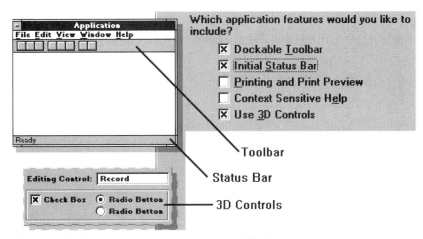

Figure 1-10: The Toolbar, Status Bar and 3D Controls features.

○ *Initial Status Bar.* The initial status bar appears at the bottom of the main window. In fact you can see one at the bottom of the Visual C++ main window. AppWizard builds in automatic indicators for Caps Lock, Num Lock and Scroll Lock. It also includes a message line for help strings that describe menu commands and toolbar buttons. Finally, AppWizard adds a menu command for hiding and displaying the status bar.

○ *Printing and Print Preview.* AppWizard includes code for the commands Print, Print Setup and Print Preview and displays them in the File menu.

○ *Context Sensitive Help.* If you select this option, AppWizard does the following:

1. Creates a help menu with menu items for Index and Using Help.

2. Adds status bar command prompts that appear when the user clicks on the menu items.

3. Creates a MAKEHELP.BAT batch file to run the Help compiler.

4. Creates a Help project file (your project's name with an .HPJ extension).

5. Creates one or more .RTF (Rich Text Format) files with standard help contexts.

6. Creates .PCX (bitmap) files used in the help files.

7. Inserts a keyboard accelerator for F1 and Shift-F1 command keys.

Pressing F1 will bring up the help text for the currently active object. Pressing Shift-F1 will change the cursor to a help cursor (an arrow with a question mark next to it) that brings up help text for whichever object the user clicks on.

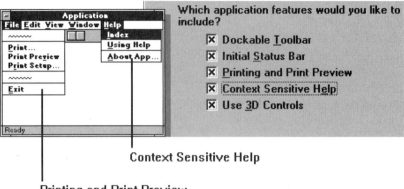

Context Sensitive Help

Printing and Print Preview

Figure 1-11: The Printing and Print Preview and Context Sensitive Help features.

○ *Use 3D Controls.* When you select this option, shading is added to the control box graphics.

How many files would you like remembered on your MRU (Most Recently Used) list? Enter a number here. Your application can keep track of up to 16 of its most recent files and display them in the File menu. Figure 1-12 shows an MRU list from Microsoft Word for Windows.

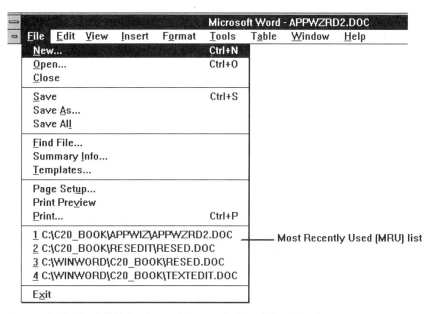

Figure 1-12: An MRU list from Microsoft Word for Windows.

Selecting Advanced Options: To complete Step 4, indicate which advanced options you would like to adjust. The Advanced button opens the new Advanced Options dialog box, shown in Figure 1-13. When your application creates or looks for a document, it needs guidelines for naming and storing the file. If you selected this option, MFC looks for information about your application, its documents, and OLE automation in the Document Template Strings resource file.

There are actually three pages to this box, and you move through them by clicking on the tabs at the top: Document Template Strings, Main Frame and MDI Child Frame.

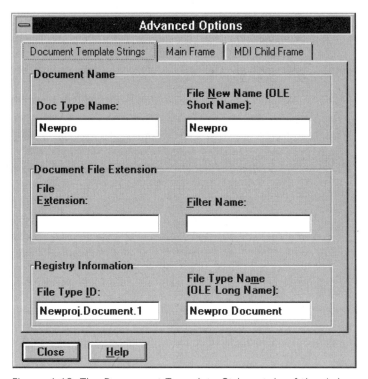

Figure 1-13: The Document Template Strings tab of the Advanced Options dialog box.

The Document Template Strings Tab: The first tab, Document Template Strings, lets you give AppWizard a little guidance on naming conventions:

○ *Doc Type Name.* Type in the default root name for new documents of a particular type. For example, when you open a new spreadsheet in Microsoft Excel, the spreadsheet's default name is sheet1.xls. The root name (what you would enter at Doc Type Name) is "sheet."

○ *File New Name (OLE Short Name).* Enter a description of the type of document, such as Project. For example, after selecting File New in Visual C++, you selected Project from a list of file types to wake up AppWizard. In this case, the File New name was "Project."

○ *Document File Extension.* When you create a document, your application can automatically append an extension of your choice, like the.doc extension used in MS Word. The application will look for this extension when opening files from the file menu.

○ *Filter Name.* The Filter Name is used in client server transactions. When a client wants data, it sends a message to the DDEML (the Dynamic Data Exchange Management Library), which solicits a response from the server. If the client has submitted a name that matches the filter name, the server indicates that it is available for the data exchange. In a way, this is how the server keeps out unwanted guests, since the client needs to know the filter name to get in. The server can turn off its filter name to indicate it is available to all comers.

○ *Registry Information.* The registry is a binary database structure that can be used to store files containing initialization and configuration data. The registry has been designed to be used instead of initialization configuration files, which are subject to conflict and corruption. Applications do not write directly to the registry, but use a registry API instead. The information you provide in these two fields is used to store data in the registry:

1. *File Type ID.* This is the file extension Windows will use to associate applications and data for in-place activation.

2. *File Type Name (OLE Long Name).* This is a string that identifies the application that created a data file.

The Main Frame Tab: The Main Frame tab, shown in Figure 1-14, lets you select characteristics for your application, or *main frame*, window. Select as many or as few as you like:

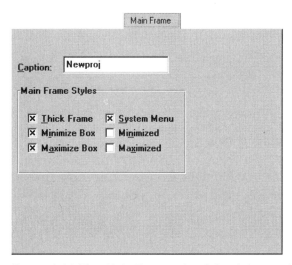

Figure 1-14: The Main Frame tab of the Advanced Options dialog box.

○ *Thick Frame*. This option makes the frame resizable.

○ *Minimize Box*. Choose this to include the Minimize box (the button with a down arrowhead, located at the upper right corner of the frame). It reduces your application to an icon.

○ *Maximize Box*. Choose this to include the Maximize box (the button with an up arrowhead, located at the upper right corner of the frame). It enlarges your application to fill all the screen.

○ *System Menu*. Choose this to include the menu box containing a dash, located in the upper left-hand corner of the frame. It displays commands relating to your application's presentation on the screen, including closing it.

○ *Minimized*. Selecting Minimized makes your application appear as an icon when it first opens.

○ *Maximized*. Selecting Maximized makes your main window fill the screen when the application opens.

○ *Use Splitter Window*. The splitter window option lets you divide a window into two stacked sections, each with its own vertical scroll bars. These two windows are open to the same document, but allow you to scroll to different parts of the same document. (This option won't appear if you selected the Single Document application type back in Step 1.)

The MDI Child Frame Tab: The MDI Child Frame tab is exactly the same as the Main Frame Tab, except that it doesn't have the System Menu option (see Figure 1-15). Use it to select characteristics for your application's child frames.

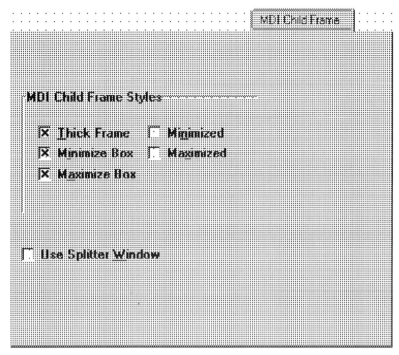

Figure 1-15: This is the same as the Main Frame tab, minus the System Menu option.

Selecting Application Features for Dialog-Based Applications: As promised earlier, here is the discussion of the abbreviated dialog-based version of the application features dialog box. The Step 2 of 4 dialog box, shown in Figure 1-16, lets you choose from among the following options:

○ *About Box.* This option puts an About command in the Systems Menu for your application. The command will open the About dialog, which you can use to include version, copyright and other information about the application.

○ *Context Sensitive Help.* This option adds context-sensitive help, accessible though a button.

○ *Use 3D Controls.* Using 3D controls adds shading and gives depth to the application's boxes.

You are also asked to provide a title to appear in the application's title bar. AppWizard defaults to your project name.

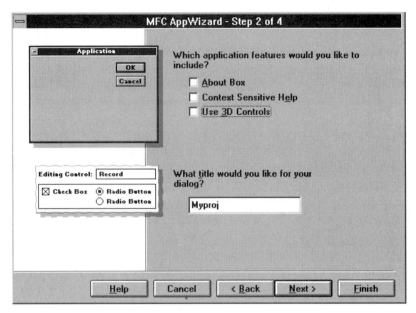

Figure 1-16: The Step 2 of 4 dialog box for dialog-based applications.

Step 5: Generating Source File Comments

In Step 5, AppWizard asks three questions. It first asks whether to generate comments in the source file it creates. If you select "Yes, please," AppWizard inserts comments into the source code to show where you need to add your own code. If you answer "No comments," you are on your own.

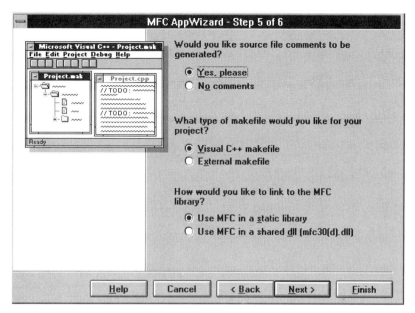

Figure 1-17: The Step 5 of 6 dialog box.

Next you're asked what type of makefile you would like. You have the following options:

○ *Visual C++ makefile*. The makefile contains the description blocks, commands, macros, inference rules, dot directives and preprocessing directives that are needed to compile and link your application code. Visual C++ AppWizard will generate the files you need and create the makefile needed to process them.

○ *External makefile*. Select this if you intend to create your own makefile, or are using a makefile from an earlier version of C++.

Finally, AppWizard asks how you would like to link to the MFC library. You have the following options:

○ *Use MFC in a static library*. This option has AppWizard create a makefile that will link the portions of MFC library that your application uses to your application's code at build time in order to create the executable.

○ *Use MFC in a shared dll (mfc30(d).dll)*. This option does not link the MFC library at build time. Linkage occurs during run-time.

Step 6: Creating Classes

Step 6 is your last chance to make any changes in either the Step 6 of 6 dialog box (shown in Figure 1-18) or any previous one. The dialog box lists the classes AppWizard will create. In the four fields below, it displays information about each class as the class is selected (use the arrow keys or the mouse). You can change this information if it is not dimmed.

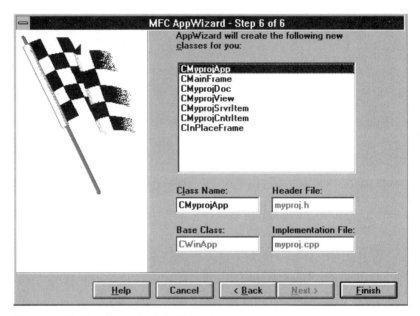

Figure 1-18: The Step 6 of 6 dialog box.

The Step 6 of 6 dialog box contains the following text boxes:

○ *Class Name.* This just repeats the name of the class selected in the list above. If you change the name, the new name appears in the list when you move to a different field.

○ *Header File.* The Header File is where the definition for the selected class resides. If it is dimmed, you cannot change it. If it is not, you can change it.

○ *Base Class.* Generally the Base Class is dimmed and fixed. But in some instances, as in the example below, you can choose a different base class on which to base your projects class. If you have this option, the type is darkened and an arrow appears, which will open the list box when clicked. You can only change to one of the classes from this list. This is another opportunity to do a bit of fine-tuning by selecting a base class with functions more suited to your needs.

○ *Implementation File*. This is the source file that contains the function body code.

The Creation

All that is left before AppWizard actually does its work is to get your final approval. The New Project Information dialog box, shown in Figure 1-19, summarizes what is to be created.

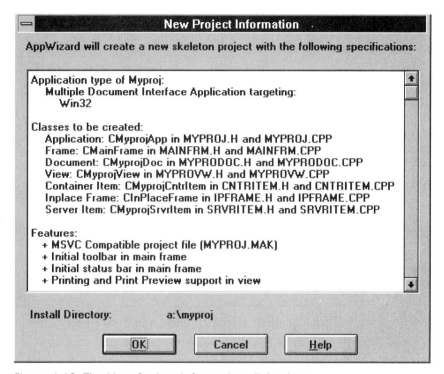

Figure 1-19: The New Project Information dialog box.

The New Project Information dialog box contains the following information:

○ A type and target.

○ A list of Classes, with focus, class name, header file and implementation file.

○ A list of features.

At this point you can accept or reject, but you cannot make any changes. If you bail out at this point, you will need to start the new project process over. To accept the application, click OK. Wait a bit, and a project window (projectname.mak) opens. Now you are ready to code. To open a folder, click on the + sign to its left or double-click on the folder itself.

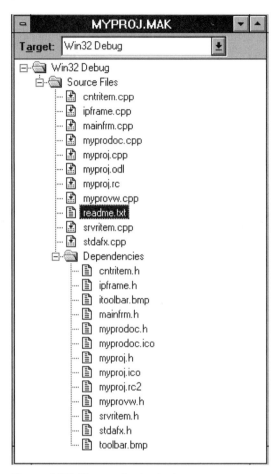

Figure 1-20: The project window.

File types that may be listed are as follows:

○ .cpp (a C++ source code file)

○ .odl (object description language, which describes an application's interface)

○ .rc (resource file)

○ .txt (text file)

○ .h (header file)

○ .pcx (bitmap file)

○ .ico (icon file)

○ .cur (cursor file)

○ .rc2 (an additional resource file for resources not editable in C++)

Readme.txt

Finally, notice the highlighted readme.txt, a copy of which is reproduced below. DON'T READ IT! That is unless you have trouble getting to sleep. Just make a note of what a useful reference it is. It contains a description of all the AppWizard-created files.

MICROSOFT FOUNDATION CLASS LIBRARY : MYPROJ

AppWizard has created this MYPROJ application for you. This application not only demonstrates the basics of using the Microsoft Foundation classes but is also a starting point for writing your application.

This file contains a summary of what you will find in each of the files that make up your MYPROJ application.

MYPROJ.MAK

This project file is compatible with the Visual C++ development environment. It is also compatible with the NMAKE program provided with Visual C++.

To build a debug version of the program from the MS-DOS prompt, type:

    nmake /f MYPROJ.MAK CFG="Win32 Debug"

Or to build a release version of the program, type:

    nmake /f MYPROJ.MAK CFG="Win32 Release"

MYPROJ.H

This is the main header file for the application. It includes other project specific headers (including RESOURCE.H) and declares the CMyprojApp application class.

MYPROJ.CPP

This is the main application source file that contains the application class CMyprojApp.

MYPROJ.RC

This is a the definition of the resources that the program uses. It includes the icons, bitmaps, and cursors that are stored in the RES

25

subdirectory. This file is generated for you when you use the tools of the Visual C++ development environment.

RES\MYPROJ.ICO
This is an icon file, which is used as the application's icon. This icon is included by the main resource file MYPROJ.RC.

RES\MYPROJ.RC2
This file contains resources that are not edited by the Visual C++ development environment. You should place all resources not editable by the resource editor in this file.

MYPROJ.CLW
This file contains information used by ClassWizard to edit existing classes or add new classes. ClassWizard also uses this file to store information needed to create and edit message maps and dialog data maps and to create prototype member functions.

///

For the main frame window:

MAINFRM.H, MAINFRM.CPP
These files contain the frame class CMainFrame, which is derived from CMDIFrameWnd and controls all MDI frame features.

RES\TOOLBAR.pcx
This bitmap file is used to create tiled images for the toolbar. The initial toolbar and status bar are constructed in the CMainFrame class. Edit this toolbar bitmap along with the array in MAINFRM.CPP to add more toolbar buttons.

RES\ITOOLBAR.pcx
This bitmap file is used to create tiled images for the toolbar when your server application is in-place activated inside another container. This toolbar is constructed in the CInPlaceFrame class. This bitmap is similar to the bitmap in RES\TOOLBAR.pcx except that it has many non-server commands removed.

///

AppWizard creates one document type and one view:

MYPRODOC.H, MYPRODOC.CPP - the document
These files contain your CMyprojDoc class. Edit these files to add your special document data and to implement file saving and loading (via CMyprojDoc::Serialize).

MYPROVW.H, MYPROVW.CPP - the view of the document
These files contain your CMyprojView class. CMyprojView objects are used to view CMyprojDoc objects.

RES\MYPRODOC.ICO
This is an icon file, which is used as the icon for MDI child windows for the CMyprojDoc class. This icon is included by the main resource file MYPROJ.RC.

MYPROJ.REG
This is an example .REG file that shows you the kind of registration settings the framework will set for you. You can use this as a .REG file to go along with your application or just delete it and rely on the default RegisterShellFileTypes registration.

MYPROJ.ODL
This file contains the Object Description Language source code for the type library of your application.

//

AppWizard has also created classes specific to OLE Linking and Embedding:

CNTRITEM.H, CNTRITEM.CPP
This class is used to manipulate OLE objects. They are usually displayed by your CMyprojView class and serialized as part of your CMyprojDoc class.

SRVRITEM.H, SRVRITEM.CPP
This class is used to connect your CMyprojDoc class to the OLE system, and optionally provide links to your document.

IPFRAME.H, IPFRAME.CPP
This class is derived from COleIPFrameWnd and controls all frame features during in-place activation.

//

Help Support:

MAKEHELP.BAT
Use this batch file to create your application's Help file, MYPROJ.HLP.

MYPROJ.HPJ
This file is the Help Project file used by the Help compiler to create your application's Help file.

HLP*.pcx
These are bitmap files required by the standard Help file topics for Microsoft Foundation Class Library standard commands.

HLP*.RTF
This file contains the standard help topics for standard MFC commands and screen objects.

//

Other standard files:

STDAFX.H, STDAFX.CPP
These files are used to build a precompiled header (PCH) file named MYPROJ.PCH and a precompiled types file named STDAFX.OBJ.

RESOURCE.H
This is the standard header file, which defines new resource IDs. Visual C++ reads and updates this file.

//

Other notes:

AppWizard uses "TODO:" to indicate parts of the source code you should add to or customize.

///

Moving On

AppWizard provides the skeleton of a Windows program. Most of the generic functionality is in place and correctly tied to the related application elements. This saves time and removes the opportunity for error.

The best part about AppWizard is that the job it does relieves you, the programmer, of hours of tedium. You can get directly to the task of coding application-specific functionality. In Section II, we explore the various resource editors in the Visual C++ integrated development environment.

SECTION II

. . . .

USING THE INTEGRATED DEVELOPMENT ENVIRONMENT TOOLS

. . . .

USING THE INTEGRATED DEVELOPMENT ENVIRONMENT TOOLS

One of the best reasons to choose Visual C++ 2.0 over another C++ language product is that it provides a spectrum of powerful tools that are both easy to learn and easy to use. If you have been working with Microsoft Visual C++ 1.5, you are in for a pleasant surprise with this version. Many tools are greatly improved, and all are more seamlessly integrated than ever.

This section of the book gives you the most graphically rich, detailed tour of the development environment you will find anywhere. First, we show how to get into an existing resource or create a new one. We then explore the various resource editors.

Resources include:

○ Accelerator tables, containing lists of shortcut keys

○ Bitmaps

○ Cursors

○ Dialog boxes

○ Icons

○ Menus

○ String Tables

○ Version information

To build and manipulate resources, you use resource editors. These include:

○ Accelerator editor, for Accelerator tables

○ Binary editor, for minor changes to custom resources and non-C++ resources

○ Dialog editor, for dialog boxes

○ Graphics editor, for bitmaps, icons and cursors

○ Menu editor, for menus

○ String Table editor, for String Tables

Where Do You Find Resources?

Find resources with the Resource Browser window. This is the
entry point for resource editing, whether you are creating a new
resource or editing an existing one. It is not an editor itself, but any
time you go to an editor you pass through this window, which
displays files and the resources they contain.

   Resources are saved in files and may show up (or be saved) with
any of the following extensions:

.C	C source files
.CPP	application source code
.H	application include file
.RC	resource list file
.RES	compiled resource file (opens as a binary data file; not very useful for editing or copying)
.PCX	bitmap
.DIB	device-independent bitmap
.ICO	icon
.CUR	cursor

Getting Into a Resource Editor

How you get into a resource editor depends partly on whether you
are creating a new resource or editing an existing one. To create a
new resource from the Resource menu, follow these steps:

   1. Pull down the Resource menu.

   2. Select New.

Figure 2-1: The New Resource dialog box.

3. Choose the type of resource to create, and the editor automatically opens.

To create a new resource from the Resource toolbar, follow these steps:

1. Pull down the Tools menu.

2. Select Toolbars.

3. Check the box for Resource, and the Resource toolbar appears.

4. Close the dialog box and click the toolbar button for the resource you want to create.

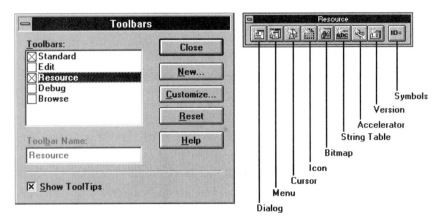

Figure 2-2: Toolbars dialog box with Resource toolbar and button labels.

To edit an existing resource, enter from the resource itself:

1. Get to a resource by opening the file that contains it. For example, pull down the File menu, select Open, and then select and open a .MAK file. This opens a project window with .MAK in the title—in this example, HELLO.MAK.

Figure 2-3: The HELLO.MAK window.

2. To open the project folder, click on the + sign next to it or double-click on the folder. Open the Source Files folder the same way. Then select the .RC file and double-click on it to open the Resource Browser window.

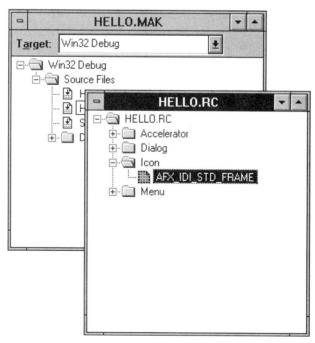

Figure 2-4: The HELLO.RC window.

3. Open one of the resource folders. In our example it is the Icon folder. Open the resource by double-clicking. This automatically opens the appropriate resource editor—in this instance, the Graphics editor.

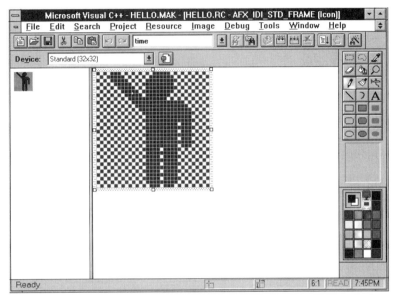

Figure 2-5: The Graphics editor with an icon resource.

The essential bit of information above is that you start with the *projectname*.MAK file. As an alternative, you can go directly to a .RC file, double-click, and open into the Resource Browser.

There always seems to be an exception. In this case it is the Binary editor. To use the Binary editor, step through the folders as explained above to select the the resource you wish to edit. But don't double-click to open it. Instead, go to the Resource menu and select Open Binary Data. The new window shows both the hexadecimal code and the ASCII format for the resource. You move from one to the other by pressing Tab. Remember, handle with care— changes in data are very risky here.

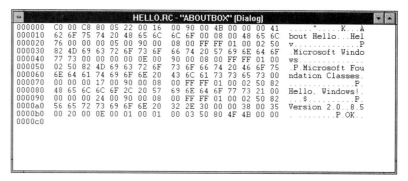

Figure 2-6: The Binary editor displays both the hexadecimal code and the ASCII format for the resource.

Using the Editors

Now that you know how to get into an editor, you are ready to express your creativity. We start by examining the basic features all editors have in common. Then we discuss each editor in turn, from the simpler editors to the more feature-laden.

Common Features of the Editors

All the editors support certain basic file-handling commands:

Copy	From the Resource Browser window, select the resource and choose Copy from the Edit menu (Ctrl-C). Move to another Resource Browser window (several can be open at the same time) and select Paste from the Edit menu.
Paste	You can paste a copied resource into a Resource Browser Window using the Paste command from the Edit menu (or use Ctrl-V from the keyboard).
Save	Select Save from the Edit menu or use Ctrl-S from the keyboard.
Delete	Make the resource active by selecting it. Select Delete from the Edit menu or use the Del key.
Import	This is a way to copy a resource out of an unopened file. You need to be in the Resource Browser. Make sure the file that will receive the resource is open and active. Choose Import from the Resource menu, and move through the directories until you find the file with the resource you want. Select the resource and click OK.

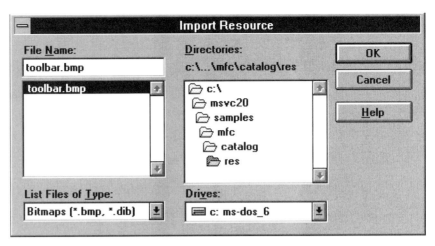

Figure 2-7: In this example, toolbar.bmp would be imported from the catalog resource file into your open resource file.

Export
Like Import, Export is a way to copy a resource to an opened file. You must have the resource selected in the Resource Browser window. Select Export from the Resource menu, and move through the directories until you find your target. Then click OK.

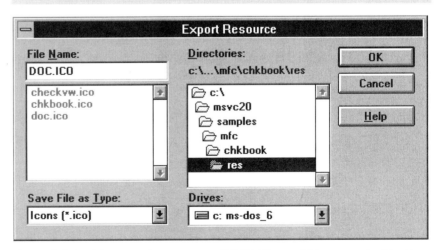

Figure 2-8: In this case, the resource DOC.ICO would be exported to the chkbook resource file.

Drag-and-drop
Really, this is just another way to copy. With two Resource Browser windows open, select a resource in one window and drag it to the other. That's it. A copy will find its own way into the appropriate folder.

Shortcut menus

Here is an opportunity to use the almost vestigial right mouse button. From inside an editor, put the arrow on an object you wish to edit and then press the right button. In many cases, a shortcut menu will appear from which you can select a command.

The Dialog Editor

If you have worked with a drawing program before, putting together a dialog box will seem pretty basic. Many elements can go into a box, and you'll want to play around a bit with layout using pencil and paper. But the features of the Dialog editor make it easy to construct, modify and fine-tune the final product. (***Note:*** A dialog box resource must be created before ClassWizard can create the class to be associated with it. For other resources, the class can be created first.)

Let's take a brief interlude to talk about a new unit of measurement, the *dialog box unit*, or DBU. There is such a variety of monitors, resolutions and refresh rates in the marketplace that Microsoft went to great pains to come up with a device-independent way to scale dialog boxes. It did this by inventing the DBU, which is based on the size of the installed system font. A *vertical dialog box unit* (VDBU) is equal to 1/8 of the average character height of the system font. A *horizontal dialog box unit* (HDBU) is 1/4 the size of the VDBU. You will see occasional references to the DBU in the Visual C++ reference material and less frequent references in this book.

Now, back to creating a new dialog box. When you select New from the Resource menu and choose Dialog from the box, you get the following picture:

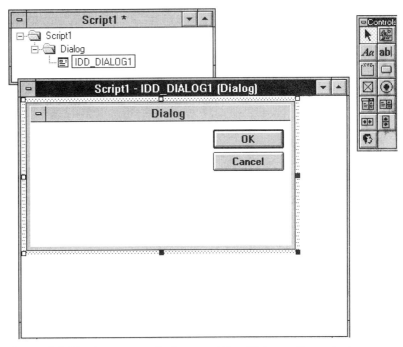

Figure 2-9: The browser window and the Dialog editor window.

The small box labeled Script1* is the browser window, and the large box labeled Script1-IDD_DIALOG1 (Dialog) is the Dialog editor window. Off to the side is the Controls toolbar. If the toolbar isn't visible, go to the Tools menu, select Toolbars and check the box beside Controls.

The first step in building a dialog box is setting up the box itself. Double-click the box, and a Properties box appears (you can also get the Properties box by selecting Properties from the Edit menu or pressing Alt-Enter).

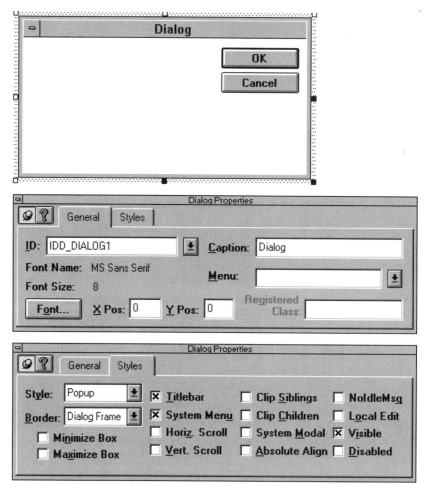

Figure 2-10: The dialog box as it first appears and the two tab pages of the Dialog Properties box.

Let's step through our options:

General Properties	Description
ID	A default ID for the box is already created for you. Pull down the list to see alternatives or create your own.
Font Name, Font Size	Display the currently selected font and size. To change them, click the Font button.
Font	Takes you to another pretty standard dialog box where you can change the font and size.
X pos, Y pos	Show the postion of the upper-left corner of the dialog box. The position is relative to the parent window and is measured in dialog box units.

General Properties	Description
Caption	The title of your dialog box. It will appear, as typed, in the center of the title bar, unless you choose not to have a title bar on the Styles tab page.
Menu	Normally, a dialog has no menu other than the system menu. But in the odd event that you decide to include one, enter the resource identifier of the menu in this box so it can be included.
Registered Class	If you are using the MFC library, this box is disabled. But if you intend to use a C language registered dialog class, put its identifier here. If the identifier is a string, be sure to enclose it in double quotes.

Style Properties	Description
Style	You have three choices of style: ○ *Overlapped.* An overlapped window is meant to be an application's main window, with such things as a title bar, border, client area, system menu, minimize and maximize boxes, and scrollbars. ○ *Pop-up.* This is the default and the most common style of a dialog box. It is, in fact, a special type of Overlapped window in which the title bar is optional. ○ *Child.* A child window is confined to the client area of its parent window. If you try to move it beyond the boundaries, it gets clipped. The one thing a child window always has is a client area. You can add a title bar, a system menu, minimize and maximize boxes, a border and scrollbars, but not a menu. A child window shows it dependency in other ways: it is destroyed before a parent, hides when a parent hides, moves when a parent moves and shows up only after a parent shows.
Border	You have four choices of border: ○ *None.* No border, no title bar. ○ *Thin.* A non-resizable border, with a title bar. ○ *Resizable.* The standard border for application windows.
Dialog Frame	A dialog frame is just like the thin frame, except gray shading is used to add body.
Minimize Box	The minimize box is available only if there is a title bar. It's the little box in the upper-right corner that reduces your window to an icon.
Maximize Box	Like the minimize box, the maximize box is located in the upper-right corner and is available only if is there is a title bar. Clicking it expands the window to fill the available screen.
Titlebar	The title bar is available only when a border is used.

Style Properties	Description
System Menu	This is the little box in the upper-left corner of the window that you double-click to close your window.
Horiz. Scroll, Vert. Scroll	These options add a horizontal and vertical scrollbar to the window. Don't use these with the default dialog frame border. If you do, they overlap the borders instead of lying within them, and the client area isn't clipped correctly.
Clip Siblings	Check this only if you have chosen the child window style. When selected, this window clips the windows of any other child windows whenever it gets repainted. Without it, the painting can occur in the sibling's client area. You are messing with someone else's space.
Clip Children	This option prevents a parent from drawing inside a child's window. Don't use it if your dialog box has a group box (see the group box control in the section just after this one).
System Modal	You know those warning boxes that won't go away until you click on them? They won't go away because they are modal. The modal setting prevents the user from switching to another window as long as the modal window is active. Microsoft recommends that modal dialog boxes be pop-up style, with a system menu, a title bar and a thick border. Microsoft insists that they not be child windows, mainly because this style will block any further communication with the application.
Absolute Align	Absolute align means that your dialog box will align itself to the upper-left corner of the screen rather than the upper-left corner of the parent window.
NoIdleMsg	When a dialog box has no more messages to send, it sends the WM_EnterIDLE message. This message lets the application do background computing even when the dialog box is open. Checking the NoIdleMsg box blocks the message so that the application will wait. You may want to use this in a System Modal dialog box.
Local Edit	Edit-box controls normally use memory outside of the application's allotted memory. Check this box if you want the controls to use memory inside the application memory.
Visible	Check Visible if the dialog box should appear to users. Leave it unchecked for form views and dialog bar templates, when you want the controls but not the box to appear.
Disabled	Check Disabled to create a dialog that initially accepts no input.

Control Toolbox

The elements of a dialog box are windows called controls. There are 11 standard controls, as well as one control that can be defined by the programmer. All controls share certain features accessible through the Properties dialog box. To open the Properties dialog box, double-click on the installed control, select Properties from the Edit menu, or press Alt-Enter.

Controls share these basic properties:

ID	A symbol or integer identifier (usually a symbol provided by Visual C++) defined in the project's .H file. If you don't like the default, select one from the list or type your own.
Visible	When Visible is checked, the control is visible from the time an application opens.
Disabled	When Disabled is checked, the control is disabled (dimmed) when the dialog box opens.
Group	A group is a collection of controls that you can move through with the arrow keys or with the Tab key. The Group value identifies where one group begins and another ends. It works like this: A true value starts the group. All the following controls that are set to false are part of that group. The next true value starts a new group.
Tabstop	When Tabstop is selected, the user can move to this control using the Tab key.

The Toolbar

Now, on to the toolbar. Use the toolbar to install controls in the dialog box. Doing so is relatively simple: just click the toolbar button for the control you want to install, place the crosshairs on a spot in the dialog box and click again. We'll talk about resizing, aligning and layout after we have introduced each control and its properties.

Let's run through the toolbar control buttons one by one, starting on the left side and running down, then moving down the right side. Each illustration that follows shows the button and its associated Properties box and an example of the control itself. With each illustration is an explanation of the control properties that are special for that control. We won't repeat the common properties that were listed above.

Selection Arrow: If you need to get back to the arrow after selecting a control, click here. You almost never need this button, since you return to the arrow automatically after installing a control.

Figure 2-11: The selection arrow.

Static Text: The *static text* control is fixed text that you place in the dialog box, such as a caption for a field. The text is entered into the Properties box Caption field. (If your static text control is selected, just start typing; the box automatically opens and the text is entered into the proper field.) Text will wrap to fit the shape of the box if it is resized.

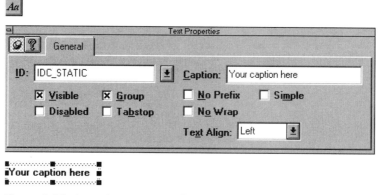

Figure 2-12: A static text control.

The text properties are as follows:

Caption	This is just the text you want to appear. In Figure 2-12, "Your caption here" appears in the field and in the control itself.
No Prefix	No Prefix prevents ampersands (&) in the text from being interpreted as control characters. If you check this box, the ampersand appears as an ampersand. If you don't check it, the ampersand is not printed and the character following the ampersand is underlined.
Simple	Simple prevents text wrapping and text alignment. Basically, it disables the next two properties. It also means that if you override WM_CTLCOLOR in the parent window, it has no effect on the control.

| No Wrap | Normally, text wraps to fit the control as you resize it. Select this property if you do not want text to wrap. |
| Text Align | You have three choices from the drop-down list: Left, Center and Right. The default is Left. |

Group Box: The *group box* is another static feature, designed to be resized and placed around a group of controls such as a column of radio buttons.

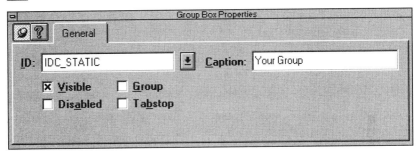

Figure 2-13: A group box control.

Properties Box: The Properties box has only one nonstandard field:

| Caption | Type the title of the group box. The text will be center-aligned and will not wrap. |

47

Check Box: A *check box* is used to turn an option on or off.

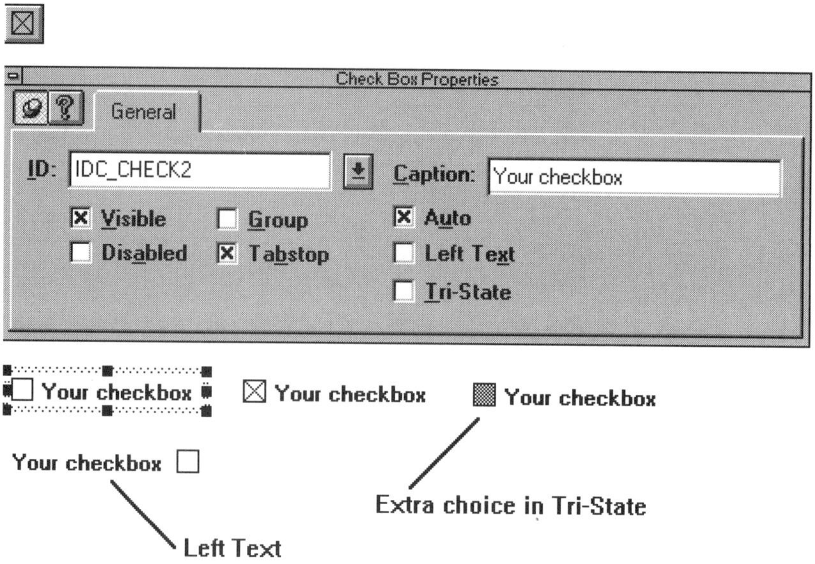

Figure 2-14: Check box controls.

The check box-specific properties are as follows:

Caption	The caption you type will appear to the right of the check box (or at left, if the Left Text property is selected).
Auto	When Auto is set, the check box automatically toggles to the alternate state when a check box is clicked.
Left Text	This simply flips the positions of text and box, as you can see in Figure 2-14.
Tri-State	This is not the tollway that connects Indiana, Illinois and Wisconsin. If you select Tri-State, there is a third state of the check box: gray filled. It represents an indeterminate state.

Combo Box: The ID field in the Properties dialog box is an example of the *combo box* control: Hit the arrow, and a list drops down. Select an item from the list, and it appears in the top box as your choice. If the list is too long for the box as you've sized it, vertical scrollbars are automatically included (unless you purposely choose not to have them, as explained below).

When you install a combo box control in a dialog box, you see a control like the one at bottom left in Figure 2-15. Notice that only the left and right sizing handles are filled. These are the only two that work, stretching the box to the right or left. Click the arrow to get the control at the bottom right of Figure 2-15, which shows the box's dimensions when its list is dropped. The single active sizing handle on the bottom allows you to lengthen the box.

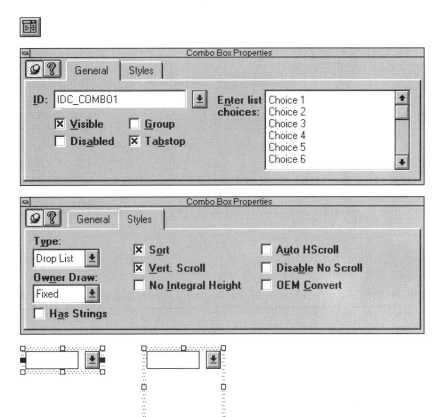

Figure 2-15: A combo box control.

There are two tabs to this Properties box, General and Styles:

General Tab	Description
Enter List Choices	Enter the text for your choices. The tricky part is moving to the next line—you must use Ctrl-Enter. If you just use Enter, the Properties dialog box closes.

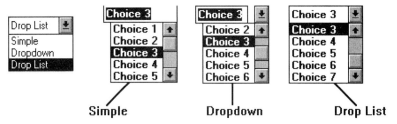

Figure 2-16: Combo box list choices.

Styles Tab	Description
Type	There are three types of list to choose from:
	○ *Simple.* A simple list is always visible and has no drop-down arrow. Users can select an item or type their own.
	○ *Dropdown.* The default, the dropdown list, includes an arrow that opens and closes the list. Users can select an item or type their own.
	○ *Drop List.* The drop list is just like the Dropdown except that users must select from the list and cannot type their own strings.
Owner Draw	The Owner Draw property determines whether the application assumes responsibility for maintaining the control's appearance. There are three options:
	○ *No.* The default, No, means the list is not owner drawn but self-drawn from the control window. The choice list will all be strings.
	○ *Fixed.* The term Fixed refers to the "fixed" height of the list items. Because it is owner-drawn, you must call CWnd::OnMeasureItem when the list box is created, and call CWnd::OnDrawItem when the box changes its appearance.
	○ *Variable.* Again, a reference to the height. The list items are owner-drawn, and their heights will be variable. CWnd::OnDrawItem must be called on each item when creating the list.
Has Strings	Check this box to alert Visual C++ that there are strings in the list, so they can be handled as text. If No was selected for the Owner Draw field, the presence of strings is assumed and this check box is disabled.
Sort	Select this check box to sort your list alphabetically.
Vert. Scroll	The default is to provide a vertical scrollbar for the drop list, if needed. Deselecting this option eliminates scrollbars, even if your list is too long for the list box.

No Integral Height	Windows will automatically resize a combo box to prevent items from being cut off. Selecting this box will turn off that feature, and you must ensure that the combo box has adequate dimensions. Figure 2-17 shows an example of No Integral Height.

Figure 2-17: An example of No Integral Height.

Auto HScroll	If the simple or dropdown list type is selected, users may type in strings. Select Auto Hscroll for automatic scrolling when the user types an entry longer than the available space.
Disable No Scroll	If all the list's items fit in the drop box, the vertical scrollbar is normally eliminated. Select this option to display the scrollbar even though it won't actually scroll.
OEM Convert	This one is a little wild. If this option is set, text entered into the combo box will be converted from the Windows character set to the Original Equipment Manufacturer's (OEM) character set and back again. This bit of reverse engineering ensures that calls to AnsiToOem properly convert Windows characters to OEM characters.

Horizontal & Vertical Scrollbars: The standard scrollbar is part of the nonclient area of a window and has no independence. It always appears with the window and always serves to scroll the window's contents.

The scrollbar *control*, on the other hand, is a window unto itself. It has direct input focus and a built-in keyboard interface for direct scrolling. While you may have only one set of standard scrollbars per window, you can install as many control scrollbars as you like. And they can be used for purposes other than scrolling—as volume controls, for instance, or for changing color parameters in an image.

The *horizontal scrollbar* and *vertical scrollbar* controls are essentially the same.

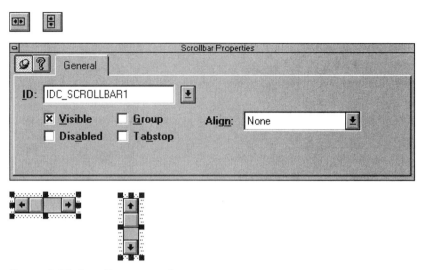

Figure 2-18: Scrollbar controls.

There is only one property to discuss—Align—with only three options:

None	The scrollbar's size remains the size that you define in Visual C++.
Top/Left	The upper-left corner of the scrollbar is aligned with the upper-left corner of the window that contains it.
Bottom/Right	The bottom-right corner of the scrollbar is aligned with the bottom-right corner of the window.

User-Defined Controls: *User-defined* controls are a blank slate. The Dialog editor does little more than reserve space for the control by making the control window. What goes into the window and what it does is entirely in your hands.

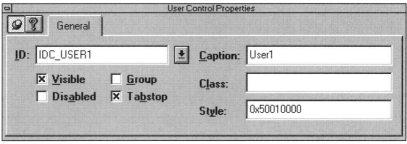

Figure 2-19: A user-defined control.

Caption	This is the label for the control.
Class	Class is the name of the windows class that must be registered before the control is created.
Style	The lower 16 bits of this 32-bit hexadecimal identify the user control's substyle. Use hex digits or predefined window style constants here.

Picture Control: The *picture* control, another static control, doesn't do anything but display. You can create your own graphic displayed as an icon or as a simple rectangle, filled or unfilled.

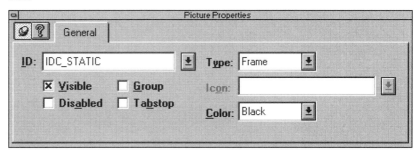

Figure 2-20: A picture control.

Its properties are as follows:

Type	Choose one of these types:
	○ *Frame.* You get a frame, in the color set in the Color property field.
	○ *Icon.* The icon you identify in the Icon property field will be displayed.
	○ *Rectangle.* The rectangle is filled with the color from the Color property field.
Icon	If you choose the Icon type above, put the icon identifier here.
Color	Choose from black, white or gray. You don't get a choice when the type is Icon.

Text Box: The *text box* control accepts text entry for everything from entering a password to finding a file. Its General properties are the basic five that all controls have.

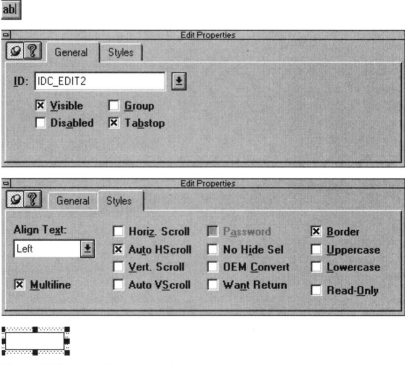

Figure 2-21: A text box control.

The Style properties are more diverse:

Align Text	If you have selected the Multiline check box just below this field, you can choose here to align text at left, right or center.
Multiline	Select this option to let the user enter more than one line in the text box. But it won't work unless you do one or more of the following:
	○ Make the box big enough for several lines. If this is all you do, the user can type more than one line but no more than will fit in the box.
	○ Check the Auto Vscroll box.
	○ Check the Vert. Scroll box.
	(These last two choices have idiosyncrasies, so be sure to read about the Auto Hscroll, the Auto Vscroll and the Want Return check boxes.)
	How the box handles multiline text entry depends on the check boxes selected. Select Auto Hscroll and Want Return (discussed below) to require the user to press Enter to get to a new line; there will be no automatic wraparound because there is no effective end to the box. For automatic wraparound, *do not* select Auto Hscroll. For automatic wraparound that also permits the user to press Enter to start a new line, select both AutoHscroll and Want Return.
	Selecting Multiline affects the availability of other check boxes:
	○ Align Text becomes available.
	○ Horiz. Scroll becomes available.
	○ Vert. Scroll becomes available.
	○ Auto Vscroll becomes available.
	○ Password is not available.
Horiz Scroll	Available when Multiline is selected, this option provides horizontal scrolling with a scrollbar.
Auto HScroll	If Auto HScroll is checked, text automatically scrolls left when the user tries to type beyond the end of the box.
Vert. Scroll	Available when Multiline is selected, this option provides vertical scrolling with scrollbars.
Auto VScroll	Auto VScroll is available only when Multiline is selected. Select AutoVScroll—and deselect AutoHScroll—to provide wrap-around and automatic vertical scrolling when the user tries to type beyond the end of the box. You can select Want Return (whether Auto Hscroll is selected or not) to also enable the user to move to the next line by pressing Enter.
Password	Check Password to have typed characters appear as asterisks (*). This is not available when Multiline is selected.

No Hide Sel	Select this option to keep highlighted text highlighted when the user moves the focus out of the text box. Normally, the highlighting disappears.
OEM Convert	We covered this with the combo box control. But we'll repeat it. If OEM Convert is selected, text will be converted from the Windows characters set to an OEM character set and back again. This prevents surprises when AnsiToOem is called to convert Windows characters to OEM characters.
Want Return	Want Return is important only if you have selected Multiline. Normally when you press Enter in a dialog box you are, in effect, pushing the default push-button— usually the OK button, which causes your dialog box to close. This is a problem if you want to go to a new line in a Multiline text box. Want Return makes Enter nothing more than a carriage return and prevents the dialog box from disappearing.
Border	Border puts a border around the text box.
Uppercase	Uppercase changes all characters to uppercase.
Lowercase	Lowercase changes all characters to lowercase.
Read Only	Read Only prevents typing or editing. The user can read text in the box, but can't change it.

Push Button: A *push button* invokes a single action. It is on or off, and clicking a push button typically results in an immediate action. Here are your options for the push buttons generated by the Dialog editor:

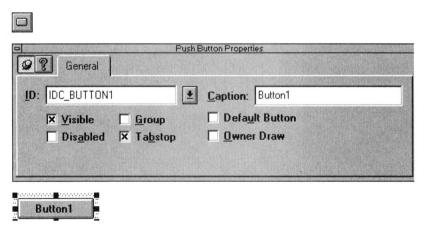

Figure 2-22: A push button control.

Caption	The caption you enter will appear centered in the button.
Default Button	Select this check box to make the push button the default when the dialog box first opens. There can be only one default button. The default button, indicated by a heavy border, is activated by pressing Enter. Once the dialog box is open, tabbing through the controls can shift the default. Note that checking Default Button automatically deselects Owner Draw.
Owner Draw	Owner Draw creates a button whose style you will provide. Selecting Owner Draw automatically deselects Default Button.

Radio Button: *Radio buttons* are so called because within a group you always have one, but only one, selected at a time, like the buttons on your car radio. The selected button is always marked by a black dot within the circle, as you can see in Figure 2-23. Radio buttons are automatically installed so only one can be selected at a time. It is a handy way of forcing a user to choose one option from a list.

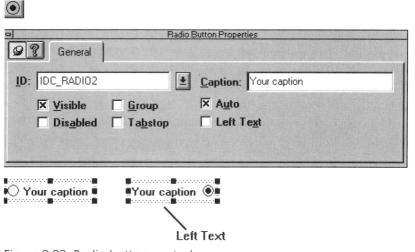

Figure 2-23: Radio button controls.

With the help of the Group property, described below, you can include more than one group of radio buttons in a dialog box.

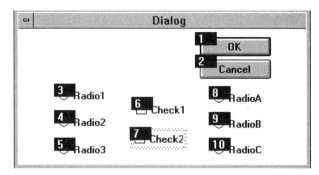

Figure 2-24: Sequencing a group of radio button controls.

Radio button properties include the following:

Group	Use the Group option if you want to install more than one group of radio buttons in the dialog box. Here's how: Let's say you want two groups of three buttons, one with labels 3, 4 and 5 and the other with labels 8, 9 and 10. First, set the tab order. Select Tab Order from the Layout menu. This will show you the current tab order of controls in the dialog box, as shown in Figure 2-24. If the items are not in the right order, click on each control in the order you want them to appear. Then set the Group property to true for the first item in each group (3 and 8, in our example) and set it to false for the rest.
Auto	Auto simply means that the button will automatically toggle on and off whenever the control is selected and that any other radio button in the group that was on will now be off. You must select this if you are using Dynamic Data Exchange.
Left Text	This selection puts the text to the left of the button, as you can see in Figure 2-23.

List Box: A *list box* contains items that the user can select, but unlike the combo box, it permits no additions to the list. There are two basic list types: a list in which only one item can be selected, and a list in which several items can be selected.

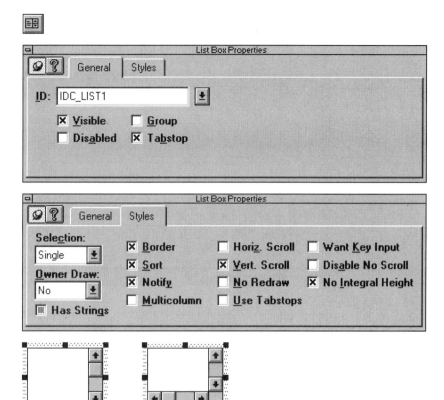

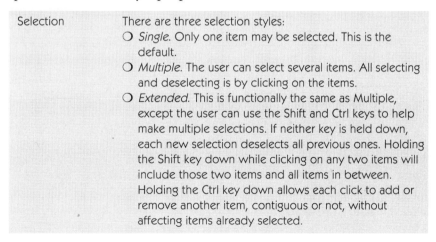

Figure 2-25: List box controls.

The General properties for a list box are standard, but there are quite a number of Style properties:

Selection	There are three selection styles:
	○ *Single*. Only one item may be selected. This is the default.
	○ *Multiple*. The user can select several items. All selecting and deselecting is by clicking on the items.
	○ *Extended*. This is functionally the same as Multiple, except the user can use the Shift and Ctrl keys to help make multiple selections. If neither key is held down, each new selection deselects all previous ones. Holding the Shift key down while clicking on any two items will include those two items and all items in between. Holding the Ctrl key down allows each click to add or remove another item, contiguous or not, without affecting items already selected.

Owner Draw	You have three choices: ○ *No.* This is the default. No owner-drawn items are in the list; all are strings. ○ *Fixed.* The owner window draws the list items, but they are all the same height. This means you must call CWnd::OnMeasureItem when the list box is created, and call CWnd::OnDrawItem when the box changes its appearance ○ *Variable.* The list is owner-drawn, and the items vary in height. This means CWnd::OnDrawItem must be called on each item when creating the box.
Has Strings	This box is automatically selected if No Owner Draw is selected, since the box must contains strings in that case. However, if the items are Fixed Owner Draw or Variable Owner Draw, selecting Has Strings will insure that strings are handled as strings and the text can be retrieved.
Border	Check this option if you want the list box to have a border.
Sort	Select this check box if you want the list sorted alphabetically.
Notify	Select Notify to notify the parent window each time an item is clicked or double-clicked.
Multicolumn	This creates a multicolumn list box that can be scrolled horizontally. Column width is set with LB_SETCOLUMNWIDTH.
Horiz. Scroll	Check this if you have multicolumns. It creates a horizontal scroll box.
Vert. Scroll	This creates a vertical scroll box.
No Redraw	If you don't want the list box's appearance updated every time there is a change, select this. You can override No Redraw at any time by sending a WM_SETREDRAW message.
Use Tabstops	This allows the list to recognize tabs and gives them a value of 32 DBUs. (As noted earlier, a DBU is a Dialog Box Unit, and 32 horizontal DBUs are equal to the height of the average system font character.)

Aligning Controls

When your controls are in place, use the Alignment controls at the bottom of the Visual C++ window to clean up their appearance. These controls simplify the task of lining up controls and getting the proper spacing.

Selecting Multiple Controls: To select multiple controls, hold down the Shift key while clicking on controls. Each click selects (or deselects) an additional control. The last one selected is the *dominant* control.

Alternatively, you can drag a selection box around a cluster of controls to select them all, as in Figure 2-26. The control closest to your starting point for the selection box becomes the dominant control.

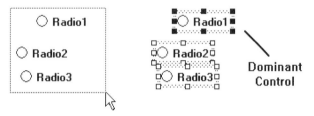

Figure 2-26: Selecting multiple controls.

The dominant control is very important. It is the reference point for all alignments that occur using the alignment toolbar. When several controls are selected at once, the one with filled resizing handles is the dominant control.

If you want a control outside the dialog box, move it beyond the box boundaries by holding down the Alt key as you drag.

The Alignment Toolbar: Figure 2-27 shows the Alignment toolbar. The table that follows describes the toolbar buttons from left to right.

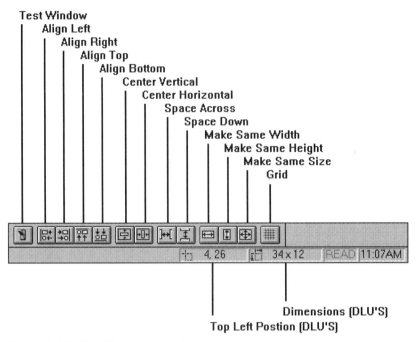

Figure 2-27: The Alignment toolbar.

Test window	As you put a dialog box together, use the Test window to see how well things work. Do you have your radio buttons grouped properly? Would it be better to have a simple combo box style, or do you need the drop list style? Did you remember to include horizontal scrolling in the text box? The test window will tell you if controls work the way you intended, without having to compile the whole mess each time you make a change. You can get to the Test window quickly by simply clicking the light switch.
Left Align	To align a group of controls with the left side of the dominant control, select the controls you want aligned. Then select Left Align. The controls will line up with their left sides even with the left side of the dominant control. The distance between controls does not change.
Right Align	The selected controls will line up with their right sides even with the right side of the dominant control. The distance between controls does not change.

Align Top	The selected controls will line up with their top edges even with the top edge of the dominant control. The space between controls is unchanged.
Align Bottom	The selected controls will line up with their bottom edges even with the bottom edge of the dominant control. The space between controls is unchanged.
Center Vertical	The entire selection of one or more controls is centered. The top edge of the top control is the same distance from the center as the bottom edge of the bottom control.
Center Horizontal	The entire selection of one or more controls is centered. The left edge of the left control is the same distance from the center as the right edge of the right control.
Space Across	The left and right controls of the selection group don't move, but the controls between them shift so that they are evenly spaced horizontally.
Space Down	The top and bottom controls of the selection group don't move. All the controls between them shift so that they are evenly spaced vertically.
Make Same Width	All selected controls become the same width as the dominant control.
Make Same Height	All selected controls become the same height as the dominant control.
Make Same Size	All selected controls become the same width and height as the dominant control.
Grid	Select this, and a grid appears. As you move or resize controls, they are constrained to the grid.

Position & Dimension Information: Just below the Alignment toolbar is the status bar. When you are in the Dialog editor, there are two information boxes. The first shows the top left position, in DBUs, of the selected item. The second shows the dimensions of the selected item in DBUs. These can be a helpful reference when placing controls.

The Graphics Editor

The Graphics editor has a lot of features but is quite simple to use. If you are used to painting or drawing programs, you shouldn't have much trouble. You get into the Graphics editor by opening a Bitmap, Cursor or Icon resource. The editor changes slightly with each resource, and these differences are discussed later in this section. But all three look much like the Bitmap editor shown in Figure 2-28.

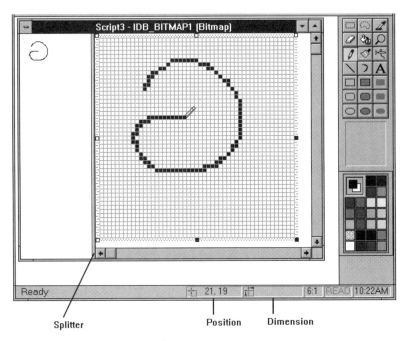

Figure 2-28: The Bitmap editor.

The image is divided into two panes. On the left you see the bitmap at actual size. On the right you see it magnified six times. In this example, each pixel is outlined in a pixel grid. You can draw or paint in either pane and see the results in both simultaneously. The vertical border that separates the two panes is called the *splitter*, and it can be dragged left or right to resize both panes. You can change the magnification in either window and even set them the same so that you are looking at two different parts of the same bitmap.

In the status bar at the bottom are two information boxes. The one on the left shows the position of the cursor (in this case, the pencil) relative to the upper-left corner of the bitmap. As you can see, the pencil is 21 pixels right and 19 pixels down from the corner. The second box shows the current dimensions of the bitmap, as in Figure 2-29, whenever you resize the image.

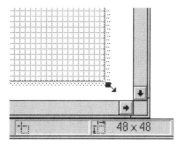

Figure 2-29: The current dimensions of the image.

To the right of the bitmap panes are the toolbar, the option selection box and the colors palette. The toolbar contains standard drawing and painting tools, many of which have options. When a tool is selected, the options automatically show up in the option selection box. Simply click the one you wish to use. The current option is highlighted. In Figure 2-30, the paintbrush is the selected tool, and the option selection box shows the different brush shapes available. The colors palette simply shows the colors available for drawing and painting.

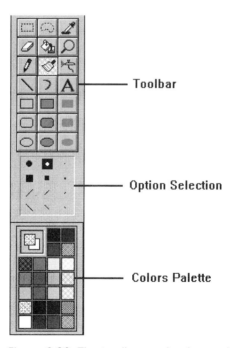

Figure 2-30: The toolbar and colors palette.

In effect, the colors palette lets you have two colors chosen at once. Look at the overlapping squares in the upper-left corner of the palette. The top square is the foreground, and the overlapped square is the background. Foreground color is selected with the left mouse button, and background color with the right. Furthermore, any drawing tool will draw in the foreground color when you hold down the left button and the background color when you hold down the right.

The eraser, brush, rectangle tools, ellipse tools and airbrush can be increased or decreased in size a pixel at a time by hitting the + (plus) or - (minus) key. The brush and eraser can be reduced to a single pixel by pressing the period key.

The rectangle, selection tools and ellipse tools have cross hairs that appear in the pane you are working in, to help you line up edges of the closed figures.

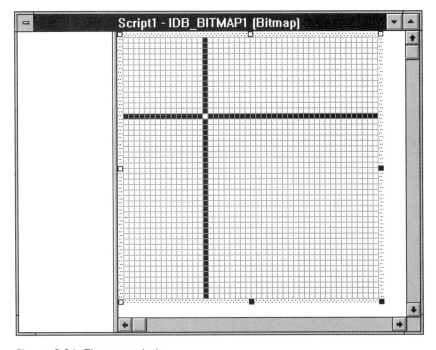

Figure 2-31: The cross hairs.

The Tools

Here is a brief description of each tool in the Graphics editor toolbar. In all cases, using the left mouse button draws in the foreground color while the right button draws in the background color. These colors are shown at top left of the colors palette; the option box shows only the current *foreground* color.

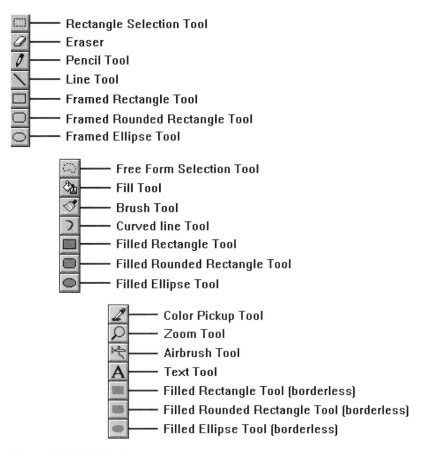

Figure 2-32: The tools.

   Use the *rectangle selection* tool to drag a selection box around part of the image for cutting, copying and dragging that part of the image. Notice the options box. The top option is an opaque selection. No background will show through white parts of the selection if it is moved to a different part of the image. The bottom option is a transparent selection box, and in this option any white pixels allow background image to show through.

   The *eraser* erases when you hold down the left mouse button. There are several sizes to choose from. The *pencil tool* draws a line of the chosen color that is a single pixel wide.

   The *line tool* draws a straight line. Click and hold down the mouse button to anchor one end of the line. Drag to produce the line (it will pivot on the anchor point as you move). When you have the line you want, click again to lock it in place. There are several drawing shapes to choose from.

To use the *framed rectangle tool, framed rounded rectangle tool* or *framed ellipse tool,* hold down the mouse button and drag from one corner to the opposite corner. This creates an unfilled rectangle or ellipse in the chosen color. Use the cross hairs to line up the sides. The option box has a number of line thicknesses to choose from.

The *free form selection tool* works like the rectangle selection tool, except that the selection is free form. You drag a line around the area you wish to select as if you were drawing with the pencil.

To use the *fill tool*, click inside a closed figure. The figure fills with the current drawing color. If the figure isn't truly closed, the color will spill into the entire image.

The *brush tool* draws like the pencil but with broader strokes. The options box gives you several brush shapes to choose from. You can also make a custom brush shape by selecting part of the image and pressing Ctrl-B. The selected area is now a brush tool. This is handy when you need to "rubber stamp" a pattern repeatedly.

To use the *curved tool*, click and hold a mouse button to anchor one end of the curve. Now drag to the other end of the curve and release. Next, move the mouse to get the curve shape you want and click again. If you want a double curve, move the mouse one more time and click again. If you begin with a click and release, then move the mouse and click again, you get a closed curve. You can then move the mouse around to get the shape you want and click again to lock it in. The curved tool comes with the usual drawing tool assortment in the options box.

The *filled rectangle tool, filled rounded rectangle tool* and *filled ellipse tool* are just like the framed rectangle tool. The difference is that you get a rectangle or ellipse drawn in the background color and filled with the foreground color if you use the left button, and vice versa with the right. The options box has an assortment of thickness lines to choose from.

The *color pickup tool* is an eyedropper used to pick up a color from another part of the bitmap. To shift to the desired color, just select the eyedropper and click on the color in the bitmap (the left mouse button will shift the foreground color and the right button will shift the background color). The last drawing tool you used is then automatically reselected for you.

To use the *zoom tool*, choose the magnification in the option box and click on the image of either pane. It will toggle back or forth between magnified and normal size. After a click you are automatically returned to the last tool you were using. You can use the zoom tool on either pane.

The *airbrush tool* sprays a random distribution of diffuse foreground color when you hold down a mouse button. The options box has several sizes to choose from.

    When you select the *text tool* an extra little window pops up (see Figure 2-33). As you type, text appears simultaneously in the Text Tool window and both pane images. If you don't like the font or size, change it by clicking the font button and changing the selection in the dialog box that appears. The options box has an opaque versus transparent choice. *Opaque* means the text, which is in the foreground color, is embedded in the background color as it is typed.

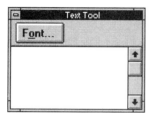

Figure 2-33: Using the text tool.

    To use the *filled rectangle tool* (borderless), *filled rounded rectangle tool* (borderless) or *filled ellipse tool* (borderless), drag from one corner to the other to draw a borderless solid rectangle or ellipse.

The Color Palette

As explained earlier, clicking on a color with the left mouse button selects it as the foreground color and clicking with the right selects it for the background. There are two ways to change the palette. If you want to change just one color, double-click it and a Custom Color Selector box appears.

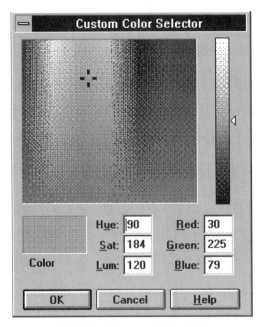

Figure 2-34: The Custom Color Selector.

You can change color by the numbers if you like, by resetting hue, saturation, luminosity and color proportions. Or simply click the cross hairs to a color you like in the left control and slide to a contrast you like in the right control. When you have created a color you like in the Color box at lower left, click OK.

Alternatively, you can change the entire palette by going to the Bitmap Properties box (select Properties from the Edit menu). Click the Palette tab and go through the colors, changing each one by double-clicking to open the Custom Color Selector and then making your changes.

The Image Menu

You may not have noticed it, but when you opened the Graphics editor, a new menu, the Image menu, popped into the menu bar right between the Resource menu and the Debug menu.

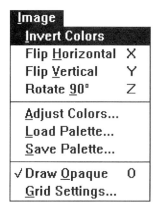

Figure 2-35: The Image menu.

Let's look at the menu commands:

❍ *Invert Colors*. This option inverts all the colors in your image.

❍ *Flip Horizontal*. Right becomes left, and left becomes right.

❍ *Flip Vertical*. Top becomes bottom, and bottom becomes top.

❍ *Rotate 90°*. Your image rotates 1/4 turn clockwise.

❍ *Adjust Colors*. This opens the Custom Color Selector for the foreground color. Any changes you make affect only that color.

❍ *Load Palette, Save Palette*. These two are related. If you have created a palette that might be useful again, save it as a file with Save Pallete. This command opens a dialog box like the one you get when you select Save As from the File menu. When you want to retrieve a saved palette, choose the Load Pallete command, track it down through the directories and click OK, and it's loaded.

❍ *Draw Opaque*. If this is selected, there will be a check mark next to the command, as shown in Figure 2-35. This means that any white pixels in your brush or pasted image act as though they are opaque white. If Draw Opaque is not selected, white pixels are considered transparent and the colors already present will show through a pasted selection.

❍ *Grid Settings*. As shown in Figure 2-36, the little squares are in the Pixel Grid. The larger squares are the Tile Grid, and you can set the dimensions to these yourself in the Width and Height boxes.

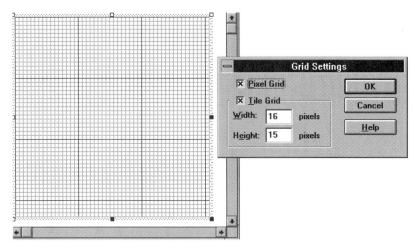

Figure 2-36: The Grid Settings dialog box.

Differences in the Graphics Editor for Bitmaps, Cursors & Icons

The differences between the Graphics editors for bitmap, cursor and icon resources are minor but worth pointing out. First we'll show the Properties differences. Then we'll explain the differences in the editors themselves. (We covered the Bitmap editor in detail above, so just keep that discussion in mind as we explain the differences in the other two editors.)

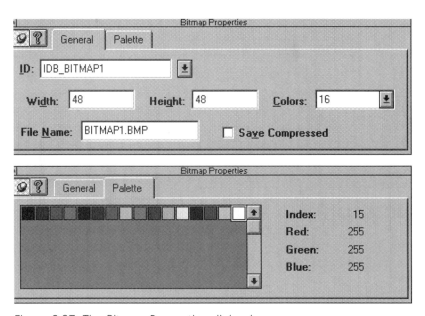

Figure 2-37: The Bitmap Properties dialog box.

The General tab of the Bitmap Properties dialog box includes the following properties:

ID	The resource identifier is a symbol created by C++ and defined in a .H file.
Width, Height	These are the image's width and height in pixels. Both default to 48.
Colors	This is a drop list box with choices of 2, 16 or 256 colors.
File Name	This is the file that contains the bitmap resource.
Save Compressed	You can save some disk space by checking this, especially if your bitmaps are larger than the default.

The Palette tab of the Bitmap Properties dialog box shows what colors are available. Double-click on a color to open the Custom Color Selector, and you can change the color. The right side of the box displays the color's number and the proportions of red, green and blue.

Notice that as you select different colors, the foreground color on the toolbar palette also changes. If you are working with 256 colors, you can choose from all of them for the foreground and background.

The General tab of the Cursor Properties dialog box is shown in Figure 2-38.

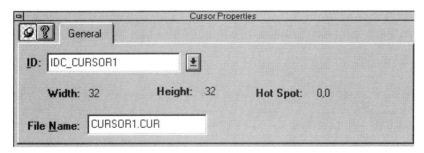

Figure 2-38: The General tab of the Cursor Properties dialog box.

The General tab of the Cursor Properties dialog box contains the following properties:

ID	The ID is the resource identifier.
Width, Height	You can't change these yourself. They are determined by the target-device of your project.
Hot Spot	The hot spot is is set from within the editor. The position is given, in pixels, relative to the upper-left corner of the image.
File Name	This is the file where the resource is stored.

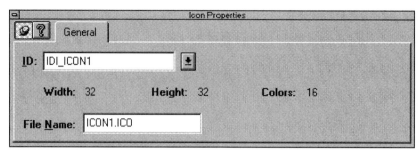

Figure 2-39: Icon General properties.

The General tab of the Icon Properties dialog box (see Figure 2-39) contains the following properties:

ID	The resource identifier.
Width, Height	You can't change these yourself. They are determined by the target-device of your project.
Colors	Colors, too, are determined by the target-device of your project and can't be changed.
File Name	This is the file where the resource is stored.

The Cursor Editor: The Hotspot button in the Cursor editor (see Figure 2-40) activates the hot spot cross hairs. Click the cross hairs on the pixel where you want your hot spot, and it is so. Click the button again to return to the previous tool in use.

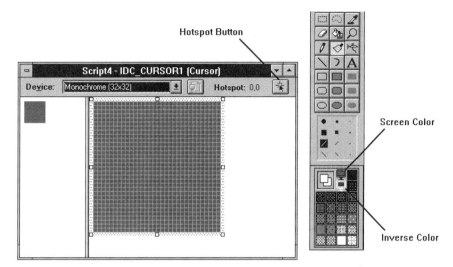

Figure 2-40: The Cursor editor.

The Screen Color and Inverse Color tools are meant to represent the screen background color. In effect, drawing on the cursor with the Screen Color creates a transparent part of the cursor. Wherever this color shows on your image, the screen will show through the cursor in your application. Just click on the little monitor to draw with the screen color. If you want the screen image to show through in inverse color, click on the inverted monitor instead.

Since these are not the true colors that will be in the cursor, you can use different colors to represent transparency, inverted or not. To do this, select one of the colors. The current selection appears in the options box. Then go to the Adjust Colors command in the Image menu and open the Custom Color Selector dialog box, where you can change the color as you wish.

The Icon Editor: The Icon editor is almost identical to the Cursor editor, with the same size image and the same Screen Color/Inverse Color feature. It differs only in the lack of a Hotspot button, and the presence of a New Icon Image button.

Click the New Icon Image button to open the New Icon Image dialog box (see Figure 2-41). This gives you a chance to change the target device for the icon image. Now here is the unusual part. When you make a selection from the list, say Small (16x16), it is removed from this list and added to the Device list in the editing window. If you select all the options from the New Icon Image box, one at a time, the button is dimmed because the list is empty, and all the list's items are now in the Device list of the editor.

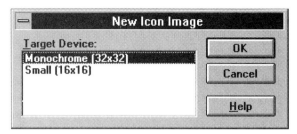

Figure 2-41: The New Icon Image dialog box.

The Menu Editor

Building a new menu bar, complete with menus, menu items and cascading menus, is easy. There's not much more to it than typing in names.

Figure 2-42 shows what you see when you open a new Menu resource. There's a window with a blank menu bar at the top. Inside the Menu bar is a highlighted New Item box.

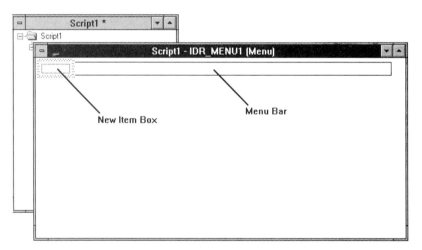

Figure 2-42: A new Menu resource.

The Menu bar has no general properties to deal with except an ID (see Figure 2-43).

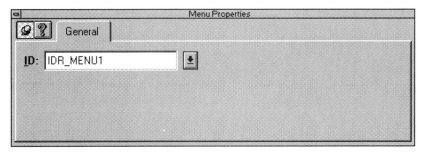

Figure 2-43: The General tab of the Menu Properties dialog box.

The New Item box (see Figure 2-42) indicates where the next menu title will appear. Just type the title. The Properties box automatically opens, and the text goes straight into the Captions field of the Menu Item Properties box as well as the menu itself.

You can, of course, open the Properties box first. To do this, double-click the New Item box, select Properties from the Edit menu, or press Alt-Enter.

The Menu Item Properties box is identical for menu titles and menu items, except that for menu titles, the separator check box and ID list box are dimmed. The properties are as follows:

ID	This is the resource identifier, usually a symbol created by C++ and stored in the appropriate .H file.
Caption	Caption is the menu item title, the text that appears in the menu itself. If you want to use a mnemonic for a particular item, insert an ampersand (&) in front of the letter that will be the mnemonic. It will be underlined in the menu.
Separator	The separator is a horizontal line that visually separates parts of the menu. It cannot be selected by a user and cannot send a message.
Checked	If you select this check box, the menu item will already be checked when the application opens.
Pop-up	Set this to true for the menu title and for any menu items for which you want to generate a cascading submenu.
Grayed	Set this option to dim an item that is is inactive when the application starts.
Inactive	Yes, you can have an inactive item that is not grayed. Just select this box. (If you have already selected grayed, than this box is forced to be true.)
Help	The Help setting justifies the menu item in the menu at run time.

Break	There are three ways to handle breaks in the menu: ○ *None*. None, the default, includes no breaks. ○ *Column*. For static menu-bar items, the Column setting places the breaking item on a new line. For pop-up menus, it places the item in a new column with no dividing line between the columns. This property affects the appearance of the menu only at run time, not in the Menu editor. ○ *Bar*. This setting has the same effect as Column except for pop-up menus. With these it separates the new column from the old column with a vertical line. Setting this property affects the appearance of the menu at run time. You can't see how it looks in the Menu editor.
Prompt	This is text that goes into the status bar message area when the menu item is highlighted. The message goes into the string table with the same ID as the menu item. This is not available without MFC support.

Making a New Menu

Making a new menu is easy. First make sure the New Item box is selected. Then type the name of the menu. (If you want a letter to be mnemonic, type an ampersand (&) in front of it.)

When you press Enter, the selection moves to the menu's New Item box, where you can type the first item of the menu. Press Enter again to move to the next new item, and type again.

This is pretty slick, but it only works when you are creating the menu the first time. If you edit the menu later, Enter doesn't take you anywhere. At that point, you need to use the mouse to select the next item to edit.

To create the next menu, just select the New Item box to the right of the first menu and repeat what you've done.

Cascading Menus

Creating a *cascading* (hierarchical) menu is almost as easy as creating a regular menu. Just select the menu item that will generate your cascading menu. Open the Properties dialog box (double-click the menu item, or select Properties from the Edit menu, or press Alt-Enter). Check the Pop-up box. As soon as you do, a New Item box buds off to the right. You can see one in Figure 2-44 coming out of the side of Item 3. Now just type the item name and press Enter to get to the next item. If you now inactivate Item 3 by selecting something else, the cascading menu collapses and that little triangle next to the menu item appears.

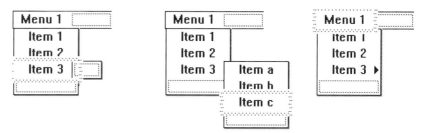

Figure 2-44: Creating a cascading menu.

Accelerator Keys

You can easily specify an accelerator key for a menu item. Create the menu item first so that it is assigned a Resource Identifier. Then select the identifier (the ID on the General tab of the Properties box) and enter the accelerator key at Caption, as shown in Figure 2-45. By putting \t, the escape sequence for a tab, between the caption and the key combination, you can align the key combinations on the left.

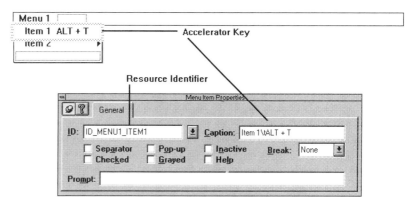

Figure 2-45: Specifying an accelerator key.

Shortcut Menus

Shortcut menus are the menus that show up in midscreen when you click the right mouse button. They usually relate to the object onscreen that the pointer is on. To create a shortcut menu, perform the following steps:

1. Start a new menu, but leave the Menu bar empty (that is, don't enter a menu title).

2. Create the menu items as usual.

3. Save the menu.

4. Connect the menu to your application by inserting this code:

```
Cmenu menu;
menu.LoadMenu (IDR_MENU1);
Get subMenu (0) ._TrackPopupMenu (IDM_LEFTALIGN, \
    x, y, theApp.m_pMainWnd
```

View as Popup

The View as Popup command is a new command in the Resource menu (see Figure 2-46).

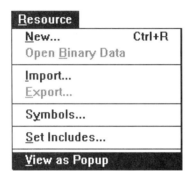

Figure 2-46: The Resource menu.

Select View as Popup to change the menu's appearance as shown in Figure 2-47. To change back again, just reselect the same command.

Figure 2-47: The menu viewed as a pop-up.

Moving & Copying

You can use the Tab key to move between titles in the menu bar. Use the arrow keys to move between items in a menu or to jump to and from a cascading menu.

You can drag and drop a menu item into a different location in its own menu, or even into another menu. To copy the item instead of moving it, hold down the Ctrl key while you drag and drop. Of course, if you prefer, you can always use the edit commands to copy, cut and paste a selected object.

The Accelerator Editor

An accelerator is a keyboard shortcut for a command. Let's take a brief timeout to explain *virtual* keys, because the concept is central to understanding accelerators. The impression you have when you type on a keyboard is that you strike the X key and *x* gets sent by the keyboard to the computer. It isn't quite that simple. What really happens explains a lot of the flexibility of keyboard input, like accelerator keys. When you press a key, a value called a scan code is sent to the computer. When you release the key yet another scan code value is sent. These code values go to a virtual key code table where they are translated into the proper ASCII value, or whatever else may be mapped to that value.

So when Microsoft talks about virtual keys, they mean the value in that translation table, not the actual keys on the keyboard. Now the presence of a scan code from a pressed-down Shift, Ctrl or Alt can, in effect, change the virtual table. That is how an *x* can become the command for *cut*. So when you create or modify an Accelerator table, you are just supplementing the virtual key translation table.

Properties

First let's look at the Accel Properties dialog box, through which you'll make most of your additions or corrections to the Accelerator table.

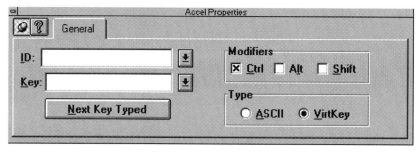

Figure 2-48: The Accel Properties dialog box.

The Accel Properties dialog box (see Figure 2-48) includes the following properties:

Type

This designates whether the value is to be an ASCII value or a virtual key value.

ID

As always, the ID is the symbol assigned by Visual C++ or yourself to the resource object. It plays particular importance in the Accelerator table because it provides the link between the accelerator keys and the menu or toolbar commands they are meant to invoke. The link comes from using the same resource identifier for the Accelerator as you did for the menu command.

Key

This is the accelerator key. It may be any of the following:

O 000 to 255. This is interpreted as code, either ASCII or virtual key, depending on what Type you select. If you try to enter a single digit, like 7, it will be interpreted as the key 7, not the number. The solution is to always use triple digits, like 007.

O A single keyboard character. A–Z (uppercase), and 0–9 can be either ASCII or virtual key. Any other character is considered a virtual key.

O ^ (caret) followed by a single character in the range A–Z (uppercase). This is interpreted as the ASCII value of key when the Ctrl key is held down.

O Any entry from the drop list. These are all virtual key identifiers.

O Next Key Typed. If you are lazy, click this button, and the next key combination you type is automatically entered into the Key and Modifiers boxes. Where there is a choice, a key is always interpreted as a virtual key.

Modifiers

These are the three standard modifier keys for creating key combinations: Alt, Shift and Ctrl. If the accelerator key is to be an ASCII value, then you can only use the Alt key. You will see that Ctrl and Shift are dimmed when the ASCII type is selected.

Editing the Accelerator Table

To edit the Accelerator table, select an entry and open its Properties dialog box. The quick way is to just double-click the entry and then change it as you see fit. Remember, though, that you are not protected against multiple definitions for the same key combination. Visual C++ will just use the first one it encounters and ignore the rest.

ID	Key	Type
ID_EDIT_COPY	Ctrl + C	VIRTKEY
ID_EDIT_PASTE	Ctrl + V	VIRTKEY
ID_EDIT_UNDO	Alt + VK_BACK	VIRTKEY
ID_EDIT_CUT	Shift + VK_DELETE	VIRTKEY
ID_NEXT_PANE	VK_F6	VIRTKEY
ID_PREV_PANE	Shift + VK_F6	VIRTKEY
ID_EDIT_COPY	Ctrl + VK_INSERT	VIRTKEY
ID_EDIT_PASTE	Shift + VK_INSERT	VIRTKEY
ID_EDIT_CUT	Ctrl + X	VIRTKEY
ID_EDIT_UNDO	Ctrl + Z	VIRTKEY

CATALOG.RC - IDR_MAINFRAME (Accelerator)

Figure 2-49: The Accelerator table.

There is always a new entry box at the end of the Accelerator table. You can select the new entry box in any of the following ways:

❍ Click on the new entry box.

❍ Press the Ins key.

❍ Select New Accelerator from the shortcut menu (opened by pressing the right mouse button).

❍ Select New Accelerator from the Resource menu in the menu bar.

Once the new entry box is selected you can open its Properties dialog box and create your key combination.

If you are defining an accelerator as a menu item shortcut, give it the same resource identifier as the menu item. If you are defining an accelerator to perform an action that is not already a menu resource, you will need to use ClassWizard to associate the accelerator with your code (see Section 3 for instructions on using ClassWizard).

The virtual key codes list is about three pages long. But if you would like to see it, select Books Online from the Help menu and open any document from the Table of Contents. At the top of the document is a dialog bar. Click Search Plus in the bar. Fill out the dialog box as shown in Figure 2-50—checking Topic Titles Only and User's Guides—and it will take you to the list.

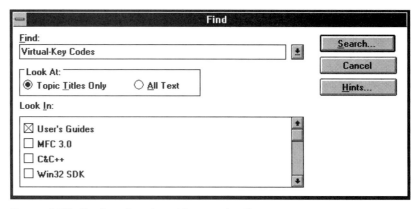

Figure 2-50: Finding the virtual key codes list.

The String Table Editor

So, you have built, debugged and brought to market your new application. Out of the blue, the marketing department decides it would be the perfect product for a new sales campaign in Germany. How do you get all those strings translated in time for the deadline? Use the String Table editor.

All the strings in your resources are in one place: the String Table, located in your .RC file and put there by AppWizard and the resource editors. Just open your .RC file and double-click the String Table folder. It opens into the String Table editor, as you can see in Figure 2-51.

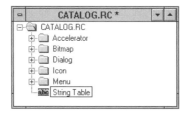

ID	Value	Caption
IDR_MAINFRAME	2	Catalog Windows Application\nCatalo\nCatalo Document\n\n\r
IDP_FAILED_OPEN_DATABA	103	Cannot open database.
AFX_IDS_APP_TITLE	57344	Catalog Windows Application
AFX_IDS_IDLEMESSAGE	57345	Ready
ID_FILE_MRU_FILE1	57616	Open this document
ID_FILE_MRU_FILE2	57617	Open this document
ID_FILE_MRU_FILE3	57618	Open this document

Figure 2-51: The String Table editor.

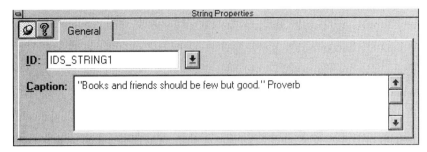

Figure 2-52: The String Properties dialog box.

As shown in Figure 2-52, there are only two fields in the String Properties dialog box:

ID	ID is the symbol identifying the string. Use this field to change the identifier or value of a string.
Caption	Caption is the string itself. You can use the standard editing commands with some exceptions, as explained below.

There are three fields in each record of the String Table (see Figure 2-51).

ID	The ID is the symbol assigned to the resource. You may or may not be able to change it in the String Table editor. If it is a shared resource, you must go to the header file (.H) where it is defined and change it there. To make a change, open the String Properties box (double-click the record in the String Table, select Properties from the Edit menu, or press Alt-Enter), and change the value in the ID field.
Value	Value is the integer constant assigned to the ID. The same restrictions that apply to the ID apply here. Values for shared resources are editable only in the header file. If you can change it, and want to, here's how: Open the Properties dialog box. Add an equals sign after the ID, and follow it with the new Value integer, like this:

IDS_YOURSTRING=357

357 will now be the new value of the string.

Caption	You can always change the caption. Again, go to the Properties box. Then make the desired changes in the Caption field. Occasionally you may want to put in some special characters, like *new line* or Tab. Here's how to represent them in a string:

To Insert	Use
New line	\n (or press Ctrl-Enter)
Carriage return	\r
Tab	\t (or press Ctrl-Tab)
Backslash	\\
ASCII character	\nnn (where nnn represents the octal notation for the character)
Bell	\a

Moving & Copying Using Drag & Drop

If you need to *move* a record from one String Table to another, this is the easy way to do it. Open both String Tables at the same time. Select the string record, drag it to the second table and let it go. It will place itself in the table according to the integer value. If you need to *copy* from one table to another, do the same thing but hold down the Ctrl key while you do it. You can always use cut, copy and paste from the Edit menu if you prefer.

Finding a Particular String in a Table

To find a particular string in a table, just use the Find command in the Search menu.

The Shortcut Menu

To use the String Table editor's handy shortcut menu, shown in Figure 2-53, just click the right mouse button.

Figure 2-53: The String Table editor's shortcut menu.

Almost everything you need to do in the String Table editor can be done with the shortcut menu:

○ *Cut*, *Copy* and *Paste*. These are the standard commands and work as you would expect them to.

○ *New String*. First select a record. Then open the shortcut menu and select New String. This inserts a blank record after the selected record. If the next integer value is already taken, the blank keeps moving down the list until it finds an integer value. Then the Properties dialog box opens.

○ *Properties*. This is yet another way into the Properties box. (Other ways to open the Properties box are to double-click the record in the String Table, press Alt-Enter, or select Properties from the Edit menu. You also open a Properties box when you select New String or press Ins. But these are only for new, blank records.)

Grouping String Segments

You may have noticed that strings in the String Table are divided into groups. These groups are called *segments,* and a segment can have up to 16 strings. When they are needed, strings are loaded into memory by segment, rather than individually. You can speed up your application by grouping related strings into the same segment so they will load together.

To move a string, change its value. For instance, if you want to move the string IDS_YOURSTRING into a particular segment, pick a number that falls within that segment—for example, the integer 2,345. Then just enter it in the ID field of the Properties dialog box like so:

```
IDS_YOURSTRING=2345
```

The Binary Editor

The Binary editor can corrupt a resource quite handily. As Microsoft says, "A corrupted resource can cause Visual C++ and Windows NT to behave in unexpected ways." This is a nicely understated way of saying you may be courting disaster. So use the Binary editor sparingly.

The Binary editor is useful for viewing the binary data in a resource or for making minor changes in custom resources or resource types not supported by Visual C++. In fact, if you try to open such a resource type from the Resource Browser window, it will automatically open in the Binary editor (see Figure 2-54).

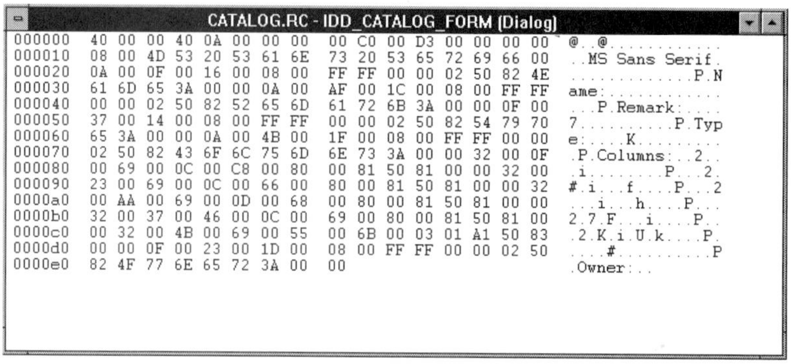

```
□                  CATALOG.RC - IDD_CATALOG_FORM (Dialog)            ▼ ▲
000000   40 00 00 40 0A 00 00 00   00 C0 00 D3 00 00 00 00    @..@...........
000010   08 00 4D 53 20 53 61 6E   73 20 53 65 72 69 66 00    ..MS Sans Serif.
000020   0A 00 0F 00 16 00 08 00   FF FF 00 00 02 50 82 4E    .............P.N
000030   61 6D 65 3A 00 00 0A 00   AF 00 1C 00 08 00 FF FF    ame:...........
000040   00 00 02 50 82 52 65 6D   61 72 6B 3A 00 00 0F 00    ...P.Remark:....
000050   37 00 14 00 08 00 FF FF   00 00 02 50 82 54 79 70    7..........P.Typ
000060   65 3A 00 00 0A 00 4B 00   1F 00 08 00 FF FF 00 00    e:....K.........
000070   02 50 82 43 6F 6C 75 6D   6E 73 3A 00 00 32 00 0F    .P.Columns:..2..
000080   00 69 00 0C 00 C8 00 80   00 81 50 81 00 00 32 00    .i........P...2.
000090   23 00 69 00 0C 00 66 00   80 00 81 50 81 00 00 32    #.i...f....P...2
0000a0   00 AA 00 69 00 0D 00 68   00 80 00 81 50 81 00 00    ...i...h....P...
0000b0   32 00 37 00 46 00 0C 00   69 00 80 00 81 50 81 00    2.7.F...i....P..
0000c0   00 32 00 4B 00 69 00 55   00 6B 00 03 01 A1 50 83    .2.K.i.U.k....P.
0000d0   00 00 0F 00 23 00 1D 00   08 00 FF FF 00 00 02 50    ....#..........P
0000e0   82 4F 77 6E 65 72 3A 00   00                         .Owner:..
```

Figure 2-54: The Binary editor.

Figure 2-54 shows what you get in the Binary editor. The left side shows the data in its hexadecimal format, which is edited one byte at a time. The right side displays the same data in its ASCII format, and is also editable. Any changes are reflected in the other half of the window as they occur. To make changes, just go in and type what you want. You can get quick access to Cut, Copy and Paste by pressing the right mouse button, which produces a pop-up menu. Pressing Ins toggles between insert and overstrike typing, if you have a preference. Use Tab to move between the hexadecimal and ASCII formats.

To create a new resource, take these steps:

1. Go to the File menu. Select New and then select Binary File. This opens the Binary editor.

2. Enter your data and save it as an .RC file.

To incorporate the new resource into a project, do this:

1. Choose the Set Includes command from the Resource menu.

2. When the Set Includes dialog box opens, add the name of this .RC file to the Compile-Time Directives box (it should be a new line with *#include* followed by the name of your file).

To open an existing resource, do this:

1. Open a resource file and select the resource you want to edit.

2. Select the Open Binary Data command from the Resource menu.

Moving On

In this section we took a detailed tour of the powerful tools available to you in the Visual C++ integrated development environment. We saw how to get into an existing resource and how to create a new one, and we explored the editors that are used to build and manipulate the various resources.

In the next section, "A Cookbook Approach to Creating Windows Applications," we'll look at the basics of starting a real-life project using Visual C++. After using AppWizard to create the skeleton code for your base application, we'll look at a series of "recipes" that show you the code you'll need to add to the application skeleton, where it should go, and what it does.

SECTION III

A COOKBOOK APPROACH TO CREATING WINDOWS APPLICATIONS

A COOKBOOK APPROACH TO CREATING WINDOWS APPLICATIONS

Visual C++ is a rich and powerful programming environment that can accomplish a great deal of the routine work of Windows programming automatically, but it is also true that there is a lot to know about the tools it provides. This stems from the fact that it is a confluence of three complex technologies: Windows, C++ and the Microsoft Foundation Classes. Let's take a look for a second at what this means in terms of getting started on a real-life project using Visual C++.

The MFC Cookbook

In the previous section of this book, you got a detailed tour through the landscape of the Visual Workbench tools. Even if you just flipped through the pages devoted to the integrated development environment, it was probably apparent that putting the predictable elements of a Windows program in place is a highly automated procedure. In fact, this tool set is so complete that you can more or less check off the "learn basic Windows programming concepts" item on your to-do list. Much of what occupied C language/SDK Windows programmers is abstracted in the classes of the MFC library, and you may never need to concern yourself with such details as micro-managing printing or putting up a toolbar. You'll find that as you use the tools you absorb a great deal simply by seeing the code the workbench generates for you.

Another thing you'll notice as you begin to use the Visual C++ tools is that you certainly don't have to be a C++ *expert* to make progress. This, again, is because the people who built the development environment and MFC *are* experts, and much of what they know and have done has been placed at your disposal in the class libraries and development tools. You can build your C++ skills as you go, but to start with, if you are a good C programmer you can take a cookbook approach to creating Windows applications with the Microsoft Foundation Classes and get a huge amount of leverage out of them.

This section of the book is meant to provide you with the basic recipes you need to get (well, we have to say it...) cooking on code of your own. The format and concept here is a little bit different than that used in most programming books, and here's why: A typical programming treatise will take a concept and devote a chapter of 20 to 40 pages to an example that illustrates the subject in detail. The disadvantage of this approach with MFC, and Windows in general, is that you may have to read and study a great deal of material you are not interested in to get to the information you want. What we want to accomplish with this recipe format is to make examples much smaller, and more granular. Because so much work is done for you both by AppWizard and the framework, you can get started more quickly by agreeing to take the part provided by Visual C++ on faith and initially learning only about the parts you must supply. As your understanding grows, you can investigate the nuances of the framework more deeply.

How to Use the Cookbook

For beginning MFC programmers, there are two basic questions about how to get a particular thing working. The first is *what* code to write, but the second is *where* does that code belong. By now you'll probably have noticed that if you go through AppWizard's sequence of New Project screens and let it generate code for your base application, what you start with may run to a dozen or more files, each of which contains many functions and/or data structures. Given this starting point, the *where* part of the question can seem overwhelming. Here's how you can use the recipes to get started writing real code of your own, right off the bat.

First, all the recipes will list the sequence of steps used in AppWizard to generate the skeleton code you'll need to begin. Next, they show the code you need to add and where it should go, and they explain what it does. The recipes are grouped by topic. Some of them deal with specific single-step jobs, such as how to create, use and destroy a brush. To create your own applications, generate a skeleton using AppWizard, plug in recipe code for the features you want to implement using MFC, and add application-specific logic of your own where it is needed. Though it doesn't cover every corner of the MFC classes, the collection is complete enough to get you moving toward creating useful, full-featured applications very quickly.

You'll find the code examples from this section of the book, as well as the MFC C++ Library function prototypes included in Section IV, on the *Visual Guide to Visual C++ Companion Disk* at the back of this book.

Creating an SDI Skeleton

Use the following steps to generate the framework code for a single document interface application:

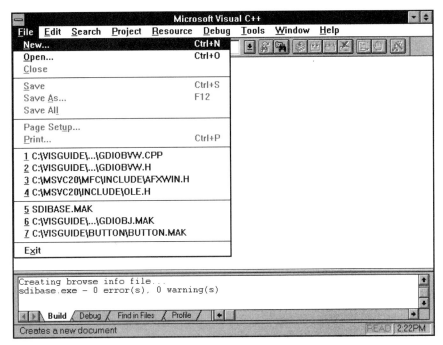

Figure 3-1: From the File menu, choose New.

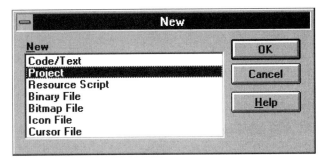

Figure 3-2: Choose Project from the list of new file types.

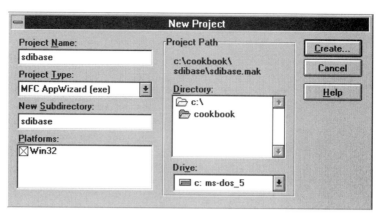

Figure 3-3: Fill in the Project Name edit control, and accept the default Project Type and New Subdirectory choices. Click the Create button.

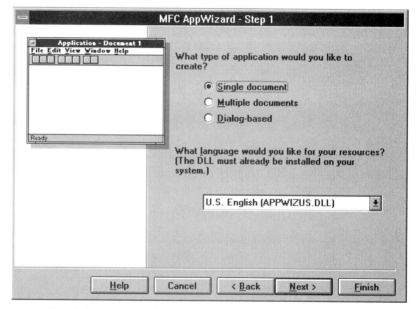

Figure 3-4: Select the Single document application type, and accept the default for language locality. Click the Next button.

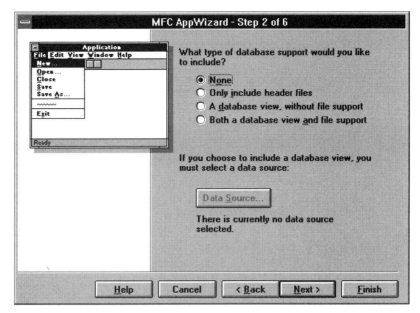

Figure 3-5: Choose None to omit database support from your application skeleton code. (This is the default.) Click the Next button.

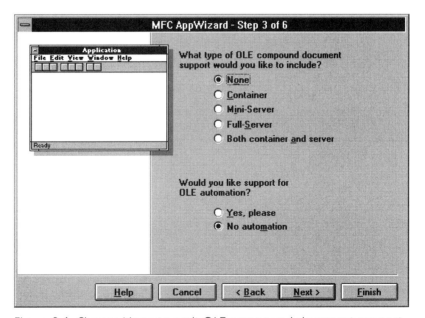

Figure 3-6: Choose None to omit OLE compound document support from your application skeleton code. Choose No automation to omit OLE automation from your application skeleton code. (These are the defaults.) Click the Next button.

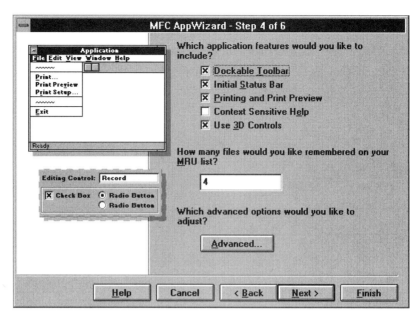

Figure 3-7: Accept the defaults for application features including dockable toolbars, the initial status bar, print preview, 3D controls, and 4 files in the MRU (most recently used) list of the File menu. Skip the advanced options for now, and click the Next button.

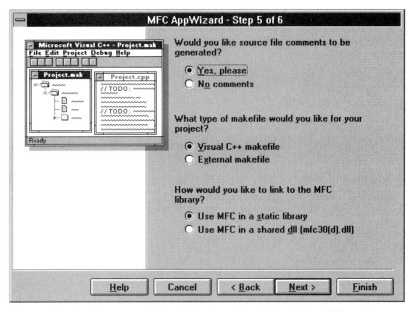

Figure 3-8: Again, accept the defaults, which direct AppWizard to generate comments in the source it writes for you, to create a Visual C++ makefile, and to link to the static version of the MFC libraries. Click the Next button.

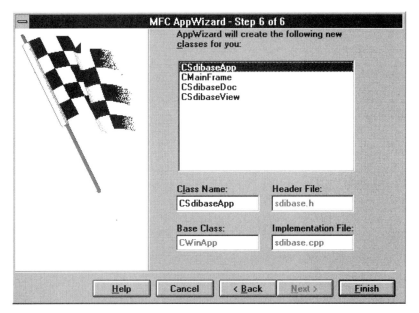

Figure 3-9: This last screen shows you the names of the classes that AppWizard is going to create for you, along with the names of the associated header and implementation files.

If you experiment a bit here by clicking on different class names, you'll notice that the string displayed in the Base Class control is grayed for all of the classes except the one associated with your view. This is because there is only one possible base class provided by the framework for the classes that were derived for you by AppWizard. For the view, however, there are several alternatives. In this case we take the default.

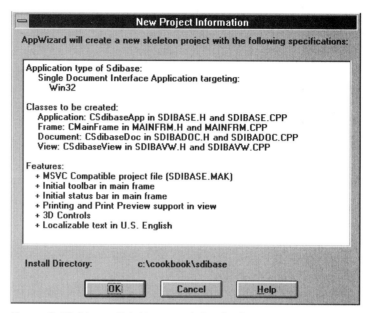

Figure 3-10: Now click Next, and the final screen of the skeleton code generation process will give you complete information about the code that is going to be created for you. Click OK to generate the project files.

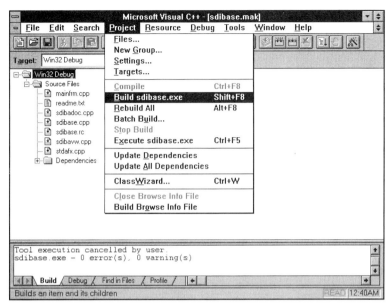

Figure 3-11: You now have an SDI skeleton application that you can compile and examine. Go to the Project menu and select Build sdibase.exe.

Now you can execute the code that you just built by choosing the Execute sdibase.exe item from the Project menu.

When you experiment with the application, notice that most of the things you associate with a Windows application's initial appearance are present and functioning. Menus pull down and highlight selections, the system menu does the usual tasks, such as closing or minimizing the application window, and so on.

All you have to do now is add application-specific features and functionality. Before you go on to do this, however, here is a bit of background on the application you just created. The Single Document Interface application takes its name from a concept at the heart of the MFC application framework: the Document/View architecture. The basic idea is that an application has data, which it stores in a *document*. It displays the data to the world by showing a *view* of the data. An SDI application has only one document active at a time, though it can display one or more views of the document. For example, if the data were polar bear reproductive success statistics, a bar chart view could show live births by region and a line graph view could show live births versus maternal age. The two views receive data from the document, but neither of the views necessarily knows how the data are really stored in the document.

The key thing about an SDI application is that there can be no more than one document object supplying data to the views at a time. It is possible to use more than one document in an SDI application, and even more than one type of document by alternating between them. In general, though, if you plan to use more than one source of data, start out with an MDI skeleton.

Creating an MDI Skeleton

Use the following steps to generate the framework code for a multiple document interface application:

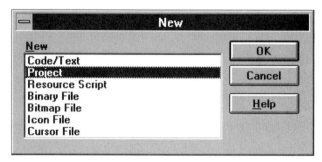

Figure 3-12: From the File menu, choose New, Project.

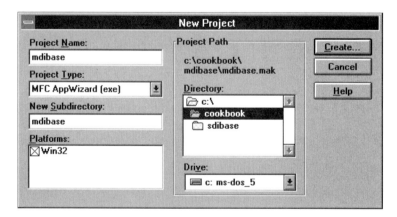

Figure 3-13: Fill in the Project Name edit control, and accept the default Project Type and New Subdirectory choices. Click the Create button.

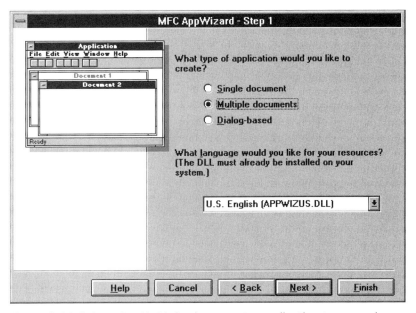

Figure 3-14: Select the Multiple documents application type, and accept the default for language locality. Click the Next button.

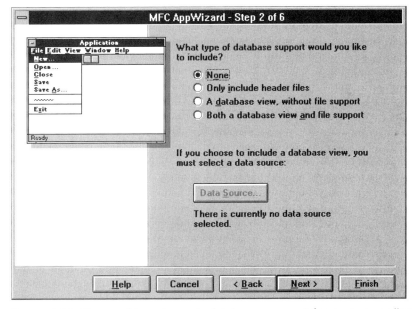

Figure 3-15: Choose None to omit database support from your application skeleton code. (This is the default.) Click the Next button.

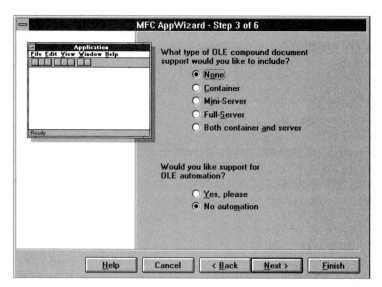

Figure 3-16: Choose None to omit OLE compound document support from your application skeleton code. Choose No automation to omit OLE automation from your application skeleton code. (These are the defaults.) Click the Next button.

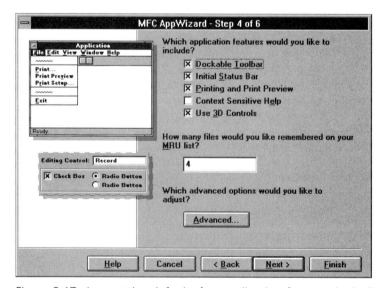

Figure 3-17: Accept the defaults for application features including dockable toolbars, the initial status bar, print preview, 3D controls, and 4 files in the MRU (most recently used) list of the File menu. Skip the advanced options for now, and click the Next button.

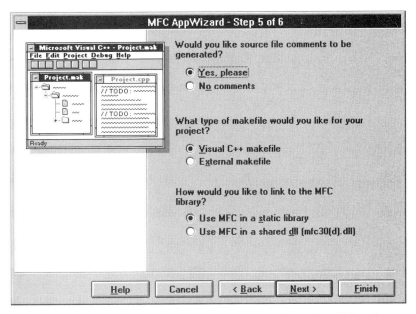

Figure 3-18: Again, accept the defaults, which direct AppWizard to generate comments in the source it writes for you, to create a Visual C++ makefile, and to link to the static version of the MFC libraries. Click the Next button.

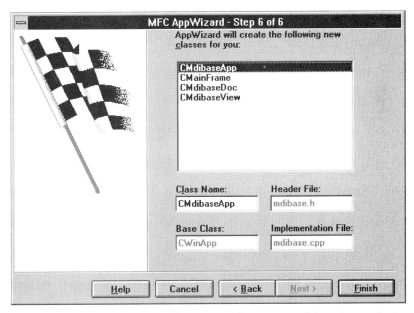

Figure 3-19: This last screen shows you the names of the classes that AppWizard is going to create for you, along with the names of the associated header and implementation files.

If you experiment a bit here by clicking on different class names, you'll notice that the string displayed in the Base Class control is grayed for all of the classes except the one associated with your view. This is because there is only one possible base class provided by the framework for the classes that were derived for you by AppWizard. For the view, however, there are several alternatives. In this case we take the default, but we will use the edit and form views in other recipes.

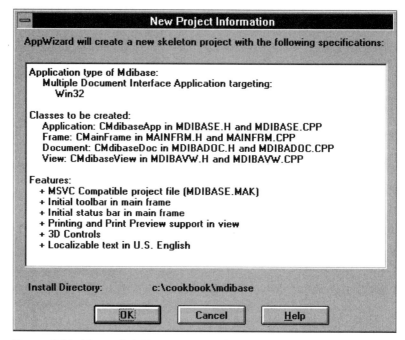

Figure 3-20: Now click Next, and the final screen of the skeleton code generation process will give you complete information about the code that is going to be created for you. Click OK to generate the project files.

You now have an MDI skeleton that you can compile and examine. Go to the Project menu and select the Build mdibase.exe item.

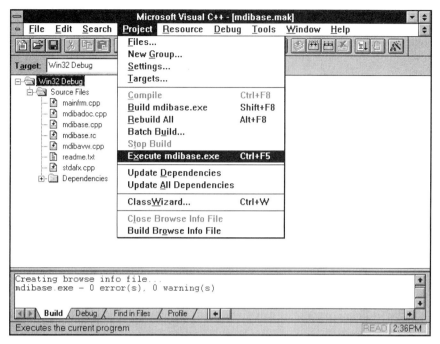

Figure 3-21: Now execute the code that you just built by choosing the Execute item from the Project menu.

Experiment with the application, and notice that most of the things you associate with a Windows application's initial appearance are present and functioning. Menus pull down and highlight selections, the system menu does the usual tasks, such as closing or minimizing the application window, and so on. If you tried building the basic SDI skeleton code, you'll notice that the MDI window has an additional item on the menu bar: the Window item.

Because the MDI application expects that it will have to handle more than one source of data at a time, its default functionality provides management of multiple view windows in the client area of the main frame window. Using the Window menu you can open and close views, make them iconic, and cascade and tile them.

All you have to do now is add application-specific features and functionality. Before you go on to do this, however, here is a bit of background on the application you just created. The Multiple Document Interface application takes its name from a concept at the heart of the MFC application framework: the Document/View architecture. The basic idea is that an application has data, which it stores in a *document*. It displays the data to the world by showing a *view* of the data. An MDI application may have one *or more* documents active at a time, and it can display one or more views of each document. For example, it could incorporate weather data in one document, projected crop yields data in another, and the output of a model that predicts commodity futures prices in a third. Each of the documents' data is displayed in its own view window.

The key thing about an MDI application is that an application can use multiple sources of data simultaneously, and the framework will manage the child windows that contain the views for you by tiling, cascading, resizing and so on. It is possible to have more than one view connected to each of the documents, just as in an SDI application. The MDI application structure is more complex than that of the SDI, so if you don't require more than one source of data at a time, use SDI.

Drawing in the Client Area

There are exceptions, but applications almost always do their drawing operations in the **OnDraw** member function of their application's view class. The implementation of this member looks like this in our **sdibase** view class, and is contained in the file sdibavw.cpp. The italic comments have been added.

```
//CSdibaseView drawing
void CSdibaseView::OnDraw(CDC* pDC)
//At the time we enter this function, all the preliminary
//housekeeping necessary to drawing has been done. We are
//passed a pointer to a device context ( pDC ), and we can use
//it to access all of the functions of the CDC class. Numbering
//over 100, these handle most aspects of creating graphics.
{
    CSdibaseDoc* pDoc = GetDocument();
    //This gets a pointer to our application's one and only
    //document. The document contains an application's data.
    //Note that in addition to data such as stock prices or
    //employee lists, we could also be talking about information
    //that we gathered at runtime which in some way records our
    //application's state.
    ASSERT_VALID(pDoc);
    //Here we are checking to see if the pointer to the
    //document is valid
    //TODO: add draw code for native data here
    //AppWizard leaves these clues behind when it generates
    //skeleton code to tell us where to add our own code. To draw
    //in the client area, we add code here.
}
```

Graphic Output: Lines, Rectangles, Polygons, Ellipses

Start by creating an SDI skeleton, as described in the basic recipes. Windows has set the default characteristics of the the drawing environment before it calls the **OnDraw** member of our view class. Unless we change them by using the coordinate mapping functions (see the "Coordinate Systems & Mapping" section for information on how to do this), x coordinates increase to the right, and y coordinates increase going down. The boundaries in both the x and y directions will depend on the resolution of the display. If you draw beyond the edge of the coordinate system, it won't cause an error, but the part of the drawing that extends beyond the boundaries won't be visible. Here we use these defaults.

The width and style of a line drawn in the client area depends on the pen that is selected in the DC when drawing is performed. By default, it is black, a single pixel wide, and draws a solid line. If you are drawing a closed figure, the color and pattern that fill its interior depend on the selected brush. By default, the brush is solid white. To see how to change either the brush or pen, see the "Pens & Brushes" section later.

Where to Add Code: The application's view class, in the **OnDraw** member function.

Files to Modify: sdibavw.cpp

```
/////////////////////////////////////////////////////////
//CSdibaseView drawing
    void CSdibaseView::OnDraw(CDC* pDC)
{
    CSdibaseDoc* pDoc = GetDocument();
    ASSERT_VALID(pDoc);
    //TODO: add draw code for native data here
    //Draw a line, using the default pen and coordinate
    //system mapping
    //MoveTo sets the initial position of the pen.
pDC->MoveTo ( 50, 50 );
    //LineTo Draws the line and updates the position of the pen.
pDC->LineTo ( 100, 50 );
    //Subsequent lines are drawn using the last point of the
 previous line as a starting point
pDC->LineTo ( 100, 100 );
pDC->LineTo ( 50, 50);
    }
```

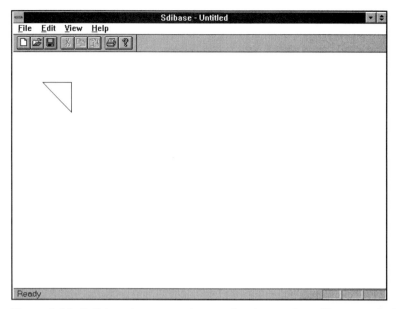

Figure 3-22: Build and execute the application and you'll see a window that looks something like this.

Any basic figure encapsulated in the **CDC** class can be drawn in the client area this way. Following are some further examples.

Rectangle

```
void CSdibaseView::OnDraw(CDC* pDC)
{
CSdibaseDoc* pDoc = GetDocument();
ASSERT_VALID(pDoc);
    //TODO: add draw code for native data here
    //Draw a rectangle, using the default pen for its outline,
    //the default brush to fill it's interior, and default
    //coordinate system mapping
    //The parameters give the x y coordinates of the upper left
    //and lower right corners
pDC->Rectangle(50, 50, 350, 350 );
    }
```

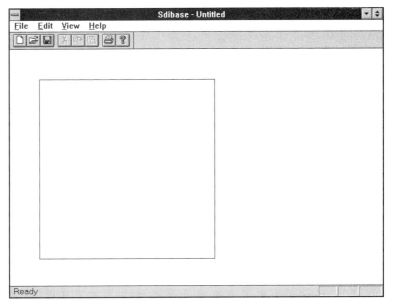

Figure 3-23: A rectangle.

Ellipse

```
void CSdibaseView::OnDraw(CDC* pDC)
{
CSdibaseDoc* pDoc = GetDocument();
ASSERT_VALID(pDoc);
    //TODO: add draw code for native data here
    //Draw an ellipse, using the default pen for its outline,
    //the default brush to fill it's interior, and default
    //coordinate system mapping
    //The parameters give the x y coordinates of the upper left
    //and lower right corners of its bounding rectangle
pDC->Ellipse(50, 50, 350, 350 );
    }
```

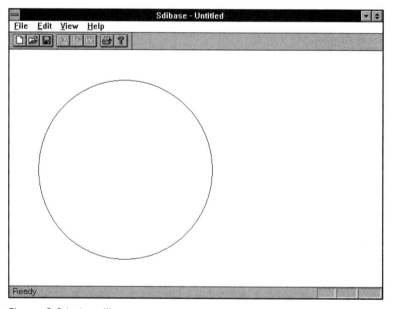

Figure 3-24: An ellipse.

Rectangle With Rounded Corners

```
void CSdibaseView::OnDraw(CDC* pDC)
{
CSdibaseDoc* pDoc = GetDocument();
ASSERT_VALID(pDoc);
    //TODO: add draw code for native data here
    //Draw a rectangle with rounded corners
    //using the default pen for its outline,
    //the default brush to fill its interior, and default
    //coordinate system mapping
    //The parameters give the x y coordinates of the upper left
    //and lower right corners, and the height and width of
    //the ellipse used to round its corners
    pDC->RoundRect(50, 50, 350, 350, 100, 100 );
    }
```

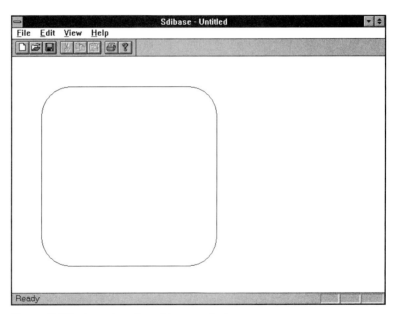

Figure 3-25: A rectangle with rounded corners.

Arc

```
void CSdibaseView::OnDraw(CDC* pDC)
{
CSdibaseDoc* pDoc = GetDocument();
ASSERT_VALID(pDoc);
    //TODO: add draw code for native data here
    //Draw an arc using the default pen for its outline,
    //and default coordinate system mapping
    //The parameters give the x y coordinates of the upper left
    //and lower right corners of a bounding rectangle
    //and the start and end points of the arc
    pDC->Arc(50, 50, 350, 350, 50, 350,350, 350 );
    }
```

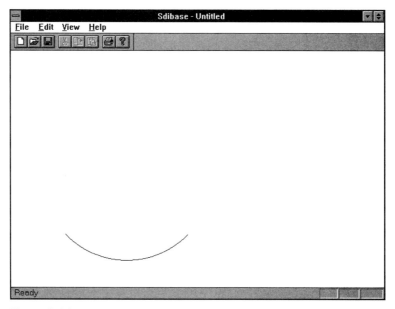

Figure 3-26: An arc.

Chord

```
void CSdibaseView::OnDraw(CDC* pDC)
{
CSdibaseDoc* pDoc = GetDocument();
ASSERT_VALID(pDoc);
    //TODO: add draw code for native data here
    //Draw a chord using the default pen for its outline,
    //and default coordinate system mapping
    //A chord is an arc that it is closed with a line
    //connecting its endpoints
    //The parameters give the x y coordinates of the upper left
    //and lower right corners of a bounding rectangle
    //and the start and end points of the arc
    pDC->Chord(50, 50, 350, 350, 50, 350,350, 350);
}
```

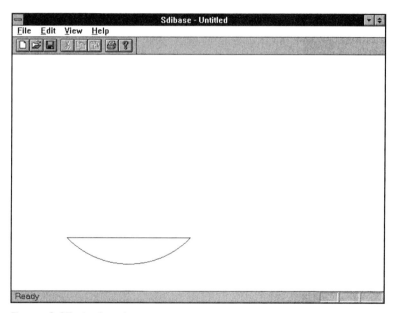

Figure 3-27: A chord.

Polygon

```
void CSdibaseView::OnDraw(CDC* pDC)
{
CSdibaseDoc* pDoc = GetDocument();
ASSERT_VALID(pDoc);
    //TODO: add draw code for native data here
    //Draw a closed figure using the default pen for its outline,
    //the default brush to paint its interior,
    //and default coordinate system mapping
    //Declare and initialize an array to store the coordinates of
    //vertices of the polygon. Notice that the start and end points
    //of the the vertex list are not equal. The Polygon function will
    //detect this and close the figure for you automatically
POINT ptPoly[4] = { 50, 50, 200, 50, 200, 200, 50, 200 };
    //The Polygon function takes a pointer to an array of vertex
    //points and a count of the vertices as parameters.
pDC->Polygon( (LPPOINT)&ptPoly, 4 );
}
```

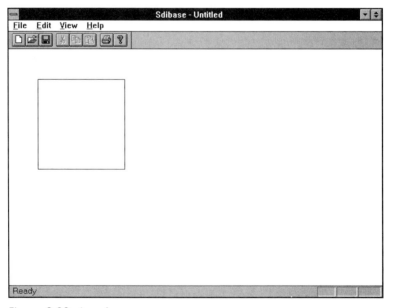

Figure 3-28: A polygon.

PolyPolygon

```
void CSdibaseView::OnDraw(CDC* pDC)
{
CSdibaseDoc* pDoc = GetDocument();
ASSERT_VALID(pDoc);
    //TODO: add draw code for native data here
    //Draw a series of closed figures using the default pen for its
    //outline, the default brush to paint its interior,
    //and default coordinate system mapping
    //The figures don't necessarily have to be the same shape or
    //have the same number of vertices
    //Declare and initialize an array to store the coordinates of
    //vertices of the polygon. Notice that the start and end points
    //of the the vertex list are equal. The PolyPolygon function
    //requires each polygon to be explicitly closed in this way
POINT ptPolyPoly[10] =
    { 50, 50, 200, 50, 200, 200, 50, 200, 50, 50,
     150, 150, 300, 150, 300, 300, 150, 300, 150, 150};
    //This array stores the vertex count for each individual polygon
int nPolyVertex[2] = { 5, 5 };
    //The PolyPolygon function takes a pointer to an array of vertex
    //points an array containing the count of the vertices for each
    //polygon, and a count of the entries in the nPolyVertexArray.
pDC->PolyPolygon( pptPolyPoly, ptnPolyVertex, 2 );
}
```

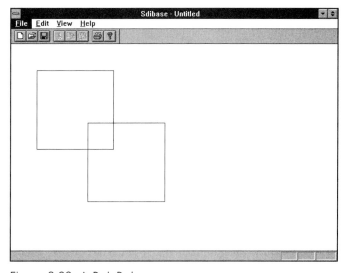

Figure 3-29: A PolyPolygon.

Adding & Initializing View Class Data Members

The examples of the native drawing functions all use hard coded data to draw the figures, which in actual practice would not be useful very often. Using the "Rectangle" example, we'll add member variables to our View class and use them to draw the figure.

Where to Add Code: The application's view class, in the header file and the **CSdibaseView::CSdibaseView** view class constructor function.

Files to Modify: sdibavw.cpp, sdibavw.h

We add several public data members to the file sdibavw.h. The Rectangle function will accept either a pointer to a **CRect** object, or two pairs of integer coordinates that specify the upper left and lower right corners of the rectangle. Note that we have data items, but they are not initialized yet.

```
//sdibavw.h : interface of the CSdibaseView class
//
//////////////////////////////////////////////////////////
    class CSdibaseView : public CView
{
//We add the lines in bold italics
public:
    CRect rectData;
    int ULeft, XULeftY, LRightX, LRightY;
    protected: //create from serialization only
    CSdibaseView();
    DECLARE_DYNCREATE(CSdibaseView)
    //Attributes
public:
    CSdibaseDoc* GetDocument();
    //Operations
public:
    //Overrides
    //ClassWizard generate virtual function overrides
    //{{AFX_VIRTUAL(CSdibaseView)
    public:
    virtual void OnDraw(CDC* pDC);
```

```
    //overridden to draw this view
    protected:
    virtual BOOL OnPreparePrinting(CPrintInfo* pInfo);
    virtual void OnBeginPrinting(CDC* pDC, CPrintInfo* pInfo);
    virtual void OnEndPrinting(CDC* pDC, CPrintInfo* pInfo);
    //}}AFX_VIRTUAL
    //Implementation
public:
    virtual ~CSdibaseView();
#ifdef _DEBUG
    virtual void AssertValid() const;
    virtual void Dump(CDumpContext& dc) const;
#endif
    protected:
    //Generated message map functions
protected:
    //{{AFX_MSG(CSdibaseView)
    afx_msg void OnLButtonDown(UINT nFlags, CPoint point);
    //}}AFX_MSG
    DECLARE_MESSAGE_MAP()
};
    #ifndef _DEBUG //debug version in sdibavw.cpp
inline CSdibaseDoc* CSdibaseView::GetDocument()
 { return (CSdibaseDoc*)m_pDocument; }
    #endif
////////////////////////////////////////////////////////////////
```

Now we want to give the data initial values. We do this in the view's constructor, **CSdibaseView::CSdibaseView**, which is in the file sdibavw.cpp. Here are two different ways to perform the initialazation. To initialize a data member, use one or the other of the methods, but not both.

```
/////////////////////////////////////////////////////
//CSdibaseView construction/destruction
    CSdibaseView::CSdibaseView() : rectData( 50, 50, 275, 275 )
    //You can initialize a class data member
    //in this way
{
    //TODO: add construction code here
    //You can also explicitly initialize data members in the class
    //constructor
m_nULeftX = 250;
m_nULeftY = 250;
m_nLRightX = 475;
m_nLRightY = 475;
    }
```

If you build and execute this example, you'll get a window more or less like the one below. Notice that where the rectangles overlap, the second one overdraws the lower right corner of the first. This is because rectangles, like the other closed figures you can draw with the class libraries, are filled with the current brush. The default white brush is opaque, so it obscures some of the first rectangle that was drawn when it fills the second rectangle.

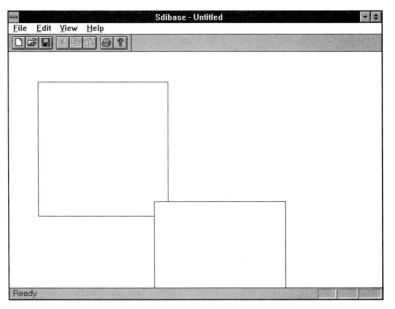

Figure 3-30: The default brush is opaque white, so it obscures the previously drawn rectangle.

Next Steps

To see how to draw and paint in color, refer to the examples in the "Pens & Brushes" section and the "Color" section.

To see examples of how to change the units, the scale of the coordinate system, or orientation of coordinate system axes, see the "Coordinate Systems & Mapping" section.

To see how to cue redrawing of your view, see the "Capturing Mouse Input" section.

Pens & Brushes

Pens and brushes are used to draw in Windows applications. Pens may draw thin or thick lines of various styles (solid, dashed and dotted, for example), but they are always used to create the outline of a figure. Brushes are used to fill an area of the screen with a color or pattern.

Before we actually try creating custom pens and brushes, we need a little bit of background on the *Device Context*. Device Contexts keep track of two kinds of things: GDI objects and drawing attributes. GDI objects are items such as pens, brushes, fonts and bitmaps. GDI objects currently in use are said to be selected into the DC. If you want to use a different pen or brush, you must interact with the DC to make it available to your application. Here are the steps.

Start by creating an SDI skeleton, as described in the basic recipes. Then you must either create a new drawing object or retrieve a stock object. Next, you have to select the new object into the DC, saving the returned handle to the old object. After you are finished using your custom object, it must be selected out of the DC and replaced with the original object. If the object you used was a stock object, then your work is done at this point. Otherwise, if you created the object, you must destroy it *after it is no longer selected in the DC*. This last step is critical. Never attempt to destroy an object that is selected in the DC.

When you enter the **OnDraw** function of your view class, you receive a pointer to it as a parameter to add code to the **OnDraw** member of your application's view class, you already have access to a DC equipped with the standard items: a black pen and an opaque white brush, among other things.

Where to Add Code: The application's view class, **OnDraw** member function.

Files to Modify: sdibavw.cpp

Creating & Using Pens

Windows has two kinds of pens. Stock pens are available for the asking and custom pens are created based on a definition supplied by the programmer. First we will get a stock pen, select it into the DC, draw a line with it, and repace the pen originally selected in the DC.

Creating a Custom Pen to Draw a Dashed Line:

```
//CSdibaseView drawing
    void CSdibaseView::OnDraw(CDC* pDC)
{
    CSdibaseDoc* pDoc = GetDocument();
    ASSERT_VALID(pDoc);
    //TODO: add draw code for native data here
    //First we create a CPen object. The CPen constructor
    //takes three parameters. The first is the pen style. To take
    //advantage of styles other than solid, the second argument,
    //pen width, must be 1. The last argument gives the color of
the
    //pen. In this example the color is black, the COLORREF value
    //for black being 0
CPen penBlackDash( PS_DASH, 1, (COLORREF) 0);
    //We select our new pen into the DC, saving the handle
    //of the currently selected pen
CPen *ppenDefault = pDC->SelectObject( & penBlackDash );

    //We use the pen to draw a triangle
pDC->MoveTo ( 50, 50 );
pDC->LineTo ( 300, 50 );
pDC->LineTo ( 300, 300 );
pDC->LineTo ( 50, 50);
    //When we are finished, we select the original pen back into
    //the DC. Notice that we don't bother capturing the handle of
    //our custom pen.
pDC->SelectObject(ppenDefault );
    //penBlackDash is automatically destroyed when this
    //function terminates
}
```

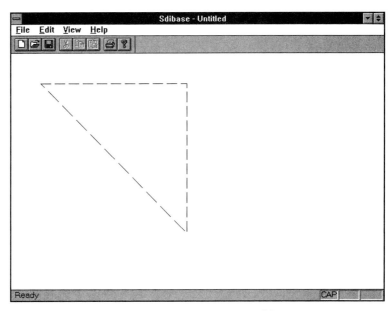

Figure 3-31: A custom pen to draw a dashed line.

Creating a Custom Pen to Draw a Thick Line:

```
//CSdibaseView drawing
    void CSdibaseView::OnDraw(CDC* pDC)
{
    CSdibaseDoc* pDoc = GetDocument();
    ASSERT_VALID(pDoc);
    //TODO: add draw code for native data here
    //First we create a CPen object. The CPen constructor
    //sets the first parameter, pen style, to PS_SOL:ID
    //if the second argument, pen width, is greater than 1. Here we
    //specify the PS_SOLID style, but any other style would give
    //the same result because of the value we pass for width. The
    //last argument gives the color of the pen. In this example the
    //color  is black, the COLORREF value for black being 0
CPen penWideBlack( PS_SOLID, 15, (COLORREF) 0);
    //We select our new pen into the DC, saving the handle
    //of the currently selected pen
CPen *ppenDefault = pDC->SelectObject( & penWideBlack );
```

123

```
//We use the pen to draw a triangle
pDC->MoveTo ( 50, 50 );
pDC->LineTo ( 300, 50 );
pDC->LineTo ( 300, 300 );
pDC->LineTo ( 50, 50);
    //When we are finished, we select the original pen back
    //into the DC
    //Notice that we don't bother capturing the handle of our
    //custom pen.
pDC->SelectObject(ppenDefault );
    //penWideBlack is automatically destroyed when this
    //function terminates
}
```

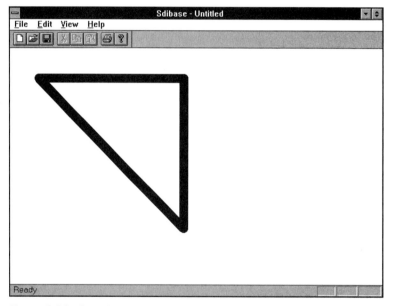

Figure 3-32: Creating a custom pen to draw a thick line.

Using the Stock Pens: Windows has a set of stock pen that you can acess simply by using the **CDC::SelectStockObject** member function. **SelectStockObject** is a function that is used to select standard, pre-existing pens and brushes into the DC. It is by far the easiest and most surefire way to select a pen, but it provides only three pens: black, white and null solid pens, 1 pixel wide.

To see how the stock pens look, we need to jump ahead a bit and use a stock brush to paint the interior of a rectangle black. See the next section for more on using brushes.

```
//CSdibaseView drawing
void CSdibaseView::OnDraw(CDC* pDC)
{
    CSdibaseDoc* pDoc = GetDocument();
    ASSERT_VALID(pDoc);
    //TODO: add draw code for native data here
    //First select the stock black pen and draw a rectangle
pDC->SelectStockObject( BLACK_PEN );
    //The default white brush will be used to fill the rectangle
pDC->Rectangle ( 10,10, 375,375 );
    //Next we select a stock brush to fill another rectangle
pDC->SelectStockObject( BLACK_BRUSH );
//The new brush will be used to fill the rectangle
pDC->Rectangle ( 50,50, 275,275 );
    //Now select the white pen and draw a diagonal line
 pDC->SelectStockObject(WHITE_PEN);
pDC->MoveTo( 50,50);
pDC->LineTo( 275, 275 );
    //Select the null pen and draw another diagonal line
    //Notice that the pen has no visible effect—the line does not
    //appear in either rectangle
 pDC->SelectStockObject(NULL_PEN);
pDC->MoveTo( 375,10);
pDC->LineTo( 100, 375 );
    }
```

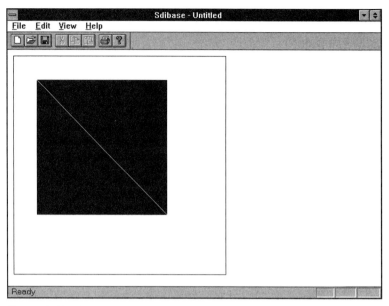

Figure 3-33: The stock pens.

Creating & Using Brushes

Creating and using a brush is similar in most respects to using a pen. Brushes have color and style attributes associated with them, and there is a set of stock brushes that can be selected using the **SelectStockObject** function. The stock brushes are more varied and useful than the stock pens.

Brushes are actually small bitmaps that are combined with the image on the screen and the current background brush for a given window. The exact way the bits of the three are combined is set by the Raster Operation Code (ROP code). By default, the brush paints an opaque layer over the area to which it is applied. (For more on ROP codes, see the "Using ROP Codes" section.)

Brushes can be solid, use pre-established patterns, or you can supply a bitmap for the brush pattern.

Where to Add Code: The application's view class, **OnDraw** member function.

Files to Modify: sdibavw.cpp

Using Stock Brushes:

```
//CSdibaseView drawing
    void CSdibaseView::OnDraw(CDC* pDC)
{

    CSdibaseDoc* pDoc = GetDocument();
    ASSERT_VALID(pDoc);
    //TODO: add draw code for native data here
    //All we have to do is select a stock brush into the
    //DC

    pDC->SelectStockObject( BLACK_BRUSH );
//The new brush will be used to fill the rectangle
    pDC->Rectangle ( 10,10, 75,75 );
    pDC->SelectStockObject( DKGRAY_BRUSH );
//The new brush will be used to fill the rectangle
    pDC->Rectangle ( 60,60, 125,125);
    pDC->SelectStockObject( GRAY_BRUSH );
//The new brush will be used to fill the rectangle
    pDC->Rectangle ( 115,115, 180,180 );
    pDC->SelectStockObject( HOLLOW_BRUSH );
//The new brush will be used to fill the rectangle. Notice that it
//doesn't obscure the rectangles it is painting over
    pDC->Rectangle ( 165, 165, 250,250 );
    pDC->SelectStockObject( LTGRAY_BRUSH );
//The new brush will be used to fill the rectangle
    pDC->Rectangle ( 15,15, 10,380 );
    pDC->SelectStockObject( NULL_BRUSH );
//The new brush will be used to fill the rectangle. Notice that it
//doesn't obscure the rectangles it is painting over
    pDC->Rectangle ( 0, 0, 25,125);
    }
```

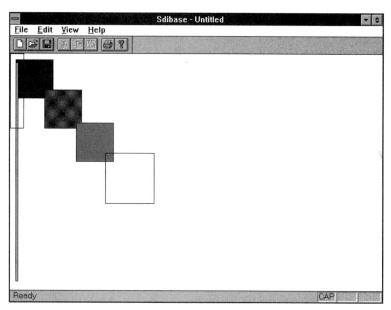

Figure 3-34: Stock brushes.

Creating Custom Brushes: You can create brushes in colors and patterns using the **CBrush** member functions.

```
//CSdibaseView drawing
    void CSdibaseView::OnDraw(CDC* pDC)
{
    CSdibaseDoc* pDoc = GetDocument();
    ASSERT_VALID(pDoc);
    //TODO: add draw code for native data here
    //the color of the brush
CBrush brushSolidRed( RGB( 255,0,0) );
    //We select the brush into the
    //DC, saving the handle of the previous brush
    //We need to cast the return to the appropriate type or
    //a compilation error results

CBrush* pbrushDefault = (CBrush* ) pDC->SelectObject(
&brushSolidRed );
    //The new brush will be used to fill the rectangle
pDC->Rectangle ( 10,10, 75,75 );
    //Now we create a green hatched brush
CBrush brushHatchedGreen( HS_CROSS, RGB( 0, 255,0) );
    //We select the brush into the DC,
```

```
pDC->SelectObject( &brushHatchedGreen);
    //The green hatched brush will be used to fill the rectangle
pDC->Rectangle ( 80,80, 175, 175 );
    //Now we replace the original brush
pDC->SelectObject( pbrushDefault );
    //The custom brushes were created on the stack, so they are
    //destroyed automatically when they go out of scope
}
```

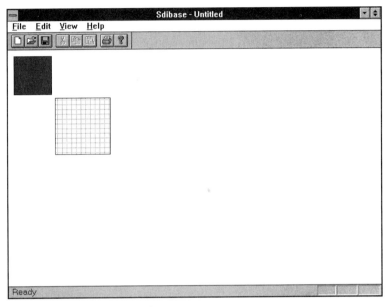

Figure 3-35: Custom brushes.

Color

One of the most important achievements of Windows, dating back to its earliest versions, is the fact that it largely eliminated the need for an application to explicitly support display hardware. One of the trickiest aspects of dealing with device dependencies is the way in which color is handled. There are numerous schemes for organizing color information in display memory, but in the Windows environment, you don't necessarily need to know the details. It can be astonishingly simple to write an application that uses color freely, provided you observe a few basic caveats.

In Windows, we specify colors using the COLORREF data type. To create a COLORREF, we use the RGB macro. RGB takes 3 arguments of 8 bits each for the red, green and blue components of a given color, and combines them into a single 24 bit color value. A color component value of 0 means to add none of that color to the mixture, and a value of 255 means to add the full intensity of that component to the final color. This means that RGB(0,0,0) gives a display color of black on all display devices, and RGB(255,255,255) gives a display color of white on all display devices. You can retrieve the red, green and blue components of a COLORREF using the SDK functions **::GetRValue**, **::GetGValue** and **::GetBValue**.

Keep in mind that the world of the desktop computer ranges from machines that can display 16 colors to those that can display 16 million colors. When you request a brush or pen of a particular color, Windows has an elaborate strategy for trying to provide your application with a color as near as possible to what you specify in the COLORREF. If you request a color that the device is capable of displaying, known as a *pure color*, then the pen or brush Windows creates for you'll match your COLORREF exactly. If not, then color matching depends on whether you are creating a pen or a brush.

If Windows can't match a COLORREF for a pen exactly, then it can create a pen of the nearest pure color available. If a COLORREF for a brush can't be matched exactly, then Windows may create a *dithered* brush to simulate the COLORREF as closely as possible. Dithering involves using patterns composed of pixels of different pure colors to simulate a mixture of them. (This is the method used to color newspaper images, and the individual dots are often large enough to be visible to the naked eye.)

The discussion in the preceding paragraph may sound a little tentative, and there is a reason for this. In an environment where color-intensive applications are competing for control of the number and kind of colors that will be displayed, a great deal of influence can be exerted on color matching by an application. It may direct that actual display colors be mapped to COLORREFs in a particular fashion by using *palettes*. If color precision matters a lot to your application, you'll need to look into using the **CPalette** member functions to construct and manage a color palette for your application. In most cases, it is a safe bet to leave the mapping of system colors to COLORREFs in the care of Windows.

Where to Add Code: The application's view class, **OnDraw** member function.

Files to Modify: sdibavw.cpp

Defining & Using Custom Color Brushes

```
//////////////////////////////////////////////////////
//CSdibaseView drawing
    void CSdibaseView::OnDraw(CDC* pDC)
{

    CSdibaseDoc* pDoc = GetDocument();
    ASSERT_VALID(pDoc);
    //TODO: add draw code for native data here
    //First we create a solid red brush. The RGB
    //macro takes red, green, and blue color components
    //All color monitors can display pure red,
    //so this request will be satisfied with an exact match
    //on a color screen
CBrush brushSolidRed( RGB( 255,0,0) );
    //We select the brush into the
    //DC, saving the handle of the previous brush

CBrush* pbrushDefault = (CBrush* ) pDC->SelectObject(
&brushSolidRed );
    //The new brush will be used to fill the rectangle
pDC->Rectangle ( 0,0, 175,475 );
    //Now ask to create a brush that a 16 color
    //monitor cannot display as a pure color
CBrush brushNearBlack( RGB( 5, 5, 5) );
    //We select the brush into the DC,
pDC->SelectObject( &brushNearBlack);
    //The rectangle is filled the nearest dithered color
    //the 16 color monitor could render
pDC->Rectangle ( 175,0, 375, 375 );
    //Now we replace the original brush
 pDC->SelectObject( pbrushDefault );
    //The custom brushes were created on the stack, so they are
    //destroyed automatically when they go out of scope
}
```

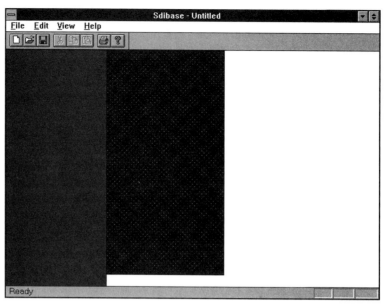

Figure 3-36: Custom color brushes.

Coordinate Systems & Mapping

Of all the aspects of drawing in the client area, the topic of coordinate systems is easily the one most likely to engender confusion. The probable cause of this is that coordinate system mapping is 100 percent visual. It's hard to describe in words, but pictures make it abundantly clear, so this is actually one topic that benefits from less rather than more explanation. The rules are few, absolute, and easy to remember. We will be taking the visual approach to demonstrating them.

*Rule 1: There are two coordinate systems: the **logical** one and the **physical** one.*

The logical coordinate system is the one your application defines to match its drawing requirements. It can be up to 32k in the x and y directions. Coordinates can be negative, but they must be whole numbers. *Graphic output operations use logical coordinates.*

The physical coordinate system is the one that overlays the presentation surface, that is, the one that corresponds to the screen of a monitor or a piece of paper on the printer. For a monitor, one pixel equals one physical unit, and for a printer, one dot equals one physical unit. There are no negative units, no fractional units, and the overall size of the physical coordinate system depends on the resolution of the device. *Mouse position is always reported to the application in physical units.*

*Rule 2: You can send output to only the part of the physical coordinate system that is inside the application's **viewport**. You can display only the part of the logical coordinate system that is inside the application's **logical window**.*

An application defines the part of the screen real estate that can be used for graphic output by setting the size and location of the viewport. In other words, a viewport encloses drawing on the screen or printed page. By default, the viewport exposes the entire client area.

The logical window is a boundary in the abstract coordinate system that has dimensions and units assigned by the application. It defines the part of the logical coordinate space that is available for display on the screen or printer. In other words, anything drawn in the logical window is visible in the viewport

Notice that we called this the *logical window*. Unfortunately, the word *window* is a somewhat overladen noun in the Windows environment. When we are talking about coordinate systems, the terms *window* and *logical window* refer only to the part of our drawing that we are going to allow to be displayed in the viewport. *Window* in this case does not mean the application's frame window.

Rule 3: The logical coordinate system is mapped onto the physical coordinate system by aligning origins of the two systems, setting the extent of x and y axes, and defining the direction of increase for the x and y axes.

By default, the physical and logical coordinate systems are expressly set to be equal in x and y extent, to have an origin at the upper left-hand corner, and to have x axes that increase to the right and y axes that increase in the downward direction. This mirrors the "coordinate system" of a page of text.

In many cases, the size and number of units we need in the logical coordinate sytem does not equal the size and number of units in the physical coordinate system. If this is the case, we can use **CDC** member functions to define our own x and y dimensions, called *extents*, for the logical window. We can also set the logical window origin to be anywhere within the limits of the logical coordinate space. A key thing to note here is that there is no second guessing or sanity checking done for you when you set the coordinate system parameters. If the origin and extents of a window are set to exclude a region, anything drawn there won't appear on the viewport. Put another way, drawing outside the logical window does not produce any runtime errors, but the drawing isn't visible until the logical window is adjusted to allow excluded areas to display in the viewport.

Rule 4: To change the direction of increase of an axis, make the sign of the window extent opposite the sign of the viewport extent.

Making the x and y axes increase in the direction you wish is by far the most confusing aspect of customizing the coordinate systems. This is probably because there is no SetWindowAxis function. The orientation of the axes is determined by the values used to set the window and viewport extents. There are two basic facts you need to keep in mind to completely understand the way the orientation of an axis is set.

Fact 1: The viewport x axis increases as you go right, and the viewport y axis increases as you go down. By default, the axes of the logical coordinate system do the same.

Fact 2: To reverse the direction of increase of an axis, you set a negative value for its window extent and a positive value for its viewport extent. For example, if you want to draw an x-y plot of some data, you set a negative value for the window extent of the y axis so it will increase going upward since this is how we expect x=y graphs to look. To draw a map using latitude and longitude coordinates from North America, you set a negative value for the window extents of the x and y axes so y will increase going upward, like northern latitude values, and x will increase going left, like western longitude values.

Rule 5: The mapping mode defines the units of measure in the logical coordinate system.

When you set a mapping mode, you define whether x and y units are of equal size, whether the units closely approximate some commonly used real world units of measure, and in the case of the MM_TEXT, MM_LOENGLISH, MM_HIENGLISH, MM_LOMETRIC, and MM_HIMETRIC modes, the orientation of the axes is set also. You can get a full description of the mapping modes in the function reference under **CDC::SetMapMode**.

Coordinate Mapping Defaults

The following code writes the default logical window and viewport origins and extents to the client area. Notice in Figure 3-37 that the extents are set to 1 for both dimensions of the window and the viewport. If you have looked through the simple drawing examples, you know that we have used logical coordinates in the range from 0 to 475 to draw various shapes, and these have been displayed in the client area with no apparent difficulty. This is because when the default mapping mode, MM_TEXT, is in effect the extents of the logical coordinate system match the extents of the physical coordinates exactly. The values of 1 for all the extents here don't mean we have a drawing space that is 1 by 1. They signify that there is a 1 to 1 correspondence between the logical and physical units, and make the coordinate transformation equations work out correctly.

```
/////////////////////////////////////////////////////
//CSdibaseView drawing
    void CSdibaseView::OnDraw(CDC* pDC)
{
    CSdibaseDoc* pDoc = GetDocument();
    ASSERT_VALID(pDoc);
    //TODO: add draw code for native data here
    //Create some local variables to help us space multiline text in
    //the client area
    //The first line is 10 pixels from the top of the client area
int nFirstLine = 10;
TEXTMETRIC tmTextMetrics;
    //Get the text metrics for the current font so we can calculate
    //the height of a line
pDC->GetTextMetrics( &tmTextMetrics );
    //Write this heading
pDC->TextOut( 10, nFirstLine, "Default Window and Viewport
Settings",
    strlen( "Default Window and Viewport Settings" ) );
    //Increment the y coordinate to write the next line of text
nFirstLine += 2 * (tmTextMetrics.tmHeight +
tmTextMetrics.tmExternalLeading);
    //We want to save the window and viewport origins in a CPoint
CPoint ptCoord;
    //We want to save the window and viewport extents in a CSize
CSize sizeExtents;
    //We need a pair of CStrings to print the coordinate parameters
    //to the screen
CString strMappingParms;
CString strCoords;
    //Get the default viewport origin
ptCoord = pDC->GetViewportOrg( );
strMappingParms = "Viewport Origin";
    //Format the viewport coordinates for printing
strCoords.Format("%s%i%s%i", " x = ",ptCoord.x, " y = ",ptCoord.y );
    //Catenate the two strings, letting the first one grow to
    //accomodate the coordinates
```

```
strMappingParms += strCoords;
    //Write out the viewport origin.
pDC->TextOut( 10, nFirstLine, strMappingParms );
    //Move down two lines
nFirstLine += 2 * (tmTextMetrics.tmHeight +
tmTextMetrics.tmExternalLeading);
    //Get the default window origin
ptCoord = pDC->GetWindowOrg( );
strMappingParms = "Logical Window Origin";
    //Format the window coordinates for printing
strCoords.Format("%s%i%s%i", " x = ",ptCoord.x, " y = ",ptCoord.y );
    //Catenate the two strings, letting the first one grow to
    //accomodate the coordinates
strMappingParms += strCoords;
    //Write out the window origin.
pDC->TextOut( 10, nFirstLine, strMappingParms );
    //Move down two lines
nFirstLine += 2 * (tmTextMetrics.tmHeight +
tmTextMetrics.tmExternalLeading);
    //Get the default viewport extent
sizeExtents = pDC->GetViewportExt( );
strMappingParms = "Viewport Extents";
    //Format the viewport coordinates for printing
strCoords.Format("%s%i%s%i", " x = ",sizeExtents.cx,
    " y = ",sizeExtents.cy );
    //Catenate the two strings, letting the first one grow to
    //accomodate the coordinates
strMappingParms += strCoords;
    //Write out the viewport extents.
pDC->TextOut( 10, nFirstLine, strMappingParms );
    //Move down two lines
nFirstLine += 2 * (tmTextMetrics.tmHeight +
tmTextMetrics.tmExternalLeading);
    //Get the default window extent
sizeExtents = pDC->GetWindowExt( );
strMappingParms = "Logical Window Extents";
    //Format the window coordinates for printing
strCoords.Format("%s%i%s%i", " x = ",sizeExtents.cx,
    " y = ",sizeExtents.cy );
```

```
    //Catenate the two strings, letting the first one grow to
    //accomodate the coordinates
strMappingParms += strCoords;
    //Write out the window extent.
pDC->TextOut( 10, nFirstLine, strMappingParms );
}
```

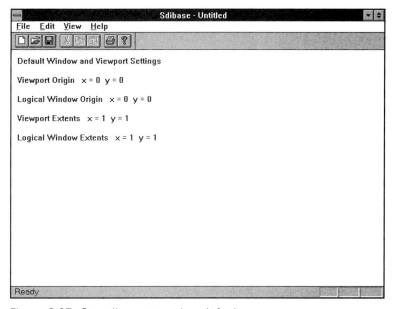

Figure 3-37: Coordinate mapping defaults.

Using Custom Units

If you need to use application-specific units in your logical coordinate system or control the orientation of the axes, there are two mapping modes that let you do this. In the *unconstrained* MM_ANISOTROPIC mapping mode, x and y units can be of different sizes. In the MM_ISOTROPIC mapping mode units are said to be *constrained,* because they must be the same size in the x direction as in the y direction.

These two mapping modes also give you the freedom to set the orientation of the axes of the logical coordinate system.

137

```
/////////////////////////////////////////////////////////////
//CSdibaseView drawing
    void CSdibaseView::OnDraw(CDC* pDC)
{
    CSdibaseDoc* pDoc = GetDocument();
    ASSERT_VALID(pDoc);
    //TODO: add draw code for native data here
CRect rectClient;
GetClientRect( &rectClient );
    pDC->SetMapMode( MM_ANISOTROPIC );
pDC->SetWindowOrg( 0, 0 );
pDC->SetWindowExt( 20000, 20000 );
pDC->SetViewportOrg( 0, 0 );
pDC->SetViewportExt( rectClient.right, rectClient.bottom );
    //Write this heading
pDC->TextOut( 1000, 19000, "Anisotropic Map Mode Demo",
    strlen( "Anisotropic Map Mode Demo" ) );
    pDC->MoveTo( 18000, 500        );
pDC->LineTo( 18000, 18000);
pDC->TextOut( 15000, 19000, "x = 18000, y = 18000",
    strlen( "x = 18000, y = 18000" ) );
    pDC->LineTo( 1000, 500   );
pDC->TextOut( 2000, 1500, "x = 1000, y = 500",
    strlen( "x = 1000, y = 500") );
    pDC->LineTo( 18000, 500 );
pDC->TextOut( 15000, 1500, "x = 18000, y = 500",
    strlen("x = 18000, y = 500" ) );


}
```

Notice that the three screen shots, Figures 3-38, 3-39 and 3-40, all show the complete triangle, and the coordinates of the vertices are the same for each. The proportions of the three triangles are very different, though the coordinates have not changed. This is because in the unconstrained MM_ANISOTROPIC map mode, the relative sizes of x and y units change as the frame window is resized. There will always be 20,000 units in each direction, and they will be distributed over the x and y dimensions of the client area independently of each other.

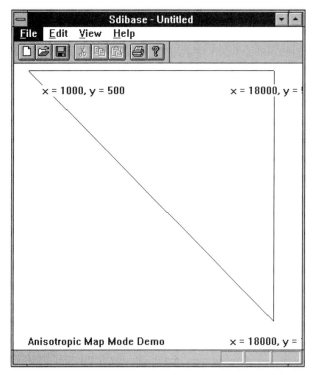

Figure 3-38: First triangle in MM_ANISOTROPIC mapping mode.

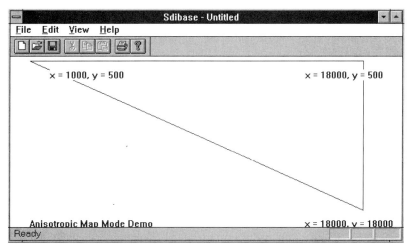

Figure 3-39: Second triangle in MM_ANISOTROPIC mapping mode.

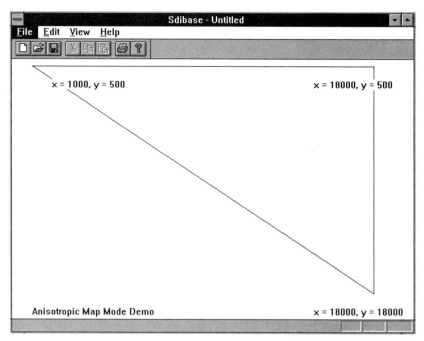

Figure 3-40: Third triangle in MM_ANISOTROPIC mapping mode.

Now look at the difference if we set the mapping mode to MM_ISOTROPIC.

```
/////////////////////////////////////////////////////////
//CSdibaseView drawing
    void CSdibaseView::OnDraw(CDC* pDC)
{
    CSdibaseDoc* pDoc = GetDocument();
    ASSERT_VALID(pDoc);
    //TODO: add draw code for native data here
CRect rectClient;
GetClientRect( &rectClient );
    pDC->SetMapMode( MM_ISOTROPIC );
pDC->SetWindowOrg( 0, 0 );
pDC->SetWindowExt( 20000, 20000 );
pDC->SetViewportOrg( 0, 0 );
pDC->SetViewportExt( rectClient.right, rectClient.bottom );
    //Write this heading
pDC->TextOut( 1000, 19000, "Isotropic Map Mode Demo",
    strlen( "Isotropic Map Mode Demo" ) );
    pDC->MoveTo( 18000, 500 );
```

```
pDC->LineTo( 18000, 18000);
pDC->TextOut( 15000, 19000, "x = 18000, y = 18000",
    strlen( "x = 18000, y = 18000" ) );
    pDC->LineTo( 1000, 500   );
pDC->TextOut( 2000, 1500, "x = 1000, y = 500",
    strlen( "x = 1000, y = 500") );
    pDC->LineTo( 18000, 500 );
pDC->TextOut( 15000, 1500, "x = 18000, y = 500",
    strlen("x = 18000, y = 500" ) );


}
```

Notice that the proportions of the three triangles are *constant*, no matter how the frame window is sized. This is because in the constrained MM_ISOTROPIC map mode, the size of x and y units are held equal as the frame window is resized. The drawing in the client area is not distorted when the frame window changes shape.

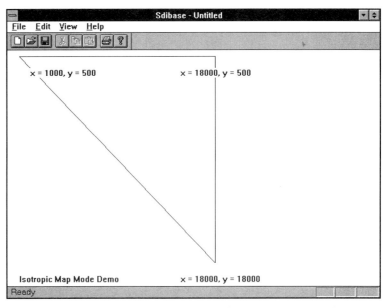

Figure 3-41: First triangle in MM_ISOTROPIC mapping mode.

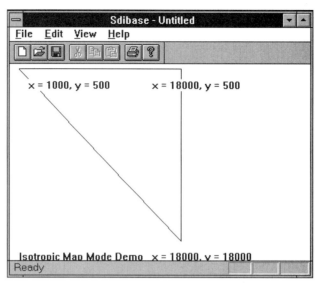

Figure 3-42: Second triangle in MM_ISOTROPIC mapping mode.

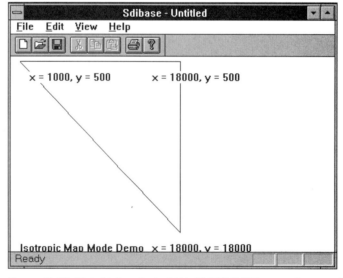

Figure 3-43: Third triangle in MM_ISOTROPIC mapping mode.

Changing the Orientation of the Axes

If you want to change the orientation of the axes, you need to do three things. First, set the map mode to either MM_ANISOTROPIC or MM_ISOTROPIC. Next, *set the logical window extent of the axis you wish to invert to a negative value*. Finally, you must align the viewport origin with the origin of the logical window.

Changing the Orientation of the Y Axis:

```
//////////////////////////////////////////////////////////
//CSdibaseView drawing
    void CSdibaseView::OnDraw(CDC* pDC)
{
    CSdibaseDoc* pDoc = GetDocument();
    ASSERT_VALID(pDoc);
    //TODO: add draw code for native data here
    //We need the dimensions of the viewport so that we can set
    //the origin of the viewport coordinate system to the lower
    //right hand corner
    //GetClientRect returns the coordinates of the upper left and
    //lower right corners by filling in a CRect
CRect rectClient;
GetClientRect( &rectClient );
    //We could use either MM_ANISOTROPIC or MM_ISOTROPIC
    //map modes here, depending on whether or not we want
    //units to be of equal size in the x and y direction. If we use
    //MM_ISOTROPIC
    //we must set the window extents before the viewport extents.
pDC->SetMapMode( MM_ANISOTROPIC );
    //The origin of the logical coordinate system is at x = 0, y = 0
pDC->SetWindowOrg( 0, 0 );
    //The logical coordinate system extends 20000 units in the x
    //direction and 20000 units in the y direction.
    //The negative y extent means that we want the y axis to
    //increase going upward
pDC->SetWindowExt( 20000, -20000 );
    //We want the viewport origin to align with the logical
    //window origin.
    //We have set up a logical coordinate system where the lower
    //left corner ( x = 0, y = 0 ) is the origin. Now we have to make
    //the lower left corner of the viewport the origin of the
    //viewport coordinate system.
```

```
        //We supply an x coordinate of zero, to designate the farthest
        //left position.
        //For the y coordinate, we use the value returned by
        //GetClientRect in the rectClient.bottom member. Recall that by
        //default, the viewport y coordinates increase going
        //downward. Therefore the pair x = 0, y = rectClient.bottom
        //locates the lower left corner of the viewport.
        //Now both coordinate system have set their origins to the
        //lower left corner.
    pDC->SetViewportOrg( 0, rectClient.bottom);
        //We use the values returned by GetClientRect to set the
        //viewport to cover the entire client area. GetClientRect returns
        //the dimensions of the client area in device units, which are
        //always positive.
        //The key to inverting the y axis is using values for logical and
        //viewport y extents that are of opposite signs. It is a good
        //practice to change the sign of the logical extent and always
        //use positive values for the viewport extent.
    pDC->SetViewportExt( rectClient.right, rectClient.bottom );
        //Write this heading
    pDC->TextOut( 1000, 19000, "The y axis increases going upward",
        strlen( "The y axis increases going upward" ) );
        //Draw the triangle
    pDC->MoveTo( 18000, 500);
    pDC->LineTo( 18000, 18000);
    pDC->TextOut( 15000, 19000, "x = 18000, y = 18000",
        strlen( "x = 18000, y = 18000" ) );
        pDC->LineTo( 1000, 500   );
    pDC->TextOut( 2000, 1500, "x = 1000, y = 500",
        strlen( "x = 1000, y = 500") );
        pDC->LineTo( 18000, 500 );
    pDC->TextOut( 15000, 1500, "x = 18000, y = 500",
        strlen("x = 18000, y = 500" ) );


    }
```

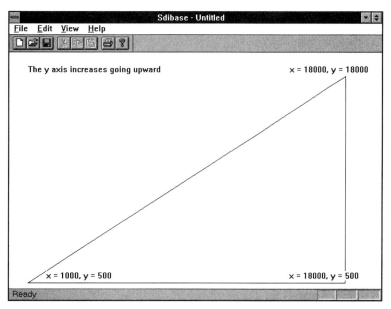

Figure 3-44: The y axis increases going upward.

Changing the Orientation of Both Axes: To draw a map using coordinates in the northwestern quadrant of the globe, you need a coordinate system in which y increases going upward and x increases going left, just as latitude and longitude do.

```
/////////////////////////////////////////////////////
//CSdibaseView drawing
    void CSdibaseView::OnDraw(CDC* pDC)
{
    CSdibaseDoc* pDoc = GetDocument();
    ASSERT_VALID(pDoc);
    //TODO: add draw code for native data here
CRect rectClient;
GetClientRect( &rectClient );
    //We could use either MM_ANISOTROPIC or MM_ISOTROPIC
    //map modes here, depending on whether or not we want
    //units to be of equal size in the x and y direction. If we use
    //MM_ISOTROPIC we must set the window extents before the
    //viewport extents. Most map data has already been
    //"projected" so that in the translation from 3 dimensional real
    //world coordinates to 2 dimensional display coordinates
    //some acceptable distortion has occurred. MM_ISOTROPIC
```

```
        //would preserve the areal proportions of the map as
        //projected
pDC->SetMapMode( MM_ANISOTROPIC );
        //The origin of the logical coordinate system is at x = 0, y = 0
pDC->SetWindowOrg( 0, 0 );
        //The logical coordinate system extends 20000 units in the x
        //direction and 20000 units in the y direction.
        //The negative y extent means that we want the y axis to
        //increase going upward
        //The negative x extent means that we want the x axis to
        //increase going left
pDC->SetWindowExt( -20000, -20000 );
        //We want the viewport origin to align with the logical
        //window origin.
        //We have set up a logical coordinate system where the
        //lower right corner ( x = 0, y = 0 ) is the origin. Now we have
        //to make the lower right corner of the
        //viewport the origin of the viewport coordinate system.
        //For the x coordinate, we use the value returned by
        //GetClientRect in the rectClient.right member.
        //For the y coordinate, we use the value returned by
        //GetClientRect in the rectClient.bottom member. Recall that by
        //default, the viewport x coordinates increase going right and
        //the viewport y coordinates increase going downward.
        //Therefore the pair x = rectClient.right, y = rectClient.bottom
        //locates the lower right corner of the viewport.
        //Now both coordinate system have set their origins to the
        //lower right corner.
pDC->SetViewportOrg( rectClient.right, rectClient.bottom);
        //We use the values returned by GetClientRect to set the
        //viewport to cover the entire client area. GetClientRect returns
        //the dimensions of the client area in device units, which are
        //always positive.
        //The key to inverting the y axis is using values for logical and
        //viewport y extents that are of opposite signs. It is a good
        //practice to change the sign of the logical extent and always
        //use positive values
        //for the viewport extent.
pDC->SetViewportExt( rectClient.right, rectClient.bottom );
        //Write this heading
pDC->TextOut( 19000, 19000, "The y axis increases upward, x
        increases to the right",
```

```
        strlen( "The y axis increases upward, x increases to the right" ) );
        //Draw the triangle
    pDC->MoveTo( 18000, 500    );
    pDC->LineTo( 18000, 18000);
    pDC->TextOut( 17500, 16500, "x = 18000, y = 18000",
        strlen( "x = 18000, y = 18000" ) );
        pDC->LineTo( 1000, 500    );
    pDC->TextOut( 8000, 1500, "x = 1000, y = 500",
        strlen( "x = 1000, y = 500") );
        pDC->LineTo( 18000, 500 );
    pDC->TextOut( 17500, 1500, "x = 18000, y = 500",
        strlen("x = 18000, y = 500" ) );
        }
```

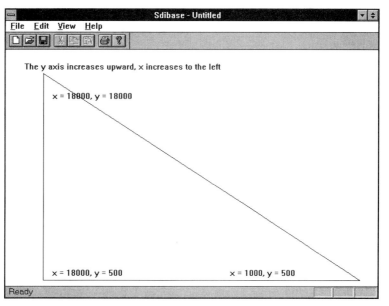

Figure 3-45: The y axis increases upward, x increases to the left.

Using Negative Coordinates: If we use the signs of the logical and viewport extents to set the orientation of the axes, then we have to have another means of defining a coordinate system that uses negative units. We do this by setting the origin of the logical coordinate system to a point where x and/or y are negative.

There is a potential point of confusion here, so let's reiterate that extents give the absolute dimensions of the logical coordinate space and, based on their signs, determine the orientation of the axes. You can set the axes to increase in either direction if you are using negative coordinates, just as you can if you are using positive coordinates. The origin of the coordinate space determines the sign of the units.

```
/////////////////////////////////////////////////////////
//CSdibaseView drawing
    void CSdibaseView::OnDraw(CDC* pDC)
{
    CSdibaseDoc* pDoc = GetDocument();
    ASSERT_VALID(pDoc);
    //TODO: add draw code for native data here
CRect rectClient;
GetClientRect( &rectClient );
    //We could use either MM_ANISOTROPIC or MM_ISOTROPIC
    //map modes here, depending on whether or not we want
    //units to be of equal size in the x and y direction. If we use
    //MM_ISOTROPIC we must set the window extents before the
    //viewport extents.
pDC->SetMapMode( MM_ANISOTROPIC );
    //The origin of the logical coordinate system is at x = -20000,
    //y = -20000
pDC->SetWindowOrg( -20000, -20000);
    //The logical coordinate system extends 20000 units in the x
    //direction and 20000 units in the y direction.
    //The negative y extent means that we want the y axis to
    //increase going upward. In this case, "increase" means become
    //less negative.
pDC->SetWindowExt( 20000, -20000 );
    //We want the viewport origin to align with the logical
    //window origin.
    //We have set up a logical coordinate system where the
    //lower left corner
    //( x = -20000, y = -20000 ) is the origin.
```

```
        //Now we have to make the lower left corner of the
        //viewport the origin of the viewport coordinate system.
        //For the x coordinate, we use 0.
        //For the y coordinate, we use the value returned by
        //GetClientRect in the rectClient.bottom member.
        //Now both coordinate system have set their origins to the
        //lower right corner.
    pDC->SetViewportOrg( 0, rectClient.bottom);
        //We use the values returned by GetClientRect to set the
        //viewport to cover the entire client area.
    pDC->SetViewportExt( rectClient.right, rectClient.bottom );
        //Write this heading
    pDC->TextOut( -19000, -19000, "The y axis increases upward, x
        increases to the left",
        strlen( "The y axis increases upward, x increases to the left" ) );
        //Draw the triangle
    pDC->MoveTo( -18000, -500  );
    pDC->LineTo( -18000, -18000);
    pDC->TextOut( -17500, -16500, "x = -18000, y = -18000",
        strlen( "x = -18000, y = -18000" ) );
        pDC->LineTo( -1000, -500  );
    pDC->TextOut( -8000, -1500, "x = -1000, y = -500",
        strlen( "x = -1000, y = -500") );
        pDC->LineTo( -18000, -500          );
    pDC->TextOut( -17500, -1500, "x = -18000, y = -500",
        strlen("x = -18000, y = -500" ) );
        }
```

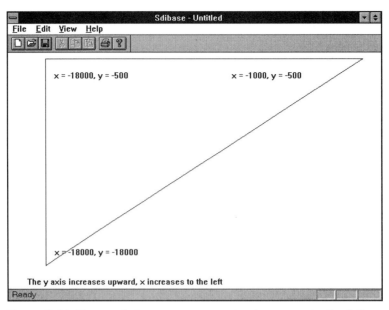

Figure 3-46: The y axis increases upward, x increases to the left.

Fonts & Text Output

Programmers generally take text output for granted, assuming it to be the simplest of tasks. As we have seen in previous examples, it isn't necessarily difficult in Windows if you want to use the default font and coordinate systems. However, if you have something more distinctive in mind, Windows has a remarkably comprehensive set of tools available.

You create a custom font by providing a description of the new font in a LOGFONT structure. This is used to construct a font object matching your requested characteristics as closely as possible. If you examine the structure definition, the first thing you will notice is that it is quite large and contains a somewhat arcane selection of data. Don't be put off by this. You can retrieve most of the information needed to fill in the LOGFONT from an existing font and modify the particular features, such as character height, that you'd like to change.

You can also control the certain aspects of the way in which the default font is displayed. You may set its color, justification, and whether it paints over the background or lets the original background show through between and underneath characters.

Where to Add Code: The application's view class, in the **OnDraw** member function.

Files to Modify: sdibavw.cpp

Changing Color & Background Mode for Text Output

```
/////////////////////////////////////////////////////
//CSdibaseView drawing
    void CSdibaseView::OnDraw(CDC* pDC)
{
    CSdibaseDoc* pDoc = GetDocument();
    ASSERT_VALID(pDoc);
    //TODO: add draw code for native data here
    //We use the default MM_TEXT map mode and navigate the
    //client area in viewport units; We retrieve the dimensions
    //of the screen with GetClientRect
CRect rectClient;
GetClientRect( &rectClient );
    //The TEXTMETRIC structure contains detailed information
    //about the current font. Below we use the tmMaxCharWidth
    //field, which is the width in device units of the widest
    //character in the font, and the tmHeight and tmExternalLeading
    //fields together to give the height of a line of text. The
    //tmHeight field gives the height in device units of the tallest
    //character in the font.
    //
    //The tmExternalLeading field has an archaic name. It is a
    //remnant of terminology from the time when type was cast in
    //lead. Individual characters included an upper and lower
    //margin so that lines of type would have proper vertical
    //spacing.
    //We use the tmExternalLeading field in calculating vertical line
    //position for the same reason.
    TEXTMETRIC tmTextMetrics;
    //Get the text metrics for the current font so we can calculate
    //the height of a line
pDC->GetTextMetrics( &tmTextMetrics );
    //We set up these three variables to make out TextOut calls
    //look a bit tidier
int nThisCol = rectClient.left + tmTextMetrics.tmMaxCharWidth;
int nThisLine = rectClient.top + tmTextMetrics.tmHeight +
    tmTextMetrics.tmExternalLeading;
```

```
int nOneLineDown = tmTextMetrics.tmHeight +
tmTextMetrics.tmExternalLeading;
    //Write this sample
pDC->TextOut( nThisCol, nThisLine, "This is the default font",
      strlen( "This is the default font" ) );
    //Move down one line
nThisLine += nOneLineDown;
    //Set the text color to red
pDC->SetTextColor( RGB( 255, 0, 0) );
    //Write this sample
pDC->TextOut( nThisCol, nThisLine, "This is the default font in red",
        strlen( "This is the default font in red" ) );
    //Move down one line
nThisLine += nOneLineDown;
      //Select the stock gray brush to fill the rectangle so we can
      //experiment with background modes;
      //Save the default Brush so we can replace it when
      //we are done
CBrush* pDefaultBrush = ( CBrush* ) pDC->SelectStockObject(
GRAY_BRUSH );
    //Draw a rectangle and fill it with the gray brush
pDC->Rectangle( nThisCol, nThisLine, rectClient.right, nThisLine * 4 );
    //Now set the background mode to OPAQUE
pDC->SetBkMode( OPAQUE );
    //Move down into the rectangle
nThisLine += 2 * nOneLineDown;
    //Write the sample
pDC->TextOut( nThisCol, nThisLine, "This is the OPAQUE
        background mode",
        strlen( "This is the OPAQUE background mode" ) );
    //Move down into the rectangle
nThisLine += 2 * nOneLineDown;
    //Now set the background mode to TRANSPARENT
pDC->SetBkMode( TRANSPARENT );
    //Write the sample
pDC->TextOut( nThisCol, nThisLine, "This is the TRANSPARENT
        background mode",
        strlen( "This is the TRANSPARENT background mode" ) );
    //Replace the default brush
 pDC->SelectObject( pDefaultBrush );
    }
```

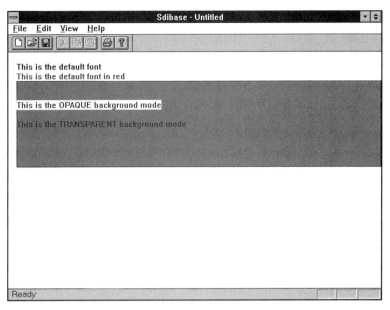

Figure 3-47: Changing color and background mode for text output.

Changing the Alignment of Text Output

When you use the **TextOut** function to display text, the default is to align the upper left corner of the bounding rectangle with the point specified by the first two parameters. You can change the alignment with **CDC::SetTextAlign**.

```
/////////////////////////////////////////////////////////
//CSdibaseView drawing
    void CSdibaseView::OnDraw(CDC* pDC)
{
    CSdibaseDoc* pDoc = GetDocument();
    ASSERT_VALID(pDoc);
    //TODO: add draw code for native data here
    //We use the default MM_TEXT map mode and navigate the
    //client area in viewport units; We retrieve the dimensions
    //of the screen with GetClientRect
CRect rectClient;
GetClientRect( &rectClient );
    //The TEXTMETRIC structure contains detailed information
    //about the current font. Below we use the tmMaxCharWidth
    //field, which is the width in device units of the widest
    //character in the font, and the tmHeight and tmExternalLeading
```

153

```
        //fields together to give the height of a line of text. The
        //tmHeight field gives the height in device units of the tallest
        //character in the font.
        //
        //The tmExternalLeading field has an archaic name.
        //It is a remnant of terminology from the time when type was
        //cast in lead.
        //Individual characters included an upper and lower margin so
        //that lines of type would have proper vertical spacing.
        //We use the tmExternalLeading field in calculating vertical line
        //position for the same reason.
        //Get the text metrics for the current font so we can calculate
        //the height of a line
    TEXTMETRIC tmTextMetrics;
    pDC->GetTextMetrics( &tmTextMetrics );
        //We set up these three variables to make out TextOut calls
        //look a bit tidier
    int nThisCol = rectClient.left + tmTextMetrics.tmMaxCharWidth;
    int nThisLine = rectClient.top + tmTextMetrics.tmHeight +
        tmTextMetrics.tmExternalLeading;
    int nThreeLinesDown = 3 *
        (tmTextMetrics.tmHeight + tmTextMetrics.tmExternalLeading);
        pDC->SetBkMode( TRANSPARENT );
        //Select the stock gray brush to fill the rectangle
        //so we can experiment with background modes;
        //Save the default Brush so we can replace it when we
        //are done
    CBrush* pDefaultBrush = ( CBrush* ) pDC->SelectStockObject(
    LTGRAY_BRUSH );
        //We create a dashed pen to draw the bounding rectangle
        //around text samples
    CPen penDashedBoundingRect( PS_DASH, 1, RGB( 0,0,0 ));
        //Select the pen into the DC, saving the default pen so we can
        //replace it later
    CPen * pDefaultPen =
        ( CPen* )pDC->SelectObject( &penDashedBoundingRect );
        //Draw a small rectangle at the text anchor point
        //and fill it with the gray brush
    pDC->Rectangle( nThisCol - 3, nThisLine - 3, nThisCol + 3,
        nThisLine + 3 );
        //Get the dimensions of the text string's bounding rectangle
    CSize sizeBoundingRect=
```

```
            pDC->GetTextExtent( "Text aligned left is the default",
            strlen( "Text aligned left is the default" ) );
        //Draw the bounding rectangle of the text
pDC->Rectangle( nThisCol, nThisLine,
        nThisCol + sizeBoundingRect.cx,
        nThisLine + sizeBoundingRect.cy );
        //Write this sample
pDC->TextOut( nThisCol, nThisLine, "Text aligned left is the default",
        strlen( "Text aligned left is the default" ) );
        //Now we align the string to the right
pDC->SetTextAlign( TA_RIGHT );
        //Move down three lines
nThisLine += nThreeLinesDown;
        //Get the dimensions of the text string's bounding rectangle
sizeBoundingRect=
        pDC->GetTextExtent( "Text horizontally aligned using right of
        bounding rect",
        strlen( "Text horizontally aligned using right of bounding rect" ) );

        //Draw the anchor point
pDC->Rectangle( nThisCol + sizeBoundingRect.cx - 3, nThisLine - 3,
        nThisCol + sizeBoundingRect.cx + 3, nThisLine + 3 );
        //Draw the bounding rectangle
pDC->Rectangle( nThisCol, nThisLine,
        nThisCol + sizeBoundingRect.cx,
        nThisLine + sizeBoundingRect.cy );
        //Write this sample
pDC->TextOut( nThisCol + sizeBoundingRect.cx, nThisLine,
    "Text horizontally aligned using right of bounding rect",
     strlen( "Text horizontally aligned using right of bounding rect" )
    );

        //We horizontally align text using
        //the center of a bounding rect
pDC->SetTextAlign( TA_CENTER );
        //Move down three lines
nThisLine += nThreeLinesDown;
        //Get the dimensions of the bounding rect of the text
sizeBoundingRect=
        pDC->GetTextExtent( "Text horizontally aligned using center of
        bounding rect",
        strlen( "Text horizontally aligned using center of bounding rect" )
        );
```

155

```
    //Draw the anchor point
pDC->Rectangle(( rectClient.right / 2 ) - 3, nThisLine - 3,
    ( rectClient.right / 2 ) + 3, nThisLine + 3 );
    //Draw the bounding rectangle
pDC->Rectangle( rectClient.right / 2 - sizeBoundingRect.cx / 2,
    nThisLine,
    rectClient.right / 2 + sizeBoundingRect.cx / 2,
    nThisLine + sizeBoundingRect.cy );
    //Write this sample
pDC->TextOut( rectClient.right / 2, nThisLine,
    "Text horizontally aligned using center of bounding rect",
    strlen( "Text horizontally aligned using center of bounding rect" )
    );

    //This text is vertically aligned to the baseline of the font
    //The baseline is the imaginary line on which characters "sit,"
    //and which descenders, (for example the bottom part of a
    //lowercase y) fall below
pDC->SetTextAlign( TA_BASELINE );
    //Move down three lines
nThisLine += nThreeLinesDown;
    //Get the dimensions of the bounding rectangle of the text
sizeBoundingRect=
    pDC->GetTextExtent( "Text aligned vertically to font baseline",
    strlen( "Text aligned vertically to font baseline" ) );

    //Draw the anchor point
pDC->Rectangle( nThisCol - 3, nThisLine, nThisCol +3, nThisLine + 3 );
    //Draw the bounding rectangle
pDC->Rectangle( nThisCol,
        nThisLine - sizeBoundingRect.cy,
        nThisCol + sizeBoundingRect.cx,
        nThisLine );
    //Write this sample
pDC->TextOut( nThisCol, nThisLine,
        "Text aligned vertically to font baseline",
        strlen( "Text aligned vertically to font baseline" ) );
    //Text vertically aligned using the bottom of an enclosing
    //rectangle
    pDC->SetTextAlign( TA_BOTTOM );
    //Move down three lines
nThisLine += nThreeLinesDown;
```

156

```
    //Get the dimensions of the bounding rectangle of the text
sizeBoundingRect=
    pDC->GetTextExtent( "Text aligned vertically to bottom of
    bounding rect",
    strlen( "Text aligned vertically to bottom of bounding rect" ) );

    //Draw the anchor point
pDC->Rectangle( nThisCol - 3, nThisLine, nThisCol +3, nThisLine + 3 );
    //Draw the bounding rectangle
pDC->Rectangle( nThisCol,
        nThisLine - sizeBoundingRect.cy,
        nThisCol + sizeBoundingRect.cx,
        nThisLine );
    //Write this sample
pDC->TextOut( nThisCol, nThisLine,
        "Text aligned vertically to font baseline",
        strlen( "Text aligned vertically to font baseline" ) );
    //Replace the default brush in the DC
pDC->SelectObject( pDefaultBrush );
}
```

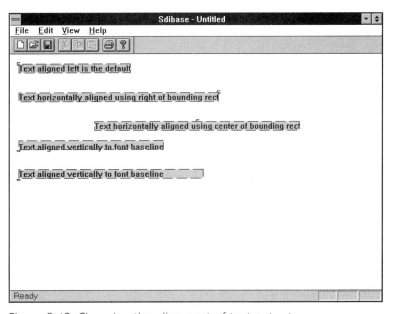

Figure 3-48: Changing the alignment of text output.

Creating Custom Fonts

Windows allows you to create a new font literally from the ground up if you need to do so. However, in practice, what most often happens is that you base a custom font on an existing font. To do this, you create a LOGFONT structure and fill it with data describing an existing font, change the values of some members of the LOGFONT structure, and then pass it to CreateFont. CreateFont will attempt to match your specifications as closely as possible and manufacture a custom font. To use the custom font, you select it into the DC, just as you would a pen or brush.

Creating a Large Font: The first step to creating a large custom font is to get a basic font description for the current default font. The font description information is copied to a LOGFONT structure. We modify the height, width and typeface name members, and use the structure to initialize a **CFont** object. We select our custom font into the DC after it is successfully initialized.

```
////////////////////////////////////////////////////////
//CSdibaseView drawing
    void CSdibaseView::OnDraw(CDC* pDC)
{
    CSdibaseDoc* pDoc = GetDocument();
    ASSERT_VALID(pDoc);
    //TODO: add draw code for native data here
    //We use the default MM_TEXT map mode and navigate the
    //client area in viewport units; We retrieve the dimensions
    //of the client area with GetClientRect
CRect rectClient;
GetClientRect( &rectClient );
    //We get a pointer to the currently selected font. This may be a
    //temporary pointer, so never store it for later use. Assume that
    //when this function exits, the pointer to the current font has
    //become invalid
CFont * pfontCurrent = pDC->GetCurrentFont( );
    //Now we are going to retrieve the data used to specify the
    //font
    //First, we declare a LOGFONT structure to hold the info.
LOGFONT lfCurrentFont;
    //Then we use GetObject to copy the info to our LOGFONT
    //GetObject is a member of the CGdiObject class, from which
    //CFont, CBrush, CPen and the rest of the classes that
    //encapsulate GDI objects are derived. You can use it
    //to copy descriptive information to the appropriate
```

```
        //structures for these other types of GDI objects also
pfontCurrent->GetObject(sizeof(LOGFONT), &lfCurrentFont);
        //Now we are going to create our custom font's encapsulating
        //object
CFont fontBig;
        //We change some of the fields in the LOGFONT structure
        //to provide custom specifications for our font
lfCurrentFont.lfHeight = rectClient.bottom / 5;
lfCurrentFont.lfWidth = rectClient.right / 10;
strcpy( lfCurrentFont.lfFaceName, "Times New Roman" );
        //When we pass the LOGFONT to CreateFontIndirect, the
        //Windows font mapping algorithm will try to match our
        //specification as closely as possible, but the result may not be
        //exactly what we request.
        //To achieve the best looking results, especially if you are doing
        //something drastic to the size of the font, always specify
        //the facename of a TrueType font in the lfFaceName.
        //TrueType fonts are vector fonts, and so are continuously
        //scalable. The default system font is often a raster font and has
        //a rather hideous blocky appearance when greatly enlarged.
fontBig.CreateFontIndirect(&lfCurrentFont);
        //Select the custom font
CFont* defaultFont = (CFont*)pDC->SelectObject( &fontBig );
        //Write some text
pDC->TextOut( 10, 50, "Wow!", strlen( "Wow!" ) );
        //Replace the default font
pDC->SelectObject( defaultFont );
}
```

Figure 3-49: Creating a large font.

Creating an Italic Font: Italic, strikeout and underline font attributes are set by Boolean fields in the LOGFONT structure.

```
//////////////////////////////////////////////////////
//CSdibaseView drawing
    void CSdibaseView::OnDraw(CDC* pDC)
{
    CSdibaseDoc* pDoc = GetDocument();
    ASSERT_VALID(pDoc);
    //TODO: add draw code for native data here
    //We use the default MM_TEXT map mode and navigate the
    //the client area in viewport units; We retrieve the dimensions
    //of the client area with GetClientRect
CRect rectClient;
GetClientRect( &rectClient );
    //We get a pointer to the currently selected font. This may be a
    //temporary pointer, so never store it for later use. Assume that
    //when this function exits, the pointer to the current font has
    //become invalid
```

```
CFont * pfontCurrent = pDC->GetCurrentFont( );
    //Now we are going to retrieve the data used to specify the
    //font
    //First, we declare a LOGFONT structure to hold the info.
LOGFONT lfCurrentFont;
    //Then we use GetObject to copy the info to our LOGFONT
pfontCurrent->GetObject(sizeof(LOGFONT), &lfCurrentFont);
    //Now we are going to create our custom font's encapsulating
    //object
CFont fontItalic;
    //We change some of the fields in the LOGFONT structure
    //to provide custom specifications for our font
lfCurrentFont.lfHeight = rectClient.bottom / 5;
lfCurrentFont.lfWidth = rectClient.right / 10;
lfCurrentFont.lfItalic = TRUE;
strcpy( lfCurrentFont.lfFaceName, "Times New Roman" );
    //When we pass the LOGFONT to CreateFontIndirect, the
    //Windows font mapping algorithm will try to match our
    //specification as closely as possible, but the result may not be
    //exactly what we request.
fontItalic.CreateFontIndirect(&lfCurrentFont);
    //Select the custom font
CFont* defaultFont = (CFont*)pDC->SelectObject( &fontItalic );
    //Write some text
pDC->TextOut( 10, 50, "Italic", strlen( "Italic" ) );
    //Replace the default font
pDC->SelectObject( defaultFont );
}
```

Figure 3-50: Creating an italic font.

Creating a Rotated Font: The rotation of output text strings is controlled by the **lfEscapement** member of the LOGFONT structure.

```
/////////////////////////////////////////////////////////
//CSdibaseView drawing
    void CSdibaseView::OnDraw(CDC* pDC)
{
    CSdibaseDoc* pDoc = GetDocument();
    ASSERT_VALID(pDoc);
    //TODO: add draw code for native data here
    //We use the default MM_TEXT map mode and navigate the
    //client area in viewport units; We retrieve the dimensions
    //of the client area with GetClientRect
CRect rectClient;
GetClientRect( &rectClient );
    //We get a pointer to the currently selected font. This may be a
    //temporary pointer, so never store it for later use. Assume that
    //when this function exits, the pointer to the current font has
    //become invalid
CFont * pfontCurrent = pDC->GetCurrentFont( );
    //Now we are going to retrieve the data used to specify the
    //font
```

```
    //First, we declare a LOGFONT structure to hold the info.
LOGFONT lfCurrentFont;
    //Then we use GetObject to copy the info to our LOGFONT
pfontCurrent->GetObject(sizeof(LOGFONT), &lfCurrentFont);
    //Now we are going to create our custom font's encapsulating
    //object
CFont fontTilt;

    //We change some of the fields in the LOGFONT structure
    //to provide custom specifications for our font. Escapement
    //gives the angle, measured in 10ths of degrees,
    //counterclockwise from the x axis between the axis and the
    //bottom of a bounding rectangle of the output text string
lfCurrentFont.lfEscapement = 450;
    //Rotated fonts have to be vector based, the easiest way to
    //make sure you have a vector font is to use the name of a
    //TrueType typeface.
strcpy( lfCurrentFont.lfFaceName, "Times New Roman" );
    //When we pass the LOGFONT to CreateFontIndirect, the
    //Windows font mapping algorithm will try to match our
    //specification as closely as possible, but the result may not be
    //exactly what we request.
fontTilt.CreateFontIndirect(&lfCurrentFont);
    //Select the custom font, but save a pointer to the default font
    //so you can replace it in the DC
CFont* defaultFont = (CFont*)pDC->SelectObject( &fontTilt );
    //Write some text
pDC->TextOut( 10, 3 * ( rectClient.bottom / 4),
        "Escapment specifies rotation for the entire string",
        strlen( "Escapment specifies rotation for the entire string" ) );
    //Replace the default font
pDC->SelectObject( defaultFont );}
}
```

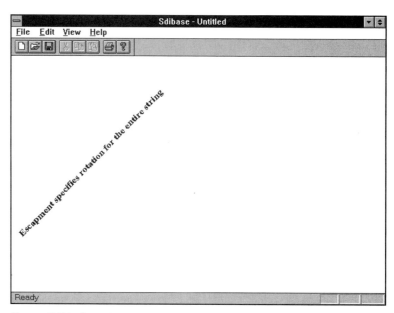

Figure 3-51: Creating a rotated font.

Bitmaps

Bitmap graphics is probably one of the more complicated aspects of drawing in Windows for two reasons. First, bitmaps are subject to so many device limitations that their implementation is not as cleanly abstract as other GDI primitive objects such as pens and brushes. Second, you can't simply load bitmap data and select a bitmap object into the DC the way you select a pen or brush. There is no default bitmap in the DC when you enter your view's **OnDraw** function. The key thing to understand about displaying bitmaps is that the bitmap output functions require that the bitmap be *transferred from a DC in memory to the DC that is managing the current output device.* You could think of it as a copy and paste kind of situation.

Using Bitmaps to Copy One Part of the Screen to Another

We mentioned above that to display a bitmap, you must copy the image from a source DC to a destination DC. When you copy a bitmap from one part of the screen to another, the source and destination DCs are one in the same. All that you need to do is specify the upper left corner and dimensions of the rectangle bounding the bitmap you wish to copy, the point to use as the upper left corner of the destination rectangle, and the raster operation that you should use to combine the bits of the source and destination bitmaps. All coordinates are in logical units. (For more information on logical coordinates, look at the examples under the "Coordinate Systems & Mapping" heading.)

```
/////////////////////////////////////////////////////
//CSdibaseView drawing
    void CSdibaseView::OnDraw(CDC* pDC)
{
    CSdibaseDoc* pDoc = GetDocument();
    ASSERT_VALID(pDoc);
    //TODO: add draw code for native data here
    //We use the default MM_TEXT map mode and navigate the
    //client area in viewport units; We retrieve the dimensions
    //of the client area with GetClientRect
CRect rectClient;
GetClientRect( &rectClient );
    //To provide contrast between the area the source bitmap
    //comes from and the destination, we will paint the left half of
    //the screen gray. Select a stack brush and save the handle of
    //the default brush.
CBrush* pDefaultBrush = ( CBrush* ) pDC->SelectStockObject(
    LTGRAY_BRUSH );
    //Shade the left half of the client area
pDC->Rectangle( rectClient.left,
        rectClient.top,
        rectClient.right / 2,
        rectClient.bottom / 2);

    //We will draw an ellipse and fill it with the black brush — this is
    //our "source" bitmap.
    //Select the stock black brush to fill the ellipse
    //Save the default Brush so we can replace it when we are
    //done
pDC->SelectStockObject( BLACK_BRUSH );
pDC->Ellipse( rectClient.right / 4,
        rectClient.bottom / 4,
        2 * rectClient.right / 4,
        2 * rectClient.bottom / 4);
    //We create a dashed pen to draw the bounding rectangle so
    //that we can see what we are copying
CPen penDashedBoundingRect( PS_DASH, 1, RGB( 0,0,0 ));
```

```
    //Select the pen into the DC, saving the default pen so we can
    //replace it later
CPen * pDefaultPen = ( CPen* )pDC->SelectObject(
    &penDashedBoundingRect );
    //Select the hollow brush. This allows us to draw the dashed
    //rectangle without obliterating the gray background or the
    //ellipse. It essentially fills a closed shape like a rectangle with a
    //transparent background.
pDC->SelectStockObject( HOLLOW_BRUSH );
    //Draw the bounding rectangle of the ellipse
pDC->Rectangle( rectClient.right / 4,
        rectClient.bottom / 4,
        2 * rectClient.right / 4,
        2 * rectClient.bottom / 4);
    //Replace the original brush and pen in the DC
pDC->SelectObject( &pDefaultPen );
pDC->SelectObject( &pDefaultBrush );
    //Now transfer the bits using BitBlt. This function assumes that
    //the source DC is the object to which pDC points
pDC->BitBlt(   3 * (rectClient.right / 4),        //Upper left x coord
                                                  //of the destination
        3 * (rectClient.bottom / 4),              //Upper left y coord
                                                  //of the destination
    rectClient.right / 4,      //Width of the destination
    rectClient.bottom / 4,  //Height of the destination
    pDC,      //Pointer to SOURCE DC
            //In this case the source and
            //destination DC are the same
    rectClient.right / 4,      //Upper left x coord of source
    rectClient.bottom / 4,  //Upper left y coord of source
    SRCCOPY);                 //The raster operation that combines
                              //the bits ( ROP code )
    //ROP codes are demonstrated in an example that follows
}
```

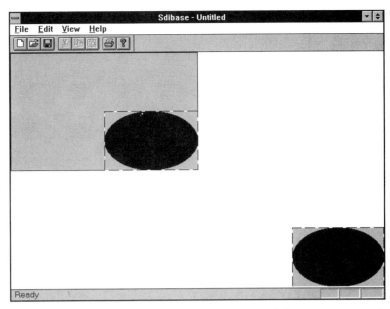

Figure 3-52: Using bitmaps to copy one part of the screen to another.

Creating a Bitmap in Memory & Displaying It on the Screen

If you want to display a bitmap that comes from a source other than the current DC, there are more steps involved. Recall that one of **BitBlt's** arguments is a pointer to the source DC for the bitmap. To create original bitmaps, either by drawing them on the fly at runtime or loading them from disk, you need a second DC. This DC exists in memory, solely to hold your source bitmap. Here is how to use a memory DC to draw and display an original bitmap.

```
/////////////////////////////////////////////////////////
//CSdibaseView drawing
   void CSdibaseView::OnDraw(CDC* pDC)
{
   CSdibaseDoc* pDoc = GetDocument();
   ASSERT_VALID(pDoc);
   //TODO: add draw code for native data here
   //We use the default MM_TEXT map mode and navigate the
   //client area in viewport units; We retrieve the dimensions
   //of the client area with GetClientRect
CRect rectClient;
GetClientRect( &rectClient );
```

```
        //To provide contrast between the background of the source
        //bitmap and the destination, we will paint the client area gray.
        //Select a stock brush and save the handle of the default brush.
CBrush* pDefaultBrush =
        ( CBrush* ) pDC->SelectStockObject( LTGRAY_BRUSH );
        //Shade the client area
pDC->Rectangle( rectClient.left,
        rectClient.top,
        rectClient.right,
        rectClient.bottom );
        //Replace the default brush
pDC->SelectObject( pDefaultBrush );
        //We need another DC to hold the bitmap we are going to
        //draw so we create it on the heap using the new operator.
        //This will have to be explicitly deleted when we are done with
        //it. Only stack based objects are automatically destroyed
        //when the function exits
CDC * pMemoryDC = new CDC;
        //Creating the object does not give us an initialized DC; A DC
        //can identify all sorts of display devices, so we need to
        //explicitly initialize ours to be compatible with the one the
        //manages the client area of the screen.
        //We do this with the CreateCompatibleDC function
pMemoryDC->CreateCompatibleDC( pDC );
        //We can't use the memory DC we just created
        //to draw any output until we initialize it with a bitmap
        //First we create the bitmap object
CBitmap * pMemoryBitmap = new CBitmap;
        //Then we initialize the object with a bitmap
        //that is 1/4 the width of the client area,
        //1/4 the height of the client area
        //has one color plane, one color bit for each pixel
        //and has no initial image data
pMemoryBitmap->CreateBitmap(
        rectClient.right / 4,
        rectClient.bottom / 4, 1, 1, NULL );
```

```
                //We select the initialized bitmap object into the DC,
                //and now we can do output operations referencing the
                //memory DC
        CBitmap * pOldBitmap =
                ( CBitmap * ) pMemoryDC->SelectObject( pMemoryBitmap );
                //Since our bitmap object had no initial image data,
                //it starts out filled with whatever random garbage existed in
                //the memory it now occupies. PatBlt allows us to fill a
                //rectangle specified by the first four parameters with a pattern.
                //The constant we use here, BLACKNESS, is a ROP
                //code that causes the rectangle to be painted black.
        pMemoryDC->PatBlt( 0, 0,
                rectClient.right,
                rectClient.bottom,
                BLACKNESS );
                //Then we draw an ellipse and fill it with the standard white
                //brush— this is our "source" bitmap.
        pMemoryDC->Ellipse(0, 0,
                rectClient.right / 4,
                rectClient.bottom / 4);

                //Now transfer the bits from the memory DC to the screen
                //DC using BitBlt.
        pDC->BitBlt(   3 * rectClient.right / 8,        //Upper left x coord
                                                        //of the dest
                3 * rectClient.bottom / 8,              //Upper left y coord
                                                        //of the dest
                rectClient.right / 4,           //Width of the dest
                rectClient.bottom / 4,          //Height of the dest
                pMemoryDC,                      //Pointer to SOURCE DC
                0,      //Upper left x coord of SOURCE
                0,      //Upper left y coord of SOURCE
                SRCCOPY);      //The raster operation that combines
                                //the bits of source,
                                //destination, and background
                                //brush ( ROP code )
```

```
//Both the memory DC and the bitmap
//we used to initialize it were created on the heap using the
//new operator, so they must be explicitly deleted.
//First, we must select the bitmap out of the memory DC, and
//replace the pointer to the "old bitmap." Never delete any
//object that is currently selected in a DC.
//Selecting the pointer to the old bitmap returns a pointer to
//our bitmap object, which in turn is deleted.
delete pMemoryDC->SelectObject( pOldBitmap );
//After dispatching the bitmap, we can delete the DC
delete pMemoryDC;
}
////////////////////////////////////////////////////////////
```

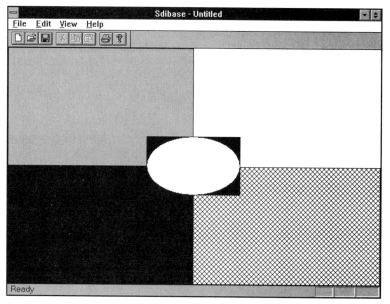

Figure 3-53: Creating a bitmap in memory and displaying it on the screen.

Using ROP Codes

The ROP codes are sets of Boolean operations that govern the way the bits of the source bitmap, the destination bitmap, and the current brush, called the pattern, are combined to create the image displayed. The most commonly used ROP codes have symbolic names, and each of these is shown below.

```
//////////////////////////////////////////////////////
//CSdibaseView drawing
    void CSdibaseView::OnDraw(CDC* pDC)
{
    CSdibaseDoc* pDoc = GetDocument();
    ASSERT_VALID(pDoc);
    //TODO: add draw code for native data here
    //We use the default MM_TEXT map mode and navigate the
    //the client area in viewport units; We retrieve the dimensions
    //of the client area with GetClientRect
CRect rectClient;
GetClientRect( &rectClient );
    //To provide an illustration of what various ROP codes do,
    //we paint the client area in quadrants: black, white, gray and
    //cross hatched
CBrush* pDefaultBrush =
    ( CBrush* ) pDC->SelectStockObject( LTGRAY_BRUSH );
    //Shade the upper left quadrant of the client area
pDC->Rectangle( rectClient.left,
        rectClient.top,
        rectClient.right / 2,
        rectClient.bottom / 2);
    pDC->SelectStockObject( BLACK_BRUSH );
    //Paint the lower left quadrant of the client area black
pDC->Rectangle( rectClient.left,
        rectClient.bottom / 2,
        rectClient.right / 2,
        rectClient.bottom);
    //Create a cross hatched brush and select it into the DC
CBrush brushHatch( HS_DIAGCROSS, RGB( 0, 0, 0 ) );
pDC->SelectObject( &brushHatch );
    //Paint the lower right quadrant of the client area with the cross
    //hatch brush
```

```
            pDC->Rectangle( rectClient.right / 2,
                rectClient.bottom / 2,
                rectClient.right,
                rectClient.bottom);
            pDC->SelectObject( pDefaultBrush );
            //We need another DC to hold the bitmap we are going to
            //draw so we create it on the heap using the new operator.
            //This will have to be explicitly deleted when we are done with
            //it. Only stack based objects are automatically destroyed
            //when the function exits
        CDC * pMemoryDC = new CDC;
            //Creating the object does not give us an initialized DC; A DC
            //can identify all sorts of display devices, so we need to
            //explicitly initialize ours to be compatible with the one the
            //manages the client area of the screen.
            //We do this with the CreateCompatibleDC function
        pMemoryDC->CreateCompatibleDC( pDC );
            //We can't use the memory DC we just created
            //to draw any output until we initialize it with a bitmap
            //First we create the bitmap object
        CBitmap * pMemoryBitmap = new CBitmap;
            //Then we initialize the object with a bitmap
            //that is 1/4 the width of the client area,
            //1/4 the height of the client area
            //has one color plane, one color bit for each pixel
            //and has no initial image data
        pMemoryBitmap->CreateBitmap(
                rectClient.right / 4,
                rectClient.bottom / 4, 1, 1, NULL );

            //We select the initialized bitmap object into the DC,
            //and now we can do output operations referencing the
            //memory DC
        CBitmap * pOldBitmap =
            ( CBitmap * ) pMemoryDC->SelectObject( pMemoryBitmap );
            //PatBlt allows us to fill a rectangle specified by the
            //first four parameters with a pattern. The constant we use
            //here, BLACKNESS, is a ROP code that causes the rectangle to
            //be painted black.
        pMemoryDC->PatBlt( 0, 0,
                rectClient.right,
                rectClient.bottom,
                BLACKNESS );
```

```
    //Then we draw an ellipse and fill it with the standard white
    //brush— this is our "source" bitmap.
pMemoryDC->Ellipse(0, 0,
    rectClient.right / 4,
    rectClient.bottom / 4);
    //Annotate the screen with symbolic constant for this ROP
    //code
pDC->TextOut( 3 * rectClient.right / 5, rectClient.bottom / 8,
    "SRCCOPY", strlen( "SRCCOPY" );
    //Now transfer the bits from the memory DC to the screen
    //DC using BitBlt.
pDC->BitBlt(   3 * rectClient.right / 8,          //Upper left x coord
                                                  //of the dest
        3 * rectClient.bottom / 8,                //Upper left y coord
                                                  //of the dest
    rectClient.right / 4,          //Width of the dest
    rectClient.bottom / 4,         //Height of the dest
    pMemoryDC,                     //Pointer to SOURCE DC
    0,        //Upper left x coord of SOURCE
    0,        //Upper left y coord of SOURCE
    SRCCOPY);      //The raster operation that combines
                   //the bits of source,
                   //destination, and background
                   //brush ( ROP code )

    //Both the memory DC and the bitmap we used to initialize it
    //were created on the heap using the new operator, so they
    //must be explicitly deleted.
    //First, we must select the bitmap out of the memory DC, and
    //replace the pointer to the "old bitmap." Never delete any
    //object that is currently selected in a DC.
    //Selecting the pointer to the old bitmap returns a pointer to
    //our bitmap object, which in turn is deleted.
delete pMemoryDC->SelectObject( pOldBitmap );
    //After dispatching the bitmap, we can delete the DC
delete pMemoryDC;
}
/////////////////////////////////////////////////////////////
```

The following illustrations show some examples of the named ROP codes.

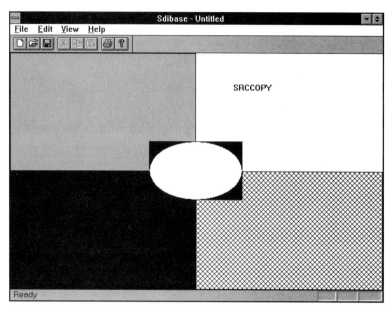

Figure 3-54: SRCCOPY.

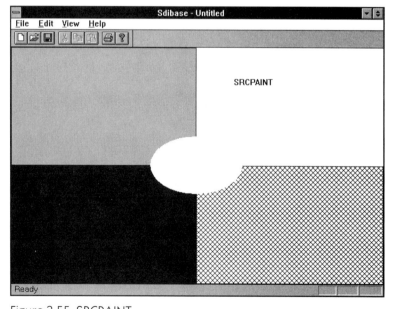

Figure 3-55: SRCPAINT.

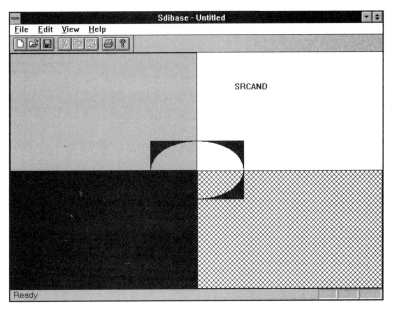

Figure 3-56: SRCAND.

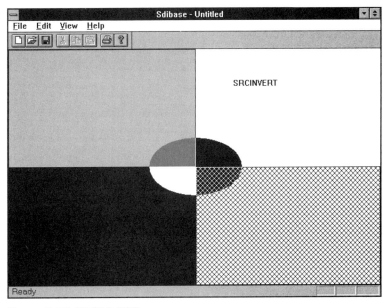

Figure 3-57: SRCINVERT.

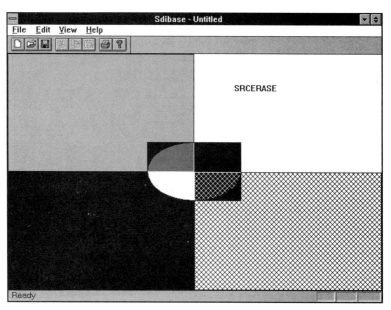

Figure 3-58: SRCERASE.

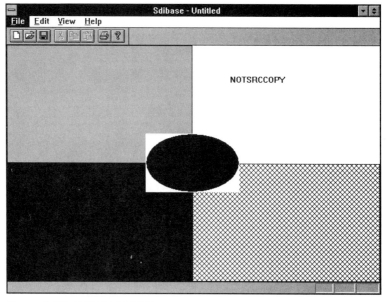

Figure 3-59: NOTSRCCOPY.

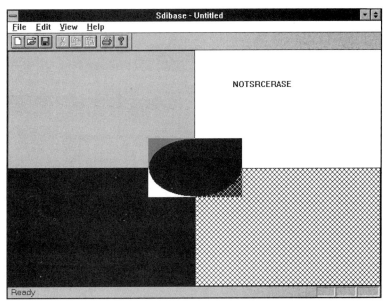

Figure 3-60: NOTSRCERASE.

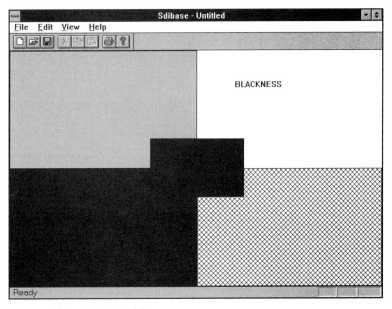

Figure 3-61: BLACKNESS.

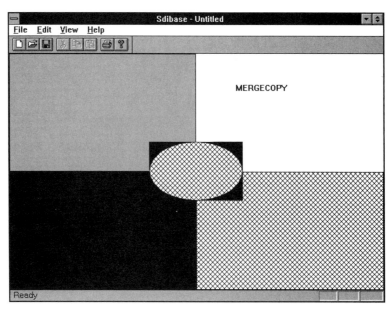

Figure 3-62: MERGECOPY.

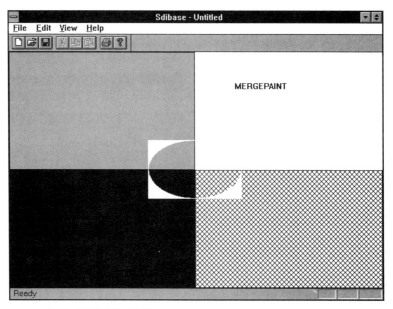

Figure 3-63: MERGEPAINT.

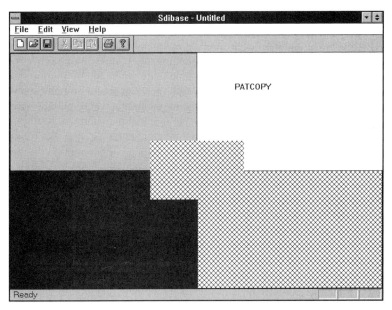

Figure 3-64: PATCOPY.

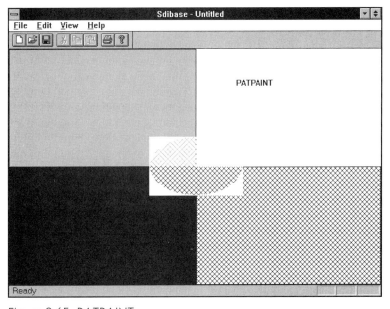

Figure 3-65: PATPAINT.

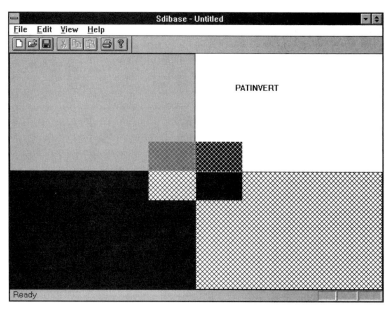

Figure 3-66: PATINVERT.

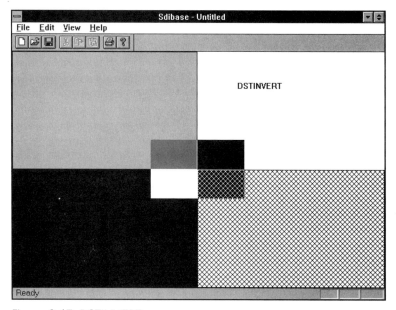

Figure 3-67: DSTINVERT.

Stretching & Compressing Bitmaps

If the dimensions of your source and destination bitmaps don't match exactly, then they are stretched or compressed until they fit. This happens transparently if you use **BitBlt** for bitmaps of unequal sizes. If you use the **StretchBlt** function, you can control stretching and placement explicitly.

```
//////////////////////////////////////////////////////////
//CSdibaseView drawing
    void CSdibaseView::OnDraw(CDC* pDC)
{
    CSdibaseDoc* pDoc = GetDocument();
    ASSERT_VALID(pDoc);
    //TODO: add draw code for native data here
    //We use the default MM_TEXT map mode and navigate the
    //client area in viewport units; We retrieve the dimensions
    //of the client area with GetClientRect
CRect rectClient;
GetClientRect( &rectClient );
    //To provide contrast between the background of the source
    //bitmap and the destination, we will paint the client area gray.
    //Select a stock brush and save the handle of the default brush.
CBrush* pDefaultBrush =
    ( CBrush* ) pDC->SelectStockObject( LTGRAY_BRUSH );
    //Shade the client area
pDC->Rectangle( rectClient.left,
        rectClient.top,
        rectClient.right,
        rectClient.bottom );
    //Replace the default brush
pDC->SelectObject( pDefaultBrush );
    //We need another DC to hold the bitmap we are going to
    //draw so we create it on the heap using the new operator.
    //This will have to be explicitly deleted when we are done with
    //it. Only stack based objects are automatically destroyed
    //when the function exits
CDC * pMemoryDC = new CDC;
```

```
                //Creating the object does not give us an initialized DC; A DC
                //can identify all sorts of display devices, so we need to
                //explicitly initialize ours to be compatible with the one the
                //manages the client area of the screen.
                //We do this with the CreateCompatibleDC function
        pMemoryDC->CreateCompatibleDC( pDC );
                //We can't use the memory DC we just created
                //to draw any output until we initialize it with a bitmap
                //First we create the bitmap object
        CBitmap * pMemoryBitmap = new CBitmap;
                //Then we initialize the object with a bitmap
                //that is 1/4 the width of the client area,
                //1/4 the height of the client area
                //has one color plane, one color bit for each pixel
                //and has no initial image data
        pMemoryBitmap->CreateBitmap(
                rectClient.right / 4,
                rectClient.bottom / 4, 1, 1, NULL );


                //We select the initialized bitmap object into the DC,
                //and now we can do output operations on the
                //memory DC
        CBitmap * pOldBitmap =
                ( CBitmap * ) pMemoryDC->SelectObject( pMemoryBitmap );
                //Since our bitmap object had no initial image data,
                //it starts out filled with whatever random garbage existed in
                //the memory it now occupies. PatBlt allows us to fill a
                //rectangle specified by the first four parameters with a pattern.
                //The constant we use here, BLACKNESS, is a ROP code that
                //causes the rectangle to be painted black.
        pMemoryDC->PatBlt( 0, 0,
                rectClient.right,
                rectClient.bottom,
                BLACKNESS );
                //Then we draw an ellipse and fill it with the standard white
                //brush— this is our "source" bitmap.
        pMemoryDC->Ellipse(0, 0,
                rectClient.right / 4,
                rectClient.bottom / 4);
```

```
//Transfer the bits from the memory DC to the screen
//DC using BitBlt. The sizes of the source and destination match
//exactly so there will be no distortion of the source when it is
//painted on the destination
pDC->BitBlt( rectClient.right / 8,        //Upper left x coord
                                          //of the dest
        rectClient.bottom / 8,            //Upper left y coord
                                          //of the dest
        rectClient.right / 4,             //Width of the dest
        rectClient.bottom / 4,            //Height of the dest
        pMemoryDC,                        //Pointer to SOURCE DC
        0,      //Upper left x coord of SOURCE
        0,      //Upper left y coord of SOURCE
        SRCCOPY);                 //The raster operation that combines
                                  //the bits of source,
                                  //destination, and background
                                  //brush (ROP code)


//Now transfer the bits from the memory DC to the screen
//DC using StretchBlt to squeeze the bitmap. We are making it
//half as wide on the destination as it was in the source. We do
//this by reducing the width of the destination rectangle to
rectClient.right / 8
pDC->StretchBlt ( 5 * rectClient.right / 8,    //Upper left x coord
                                               //of the dest
        rectClient.bottom / 8,            //Upper left y coord
                                          //of the dest
        rectClient.right / 8,             //Width of the dest
        rectClient.bottom / 4,            //Height of the dest
        pMemoryDC,                        //Pointer to SOURCE
                                          //DC
        0,      //Upper left x coord of SOURCE
        0,      //Upper left y coord of SOURCE
        rectClient.right / 4,             //Width of the source
        rectClient.bottom / 4,            //Height of the source
        SRCCOPY);                 //The raster operation that combines
                                  //the bits of source,
                                  //destination, and background
                                  //brush (ROP code)
```

```
    //Both the memory DC and the bitmap we used to initialize it
    //were created on the heap using the new operator, so they
    //must be explicitly deleted.
    //First, we must select the bitmap out of the memory DC, and
    //replace the pointer to the "old bitmap." Never delete any
    //object that is currently selected in a DC.
    //Selecting the pointer to the old bitmap returns a pointer to
    //our bitmap object, which in turn is deleted.
delete pMemoryDC->SelectObject( pOldBitmap );
    //After dispatching the bitmap, we can delete the DC
delete pMemoryDC;
}
/////////////////////////////////////////////////////////////////
```

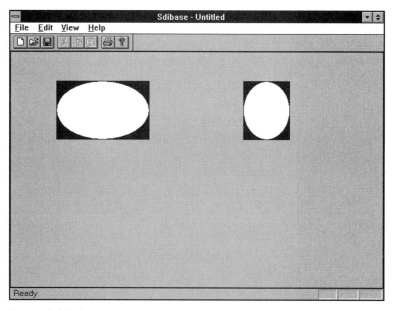

Figure 3-68: Stretching and compressing bitmaps.

Device Dependent Drawing Attributes

The device independent drawing environment of Windows shields you from the need to accomodate all kinds output devices specifically, but sometimes you need to be able to make allowances for the idiosyncracies of a device. For example, many pen plotters can't render bitmaps, so you probably wouldn't want your application to attempt to send documents with embedded bitmaps to them.

The **GetDeviceCaps** function can retrieve a great variety of information about the capabilities of a particular device. This gives you a way to test for device dependencies at runtime so that you don't have to make restrictive assumptions at design time. It can provide many more kinds of information than are shown here. See the **CDC::GetDeviceCaps** heading in the function reference section for more detail.

```
/////////////////////////////////////////////////////////
//CSdibaseView drawing
    void CSdibaseView::OnDraw(CDC* pDC)
{
    CSdibaseDoc* pDoc = GetDocument();
    ASSERT_VALID(pDoc);
    //TODO: add draw code for native data here
    //We use the default MM_TEXT map mode and navigate the
    //client area in viewport units; We retrieve the dimensions
    //of the screen with GetClientRect
CRect rectClient;
GetClientRect( &rectClient );
    //The TEXTMETRIC structure contains detailed information
    //about the current font. Below we use the tmMaxCharWidth
    //field, which is the width in device units of the widest
    //character in the font, and the tmHeight and tmExternalLeading
    //fields together to give the height of a line of text. The
    //tmHeight field gives the height in device units of the tallest
    //character in the font.
TEXTMETRIC tmTextMetrics;
    //Get the text metrics for the current font so we can calculate
    //the height of a line
pDC->GetTextMetrics( &tmTextMetrics );
```

```
    //We set up these three variables to make out TextOut calls
    //look a bit tidier
int nThisCol = rectClient.left + tmTextMetrics.tmMaxCharWidth;
int nThisLine = rectClient.top + tmTextMetrics.tmHeight +
    tmTextMetrics.tmExternalLeading;
int nOneLineDown = tmTextMetrics.tmHeight +
tmTextMetrics.tmExternalLeading;
    //Write a heading for our column of device raster capabilities
pDC->TextOut( nThisCol, nThisLine, "Raster Capabilities",
     strlen( "Raster Capabilities" ) );
    //Move down two lines
nThisLine += 2 * nOneLineDown;
    //Call GetDeviceCaps to get the raster capabilities
int nRasterCaps = pDC->GetDeviceCaps( RASTERCAPS );
    //Compare the value returned by GetDeviceCaps
    //to the named constants to see if the device supports a
    //particular raster capability
if( nRasterCaps & RC_BITBLT )
 pDC->TextOut( nThisCol, nThisLine += nOneLineDown,
    "Can do standard BLT",
    strlen( "Can do standard BLT" ) );
    if( nRasterCaps & RC_BANDING )
pDC->TextOut( nThisCol, nThisLine += nOneLineDown,
    "Device requires banding support",
    strlen( "Device requires banding support" ) );
    if( nRasterCaps & RC_SCALING )
pDC->TextOut( nThisCol, nThisLine += nOneLineDown,
    "Device requires scaling support",
    strlen( "Device requires scaling support" ) );
    if( nRasterCaps & RC_PALETTE )
pDC->TextOut( nThisCol, nThisLine += nOneLineDown,
    "supports a palette ",
    strlen( "supports a palette " ) );
    if( nRasterCaps & RC_BIGFONT )
pDC->TextOut( nThisCol, nThisLine += nOneLineDown,
    "supports >64K fonts ",
    strlen( "supports >64K fonts " ) );
    if( nRasterCaps & RC_STRETCHBLT )
pDC->TextOut( nThisCol, nThisLine += nOneLineDown,
    "supports StretchBlt ",
    strlen( "supports StretchBlt " ) );
    if( nRasterCaps & RC_FLOODFILL )
```

```
    pDC->TextOut( nThisCol, nThisLine += nOneLineDown,
        "supports FloodFill ",
        strlen( "supports FloodFill " ) );


    //Move over and start a new column for polygonal capabilities
nThisCol += rectClient.right / 2;
nThisLine = rectClient.top + tmTextMetrics.tmHeight +
        tmTextMetrics.tmExternalLeading;
    //Write out a heading for the column
pDC->TextOut( nThisCol, nThisLine,
        "Polygon Capabilities", strlen( "Polygon Capabilities" ) );
    //Move down two lines
nThisLine += 2 * nOneLineDown;


    //Call GetDeviceCaps to get the polygon capabilities
int nPolygonCaps = pDC->GetDeviceCaps( POLYGONALCAPS );
    //Compare the value returned by GetDeviceCaps
    //to the named constants to see if the device supports a
    //particular polygonal capability
    if( nPolygonCaps & PC_POLYGON )
pDC->TextOut( nThisCol, nThisLine += nOneLineDown,
        "Can do polygons ",
        strlen( "Can do polygons " ) );
    if( nPolygonCaps & PC_RECTANGLE )
pDC->TextOut( nThisCol, nThisLine += nOneLineDown,
        "Can do rectangles",
        strlen( "Can do rectangles" ) );
    if( nPolygonCaps & PC_WINDPOLYGON )
pDC->TextOut( nThisCol, nThisLine += nOneLineDown,
        "Can do winding polygons",
        strlen( "Can do winding polygons" ) );

if( nPolygonCaps & PC_TRAPEZOID )
pDC->TextOut( nThisCol, nThisLine += nOneLineDown,
        "Can do trapezoids",
        strlen( "Can do trapezoids" ) );
```

```
if( nPolygonCaps & PC_SCANLINE )
pDC->TextOut( nThisCol, nThisLine += nOneLineDown,
    "Can do scanlines",
    strlen( "Can do scanlines" ) );

if( nPolygonCaps & PC_WIDE )
pDC->TextOut( nThisCol, nThisLine += nOneLineDown,
    "Can do wide borders ",
    strlen( "Can do wide borders " ) );

if( nPolygonCaps & PC_STYLED )
pDC->TextOut( nThisCol, nThisLine += nOneLineDown,
    "Can do styled borders ",
    strlen( "Can do styled borders " ) );

if( nPolygonCaps & PC_WIDESTYLED )
pDC->TextOut( nThisCol, nThisLine += nOneLineDown,
    "Can do wide styled borders",
    strlen( "Can do wide styled borders" ) );

if( nPolygonCaps & PC_INTERIORS )
pDC->TextOut( nThisCol, nThisLine += nOneLineDown,
    "Can do interiors ",
    strlen( "Can do interiors " ) );
    //Get the horizontal and vertical resolution of the output device
int nPixelsX = pDC->GetDeviceCaps( HORZRES );
int nPixelsY = pDC->GetDeviceCaps( VERTRES );
    //Create a string object to hold the caption
CString stringResolution;
    //Use the format function to concatenate and format the
    //message
stringResolution.Format( "%s%i", "Horizontal Resolution: ", nPixelsX );
    //Write out the horizontal resolution message
pDC->TextOut( rectClient.left, rectClient.bottom - 5 *
        nOneLineDown,
        stringResolution );
```

```
            //Do it again for the vertical resolution
        stringResolution.Format( "%s%i", "Vertical Resolution: ", nPixelsY );
        pDC->TextOut( rectClient.left, rectClient.bottom - 3 *
                nOneLineDown,
                stringResolution );


    }
```

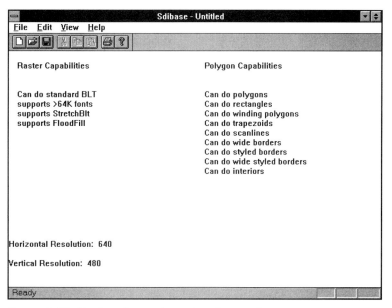

Figure 3-69: Device dependent drawing attributes.

One of the things with which Windows programmers learn to cope is the fact that there are some kinds of things your application just can't determine in advance. Luckily, Windows is replete with information retrieval interfaces that will help your application to decide at runtime whether a particular display device can do interior fills of graphics, the aspect ratio of the screen, the color of the background brush, and dozens of other things as well.

Dialogs & Controls

In most cases, controls such as buttons and list boxes exist inside dialog boxes. Visual C++ provides services and tools that make creating and programming dialogs and the controls they manage a snap. To use the following examples, begin by generating a basic skeleton for a project. Below we will use the SDI project that was the basis of the examples we looked at in the "Drawing in the Client Area" section.

Creating a New Dialog

Before creating controls, we need to create a dialog box in which the controls are to be displayed. To do this, complete the following steps.

First, select the Files item under the Project menu. Now you see a tree diagram of the files in the project. Click the left mouse button over the file that has the extension .rc. This is the resource file, which contains definitions of the application's resources like dialogs, bitmaps, icons and so on. Double-clicking it wakes up the resource editor. If you click the left mouse button twice over the dialog folder, it will show you the dialogs your application already has.

A brand new application generated by the AppWizard includes an About dialog box, which may be used to display version and copyright information. If we had other dialogs, they would appear in this list, and we could access them by clicking over them.

We want to create a new dialog. Click the right mouse button over the Dialog file folder, and a floating menu will appear. Choose New Dialog. The palette displayed on the right gives us a selection of controls that we can drop on the dialog. A right-click over the dialog brings up a floating menu that has two enabled menu items. Ignore ClassWizard for the time being, and choose Properties.

The Properties box is a tabbed dialog that allows us to define the appearance and behavior of our dialog. Change the caption of the dialog by typing **Dialog Recipes: Using Dialog Based Controls** in the Caption edit control.

Click on the tab titled Styles. We will use the default styles, but you can experiment with the check boxes to alter the appearance and behavior of your dialog. For a full description of what these styles do, see the guided tour of the resource editors in Section 2 of this book.

Buttons

Next to static text, buttons are the simplest controls to create and employ. We don't really need any introduction, so we'll press on with the example. If you haven't already created a dialog box to contain the button, follow the steps in the "Creating a New Dialog" section above.

Next, select the button control from the palette at the right of the empty dialog box. Click over the dialog to drop the button. Move the button by holding down the left mouse button while the cursor is over it and then dragging.

The new button is automatically selected when it is dropped on the dialog. (To select another control, click once over it with the left mouse button.) The little rectangular handles that appear around its frame when it is selected allow you to move or size the button.

Click the right mouse button over the button, and you'll see a floating menu that includes several enabled choices. Select the Properties item. The button's properties define certain aspects of its behavior and appearance. We'll be using some of the default properties for this button. Notice that it is automatically assigned a resource ID of IDC_BUTTON1. Allowing the resource editor to assign the constants associated with IDs ensures that they will be unique, and that the ID will be properly added to all of the files in which it needs to exist. We can change the ID's name to something more meaningful to our application and still take advantage of these features.

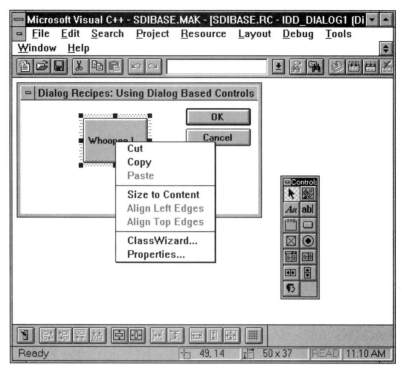

Figure 3-70: We want the button to be initially visible in the dialog, and we want the user to be able to navigate to the button with the Tab key, so the only change we make is to the button's caption.

Now we are ready to do some coding, but first, lets review what we have done to this point. We have a created the visual elements of a dialog box including standard OK and Cancel buttons, and a push button interface element inside the dialog. To this point, most of what we have done (and what has been done on our behalf) establishes the visual location and appearance of the dialog and the new button.

The next step is to connect the visual interface element of our button to the code that will actually implement its behavior. Sometimes this is called "plumbing" the interface elements to the handler code. Select the dialog frame by clicking at any point that is not occupied by a control with the left mouse button. Next, click the right mouse button and a pop-up menu will appear.

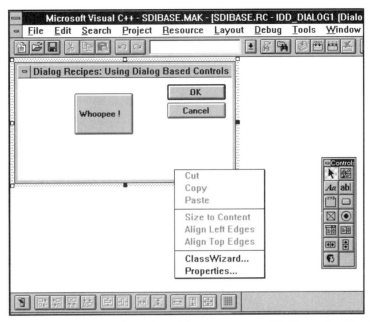

Figure 3-71: Select ClassWizard from the menu. We'll use the ClassWizard dialog to create a class for the dialog and a handler function for each of the messages the button will process.

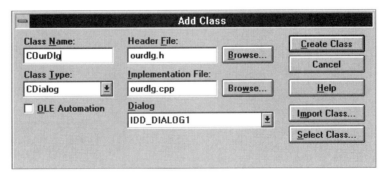

Figure 3-72: We provide a name for our dialog box class, and the names for the support files are automatically synthesized by the Add Class dialog. Click Create Class to generate a skeleton class.

Notice a few things about the Message Maps page of the ClassWizard dialog (see Figure 3-73). At the upper left is a list of objects, including the name of the class we just created for the dialog frame and the IDs of all of the controls in the dialog. If you select any of these objects, a list of Windows messages appears in the listbox to the right. It includes all of the system messages a control is capable of processing. The important thing about this is that it means that you and I don't have to determine which messages are appropriate to a given interface element.

Also note that the only member function we have at this point, **DoDataExchange**, is preceded by a *V*. This means that this particular member is a virtual function. The framework provides us with a default implementation, but we can replace it with a function of our own by the same name. We would do this to implement application-specific logic when the dialog passes the input it gathered from the the user to the application.

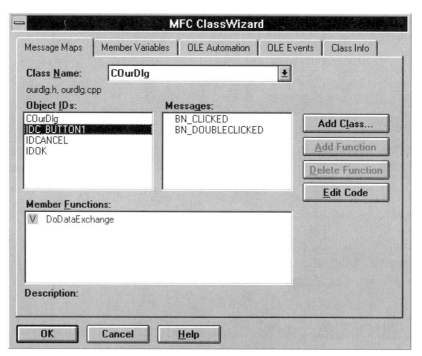

Figure 3-73: The Message Maps page of the MFC ClassWizard dialog box.

When we select our control, IDC_BUTTON1, from the list on the left, and then select the BN_CLICKED message, the Add Member Function box is displayed. It displays a default name for the member function we will complete. The member function will take action as necessary when the button receives this message, and it is called a *handler*.

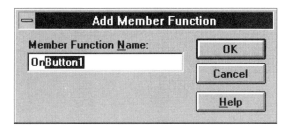

Figure 3-74: The Add Member Function dialog box.

After we add the member function, it is appended to the list in the lower right corner of the ClassWizard dialog. The BN_CLICKED message in the message listbox is preceded by a small image of a hand, signifying that the application has implemented a handler function for it. We can use either the Edit Code button or double-click on the handler function name in the dialog to open the text editor and display the code that has been generated for this function. The code is an empty function body, to which we will add logic to display a message box.

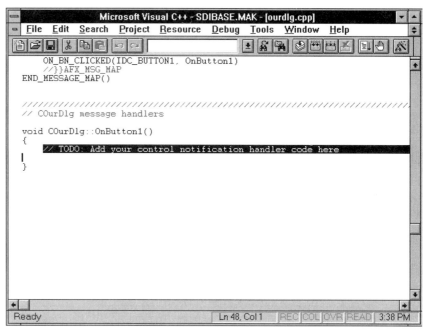

Figure 3-75: The code generated for the ON_BN_CLICKED function.

Where to Add Code: The BN_CLICKED handler is in the dialog implementation file, ourdlg.cpp.

The header for the dialog class our application derived, **COurDlg**, must be **#included** at the top of the view class implementation file. We used the generic SDI base application in this example, so that file is named sdibavw.cpp.

The code that creates and displays the dialog is placed in the view's constructor function, **SdibaseView**. (This is unusual in that it causes the dialog to be displayed immediately when the application wakes up. It allows us to demonstrate the modal dialog box without using menus or capturing mouse input, however.)

```
///////////////////////////////////////////////////////
//COurDlg message handlers
    void COurDlg::OnButton1( )
    //This is the function generated by ClassWizard
{
    //This line displays a message box when we click on the button
    //in our dialog
    MessageBox( "Whoopee, it's recess!" );
```

```
//This line calls the CDialog base class function which terminates
//the dialog
CDialog::OnCancel();
}
```

In order to create a dialog in the view class, we have to include the header for the dialog class in the view's implementation file. This line is inserted immediately after the one that includes the view's header.

```
//Include the class declaration for COurDlg
#include "ourdlg.h"
```

To create the dialog, we add two lines to the application's view class constructor.

```
/////////////////////////////////////////////////////////////
//CSdibaseView construction/destruction
    CSdibaseView::CSdibaseView()
{
    //Now we create a dialog object on the stack.
    //Putting the creation here makes our dialog
    //appear as soon as the application is opened.
    COurDlg OurButtonDemoDlg;

    //Calling this member function makes the modal dialog visible. It
    //doesn't return until the dialog has been destroyed.
    int dlgReturn = OurButtonDemoDlg.DoModal();
    }
```

Bitmapped Buttons

Bitmap buttons differ from ordinary push buttons in that they allow you to associate up to four bitmaps with a button in place of a text caption. Generally, the four bitmaps represent the button's appearance when the button is up, down, has the focus, or is disabled. We use the up bitmap when the button has not been clicked, and the down bitmap to show that the button has been depressed by the user.

Occasionally a button's bitmap means that whatever it controls is in an indeterminate state. You can see an example of the indeterminate state in Microsoft Word, when you select a passage of text that includes some words in italics. The italics button on the speedbar assumes its indeterminate state because the text selection is neither exclusively italic nor exclusively non-italic.

197

Our example uses two bitmaps: one for the up state and one for the down state of the push button. We'll use the basic SDI application, and follow the same basic steps to create the dialog box template that were listed in the recipe for push buttons, except that when you create a bitmap button you check the Owner Draw box of its Properties dialog.

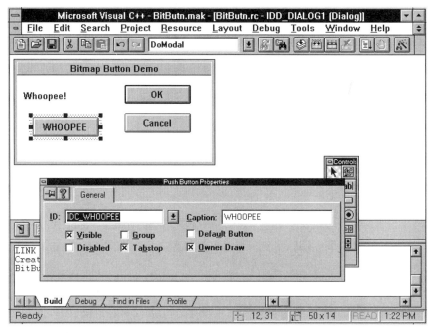

Figure 3-76: When you create a bitmap button, check the Owner Draw check box in the Properties dialog box.

Notice also that we have changed the default name for the bitmap button's constant to IDC_WHOOPEE, and changed its caption to WHOOPEE. (We never want to let ourselves forget how much fun this all can be...)

Bitmaps are associated with their bitmap button by the button's caption. This is a bit of a sleight of hand, because, obviously, a button that displays a bitmap can't also have a caption. The button's caption will be used at run time to find the bitmap that reflects the button's state. In this case we are using two bitmaps and must name them as follows. The up bitmap is named WHOOPEEU.BMP, which is the button's caption with a *U* appended. The down bitmap is named WHOOPEED.BMP, or the button's caption plus a *D*. If we were using the additional bitmaps, we would name them in the same way, appending an *F* for focus and an *X* for disabled.

The next step is finding or creating the bitmaps. We will make our own using the Resource editor. From the Resource menu, choose New, which will display a dialog listing the resource types. Select Bitmap from the list, and do a little bit of doodling. Save the two bitmaps using the File Save command.

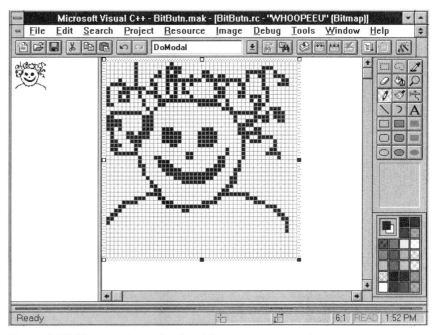

Figure 3-77: You see here the first bitmap we created.

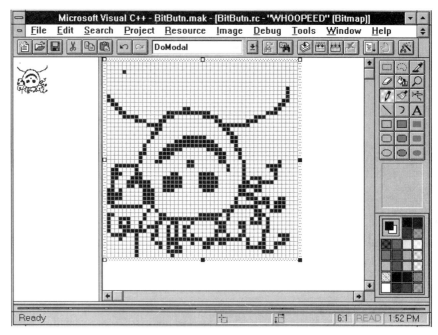

Figure 3-78: Here's the second bitmap we created.

You can also import existing bitmaps and use them in your applications, but exercise a bit of caution. Many that you find by browsing your system will be under the protection of copyright.

After we have the two bitmaps, we want to modify their IDs. Normally bitmap resources are identified by constants (IDC_BITMAP1, for example) but *bitmap button bitmaps are an exception*. In place of an ID, they are represented by double quoted strings that are exactly the same as the fictitious caption for the button, except that either a *U*, a *D*, an *X* or an *F* is appended. Under Resources, select the Set Symbols menu item. The Symbol Browser dialog (see Figure 3-79) lists all of your application's resource-related symbols. To make the list a bit less confusing, uncheck the Show Read-Only Symbols box. That way only the symbols specific to your application will be listed. Select the bitmap resource you just created from the list and click the Change button to display the Change Symbol dialog box (see Figure 3-80).

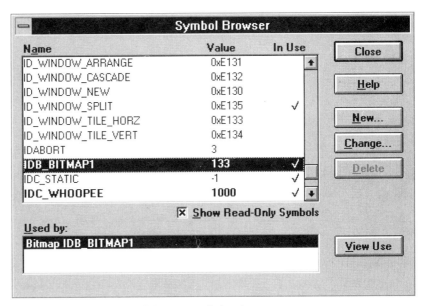

Figure 3-79: The Symbol Browser dialog box.

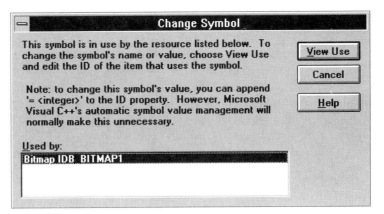

Figure 3-80: The Change Symbol dialog box.

Now click the View Use button to open the bitmap's Properties dialog.

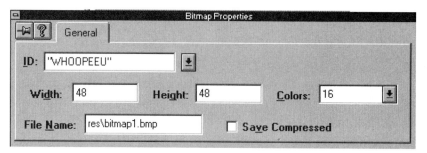

Figure 3-81: The Bitmap Properties dialog box.

This is where we exchange the IDC_BITMAP1 ID for WHOOPEEU. *Make sure to use all uppercase letters, and to enclose the new name in double quotes.* After you make this change, the constants for the bitmaps will no longer appear in the list of symbols. Don't let this confuse you. If you need to get to the bitmaps again, you can access them through the Project.Files window. Click on the application's resource file (the one that has the file suffix .rc) and a list will appear that includes the renamed bitmap resources.

Where to Add Code: We have constructed the visual interface elements, so now we can turn our attention to creating a class to manage the dialog and its controls. From the Project menu, Select ClassWizard. First we create a class, which we name **CWhoopee**. Next, for each of the object IDs we select the message types we wish to handle. (For a detailed discussion of using the ClassWizard to plumb visual interface elements to handler code, look at the recipe for ordinary push buttons in the previous section.)

By default, our dialog class includes a handler for **DoDataExchange**. This example doesn't collect any data from the user, so we will ignore this function, and just accept the default implementation. We select **CWhoopee** and add a handler for the WM_INITDIALOG message. This is the point at which we must associate the bitmaps with our bitmap button, so use the Edit Code button to drop into this function. Here is what we want to add.

```
/////////////////////////////////////////////////////
//CWhoopee message handlers
    BOOL CWhoopee::OnInitDialog()
{   //This is the code that loads all of the bitmaps associated
    //with the bitmap button.
    m_BitmapButton.AutoLoad(IDC_WHOOPEE, this );
    //Everything below these comments was automatically
    //generated
    CDialog::OnInitDialog();

    return TRUE;
    //return TRUE unless you set the focus to a control
    //EXCEPTION: OCX Property Pages should return FALSE
}
```

Next we visit the header file for our dialog class, whoopee.h, and add these lines:

```
    //This gives the view access to CWhoopee member functions
    //and data
friend class CBitButnView;
    //This creates our bitmap button object
private:
    CBitmapButton m_BitmapButton;
```

We make two changes to the implementation file of the view, bitbuvw.cpp. First, we include the dialog class header after the other **#includes** in the implementation of the view.

```
#include "whoopee.h"
```

In the constructor of the view, we set a member variable, m_FirstPaint, to equal TRUE. We do this because in this example we want our dialog to be displayed only the first time the window is painted.

```
/////////////////////////////////////////////////////
//CBitButnView construction/destruction
    CBitButnView::CBitButnView()
{
    //Set the member to true so that the dialog will
    //be displayed the first time the window is painted.
  m_FirstPaint = TRUE;
}
```

Next, we modify the **OnDraw** member function of the view.

```
    void CBitButnView::OnDraw(CDC* pDC)
{
    CBitButnDoc* pDoc = GetDocument();
    ASSERT_VALID(pDoc);
    //We create a CWhoopee dialog object and show it with
    //DoModal if this is the first time the window has been painted.
    //After the dialog returns, we set m_FirstPaint to FALSE
    CWhoopee BitButtonDlg;
    if( m_FirstPaint )
    {
        BitButtonDlg.DoModal();
        m_FirstPaint = FALSE;
    }
    }
```

The final step is adding a member variable to the view, which we place in bitbuvw.h.

```
    private:
        BOOL m_FirstPaint;
```

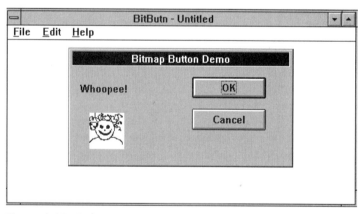

Figure 3-82: Our bitmap button looks like this when it is "up."

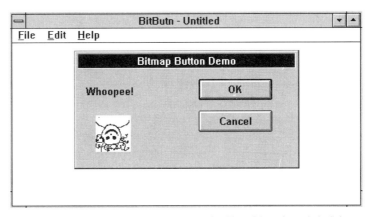

Figure 3-83: Our bitmap button looks like this when it is "down."

Check Boxes

We have shown how to create visual interface elements using the dialog editor in the two previous recipes. Let's assume that for the sake of this example, we have a basic SDI application and a dialog template with the three check boxes shown below. We accepted all of the default properties for the check boxes, so they are initially visible and can be reached by using the Tab key to navigate through the dialog. We set the IDs of the check boxes to IDC_TRAIN, IDC_DOOR and IDC_MAYO, using the ID control of the Properties box for each.

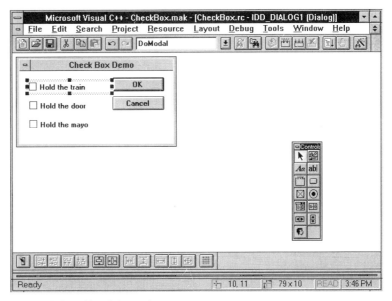

Figure 3-84: Check box demo.

Now we will use ClassWizard to generate a class for this dialog. Click on any unused area of the dialog to select the dialog frame, then click the right mouse button and select ClassWizard from the floating menu. We create a class called **CCheckBoxDemo** when the Add Class dialog is displayed.

Next we use ClassWizard to add member variables to the dialog class so that we can record the state of each of the check boxes. Click the dialog's Member Variables tab, select the ID of a check box control from the list, and click the Add Variable button. All that is necessary here is to supply a name that reflects the correspondence of the member variable to the control. We use **m_bTrain** as the name for the variable that will record the state of the Hold the train check box. Notice that the default type of the variable is BOOL. ClassWizard has made an assumption on our behalf that we will want to record a value of either TRUE or FALSE when we collect data from this control.

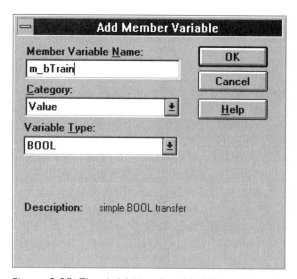

Figure 3-85: The Add Member Variable dialog box.

We add more or less the same code to the view to launch the dialog that we did in the bitmap button recipe, modified to reflect the names and types used in the check box dialog.

In the constructor of the view, we set a member variable, **m_FirstPaint**, to equal TRUE. We do this because in this example we want our dialog to be displayed only the first time the window is painted.

```
/////////////////////////////////////////////////////////
//CCheckBoxView construction/destruction
    CCheckBoxView::CCheckBoxView()
{
    //Display the dialog only the first time the client area is painted
    m_FirstPaint = TRUE;
}
```

Next, we modify the OnDraw member function of the view.

```
/////////////////////////////////////////////////////////
//CCheckBoxView drawing
    void CCheckBoxView::OnDraw(CDC* pDC)
{
    CCheckBoxDoc* pDoc = GetDocument();
    ASSERT_VALID(pDoc);
    //We create a CCheckBoxDemo dialog object and show it with
    //DoModal if this is the first time the window has been painted.
    //After the dialog returns, we set m_FirstPaint to FALSE
CCheckBoxDemo CheckBoxDlg;
if( m_FirstPaint )
{
    //Here we set the initial value of the controls
    CheckBoxDlg.m_bTrain = FALSE;
    CheckBoxDlg.m_bDoor = FALSE;
    CheckBoxDlg.m_bMayo = FALSE;
    CheckBoxDlg.DoModal();
    m_FirstPaint = FALSE;
}
    }
```

The final step is adding a member variable to the view, which we place in checkvw.h.

```
private:
    BOOL m_FirstPaint;
```

If we build the application at this point, we get a functioning dialog box that includes the check box controls. The controls handle checking and unchecking themselves with no help from us! What is more surprising, but not altogether obvious, is that the dialog also updates the member variables we linked to the controls in the previous step using the ClassWizard Member Variable page.

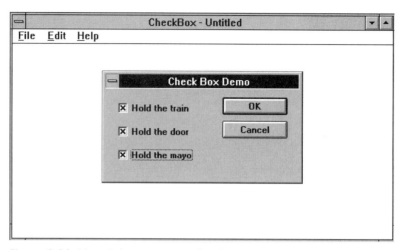

Figure 3-86: Here is how our application looks.

Just how does the group of member variables get updated when the boxes are checked and unchecked? ClassWizard generates two sets of maps that handle the transfer of data between member variables and dialog box controls. One of them is in the dialog box constructor function, and the other is in the **DoDataExchange** function. Their listings appear below.

```
CCheckBoxDemo::CCheckBoxDemo(CWnd* pParent /*=NULL*/)
    : CDialog(CCheckBoxDemo::IDD, pParent)
{
    //{{AFX_DATA_INIT(CCheckBoxDemo)
    m_door = FALSE;
    m_mayo = FALSE;
    m_train = FALSE;
    //}}AFX_DATA_INIT
}

void CCheckBoxDemo::DoDataExchange(CDataExchange* pDX)
{
    CDialog::DoDataExchange(pDX);
    //{{AFX_DATA_MAP(CCheckBoxDemo)
    DDX_Check(pDX, IDC_DOOR, m_door);
    DDX_Check(pDX, IDC_MAYO, m_mayo);
    DDX_Check(pDX, IDC_TRAIN, m_train);
    //}}AFX_DATA_MAP
}
```

Both of these functions were generated in their entirety by ClassWizard. Notice what appear to be commented macro calls at the beginning and end of the blocks of statements in the two functions. These are not really comments. You could think of them as being more along the lines of guards around the ClassWizard-generated data exchange maps. Everything between the opening and closing curly braces is maintained by ClassWizard, so you should never attempt to modify data exchange mapping by editing the code in these places directly. If you need to add or delete a variable, use the Member Variables page of ClassWizard to do so.

Radio Buttons

Radio buttons are groups of controls where only one of the group may be selected at a time. Once again, we will assume that we start with a basic SDI application skeleton and a dialog box template that includes three radio buttons. The dialog template is shown below.

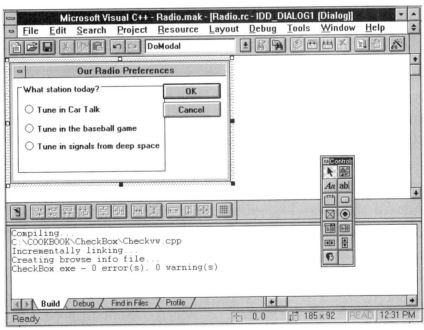

Figure 3-87: A dialog box template that includes three radio buttons.

For radio buttons there is one detail to which you must pay special attention on the Properties box. The first button of the group must have its Group box checked, and all other buttons in the group must have this property cleared.

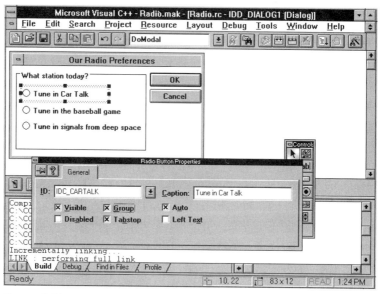

Figure 3-88: The Radio Button Properties dialog box.

Next we generate a class, **CRadioDlg**, for our dialog, using ClassWizard. Now we need a member variable to record the selection state of the radio buttons. Recall that individual radio buttons are part of a group, and only one of the group may be selected at any given time. For this reason, we need a *single* member variable that records which button is selected rather than a member for each control. When the ClassWizard displays the Member Variables page for **CRadioDlg**, it shows only the first control, IDC_CARTALK, in the list of objects. The key idea here is that it is treating the entire group of radio buttons as an indivisible object.

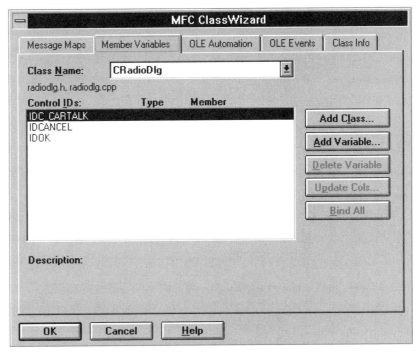

Figure 3-89: The Member Variables page of the MFC ClassWizard dialog box.

We create a member variable, **m_nRadioPreference**, to record which of the group is selected. The framework automatically assigns 0 to this variable if the first radio button is selected, 1 if the second button is selected, and so on.

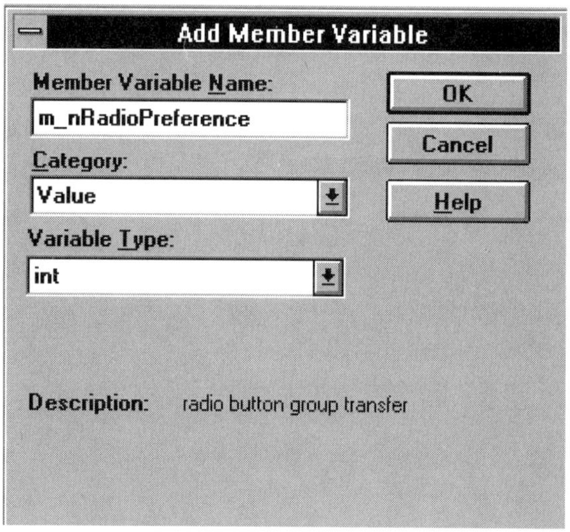

Figure 3-90: The Add Member Variable dialog box with the variable
m_nRadioPreference added.

Now all we have to do is add some code to the application's view
class that allows us to launch the dialog. We make two changes to
the implementation file of the view, **radiow.cpp**. First, we include
the dialog class header after the other **#includes** in the implementation of the view.

```
#include "radio.h"
```

In the constructor of the view, we set a member variable,
m_FirstPaint, to equal TRUE. We do this because in this example
we want our dialog to be displayed only the first time the window
is painted.

```
/////////////////////////////////////////////////////////
//CRadioViewconstruction/destruction
    CRadioView::CRadioView()
{
    //Set the member to true so that the dialog will
    //be displayed the first time the window is painted.
  m_FirstPaint = TRUE;
}
```

Next, we modify the **OnDraw** member function of the view.

```
    void CRadioView::OnDraw(CDC* pDC)
{

    CRadioDoc* pDoc = GetDocument();
    ASSERT_VALID(pDoc);
    //We create a CRadioDlg dialog object and show it with
    //DoModal if this is the first time the window has been painted.
    //After the dialog returns, we set m_FirstPaint to FALSE
    CRadioDlg RadioDlg;
if( m_FirstPaint )
{
    //Here we set the initial value of the controls
    //Radio buttons in a group are numbered 0 thru n-1
    //The statement below initially selects the third button in the
    //group
    RadioDlg.m_nRadioPreference = 2;
    RadioDlg.DoModal();
    m_FirstPaint = FALSE;
}
}
```

The final step is adding a member variable to the view, which we place in radiovw.h.

```
    private:
    BOOL m_FirstPaint;
```

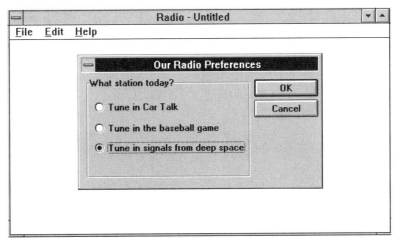

Figure 3-91: Here is how our radio button demo looks.

Edit Controls

Edit controls accept text input from the user. In most respects they are similar to the dialog box controls already described. Let's again assume that we have a basic SDI application skeleton, and a dialog template created that looks like Figure 3-92.

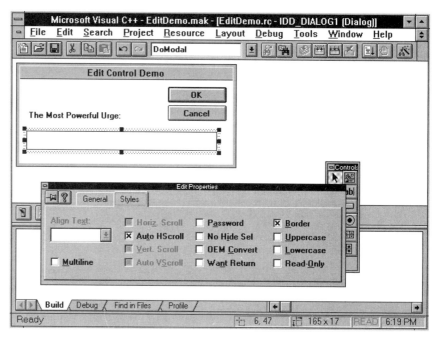

Figure 3-92: The Dialog editor.

The next step is to create a member variable to hold the contents of the edit control. We do this from the ClassWizard Member Variables page.

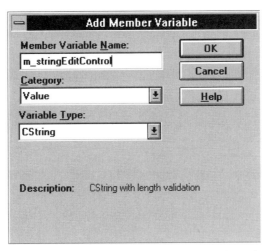

Figure 3-93: Creating a member variable to hold the contents of the edit control.

Notice that for this control we have specified that we will accept a maximum of 48 characters by filling in the maximum length control of the ClassWizard Member Variables page. When the framework data exchange mechanism is invoked it will check the length of the input string and display a message box if the input string is too long.

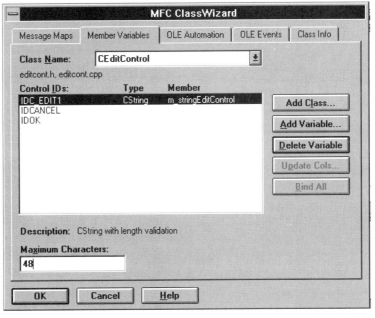

Figure 3-94: The Member Variables page of the ClassWizard dialog.

Here is the code we add to the view's implementation file:

```
#include "Editcont.h"
/////////////////////////////////////////////////////////
//CEditDemoView construction/destruction
    CEditDemoView::CEditDemoView()
{
    //Set the member to true so that the dialog will
    //be displayed the first time the window is painted.
  m_FirstPaint = TRUE;
    }
/////////////////////////////////////////////////////////
//CEditDemoView drawing
    void CEditDemoView::OnDraw(CDC* pDC)
{
    CEditDemoDoc* pDoc = GetDocument();
    ASSERT_VALID(pDoc);
    //We create a CEditControl dialog object and show it with
    //DoModal if this is the first time the window has been painted.
    //After the dialog returns, we set m_FirstPaint to FALSE
    CEditControl EditControl;
if( m_FirstPaint )
{
    EditControl.m_stringEditControl =
    "Is to edit another person's copy";
    EditControl.DoModal();
    m_FirstPaint = FALSE;
}
    }
```

And again, we add these lines to the header file of the view, editdvw.h:

```
private:
BOOL m_FirstPaint;
```

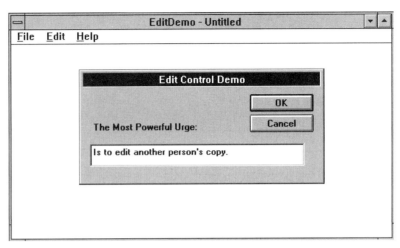

Figure 3-95: Here is how the edit control demo looks.

Dropdown Lists

Dropdown list controls provide a way to prompt the user to make a choice from a pre-established set of alternatives. (The list of disk drives in the common File dialog is a dropdown list.) To create a dropdown control, start by selecting the combo box control from the Dialog editor's tool palette. Drop the control on the dialog, size it, and then open its property box. Select Drop List from the list of control types on the Styles page.

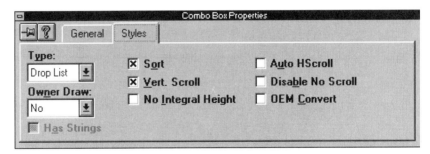

Figure 3-96: Select Drop List from the list of control types on the Styles page.

Click the tab for the General properties, and here we will enter the list of choices that will appear when the list drops down. If you want to type in more than one choice, there is a bit of a trick to it. *For each new line, hold down the Ctrl key as you press Enter.* If you forget and simply hit the Enter key, you'll dismiss the Properties box.

217

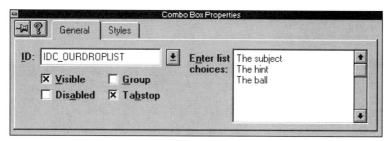

Figure 3-97: Enter the list of choices.

Next we will follow the familiar route, by adding a member variable to the dialog class we generate for this dialog template. We will call it **m_stringDropChoice**.

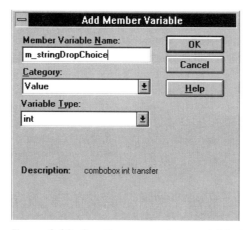

Figure 3-98: Creating a member variable to hold the contents of the edit control.

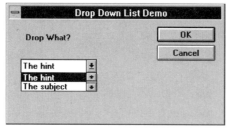

Figure 3-99: If we add the now-familiar code that launches the dialog from the view the first time the view is painted, we get something that looks like this.

This type of dropdown does not allow the user to select anything that is not in the list of choices presented by the list. If you need a dropdown list that allows users to supply their own choices as well as pick from your list, then you can use the dropdown combo box control. These behave in much the same way as combo boxes (which we touch on in the next recipe), and you can select this style from the type list in the Properties box.

List Boxes & Combo Boxes

List boxes and combo boxes are closely related. List boxes, sensibly enough, present the user with a list of choices. Depending on the properties selected for the control, the list may allow multiple item selection and even multiple columns. A special type, the Owner Draw List, allows you to insert graphics as list elements (a map key might make use of this feature), though much of the responsibility for updating falls on the application with this sort of list box. Combo boxes simply couple an edit control with a list box, so that users may select from the list or use the edit control to specify their selection.

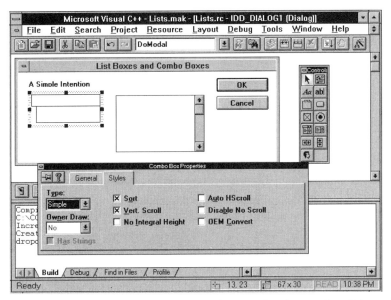

Figure 3-100: Let's start with a basic SDI application and a dialog template that looks like this. The first thing to notice here is that we have specified the type of the combo box control as Simple.

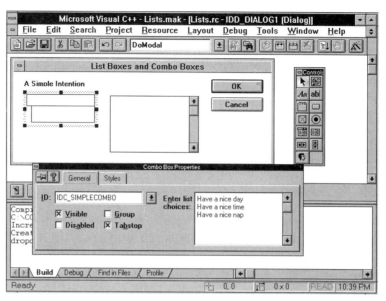

Figure 3-101: Again, we specify the list of choices that will appear in the combo box by typing them one per line and pressing Ctrl and Enter keys at the same time to move from line to line.

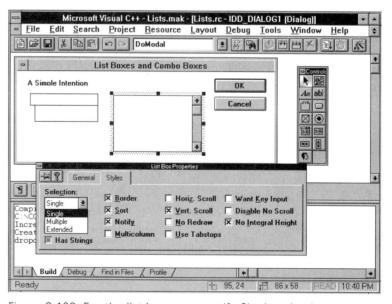

Figure 3-102: For the list box, we specify Single selection, meaning that only one list entry can be selected at a time.

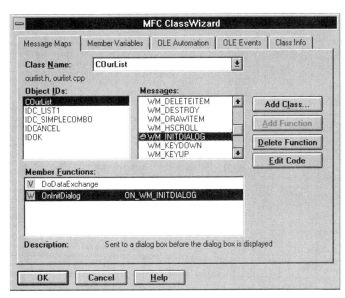

Figure 3-103: Unlike some of the other controls, list boxes must be initialized with the strings they will contain in the OnInitDialog function. Now we'll use ClassWizard to create a handler for the WM_INITDIALOG message.

Dropping into the code with the Edit Code button, we add these lines to put our strings in the dialog.

```
//////////////////////////////////////////////////////
//COurList message handlers
    BOOL COurList::OnInitDialog()
{
    CListBox* pListBox = (CListBox *) GetDlgItem(IDC_LIST1 );
    pListBox->InsertString( -1, "Left Handed" );
    pListBox->InsertString( -1, "Right Handed" );
    pListBox->InsertString( -1, "Ambidextrous " );

    return   CDialog::OnInitDialog();
    }
```

The first gets a pointer to the list box object by passing its ID to GetDlgItem. Using this pointer, we add strings to the list box with InsertString. Finally we call the base class function to complete initialization. This is how the dialog looks.

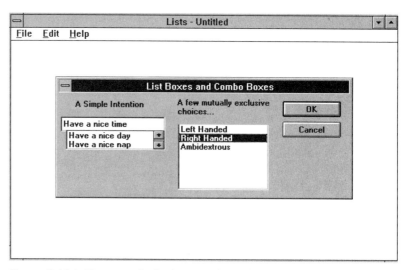

Figure 3-104: The sample list box and combo box.

Notice that even though we specified Sort in the Styles page of the list box's Properties dialog, the strings appear in exactly the order in which we made the insertion calls, rather than in alphabetical order. This is because we used -1 as the first argument to InsertString. This value directs the function to insert each new string at the end of the list.

Getting Input

Most programs need input from the user to do useful work. In this section we provide recipes for capturing input from the mouse and using Windows menus.

Capturing Mouse Input

Of all the things that generate messages, the mouse is responsible for by far the greatest number of them. Mouse messages are sent every time a mouse button goes up or down, and every time the user moves the mouse, and in all but a very few cases, your application has nothing to gain from knowing about it. For this reason, an application doesn't normally see the mouse messaging traffic. The example below captures the mouse when the user clicks the left button and then prints the coordinates at which the mouse-click occurred.

Let's assume we are starting out with the basic SDI application we have used in other recipes. The first thing we are going to do is add two variables to the header file of our view class **CMouseView**. One will record the location at which the user pressed the left mouse button, and the other will tell us whether the mouse message stream is currently captured by our application. They are in the file mousevw.h and look like this:

```
private:
    BOOL   m_bMouseCaptured;
    CPoint m_MousePoint;
```

Next we will use ClassWizard to create handlers for the WM_LBUTTONUP and WM_LBUTTONDOWN mouse events. We choose the view class from the project files window, and then select the Project menu's ClassWizard item. From the list on the left, select the **CMouseView** class, which implements the application's view. From the list of messages, select WM_LBUTTONUP and WM_LBUTTONDOWN.

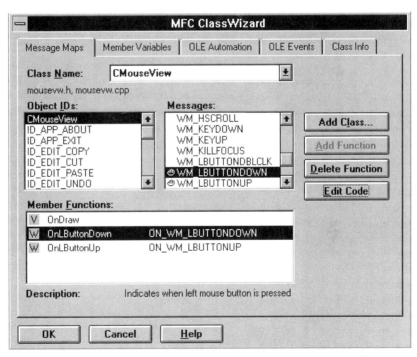

Figure 3-105: Use ClassWizard to create the mouse event handlers.

Now that we have handlers mapped to the left button events, let's add code to capture the mouse message stream when the button goes down, and save the location at which this occurred.

```
void CMouseView::OnLButtonDown(UINT nFlags, CPoint point)
{
    //First we say that we want to recieve mouse messages
    SetCapture();
    //Next we set our member variable to record mouse capture
    //state
    m_bMouseCaptured = TRUE;
    //We want to know where it was captured—this information is
    //passed to us in the parameters to OnLButtonDown
    m_MousePoint = point;
    //We cause the OnDraw member function to be called
    InvalidateRect(NULL, FALSE);
    CView::OnLButtonDown(nFlags, point);
}
```

When the client area is invalidated, **OnDraw** is called. Here is the code that prints the location of the mouse.

```
void CMouseView::OnDraw(CDC* pDC)
{
    //Our buffer for formatting the string we print
    char  szMouseLocation[24];

    CMouseDoc* pDoc = GetDocument();
    ASSERT_VALID(pDoc);
    //Is the mouse captured?
    if(m_bMouseCaptured)
    {   //If so, print the location at which the user clicked
        //the left button
        sprintf(szMouseLocation, "%s%i%s%i","Mouse Click At:  ",
                m_MousePoint.x, ",", m_MousePoint.y);
        pDC->TextOut(m_MousePoint.x,
        m_MousePoint.y,szMouseLocation);

    }
}
```

We want to terminate the flow of mouse messages if the user releases the left button. We do this in the handler for WMLBUTTONUP.

```
void CMouseView::OnLButtonUp(UINT nFlags, CPoint point)
{
    //We don't want to see the mouse message stream any more
    ReleaseCapture();
    //Record the new capture state in our data member
    m_bMouseCaptured = FALSE;

    CView::OnLButtonUp(nFlags,  point);
}
```

If you build the application and click a few times in the client area, you'll get a pair of coordinates for each point at which a click occurred.

Using Menus

Many user commands are initiated by choosing menu items. One of the advantages of the MFC way of doing things is that it automates so much menu processing. We will add an item to the system menu bar to trigger display of a message box.

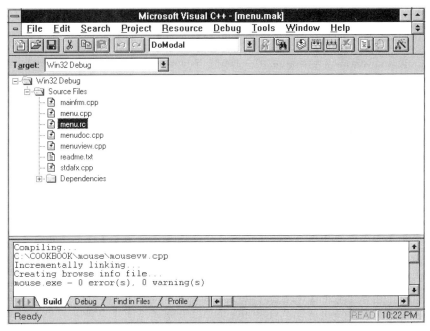

Figure 3-106: Assume we have an SDI application, and this is its project manager window. Select the resource file by clicking over its folder.

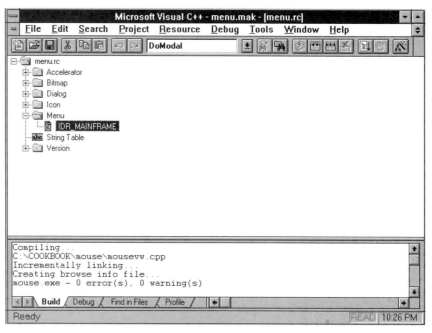

Figure 3-107: We want to edit the system menu, so select
IDR_MAINFRAME and double-click.

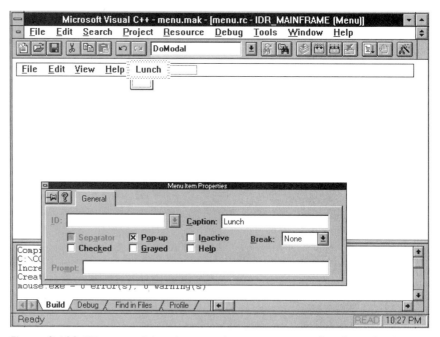

Figure 3-108: We can add an item to the system menu bar by selecting
the highlighted box and typing in a menu item name.

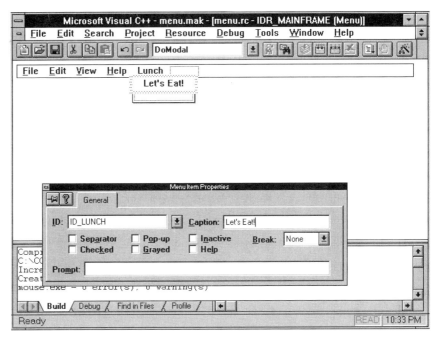

Figure 3-109: Next we add an item to the dropdown below the system menu, and use the Properties box to set its ID.

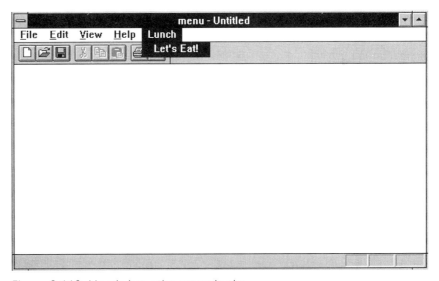

Figure 3-110: Here's how the menu looks.

Moving On

In the first two sections of this book we presented an introduction to using the Visual C++ AppWizard, as well as the various resource editors that make up the Visual C++ integrated development environment. And in this section we explored a series of code "recipes" that you can use to add specific features and functionality to your application skeletons.

In the next and final section of the book, you'll find a handy alphabetical reference, including descriptions and function prototypes, of the Microsoft Foundation Classes C++ Library, version 3.0. This reference will serve as a valuable aid as you add and modify code in your Visual C++ applications.

SECTION IV

ALPHABETICAL REFERENCE TO THE MICROSOFT FOUNDATION CLASSES C++ LIBRARY

CArchive

Description   The class **CArchive** is used to transfer objects between disk and memory in binary format. A **CArchive** object is most often used in conjunction with the **Serialize** methods of a user-defined type derived from **CObject**. It can also be used with objects of the **CFile** class to implement serialization of binary or special format objects. Applications that use the **CArchive** class to serialize objects in conjunction with the standard **OnFileOpen** supplied by MFC don't have to create or manipulate **CFile** objects directly because archival services are handled transparently by the framework. Otherwise, they must open a **CFile** object, and create a **CArchive** object from it before using it as an archive. The application's **Serialize** function loads data into the archive object, and the **CArchive** object buffers the data as it is being transferred to the **CFile** object. The application framework handles the connection between the application's **Serialize** function, the **CArchive** object, and the **CFile** object, which is responsible for storing the data.

Serialization is one of the most difficult concepts for people new to object-oriented technologies to grasp. In MFC, serialization is implemented primarily through **CArchive** objects. It implements the concept of "persistent objects," or objects that retain their state across disjoint executions of the program. The key to this is that the object is recreated when deserialized exactly as it was when last seen.

There is no particular magic to this, as the user provides the semantics that define what state must be retained. Of particular interest to the new user of these classes is the fact that deserializing an object from an archive actually *creates* the object. This is a key concept, because it clarifies a number of issues that will be encountered later on.

Member Functions

CArchive   FUNCTION

Description   **CArchive** constructs an object and specifies whether it will be used to store data to disk or load data into memory. Don't explicitly destroy this object. Let scope destruct it or allocate it on the heap and delete it. The compiler has no way of knowing you did this and will try to destruct the object *again* as it goes out of scope.

Prototype

```
//Function Prototype
//CArchive(CFile* pFile, UINT nMode, int nBufSize  = 512, void
FAR* lpBuf = NULL );
```

Example

```
//Alternative 1
TRY{
CArchive loadArchive(&file, CArchive::load |
CArchive::bNoFlushOnDelete);
    //Call the Serialize function and try to load the data
  Serialize(loadArchive);
    //Close the archive and its associated file object
  loadArchive.Close();
  file.Close();
} //Destructor for loadArchive implicitly called here.
CATCH(CArchiveException e){
    //Handle the exception
#ifndef _CPPUNWIND
    //For compilands that don't do C++ stack unwinding
    //explicitly destruct the object.
    loadArchive::~CArchive();
#endif
} END_CATCH
//Alternative 2
TRY{
CArchive *pLoadArchive = new CArchive(&file, CArchive::load |
CArchive::bNoFlushOnDelete);
    //Call the Serialize function and try to load the data
  Serialize(*pLoadArchive);
    //Close the archive and its associated file object
  pLoadArchive->Close();
  file.Close();
    delete pLoadArchive;
CATCH(CArchiveException e){
    //Destroy the archive object
    delete pLoadArchive;
}
```

~CArchive   FUNCTION

Description   **~CArchive** deletes the **CArchive** object. Before deleting the object, the application should flush the archive buffer and close the associated file. This can be done by calling the **Close** member function. This function is called implicitly when the archive object goes out of scope or when it is deleted (if it is allocated on the heap using the new operator). *See CArchive for a usage example.*

Prototype
```
//Function Prototype
//~CArchive( )
```

Close   FUNCTION

Description   **Close** flushes the archive buffer and closes the file associated with the object. *See CArchive for a usage example.*

Prototype
```
//Function Prototype
//void Close( );
```

Flush   FUNCTION

Description   **Flush** forces the data in the archive buffer to be written to the file associated with the archive. *See GetFile for a usage example.*

Prototype
```
//Function Prototype
//void Flush( );
```

GetFile   FUNCTION

Description   **GetFile** gets the **CFile** pointer to the file object associated with the archive.

Prototype
```
//Function Prototype
    //CArchive::Read only lets us read 64K or less at a time
if (dwBytes >= 0x10000)
{
    //If we want to read more than 64K,
    //use CFile interface for huge Read
    //First flush all outstanding archive
    //buffer data to the archive
    ar.Flush( );
```

```
        //Then get a pointer to the CFile object
        //and read a huge chunk
        CFile* pFile = ar.GetFile();
        dwBytesRead = pFile->ReadHuge(lpBuf, dwBytes);
    }
    else
    {
        //Otherwise, just use the Read member function
        dwBytesRead = ar.Read(lpBuf, (UINT)dwBytes);
    }
```

IsLoading   FUNCTION

Description   **IsLoading** returns TRUE if the archive is reading data from disk to memory.

Prototype
```
//Function Prototype
//BOOL IsLoading( )const;
    //Is the archive loading to memory?
if (ar.IsLoading( ))
{
    //If so, use the extraction
    //operator to load the item from disk
    ar >> m_MemberData;
}
```

IsStoring   FUNCTION

Description   **IsStoring** returns TRUE if the archive is reading data from memory to disk.

Prototype
```
//Function Prototype
//BOOL IsStoring( )const;
    //Is the archive storing to disk?
if (ar.IsStoring( ))
{
    //If so, use the insertion operator to send this item to disk
    ar << m_MemberData;
}
```

Read
FUNCTION

Description **Read** does a byte-for-byte read of an archive and returns the number of bytes read. If the return is less than the requested amount of bytes, the archive has reached the end of the file. *See **GetFile** for a usage example.*

Prototype
```
//Function Prototype
//UINT Read(void FAR* lpBuf, UINT nMax);
```

ReadObject
FUNCTION

Description **ReadObject** calls an object's **Serialize** function to read data from the archive file and constructs an object of the appropriate type. If the object contains embedded pointers to other **CObject**-derived objects, they are constructed as needed, and the embedded object pointers are initialized with valid values.

Prototype
```
//Function Prototype
//CObject* ReadObject(const CRuntimeClass*
    //pClassRefRequested);
CMyObject *pMyObject;
pMyObject = (CMyObject *)
ar.ReadObject(RUNTIME_CLASS(CMyObject));
    //Note that the key here is that a
    //fully-constructed object is returned from this function.
```

Write
FUNCTION

Description **Write** does a byte-for-byte write to an archive.

Prototype
```
//Function Prototype
//void Write(const void FAR* lpBuf, UINT nMax);
    //Write the string to the archive;
    //its length is given by the second parameter
ar.Write(lpszText, strlen(lpszText)*sizeof(TCHAR));
```

WriteObject   FUNCTION

Description   **WriteObject** calls an object's **Serialize** function to write an object to a disk file. **WriteObject** preserves information about the object's class name and the classes of objects for which it includes embedded pointers. How you use the **Serialize** function determines whether the object is deserialized from the inside out (as you might expect). The right way to serialize an object is to

1. Serialize/deserialize the base class.
2. Serialize/deserialize any embedded objects.
3. Serialize/deserialize any state scalars.

By strictly observing this symmetry, you can be sure you'll get a completely initialized persistent object.

Prototype

```
//Function Prototype
//void WriteObject(const CObject* pOb);
```

Operators

operator >>   OPERATOR

Description   **operator >>** is the overloaded archive-storage insertion operator. The insertion operator stores fundamental data types and **CObject**-derived objects to disk. Types supported by the **CArchive** insertion and extraction operators are as follows:

```
CObject *          (any type derived from CObject)
BYTE
WORD
LONG
DWORD
float
double
```

*See **IsStoring** for a usage example.*

operator <<   OPERATOR

Description   **operator <<** is the overloaded archive-loading extraction operator. The extraction operator loads fundamental data types and **CObject**-derived objects to disk. See the previous topic regarding types supported by MFC. *See **IsLoading** for a usage example.*

ArchiveException

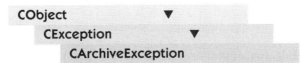

Derivation

CObject ▼
   CException ▼
      CArchiveException

Description The **CArchiveException** class provides objects that signal serialization I/O-related failures. Its public data member records the generic, and therefore portable, exception descriptor code. The **CArchiveException** group of conditions is thrown from **CArchive**-class member functions. The constructor for this class is never called directly. Instead, the global function **AfxThrowArchiveException** is used. The **CArchiveException** object is accessible from within the handler that catches it. The most interesting of all of these to work with is **CArchiveException::BadSchema**, as it indicates a downlevel version of an archive. When upgrading an archive format, it is advisable to upgrade its schema; you can then keep code around to trap this exception and convert old-style archives to new formats.

Public Data Members

m_cause

MEMBER

Description **m_cause** is the portable cause code for the exception. The following table lists the correspondence between specific error messages and the possible values of the **CArchiveException** enumeration for portable error identification.

237

Reported Serialization Error	Portable Enumeration
CArchiveException::none	No errors.
CArchiveException::generic	Error does not map to a pre-established CArchiveException category.
CArchiveException::readOnly	Tried to write to an archive opened for reading.
CArchiveException::endOfFile	End of file encountered during read
CArchiveException::writeOnly	Tried to read from an archive opened for reading.
CArchiveException::badIndex	Invalid file format.
CArchiveException::badClass	Tried to read an object of the wrong type.
CArchiveException::BadSchema	Tried to read an object by using the wrong version of the class.

Member Functions

CArchiveException FUNCTION

Description **CArchiveException** constructs an object of this type and stores the portable cause code in its member variable. This function is never called directly. Instead, the global function **AfxThrowArchiveException** is used. More commonly, you will do something like derive a class from **CArchive**, then throw **CArchiveExceptions** from any customized functions.

Prototype
```
//Prototype
//CArchiveException( int cause = CArchiveException::none );
```

Example
```
    //Read in raw data from an archive in MAX_LEN bytes-size
    //chunks
if (ar.Read(lpszBuffer, MAX_LEN) != MAX_LEN )
    //If we get less than MAX_LEN bytes, we are at the end of the
    //file
    AfxThrowArchiveException(CArchiveException::endOfFile);
```

CBEdit
CLASS

Derivation

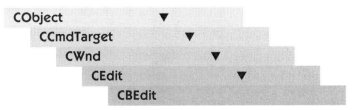

CObject ▼

CCmdTarget ▼

CWnd ▼

CEdit ▼

CBEdit

Description The **CBEdit** class implements the Windows handwriting-recognition boxed-edit controls used by the Windows pen interface. It differs from the **CHEdit** class handwriting-recognition edit control in that it displays a "comb" that forces the user to space characters in a predetermined way. The forced placement of characters improves recognition performance of the engine. The **CBEdit** control inherits the functionality of both the **CEdit** and the **CHEdit** classes, adding member functions that deal with the individual input characters. Pen-based APIs are not available for Win32 or Win32s.

Member Functions

CBEdit
FUNCTION

Description **CBEdit** constructs a **CBEdit** object, but does not create, attach or initialize its accompanying edit control window.

Example
```
//Construct an edit control in the frame window's client area
CBEdit edOurEdit;
//Then specify its style, location, parent, and control ID
edOurBEdit.Create( WS_CHILD | WS_VISIBLE | ES_AUTOVSCROLL,
rect, this, ID_OUREDITCTRL);
```

Create
FUNCTION

Description **Create** creates a Windows boxed handwriting edit control, attaches it to the **CBEdit** object, and shows it. Like edit controls, handwriting edit control properties are determined by style constants, which may be combined with one another. They are listed in the **Create** member function entry of the **CEdit** class. *See **CBEdit** for a usage example.*

CharOffset   FUNCTION

Description   **CharOffset** returns the offset in the *text buffer* of the character that was developed from the ink in the comb position specified by the parameter. If the parameter passed is greater than the total length of the text buffer, the return has -1 in the high word and the length of the text in bytes of the translated string. Note that there is not always a 1:1 mapping between character cells in the control and characters.

Prototype
```
//Function Prototype
//DWORD CharOffset( UINT nCharPos );
```

CharPosition   FUNCTION

Description   **CharPosition** returns the offset in the *edit control comb* of the text buffer position specified by the parameter. If the parameter passed is greater than the total length of the text buffer, the return has -1 in the high word and the length of the edit control in logical positions. This function maps from physical to logical position (that is, byte offset in the buffer to position in the comb). By contrast, the previous function **CharOffset** maps from logical to physical.

Prototype
```
//Function Prototype
//DWORD CharPosition( UINT nCharPos );
```

DefaultFont   FUNCTION

Description   **DefaultFont** resets the font of the edit control to the default and optionally repaints it.

Prototype
```
//Function Prototype
//BOOL DefaultFont( BOOL bRepaint );
```

GetBoxLayout   FUNCTION

Description   **GetBoxLayout** fills in a structure that defines the way in which a boxed handwriting edit control is laid out. Below is the structure declaration and a description of its fields.

```
typedef struct{        int cyCusp;
        int cyEndCusp;
        UINT style;
        DWORD rgbText;
        DWORD rgbBox;
        DWORD rgbSelect;} BOXLAYOUT;
```

cyCusp	Height (in pixels) of the box when the BXS_RECT style is specified, otherwise the height of the comb. This is the equivalent in pixels of BXD_CUSPHEIGHT in dialog units.
cyEndCusp	Height (in pixels) of the cusps at the ends of the box. This is the equivalent in pixels of BXD_ENDCUSPHEIGHT in dialog units.
style	0 for a single-line boxed edit control, BXS_ENDTEXTMARK for a multiline boxed edit control, or BXS_RECT for a boxed-edit control that uses rectangular boxes instead of a comb.
rgbText	If -1, the color of the window text is used; otherwise, this member specifies the RGB color to use for text.
rgbBox	If -1, the color of the window frame is used; otherwise, this member specifies the RGB color to use for the boxes.
rgbSelect	If -1, the color of the window text is used; otherwise, this member specifies the RGB color to use for the selection.

Prototype   //Function Prototype
//void GetBoxLayout(LPBOXLAYOUT lpBoxLayoutStruct);

SetBoxLayout   FUNCTION

Description   **SetBoxLayout** specifies new parameters for the layout of the boxes in the control.

Prototype   //Function Prototype
//BOOL SetBoxLayout(LPBOXLAYOUT lpBoxLayoutStruct);

CBitmap

CLASS

Derivation

CObject ▼

    CGdiObject ▼

        CBitmap

Description   **CBitmap** encapsulates the Windows GDI bitmap. Used with **CDC** member functions for bitmap manipulation. **CBitmap** is not used with **CBitmapButton**.

Member Functions

CBitmap   FUNCTION

Description   This constructor creates an uninitialized **CBitmap** object. The object must be initialized with a bitmap before it can be used.

Prototype
```
//Function Prototype
//CBitmap( );
CBitmap  theBitmapObject;   //creates a bitmap object, but
                            //it is not initialized
                            //with a bitmap resource
```

CreateBitmap   FUNCTION

Description   **CBitmap::CreateBitmap** initializes a **CBitmap** object with a memory-resident, device-dependent bitmap. Device-dependent bitmaps are provided for compatibility with older Windows applications. New applications should use the device-independent bitmap format (DIB). A bitmap created using this function must be deleted when the application is finished using it. It must not be selected in a device context at the time it is deleted. Bitmap widths must always be an even multiple of 16 because GDI handles bitmaps as arrays of two-byte integer values. When an application constructs a bitmap on its own or takes a bitmap from some non-Windows source, the bitmap rows may need to be padded if they don't satisfy this rule. Bitmaps copied between Windows device contexts (DCs) always obey this rule, so it is not a problem in that case. The return from **CreateBitmap** is non-zero if the function is successful; otherwise, it's zero.

Prototype
```
//Function Prototype
//BOOL CreateBitmap( int nWidth, int nHeight,
//UINT nPlanes, UINT nBitcount, const void FAR* lpBits );

CBitmap theBitmapObject;    //creates a bitmap object, but
                            //it is not initialized with
                            //a bitmap
theBitmapObject.CreateBitmap( nWidth, nHeight, nPlanes,
nBitcount, lpBits );    //initialize the bitmap:
                        //width and height are in
                        //pixels, how many color planes
                        //does the device have?
                        //How many bits give the color
                        //of a pixel?
                        //long pointer to the actual
                        //array of bits
```

CreateBitmapIndirect   FUNCTION

Description **CBitmap::CreateBitmapIndirect** initializes a **CBitmap** object with a memory-resident, device-dependent bitmap. The bitmap dimensions and format are defined in a structure passed to the function. Device-dependent bitmaps are provided for compatibility with older Windows applications. New applications should use the device-independent bitmap format (DIB). A bitmap created using this function must be deleted when the application is finished using it. It must not be selected in a device context at the time it is deleted. Bitmap widths must always be an even multiple of 16 because GDI handles bitmaps as arrays of two-byte integer values. When an application constructs a bitmap on its own or takes a bitmap from some non-Windows source, the bitmap rows may need to be padded if they don't satisfy this rule. Bitmaps copied between Windows DCs always obey this rule, so it is not a problem in that case. The return from **CreateBitmapIndirect** is non-zero if the function is successful, otherwise, it's zero.

Prototype
```
//Function Prototype
//BOOL CreateBitmapIndirect( LPBITMAP lpBitmapStruct );

CBitmap  theBitmapObject;   //creates a bitmap object, but
                            //it is not initialized with
                            //a bitmap
theBitmapObject.CreateBitmapIndirect( LPBITMAP lpBitmapStruct );
                //initialize the bitmap:
                //all the descriptors are
                //in the BITMAP struct
```

CreateCompatibleBitmap   FUNCTION

Description   **CBitmap::CreateCompatibleBitmap** initializes a **CBitmap** object. It establishes the color, format, and dimension of the new bitmap. These settings are compatible with those of the bitmap currently selected in the device context (DC), which is identified by the pointer to the DC object passed to the function.

   CreateCompatibleBitmap initializes a **CBitmap** object with an empty bitmap, which is to say that even though it is defined as being of a given size and color format, it contains no "picture" at this point. The application can select this initialized bitmap into a memory device context and direct GDI output to it. It can also be the source or destination for bit block transfer operations. A bitmap created using this function must be deleted when the application is finished using it. It must not be selected in a device context at the time it is deleted. The return from **CreateCompatibleBitmap** is non-zero if the function is successful; otherwise, it's zero.

Prototype
```
//Function Prototype
//BOOL CreateCompatibleBitmap( CDC* pDC, int nWidth,
//int nHeight);

CBitmap  theBitmapObject;   //creates a bitmap object, but
                            //it is not initialized with
                            //a bitmap
theBitmapObject.CreateCompatibleBitmap
            ( CDC* pDC, int nWidth, int nHeight );
                //initialize the bitmap object
                //with a bitmap compatible with
                //the memory, display, or printer
                //DC pointed to by pDC
```

CreateDiscardableBitmap

Description   **CBitmap::CreateDiscardableBitmap** initializes a **CBitmap** object. It establishes the color, format, and dimension of the new bitmap. These settings are compatible with those of the bitmap currently selected in the device context (DC), which is identified by the pointer to the DC object passed to the function.

       CreateDiscardableBitmap initializes a **CBitmap** object with an empty bitmap, which is to say that even though it is defined as being of a given size and color format, it contains no "picture" at this point. The bitmap can be discarded from memory by Windows if the bitmap is not currently selected in a device context and memory is low. The application can select this bitmap into a memory device context and direct GDI output to it. This function can also be the source or destination for bit block transfer operations. Device-dependent bitmaps are provided for compatibility with older Windows applications. New applications should use the device-independent bitmap format (DIB). A bitmap created using this function must be deleted when the application is finished using it. It must not be selected in a device context at the time it is deleted. Windows can optionally discard this bitmap from memory if it is not currently selected in a device context. The return from **CreateDiscardableBitmap** is non-zero if the function is successful; otherwise, it's zero.

Prototype
```
//Function Prototype
//BOOL CreateDiscardableBitmap( CDC* pDC, int nWidth,
//int nHeight);

CBitmap  theBitmapObject;   //creates a bitmap object,
                            //but it is not initialized
                            //with a bitmap
theBitmapObject.CreateDiscardableBitmap( CDC* pDC, int nWidth,
int nHeight );  //initialize the bitmap object
                //with a discardable bitmap
                //compatible with the memory,
                //display, or printer DC pointed
                //to by pDC
```

FromHandle   FUNCTION

Description   **CBitmap::FromHandle** returns a pointer to a temporary **CBitmap** object. The handle of the bitmap is attached to the **CBitmap** object. Internally, tracking of most Windows GDI objects is done using a table of handles. MFC provides classes to wrap the handles in objects, making the member functions of the class available to act on the object identified by the handle. Not all handles have wrappers, however, so the **FromHandle** family provides a quick and convenient way to package the handle temporarily in an object. An object pointer returned by any of the **FromHandle** family has a life cycle of approximately one Windows message-passing cycle, so when a function that uses this call exits, the object goes out of scope and is destroyed. It is therefore not necessary for an application to destroy an object returned by **FromHandle**. This process is taken care of during the idle-time processing of **CWinApp**. The object identified by the handle is not deleted along with the temporary object. **FromHandle** returns a valid pointer to the previously selected bitmap if successful, or NULL if unsuccessful.

      FromHandle is used with **CDC** member functions that do drawing, to quickly create an initialized **CBitmap** object.

      The lifetime of the object referenced by the pointer is very brief, so don't store the pointer for later use. It will be invalid.

Prototype

```
//Function Prototype
//static CBitmap* PASCAL FromHandle( HBITMAP hBitmap );
CBitmap* pThePreviousCBitmap;        //Save the pointer to the
                                     //currently selected object
                                     //in the DC; assume we have
                                     //a valid pointer to a CDC
                                     //object called pDC
pThePreviousCBitmap =
pDC->SelectObject(CBitmap::FromHandle(m_hObject));

        //Select a new bitmap that is identified
        //by the handle in the public member variable
        //of the CGdiObject base class
```

GetBitmapBits · FUNCTION

Description   **CBitmap::GetBitmapBits** copies the actual bit array for a
CBitmap object into a buffer supplied by the application. To
determine the size of the array, the application can call the
CGdiObject class member function **GetObject**. **GetObject** returns
the width, height and color format of the bitmap. From this information, you can calculate the array size. Bitmap arrays must always
be even multiples of bytes. **GetBitmapBits** returns the actual
number of bytes in the bitmap if successful, or returns zero if not
successful.

Prototype

```
//Function Prototype
//DWORD GetBitmapBits( DWORD dwCount, LPVOID lpBits );

CBitmap  theBitmapObject;   //creates a bitmap object, but
                            //it is not initialized with
                            //a bitmap
theBitmapObject.GetBitmapBits( dwCount, lpBits );
            //get a bit array from the bitmap
            //object by passing the number of
            //bytes our buffer can hold and a
            //long pointer to it
```

GetBitmapDimension · FUNCTION

Description   **CBitmap::GetBitmapDimension** retrieves the width and height
of a bitmap in .1-millimeter units, if they have been previously set
by calling **CBitmap::SetBitmapDimension**. If the bitmap dimensions have not previously been set using
CBitmap::SetBitmapDimension, the function returns 0.

Prototype

```
//Function Prototype
//CSize GetBitmapDimension( ) const;
CSize  sizeBitmap
CBitmap  theBitmapObject;   //creates a bitmap object,
                            //but it is not initialized
                            //with a bitmap
sizeBitmap = theBitmapObject.GetBitmapDimension( );
            //assume the size was previously
            //set using SetBitmapDimension;
            //sizeBitmap holds x and y in .1 mm units
```

LoadBitmap

FUNCTION

Description **CBitmap::LoadBitmap** loads a bitmap resource by name or ID from an application's executable file and attaches it to the current bitmap object. Bitmaps loaded using this function should be deleted using the **CGdiObject::DeleteObject** function. As contrasted with the functions in **CBitmapButton**, **LoadBitmap** can load bitmaps by both name (a string) or manifest constant.

Prototype
```
//Function Prototype
//BOOL LoadBitmap( LPCSTR lpszBitmapResourceName );
//BOOL LoadBitmap( UINT BITMAP_RESOURCE_ID );

CBitmap  theBitmapObject;   //creates a bitmap object, but
                            //it is not initialized with
                            //a bitmap
theBitmapObject.LoadBitmap(lpszBitmapResourceName);
                //assume we have initialized
                //the string with the name
                //of the bitmap used in the
                //resource file
theBitmapObject.LoadBitmap(IDR_OURBITMAP);
                //assume we have a resource ID for
                //the bitmap in our resource file
```
The return from **LoadBitmap** is non-zero if the function is successful; otherwise, it's zero.

LoadOEMBitmap

FUNCTION

Description **CBitmap::LoadOEMBitmap** loads a predefined Windows bitmap resource by name and attaches it to the current bitmap object. Bitmaps loaded using this function should *not* be deleted using the **CGdiObject::DeleteObject** function. The return from **LoadOEMBitmap** is non-zero if the function is successful; otherwise, it's zero.

The following list provides the names of predefined Windows bitmap resources.

OBM_BTNCORNERS	OBM_BTSIZE	OBM_CHECK
OBM_CHECKBOXES	OBM_CLOSE	OBM_COMBO
OBM_DNARROW	OBM_DNARROWD	OBM_DNARROWI
OBM_LFARROW	OBM_LFARROWD	OBM_LFARROWI
OBM_MNARROW	OBM_OLD_CLOSE	OBM_OLD_DNARROW
OBM_OLD_LFARROW	OBM_OLD_REDUCE	OBM_OLD_RESTORE
OBM_OLD_RGARROW	OBM_OLD_UPARROW	OBM_OLD_ZOOM
OBM_REDUCE	OBM_REDUCED	OBM_RESTORE
OBM_RESTORED	OBM_RGARROW	OBM_RGARROWD
OBM_RGARROWI	OBM_SIZE	OBM_UPARROW
OBM_UPARROWD	OBM_UPARROWI	OBM_ZOOM
OBM_ZOOMD		

Prototype

```
//Function Prototype
//BOOL LoadOEMBitmap( UINT BITMAP_RESOURCE_ID );

CBitmap  theBitmapObject;   //creates a bitmap object, but
                            //it is not initialized with
                            //a bitmap
theBitmapObject.LoadOEMBitmap( OBM_DNARROW );
            //This function accepts only
            //predefined Windows bitmap IDs
```

SetBitmapBits   FUNCTION

Description   **CBitmap::SetBitmapBits** sets the actual bit array for a **CBitmap** object. It is used with **CBitmap** class functions for creating and initializing bitmaps, **CDC** member functions that manipulate bitmaps, and **CBitmapButton** member functions. Bitmap arrays must always be even multiples of bytes. **SetBitmapBits** returns the number of bytes used in setting the bitmap bits or 0 if the function fails.

Prototype

```
//Function Prototype
//DWORD SetBitmapBits( DWORD dwCount,
//const VOID FAR* lpBits );

CBitmap  theBitmapObject;   //creates a bitmap object,
                            //but it is not initialized
                            //with a bitmap
```

```
theBitmapObject.SetBitmapBits( dwCount, lpBits );
                    //put a bit array in the bitmap
                    //object by passing the count of
                    //bytes and a long pointer to the
                    //buffer that holds them
```

SetBitmapDimension FUNCTION

Description **CBitmap::SetBitmapDimension** sets the width and height of a bitmap in .1-millimeter units. If the bitmap dimensions are not set using **CBitmap::SetBitmapDimension**, the function **CBitmap::GetBitmapDimension** returns a zero size.

Prototype
```
//Function Prototype
//CSize SetBitmapDimension( int nWidth, int nHeight );

CBitmap  theBitmapObject;   //creates a bitmap object,
                            //but it is not initialized
                            //with a bitmap
theBitmapObject.SetBitmapDimension
       ( int nMillimeterXin100ths, int nMillimeterXin100ths );
                    //assume we have x and y
                    //measurements in 100ths of
                    //millimeters
```

BitmapButton CLASS

Derivation

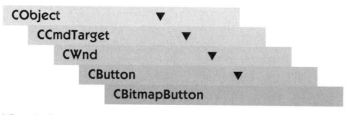

Description The **CBitmapButton** class implements a button control that displays a bitmap rather than a text caption. The button needs at least one bitmap and optionally as many as four to display itself in various selection states. The bitmaps represent the button's up, down, focused and disabled states. The dimensions of the bitmaps do not have to be identical, but only the portion of each bitmap that corresponds to the dimensions of the "up" bitmap are used to paint the button.

Bitmap buttons are constructed differently in dialog boxes than in an application's client area.

Member Functions

AutoLoad — FUNCTION

Description **AutoLoad** connects a button in a dialog box with a **CBitmapButton** object, loads its bitmaps, and sizes the button to fit the first bitmap. To create the connections between the control and the necessary bitmaps, create a push-button control in the dialog and set a caption for it. Use AppStudio to create and name bitmap resources that will be displayed on the push-button. The bitmap resources are named by combining the button's caption and one-letter suffixes: *U* for up, *D* for down, *F* for focused, and *X* for disabled. Also, emphasize that if you set the ID to IDB_FOOU, the bitmap isn't drawn. You must set the ID to "IDB_FOOU."

Add a **CBitmapButton** member to the application-derived **CDialog** object, and use it to call **AutoLoad** in the **OnInitDialog** handler with the button ID as the first parameter.

Example
```
//Example
}
//Function Prototype
//BOOL AutoLoad(UINT nID, CWnd* pParent);
    //We have a dialog that contains bitmapped buttons
BOOL BitButtonDlg::OnInitDialog( )
{
    //Load bitmaps for all the bitmap buttons
StereoButton.AutoLoad(ID_STEREO, this));
DolbyFilterButton.AutoLoad(ID_DOLBY, this);
return TRUE;
```

CBitmapButton — FUNCTION

Description **CBitmapButton** constructs a button object, but it does not initialize it with a bitmap or display it.

Example

```
//Create a bitmap button object
CBitmapButton m_OurBitmapButton;
    //Load it with two bitmaps
m_OurBitmapButtonl.LoadBitmaps(lpszUpPicture,
lpszDownPicture);
    //Force the button to be the size of the Up bitmap
m_OurBitmapButton.SizeToContent( );
```

LoadBitmaps   FUNCTION

Description   **LoadBitmaps** loads from one to four bitmaps used to paint a
bitmap button. **LoadBitmaps** is used for buttons created in a
window's client area, independently of a dialog box. Dialog bitmap
buttons load their bitmaps with the **AutoLoad** member function.

The first argument to **LoadBitmaps** identifies the bitmap that is
displayed when the button is in its normal "up" state, and it is
required to be present. The other three bitmaps are optional and
are used in the following ways: The second bitmap may be used to
display the button when it is pressed "down," the third is used to
display the button when it has the focus, and the fourth is displayed
when the button is disabled. The return value is non-zero if
LoadBitmaps succeeds; otherwise, it is zero.

It's important to note that, as distinct from the way AutoLoad
works, **LoadBitmaps** can load by resource ID, using arbitrary
identifiers. Equally important is that AppStudio, by default, gives
you a #define identifier to associate with each resource. These can't
be synthesized on the fly (at runtime), so you must make the ID a
string in the property page for each individual bitmap. You do this
by surrounding the identifier with quotes.

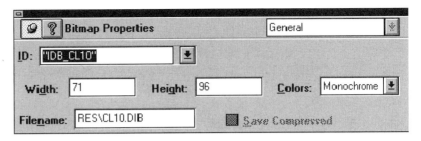

Figure B-1: Surround the identifier (IDB_CL10 in this example) with quotes.

See ***CBitmapButton*** *for a usage example.*

SizeToContent   FUNCTION

Description   **SizeToContent** forces a bitmap button window to resize itself to fit the bitmap. Use this function only for client-area bitmap buttons. Dialog bitmap buttons are automatically sized as a function of **AutoLoad**. *See* ***CBitmapButton*** *for a usage example.*

Prototype
```
//Function Prototype
//void SizeToContent( );
```

⟨ Brush   CLASS

· ·

Derivation

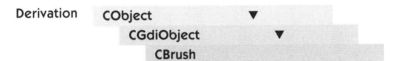

CObject   ▼
      CGdiObject   ▼
          CBrush

Description   **CBrush** encapsulates the Windows GDI brush. Used with **CDC** member functions for drawing and painting.

Member Functions

CBrush   FUNCTION

Description The **CBrush** class has four overloaded constructors to provide flexibility and convenience in constructing and initializing an application's brushes.

The following table shows the four constructors and when they are used.

Constructor Prototype	Description
CBrush( )	Use this when the constructor call can't be allowed to throw an exception; it delivers an uninitialized CBrush.
CBrush(COLORREF crColor)	Creates a CBrush object initialized with a solid brush of the specified color.
CBrush(int nIndex, COLORREF crColor)	Creates a CBrush object initialized with a brush of the specified hatching and color.
CBrush(CBitmap* pBitmap)	Creates a CBrush object initialized with a patterned bitmap.

Color requests are subject to palette matching. Palette matching means that on a given display device, only a certain number of colors is available. If the requested color is not available—that is, all slots in the palette are used or the device can't provide the exact color requested—then Windows uses the closest approximation from colors already in the palette.

The bitmap used to create a patterned brush must already exist. Hatching style constants include **HS_DIAGONAL**, **HS_CROSS**, **HS_DIAGCROSS**, **HS_FDIAGONAL**, **HS_HORIZONTAL**, **HS_VERTICAL**.

Example
```
//Example
CBrush theBrush;
        //create an unitialized CBrush object
CBrush theBrush( RGB(0,0,0));
        //create a solid brush in the color black
CBrush theBrush(HS_CROSS, RGB(0,0,0));
        //create a cross-hatched black brush
CBrush theBrush( pBrushBitmap);
        //assume we have a valid pointer to a bitmap,
        //and create the patterned brush
```

CreateBrushIndirect   FUNCTION

Description **CreateBrushIndirect** initializes a brush object by drawing style; color and hatching information form a LOGBRUSH structure. Color requests are subject to palette matching. Hatching style constants include **HS_DIAGONAL, HS_CROSS, HS_DIAGCROSS, HS_FDIAGONAL, HS_HORIZONTAL** and **HS_VERTICAL**. **CreateBrushIndirect** returns non-zero if the function is successful; otherwise, zero.

Prototype
```
//Function Prototype
//BOOL CreateBrushIndirect(LOGBRUSH lpLogBrush );
LOGBRUSH lbTheBrush;

lbTheBrush.lbStyle = BS_HATCH;
        //describe a hatched brush
lbTheBrush.lbColor = RGB(0,0,0);
        //black
lbTheBrush.lbHatch = HS_CROSS;
        //cross-hatch pattern

CBrush theBrush;
        //create an unitialized brush object
theBrush.CreateBrushIndirect( &lbTheBrush);
        //initialize the brush with a hatched black brush
```

CreateDIBPatternBrush   FUNCTION

Description **CreateDIBPatternBrush** initializes a **CBrush** object with an application-specific, device-independent bitmap pattern so that it can be selected into a device context and used for painting. Color requests are subject to palette matching. The bitmap used to initialize the brush must exist before this function is called. This bitmap may be any size, but Windows will use only the 8-by-8 grid of bits in the upper left corner. A brush initialized using this function should be selected out to the device context after the application is finished using it. Also, storage associated with the bitmap must be explicitly freed.

Prototype
```
//Function Prototype
//BOOL CreateDIBPatternBrush( HGLOBAL hPackedDIB,
//UINT uUsage );
```

255

```
CVentana::DoDIBPatternBrush( HGLOBAL hPackedDIB, UINT uUsage)
{
        //our function was passed a global handle
        //to a packed DIB
        //and DIB color use information....
CBrush theBrush;
        //create an unitialized Brush object
theBrush.CreateDIBPatternBrush( HGLOBAL hPackedDIB,
UINT uUsage );
        //initialize the brush with a device-
        //independent bitmap
```

The reason the first argument in the preceding example is of type HGLOBAL, a rather anonymous type, is that your application must explicitly allocate global memory by using the Windows API **::GlobalAlloc**. The DIB is then copied into this memory, and it can be used in **CreateDIBPatternBrush**.

The second argument is either DIB_PAL_COLORS or DIB_RGB_COLORS. It specifies whether the color table contains an array of color indexes or an array of RGB colors.

This function returns non-zero if successful; otherwise, zero.

CreateHatchBrush   FUNCTION

Description   **CreateHatchBrush** initializes a **CBrush** object so that it can be selected into a device context and used for painting. Color requests are subject to palette matching. A brush initialized using this function should be selected out to the device context after the application is finished using it.

This function returns non-zero if successful; otherwise, zero.

Prototype
```
//Function Prototype
//BOOL CreateHatchBrush( int nIndex, COLORREF crColor );
LOGBRUSH lbTheBrush;

CBrush theBrush;              //create an uninitialized brush object
theBrush.CreateHatchBrush( HS_VERTICAL, RGB( 0,0,0));
        //initialize the brush object
        //with a hatched black brush
```

The allowable values for nIndex are shown in this table:

HS_BDIAGONAL	Downward hatch (left to right) at 45 degrees
HS_CROSS	Horizontal and vertical crosshatch
HS_DIAGCROSS	Crosshatch at 45 degrees
HS_FDIAGONAL	Upward hatch (left to right) at 45 degrees
HS_HORIZONTAL	Horizontal hatch
HS_VERTICAL	Vertical hatch

CreatePatternBrush   FUNCTION

Description   **CreatePatternBrush** initializes a **CBrush** object with an application-specific bitmap pattern so that it can be selected into a device context and used for painting. Color requests are subject to palette matching. The bitmap used to initialize the brush must exist before this function is called. This bitmap may be any size, but Windows will use only the 8-by-8 grid of bits in the upper left corner. A brush initialized using this function should be selected out to the device context after the application is finished using it. Also, storage associated with the bitmap must be explicitly freed.

Prototype
```
//Function Prototype
//BOOL CreatePatternBrush( CBitmap* pBitmap )

CVentana::DoPatternBrush( CBitmap* pBitmap )
{
        //our function was passed a pointer to a CBitmap object
CBrush theBrush;      //create an uninitialized brush object
theBrush.CreatePatternBrush( CBitmap* pBitmap );
            //initialize the brush with a device-dependent bitmap
```

If a monochrome bitmap is supplied as an argument to this function, the pattern is drawn by using the current text color and background color.

This function returns non-zero if successful; otherwise, zero.

CreateSolidBrush   FUNCTION

Description   **CreateSolidBrush** initializes a **CBrush** object so that it can be selected into a device context and used for painting. Color requests are subject to palette matching. A brush initialized using this function should be selected out of the device context after the application is finished using it. This function returns non-zero if successful; otherwise, zero.

Prototype

```
//Function Prototype
//BOOL CreateSolidBrush( COLORREF crColor );
LOGBRUSH lbTheBrush;

CBrush theBrush;              //create an uninitialized brush object
theBrush.CreateSolidBrush( RGB( 0,0,0));
                //initialize the brush object with
                //a solid black brush
```

FromHandle   FUNCTION

Description   **CBrush::FromHandle** returns a pointer to a temporary **CBrush** object. The handle of the brush is attached to the **CBrush** object. Internally, tracking of most Windows GDI objects is by using a table of handles. MFC provides classes to wrap the handles in objects, making the member functions of the class available to act on the object identified by the handle. The **FromHandle** API provides a quick and convenient way to package the handle temporarily in an object. An object pointer returned by any of the **FromHandle** family has a life cycle of approximately one Windows message-passing cycle, so when a function that uses this call exits, the object goes out of scope and is destroyed. It is therefore not necessary for an application to destroy an object returned by **FromHandle**. Disposing of the object and freeing the memory used by it is taken care of during the idle-time processing of **CWinApp**. The object identified by the handle is *not* deleted along with the temporary object. The lifetime of the object referenced by the pointer is brief, so don't store the pointer for later use. It will be invalid. This function returns a pointer to a **CBrush** object if successful; otherwise, NULL.

Prototype

```
//Function Prototype
//static CBrush* PASCAL FromHandle( HBRUSH hTheBrush );
CBrush* pThePreviousCBrush;
                //Save the pointer to the
                //object we are selecting
                //out of the DC; assume we have a
                //valid pointer
                //to a CDC object called pDC
pThePreviousCBrush =
pDC->SelectObject(CBrush::FromHandle(m_hObject));
                //Select a new brush, which is identified by the handle
                //in the public member variable of the CGdiObject
                //base class
```

CButton

Derivation	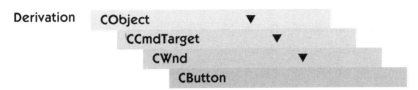

Derivation

CObject ▼
CCmdTarget ▼
CWnd ▼
CButton

Description The **CButton** class encapsulates a button control. Button controls may behave as toggle state push-buttons, check boxes, radio buttons or three-state buttons, depending on the style with which they are created. If an application creates button controls independent of a dialog box, form view or dialog bar, steps must be taken to ensure that the object associated with the control is properly destroyed. **CButton** objects created on the heap with **new** should be deleted with **delete**. Frame-based **CButton** objects are destroyed when they go out of scope, which is always between the beginning and end of a given function. These objects are of limited usefulness because it is unlikely that the function that creates a button will be able to process messages from that button before it is destroyed. In short, frame-based **CButton** objects are essentially useless.

Overrides

Function Name	Triggering Event
DrawItem	Called when a button that specified BS_OWNERDRAW style needs to be repainted.

Member Functions

CButton   FUNCTION

Description   **CButton** constructs a button object, but it does not initialize or display it.

Example

```
//Example
 class CMyView : public CView
 {
    CButton m_OurButtonControl;
                          //declaration of the button
                          //in the view class.
                          //The control will have the
                          //lifespan of the view
 };
 int CMyView::Create(LPCREATESTRUCT lpcs)
 {
    if(CView::Create(lpcs))
                          //Create the view that contains
                          //the button control
        return -1;
                          //If Create fails, return -1

    m_OurButtonControl.Create("Panic Button:",
       WS_VISIBLE | WS_CHILD | BS_PUSHBUTTON,
       rectPanicButton, this, ID_PANICBUTTON);
                          //Create a button that is
                          //initially visible, a child
                          //of this view, with the
                          //BS_PUSHBUTTON style, at the
                          //location given by
                          //rectPanicButton
                          //All button notifications
                          //from the button will have
                          //the ID ID_PANICBUTTON.
 }
```

In the preceding example, the button object persists as long as the view does.

Create

Description **Create** builds and initializes a button window, connects it to the **CButton** object, and then shows the control. **Create** initializes the button control with the caption passed as its first parameter. Possible styles for button controls are listed in the following table. *See **CButton** for a usage example.*

Button Style	Meaning
BS_PUSHBUTTON	Push-button.
BS_DEFPUSHBUTTON	Default push-button; user pressing Enter is the same as user clicking the button.
BS_CHECKBOX	Control is a check box.
BS_AUTOCHECKBOX	Check box that inverts its check state every time it is clicked.
BS_RADIOBUTTON	One of a group of buttons; only one of the group at a time can be selected.
BS_3STATE	Push-button that has On, Off and Indeterminate states. Indeterminate often means disabled or "not applicable."
BS_AUTO3STATE	Push-button that has On, Off and Indeterminate states; cycles through the states as the control is clicked.
BS_GROUPBOX	Rectangular frame enclosing grouped controls.
BS_AUTORADIOBUTTON	One of a group of buttons; only one of the group at a time can be selected; selection state is updated automatically, so that when a new button is selected, the button that was previously selected is deselected. In other words, when one button is selected, the button that was previously selected is deselected. (It sort of resembles the buttons on old car radios; hence, the name radio button.)
BS_OWNERDRAW	Application is responsible for drawing the button; cannot be combined with other button styles. For owner draw buttons, MFC calls the DrawItem member function to perform the actual drawing of the image. You override this function in your derived class to implement the owner draw button.
BS_LEFTTEXT	Aligns the caption to the left.

Prototype
```
//Function Prototype
//BOOL Create(LPCTSTR lpszText, DWORD dwStyle,
//    const RECT& rect, CWnd* pParentWnd, UINT nID);
```

GetButtonStyle   FUNCTION

Description   **GetButtonStyle** retrieves the button-specific style parameters of the control. See the table in the **Create** member function section for a list of styles.

Prototype
```
//Example
//Function Prototype
//UINT GetButtonStyle( )const;
    //Test to see whether this is a push-button
    //Mask to do a test for one of these styles
    //because windows have multiple styles,
    //only one of which is set by the BS_PUSHBUTTON bit.



if ( m_OurButtonControl.GetButtonStyle( ) & BS_PUSHBUTTON )
    //If so, highlight it
    m_OurButtonControl.SetState( TRUE );
```

GetCheck   FUNCTION

Description   **GetCheck** retrieves the current check state for a check box, radio button, or three-state push-button control. Check boxes and push-buttons set themselves on and off by using the values 1 and 0, respectively. A three-state control can set an indeterminate state by using the value 2.

Prototype
```
//Function Prototype
//UINT GetCheck( ) const;
```

GetState **FUNCTION**

Description   **GetState** retrieves the state of a button control. The return value must be masked to extract information about the state of the button. The following table lists masks and the information they isolate.

Mask	Meaning of Result
0x0003	0 = unchecked
	1 = checked
	2 = indeterminate (three-state controls only)
0x0004	Non-zero if button is highlighted
0x0008	Non-zero if button has input focus

Prototype

```
//Function Prototype
//UINT GetState( ) const;
    //Test to see whether the user pushed the Panic Button

UINT nCheckState = m_OurButtonControl.GetState() & 0x0003;
UINT nState = m_btn.GetState() & 0x0003;
CString strMsg("The button is: ");
strMsg += (nState == 1) ? CString("Checked") :
                CString("Unchecked");
MessageBox(strMsg);
```

SetButtonStyle **FUNCTION**

Description   **SetButtonStyle** changes the button style and optionally redraws it.

Prototype

```
//Function Prototype
//void SetButtonStyle( UINT nStyle, BOOL bRedraw = TRUE )const;
    //Change the button to an auto-check box
m_OurButtonControl.SetButtonStyle( BS_AUTOCHECKBOX, TRUE );
    //If you omit the second argument,
    //the default is to redraw the control;
    //otherwise, the control is not redrawn
    //until its rectangle is invalidated.
```

SetCheck   FUNCTION

Description **SetCheck** sets the check state for a button. Check boxes and push-buttons set themselves on and off by using the values 1 and 0, respectively. A three-state control can set an indeterminate state by using the value 2. The indeterminate state often means that a control is disabled or inapplicable to the current operations.

Prototype
```
//Function Prototype
//void SetCheck( int nCheck );
    //Create a button control
CStatic m_OurButtonControl;
m_OurButtonControl.Create("CheckBox:",
    WS_VISIBLE | WS_CHILD | BS_AUTOCHECKBOX,
    rectCheckBox, this, ID_OURCHECKBOX );
    //Check the check box
m_OurButtonControl.SetCheck( 1 );
```

SetState   FUNCTION

Description **SetState** changes the appearance of a push-button by adding or removing a highlight around its perimeter. SetState affects check boxes as well as push-buttons. For push-buttons, SetState(TRUE) actually presses the button and leaves it down. For check boxes, the check box is given a heavy border (and SetState(FALSE) restores the 1-pixel, light border).

Prototype
```
//Function Prototype
//UINT SetState( BOOL bHighlight );
    //Highlight the Panic Button
m_OurButtonControl.SetState( TRUE );
```

CByteArray

See **CObArray**.

ClientDC

Derivation

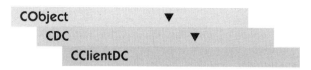

CObject	▼	
CDC	▼
CClientDC	

Description The **CClientDC** class takes most of its characteristics from the **CDC** base class. Its basic function is to acquire a DC for painting the application's client area by calling the SDK functions **::GetDC** in its constructor and **::ReleaseDC** in its destructor. As with most of the classes derived from **CDC**, it differs only in constructor and destructor functions. The constructor throws an exception if the **::GetDC** call fails.

Also note that before you allow a **CClientDC** (or a *Canything*DC) to be destroyed, you should restore it to its stock state. All of the GDI objects created or retrieved by the application and selected into the DC must have been selected out and replaced with the DC's original GDI tools. That is, no dead GDI objects should still be selected when the **CClientDC** object is destroyed.

Protected Data Member

m_hWnd

Description Identifies the window for which this **CClientDC** object is valid.

Member Functions

CClientDC

Description **CClientDC::CClientDC** constructs a **CClientDC** object for the application's **CWnd** object by calling **::GetDC** and then attaches it to the **CWnd** object. This DC is used to access the window's client area.

CClientDC::~CClientDC destroys a **CClientDC** object for the application's **CWnd** object by calling **::ReleaseDC**.

Example   Here we construct a **CClientDC** object on the stack inside an application's view message handler, using the *this* pointer. If we get a "right mouse button up" message, this handler is called. It is not passed a pointer to a DC as a parameter, so we have to construct a **CClientDC** object before we can use **CDC::TextOut** to put our snappy message in the application's client area. Because the DC we construct is a local object, its destructor is automatically called when it goes out of scope.

Prototype
```
//Function Prototype
//CClientDC( CWnd* pWindowOwnsClientArea )
void CVentanaView::OnRButtonUp( UINT nFlags, CPoint point)
{
CClientDC dc(this);                    //Construct the DC
dc.TextOut(point.x, point.y , "Hello World");
    //Use it to write some text....
}
```

CmdTarget   CLASS

Derivation

CObject ▼
CCmdTarget

Description   **CCmdTarget** provides the base class for the MFC message map architecture. The class is rarely used directly by applications, but the classes derived from it are the flesh and blood of windowing. (OLE automation classes are often directly derived from **CCmdTarget** because no UI is involved.)

The important thing to understand about this class is what message mapping is and why the foundation class relies on it. *Message mapping* is a scheme by which the foundation class delivers a Windows message directly to a class member function. Based on the table generated by the workbench tools, specific messages are targeted to handler functions. Messages are delivered to the handlers by special macros. This scheme is efficient because it does not require a significant record-keeping burden for derived classes of the class that implements message handlers, allows for future expansion of the message list without a serious impact on existing code and best of all, requires no proprietary extensions to the C++ language.

Derived Classes

CWnd
CWinApp
CDocTemplate
CDocument

Member Functions

BeginWaitCursor `FUNCTION`

Description   **BeginWaitCursor** displays the hourglass cursor, which is typically used to show the user that an operation will take a discernible time to complete. To restore the cursor that the application displayed before the call to **BeginWaitCursor**, call the companion function **EndWaitCursor**.

Under NT, you should avoid doing such tasks synchronously (if possible). Rather, use a **CWinThread** to perform the task while leaving the UI responsive to the user. This behavior can be imitated to some degree in 16-bit Windows by using **CWinApp::OnIdle** and **CWnd::OnEnterIdle**.

Prototype
```
//Function Prototype
//void BeginWaitCursor( );
    //Display the hourglass cursor
BeginWaitCursor( );
    //Do some long job, like adding database records....
    //Then restore the previous cursor
EndWaitCursor( );
```

EndWaitCursor `FUNCTION`

Description   **EndWaitCursor** restores the cursor the application displayed before the call to **BeginWaitCursor**. *See BeginWaitCursor for a usage example.*

Prototype
```
//Function Prototype
//void EndWaitCursor( );
```

OnCmdMsg   FUNCTION

Description   **OnCmdMsg** is called by the framework to route command messages to handlers and update messages to command user interface
objects. Command messages are generated by menu items. This
function does the lookup and dispatch based on the application's
message map. Although **OnCmdMsg** is a virtual function, it is not
likely that an application would want to override it.

 CmdUI   CLASS

. . . .

Description   **CCmdUI** is a special purpose support class that is used only in the
ON_UPDATE_COMMAND_UI handler function of classes derived
from **CCmdTarget**. The function of this class is to make it easier
for an application to synchronize application modes and corresponding command user interface item states when the user can
select a mode from more than one place in the application's interface. For example, if a particular graphic editing mode can be
chosen either from a tool bar button or a pop-up menu item, it can
be difficult for the application to keep the state of the menu item in
sync by checking and unchecking it at appropriate times. In the
application's message map entries, the ON_UPDATE_COMMAND_UI
entry specifies a triggering message and a handler that updates the
command user interface object to be checked, unchecked, grayed,
or to have its displayed text changed. Another entry in the message
map links the triggering event with a handler that actually implements the functionality of the command. The beauty of the
ON_UPDATE_COMMAND_UI architecture is that the same handler
can map to a button, a menu item, a status bar pane or a dialog bar
control. All of the user interface command elements for a given
triggering event can be managed in response to a single message
type.

It is not necessary to use the **CCmdUI** top level menu items or
other command interface elements if the user can only issue the
command from one place in the application. Menu, toolbar and
control classes include member functions that directly manipulate
the state of their interface elements.

Member Functions

ContinueRouting   FUNCTION

Description **ContinueRouting** tells the framework that this class declines to handle the message, and tells it to look for another class that can handle the message. This function is used with the ON_COMMAND_EX macro.

Enable   FUNCTION

Description **Enable** toggles the enabled status of a user interface element. A disabled control is grayed and a disabled status pane is displayed without text. A disabled menu item is grayed; a disabled toolbar button is grayed; a disabled status pane is displayed without text.

Prototype
```
//Function Prototype
//virtual void Enable(BOOL bOn = TRUE );
void CMyPaint::OnUpdateNullPen(CCmdUI* pCmdUI)
{
    //Toggle the state of the command user interface object
    //(menu item or tool bar button) as recorded in the member
    //data item m_PenIsNull.
    pCmdUI->Enable(!m_PenIsNull);
}
```

SetCheck   FUNCTION

Description **SetCheck** toggles the appearance of a check mark on a menu item, draws a pop-out or normal border around a status pane and makes a toolbar button selected, unselected or indeterminate. A parameter value of 0 unchecks, 1 checks and 2 sets the control state as indeterminate.

Prototype
```
//Function Prototype
//virtual void SetCheck( int nCheck = 1 );
void CMyComms::OnUpdateDialNow()
{
    //Add check mark to Dial Number menu item, if the member
    //variable m_bDialNow is set to TRUE.
    pCmdUI->SetCheck(m_bDialNow);
}
```

SetRadio   FUNCTION

Description   **SetRadio** sets the selection state of a control that is part of a "radio" group. Like the buttons on an automobile radio, only one of the controls can be set at a time. The **CCmdUI::SetRadio** function does not unset any currently "pressed" controls in the radio group, in contrast to dialog functions which manage radio controls. If you update the command UI object using the pointer passed to the **CCmdUI** handler, you must explicitly unset radio group control items as well as setting the new control. To accomplish this, each element in the radio group must have an ON_UPDATE_COMMAND_UI handler.

Prototype
```
//Function Prototype
//virtual void SetRadio( BOOL bOn = TRUE );
void CScribDoc::OnUpdateRadioPaperSize(CCmdUI* pCmdUI)
{
    //Set the radio button according to status recorded in member
    //variable m_bSmallPaperSize;
    pCmdUI->SetRadio( m_bSmallPaperSize);
}
```

SetText   FUNCTION

Description   **SetText** sets menu item text, status bar pane text, button text in a dialog bar button or window text in a dialog bar control.

Prototype
```
//Function Prototype
//virtual void SetText( LPCSTR lpszText );
void CMyEditorView::OnUpdatePageNumber(CCmdUI* pCmdUI)
{
    //Set a new page number in the status bar pane,
    //based on a member variable m_szCurrentPage
  pCmdUI->SetText(m_szCurrentPage);
}
```

ColorDialog

Derivation

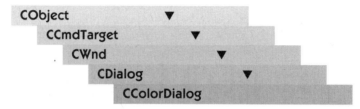

Description The **CColorDialog** class encapsulates the Windows common dialog box for color selection that displays a list of system colors. Its public data member **m_cc** is a CHOOSECOLOR data structure that the application can use to modify the way in which the dialog is displayed.

Like other modal dialogs provided by the framework, **CColorDialogs** are created by constructing the dialog object and calling the member function **DoModal**. **DoModal** handles all interface updating and data exchange, returning either **IDOK** or **IDCANCEL**. After **DoModal** returns, the **CColorDialog** member functions are used by the application to retrieve information about the user's color selection.

Overrides

Function Name	Triggering Event
OnColorOK	Validation of the user's color choice

Public Data Members

m_cc	MEMBER

Description **m_cc** is a **CHOOSECOLOR** structure used to pass information between the dialog and the application. Field values that control the way in which the dialog is displayed must be set before **DoModal** is called.

Field Name	Type	Meaning
lStructSize	DWORD	Size of the structure in bytes.
hwndOwner	HWND	Handle of the window that owns the dialog.
hInstance	HWND	Handle to memory containing an application-specific dialog template that will be used to construct the dialog; requires the CC_ENABLETEMPLATE flag.
rgbResult	COLORREF	Specifies the color selected when the dialog opens and the user's color choice when DoModal returns.
lpCustColors	COLORREF	Points to an array of 16 custom colors displayed in the color boxes of the dialog; if the user modifies the colors, the modified values are stored back to this array. (The variable we are talking about is actually a pointer to a structure of type COLORREF.)
Flags	DWORD	Controls the way in which the dialog is displayed and optionally enables custom features (see the Flags table below).
lCustData	LPARAM	Pointer to application-specific data to be passed to the hook function.
lpfnHook	LPCCHOOKPROC	Pointer to an application-supplied function that hooks the dialog message stream to do custom processing.
lpTemplateName	LPCSTR	Name of the dialog template that will be used to build the application's custom dialog.

The possible meanings of the Flags field are shown below:

Flag	Meaning
CC_RGBINIT	Use rgbResult to set the initially selected color.
CC_FULLOPEN	Initial display of the dialog includes the controls that allow the user to create custom colors; if this flag is not set, the user must click the DefineCustomColors push-button to get to custom color controls.
CC_PREVENTFULLOPEN	Display of the dialog omits the controls that allow the user to create custom colors.
CC_SHOWHELP	Shows the Help button.
CC_ENABLEHOOK	Enables an application-supplied function that hooks the dialog message stream to do custom processing.
CC_ENABLETEMPLATE	Creates the dialog from an application-supplied template.
CC_ENABLETEMPLATEHANDLE	Indicates that the hInstance member is a handle to a data block that contains a dialog template (this must be a preloaded template). lpTemplateName is ignored when this flag is specified.

static COLORREF clrSavedCustom[16]   MEMBER

Description   **static COLORREF clrSavedCustom[16]** is an array of 16 COLORREF values. **CColorDialog** provides this array to allow the user to save custom colors between invocations of the dialog during an application session. The values may be retrieved after **DoModal** returns. For version 2.0, use **GetSavedCustomColors** to access this table.

```
static COLORREF * GetSavedCustomColors();
```

Member Functions

CColorDialog   FUNCTION

Description   **CColorDialog** constructs the **CColorDialog** object.

Prototype
```
//Function Prototype
//CColorDialog(COLORREF clrInit = 0 ,
//DWORD dwFlags = 0 ,
```

```
//CWnd* pParentWnd = NULL );
//Create a color choice dialog:
//black is the initially selected color
//Show the Define Custom Color controls, pParentWnd owns
//this dialog
CColorDialog dlgColor(RGB( 0,0,0 ), CC_FULLOPEN, this);
    //Let CColorDialog handle dialog display and data collection
dlgColor.DoModal( );
    //Get the user's color choice
COLORREF crColorChoice = dlgColor. GetColor( );
```

DoModal   FUNCTION

Description   **DoModal** initiates and manages the **CColorDialog** box. **DoModal** returns IDOK or IDCANCEL if the dialog box was displayed. It returns NULL for errors. Any **m_cc** flags that affect the appearance or behavior of the dialog must be set before calling **DoModal**. *See **CColorDialog** for a usage example.*

Prototype
```
//Function Prototype
//int DoModal( );
```

GetColor   FUNCTION

Description   **GetColor** retrieves the COLORREF for the color selected in the dialog box. *See **CColorDialog** for a usage example.*

Prototype
```
//Function Prototype
//COLORREF GetColor( )const;
```

SetCurrentColor   FUNCTION

Description   **SetCurrentColor** is used in derived classes that override the **OnColorOK** member function to validate the user's color selection. For example, you might want to round to the nearest solid color your application can understand.

Prototype
```
//Function Prototype
//void SetCurrentColor(COLORREF clr);
```

275

ComboBox

Derivation

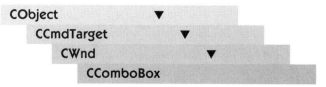

CObject ▼

    CCmdTarget ▼

        CWnd ▼

            CComboBox

Description   The **CComboBox** class encapsulates the Windows combo box, which combines an edit control or static control with a list box. The combo box can optionally be a drop-down list or a fully displayed list box. When the user types in the edit control, the list box will highlight a matching item. Combo boxes can be constructed in an application's client area by constructing a combo box object and calling the **Create** member function to build and attach a combo box window. Dialogs construct combo box controls based on their template.

    If an application creates combo box controls independently of a dialog box, form view or dialog bar, then steps must be taken to assure that the object associated with the control is properly destroyed. **CComboBox** objects created on the heap with **new** should be deleted with **delete**.

Overrides

Function Name	Triggering Event.
DrawItem	An OWNERDRAW combo box needs to be repainted
MeasureItem	An OWNERDRAW combo box is being drawn; the application must fill in a MEASUREITEM structure to define how list items are drawn.
CompareItem	A sorted OWNERDRAW combo box is inserting an item.
DeleteItem	An OWNERDRAW combo box is deleting an item.

Member Functions

CComboBox

Description   **CComboBox** constructs a **CComboBox** object, but does not create, attach or initialize its accompanying combo box control window.

Prototype

```
//Function Prototype
    //Construct a combo box in the frame window's client area
CComboBox ComboOur;
    //Then specify its style, location, parent and control ID
ComboOur.Create( WS_CHILD | WS_VISIBLE | CBS_SIMPLE, rect,
this, ID_OURCOMBO);
    //After the combo box is created, initialize it with list items
ComboOur.AddString("First Choice");
ComboOur.AddString("Next Choice");
    //The return from the GetCount Call is 2
int iNumberListItems = ComboOur.GetCount( );
```

Clear · FUNCTION

Description **Clear** removes a selection highlight from the edit control text, but does not remove the text itself. Use **Cut** to remove both text and highlight.

Prototype

```
//Function Prototype
//void Clear( );
    //Find this string in the list box, highlight it, and copy it to the
    //edit control
cbOurCombo.SelectString( "Tennis");
    //Highlight the whole string
cbOurCombo.SetEditSel( 0, -1 );
    //Copy it to the clipboard
cbOurCombo.Copy( );
    //Remove the highlight
cbOurCombo.Clear( );
```

Copy · FUNCTION

Description **Copy** copies the selected text from an edit control and places it in the Windows clipboard in CF_TEXT format. *See **Clear** for a usage example.*

Prototype

```
//Function Prototype
//void Copy( );
```

Create `FUNCTION`

Description **Create** creates a Windows combo box, attaches it to the **CComboBox** object and shows it. Combo box properties are determined by style constants, which may be combined with one another. They are listed in the table below. *See **CComboBox** for a usage example.*

Combo Box Style	Meaning
CBS_SIMPLE	List box is always displayed.
CBS_DROPDOWN	The list is displayed when the user selects an icon next to the edit control.
CBS_DROPDOWNLIST	Like CBS_DROPDOWN, but edit control is replaced by static control set to current list selection.
CBS_OWNERDRAWFIXED	List box is OWNERDRAW, with all items equal height.
CBS_OWNERDRAWVARIABLE	List box is OWNERDRAW, with items of variable height.
CBS_AUTOHSCROLL	Set automatic horizontal scrolling on the edit control.
CBS_OEMCONVERT	ANSI/OEM conversion for edit control text.
CBS_SORT	List box strings are alphabetically sorted.
CBS_HASSTRINGS	List box items are strings.
CBS_DISABLENOSCROLL	Scroll bar is disabled when not enough items populate the listbox to require scrolling. Behavior without this style bit is to hide the scroll bar in this case.
CBS_NOINTEGRALHEIGHT	Use exact coordinates specified by rect to size the combo box. Behavior without this style bit is for the listbox part of the combo box to be adjusted so that no partial items are displayed.

Prototype
```
//Function Prototype
//BOOL Create(DWORD dwStyle, const RECT& rect, CWnd*
//pParentWnd, UINT nID);
```

Cut `FUNCTION`

Description **Cut** removes the selected text from an edit control and places it in the Windows clipboard in CF_TEXT format.

Prototype
```
//Function Prototype
//void Cut( );
    //Find this string in the list box, highlight it and copy it to the
    //edit control
cbOurCombo.SelectString( "Winter Sports");
    //Highlight "Winter"
cbOurCombo.SetEditSel( 0, strlen("Winter") );
    //Cut "Winter" from the edit control to the clipboard
cbOurCombo.Cut( );
    //Paste it back again
cbOurCombo.Paste( );
```

GetCount   FUNCTION

Description **GetCount** returns a *count,* or the index +1, of all of the combo box items. *See CComboBox for a usage example.*

Prototype
```
//Function Prototype
//int GetCount( )const;
```

GetCurSel   FUNCTION

Description **GetCurSel** retrieves the zero-based index of a the current selection in a single selection combo box. The function returns **CB_ERR** if there is no current selection.

Prototype
```
//Function Prototype
//int GetCurSel( )const;
    //If there is no current selection
if ( LB_ERR == cbOurCombo.GetCurSel( ) )
    //Select the topmost visible item
 cbOurCombo.SetCurSel( cbOurCombo.GetTopIndex( ) );
```

GetEditSel   FUNCTION

Description **GetEditSel** reports the zero-based starting and ending character positions of text selected in the edit control. The ending position is the first *unselected* character after the selected string.

Prototype
```
//Function Prototype
//DWORD GetEditSel( )const;
    //If there is no currently selected text in the edit control
if ( NULL == cbOurCombo.GetEditSel( ))
```

```
//Select the whole string
cbOurCombo.SetEditSel( 0, -1);
```

GetItemData   FUNCTION

Description **GetItemData** is the companion function to **SetItemData**.
SetItemData associates an application-supplied 32-bit **DWORD**
with a given combo box item. **GetItemData** retrieves the value.

Prototype
```
//Function Prototype
//DWORD GetItemData(int nIndex );
    //Get the index of the first visible list box item
int iTopItem = cbOurCombo.GetTopIndex( );
    //Get the item data associated with it
DWORD dwTopItemData = cbOurCombo.GetItemData( iTopItem );
    //Test to see if the datum is NULL
if( NULL != dwTopItemData )
    //If not, set item data to NULL
cbOurCombo.SetItemData( iTopItem, NULL );
    //Get the pointer associated with the next list item
void* pTopItemData = cbOurCombo.GetItemData( iTopItem + 1 );
    //Set the next item's pointer to the one we retrieved
cbOurCombo.SetItemDataPtr( iTopItem + 3, pTopItemData );
```

GetItemDataPtr   FUNCTION

Description **GetItemDataPtr** is the companion function to **SetItemDataPtr**.
SetItemDataPtr associates an application-supplied 32-bit **void ***
with a given combo box item. **GetItemDataPtr** retrieves the
pointer. *See **GetItemData** for a usage example.*

Prototype
```
//Function Prototype
//void* GetItemDataPtr(int nIndex );
```

GetLBText   FUNCTION

Description **GetLBText** returns the text string associated with a list box index.

Prototype
```
//Function Prototype
//int GetLBText( int nIndex, LPSTR lpszText );
//int GetLBText( int nIndex, CString rString );
    //Get the length of the first list box string and see if it is
    //less than the size of our
```

```
//buffer—we have to leave room for a terminal NULL, because
//it is not included
//in the count returned by GetLBTextLen
if( cbOurCombo.GetLBTextLen( 0 ) < sizeof ( szItemBuffer ) )
    //Copy the list box string
cbOurCombo.GetLBText( 0, szItemBuffer )
```

GetLBTextLen   FUNCTION

Description **GetLBTextLen** returns the length in bytes of the text string associated with a combo box index, *excluding the terminal* NULL. *See **GetLBText** for a usage example.*

Prototype
```
//Function Prototype
//int GetLBTextLen( int nIndex);
```

LimitText   FUNCTION

Description **LimitText** limits the amount of text a user can put into the text from the keyboard, if the combo box has set the CBS_DROPDOWNLIST, but has not set the **CBS_AUTOHSCROLL** style. **LimitText** does not limit the amount of text that can be copied to the control when a list box string is selected, so it cannot be used to ensure that an edit string will not be less than the given size.

Prototype
```
//Function Prototype
//BOOL LimitText( int nMaxChars );
    //We are accepting the user's file name extension choice,
    //and want to make
    //sure it is no more than 3 characters long
cbOurCombo.LimitText( 3 );
    //After we get the input, we reset the limit to
    //65,535 chars like this:
    //cbOurCombo.LimitText( 0 );
```

Paste   FUNCTION

Description **Paste** copies the selected text from the Windows clipboard into an edit control at the current insertion point. *See **Cut** for a usage example.*

Prototype
//Function Prototype
//void Paste( );

SetCurSel FUNCTION

Description **SetCurSel** selects the item identified by the zero-based index in a single selection combo box. *See **GetCurSel** for a usage example.*

Prototype
//Function Prototype
//int SetCurSel(int nSelect);

SetEditSel FUNCTION

Description **SetEditSel** sets the zero-based starting and ending character positions of text selected in the edit control. The ending position is the first *unselected* character after the selected string. To remove the selection highlight, pass -1 as the starting position. To select the whole string, pass 0 as the starting position and -1 as the ending position. *See **GetEditSel** for a usage example.*

Prototype
//Function Prototype
//BOOL SetEditSel(int nStartChar, int nEndChar);

SetItemData FUNCTION

Description **SetItemData** associates an application-supplied 32-bit **DWORD** with a given combo box item. It returns **CB_ERR** if the operation fails. *See **GetItemData** for a usage example.*

Prototype
//Function Prototype
//int SetItemData(int iItemIndex, DWORD dwAppData);

SetItemDataPtr FUNCTION

Description **SetItemDataPtr** associates an application-supplied 32-bit **void*** with a given combo box item. It returns **LB_ERR** if the operation fails. *See **GetItemData** for a usage example.*

Prototype
//Function Prototype
//int SetItemDataPtr(int nIndex, void* pData);

ShowDropDown   FUNCTION

Description   **ShowDropDown** shows or hides the drop-down list box part of a combo box that has set the **CBS_DROPDOWN** or **CBS_DROPDOWNLIST** style.

Prototype
```
//Function Prototype
//void ShowDropDown( BOOL bShowIt = TRUE );
```

List Box String Operations

AddString   FUNCTION

Description   **AddString** adds a string to a combo box. If the combo box has set **CBS_SORT**, then the new string is inserted in the list at its alphabetical rank. If it is unsorted, the string is appended to the list. To explicitly control the insertion point, use the **InsertString** member function. *See **CComboBox** for a usage example.*

Prototype
```
//Function Prototype
//int AddString( LPCSTR lpszString );
```

DeleteString   FUNCTION

Description   **DeleteString** removes the string at the zero-based index from the combo box.

Prototype
```
//Function Prototype
//int DeleteString( int nIndex );
    //Delete the currently selected string
cbOurCombo.DeleteString( cbOurCombo.GetCurSel( ) );
```

Dir   FUNCTION

Description   **Dir** adds a list of file and directory names to the combo box, filtering by file attribute and a wildcard string. Possible file attribute flags are listed in the table below. *See **ResetContent** for a usage example.*

283

Attribute Flag	Meaning
0x0000	Read write
0x0001	Read only
0x0002	Hidden
0x0004	System file
0x0010	Directory
0x0020	Archive
0x4000	Scan all drives that match the wildcard string
0x8000	Display wildcard matches only

There are constants for these:

```
DDL_READWRITE
DDL_READONLY
DDL_HIDDEN
DDL_SYSTEM
DDL_DIRECTORY
DDL_ARCHIVE
DDL_DRIVES
DDL_EXCLUSIVE
```

Prototype

```
//Function Prototype
//int Dir( UINT attr, LPCSTR lpszWildCard );
```

FindString   FUNCTION

Description   **FindString** does a case-insensitive substring search and returns the index of the first string containing a match of its initial characters and the substring or **LB_ERR** if no match is found. It starts the search after the item identified by the first parameter, continuing through the list and wrapping to the top. If the starting index is -1, the list is searched inclusively from top to bottom.

Prototype

```
//Function Prototype
//int FindString( int nStartAfter, LPCSTR lpszString );
    //Search the entire combo box for strings starting with "Old",
    //"old", "oLD", etc.
cbOurCombo.FindString(-1, "old" );
```

FindStringExact   FUNCTION

Description   **FindStringExact** is a case-sensitive version of **FindString**. *See CComboBox for a usage example.*

Prototype

```
//Function Prototype
//int FindStringExact( int nStartAfter, LPCSTR lpszString );
    //Search the entire combo box for strings starting with "old".
cbOurCombo.FindString(-1, "old" );
```

FindStringExact requires an exact case-sensitive match. **FindString** just requires that the first characters be the same.

InsertString · FUNCTION

Description   **InsertString** inserts the given string at the zero-based index.

Prototype

```
//Function Prototype
//int InsertString( int nIndex, LPCSTR lpszString );
    //Get the index of the first visible list box item
int iTopItem = cbOurCombo.GetTopIndex( );
    //Insert a string at the first visible position
cbOurCombo.InsertString( iTopItem, lpszListItem );
```

ResetContent · FUNCTION

Description   **ResetContent** removes all combo box items.

Prototype

```
//Function Prototype
//void ResetContent( );
    //Clear the combo box
cbOurCombo.ResetContent( );
    //Fill the list box exclusively with .exe filenames
cbOurCombo.Dir( 0x8000, "*.exe");
```

SelectString · FUNCTION

Description   **SelectString** behaves like **FindString**, except that it selects the first matching string, scrolling the list to bring it into view if necessary. **SelectString** does not work for combo boxes that have set the **LBS_MULTIPLESEL** style.

Prototype

```
//Function Prototype
//int SelectString( int nStartAfter, LPCSTR lpszString );
    //Search the entire combo box for strings starting with "old",
    //and select the item.
int iNewSelIndex = cbOurCombo.SelectString(-1, "old" );
```

C ControlBar CLASS

Derivation

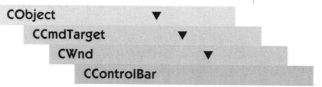

Description   **CControlBar** is the base class of framework control bar classes, which include status bars, tool bars and dialog bars. Control bars are usually the child windows of a frame and sibling windows to a view or the MDI client window in an MDI application. Control bars contain two basic kinds of controls: those that are child windows of the control bar, such as edit controls and drop-down lists, and those that are region based, like status bar panes.

   As is typical of the base classes, it is rare for applications to make direct use of **CControlBar** objects. Rather, they use the derived classes, which provide more services. There is, however, a cooperation between **CFrameWnd** and **CControlBar** such that the amount of area for the SDI client area or for MDI child windows is calculated excluding the area occupied by these control bars.

Derived Classes   CToolBar
CStatusBar
CDialogBar

Public Data Members

m_bAutoDelete MEMBER

Description   **m_bAutoDelete** is a BOOL variable that signals whether or not the control bar object should be destroyed along with the frame window's control bar.

Member Functions

GetCount FUNCTION

Description **GetCount** returns the number of control bar constituents that are not accessible through a Windows HWND. These include status bars, bitmap buttons and separators.

The following line returns a value that designates the style of the control bar:

    DWORD GetBarStyle();

This line sets the style of the control bar:

    void SetBarStyle(DWORD dwStyle);

CBRS_ALIGN_TOP	Allows the control bar to be docked to the top of the client area of a frame window.
CBRS_ALIGN_BOTTOM	Allows the control bar to be docked to the bottom of the client area of a frame window.
CBRS_ALIGN_LEFT	Allows the control bar to be docked to the left side of the client area of a frame window.
CBRS_ALIGN_RIGHT	Allows the control bar to be docked to the right side of the client area of a frame window.
CBRS_ALIGN_ANY	Allows the control bar to be docked to any side of the client area of a frame window.
CBRS_BORDER_TOP	Causes a border to be drawn on the top edge of the control bar when it would be visible.
CBRS_BORDER_BOTTOM	Causes a border to be drawn on the bottom edge of the control bar when it would be visible.
CBRS_BORDER_LEFT	Causes a border to be drawn on the left edge of the control bar when it would be visible.
CBRS_BORDER_RIGHT	Causes a border to be drawn on the right edge of the control bar when it would be visible.
CBRS_TOOLTIPS	Causes tool tips to be displayed for the control bar.
CBRS_FLYBY	Causes message text to be updated at the same time as tool tips.
CBRS_FLOAT_MULTI	Allows multiple control bars to be floated in a single mini-frame window.

The style argument in this line specifies where in the frame window this control bar can be docked:

    void EnableDocking(DWORD dwStyle)

Allowable styles are CBRS_ALIGN_TOP, CBRS_ALIGN_BOTTOM, CBRS_ALIGN_LEFT, CBRS_ALIGN_RIGHT and CBRS_ALIGN_ANY. These style constants can be combined using bitwise OR.

CreateContext

Description **CCreateContext** is a stand-alone class used at frame window creation time to establish relationships between an application's documents, views and the document template. The **CCreateContext** object also maintains data **CRuntimeClass** data, which is part of the mechanism that makes it possible for the framework to dynamically create objects.

As is typical of the abstract base classes, it is rare for applications to make direct use of **CCreateContext** objects.

Database

Derivation

CObject	
CDatabase	

Description The class **CDatabase** encapsulates an application's connection to an ODBC database. These applications include Microsoft Access, Btrieve, dBASE, FoxPro, Excel, Paradox and text files, but the list is expanding quickly. Essentially, the **CDatabase** and **CRecordset** classes allow you to design a database application program that cleaves cleanly from the system it accesses. Without dependency on the storage structure of the data, the program becomes both more portable and less vulnerable to the changes in the data-storage structure. The same application should work equally well with data stored in any ODBC-compliant system. The **CDatabase** object opens and closes a data source, establishing a connection. The application then must construct a **CRecordset** object that defines the content and organization of the data source records. At present, only SQL is shipping under NT, however, other drivers are expected very soon.

Overrides

Overridable Function Name	Triggering Event
OnSetOptions	The framework is setting connection options.
OnWaitForDataSource	The framework will yield processing during a lengthy operation.

Public Data Members

m_hdbc	MEMBER

Description **m_hdbc** is the handle to the currently opened ODBC data source, connected to the application through the **CDatabase** object.

    m_pDatabase contains a pointer to the object through which the recordset is connected to the database.

Member Functions

BeginTrans FUNCTION

Description **BeginTrans** marks the beginning of a guarded set of database operations. Everything following the **BeginTrans** and preceding the **CommitTrans** calls can be undone by the **Rollback** member. Not all data sources support transaction processing, so the application should verify support for transactions by using the **CanTransact** member function.

Prototype
```
//Function Prototype
//BOOL BeginTrans( );
    //We set a transaction at the beginning
    //of a multistep update
m_database.BeginTrans( );
TRY
{
    //Append a record to the recordset
  m_recordset.AddNew( CRecordset::dynaset);
    //Assign values to data field members
    //of the CRecordset object
  m_NameData = "Big Bill Haywood";
    //Write the changes to the data source
  m_recordset.Update( );
    //If there were no exceptions thrown,
    //commit the transaction
  m_recordset.CommitTrans( );
}
CATCH_ALL ( e )
{
    //If we threw an exception in the Update,
    //roll back the transaction
  m_recordset.RollBack( );
}
```

Cancel FUNCTION

Description **Cancel** halts an asynchronous operation on a data source. It is used to bail out of an operation that is waiting on an unavailable data source. *See **InWaitForDataSource** for a usage example.*

Prototype
```
//Function Prototype
//void Cancel( );
```

CanTransact   FUNCTION

Description   **CanTransact** tests whether the database supports transactions. Transactions are used to guard sensitive multistep updates so that partial completion of the steps can't corrupt the database. For example, an accounting application might want to ensure that when a customer payment is recorded, the customer's outstanding balance is reduced by the amount of the payment. Surrounding the receipt of the payment and the decrementing of the balance with a transaction ensures that both steps are completed successfully before the database is updated. *See **Open** for a usage example.*

Prototype
```
//Function Prototype
//BOOL CanTransact( );
```

CanUpdate   FUNCTION

Description   **CanUpdate** tests whether the **CDatabase** object allows the application to update the data source. *See **Open** for a usage example.*

Prototype
```
//Function Prototype
//BOOL CanUpdate( )const;
```

CDatabase   FUNCTION

Description   **CDatabase** constructs a **CDatabase** object and creates a connection to a data source, but does not open the associated data source. The **Open** member function opens the database.

Prototype
```
//Function Prototype
//CDatabase( );
    //Construct the CDatabase object
CDatabase m_database;
    //Set its login timeout to 30 seconds, before calling Open
m_database.SetLoginTimeout( 30 );
```

~CDatabase   FUNCTION

Description   **~CDatabase** destroys the **CDatabase** object, closing the database if necessary.

Prototype
```
//Function Prototype
//~CDatabase( );
```

Close   FUNCTION

Description   **Close** terminates a **CDatabase** object's connection to a data source, but does not destroy the object. A **CDatabase** object that has been closed can be reused to open any new data source. **Close** cancels all **AddNew** and **Edit** operations on the recordset of the data source. Incomplete transactions are automatically rolled back. You should close all recordsets prior to calling this function.

Prototype
```
//Function Prototype
//void Close( );
    //When we are finished with the data source,
    //close the connection
    //without destroying the CDatabase object
m_database.Close( );
    //Later, we can reuse the CDatabase
    //object for another connection
    //We supply a minimum of information and
    //let the system prompt
    //the user for details
 m_database.Open(NULL);
    //We retrieve the connect string built
    //in our behalf and stored in the object
CString stingNewDBConnect =  m_database.GetConnect( );
```

CommitTrans   FUNCTION

Description   **CommitTrans** is the complement of **BeginTrans**. It marks the end of a series of steps involving calls to **CRecordset** functions that modify the content of the record set. Until the **CommitTrans** function is called, any operation on the recordset since the last BeginTrans can be undone by calling **Rollback**. *See **BeginTrans** for a usage example.*

Prototype
```
//Function Prototype
//BOOL CommitTrans( );
```

ExecuteSQL   FUNCTION

Description   **ExecuteSQL** allows you to directly execute an SQL command on a data source. It is provided for situations in which the subset of SQL operations represented by the member functions of the

CRecordset class do not provide the functionality you require. **ExecuteSQL** does not return a record set object, so it is limited in what it can accomplish.

Prototype

```
//Function Prototype
//BOOL ExecuteSQL(LPCSTR lpszSQL)
```

GetConnect   FUNCTION

Description

GetConnect retrieves the "connect string" that was passed by the call to **Open**. The connect string establishes the parameters used to build the link between the database and the application. For example, a data source might be opened for reading only. The application can optionally gather other information, such as passwords, and build it into the connect string. The connect string is stored in the object. *See **Close** for a usage example.*

Prototype

```
//Function Prototype
//const CString& GetConnect( )const;
```

GetDatabaseName   FUNCTION

Description

GetDatabaseName retrieves the ODBC-registered name for a group of tables that comprise a database. This is not necessarily the data source name used for the **Open** call that connected the **CDatabase** object to the data source.

Prototype

```
//Function Prototype
//CString GetDatabaseName( ); const
    //Get a heading for the form window this way
CString stringDBName = m_database.GetDatabaseName( );
```

InWaitForDataSource   FUNCTION

Description

InWaitForDataSource is used to disable user commands until a data source responds to an application's messages.

Prototype

```
//Function Prototype
//static BOOL PASCAL InWaitForDataSource( );
    //The user doesn't want to wait for the datasource to become
    //available, so we cancel the operations
if( bNoWaiting && m_database.InWaitForDataSource( ) )
  m_database.Cancel( );
```

293

As **InWaitForDataSource** is a static member function, it can be called even when you have no instance of a **CDatabase** object. For example, in an **OnUpdate** handler:

```
//Are we waiting for some database function?
if(CDatabase::InWaitForDataSource())
    //Don't let the user open another database
    pCmdUI->Enable(FALSE);
else
    pCmdUI->Enable();
```

Actually, a smarter way to write this (slightly harder to read):

```
//Enable database open only if none currently open
pCmdUI->Enable(!CDatabase::InWaitForDataSource());
```

IsOpen — FUNCTION

Description   **IsOpen** tests whether a **CDatabase** object is connected to a data source. *See **Open** for a usage example.*

Prototype
```
//Function Prototype
//BOOL IsOpen( )const;
```

Open — FUNCTION

Description   **Open** initializes a **CDatabase** object's connection to a data source. The first parameter provides the name of an ODBC-registered database, but is not required if the database name is included in the connect string parameter. The **bExclusive** and **bReadonly** parameters default to FALSE. The connect string parameter provides the application with the means to assemble information used to open the database. The string is stored in the **CDatabase** object and can be accessed by the application to enforce access controls or perform other functions. If the **Open** function is called with a single NULL parameter, the framework displays a dialog that prompts the user for information about which database to open and how it should be accessed. Alternatively, the application may bring up a dialog to collect **Open** information and information specific to the application, such as passwords. **bExclusive** is not supported, and you'll get an **ASSERT** if you set it to TRUE.

Prototype
```
//Function Prototype
// BOOL Open( LPCSTR lpszDSN, BOOL bExclusive = FALSE,
//BOOL bReadOnly = FALSE, LPCSTR lpszConnect = "ODBC;",
//BOOL bUseCursorLib = TRUE );
```

```
                //We have a CDatabase object and
                //want to know whether it is open
            if (!m_database.IsOpen( ))
                //If not, we open it
              m_database.Open("Marine Contaminants;");
                //Now we find out which processing features it supports
            BOOL bUpdate =  m_database.CanUpdate( );
            BOOL bTransact =  m_database.CanTransact( );
                //Set 10-second timeout for recordset
                //queries before opening recordset
            m_database.SetQueryTimeout( 10 );
                //Force synchronous database operations
            m_database.SetSynchronousMode( TRUE );
```

Rollback   FUNCTION

Description **Rollback** undoes any operation on the recordset since the last **BeginTrans**. After **CommitTrans**, the **Rollback** buffer is emptied. By default, modifications to a record set are immediately committed, unless they are bracketed by a **BeginTrans**/ **CommitTrans** pair. *See **BeginTrans** for a usage example.*

Prototype
```
//Function Prototype
//BOOL Rollback( );
```

SetLoginTimeout   FUNCTION

Description **SetLoginTimeout** is called before a data source connection is opened to change the default login timeout value of 15 seconds. This function is more useful when used with remote databases than desktop databases. *See **CDatabase** for a usage example.*

Prototype
```
//Function Prototype
//void SetLoginTimeout(DWORD dwSeconds);
```

SetQueryTimeout   FUNCTION

Description **SetQueryTimeout** is called before a record set is opened to change the default query timeout value of 15 seconds. Queries time-out because of network performance or lengthy query-processing operations. Timeout values apply to recordset operations performed with the **AddNew**, **Update** and **Delete** members. This function is more useful when used with remote databases than desktop databases. *See **Open** for a usage example.*

Prototype
```
//Function Prototype
//void SetQueryTimeout(DWORD dwSeconds);
```

SetSynchronousMode   FUNCTION

Description **SetSynchronousMode** forces all database transactions to occur synchronously. This means that functions that change record sets do not return until the results of the requested change are known. The default record set update mode is asynchronous. *See **Open** for a usage example.*

Prototype
```
//Function Prototype
//void SetSynchronousMode( BOOL bSynchronous);
```

C DataExchange   CLASS

· ·

Description The **CDataExchange** is the base class that provides the data-exchange and validation services of the application framework. These services are built in to DDX/DDV-capable dialogs, but can be overridden by applications that need specialized data validation. The **CDataExchange** object does the recordkeeping needed to support DDX/DDV functions that are carried out by the **CDialog** function **DoDataExchange**. ClassWizard provides an override of **DoDataExchange** when you choose Create Class to create a class to handle dialog data. This need not be for a dialog-based application. It can be for any application—however, this particular function is part of the infrastructure that allows information to be exchanged easily between the client and the dialog.

The application's version of **DoDataExchange** includes a map that ties dialog controls to specific member variables and optionally specifies acceptable ranges for their values. Most applications don't need to extend this class.

Notes for implementing dialog data exchange and validation procedures:

○ Always start with **PrepareCtrl** or **PrepareEditCtrl.**

○ Always start with 'pDX->m_bSaveAndValidate' check.

○ pDX->Fail() will throw an exception—so be prepared to catch it.

❍ Avoid creating temporary HWNDs for dialog controls—i.e., use HWNDs for child elements.

❍ Validation procedures should only act if 'm_bSaveAndValidate' is TRUE.

❍ Use these suffixes:

❍ DDX_ = exchange procedure

❍ DDV_ = validation procedure

The application's version of **DoDataExchange** includes a map that ties dialog controls to specific member variables and optionally specifies acceptable ranges for their values.

Data Members

m_bSaveAndValidate   MEMBER

Description   This member specifies the direction of data exchange. If the flag is set to TRUE, the control's data is being saved.

m_pDlgWnd   MEMBER

Description   This member is a pointer to the dialog that is exchanging or validating its data.

Member Functions

Fail   FUNCTION

Description   **Fail** is called when data validation reports an out-of-range value. It sets the focus to the control that failed validation and throws an exception.

Prototype
```
//Function Prototype
//void Fail();
```

PrepareCtrl   FUNCTION

Description   **PrepareCtrl** retrieves a handle to the control and sets up to copy a numeric value to or from the edit control to the member variable.

Prototype
```
//Function Prototype
//HWND PrepareCtrl(int nID_CONTROL);
```

PrepareEditCtrl FUNCTION

Description **PrepareEditCtrl** retrieves a handle to the control and sets up to copy text to or from the edit control to the member variable.

Prototype
```
//Function Prototype
//HWND PrepareEditCtrl(int nID_EDITCONTROL);
```

DBException CLASS

Derivation

CObject ▼		
CException ▼		
CDBException		

Description The **CDBException** objects are thrown on **CDatabase** class member function errors that relate to failed SQL or data source operations. User code throws database exceptions by using the global function **AfxThrowDBException**. The data members of the class record error numbers and warning strings for particular exception conditions.

Public Data Members

m_nRetCode MEMBER

Description **m_nRetCode** returns the ODBC error code returned by functions in the database API. Possible values and their meanings are listed in the following table.

Error Code Constant	Meaning
AFX_SQL_ERROR_API_CONFORMANCE	The database driver does not meet ODBC API Conformance Level 1.
AFX_SQL_ERROR_CONNECT_FAIL	A CDatabase call using a NULL parameter failed in its attempt to establish a connection to a data source based on GetDefaultConnect.

Error Code Constant	Meaning
AFX_SQL_ERROR_DYNASET_NOT_SUPPORTED	An attempt to open the data source to a dynaset view of the records failed because the driver does not support dynasets.
AFX_SQL_ERROR_EMPTY_COLUMN_LIST	An attempt was made to open a table for which there are no columns listed in the application's record field exchange calls in DoDataExchange.
AFX_SQL_ERROR_FIELD_SCHEMA_MISMATCH	The record field exchange function expects a different data type than the data source declares for a column.
AFX_SQL_ERROR_ILLEGAL_MODE	The application tried to update the recordset before calling CRecordSet::AddNew or CRecordset::Edit.
AFX_SQL_ERROR_MULTIPLE_ROWS_AFFECTED	CRecordset::Update or CRecordset::Delete was called for a table that does not include a unique key, and multiple records have been modified.
AFX_SQL_ERROR_NO_CURRENT_RECORD	CRecordset::Update or CRecordset::Delete was called for a deleted record.
AFX_SQL_ERROR_NO_ROWS_AFFECTED	CRecordset::Update or CRecordset::Delete was called for a record that can no longer be found.
AFX_SQL_ERROR_ODBC_LOAD_FAILED	The ODBC DLL was not found or could not be loaded.
AFX_SQL_ERROR_RECORDSET_FORWARD_ONLY	A request was made to scroll backward on a data source that does not support that capability.

Error Code Constant	Meaning
AFX_SQL_ERROR_SNAPSHOT_NOT_SUPPORTED	An attempt to open the data source to a snapshot view of the records failed because the driver does not support snapshot.
AFX_SQL_ERROR_SQL_CONFORMANCE	The database driver does not conform to the "Minimum" SQL conformance level.
AFX_SQL_ERROR_SQL_NO_TOTAL	The ODBC driver could not report the total size of a CLongBinary object; this usually happens when memory preallocation for the object fails.
AFX_SQL_ERROR_RECORDSET_READONLY	A write was attempted on a read-only recordset.
SQL_ERROR	A function call failed, and the text error message has been stored in m_strError.
SQL_INVALID_HANDLE	A function failed because it was passed an invalid environment, connection or statement handle.

m_strError   MEMBER

Description   **m_strError** contains the text string that describes the SQL error that has occurred.

m_strStateNativeOrigin   MEMBER

Description   **m_strStateNativeOrigin** is a series of concatenated strings that give information about the source of the error that caused the exception. The format looks like this:
"State:nnnnn, Native:nnn,Origin:[name1][name2]..."
The State code is a five-character error code returned by the function **::SQLError**. The Native code is the driver-specific error code for the failure, and the Origin part of the string is built as the error is passed from the data source to the application. Each component of the database linkage appends its name as the it sees the error message.

$\bigcirc$ DC

Derivation

CObject ▼

CDC

Description In general, think of objects of the **CDC** class as the ones through which all graphical output and status reporting tasks are handled for the screen or printer. It is the largest of all the classes. It consists mostly of wrapper functions for the Graphic Device Interface of the C language API and is one of the areas of MFC in which programmers with previous experience in the Windows environment immediately feel comfortable. The benefits of using **CDC** objects rather than C language API include type-safe selection of objects, such as pens and brushes, and some automatic cleanup that helps prevent "resource leaks" caused when graphical resources are created but inadvertently left in existence after their usefulness has passed.

The **CDC** object connects a device context to a window object so that graphical output can be rendered by the view managing the application's data. All application painting is done through the use of **CDC** or derived class member functions, which encapsulate the Windows Graphic Device Interface, or GDI. An application may create and use more than one **CDC** object, but only one **CDC** object can control graphical display for a given output destination at a given time. For example, the Print Preview architecture uses two **CDC** objects. One models the output characteristics of the screen, and one models the output characteristics of the printer. By using information gathered from both **CDC** objects, Print Preview can display a document on the screen's DC, which incorporates the output metric information from the printer's DC. In this way, it uses the screen's DC to provide an accurate picture of how a document will appear in printed form.

Derived Classes **CDC** is the base class from which the special-purpose DC handling classes are derived. These include **CPaintDC**, **CClientDC**, **CWindowDC** and **CMetafileDC**.

Public Data Members

m_hAttribDC   MEMBER

By convention, calls made by an application to request attribute information on the settings of a DC should be made against the **CDC** member variable **m_hAttribDC**. This member variable is initially set to the value of **m_hDC**, the default output device context, when the **CDC** object is constructed, but may be assigned the identity of other DCs by the application. This is seldom done by user applications, but is a technique used in the application framework to implement Print Preview. Because the measurements and metrics for the screen and printer differ dramatically, being able to collect information on both is critical to creating a facsimile of the printed page on the screen.

The flexibility afforded by having more than one device context at a time available to the application comes with a bit of a hitch. Although we just said that calls for attribute information about a DC should be made using **m_hAttribDC**, there are occasions when it is necessary to get attribute information for **m_hDC**. The DC attribute function names begin with either "Get" or "GetOutput." The "Get" functions refer to the **m_hAttribDC**, and functions named with "GetOutput" collect information from the device context identified by **m_hDC**.

System Device Contexts

For the screen, Windows maintains a pool of device contexts that are automatically available to the application. These system device contexts are set up for the screen and are used incessantly while Windows is running, both by applications and by Windows itself. For this reason, it is more efficient to keep DCs around and "recycle" them than to create and destroy them on demand. Device contexts are not small items, however, and the need to have them instantly available has to be balanced against the memory they consume. A device such as a printer is seldom used, relatively speaking, so it makes sense for the application to construct the DC when it is needed, for example.

If an application uses a system device context, the device context must be released when it is no longer needed. If an application creates its own device context, the DC must be deleted when it is no longer needed. This is a very important distinction because failing to delete application-created DCs will cause serious resource leaks, but deleting a DC that came from Windows can create truly spectacular effects. Here is the rule of thumb: If the DC was obtained by a call to **CDC::CreateDC**, **CDC::CreateIC** or **CDC::CreateCompatibleDC**, it should be deleted by the application. Otherwise, it should be released when it is no longer needed.

m_hDC	MEMBER

Description   All graphical output in Windows is mediated by a *device context,* or DC, for short. The settings associated with the DC determine how coordinate systems will be scaled and oriented, where their origins will be, the degree of stretching that will be permitted when graphic data is fit to display real estate, color usage, and virtually every detail of an application's appearance. Understand the **CDC** class, and Windows graphics will be a mystery to you no more.

The **CDC** public data member **m_hDC** derives its name from the VC++ naming convention, in which all member data variables are prefixed with the "m_", and the fact that this member is used logically and semantically in pretty much the same places that a handle to a device context (hDC) would be in the C language API for Windows.

The skeleton code generated by AppWizard will have done all the legwork of creating a **CDC** object and passing a pointer to it to the **OnDraw** member function in the code that manages your application's view. You can access the initialized data member **m_hDC** through the pointer to the object. By default, all output is directed to the DC identified by **m_hDC**, and the value of **m_AttribDC**, another public data member of class **CDC**, is initially set equal to it. Only the device context identified by **m_hDC** is actually *attached* to the **CDC** object, however. In a nutshell, this means that as your application skeleton starts out, the GDI output functions that are members of the **CDC** class automatically target the device context identified by **m_hDC**.

Because **m_hDC** is the only user-accessible connection available to a **CDC** object's output DC, it must be treated with appropriate respect. You may change the value of **m_hDC** by calling the **CDC::SetOutputDC**, *if* the **CDC** object has no currently attached DC. If a DC is attached, it must be detached by a call to **CDC::Detach** before attempting to set a new one. After the new value is set in **m_hDC** by **::SetOutputDC**, the DC must be explicitly attached to the **CDC** object, with a call to **CDC::Attach**.

Member Functions

AbortDoc `FUNCTION`

Description   **CDC::AbortDoc** terminates output to a print job. It erases all output to a device since the last **CDC::StartDoc** call. The **CDC::AbortDoc** function is used to terminate printer operations that have not specified an abort procedure by calling **CDC::SetAbortProc**, and those that have not yet made a **NEWFRAME** or **NEXTBAND** escape call. This function replaces the **ABORTDOC** printer escape. It is *not* used to mop up after canceled print operations or print jobs that returned an error status. Windows cleans up in both of these situations before notifying the application that printing was suspended.

Prototype
```
//Function Prototype
//int AbortDoc( );
PrinterDC.AbortDoc( );
    //Early termination of a print job....
```

Arc `FUNCTION`

Description   **CDC::Arc** is a line-drawing function that draws a portion of an ellipse defined in the following way. A bounding rectangle for the arc is specified in its parameter list, along with a starting and ending point. From the center of the rectangle, a ray is drawn that passes through the starting point. At the point where this ray intersects the bounding rectangle, Windows begins tracing out the arc. The endpoint of the ray is located on the bounding rectangle in the same way. The arc is traced in the counterclockwise direction, and the function returns a non-zero value if it is successful. **CDC::Arc** draws a smooth curve, and because it is not a closed figure, it is not filled with the current brush. This function expects its arguments to be expressed in logical coordinates. Arc uses the currently selected pen.

Prototype
```
//Function Prototype
//BOOL Arc( int x1, int y1, int x2, int y2, int x3,
//     int y3, int x4, int y4);
//BOOL Arc( LPRECT lpRect, POINT ptStart, POINT ptEnd);
DisplayDC.Arc( lprBoundingRect, ptStartPoint, ptEndPoint);
    //Draw an arc....
```

Attach   FUNCTION

Description The **CDC::Attach** member function is one of the family of **Attach** functions implemented in several classes of the MFC application framework. This one "attaches" a Windows handle to a device context to a **CDC** object. This makes it possible to use **CDC** class member functions to act on the DC represented by a Windows handle. **CDC::Attach** sets the target **CDC** object's **m_hDC** and **m_hAttribDC** public data members equal to the handle.

In practice, **CDC** objects don't usually receive graphics output. The derived classes **CClientDC** and **CPaintDC** are the ones application programs use, and they inherit this function to attach DCs that are to be output targets for GDI commands. In most cases, initial attachment of a DC takes place during the construction of the **CDC** (or derived) object and is good for the object's lifetime.

Prototype
```
//Function Prototype
//BOOL Attach( HDC hDC );
CDC  BrandNewCDCObject;
    //CDC::CDC constructs a CDC object with a NULL
    //m_hDC and m_hAttribDC. Using Detach on this is
    //benign and a good insurance policy because if
    //you try to use Attach on an already initialized
    //CDC object (one whose m_hDC or m_hAttribDC
    //is not NULL), you get an ASSERT.

BrandNewCDCObject.Detach( );
    //We construct a new CDC object, but we don't want the
    //client window DC attached to it
    //—we got one from the Clipboard or
    //a DDE message we want to attach.
BrandNewCDCObject.Attach( hDCNew);
```

BitBlt   FUNCTION

Description **CDC::BitBlt** transfers a bitmap from a source DC to a destination DC by doing a bitwise combination of the **CDC** object's currently selected brush, the source bitmap and the bits already on the screen at the target location. The raster operation code defines the way in which the three are combined by bitwise AND, NOT, OR and XOR operations.

CDC::BitBlt is the tool used to transfer bitmapped images to the display surface. Recall that the **CDC** object's output DC has a

305

default "bitmap" object selected into it that represents either the display or the printer presentation area. (In fact, there is really not a bitmap that represents the output device. In the case of the display, output is written to display memory by Windows, and in the case of the printer, it is written to a metafile.) Each DC can have only a single bitmap selected at a time, so outputting a bitmap to either of these presentation surfaces can't be as simple as selecting a pen or brush because the transfer involves a combination of the source and the destination with the brush.

To use either of the bitmap block transfer functions, we must first create a memory DC, select into it the bitmap we want to output to the screen, and transfer our bitmap from the memory DC to the output DC. Creating the DC is accomplished by a call to **CDC::CreateDC**. We can select the bitmap into this DC by using **CDC::SelectObject**.

At this point, we are ready to transfer the bitmap with a call to **CDC:: BitBlt**.

There are 256 raster operation codes that can be used to control the result of the transfer, referred to as *ternary* ROP codes because they take into account a source bitmap, the current brush and a destination bitmap. The ROP codes combine the three by using a combination of bitwise AND, OR, XOR and NOT operations, but the most commonly used ones have descriptively named constants.

The bitmap functions are very useful in animation because the many ways in which they can be transferred to the screen make it easy to manicure images as they move, erasing shadows of previous images.

Not all output devices support bitmapped block transfers (plotters, for example), so it is advisable to use **CDC::GetDeviceCaps** with the RC_BITBLT argument to check a device's capability before using any of the bitmap functions. Also, ordinary bitmap files are very highly device dependent. In terms of proportion, resolution, and color, bitmaps may vary considerably between output devices. If the bitmaps of the source and destination have different color encoding, **CDC:: BitBlt** converts the source and the pattern (brush) bitmaps' color information to match the destination as follows:

○ If the source bitmap is monochrome and the destination is in color, white source pixels are assigned the default background color of the destination DC, and black source pixels are assigned the default foreground color.

○ If the source bitmap is in color and the display monochrome, all of the pixels in it that match the destination background color are set to white, and all other pixels are set to black.

At best, this sort of translation will look shoddy. About all that can be said for it is that it prevents a program from crashing if incompatible bitmap formats are sent to the output DC. If it is necessary to transfer bitmaps among devices, it is a good idea to use the Windows device-independent bitmap format, which provides information about color content, resolution, and aspect ratio of a bitmap. This precaution allows an application to gracefully make its own conversions.

Note: BitBlt can be made far more efficient by operating on byte-aligned areas. To do this, create your window with either the CS_BYTEALIGNWINDOW or CS_BYTEALIGNCLIENT styles. You can add these styles to your window class by using **CWnd::PreCreateWindow** as follows:

```
CMyWnd::PreCreateWindow(LPCREATESTRUCT lpcs)
{
    lpcs->style |= CS_BYTEALIGNCLIENT;
    return TRUE;
}
```

Note also that CS_BYTEALIGNCLIENT can have odd effects on some standard Windows controls (such as space between the frame and vertical scroll bar) when used in the absence of CS_BYTEALIGNWINDOW.

Prototype

```
//Function Prototype
//BOOL BitBlt( int x, int y, int nWidth, int nHeight,
        CDC* pSrcDC, int xSrc, int ySrc,
        DWORD dwRop);
CDC MemoryDC;
    //Create a new DC
MemoryDC.CreateCompatibleDC(NULL);
    //The NULL pointer to a DC tells the
    //function to create a DC compatible with the screen....
MemoryDC.SelectObject( pBitmap);
    //Assume that we have a valid pointer
    //to a bitmap object, and select it into the DC
pDC->BitBlt( iULXDest, iULYDest, iWidth, iHeight,
        &MemoryDC, 0, 0, SRCCOPY);
    //Assume that pDC points to the current
    //output DC; transfer the bitmap
    //to the screen with its corner aligned
    //to the point iULXDest. iULYDest
    //SRCCOPY make the bitmap overdraw the
    //destination pixels
```

CDC FUNCTION

Description The constructor creates a **CDC** object and attaches the handle of a device context to it, effectively wrapping it with all the member functions of the class. The **CDC** constructor is most frequently called by applications in connection with preparation for bitmap transfers (bitblts) that require a memory DC, or to wrap Windows handles passed to an application in objects.

Prototype
```
//Function Prototype
CDC MemoryDC;
        //Construct a CDC object named MemoryDC
```

Chord FUNCTION

Description **CDC::Chord** draws a closed figure, composed of a portion of an ellipse and a closing line segment. The ellipse is defined by a bounding rectangle whose upper left and lower right corners are parameters to the function. The closing line segment is passed as a set of endpoints. The ellipse is drawn with the **CDC** object's currently selected pen and filled with the currently selected brush. This function expects its arguments to be expressed in logical coordinates.

Prototype
```
//Function Prototype
//BOOL Chord( int x1, int y1, int x2, int y2, int x3,
//     int y3, int x4, int y4);
//BOOL Chord( LPRECT lpRect, POINT ptStart, POINT ptEnd);
DisplayDC.Chord( lprBoundingRect, ptStartPoint, ptEndPoint);
    //Draw chord inside the bounding
    //rectangle and fill with the current brush....
```

CreateCompatibleDC FUNCTION

Description **CDC::CreateCompatibleDC** is used mostly for transferring bitmaps from one DC to another. All output in Windows must be directed to a device context, which provides the great advantage of making graphics under Windows largely device-independent in a world of stupendous hardware variety. However, you can't directly select a bitmap of your own into a DC for an output device. You can think of the printer's or screen's output DC as having the display surface as its currently selected bitmap. (In fact, there is not really a bitmap that corresponds to the screen or page in memory. Output commands are either written directly to display memory or recorded in a metafile.)

To transfer bits to the screen, the source bitmap must first be selected in a memory DC. The output DC already holds a "bitmap" selection, so we need to construct the second DC by calling **CDC::CreateCompatibleDC**. **CDC::CreateCompatibleDC** manufactures a DC compatible in resolution and color depth with the presentation surface. We then select the source bitmap into this memory-resident, compatible DC and transfer the bitmap from one *DC to another* using one of the **CDC** bitmap functions.

Prototype

```
//Function Prototype
//virtual BOOL CreateCompatibleDC( CDC* pDC );

CDC MemoryDC;
        //Construct a memory-resident CDC object
MemoryDC.CreateCompatibleDC(pOutputDC);
        //Call the member function with a pointer to an output DC
        //we are matching
....... //do something with the DC
```

CreateDC   FUNCTION

Description **CreateDC** creates a device context, usually for a device other than the screen. In particular, **CreateDC** is used to prepare a DC for printing by setting a driver, device, and output port, and optionally applying the initialization information. Both the driver name and the output destination have the format of MS-DOS file names, except that they are appended with a colon. In fact, the colon is superfluous because Windows strips this character before using either of these parameters to construct the output environment.

There are two ways in which **CreateDC** can gather information about the specific properties of the output device, and the way in which this is done is signaled by the value of the last parameter to the function. The last parameter to **CreateDC** may optionally provide a pointer to a **DEVMODE** structure. The **DEVMODE** structure contains a lengthy list of printer-configuration parameters. This information can be retrieved for a particular device by calling the Windows SDK function **ExtDeviceMode**. This function is exported by the printer driver for the purpose of publishing information about its settings and provides a populated **DEVMODE** structure to callers.

If pointer-to-initialization data is set to NULL, **CreateDC** constructs a DC based on whatever settings the end user has specified in the Windows Control Panel.

DCs created by **CreateDC** are actual output devices, which may be the target of any of the class **CDC** GDI output functions. Because these DCs are created for specialized output, they are not returned to the system pool of DCs when the application is done with them, and they must be deleted using **CDC::DeleteDC**. It is necessary to call **CDC::DeleteDC** for any DC *created* by your application, but it is disastrous to delete a DC that was *provided* by Windows.

Prototype

```
//Function Prototype
//virtual BOOL CreateDC( LPCSTR lpszDriverName,
        //LPCSTR lpszDeviceName, LPCSTR lpszOutput,
        //const void FAR* lpInitData );
CDC PrinterDC;
    //We are going to create a special-purpose CDC object
PrinterDC.CreateDC( lpszTheDeviceDriver, TheDeviceName,
    lpszTheOutputDestination, lpInitializationInfo );
    //and initialize the DC with information from the printer
    //driver....
```

CreateIC   FUNCTION

Description   **CreateIC** is used to quickly determine the settings of parameters that define the properties of an output device. For example, if a printer must be set for a particular paper size before the application's data can be sent to it, creating an IC is faster than creating a full, output-capable DC and still provides the necessary information. Because an IC is *not* a bona fide output DC, it cannot be the target of **CDC** GDI calls. The application must delete the IC when it is no longer needed by calling **CDC::DeleteDC**. It is very important to delete any GDI objects constructed by an application, but it is just as important to make sure that an application never deletes DCs, pens, brushes, fonts and so on that it didn't create. Calls to **CDC::DeleteDC** must pair exactly with the calls that create DCs (or ICs): **CDC::CreateDC**, **CDC::CreateIC** and **CDC::CreateCompatibleDC**.

Example

```
//virtual BOOL CreateIC( LPCSTR lpszDriverName,
        //LPCSTR lpszDeviceName,
        //LPCSTR lpszOutput,
        //const void FAR* lpInitData );
CDC PrinterDC;
        //We are going to create a special-purpose CDC object
PrinterDC.CreateIC( lpszTheDeviceDriver, TheDeviceName,
        lpszTheOutputDestination, lpInitializationInfo );
        //and build an IC with information from the printer driver....
        //we can then query the IC for printer metrics and
        //capabilities.
//Delete the IC now that we're done with it.
PrinterDC.DeleteDC();
```

DeleteDC   FUNCTION

Description   **DeleteDC** is used to delete custom device contexts constructed by user applications. It deletes DCs that were constructed by calls to the **CDC** member functions **CreateDC**, **CreateIC** and **CreateCompatibleDC** *only*. **DeleteDC** deletes the device context identified by the **CDC** public data member **m_hDC** for the current **CDC** object.

A device context should not be deleted while objects created by the application are selected in it. Any custom brushes, pens, bitmaps or fonts selected into the DC must be unselected by using **SelectObject** of the previously selected object before the application-created DC is deleted. This is usually done by calling **SelectObject** with the handle of the previously selected object. Failure to do so may make it impossible to delete the GDI objects, causing memory leakage.

Prototype

```
//Function Prototype
//virtual BOOL DeleteDC( );
CDC MemoryDC;
        //Construct a memory-resident CDC object
MemoryDC.CreateCompatibleDC(pOutputDC);
        //Call the member function with a pointer to an output
        //DC we are matching

....... //do something with the DC
MemoryDC.DeleteDC( );
        //Delete the DC when we are finished with it
```

DeleteTempMap FUNCTION

Description   **DeleteTempMap** is a function seldom used in application code because it is frequently called during the idle-time processing of **CWinApp**. **DeleteTempMap** scans for temporary objects created by calls to **CDC::FromHandle**. **CDC::FromHandle** takes a Windows handle to a DC and returns a pointer to a temporary **CDC** object that has that DC attached to it. **DeleteTempMap** disposes of **CDC** objects created in this way after detaching them from the handle to the device context. This happens automatically, usually as soon as the function that called **FromHandle** returns. This system housekeeping function should not be called by application code.

The ::Attach Family of Functions

The key idea with all members of the **::Attach** family is that Windows handles can be cleanly joined to and cleaved from objects. This capability facilitates sharing of data between applications through passing of handles in DDE messages or the Clipboard, which might be difficult or impossible among anonymous partners. It provides a bridge to and from the C language API by providing a mechanism by which Windows handles may be wrapped in objects. For example, a handle to a brush passed to the application through the Clipboard can be attached to a **CBrush** object, which makes the **CBrush** member functions available to use in connection with the brush represented by the handle.

Detach FUNCTION

Description   **CDC::Detach** severs the association between a Windows handle to a device context and a **CDC** object associated with it.
CDC::Detach allows the programmer to separate a handle from the **CDC** object used to manipulate it. The advantage of this arrangement is that, if for some reason the DC identified by the handle will outlive the **CDC** object your application constructed to handle it, detaching the handle allows the object to be destroyed without affecting the DC itself. This is also useful when a **CDC** object is constructed on the fly by a call to **CDC::FromHandle**.
CDC::FromHandle returns a pointer to an object of type **CDC**,

creating the **CDC** object automatically if none exists to which the handle can be attached. Objects created in this way have a very short lifetime and must be quickly used, detached from the handle used to create them, and then allowed to be destroyed by **CWinApp** housekeeping processes.

Prototype

```
//Function Prototype
//CDC  BrandNewCDCObject;

BrandNewCDCObject.Detach( );
        //We construct a new CDC object, but we don't want the
        //client window DC attached to it — we got one from the
        //Clipboard or
        //a DDE message we want to attach.
BrandNewCDCObject.Attach( hDCNew);
```

DPtoLP   FUNCTION

Description A part of the way in which Windows provides device independence for graphics is by making use of two coordinate systems. The first is the *device* coordinate system, and the second is the *logical* coordinate system. **CDC::DPtoLP** is used by an application to translate a point or an array of points between device coordinates and logical coordinates.

Device coordinates are the physical divisions of a particular presentation surface: For a screen, device coordinates are reported in pixels. Most of the time, Windows applications are concerned with the other coordinate system, called the *logical coordinate system.* The size, orientation and location of the logical coordinate system is exclusively under the control of the application, and all its drawing operations are directed to the logical coordinate system. Sometimes, however, it is necessary to work back and forth between coordinate systems, and this situation usually comes up in connection with mouse input. The location of the mouse is reported to the application in device units, which makes sense taken in the light that it would produce a great deal of unnecessary overhead and inflexibility if Windows were to translate every mouse message into the application's own coordinates.

Device coordinates originate in the upper left corner of the screen. Moving or resizing an application's window can make device coordinates stale. If an application needs to preserve device coordinate information, it is best to save it in logical coordinates, which can be done using this function. Because an application controls the settings that apply to its logical coordinate space, it can always interpret logical coordinates correctly. User actions or other applications can affect the way screen real estate is distributed, so your application has no way of determining whether device coordinates are valid from one message processing cycle to the next.

Prototype

```
//Function Prototypes
//Translate an array of default size 1
//void DPtoLP( LPPOINT lpPoints, int nCount =1 )const;
//Translate two points using a rectangle structure
//void DPtoLP( LPRECT lpRect )const;
//Translate points using a SIZE structure
//void DPtoLP(LPSIZE lpSize) const;

DisplayDC.DPtoLP( lpArrayOfPoints );
        //We have only one point to convert,
        //perhaps a mouse click location,
        //Use the default point count of 1,
        //so we omit the point count argument
        //The point is converted in place,
        //and there is no return
```

DrawFocusRect · FUNCTION

Description **CDC::DrawFocusRect** draws a rectangle which indicates that a region of the application's client area has the input focus, showing the user that a particular control element has the input focus. The rectangle is applied to the client area by a Boolean XOR and is removed by a second call to the function by using the same rectangle coordinates.

The function arguments are expected to be in logical coordinates. If a focus rectangle is visible in the client area, the window may not be scrolled.

If you need to scroll an area that has a focus rectangle, you must take these steps in your scroll-message handler:

1. Call **DrawFocusRect** with the appropriate rectangle as an argument to remove the focus rectangle.

2. Perform the scrolling.

3. Call **DrawFocusRect** again with the appropriate rectangle as an argument to restore the focus rectangle.

Prototype

```
//Function Prototype
//void DrawFocusRect( LPRECT lpRect );

DisplayDC.DrawFocusRect( lprFocus );
    //Draw a rectangle to show the
    //user where the input focus is....
```

DrawIcon   FUNCTION

Description   **CDC::DrawIcon** paints an icon on the application's client area at the location specified in the function's argument. It is used with functions that create and manipulate icons, such as **CWinApp::LoadIcon**, **CWinApp::LoadStandardIcon**, **CWinApp::LoadOEMIcon** and Windows SDK function ::**OpenIcon**.

This function expects the location at which to draw the icon to be expressed in logical coordinates. The icon resource must have been loaded previously by the application before this function is called, and the **CDC** object's mapping mode must be set to **MM_TEXT** at the time **CDC::DrawIcon** is called.

Prototype

```
//Function Prototype
//BOOL DrawIcon( int x, int y, HICON hIcon );
//BOOL DrawIcon(POINT point, HICON hIcon );

DisplayDC.DrawIcon(ptUpperLeftCorner, hIconResource );
    //Paint the icon in the client area
    //at the specified point....
```

DrawText   FUNCTION

Description   CDC::**DrawText** draws text, using the currently selected font, into the specified clipping rectangle and can perform numerous formatting operations, such as multiline word wrapping broken at word boundaries, tab expansion, and justification. Though it takes a parameter specifying the length of the string it is to draw, if that parameter is set to -1, **DrawText** calculates the string length for you. It can optionally expand the lower boundary of the clip rectangle to accommodate text that would be clipped away; if the string is a single line, it can also adjust the right-hand boundary.

CDC::**DrawText** is a great tool for formatting the output of a moderate amount of text. The word-wrap and clipping capabilities make it unnecessary to do a great deal of information retrieval and calculations using the text metrics. Unless you need to mix fonts within the body of the text, this function can probably do most of what you need. **CDC::DrawText** is sensitive to the setting of the **TA_UPDATECP** flag, which can be set by calling **CDC::SetTextAlign**. When this flag is set, text output functions use the **CDC** object's current position to govern the point at which text output begins. If this flag is set, **CDC::DrawText** begins drawing text at the current position, ignoring the coordinates set by the rectangle in its parameter list. With this flag set, **CDC::DrawText** is not able to do automatic word wrapping, even if that format option was specified. It is not possible to override **TA_UPDATECP** by setting **CDC::DrawText** format options.

The flags for the nFormat parameter are shown in this table:

Flag	Purpose
DT_BOTTOM	Specifies bottom-justified text. This value must be combined with DT_SINGLELINE.
DT_CALCRECT	Determines the width and height of the rectangle. If there are multiple lines of text, DrawText uses the width of the rectangle pointed to by lpRect and extends the base of the rectangle to bound the last line of text. If there is only one line of text, DrawText modifies the right side of the rectangle so that it bounds the last character in the line. In either case. DrawText returns the height of the formatted text but does not draw the text.
DT_CENTER	Centers text horizontally.
DT_EXPANDTABS	Expands tab characters. The default number of characters per tab is eight.
DT_EXTERNALLEADING	Includes the font's external leading in the line height. Normally, external leading is not included in the height of a line of text.
DT_LEFT	Aligns text flush left.
DT_NOCLIP	Draws without clipping. DrawText is somewhat faster when DT_NOCLIP is used.
DT_NOPREFIX	Turns off processing of prefix characters. Normally, DrawText interprets the ampersand (&) mnemonic prefix character as a directive to underscore the character that follows, and the two-ampersand (&&) mnemonic prefix characters as a directive to print a single ampersand. By specifiying DT_NOPREFIX, this processing is turned off.
DT_RIGHT	Aligns text flush right.
DT_SINGLELINE	Specifies single line only. Carriage returns and line feeds do not break the line.

Flag	Purpose
DT_TABSTOP	Sets tab stops. The high-order byte of nFormat is the number of characters for each tab. The default number of characters per tab is eight.
DT_TOP	Specifies top-justified text (single line only).
DT_VCENTER	Specifies vertically centered text (single line only).
DT_WORDBREAK	Specifies word-breaking. Lines are automatically broken between words if a word would extend past the edge of the rectangle specified by lpRect. A carriage return-linefeed sequence will also break the line.

Note that the values DT_CALCRECT, DT_EXTERNALLEADING, DT_INTERNAL, DT_NOCLIP and DT_NOPREFIX cannot be used with the DT_TABSTOP value.

Prototype

```
//Function Prototype
//virtual BOOL DrawText( LPCSTR lpszString, int nCount,
//LPRECT lpRect,
//         UINT nFormat );
    //Assume that we have a valid pointer to a DC
    //because most drawing is done from
    //the OnDraw member function of the view....

pDC->DrawText( lpszLongString, strlen( lpszLongString ),
        lprClipRect,
        DT_CALCRECT | DT_LEFT);
    //Draw the string in the clipping rectangle,
    //but expand the clipping rectangle as
    //needed and left-align the lines of text....
```

EndDoc — FUNCTION

Description CDC::EndDoc replaces the Windows SDK **ENDDOC** printer escape under Windows 3.1, and is the preferred method of ending a print job for Win32s and Windows NT. **CDC::EndDoc** signals the device driver that a print job is complete. The **CDC::StartDoc/ CDC::EndDoc** pair brackets the pages of a multipage document as it spools, to protect it from being interspersed among pages of concurrently printing documents. This function should not be called from inside a mctafile.

Prototype
```
//Function Prototype
//int EndDoc( );
if (PrinterDC.StartDoc(&DocInfoStruct) !=ERROR)
  {
    //Do printing jobs....
  }
PrinterDC.EndDoc( );
    //Print job is finished....
```

EndPage   FUNCTION

Description **CDC::EndPage** signals the device driver that a page is complete. The **CDC::StartPage/CDC::EndPage** pair brackets the output to each page of a document as it spools. This function replaces the **NEWFRAME** printer escape. Unlike the **NEWFRAME** escape, this function should be called for every completed page. Windows disables the **CDC::ResetDC** member function between each **CDC::StartPage/CDC::EndPage** pair.

Prototype
```
//Function Prototype
//int EndPage( );
PrinterDC.StartPage( );
    //Do page drawing ....
PrinterDC.EndPage( );
```

Escape   FUNCTION

Description **CDC::Escape** allows an application to take advantage of device driver interfaces that are not covered by MFC or Windows SDK calls. Principally, the **Escape** codes are used with printers under Windows 3.*x*. Sixty-four escape codes are defined for this environment; however, all but 11 of them are made obsolete under Win32s and Windows NT. Of the 11 that remain, 10 are for backward compatibility only. In writing new applications, it is desirable to stick to this subset if possible because it makes your application more easily portable to the new environments. The 10 are shown in this list:

ABORTDOC
ENDDOC
GETPHYSPAGESIZE
GETPRINTINGOFFSET
GETSCALINGFACTOR
NEWFRAME
NEXTBAND
PASSTHROUGH
SETABORTPROC
STARTDOC

CDC::Escape allows an application to get information from and exert some control over an output device by communicating directly with the device driver. Much of the need for this has been eliminated by the printing support provided in MFC and **CDC** class member functions that wrap the escapes. An advantage of using the wrapper member functions, such as **CDC::AbortDoc** and **CDC::EndDoc**, is that they work correctly for Windows 3.1, Win32s or Windows NT. Substitute the **CDC** class member functions that wrap the major escape codes where possible. The **CDC:: Escape** function returns a positive integer if successful, and otherwise a zero. An exception is when the escape code passed to the function is QUERYESCSUPPORT. Zero is returned if the code is not implemented, and a negative value is returned if the call failed.

The function parameter that specifies the pointer to the buffer for output data should be set to NULL if the application expects no data to be returned.

Prototype

```
//Function Prototype
//virtual int Escape( int nEscape, int nCount, LPCSTR lpszInData,
//LPVOID lpOutData );

PrintDC.Escape(GETPHYSPAGESIZE, 0, NULL, sizePage);
    //Get physical page size information
    //from the device driver....
```

ExcludeClipRect   FUNCTION

Description   **CDC::ExcludeClipRect** is an inverse clipping function, in that it creates a clipping region that omits an area specified by the rectangle. *Clipping* is the process of constraining drawing to a specific area of the presentation surface. An area excluded from clipping is overdrawn by any graphic operations that are output to it. This function causes the rectangle identified by its parameter to be subject to normal redrawing when the application's client area is updated. The clipping region set after this function is called is whatever it was before, less the specified rectangle. Applications seldom do their own clipping housekeeping. **CDC::ExcludeClipRect** is used by the framework in managing repainting.

Prototype

```
//Function Prototype
//virtual int ExcludeClipRect( int x, int y,
//              int x2, int y2 );
//virtual int ExcludeClipRect( LPRECT lpRect );
DisplayDC.ExcludeClipRect( lprClientArea );
    //Prevent drawing in the application's client area....
```

ExcludeUpdateRgn   FUNCTION

Description **CDC::ExcludeUpdateRgn** removes the region of an entire window that has been identified as needing to be repainted from the **CDC** object's clipping region. Because the update region is the only area in which drawing is allowed to occur, the excluded region is not repainted, even though it has been flagged for it. Applications seldom use this function. It is invoked automatically by the framework in managing update painting.

Prototype

```
//Function Prototype
//int ExcludeUpdateRgn( CWnd* pWnd );

DisplayDC.ExcludeUpdateRgn( pAppWindow );
    //Exclude all of an application window's
    //invalid areas from the CDC
    //object's clipping region.
    //No repainting will take place....
```

ExtFloodFill   FUNCTION

Description **CDC::ExtFloodFill** fills an area by using the **CDC** object's currently selected brush. The area must currently be filled with a single color. The interior RGB color value is passed to the function as a parameter along with the point from which the fill flows outward. **CDC::ExtFloodFill** can be used to fill solid color shapes with multicolored boundaries. As long as the interior color (that is, the one over which the new color floods) occurs, the fill continues. A color boundary halts its progress. It can be used to dramatic effect because the user can usually perceive the flooding—it is rapid but not instantaneous in most cases. Its performance is highly dependent on display adapter, CPU speed, and so on. It can take place in less than one rescan on a fast machine. The point must be expressed in logical coordinates that fall within the clipping region.

The parameter **nFillType** must be either FLOODFILLBORDER or FLOODFILLSURFACE. If it's the former, the behavior is identical to FloodFill, and crColor is assumed to be the color of the border; if it's the latter, filling proceeds outward from the point defined by x and y, as long as the color remains the same as that specified by crColor. This allows for filling of areas that have different colored borders.

Prototype

```
//Function Prototype
//BOOL ExtFloodFill( int x, int y, COLORREF crColor,
//UINT nFillType );

DisplayDC.ExtFloodFill( iX, iY, crFloodColor, FLOODFILLSURFACE );
    //Fill the area starting at iX,iY
    //until we no longer encounter crFloodColor
```

ExtTextOut   FUNCTION

Description **CDC::ExtTextOut** draws a string, clipping it to a rectangle specified in the function call, optionally painting the background with the current brush and optionally setting character cell spacing. If the clipping rectangle parameter is set to NULL, it is ignored when the text is drawn.

CDC::ExtTextOut is helpful in internationalizing text or handling unusual fonts, such as scientific or mathematical symbols. It also can provide the convenience of doing the housekeeping related to text placement. A call to **CDC::ExtTextOut** can be paired with **CDC::SetTextAlign**, setting a flag instructing Windows that **CDC::ExtTextOut** will update the current position when it draws a string. The current position is then used to position the next output string. **ExtTextOut** is extremely fast and is used by some programmers with a null string argument as a way to erase a rectangular area.

Prototype

```
//Function Prototype
//virtual BOOL ExtTextOut ( int x, int y, UINT nOptions,
//          LPRECT lpRect, LPCSTR lpszString,
//          UINT nCount, LPINT lpDxWidths);
```

321

```
//Assume that we have a valid pointer to a DC
//because most drawing is done from
//the OnDraw member function of the view....
pDC->ExtTextOut( rClientArea.left, rClientArea.top, ETO_CLIPPED,
        &rClip,"Hello World!", strlen( "Hello World!" ),
        lpiCellWidths );
//Write the string in the upper left corner
//of the client area, clip it to the
//rectangle rClip, and use the array of cell widths
//to set intercharacter spacing....
```

The parameter nOptions can be 0, ETO_CLIPPED, ETO_OPAQUE, or a combination of them (ETO_CLIPPED | ETO_OPAQUE). This specifies how the rectangular area will be treated. If nOptions has the ETO_OPAQUE bit set, the rectangular area is filled with the background color. This can be handy for creating callouts that stand out from the background in a graph. Changing the intercharacter spacing by using the final argument works as follows: If the argument is NULL, the spacing is done by using the font's normal attributes; if an array is supplied, the character in a given position is spaced the number of logical units specified from the end of the previous character cell. This is primarily useful for *tracking,* a typographical technique for spreading or compressing type to fit a given area.

FillRect — FUNCTION

Description CDC::**FillRect** creates a solid, borderless rectangle. The bounds of the rectangle exclude the lower and right edges. This function expects the rectangle to be expressed in logical coordinates. The brush must exist when the function is called. Use the **CBrush** class member functions to create a custom brush, or retrieve a system brush by using the SDK function **GetStockObject**. Notice that **FillRect** does not do any "normalization" of rectangles, so if you specify the coordinates upside down or from right to left, the rectangle is not drawn. To put it another way, this function expects an "upper left" corner coordinates that are above and to the left of the coordinates for the lower right corner when the rectangle is drawn. To wit,

        pDC->FillRect(CRect(100, 10, 10, 50), pMyBrush);

is semantically the same as

        pDC->FillRect(CRect(10, 10, 100, 50), pMyBrush);

but FillRect does not draw the former rectangle.

Prototype

```
//Function Prototype
//void FillRect( LPRECT lpRect, CBrush* pBrush );
DisplayDC.FillRect( lpFillRectBoundary,  pbFillBrush );
    //Paint a solid color, borderless rectangle....
```

FillRgn   FUNCTION

Description

A *region* is an elliptical, polygonal or rounded rectangular area within an application's logical coordinate space. Creation and manipulation of regions is encapsulated in the class **CRgn**, which is derived from the GDI parent class **CGdiObject**. Regions are filled using the current polygon fill method (either ALTERNATE or WINDING) set for a **CDC** object's output DC. **CDC::FillRgn** fills the region identified by the first parameter with a brush identified by the second parameter.

The region and brush must exist before calling **CDC::FillRgn**. The brush can be created with any of the class **CBrush** member functions for brush creation or retrieved from the pool of system brushes with the Windows SDK function ::**GetStockObject**.

Note that **GetStockObject** is an external API function. When you're referring to an external API function, use the global scope resolution operator (::). It's good coding form and helps reduce name "misses" as a result of MFC's reuse of the Windows API names. What typically happens is that when you think that you're calling an API function, such as InvalidateRect(r), the compiler complains that the function doesn't take one argument. Accckkk! The rules of C++ are specific, if not very helpful: After the compiler sees the name **CWnd::InvalidateRect** (and it has to look in class scope first), it either gets a match or has to give up. What it cannot do is search the global scope. All of this is a long-winded way of saying that if you mean to use the Windows API, also use the ::.

Regions are created by using member functions of the class **CRgn**.

Prototype

```
//Function Prototype
//BOOL FillRgn( CRgn* pRgn, CBrush* pBrush );
DisplayDC.FillRgn( pRegion,
CBrush::FromHandle((HBRUSH)::GetStockObject( WHITE_BRUSH )
));
    //Fill this region with the system white brush;
    //CBrush::FromHandle returns a pointer to a
    //CBrush object, given the handle to
    //the system brush.
```

Here are a few points to keep in mind about the example. First, **CBrush::FromHandle** is a static function, and that's why it can be invoked by using the syntax shown in the example. It returns a temporary pointer to a **CBrush**. This temporary object is cleaned up in idle time by the framework. **::GetStockObject** returns a HGDIOBJ in Win32, which is an abstract type that can be coerced into types such as HBRUSH, HFONT and so on. Because of C++ type safety, you have to provide this explicit coercion by using a cast, since there is no implicit conversion from an HGDIOBJ to an HBRUSH.

FloodFill   FUNCTION

Description   **CDC::FloodFill** fills an area by using the **CDC** object's currently selected brush. The area must be bounded by a border of a single color. The border's RGB color value is passed to the function as a parameter along with the point from which the fill flows outward. **CDC::FloodFill** fills irregular shapes that were not drawn in a single operation, such as line drawings. It can be used with dramatic effect because the user can perceive the flooding—it is rapid but not instantaneous in most cases. The point from which the fill flows must be expressed in logical coordinates that fall within the clipping region. The border must be a closed boundary or the fill color will leak out. See also **CDC::ExtFloodFill**. **ExtFloodFill** is a little more flexible and much easier to use.

Prototype

```
//Function Prototype
//BOOL FloodFill( int x, int y, COLORREF crColor);
DisplayDC.FloodFill(100, 100, crBoundaryColor );
    //Fill an area containing the point 100,100 and bounded by
    //crBoundaryColor with the current brush...
```

FrameRect   FUNCTION

Description   **CDC::FrameRect** creates an unfilled rectangle by drawing a border one logical unit wide around a rectangle, using the brush specified in its argument. It has pretty much the same effect as calling **CDC::Rectangle**, except that it is more trouble because you have to supply the brush as well as a bounding rectangle.
CDC::Rectangle also provides you with more flexibility in filling the interior of the figure. The distinction between **FrameRect** and **Rectangle** is that one uses the current brush, and the other the current pen, to draw the frame. **Rectangle** fills using the current brush, and even if it is HOLLOW_BRUSH, implies more overhead.

This function expects the rectangle to be expressed in logical coordinates. The brush must exist when the function is called. Use the **CBrush** class member functions to create a custom brush, or retrieve a system brush by using the SDK function **GetStockObject**.

Prototype

```
//Function Prototype
//void FrameRect( LPRECT lpRect, CBrush* pBrush );
DisplayDC.FrameRect( lpFrameRectBoundary, pbFrameBrush );
    //Draw the outline of FrameRectBoundary,
    //using the specified brush....
```

FrameRgn   FUNCTION

Description

A region is an elliptical, polygonal or rounded rectangular area within an application's client area.

Creation and manipulation of regions is encapsulated in the class **CRgn**, which is derived from the GDI parent class **CGdiObject**. **CDC::FrameRgn** draws a border around a region. Regions are useful when comparing or highlighting irregularly shaped areas. **CDC::FrameRgn** can place a border of any size around a region. For example, a mapping application might use it to show the area taken in by a buffer zone around a lake.

Both the region and the brush passed as parameters to **CDC::FrameRgn** must exist before the call. The brush can be created with any of the class **CBrush** member functions for brush creation or retrieved from the pool of system brushes with the Windows SDK function ::**GetStockObject**. Regions are created using member functions of the class **CRgn**.

Prototype

```
//Function Prototype
//BOOL FrameRgn( CRgn* pRgn, CBrush* pBrush, int nWidth,
//       int nHeight);
DisplayDC.FrameRgn( pRegion,
    CBrush::FromHandle((HBRUSH)::GetStockObject
    ( WHITE_BRUSH ) ), 5, 5);
    //Frame this region with the system white brush;
    //CBrush::FromHandle returns a pointer
    //to a CBrush object, given the handle to
    //the system brush.
    //Make the brush used to draw the border five pixels high and
    //five pixels wide
```

Notice the type coercion that occurs in the **CBrush::FromHandle** call. See the comments in **FillRgn** for detailed comments.

FromHandle   FUNCTION

Description   **FromHandle** is one of a family of functions that is implemented in several application framework classes. In its **CDC** implementation, it provides a pointer to a **CDC** object, given a handle to a device context. If the DC identified by the handle currently has no **CDC** object attached to it, **FromHandle** manufactures a temporary one and attaches it. This makes it possible to take a handle passed in on a DDE message or from a C language API function and wrap it with an object, which provides access to member functions and framework functionality like Print Preview's. The temporary object has a life span of one Windows message-processing cycle, so the application receiving the pointer cannot use it after the function in which **FromHandle** is called returns. If it is important to preserve the object, a copy of it must be constructed. Under no circumstances should the pointer be stored for later use—it will be invalidated by normal framework garbage collection.

Prototype
```
//Function Prototype
//static CDC* PASCAL FromHandle( HDC hDC );
    CDC* pDC = CDC::FromHandle(hDeviceContext);
        //We have a handle to a device context, but we want
        //to use type-safe GDI member functions of CDC to modify
        //the DC. We call FromHandle to give us a temporary CDC
        //object
        //with this DC attached....
```

GetAspectRatioFilter   FUNCTION

Description   **CDC::GetAspectRatioFilter** retrieves the current setting for the aspect ratio filter used by the font mapper. **CDC::SetMapperFlags** sets the font-mapping flags that control the way in which a logical font is matched to a physical font for the current output device. When an application makes a request for a *logical* font, the font characteristics are compared to available *physical* fonts. Physical fonts are hardware fonts or font resources that have been loaded by the operating system or the application. The font mapper chooses a physical font that most closely matches the logical font described by the application. Mapper flags can force the font-mapping algorithm to ignore fonts that do not match exactly the aspect ratio of the target device. The aspect ratio of a device is the ratio between the width and height of a pixel for a given device.

CDC::GetAspectRatioFilter allows an application that uses raster fonts to determine whether the setting of the filter will produce font matching that is appropriate to the target display device. It is used in combination with **CDC::SetMapperFlags to** force font selections based on an exact match of a specified aspect ratio. The flag that forces aspect ratio mapping is ASPECT_FILTERING. Mapper flags are not used with TrueType fonts because they can be scaled appropriately for different aspect ratios.

Prototype

```
//Function Prototype
//CSize GetAspectRatioFilter( )const;
    //Assume that we have a valid pointer to a DC
    //because most drawing is done from
    //the OnDraw member function of the view....
CSize sizeAspectRatio = pDC->GetAspectRatioFilter( );
    //Retrieve current aspect ration filter value....
```

GetBkColor   FUNCTION

Description

CDC::GetBkColor retrieves the current background color used for client area painting. The information returned from this function references the **CDC** object's attribute DC. For the most part, the background color is simply the brush that fills in whatever pixels an application doesn't explicitly draw. Depending on the background mode, it may optionally fill in the spaces around characters and the gaps in lines drawn by dashed pens and patterned brushes.

The background color is considered when translating a bitmap from a memory DC to the screen. The way in which the composition of the background interacts with the source bitmap and the pixels currently on the screen is defined by the ROP (raster operation) code used in the bitmap transfer.

Prototype

```
//Function Prototype
//COLORREF GetBkColor( ) const;
crBackground = DisplayDC.GetBkColor( );
    //Report the current background color of the application's
    //client area....
```

GetBkMode   FUNCTION

Description

CDC::GetBkMode returns the background mode setting of the current **CDC** object's attribute device context. Background modes are **OPAQUE** and **TRANSPARENT**. **OPAQUE** mode fills the update region of the client area with the current background color before new text or a drawing is painted. This has about the same effect as pasting an update over the client area. **TRANSPARENT** mode allows a new drawing to take place without obliterating previous client area contents. This background mode lets the new drawing transparently overlay the old. The default background mode is **OPAQUE**.

Prototype

```
//Function Prototype
//int GetBkMode( ) const;
if( DisplayDC.GetBkMode( ) == OPAQUE )
  {
    //Draw over the client area....
  }
```

GetBoundsRect   FUNCTION

Description   **CDC::GetBoundsRect** retrieves an application's bounding rectangle, which is the smallest rectangle that will enclose the output operations directed to the client area of the current **CDC** object's output DC, after the most recent call to **CDC::SetBoundsRect**.

The current DC's bounding rectangle is a bit of bookkeeping Windows uses to update the client area efficiently when it is time to paint. A bounding rectangle comprises the smallest rectangle that will enclose a given drawing operation. **CDC::GetBoundsRect** retrieves the bounding rectangle for an application's client area or for Windows. The DCB_RESET flag causes the application's bounding rectangle to be cleared after it is returned. The bounding rectangle is returned in logical coordinates, and the return value specifies whether the bounding rectangle is accumulating, empty or not empty, or whether bounding is enabled or disabled. Applications seldom call this function because update management is usually best performed by Windows. Specifying DCB_WINDOWMGR gets information about the bounding rectangle for Windows's update area rather than for the application's.

Prototype

```
//Function Prototype
//UINT GetBoundsRect( LPRECT lpRectBounds, UINT flags );
UINT uiBoundingState = DisplayDC.GetBoundsRect(
    lprBoundingRect, 0 );
    //If you specify a zero, you don't do any
    //resetting of the bounding rectangle
```

GetBrushOrg   FUNCTION

Description **CDC::GetBrushOrg** retrieves the origin of the brush currently selected in the device context of the **CDC** object. The origin is an *x-y* coordinate pair, given in device units. When you consider the family of functions that change the alignment of the brush, it is helpful to remember that a "brush" is nothing more than a small bitmap combined in the way the application directs with the bits in the area it will be painting. In Windows 3.*x*, the origin of the brush bitmap is the upper left corner of the display surface. As application windows move and are resized, it is possible for this bitmap to become misaligned and produce a striping effect when the window is repainted using a patterned brush. **CDC::GetBrushOrg** has a complementary function, **CDC::SetBrushOrg**, for setting a brush origin.

Prototype
```
//Function Prototype
//CPoint GetBrushOrg( )const;
CPoint ptBrushOrg = pDisplayDC.GetBrushOrg( );
       //Retrieve the device coordinates
       //of the brush origin and save them in a
       //CPoint object
```

GetCharABCWidths   FUNCTION

Description TrueType glyphs (characters) are positioned relative to one another based on an "A+B+C" spacing formula. "A" is the white that precedes the glyph, "B" is the width of the black part of the glyph at its widest point, and "C" is the white space that follows a glyph. **CDC::GetCharABCWidths** returns the widths for a range of characters specified in the function arguments. This function provides character-by-character information to an application that exercises control over text placement by using TrueType fonts.

Prototype
```
//Function Prototype
//BOOL GetCharABCWidths( UINT nFirst, UINT nLast,
//LPABC lpabc ) const;
       //Assume that we have a valid pointer to a DC
       //because most drawing is done from
       //the OnDraw member function of the view....
pDC->GetCharABCWidths( iFirstChar, iLastChar,
                lpabcABCStructArray );
       //Copy Glyph spacing info
```

GetCharWidth — FUNCTION

Description **CDC::GetCharWidth** returns the widths for a range of characters specified in the function arguments for the currently selected font. This function provides character-by-character information to an application that exercises control over text placement by using non-TrueType fonts.

Prototype
```
//Function Prototype
//BOOL GetCharWidth( UINT nFirstChar, UINT nLastChar,
    //LPINT lpBuffer ) const;
    //Assume that we have a valid pointer to a DC
    //because most drawing is done from
    //the OnDraw member function of the view....
pDC->GetCharWidths( iFirstChar, iLastChar, lpiCharWidthArray );
    //Copy character-spacing info
```

GetClipBox — FUNCTION

Description **CDC::GetClipBox** retrieves the smallest bounding rectangle that can enclose the current clipping region as well as any overlapping windows.

It is used to limit painting to the smallest area necessary, with the effect of speeding things up a bit. Clip box coordinates are reported in logical units, and the return value gives the clipping region's type. The way this capability can speed things up is that it allows you to prune out code that might have to do lots of calculations for painting outside the clipping box. This doesn't save much Windows time, but it can save a lot of time in your application.

Possible return values are shown in this table:

Return Value	Meaning
COMPLEXREGION	Clipping region has overlapping borders.
ERROR	Device context is not valid.
NULLREGION	Clipping region is empty.
SIMPLEREGION	Clipping region has no overlapping borders.

Prototype
```
//Function Prototype
//virtual int GetClipBox( LPRECT lpRect )const;
int iClipRegionType = DisplayDC.GetClipBox( lprClipBox );
    //We retrieve the smallest rectangle
    //that will enclose the current clipping region....
```

330

GetCurrentPosition   FUNCTION

Description   **CDC::GetCurrentPosition** tells the application where the pen
will be set down in the next **CDC::LineTo** line-drawing operation.
The next line-drawing operation will begin at the current pen
position unless it is changed with a call to **CDC::MoveTo**. This
function returns a result expressed in logical coordinates.

Prototype
```
//Function Prototype
//CPoint GetCurrentPosition( )const;
CPoint ptLineStart = DisplayDC.GetCurrentPosition( );
    //Find out where a new line will begin....
```

GetDeviceCaps   FUNCTION

Description   **CDC::GetDeviceCaps** is sort of one-stop shopping for information
about what a particular output device can and cannot do. Because
it can provide such a huge variety of information, you have to be
specific about what you want. The parameter it takes tells it what
you want to know, and it provides the requested information.

    CDC::GetDeviceCaps reports on the output capabilities of
displays, printers, plotters and raster cameras. It can query a device
for driver version, the type of the device, display surface dimensions in pixels or millimeters, color-handling properties, aspect
ratio, and its capabilities to do various raster operations. Very
detailed information on graphical drawing capabilities can be
provided with respect to line, curve and polygon drawing capabilities, so that, for example, an application can decide whether to
send an image including a flood fill polygon to a pen plotter. Text
capabilities can also be minutely dissected, which is important
because display-based fonts are often much more flexibly defined
than the ones available on a low-end printer.

    The possible values for the nIndex parameter and corresponding
return values are shown in this table:

nIndex Parameter	Returns
DRIVERVERSION	Version number. Returns 3 hex digits in the form major, minor, point, so version 3.1 is represented as 0x310.
TECHNOLOGY	Device technology. Returns one of the following:
	DT_PLOTTER: Vector plotter
	DT_RASDISPLAY: Raster display
	DT_RASPRINTER: Raster printer
	DT_RASCAMERA: Raster camera
	DT_CHARSTREAM: Character stream
	DT_METAFILE: Metafile
	DT_DISPFILE: Display file

331

nIndex Parameter	Returns
HORZSIZE	Width of the physical display (in millimeters).
VERTSIZE	Height of the physical display (in millimeters).
HORZRES	Width of the display (in pixels).
VERTRES	Height of the display (in raster lines).
LOGPIXELSX	Number of pixels per logical inch along the display width.
LOGPIXELSY	Number of pixels per logical inch along the display height.
BITSPIXEL	Number of adjacent color bits for each pixel.
PLANES	Number of color planes.
NUMBRUSHES	Number of device-specific brushes.
NUMPENS	Number of device-specific pens.
NUMFONTS	Number of device-specific fonts.
NUMCOLORS	Number of entries in the device's color table.
ASPECTX	Relative width of a device pixel as used for line drawing.
ASPECTY	Relative height of a device pixel as used for line drawing.
ASPECTXY	Diagonal width of the device pixel as used for line drawing.
PDEVICESIZE	Size of the PDEVICE internal data structure.
CLIPCAPS	Clipping capabilities of the device. It can be one of the following: CP_NONE: Output is not clipped. CP_RECTANGLE: Output is clipped to rectangles. CP_REGION: Output is clipped to regions.
SIZEPALETTE	Number of entries in the system palette. This index is valid only if the device driver sets the RC_PALETTE bit in the RASTERCAPS index. It is available only if the driver is written for Windows version 3.0 or later.
NUMRESERVED	Number of reserved entries in the system palette. This index is valid only if the device driver sets the RC_PALETTE bit in the RASTERCAPS index and is available only if the driver is written for Windows version 3.0 or higher.
COLORRES	Actual color resolution of the device in bits per pixel. This index is valid only if the device driver sets the RC_PALETTE bit in the RASTERCAPS index and is available only if the driver is written for Windows version 3.0 or later.

nIndex Parameter	Returns
RASTERCAPS	Value that indicates the raster capabilities of the device. It can be a combination of the following: RC_BANDING: Requires banding support. RC_BIGFONT: Supports fonts larger than 64k. RC_BITBLT: Capable of transferring bitmaps. RC_BITMAP64: Supports bitmaps larger than 64k. RC_DEVBITS: Supports device bitmaps. RC_DI_BITMAP: Capable of supporting the SetDIBits and GetDIBits Windows functions. RC_DIBTODEV: Capable of supporting the SetDIBitsToDevice Windows function. RC_FLOODFILL: Capable of performing flood fills. RC_GDI20_OUTPUT: Capable of supporting Windows version 2.0 features. RC_GDI20_STATE: Includes a state block in the device context. RC_NONE: Supports no raster operations. RC_OP_DX_OUTPUT: Supports dev opaque and DX array. RC_PALETTE: Specifies a palette-based device. RC_SAVEBITMAP: Capable of saving bitmaps locally. RC_SCALING: Capable of scaling. RC_STRETCHBLT: Capable of performing the StretchBlt member function. RC_STRETCHDIB: Capable of performing the StretchDIBits Windows function.
CURVECAPS	The curve capabilities of the device. It can be a combination of the following: CC_NONE: Supports curves. CC_CIRCLES: Supports circles. CC_PIE: Supports pie wedges. CC_CHORD: Supports chords. CC_ELLIPSES: Supports ellipses. CC_WIDE: Supports wide borders. CC_STYLED: Supports styled borders. CC_WIDESTYLED: Supports wide, styled borders. CC_INTERIORS: Supports interiors. CC_ROUNDRECT: Supports rectangles with rounded corners.

nIndex Parameter	Returns
LINECAPS	Line capabilities the device supports. It can be a combination of the following:
	LC_NONE: Supports no lines.
	LC_POLYLINE: Supports polylines.
	LC_MARKER: Supports markers.
	LC_POLYMARKER: Supports polymarkers.
	LC_WIDE: Supports wide lines.
	LC_STYLED: Supports styled lines.
	LC_WIDESTYLED: Supports wide, styled lines.
	LC_INTERIORS: Supports interiors.
POLYGONALCAPS	Polygonal capabilities the device supports. It can be a combination of the following:
	PC_NONE: Supports no polygons.
	PC_POLYGON: Supports alternate fill polygons.
	PC_RECTANGLE: Supports rectangles.
	PC_WINDPOLYGON: Supports winding number fill polygons.
	PC_SCANLINE: Supports scan lines.
	PC_WIDE: Supports wide borders.
	PC_STYLED: Supports styled borders.
	PC_WIDESTYLED: Supports wide, styled borders.
	PC_INTERIORS: Supports interiors.
TEXTCAPS	Text capabilities the device supports. It can be a combination of the following:
	TC_OP_CHARACTER: Supports character-output precision, which indicates that the device can place device fonts at any pixel location. This is required for any device with device fonts.
	TC_OP_STROKE: Supports stroke-output precision, which indicates that the device can omit any stroke of a device font.
	TC_CP_STROKE: Supports stroke clip precision, which indicates that the device can clip device fonts to a pixel boundary.
	TC_CR_90: Supports 90-degree character rotation, which indicates that the device can rotate characters only 90 degrees at a time.
	TC_CR_ANY: Supports character rotation at any degree, which indicates that the device can rotate device fonts through any angle.
	TC_SF_X_YINDEP: Supports scaling independent of x and y directions, which indicates that the device can scale device fonts separately in x and y directions.
	TC_SA_DOUBLE: Supports doubled characters for scaling, which indicates that the device can double the size of device fonts.

nIndex Parameter	Returns
	TC_SA_INTEGER: Supports integer multiples for scaling, which indicates that the device can scale the size of device fonts in any integer multiple.
	TC_SA_CONTIN: Supports any multiples for exact scaling, which indicates that the device can scale device fonts by any amount but still preserve the x and y ratios.
	TC_EA_DOUBLE: Supports double-weight characters, which indicates that the device can make device fonts bold. If this bit is not set for printer drivers, GDI attempts to create bold device fonts by printing them twice.
	TC_IA_ABLE: Supports italics, which indicates that the device can make device fonts italic. If this bit is not set, GDI assumes that italics are not available.
	TC_UA_ABLE: Supports underlining, which indicates that the device can underline device fonts. If this bit is not set, GDI creates underlines for device fonts.
	TC_SO_ABLE: Supports strikeouts, which indicates that the device can strikeout device fonts. If this bit is not set, GDI creates strikeouts for device fonts.
	TC_RA_ABLE: Supports raster fonts, which indicates that GDI should enumerate any raster or TrueType fonts available for this device in response to a call to the EnumFonts or EnumFontFamilies Windows functions. If this bit is not set, GDI-supplied raster or TrueType fonts are not enumerated when these functions are called.
	TC_VA_ABLE: Supports vector fonts, which indicates that GDI should enumerate any vector fonts available for this device in response to a call to the EnumFonts or EnumFontFamilies Windows functions. This is significant for vector devices only (that is, for plotters). Display drivers (which must be able to use raster fonts) and raster printer drivers always enumerate vector fonts because GDI rasterizes vector fonts before sending them to the driver.
	TC_RESERVED: Reserved; must be 0.

Prototype

```
//Function Prototype
//int CDC::GetDeviceCaps( int nIndex);

int iPageWidth = pPrinterDC->GetDeviceCaps(HORZRES);
    //We want to know the width in device units for a page on
    //this printer
```

GetFontData   FUNCTION

Description   **CDC::GetFontData** retrieves information about the construction of a font from a font file. It does not require that the font presently be selected. The application must pass a parameter specifying the offset into the file at which the information it wants can be found and the length in bytes of the data that should be copied. It is used with TrueType and other scalable font files. **CDC::GetFontData** allows an application to retrieve font data so that it can be embedded in a document it is saving. Not all fonts can be embedded. **CDC::GetOutlineTextMetrics** populates the **OUTLINETEXTMETRICS** data structure that includes the field **otmfsType**. **otmfsType** has the following meanings: If bit 1 is set, embedding is not permitted; and if is cleared (that is, if it is set equal to 0) it is. If bit 2 is set, embedding is read-only.

   CDC::GetFontData returns -1 if it is called for a non-TrueType font. The names of the font data tables and other specifics of font file construction are available from Microsoft, in their TrueType font specification notes.

Prototype
```
//Function Prototype
//DWORD GetFontData( DWORD dwTable, DWORD dwOffset,
     //LPVOID lpData, DWORD cbData ) const;
     //Assume that we have a valid pointer to a DC
     //because most drawing is done from
     //the OnDraw member function of the view....
 pDC->GetFontData(   0,      //Use the first Font table
                             //in the font file
              0,             //start from the beginning
                             //of the table
              lpFontDataBuffer,  //Copy it here,
              cdDataSize );      //This many bytes
```

GetGlyphOutline   FUNCTION

Description   **CDC::GetGlyphOutline** returns the outline contour or bitmap for a character in a TrueType font. It can optionally return a bitmap of a character outline, which can be rotated using a 2-by-2 transformation matrix. Characters retrieved in native outline format are composed of a series of contours. The contour is preceded by a **TTPOLYGONHEADER** structure, followed by a series of **TTPOLYCURVE** structures. To retrieve the size of the buffer needed to hold the glyph outline, call the function with either the buffer size or pointer to the glyph buffer set to NULL.

The nFormat parameter can be either GGO_BITMAP, which instructs GetGlyphOutline to return a bitmap, or GGO_NATIVE, which returns curve data. If nFormat is 0, the **GLYPHMETRICS** structure is filled, but no data is returned.

Lpmat2 is the 2-by-2 transformation matrix.

Prototype

```
//Function Prototype
//DWORD GetGlyphOutline( UINT nChar, UINT nFormat,
    //LPGLYPHMETRICS lpgm, DWORD cbBuffer, LPVOID lpBuffer,
    //const MAT2 FAR* lpmat2 ) const;
    //Assume that we have a valid pointer to a DC
    //because most drawing is done from
    //the OnDraw member function of the view....
pDC->GetGlyphOutline( iCharConst, GGO_NATIVE,
        lpgmGlyphStruct, dwBufferSizeBytes,
        lpGlyphBuffer,  lpTransformMatrix );
    //Copy Glyph Outline info
```

GetKerningPairs   FUNCTION

Description **CDC::GetKerningPairs** retrieves the number of kerning pair structures specified by the function's argument for the currently selected font. The **KERNINGPAIR** structure contains the two characters that are to be *kerned*, or specially positioned in relation to one another (usually closer together) and the amount to move them. If an application is managing its own text justification, accounting for kerning makes the spacing more precise. The function returns the number of kerning pairs it retrieved. A 0 return indicates failure or that the font has no kerned characters. This function does not copy more than nPairs of data (thus overflowing the lpkrnpair buffer.)

If the lpkrnpair argument is in NULL, the function simply returns the number of kerning pairs in the font. You can get all kerning pairs by writing code such as this:

```
VERIFY(cdc.GetKerningPairs(cdc.GetKerningPairs(0, NULL), lpk) !=
    0);
```

Prototype

```
//Function Prototype
//int GetKerningPairs( int nPairs, LPKERNINGPAIR lpkrnpair ) const;
    //Assume that we have a valid pointer to a DC
    //because most drawing is done from
    //the OnDraw member function of the view....
```

```
pDC->GetKerningPairs(iNumberPairs, &ArrayKPStructs );
  //Copy the kerning pairs back to the
  //application's array of KERNINGPAIR structs
```

GetMapMode   FUNCTION

Description   **CDC::GetMapMode** gets the mapping mode for the current **CDC** object's attribute DC. A map mode is a set of transformation rules that specifies how the logical coordinate space will be set up for an application's drawing. It determines the units of the x and y axes, whether the axes use units of the same size, and the orientation of the axes.

For example, the default mapping mode, **MM_TEXT,** defines the x and y axes to have units of equal size, with x units increasing to the right and y axis increasing downward. This pretty much corresponds to the mental picture we all have of a piece of writing paper, and it works well for displaying text. It is a terrible way to orient axes if we want to draw a bar graph, however, because the bars generally grow upward. In the case of a bar graph, it is much more convenient for the y axis to increase going up. In the case of a map, we in the western hemisphere expect the x axis (longitude) to increase going left (west). A call to this function is almost always one of the steps required to set up a DC for non-text drawing so that you can retain information about the settings of a DC before you make changes using the **SetMapMode** function. After you are finished using a system DC, it is a good practice to reset it to its original values before releasing it.

Windows provides eight possible mapping modes, which provide for special orientations of axes and sizing of units. This function is used with other **CDC** member mapping functions, such as **SetMapMode, GetWindowOrg, GetViewportOrg, SetWindowOrg** and **SetViewportOrg**. *See **SetMapMode** for information about return values.*

Prototype
```
//Function Prototype
//int GetMapMode ( )const;
if ( DisplayDC.GetMapMode( ) == MM_ISOTROPIC )
  {
    //This mapping mode forces x and y axes
    //to have equally sized units....
  }
```

GetNearestColor   FUNCTION

Description GetNearestColor is very useful in making color-intensive applications work well across displays of varying color capabilities. It matches based on its **COLORREF** parameter and returns the nearest *solid* color the output device is capable of representing. A **COLORREF** is a 32-bit value that combines values for the red, green and blue components of a color.

Obviously, many devices have far less color capability than can be encoded in a 32-bit **COLORREF**. Device contexts for devices that have a small number of pure colors sometimes expand their color range by *dithering,* or placing small areas of pure colors next to each other in a pattern that simulates a new color. This process can be very effective in fooling the eye, but it is not taken into account by this function. **CDC::GetNearestColor** returns the closest color a device can display *without dithering.*

Prototype
```
//Function Prototype
//COLORREF GetNearestColor( COLORREF crColor ) const;
pDisplayDC->SetTextColor(
    pDisplayDC->GetNearestColor(STRANGELY_PURPLE));
        //Set the text color for the screen DC to match
        //our unusual shade as closely as possible
```

GetOutlineTextMetrics   FUNCTION

Description **CDC::GetOutlineTextMetrics** populates the **OUTLINETEXTMETRIC** structure with information about the metrics of TrueType fonts. It retrieves information that describes the characteristics of TrueType fonts and is called before attempting to save a document with an embedded font. The **OUTLINETEXTMETRIC** structure member **otmfsType** has the following meanings: If bit 1 is set, embedding is not permitted; and if it is set to 0, it is. If bit 2 is set, embedding is read-only, meaning that the font is copyrighted.

The last four members of the **OUTLINETEXTMETRIC** structure are pointers to strings of indefinite length. To allocate memory to hold these strings as well as the structure, make the first call to **CDC::GetOutlineTextMetrics** passing a NULL pointer in place of the address of the application's **OUTLINETEXTMETRIC** structure. This call causes the function to return the total amount of space needed to store the structure and the strings.

Prototype
```
//Function Prototype
//UINT GetOutlineTextMetrics( UINT cbData,
    //LPOUTLINETEXTMETRIC lpotm ) const;
    //Assume that we have a valid pointer to a DC
    //because most drawing is done from
    //the OnDraw member function of the view....
pDC->GetOutlineTextMetrics( iBufferSizeBytes, lpMetricStruct );
    //Copy the OUTLINETEXTMETRIC structure
    //to the application's buffer
```

GetOutputCharWidth   FUNCTION

Description **CDC::GetOutputCharWidth** returns the widths for a range of characters specified in the function arguments for the currently selected font in the **CDC** object's *output* DC, as opposed to **CDC::GetCharWidths**, which returns information about the current *attribute* DC. **CDC::GetOutputCharWidths** is supplied by the foundation classes for cases in which the **CDC** object's two public data members **m_hDC** and **m_hAttribDC** don't point to the same device context. This case seldom arises for applications, but it is part of the framework's implementation of Print Preview.

   This function is intended for use only with non-TrueType fonts.

Prototype
```
//Function Prototype
//BOOL GetOutputCharWidth( UINT nFirstChar, UINT nLastChar,
//LPINT lpBuffer ) const;
    //Assume that we have a valid pointer to a DC
    //because most drawing is done from
    //the OnDraw member function of the view....
pDC->GetOutputCharWidths( iFirstChar, iLastChar,
                lpiCharWidthArray  );
    //Copy character-spacing info for the current output DC
```

GetOutputTabbedTextExtent   FUNCTION

Description **CDC::GetOutputTabbedTextExtent** provides the application a means of determining the area covered by a text-drawing operation that was directed to the **CDC** object's *output* DC, as opposed to **CDC::GetTextExtent**, which reports on the *attribute* DC. If an application has set different values for its two public data members, **m_hDC** and **m_hAttribDC**, this distinction can be an important one. The framework uses this technique to implement Print Preview, but in the course of typical application programming, the two data members are set to identify the same DC.

This function does not consider the clipping region in calculating the extent of a string. It does not take kerning of characters into account, so its summing of widths of individual characters in a string may not reflect exactly the *x* extent of the string. Kerning is the portion of a typeface that projects beyond the body or shank of a character. That is, if you have two adjacent letters, such as *AW,* they can be kerned in such a way that the character cell of the *W* slightly overlaps that of the *A,* producing less space between the diagonal strokes. Another letter pair well-suited for kerning in some fonts is *fi* (lowercase). Kerning information for the current font can be obtained by calling **CDC::GetKerningPairs**. *See **GetTabbedTextExtent** for more information on how extents are calculated.*

Prototype

```
//Function Prototype
//CSize GetOutputTabbedTextExtent(LPCSTR lpszString, int nCount,
    //int nTabPositions, LPINT lpnTabPositions);

    //Assume that we have a valid pointer to a DC
    //because most drawing is done from
    //the OnDraw member function of the view....
CSize sizeTextRegion = pDC->GetOutputTabbedTextExtent(
    lpszTestString, iCount, 3, pnTabStops);
    //Report the dimensions of the rectangle
    //the text string will use on the current
    //output DC....
```

GetOutputTextExtent   FUNCTION

Description   **CDC::GetOutputTextExtent** provides the application a means of determining the area covered by a text-drawing operation that was directed to the **CDC** object's *output* DC, as opposed to **CDC::GetTextExtent,** which reports on the *attribute* DC. If an application has set different values for its two public data members, **m_hDC** and **m_hAttribDC,** this distinction can be an important one. The framework uses this technique to implement Print Preview, but in the course of typical application programming, the two data members are set to identify the same DC.

This function does not consider the clipping region in calculating the extent of a string. It does not take kerning of characters into account, so its summing of widths of individual characters in a string may not reflect exactly the *x* extent of the string. Kerning is the portion of a typeface that projects beyond the body or shank of a character. That is, if you have two adjacent letters, such as *AW,* they can be kerned in such a way that the character cell of the *W* slightly overlaps that of the *A,* producing less space between the diagonal strokes. Another letter pair that is well-suited for kerning in some fonts is *fi* (lowercase). Kerning information for the current font can be obtained by calling **CDC::GetKerningPairs.**

Prototype

```
//Function Prototype
//CSize GetOutputTextExtent( LPCSTR lpszString, int nCount );
    //Assume that we have a valid pointer to a DC
    //because most drawing is done from
    //the OnDraw member function of the view....
CSize sizeTextRegion =
    pDC->GetOutputTextExtent( lpszTestString, int iCount );
    //Report the dimensions of the rectangle
    //the text string will use on the current
    //output DC....
```

GetOutputTextMetrics   FUNCTION

Description **CDC::GetOutputTextMetrics** retrieves very detailed information about the currently selected font in a **CDC** object's *output* DC, as opposed to **CDC::GetTextMetrics,** which reports on the *attribute* DC. Character cell height, width, orientation and weight all show up here, along with more arcane things, such as metrics for "leading," and style characteristics, such as underline and italics.

CDC::GetOutputTextMetrics is supplied by the foundation classes for cases in which the **CDC** object's two public data members **m_hDC** and **m_hAttribDC** don't point to the same device context. This case seldom arises for applications, but it is part of the framework's implementation of Print Preview. Like **CDC::GetTextMetrics,** there are two common situations in which it is useful to call **CDC::GetOutputTextMetrics.** The first is when an application is doing multiline text output and needs the size information in the **TEXTMETRIC** structure to position new lines. The second is when it necessary to synthesize a font. The **CFont** class member functions that create fonts require most of the information reported in the **TEXTMETRIC** structure.

Applications that do their own text justification need the break character value (usually a space) for a given font to pass to **CDC::SetTextJustification,** which is also recorded in the **TEXTMETRIC** structure.

Prototype

```
//Function Prototype
//BOOL GetOutputTextMetrics( LPTEXTMETRIC lpMetrics);
    //Assume that we have a valid pointer to a DC
    //because most drawing is done from
    //the OnDraw member function of the view....
pDC->GetOutputTextMetrics( &tmTextMetrics );
    //Copy the current font's TEXTMETRIC structure
    //to the application's structure....
```

GetPixel   FUNCTION

Description   **CDC::GetPixel** reports the RGB color value of a pixel located at a point in the **CDC** object's logical coordinate space. **CDC::GetPixel** expects the point to be stated in logical coordinates and to be within the clipping area. Note that this function retrieves the color of only one pixel. Dithered colors extend the color range of low-end monitors by placing a pattern of differently colored pixels on the screen to simulate hues it could not otherwise represent. If the overall color of the screen area in which the point passed to **CDC::GetPixel** is located has been created by dithering, this function *does not* report the color value of the brush that painted the dithered color. In other words, if you painted an area with a brush whose color could not be represented by the device (say, RGB(11, 129, 254)), GetPixel would return the actual value of the dithered pixel and not the color value of the brush that painted that pixel (because that information is lost after the painting completes).

Prototype

```
//Function Prototype
//COLORREF GetPixel( int x, int y ) const;
//COLORREF GetPixel( POINT point ) const;
COLORREF crWhatColor = DisplayDC.GetPixel( ptColorPoint );
```

GetPolyFillMode   FUNCTION

Description   **CDC::GetPolyFillMode** retrieves the setting of the current polygon filling mode from the **CDC** object's current attribute device context. The two polygon filling modes, ALTERNATE and WINDING, identify algorithms Windows uses to fill polygonal shapes. ALTERNATE fills the area between odd and even polygon sides for each scan line. WINDING fills any region with a non-zero winding value. ALTERNATE is the default.

Prototype
```
//Function Prototype
//int GetPolyFillMode() const
if ( DisplayDC.GetPolyFillMode()== ALTERNATE )
  {
    //Do some drawing....
  }
```

GetROP2   FUNCTION

Description   **CDC::GetROP2** gets the raster operation code for the current **CDC** object's attribute DC. **ROP2** codes determine how the bits of the pen and the bits of the background will be combined in drawing. **ROP2** codes comprise all possible outcomes if the bits of the pen and the background are combined using a combination of AND, OR, XOR and NOT bitwise operations. Mnemonic constants are provided for the combinations. The constants are shown in this table:

Constant	Meaning
R2_BLACK	Pixel is always 0.
R2_WHITE	Pixel is always 1.
R2_NOP	Pixel remains unchanged.
R2_NOT	Pixel is the inverse of the screen color.
R2_COPYPEN	Pixel is the pen color.
R2_NOTCOPYPEN	Pixel is the inverse of the pen color.
R2_MERGEPENNOT	Pixel is a combination of the pen color and the inverse of the screen color.
R2_MASKPENNOT	Pixel is a combination of the colors common to both the pen and the inverse of the screen.
R2_MERGENOTPEN	Pixel is a combination of the screen color and the inverse of the pen color.
R2_MASKNOTPEN	Pixel is a combination of the colors common to both the screen and the inverse of the pen.
R2_MERGEPEN	Pixel is a combination of the pen color and the screen color.
R2_NOTMERGEPEN	Pixel is the inverse of the R2_MERGEPEN color.
R2_MASKPEN	Pixel is a combination of the colors common to both the pen and the screen.
R2_NOTMASKPEN	Pixel is the inverse of the R2_MASKPEN color.
R2_XORPEN	Pixel is a combination of the colors in the pen and in the screen, but not in both.
R2_NOTXORPEN	Pixel is the inverse of the R2_XORPEN color.

Prototype
```
//Function Prototype
//int GetROP2( )const;
if ( DisplayDC.GetROP2() == R2_XORPEN )
  {
    //Use the pen to XOR pixels in line-drawing operations....
  }
```

GetSafeHdc   FUNCTION

Description   **GetSafeHdc** is a **CDC** information function that returns the value of **m_hDC**, the handle of the default output device context. It provides a link with the C language API by allowing applications to call API routines that require a handle to a DC, but refer to the handles as framework public data members.

Prototype
```
//Function Prototype
//HDC GetSafeHdc( ) const;

::PlayEnhMetaFile( pCDC->GetSafeHdc( ), hEnhancedMetafile,
&rMetafileRect );
        //This 32-bit enhanced metafile function is
        //not yet available
        //in MFC, but you can use it
        //by passing the handle to the device
        //context using GetSafeHdc
```

GetStretchBltMode   FUNCTION

Description   **CDC::GetStretchBltMode** gets the bitmap stretching mode for the current **CDC** object's attribute DC. Bitmap stretching takes place when GDI fits a bitmap into available display real estate by resizing it. Windows can do this in three ways if the bitmap is being downsized: It can do a bitwise AND on adjacent rows or a bitwise OR on adjacent rows, or drop rows out altogether. The first two methods work best for black-and-white bitmaps because they tend to preserve detail, but the third method is preferred for color bitmaps because combining adjacent rows of color pixels can produce a garish effect. The function's argument may be any of the following constants:

```
STRETCH_ANDSCANS
STRETCH_DELETESCANS
STRETCH_ORSCANS
```

Prototype

```
//Function Prototype
//int GetStretchBltMode();
if( DisplayDC.GetStretchBltMode() == STRETCH_ANDSCANS )
  {
    //Scan lines are being ANDed, which is appropriate for
    //monochrome bitmaps....
  }
```

GetTabbedTextExtent   FUNCTION

Description **CDC::GetTabbedTextExtent** retrieves the width and height of the string specified by its parameter, using the currently selected font and logical coordinates of **CDC** object's attribute DC. This function provides the application a means of determining the area covered by a text-drawing operation. This capability is very useful in adding to the end of a line or determining the starting y position for a new line of text.

    CDC::GetTabbedTextExtent does not consider the clipping region in calculating the extent of a string. It does not take kerning of characters into account, so its summing of widths of individual characters in a string may not reflect exactly the x extent of the string. Kerning is the portion of a typeface that projects beyond the body or shank of a character. That is, if you have two adjacent letters, such as *AW,* they can be kerned in such a way that the character cell of the *W* slightly overlaps that of the *A,* producing less space between the diagonal strokes. Another letter pair well-suited for kerning in some fonts is *fi* (lowercase). Kerning information for the current font can be obtained by calling **CDC::GetKerningPairs**.

    If you supply an argument of 0 for nTabPositions and NULL for lpTabStopPositions, tabs are expanded to eight spaces, computed by taking the average character width for the current font and multiplying by eight.

    If nTabPositions is 1, lpTabStopPositions is taken to be a pointer to an int that specifies the distance between a set of regular tab stops.

    Use nTabOrigin if your application needs to make multiple calls to TabbedTextOut for a given line. This is the location from which tabs are expanded.

Prototype
```
//Function Prototype
//CSize GetTabbedTextExtent( LPCSTR lpszString, int nCount,
    //int nTabPositions, LPINT lpnTabPositions);
    //Assume that we have a valid pointer to a DC
    //because most drawing is done from
    //the OnDraw member function of the view....
CSize sizeTextRegion =
    pDC->GetTabbedTextExtent( lpszTestString, int iCount, 3,
    pnTabStops );
    //Report the dimensions of the rectangle
    //the text string will use....
```

GetTextAlign   FUNCTION

Description   **CDC::GetTextAlign** retrieves the text-alignment settings for the current **CDC** object's *attribute* DC. Text alignment determines how a text string is positioned in relation to the point passed to text output functions such as **CDC::TextOut**.

Three basic groups of flags have to do with text positioning. The ones that control horizontal placement within a bounding rectangle are **TA_LEFT**, **TA_CENTER** and **TA_RIGHT**. Vertical placement within a bounding rectangle is controlled by **TA_TOP**, **TA_BOTTOM** and **TA_BASELINE**. **TA_BASELINE** aligns the baseline of the font to the bottom of the bounding rectangle. (An *o* sits on the baseline, but a *y* descends below it.) Whether or not text output functions use the DC's current position when performing output operations is flagged by **TA_UPDATECP** or **TA_NOUPDATECP**, respectively.

Prototype
```
//Function Prototype
//UINT GetTextAlign( ) const;
    //Assume that we have a valid pointer to a DC
    //because most drawing is done from
    //the OnDraw member function of the view....
if( pDC->GetTextAlign( ) == TA_LEFT )
  {
    //If leading character cell is aligned
    //with the y value passed to TextOut, do
    //something....
  }
```

347

GetTextCharacterExtra   FUNCTION

Description   **CDC::GetTextCharacterExtra** retrieves the value set by the application for additional intercharacter white space for the current **CDC** object's attribute DC. The application can specify an amount of white space that should be inserted between characters as text is written out. This capability can be useful in making small fonts more legible on blueprint drawings or maps. It can also be of use if text is being output one character at a time, to conform to an unusual shape, such as a stream or winding road. The extra white space value must be stated in logical units.

Prototype
```
//Function Prototype
//int GetTextCharacterExtra( )const;
    //Assume that we have a valid pointer to a DC
    //because most drawing is done from
    //the OnDraw member function of the view....
int iInterCharSpacing = pDC->GetTextCharExtra();
    //Get intercharacter spacing....
```

GetTextColor   FUNCTION

Description   **CDC::GetTextColor** gets the default text color for the current **CDC** object's attribute DC. **CDC::SetBkColor** and **CDC::SetBkMode** can also influence the appearance of text drawn in the client area. The background mode determines whether the text background is erased before the text is drawn, and the background color is used to fill in the undrawn pixels of the character cell.

Prototype
```
//Function Prototype
//COLORREF GetTextColor( )const;
crTextColor = DisplayDC.GetTextColor( );
        //Report the color currently used to draw text....
```

GetTextExtent   FUNCTION

Description   **CDC::GetTextExtent** retrieves the width and height of the string specified by its parameter, using the currently selected font and logical coordinates. This function provides the application a means of determining the area covered by a text-drawing operation. This is very useful in adding to the end of a line or determining the starting y position for a new line of text.

This function does not consider the clipping region in calculating the extent of a string. It does not take kerning of characters into account, so its summing of widths of individual characters in a string may not reflect exactly the *x* extent of the string. Kerning is the portion of a typeface that projects beyond the body or shank of a character. That is, if you have two adjacent letters, such as *AW*, they can be kerned in such a way that the character cell of the *W* slightly overlaps that of the *A*, producing less space between the diagonal strokes. Another letter pair well-suited for kerning in some fonts is *fi* (lowercase). Kerning information for the current font can be obtained by calling **CDC::GetKerningPairs**.

Prototype

```
//Function Prototype
//CSize GetTextExtent( LPCSTR lpszString, int nCount);
    //Assume that we have a valid pointer to a DC
    //because most drawing is done from
    //the OnDraw member function of the view....
CSize sizeTextRegion =
    pDC->GetTextExtent( lpszTestString, iCount );
    //Report the dimensions of the rectangle the text
    //string will use....
```

GetTextFace   FUNCTION

Description   **CDC::GetTextFace** retrieves the name of the currently selected typeface for the **CDC** object's output DC and copies it into a buffer specified by a parameter to the function. In working between the screen and the printer, one of the most significant compromises an application encounters is the difference in the availability of fonts. This is one of a family of functions that provide information on typography that is helpful in font matching for the printer and in font synthesis for the display. If the typeface name is too long for the buffer, it is truncated.

Prototype

```
//Function Prototype
//int GetTextFace( int nCount, LPSTR lpszFacename);
    //Assume that we have a valid pointer to a DC
    //because most drawing is done from
    //the OnDraw member function of the view....
pDC->GetTextFace( iBufferSize, lpszTypeface);
    //Copy the typeface name to the buffer
    //identified by lpszTypeface....
```

GetTextMetrics   FUNCTION

Description   **CDC::GetTextMetrics** retrieves very detailed information about the way in which the currently selected font in a **CDC** object's *attribute* DC is constructed. Character cell height, width, orientation and weight all show up here, along with more arcane things, such as metrics for "leading," and style characteristics, such as underline and italics.

There are two commonly encountered situations in which it is useful to call **CDC::GetTextMetrics**. The first is when an application is doing multiline text output and needs the size information in the **TEXTMETRIC** structure to position new lines. The second is when it necessary to synthesize a font. The **CFont** class member functions that create fonts require most of the information reported in the **TEXTMETRIC** structure. Of course, you can also do a simple **GetObject** and synthesize a font from there.

Applications that do their own text justification need the break character value (usually a space) for a given font to pass to **CDC::SetTextJustification**, which is also recorded in the **TEXTMETRIC** structure.

Prototype

```
//Function Prototype
//BOOL GetTextMetrics( LPTEXTMETRIC lpMetrics);
    //Assume that we have a valid pointer to a DC
    //because most drawing is done from
    //the OnDraw member function of the view....
pDC->GetTextMetrics( &tmTextMetrics );
    //Copy the current font's TEXTMETRIC structure
    //to the application's structure....
```

GetViewportExt   FUNCTION

Description   **CDC::GetViewportExt** gets the viewport extents, which are *x* and *y* measurements of the bounding rectangle in which an image can be drawn on the presentation surface. The extents of a viewport determine how much presentation real estate is devoted to drawing an image and also play a role in how the *x* and *y* axes are oriented when image coordinates are mapped from the application's logical coordinate space window to the display surface.

Information about the extents is useful for fitting images to available display space. The signs of the viewport extents are compared with the signs of the window bounding the logical coordinate space when establishing the direction in which *x* and *y* coordinates increase on the axes that govern drawing. For this reason, **CDC::GetViewportOrg** can also help an application determine whether the image is properly oriented when it is displayed.

Prototype

```
//Function Prototype
//virtual CSize GetViewportExt( )const;
CSize sizeViewport = pDC->GetViewportExt( );
      //Get the absolute dimensions and
      //the signs of the viewport extents
```

GetViewportOrg   FUNCTION

Description   **CDC::GetViewportOrg** retrieves the origin of the viewport for the current **CDC** object. The viewport is the rectangular region of the display surface that will be used for graphic output. The viewport is measured in device coordinates (pixels). To translate an image from the application's logical coordinate system to the presentation surface, the Windows mapping algorithm considers the origin and x-y extents of both the viewport and the bounding window on the logical coordinate space.

Several factors influence which part of an image is displayed on a presentation surface and what its orientation will be. The viewport origin and x-y extents constrain the area on the screen or printed surface in which the image can be drawn. The bounding window of the logical coordinate space constrain the actual drawing of an image. For example, if the window origin is at 0,0 and has extents of 100 units in each direction, a rectangle whose upper left corner is at 150,150 wouldn't appear inside the application's logical window.

The orientation of an image is governed by the sense of the axes in both the logical and viewport coordinate systems. The sense of the axes is established by the relationship of the *signs* on the *x* and *y* extents of both the logical coordinate space window and the viewport. If the signs differ, the orientation of the viewport axis is reversed.

For example, in the default mapping mode MM_TEXT, the viewport's *y* axis increases going downward. If the *y* extent of the logical coordinate system window is specified as -*100,* the viewport's *y* axis increases going upward, which is convenient for drawing graphs and charts. See SctMapMode for more infomation about Windows coordinate systems and their settings.

```
//Function Prototype
//CPoint GetViewportOrg( )const;
CPoint ptViewportx0y0 = pDC->GetViewportOrg( );
    //Retrieve the physical device coordinate
    //for the 0,0 point of the application's client area
```

GetWindowExt   FUNCTION

Description   **CDC::GetWindowExt** gets the extents of the window on the logical coordinate space. The window forms the bounding rectangle of the logical coordinate space in which the application does its drawing. The units in which the window's dimensions are returned is dependent on the current mapping mode. The window on the application's coordinate system can be no more than 32k on a side, and the units must be integers, but they may be negative.

The origin and extents of the window on the application's logical coordinate space are the most important factors in how output graphics look to a user. The size of the extents should match closely the range of coordinates of an application's image uses. If, for example, an application sets the extents to their maximum possible value with an origin at 0,0 and then draws an object whose x and y coordinate maximums are 100, the rendered image will probably occupy only a couple of pixels on the viewport. See **DPtoLP** and **LPtoDP** for information on how to convert points between logical and device coordinates.

Prototype
```
//Function Prototype
//CSize GetWindowExt( )const;
CSize sizeWindow = pDC->GetWindowExt( );
        //Get the absolute dimensions and the
        //signs of the window extents
```

GetWindowOrg   FUNCTION

Description   **CDC::GetWindowOrg** gets the logical coordinate system window origin for the current **CDC** object's attribute DC. The point set as the logical window origin is aligned with the viewport origin when images are translated between the two coordinate systems. The logical coordinate system is the one defined by the application, and the viewport coordinate system covers the area of the display device in which an application can present its graphic output. The window origin may be defined anywhere within the logical coordinate system, but the overall dimensions of the system may not exceed 32k units in either the x or y direction.

This function is used with other **CDC** member mapping functions, such as **SetMapMode**, **GetWindowOrg**, **GetViewportOrg**, **SetWindowOrg** and **SetViewportOrg**. *See **SetMapMode** for more infomation about Windows coordinate systems and their settings.*

Prototype

```
//Function Prototype
//CPoint GetWindowOrg( )const;
CPoint ptLogicalCoordOrigin = pDC->GetWindowOrg( );
```

GrayString   FUNCTION

Description

In its simplest form, **CDC::GrayString** works in exactly the same fashion as the **CDC** member function **TextOut**, except that the string of text is drawn using a gray brush, signifying to the user that a feature is temporarily disabled. **CDC::GrayString** can do something that **CDC::TextOut** can't, however: It can handle strings that are represented as bitmaps. It does this by using a procedure instance address supplied by the caller, which handles output.

If the procedure instance address is set to 0, **CDC::GrayString** reverts to the behavior of **CDC::TextOut**. It optionally calculates the length of the string to be output, draws it in a memory bitmap, grays the bitmap by combining it with a brush specified by a function parameter, and then transfers the bitmap to the screen at the location given in the coordinate parameters. **CDC::GrayString** is somewhat cumbersome if the text that needs to be grayed is in string format. It is easier to use **CDC::SetTextColor** to create a gray font. If the text is already a bitmap, this function is the way to go. The procedure instance address of a callback function must be acquired by calling the SDK function **MakeProcInstance** for a function that has been exported in the module-definition file.

The callback must be prototyped in the following way:

```
BOOL CALLBACK EXPORT GrayStringCallback( HDC hDC,
                                         LPARAM lpData,
                                         int nCount);
```

This function is responsible for drawing the string and has to return TRUE if it completes its operations successfully. After the **CDC::GrayString** call returns, the procedure instance must be freed using the SDK function **FreeProcInstance**.

Does this sound like a lot of trouble, or what? There are a lot of ways you can go wrong here, starting with an extremely long and complex parameter list, a callback function that descends to the SDK, and the onus of making and freeing a procedure instance. If the text is a string, most devices will have a stock color that can be used with **CDC::SetTextColor**. If it is a bitmap, a call to **CDC::PatBlt** is a much more direct method of changing the shade.

Prototype

```
//Function Prototype
//virtual BOOL GrayString( CBrush* pBrush, BOOL ( CALLBACK
EXPORT* lpfnOutput )( HDC, LPARAM, int ), LPARAM lpData, int
nCount, int x, int y, int nWidth, int nHeight );
```

IntersectClipRgn   FUNCTION

Description **CDC::IntersectClipRgn** creates a new clipping region that is the *intersection*, or shared area, of the rectangle passed as its parameter and the existing clipping area. All the **CDC** member functions that deal with clipping share two principal uses. Either they exclude areas that need not be repainted, saving the application time and improving performance, or they protect some feature from being overdrawn. The intersect rectangle is specified in logical coordinates. It is seldom necessary for an application to manage its own clip region because this process is handled by Windows.

Prototype

```
//Function Prototype
//virtual int IntersectClipRect( int x1, int y1,
        //int x2, int y2 );
//virtual int IntersectClipRect( LPRECT lpRect );
pDC->IntersectClipRect( lprSmallRect );
    //Make a smaller clipping area,
    //by taking the intersection of the current
    //clipping area and the rectangle we pass....
```

InvertRect   FUNCTION

Description **CDC::InvertRect** inverts the color painted on a rectangle pixel by pixel, using a bitwise NOT. This has an obvious meaning for monochrome bitmaps and is used frequently by Windows for such things as depressing push-buttons. Black pixels become white and vice versa. It is much harder to figure out what "inverting" means if you are talking about a color, and it can be positively garish if colors were simulated by dithering. Unless you know for certain the color capabilities of the display that hosts your application, it is probably better to stay away from this function for rectangles that aren't strictly monochrome. However, an inverted pure colored area is clearly inverted in an unsurprising way. For a paint program, this is often exactly the behavior you want.

Prototype

```
//Function Prototype
//BOOL InvertRect( LPRECT lpRect );
pDC->InvertRect( lprRectToInvert );
    //Change the color of the rectangle,
    //pixel by pixel, using a bitwise NOT....
```

InvertRgn   FUNCTION

Description **CDC::InvertRgn** inverts the colors of a region. A *region* is an elliptical or polygonal area within an application's client area. Creation and manipulation of regions is encapsulated in the class **CRgn**, which is derived from the GDI parent class.

This function inverts, pixel by pixel, the color painted on a region. This has an obvious meaning for black-and-white regions and is used frequently by Windows for such things as setting and unsetting radio buttons. Black pixels become white and vice versa. It is much harder to figure out what "inverting" means if you are talking about a color, and it can be positively garish if colors were simulated by dithering. Unless you know for certain the color capabilities of the display that hosts your application, it is probably better to stay away from this function if regions aren't monochrome. In preference to this function, when you deal with color regions, it can be more beneficial to repaint the region for simple operations such as toggling a radio button on and off. For operations in which a true inversion is required, and particularly one that involves overlapping shapes or regions, different strategies, such as repainting the entire area, should be explored.

Prototype

```
//Function Prototype
//BOOL InvertRgn( CRgn* pRgn );
DisplayDC.InvertRgn( pMonochromeRegion );
    //Make all black pixels white and vice versa....
```

IsPrinting   FUNCTION

Description **CDC::IsPrinting**, not surprisingly, is a status-reporting function that tells whether the current **CDC** is in the process of printing itself. This function is most commonly used in the user override of **CView::OnDraw**, where a single drawing function can be used both for screen and printer output, with only minor variations. By using the **IsPrinting** function, these variations can be incorporated into the single implementation of the drawing code.

Prototype

```
//Function Prototype
//BOOL IsPrinting( );
if (pPrinterDC->IsPrinting())
   {
       //We do something if the printer DC is currently printing....
   }
```

LineTo   FUNCTION

Description   CDC::**LineTo** draws a line with the currently selected pen in the **CDC** object's output DC. The line segment begins at the DC's current pen position and ends at the point specified by the argument to **CDC::LineTo**. This function expects its arguments to be expressed in logical coordinates.

Prototype

```
//Function Prototype
//BOOL LineTo( int x, int, y );
//BOOL LineTo( POINT point );
pDC->LineTo( ptEndPoint );
   //Draw a line using the current pen
   //from the current pen position to
   //ptEndPoint....
```

LPtoDP   FUNCTION

Description   A part of the way in which Windows provides device independence for graphics is by intermediating drawing by using two coordinate systems. The first is the *device* coordinate system, and the second is the *logical* coordinate system. **CDC::LPtoDP** is used by an application to translate an array of points between device coordinates and logical coordinates.

   Device coordinates are the physical divisions of a particular presentation surface: For a screen, device coordinates are reported in pixels, and for a printer they are dots. Most of the time, Windows applications are concerned with the other coordinate system, called the *logical coordinate system.* The size, orientation and location of the logical coordinate system are exclusively under the control of the application, and all application drawing operations are directed there. Sometimes, however, it is necessary to work back and forth between coordinate systems. For example, if an application draws in a small portion of its client area, it can use the dimensions of a bounding rectangle to confine the next repaint to include only the newly drawn region. This is done by adding the freshly drawn area to the DC's invalid region using the function **InvalidateRect**. **InvalidateRect** requires that the invalid rectangle be given in device coordinates. **LPtoDP** is used to make the conversion.

Device coordinates originate in the upper left corner of the screen in Windows 3.*x*. Moving or resizing an application's window can make device coordinates stale. If an application needs to preserve coordinate information, it is best to save it in logical coordinates.

Prototype

```
//Function Prototype
//Translate an array of default size 1
//void LPtoDP( LPPOINT lpPoints, int nCount =1 )const;
//Translate two points using a rectangle structure
//void LPtoDP( LPRECT lpRect )const;
//Translate a SIZE structure
//void LPtoDP( LPSIZE lpSize ) const;
pDC->LPtoDP( lpClientAreaRect );
    //Suppose that we want to know exactly
    //which part of the screen real
    //estate our window's client area is using....
```

MoveTo

Description

CDC::MoveTo changes the current pen position of the **CDC** object's output DC, without drawing. It returns the previous pen position. **CDC::MoveTo** is used to pick up the pen when doing line drawing. For example, if the application were drawing a dashed line, each of the segments would require a call to **CDC::MoveTo** as well as a call to **CDC::LineTo**. The **MoveTo** produces a gap, and the **LineTo** produces a dash. This function expects its arguments to be expressed in logical coordinates. The position is changed without drawing *anything*.

Prototype

```
//Function Prototype
//CPoint MoveTo( int xx, int, y );
//CPoint MoveTo( POINT point );
pDC->MoveTo( ptEndDash.cx + 5, ptEndDash.cy );
    //Move five logical units past the
    //end of the last dash we drew
    //in this dashed line....
```

OffsetClipRgn FUNCTION

Description   **CDC::OffsetClipRgn** creates a new clipping region by displacing the existing clipping region a specified distance vertically and horizontally. All the **CDC** member functions that deal with clipping share two principal uses. Either they exclude areas that need not be repainted, which saves the application time and improves its performance, or they protect some feature from overdrawing. The offset distance is specified in logical coordinates. It is seldom necessary for an application to manage its own clip region because this process is handled by the framework.

Prototype
```
//Function Prototype
//virtual int OffsetClipRgn( int x, int y );
//virtual int OffsetClipRgn( SIZE size );
DisplayDC.OffsetClipRgn( 100,100 );
        //Offset the clipping region by
        //100 logical units in each direction....
```

OffsetViewportOrg FUNCTION

Description   **CDC::OffsetViewportOrg** moves the origin of the current CDC object's viewport by the number of units in the x and y directions specified by its arguments. The viewport is the rectangular area on the display surface that forms a constraining boundary for graphic output in the application's client area. The argument values are added to the current viewport origin's x and y coordinates and may be either negative or positive.

   CDC::OffsetViewportOrg is a fast way to slide the viewport to a new location on the screen or printed page. This capability can be helpful in composing a page or freeing screen real estate without much redrawing logic. The function returns the coordinates of the previous origin so that the application can easily slide the viewport back to its original position. *See **SetMapMode** for more information about Windows coordinate systems and their settings.*

Prototype
```
//Function Prototype
//CPoint OffsetViewportOrg( int nWidth, int nHeight );
pDC->OffsetViewportOrg( rClientArea.left / 2,
            rClientArea.top / 2 );
        //We just slid the viewport right and down
        //by half the size
        //of the client area
```

OffsetWindowOrg — FUNCTION

Description **CDC::OffsetWindowOrg** moves the origin of the window on the current CDC object's logical coordinate space. The window origin is offset by the number of units in the *x* and *y* directions specified by its arguments. The window is the bounding rectangle of the logical coordinate space in which the application does its logical drawing. The argument values are added to the current window origin's *x* and *y* coordinates and may be either negative or positive.

CDC::OffsetWindowOrg is a fast way to slide the window to a new location in the application's coordinate space. This capability can be helpful in quickly clipping away a part of an image without much redrawing logic. The function returns the coordinates of the previous origin so that the application can easily slide the window back to its original position. Shifting the origin of the coordinate space window incorrectly can cause some or all of the application's image to disappear from the viewport. It does not affect the extents of the window on the logical coordinate system, which is to say that it doesn't change its dimensions.

This function is used with other **CDC** member mapping functions, such as **SetMapMode**, **GetWindowOrg**, **GetViewportOrg**, **SetWindowOrg** and **SetViewportOrg**. *See **SetMapMode** for more information about Windows coordinate systems and their settings. See **DPtoLP** and **LPtoDP** for information on how to convert points between logical and device coordinates.*

Prototype
```
//Function Prototype
//CPoint OffsetWindowOrg( int nWidth, int nHeight );
OffsetWindowOrg( -100, 50 );
    //Slide the windows 100 units in the negative direction of the
    //x axis and 50 units in the positive direction of the y axis
```

PaintRgn — FUNCTION

Description **CDC::PaintRgn** paints a region with the currently selected brush of the **CDC** object's output DC. The region must exist before this function is called.

Prototype
```
//Function Prototype
//BOOL PaintRgn( CRgn* pRgn )
pDC->PaintRgn( pRegionToPaint );
    //The region is filled with the currently selected brush....
```

PatBlt | FUNCTION

Description   **CDC::PatBlt** fills a rectangular region with a pattern by doing a bitwise combination of the **CDC** object's currently selected brush and the bits already on the screen at its target location. The way in which the two are to be combined is specified to the function by a raster operation code that defines the bitwise operations that will be used. **PatBlt** can use a limited subset of the 256 raster operation codes that control the result of the combination, referred to as *ternary* **ROP** codes because they take into account a source bitmap, the current brush, and a destination bitmap. In the case of **CDC::PatBlt**, there is no source bitmap. After all that, here are the ROP codes that apply to this operation:

ROP Code	Results
PATCOPY	Copies pattern to destination bitmap.
PATINVERT	Combines destination bitmap with pattern using the Boolean XOR operator.
DSTINVERT	Inverts the destination bitmap.
BLACKNESS	Turns all output black.
WHITENESS	Turns all output white.
PATPAINT	Paints the destination bitmap.

Note: Use **CBrush::UnrealizeObject** before selecting the brush into the DC. This technique resets the brush's origin in case it was reset elsewhere.

The bitmap functions are very useful in animation because the many ways in which they can be transferred to the screen make it easy to manicure images as they move. Not all output devices support bitmapped block transfers, so it is advisable to use **CDC::GetDeviceCaps** with the RC_BITBLT argument to check a device's capability before using any of the bitmap functions. Also, ordinary bitmap files are very highly device dependent. In terms of proportion, resolution and color, bitmaps may vary considerably between output devices. If it is necessary to transfer bitmaps among devices, it is a good idea to use the Windows device-independent bitmap format.

Prototype
```
//Function Prototype
//BOOL PatBlt( int x, int y, int nWidth, int nHeight,
//DWORD dwRop );
pDC->PatBlt( iULX, iULY, iWidth, iHeight, dwROPCode );
    //Paint a rectangle identified by the first four arguments, using
    //the current brush.
    //The brush and the destination pixels are combined using the
    //raster operation specified in dwROPCode....
```

Pie   FUNCTION

Description   **CDC::Pie** draws a pie-shaped wedge with the **CDC** object's currently selected pen and fills it with the currently selected brush. The center of the ellipse from which the pie slice is taken is the center of the bounding rectangle specified in the function's arguments.

CDC::Pie, rather than **CDC::Chord**, is the obvious tool if you are drawing a pie diagram. By selecting different brushes, the slices can easily be drawn and filled with contrasting colors. All arguments are expressed in logical coordinates, and the current pen position is not used in drawing the wedge.

Prototype
```
//Function Prototype
//BOOL Pie( int x1, int y1, int x2, int y2,
    //int x3 ,int y3, int x4, int y4);
//BOOL Pie( LPRECT lpRect, POINT ptStart, POINT ptEnd);
DisplayDC.Pie( lprBoundingRect, ptStartPoint, ptEndPoint);
    //Draw and fill one pie wedge....
```

PlayMetafile   FUNCTION

Description   **CDC::PlayMetafile** plays a metafile specified by its parameter into the **CDC** object's output DC. Metafiles are a compact way to transfer graphics between applications. They can encapsulate complex lists of drawing instructions, which are accessible simply by replaying the metafile.

Metafiles can and do reset output DC parameters, such as mapping mode and windows extents. They can also replace existing GDI objects with fonts, brushes and pens of their own. To keep a metafile from playing havoc with an application's DC settings, save them before playing the metafile by calling **CDC::SaveDC**, and restore the original settings by calling **CDC::RestoreDC** after the metafile finishes.

Prototype
```
//Function Prototype
// BOOL PlayMetaFile( HMETAFILE hMF);
pDC->SaveDC( );
    //Preserve our GDI settings before playing metafile....
pDC->PlayMetaFile( hMetafileHandle );;
    // Plays metafile....
pDC->RestoreDC(-1);
    //Retrieve our GDI settings.
```

Polygon   FUNCTION

Description   **CDC::Polygon** draws a group of connected line segments, based on the array of points specified by its arguments. The line drawing begins at the first point listed in the array, and the last line segment ends on the last point. If the line segments do not create a closed figure, this function closes it automatically with a straight line between the first and last points in the array of points specified by the argument. The closed figure is filled with the **CDC** object's current brush. It does not change the current position of the pen in the **CDC** object's DC.

   CDC::Polygon is a quick way to draw a filled, closed figure of irregular shape. Even though the points are connected by straight line segments, if the points are closely spaced, it can draw smoothly curvilinear shapes. This function expects its arguments to be expressed in logical coordinates. If the application needs to know where drawing ended, it must preserve the *first point* in the array passed to **CDC::Polygon**. Take special note of this because it's easy to make the mistake of saving the last point, thinking that it's the end. Because the endpoint is not reflected in the current position of the output DC, it can't be retrieved with **CDC::GetCurrentPosition**.

Prototype
```
//Function Prototype
//BOOL Polygon( LPPOINTS lpPoints, int nCount );
pDC->Polygon( LPPOINTS lptPointArray, int iPointCount );
    //Draw and fill an irregular shape,
    //using the point array for vertices....
```

Polyline   FUNCTION

Description   **CDC::Polyline** draws a group of connected line segments, based on the array of points specified by its arguments. The line drawing begins at the first point listed in the array, and the last line segment ends on the last point. It does not change the current position of the pen in the **CDC** object's DC.

   This function expects its arguments to be expressed in logical coordinates. If the application needs to know where drawing ended, it must preserve the last point in the array passed to **CDC::Polyline**. Because the endpoint is not reflected in the current position of the output DC, it can't be retrieved with **CDC::GetCurrentPosition**.

Prototype
```
//Function Prototype
//BOOL Polyline( LPPOINTS lpPoints, int nCount );
pDC->Polyline( lptPointArray, iPointCount );
    //Draw a line using the points in
    //the array as vertices....
```

PolyPolygon   FUNCTION

Description **CDC::PolyPolygon** draws a series of polygons, based on the array of points specified by its first argument. The second argument, an integer array, tells the function how many vertices belong to each polygon, and the last argument is a count of the number of polygons. The polygons are drawn with the **CDC** object's currently selected pen and filled with the current brush.

CDC::PolyPolygon is a quick way to draw several closed figures of irregular shape. Even though the points are connected by straight line segments, if the points are closely spaced, it can draw smoothly curvilinear shapes. This function expects its arguments to be expressed in logical coordinates. If the application needs to know where drawing ended, it must preserve the first point in the array representing the last polygon passed to **CDC::PolyPolygon**. Because the endpoint is not reflected in the current position of the output DC, it can't be retrieved with **CDC::GetCurrentPosition**.

CDC::PolyPolygon does not automatically close the polygons it draws, so the list of vertices must describe a closed figure for each polygon. That is, the first and last vertex must be equal. Note that this is not a way to specify a single shape and have it propagated *n* times; rather, it is a way to specify *n* shapes in a single collection of points and then have them all drawn in one Windows API call.

Prototype
```
//Function Prototype
//BOOL PolyPolygon(LPPOINTS lpPoints, LPINT lpPolyCounts,
//int nCount );
pDC->PolyPolygon(lptPointArray, lpVertexCount, iPolyCount );
    //Draw a series of closed, filled polygons....
```

PtVisible   FUNCTION

Description **CDC::PtVisible** checks to see whether a point is within an application's visible region, or clipping area. **CDC::PtVisible** can be used by an application to see whether the result of a drawing operation will be located where output graphics are allowed to be drawn. The point is specified in logical coordinates.

<table>
<tr><td>Prototype</td><td>

```
//Function Prototype
//virtual BOOL PtVisible( int x, int y )const;
//virtual BOOL PtVisible( POINT point )const;
if( DisplayDC.PtVisible( ptTestPoint ) )
  {
     //Do some drawing if our starting point is visible....
  }
```

</td></tr>
</table>

QueryAbort (Windows 3.1 only)   FUNCTION

Description   **CDC::QueryAbort** calls a printer abort function that was previously set using **CDC::SetAbortProc**. The abort procedure allows an application user to interrupt a lengthy printing process in an orderly fashion.

It has long been a subject of concern that printing under Windows can be rather sluggish. The original architects of the system realized that this was a serious complaint for end users and provided this function as a way for an application to set up a printing process that could be terminated without catastrophe.

To take advantage of this, an application typically presents a dialog box that allows a user to cancel printing by depressing a push-button. The cancel notification routes to an abort procedure that has been exported to Windows as a callback function. This function is not necessary under Windows NT.

Prototype

```
//Function Prototype
//BOOL QueryAbort( )const;
//After printing a page (or some amount of material)
if ( PrinterDC.QueryAbort( ) )
  {
     //The user has requested termination of printing
  }
```

RealizePalette   FUNCTION

Description   An application that uses color in a precise way or needs a large range of colors can insulate itself to some degree from the variability in device color capability and the effects of other applications that make color demands on the system by constructing a list of the colors it wants to use. The colors are identified by their red, green and blue constituents, combined in a 32-bit COLORREF. Windows itself has a need for a few specific colors, and these are mapped more or less immovably onto the system palette. After that, space in the system palette is doled out to applications until the limits of the device are reached. At this point, an elaborate scheme of compromise color matching is carried out by Windows, mediating (as best it can) competing requests for color, based on the requirements an application described in its palette.

CDC::RealizePalette is the interface at which the application presents its requests, Windows attempts to satisfy them, and the success of the process is reported in the function's return value. Windows may not be able to exactly satisfy requests for color display, and it may not be able to satisfy them to the same degree every time an application gets the input focus because the color usage of applications in other windows can cause variability in color matching. **CDC::RealizePalette** returns the number of colors that were remapped to system palette entries since the last time the application realized its palette. This return value can help the application decide whether its current palette is adequate.

Prototype

```
//Function Prototype
//UINT RealizePalette( );
UINT iRemappedColors = DisplayDC.RealizePalette();
        //Find out if any color entries have been reassigned
        //since this app last realized its palette
if ( iRemappedColors == NO_CHANGE )
    pDocument->UpdateAllViews(NULL);
        //If not, trigger repainting of all of this
        //document's views
```

Rectangle   FUNCTION

Description   **CDC::Rectangle** draws a rectangle with the **CDC**'s currently selected pen and then fills it with the currently selected brush. This function uses logical coordinates and does not update the current pen position.

Description

```
//Function Prototype
//BOOL Rectangle( int x1, int y1, int x2, int y2 );
//BOOL Rectangle(LPRECT lpRect );
pDC->Rectangle(lprRectCoords );
        //Draw a rectangle filled with the current brush....
```

RectVisible

Description   **CDC::RectVisible** checks to see whether a rectangle is within an application's visible region, or clipping area. **CDC::RectVisible** can be used by an application to see whether the result of a drawing operation will be located where output graphics are allowed to be drawn. The rectangle is specified in logical coordinates. This function returns true if *any* part of the rectangle is within the clipping area.

Prototype

```
//Function Prototype
//virtual BOOL RectVisible(LPRECT lpRect )const;
if( pDC->RectVisible( ptTestRect ) )
  {
    //Do some drawing if our bounding rectangle visible....
  }
```

ReleaseAttribDC

Description   **CDC::ReleaseAttribDC** sets the **CDC** class public data member **m_hAttribDC** to NULL. **m_hAttribDC** identifies the device context referenced by **CDC** member functions that provide information about the DC settings, and initially points to the default output device context for the current **CDC** object. Setting **m_hAttribDC** to NULL effectively eliminates access to the device context information-gathering functions, but is a necessary first step to setting a new attribute display context. Before calling this function, you should delete the **AttribDC** if it was created by using **CreateIC**, **CreateDC** or **CreateCompatibleDC**. If you don't, a resource leak occurs.

Prototype

```
//Function Prototype
//virtual void ReleaseAttribDC( );

CDC  BrandNewCDCObject;
      //The constructor initialized the m_hAttribDC data member
      //with the value of the handle to the output DC;
      //We want to set a new one
BrandNewCDCObject.ReleaseAttribDC( );
```

ReleaseOutputDC   FUNCTION

Description   This function severs the connection between a DC and a **CDC** object by setting the **CDC** public data member **m_hDC** to NULL. **m_hDC** identifies the default output device context for a **CDC** object. It is used when an application wants to disconnect a device context from a **CDC** object, often in preparation for connecting a new DC to the same **CDC** object. Applications rarely use this function directly, but it is part of the strategy of the application framework's Print Preview implementation, where DCs for the printer and screen are used alternately in creating a screen-based representation of the printed page.

Before a DC is released by a call to this member function, it must first be detached from the **CDC** object, by a call to **CDC::Detach**.

Prototype
```
//Function Prototype
//virtual void ReleaseOutputDC( );
//
CDC  BrandNewCDCObject;

BrandNewCDCObject.Detach( );
      //We construct a new CDC object, but we don't want the
      //standard output DC attached to it—we will be replacing
      //it....
BrandNewCDCObject.ReleaseOutputDC();
      //We set the public data member m_hDC to NULL
```

RestoreDC   FUNCTION

Description   **CDC::RestoreDC** is the counterpart of **CDC::SaveDC**. It is used to restore information about the state of a device context after an application has completed an operation that may have altered its DC settings, such as playing a metafile. Metafiles may include commands that can reset many DC attributes, but they have histori- cally had limited capability to do queries about the settings of the DCs in which they play. In most cases, there is no attempt on the part of the metafile to leave the DC environment in the condition in which it began. The application is provided with a convenient defense against metafiles that reset DC attributes in the save and restore functions by the DC context stack maintained by Windows. The way the context stack is manipulated by **CDC::RestoreDC** is determined by its parameter. A value of -1 pops the top entry off the stack and back into the current DC. If an integer returned by a

CDC::SaveDC is passed, the entry created by that save operation is popped into the current DC. If **CDC::RestoreDC** is passed a parameter that identifies a specific saved DC, all the entries on top of it on the context stack are popped and lost when the targeted DC is restored.

Prototype

```
//Function Prototype
//virtual BOOL RestoreDC( int nSavedDC);
int iSavedDCIndex = pDC->SaveDC();
        //We save the DC on the context
        //stack and preserve the integer that
        //identifies it so that we can locate it
        //if SaveDC is called again
pDC->PlayMetafile( hMetafile );
        //We easily determine whether the metafile
        //changes DC settings
        //in advance
pDC->RestoreDC(iSavedDCIndex);
        //So we play it safe and restore the
        //DC settings from the context
        //stack after it plays.
```

RoundRect   FUNCTION

Description   **CDC::RoundRect** draws a rectangle with the **CDC**'s currently selected pen and then fills it with the currently selected brush. Its corners are rounded using segments of an ellipse whose width and height are passed to the function.

This function uses logical coordinates and does not update the current pen position.

Prototype

```
//Function Prototype
//BOOL RoundRect( int x1, int y1, int x2, int y2
//       int x3, int y3);
//BOOL RoundRect(LPRECT lpRect, POINT point);
pDC->RoundRect(lprRectCoords, ptEllipse);
    //Draw a rectangle with rounded corners,
    //and fill with the current brush....
```

SaveDC   FUNCTION

Description   **CDC::SaveDC** saves the state of the current **CDC** object's device context by copying it to a context stack maintained by Windows. **CDC::SaveDC** is used in combination with the function

CDC::RestoreDC to preserve and retrieve the application's display parameters. Saved information includes such things as selected pens, brushes and regions, as well as mapping mode and coordinate system settings. Many copies of DC information can be placed on the context stack, with the one saved by the current call identified by a positive integer returned by this function.

CDC::SaveDC is used before operations that could modify the settings of the application's DC in ways the application cannot know. This might be the case, for example, in the playing of a metafile. To properly use its complementary **CDC** member function **CDC::RestoreDC**, it is sometimes necessary to save the integer it returns. **CDC::RestoreDC** optionally restores a particular DC from the context stack, using the integer returned by **CDC::SaveDC**, or simply pops the top of the context stack. If a specific saved DC is restored, all the entries on top of it on the context stack are popped and lost when the targeted DC is restored.

SaveDC and **RestoreDC** are not a low-cost way to party on your DCs without the worry of selecting GDI objects out of them at the end. They are a firewall to be used when you know that some event will change the state of the DC and you need to restore that state after the event is over.

Prototype

```
//Function Prototype
//virtual int SaveDC( );
int iSavedDCIndex = pDC->SaveDC();
        //We are about to do something with the DC
        //identified by pDC
        //that will change its state in some way....
        //We save the DC on the context
        //stack and preserve the integer that
        //identifies it so that we can locate it if
        //RestoreDC is called
```

ScaleViewportExt   FUNCTION

Description **CDC::ScaleViewportExt** is a handy way of scaling the *viewport,* or area of the display surface to which drawing is confined. Both the x and y axes of the viewport are multiplied by fractions defined by the four arguments to the function. The first two arguments operate on the x extent. The current x extent is multiplied by the first argument and divided by the second. Fractional parts of the quotient are truncated. The result is the new x extent of the viewport. The same operations scale the *y* extent by using the next two function arguments.

The values of the scale factors can affect the signs of the viewport extents. Because the orientation of a drawing is determined by the relation of the signs of the viewport and logical coordinate system window, scaling operations that change the sign of the result can change the sense of an axis and affect the orientation of the drawn image.

This function is used with other **CDC** member mapping functions, such as **SetMapMode**, **GetWindowOrg**, **GetViewportOrg**, **SetWindowOrg** and **SetViewportOrg**.

Prototype

```
//Function Prototype
//virtual CSize ScaleViewportExt( int xNum, int xDenom,
//              int yNum, int yDenom );
pDC->ScaleViewportExt( 2, 1, 2, 1 );
    //Double the viewport height and width....
```

ScaleWindowExt   FUNCTION

Description   **CDC::ScaleWindowExt** is a very handy way of changing the proportions of the window on the application's logical coordinate space or the range of rectangular coordinates over which it can draw. Both the *x* and *y* axes of the window are multiplied by fractions defined by the four arguments to the function. The first two arguments operate on the *x* extent. The current *x* extent is multiplied by the first argument and divided by the second. Fractional parts of the quotient are truncated. The result is the new *x* extent of the window. The same operations scale the *y* extent using the next two function arguments. Note that this function and **ScaleViewportExt** both do the arithmetic *and* make the call to **Set*xxx*Ext()**, so you don't have to make two GDI calls.

The values of the scale factors can affect the signs of the window extents. Because the orientation of a drawing is determined by the relation of the signs of the viewport and logical coordinate system window, scaling operations that change the sign of the result can change the sense of an axis and affect the orientation of the drawn image or cause it to disappear from view.

Also remember that scaling the window does not affect the coordinates of the image that was drawn in the window. For example, making a larger logical window does not stretch the image to fill the newly enlarged window: It simply occupies a different proportion of the window.

This function is used with other **CDC** member mapping functions, such as **SetMapMode**, **GetWindowOrg**, **GetViewportOrg**, **SetWindowOrg** and **SetViewportOrg**. *See **DPtoLP** and **LPtoDP** for information about how to convert points between logical and device coordinates.*

Prototype

```
//Function Prototype
//virtual CSize ScaleWindowExt( int xNum, int xDenom,
//              int yNum, int yDenom );
pDC->ScaleWindowExt( 1,3,1,3 );
    //Reduce the window to one-third
    //of its former x and y extents....
```

ScrollDC   FUNCTION

Description

CDC::ScrollDC scrolls a rectangle into the application's client area vertically and horizontally. Both the rectangle to be scrolled and a clipping rectangle are taken into account by the scrolling operation. The clipping area takes precedence over the specified rectangle. To scroll the entire client area of a window, an application should use **CWnd::ScrollWindow**. **CDC::ScrollDC** does not scroll child windows that fall within its scrolling rectangle. Use **CWnd::ScrollWindow** if you need to scroll the entire client area of a window; use this function if you need to scroll only a small part of the client area. Note that if **lpRectUpdate** is NULL, Windows doesn't compute the update rectangle. If **pRgnUpdate** *and* **lpRectUpdate** are NULL, Windows doesn't compute the update region. If you pass a non-NULL value for **pRgnUpdate**, **lpRectUpdate** will contain the new invalid region and can be passed to **InvalidateRect** or **InvalidateRgn** to force that update to take place.

Prototype

```
//Function Prototype
//BOOL ScrollDC( int dx, int dy, LPCRECT
//lpRectScroll, LPCRECT lpRectClip,
//CRgn* pRgnUpdate, LPRECT lpRectUpdate );

pDC->ScrollWindow( iScrollX, iScrollY,
                //scroll this many units....
            lprScrollingRect, lprClipRect,
                //scroll the smaller of these
                //rectangles....
            pRgnNeedsUpdate,
```

371

```
                    //This region was uncovered....
                lprRectNeedsUpdate );
                    //Bounding rectangle of the
                    //area that needs
                    //repainting
```

SelectClipRgn — FUNCTION

Description **CDC::SelectClipRgn** selects a *device-dependent* clipping region
into the current **CDC** object's output DC. A NULL value selects the
entire client area. A copy of the region identified by the parameter
is made, which allows the region itself to be selected into other
DCs or destroyed. The return value specifies the type of the clipping region.

   CDC::SelectClipRgn is used most in printing, and it expects
coordinates of the region passed to it to have been stated in *device*
coordinates. It limits output to an area described by the region.
Because this function requires the region to be defined in device
units, several constraints apply. High-precision printers report their
metrics in the units used to measure text. When the printer receives graphics, such as bitmapped images, the text metrics would
make the bitmaps unacceptably small because the bitmaps usually
have much coarser resolution. The printer scales the text units to
attempt to retain the correct size for bitmaps and other graphics.
All this juggling is accomplished by the printer scaling the coordinates of graphics by a device-dependent factor. The value of the
scale factor can be retrieved from the GETSCALINGFACTOR printer
Escape function call.

Prototype
```
//Function Prototype
//virtual int SelectClipRegion( CRgn* pRgn );
int iClippingRegionType = PrinterDC.SelectClipRegion(
pNewClippingRegion );
    //Assume that we have already
    //created the region, using device-dependent coordinates.
    //Select the clipping region into the printer DC.
```

SelectPalette — FUNCTION

Description Many display devices are capable of displaying a huge range of
colors, but are limited to displaying a subset of the range at any
given time. The subset of colors that can be displayed simultaneously is recorded in the *system palette*. Windows reserves some

palette entries for its own use and then adds palette entries to the system palette as applications "realize," or make requests to install, their logical palettes. Logical palettes are specific to a given application and provide a means by which applications can define their color requirements, taking full advantage of the capability of the display device, but without having an undesirable impact on other applications' use of color. An application selects a logical palette into its device context by using **CDC::SelectPalette**. The palette is then used to mediate the application's color requests and provide reasonable compromises when they can't be satisfied exactly.

Before an application-defined palette can be selected into a device context, it must be created by a call to **CDC::CreatePalette** and then realized by **CDC::RealizePalette**. Applications that rely on a large range of colors or demand precise color rendering need to ensure both that Windows will comply as closely as possible with their color requests and that changes made to the color palette will have as little impact as possible on applications in inactive windows. Constructing and selecting an application-specific palette is the means by which this is done.

A palette may be specified as either a foreground or background palette. If the second parameter to **CDC::SelectPalette** is non-zero, the palette remains in the background, even when the window associated with its **CDC** is active. In general, applications that have the input focus request that their palettes be selected to the foreground, which gives them the greatest influence when color matching is performed. An application with multiple views might want to force to the background the palettes of all views except the active one.

A palette can be selected into more than one device context, but all of them must represent the same physical device. Any changes made to a palette shared across device contexts affects the display capabilities of the entire group.

Prototype

```
//Function Prototype
//CPalette* SelectPalette( CPalette* pPalette, BOOL
bForceBackground);
CPalette* OldPalette =
    pDC->SelectPalette(pThisPalette, FOREGROUND);
        //Select an application-specific palette,
        //saving a pointer to the palette
        //object we select out. Make this
        //the foreground palette so that its
        //color requests will be
        //considered more heavily than those
        //of inactive windows
```

373

SelectStockObject   FUNCTION

Description   **CDC::SelectStockObject** provides type-safe selection of a Windows GDI object into the device context of the current **CDC** object. Stock objects include a selection of pens, brushes, fonts and a standard palette that are provided by Windows. Stock objects are used whenever possible in graphics because they don't have to be created and destroyed by the application. When this function is successful, it returns a pointer to the previously selected object.

Functions that modify GDI objects should not be used on stock objects (for example, **CDC::SetBrushOrg**). When they are selected from the DC, they should not be destroyed.

Possible values for nIndex (in other words, the stock object names) are shown in this table:

BLACK_BRUSH	Black brush.
DKGRAY_BRUSH	Dark gray brush.
GRAY_BRUSH	Gray brush.
HOLLOW_BRUSH	Hollow brush.
LTGRAY_BRUSH	Light gray brush.
NULL_BRUSH	Null brush.
WHITE_BRUSH	White brush.
BLACK_PEN	Black pen.
NULL_PEN	Null pen.
WHITE_PEN	White pen.
ANSI_FIXED_FONT	ANSI fixed system font.
ANSI_VAR_FONT	ANSI variable system font.
DEVICE_DEFAULT_FONT	Device-dependent font.
OEM_FIXED_FONT	OEM-dependent fixed font.
SYSTEM_FONT	The system font. By default, Windows uses the system font to draw menus, dialog-box controls, and other text. In Windows versions 3.0 and later, the system font is proportional width; earlier versions of Windows use a fixed-width system font.
SYSTEM_FIXED_FONT	The fixed-width system font used in Windows prior to version 3.0. This object is available for compatibility with earlier versions of Windows.
DEFAULT_PALETTE	Default color palette. This palette consists of the 20 static colors in the system palette.

Prototype
```
//Function Prototype
//virtual CGdiObject* SelectStockObject( int nIndex );
CBrush pOldBrush = pDisplayDC->SelectStockObject(
WHITE_BRUSH );
```

```
//We select the WHITE_BRUSH stock object,
//but save a pointer to the brush
//being selected out of the DC
//so that we can replace it when we
//finish with the new one
```

SetAbortProc   FUNCTION

Description   **CDC::SetAbortProc** sets a printer abort function. The abort
procedure allows an application user to interrupt a lengthy printing process in an orderly fashion. It has long been a subject of
comment that printing under Windows can be rather sluggish. The
original architects of the system realized that this was a major
complaint for end users and provided this function as a way for an
application to set up a printing process that could be terminated
without catastrophe.

To take advantage of this, an application typically presents a
dialog box that allows a user to cancel printing by depressing a
push-button. This push-button routes the cancellation message to
an abort procedure that has been exported to Windows as a callback function. Note that this can be a C++ decorated name as long
as you pass the same thing to your **SetAbortProc** function (not
extern "C").

The abort callback function must be declared in the following
way:

```
BOOL FAR PASCAL __export MyAbortProc (HDC hPrinterDC, int
ErrCode );
```

Use of the __export keyword—or in Win32 compilers,
__declspec(dllexport)—emits the proper record in the object file to
mark the function as exported. Note that __export is not used
under Win32; you must use __declspec(dllexport) instead.

The *ErrCode* parameter notifies the abort routine if there is a
general error, not enough disk space or the user has canceled. The
function must return 0 to abort, and any non-zero value to continue
printing.

The abort procedure must be set by calling this function before
printing is started by calling **CDC::StartDoc**. The callback function
must handle any exceptions it encounters because exceptions can't
be thrown across callback boundaries.

Prototype

```
//Function Prototype
//int SetAbortProc( BOOL ( CALLBACK EXPORT* lpfn )( HDC, int )
);
//BOOL FAR PASCAL __export MyAbortProc (HDC hPrinterDC, int
ErrCode );
PrinterDC.SetAbortProc( AppAbortProc);
    //The AppAbortProc function must conform
    //to MFC callback function conventions
    //and must handle any exceptions it encounters....
```

SetAttribDC   FUNCTION

Description   The device context attached to a **CDC** object is identified by the
CDC public data member **m_hDC**. When a **CDC** object is associated with a DC, either by construction of one of the derived classes
or by using **FromHandle** or **Attach**, a complementary public data
member, **m_hAttribDC**, is initialized with the value of **m_hDC**,
but **m_hAttribDC** *is not attached to the CDC object.*
m_hAttribDC is provided to add a level of abstraction to the CDC
object. This is exploited by the application framework in the
implementation of **Print Preview**, where DCs and output metrics
are needed for the screen and printer simultaneously, so **m_hDC**
and **m_hAttribDC** reference different DCs. **CDC::SetAttribDC** is
the function used to specify a new attribute device context, the
identity of which is recorded in **m_hAttribDC**.

It can also be used when playing a metafile to set an attribute
device context for a **CMetafileDC** object. This provides the
metafile with a way to get attribute information, which is not
possible using the Windows SDK.

Prototype

```
//Function Prototype
//virtual void SetAttribDC( HDC hDC );
CDC  BrandNewCDCObject;
    //We construct a new CDC object
BrandNewCDCObject.SetAttribDC( hDCNew);
    //We set the public data member m_hAttribDC to the new
    //DC handle
```

SetBkColor   FUNCTION

Description   **CDC::SetBkColor** is used to set the background color in the output DC attached to the current **CDC** object. This setting defines the color with which the background of the application's client area will be painted and exerts an influence on the way bitmaps are displayed.

CDC::SetBkColor defines the solid brush that will be used to paint a window's client area and fill hollow shapes, such as rectangles. The background color is considered when translating a bitmap from a memory DC to the screen. The way in which the composition of the background interacts with the source bitmap and the pixels currently on the screen is defined by the ROP (raster operation) code used in the bitmap transfer.

If the background mode is OPAQUE, the background color fills in the spaces around characters and the gaps in lines drawn by dashed pens and patterned brushes.

Like all color requests in Windows, this one is subject to the availability of a system palette entry that matches the color requested and, of course, the capabilities of the display device. A failed call returns the value 0x80000000.

Prototype

```
//Function Prototype
//virtual COLORREF SetBkColor( COLORREF crColor );
    //Set the new background color, but save the old one
    //so that we can restore it later
    crOldBkColor = pDC->SetBkMode(OPAQUE);
                    //If OPAQUE, you get a bgnd
                    //color painted; otherwise,
                    //not.
    pDC->SetBkColor(RGB(0,0,128));
    pDC->SetTextColor(RGB(128,0,0));
    pDC->TextOut(400, 150, CString("Hello"));
```

SetBkMode   FUNCTION

Description   **CDC::SetBkMode** sets the background mode of the current **CDC** object's output device context. Background mode controls whether a new drawing in the client area overlays an older drawing or obliterates it. This is important in animation and in graphical applications, such as CAD, mapping and illustration, where it is necessary to add to an existing drawing without demolishing any of the existing image.

The setting of the background mode for an application is one of those things that is startlingly apparent if it isn't correct, so there is little danger of going wrong with this function. A word processor that doesn't erase its background as it draws or a CAD program that does tips you off to background mode problems right away.

Prototype

```
//Function Prototype
//int SetBkMode( int nBkMode);
CADDisplayDC.SetBkMode( TRANSPARENT );
    //We put up a new layer of a CAD drawing, without wiping out
    //the previously drawn layer....
```

SetBoundsRect   FUNCTION

Description   **CDC::SetBoundsRect** starts or stops the recording of coordinates that define the smallest rectangle which will enclose all the output operations directed to the client area of the current **CDC** object's output DC.

The current DC's bounding rectangle is a bit of bookkeeping Windows uses to update the client area efficiently when it is time to paint. A bounding rectangle comprises the smallest rectangle that will enclose a given drawing operation. **CDC::SetBoundsRect** notifies Windows to begin accumulating the bounding rectangle for an output DC when called with the flag **DCB_ENABLE**, and stops the recording when called again with the flag **DCB_DISABLE**. The bounding rectangle is returned in logical coordinates. Applications seldom use this function because it is automatically invoked in their behalf by the framework as needed.

Prototype

```
//Function Prototype
//UINT SetBoundsRect( LPRECT lpRectBound, UINT flags );
//Start accumulating bounding rectangles.
UINT nOldBoundsState = pDC->SetBoundsRect(CRect(10, 10, 100,
100), DCB_ENABLE | DCB_ACCUMULATE);
```

SetBrushOrg   FUNCTION

Description   **CDC::SetBrushOrg** relocates the origin of the brush currently selected in the device context of the **CDC** object. The origin is an *x-y* coordinate pair, given in device units. When you're considering the family of functions that change the alignment of the brush, it is helpful to remember that a "brush" is nothing more than a small bitmap combined in the way the application directs with the bits in the area it will be painting. In Windows 3.*x*, the origin of the brush bitmap is the upper left corner of the display surface. As application windows move and are resized, it is possible for this bitmap to become misaligned and produce a striping effect when the window is repainted using a patterned brush. Resetting the origin of the brush ensures that the window background is painted correctly.

It is not necessary to set brush alignment under Windows NT because NT aligns brushes based on the origin of the application window rather than on the screen.

Prototype
```
//Function Prototype
//CPoint SetBrushOrg( int x, int y );
//CPoint SetBrushOrg( POINT point );
pDisplayDC->SetBrushOrg( ptNewAlignment );
    //Make sure that the pattern brush
    //will paint the window background correctly
    //after the window has been moved or resized.
```

SetMapMode   FUNCTION

Description   **CDC::SetMapMode** sets the mapping mode for the current **CDC** object's output DC. A map mode is a set of transformation rules that specifies how the logical coordinate space will be set up for an application's drawing. It determines the units of the *x* and *y* axes, whether the axes use units of the same size, and the orientation of the axes.

CDC::SetMapMode establishes one of eight mapping modes (or transformation schemes) for an application. MM_ANISOTROPIC uses application-specific units, where the length of a unit in the *x* and *y* directions *does not have to be* equal. MM_ISOTROPIC uses application-specific units, where the length of a unit in the *x* and *y* directions *are* equal. The orientation of the axes is not fixed for either of these two.

MM_HIMETRIC and MM_LOMETRIC map units to .01 and .1 *millimeters,* respectively, *x* and *y* units are equal, and the *y* axis increases upward. MM_HIENGLISH and MM_LOENGLISH map units to .001 and .01 *inches,* respectively, *x* and *y* units are equal, and the *y* axis increases upward.

MM_TEXT relates units in both directions to the size of a pixel on the display device, with *x* increasing to the right and *y* increasing downward. MM_TWIPS relates units in both directions to the "point" (1/1440th of an inch), an important metric in typography. One TWIP is 1/20th of a typographic point, with *x* increasing to the right and *y* increasing downward.

MM_ISOTROPIC and MM_ANISOTROPIC interact with two other sets of mapping functions to determine the sense of the x and y axes. **CDC::SetWindowExt** and **CDC::SetViewportExt** determine the bounds of the logical coordinate space and the physical coordinate space the application can access. *Extents* are x and y measurements of the bounding rectangle in which an image can be drawn. *Viewport extents* define the rectangle on the presentation surface, and *window extents* define the rectangle in the logical coordinate space. If the signs of the values for x and y extents are opposite, it changes the orientation of the respective axes. Does this sound complicated? Well, yes and no. A few simple rules govern this whole business.

It is a terrific advantage to a graphical application to be able to define the orientation of its own axes, so sorting out how all this works is well worth the time. This function is used with other **CDC** member mapping functions, such as **SetMapMode**, **GetWindowOrg**, **GetViewportOrg**, **SetWindowOrg**, **SetViewportOrg**, **OffsetWindowOrg** and **OffsetViewportOrg**. Also note—and this is very important—that when you set the window extent, origin, viewport extent, origin, etc., these calls must be made after you get the DC and before you do the drawing. These settings *do not persist* in the DC, so code like this fails miserably:

```
void CMyView::OnDraw(CDC* pDC)
{
    pDC->SetMapMode(m_nMapMode);
//I cache the mapping mode
CRgn rgn;
rgn.CreateRoundRectRgn(0, 150, 150, 190, 8, 8);
pDC->FrameRgn(&rgn,
    CBrush::FromHandle(
    (HBRUSH)::GetStockObject(GRAY_BRUSH)), 2, 2);
}
void CMyView::SomeMenuTrigger()
{
    m_nMapMode = MM_ISOTROPIC; //set mapping mode
CClientDC dc(this);

dc.SetMapMode(m_nMapMode);

CRect r;
GetClientRect(r);
```

```
CPoint pt(0, 0);
dc.SetWindowOrg(pt);
dc.SetWindowExt(300, 300);
dc.SetViewportOrg(0, 0);
dc.SetViewportExt(r.right, r.bottom);

    Invalidate();
}
```

The preceding well-intentioned code fails because the coordinate system is forgotten immediately after the menu trigger message is processed and before any painting occurs (as a result of the Invalidate call).

Prototype

```
//Function Prototype
//virtual int SetMapMode( int nMapMode );
if ( pDC->GetMapMode( ) == MM_ISOTROPIC )
    //This mapping mode forces x and y axes
    //to have equally sized units....
{
    pDC->.SetMapMode( MM_ANISOTROPIC )
    //This mapping mode allows x and y
    //axes to have differently sized units....
}
```

SetMapperFlags FUNCTION

Description   **CDC::SetMapperFlags** sets the font-mapping flags that control the way in which a logical font is matched to a physical font for the current output device. When an application makes a request for a *logical* font, the font characteristics are compared to available *physical* fonts. *Physical fonts* are hardware fonts or font resources that have been loaded by the operating system or the application. The font mapper chooses a physical font that most closely matches the logical font described by the application. Mapper flags can force the font-mapping algorithm to ignore fonts that do not match exactly the *aspect ratio* of the target device. The aspect ratio of a device is the ratio between the width and height of a pixel for a given device.

    CDC::SetMapperFlags allows an application that uses raster fonts to force font selections that are appropriate to the output device. The flag that forces aspect ratio mapping is ASPECT_FILTERING. Mapper flags are not used with TrueType fonts because they can be scaled appropriately for different aspect ratios. If no physical font matches the aspect ratio specified by **CDC::SetMapperFlags**, the mapper chooses a new aspect ratio and tries again.

Prototype

```
//Function Prototype
//DWORD SetMapperFlags( DWORD dwFlag );
    //Assume that we have a valid pointer to a DC
    //because most drawing is done from
    //the OnDraw member function of the view....
pDC->SetMapperFlags( ASPECT_FILTERING );
    //Force aspect ratio matching for raster font requests....
```

SetOutputDC   FUNCTION

Description **CDC::SetOutputDC** sets the **CDC** public data member **m_hDC**, which identifies the object's default output device context. Setting the value in **m_hDC** does not attach the new device context to the **CDC** object; this must be done explicitly by calling the member function **Attach**.

Setting a new output DC on a **CDC** object that has a currently attached DC is *not allowed*. As you might have noticed, moving DCs around is a fairly granular activity, and several steps are required. First, if the **CDC** object has a currently attached DC, it must be detached using **CDC::Detach**. If it is necessary to preserve access to the detached DC, its handle is returned by this call and should be stored.

If the detached DC is no longer needed, it should be relinquished in a respectful fashion. Here are some disposal rules concerning the newly detached DC. The first concern is to ensure that any GDI objects constructed by the application (pens, brushes, bitmaps and so forth) are destroyed if they are no longer needed. They must be selected out of the DC and deleted. (For more on this, see the **CGdiObject** member function **DeleteObject**.) Return the DC to Windows by calling **CDC::ReleaseDC**. If the DC was created by the application through calls to the **CDC** member functions **CreateDC**, **CreateCompatibleDC** or **CreateIC**, it should be destroyed using **CDC::DeleteDC**.

After the old DC has been detached **CDC::SetOutputDC** resets the value of **m_hDC** if that DC is not already attached to another CDC object.

Prototype
```
//Function prototype
//virtual void SetOutputDC( HDC hDC );
CDC  BrandNewCDCObject;

BrandNewCDCObject.Detach( );
        //We construct a new CDC object, but we don't want the
        //standard attribute DC attached to it — we got one from
        //the Clipboard or a DDE message we want to attach.
BrandNewCDCObject.SetOutputDC( hDCNew);
        //We set the public data member m_hDC to the new DC
        //handle
```

SetPixel   FUNCTION

Description **CDC::SetPixel** sets the RGB color value of a pixel located at a point in the **CDC** object's logical coordinate space. **CDC::SetPixel** expects the point to be stated in logical coordinates and to be within the clipping area. A device may not be able to satisfy the color request exactly, depending on the capabilities of the devices and the state of the application and system palettes. The closest match is substituted in this case. No dithering can take place to simulate the requested color in the case of inexact matches because only one pixel is being painted.

Prototype
```
//Function Prototype
//COLORREF SetPixel( int x, int x, COLORREF crColor);
//COLORREF SetPixel( POINT point, COLORREF crColor);
DisplayDC.SetPixel( ptColorPoint, RGB( 0,0,0 ));
    //Set the pixel at ptColorPoint to black...
```

SetPolyFillMode   FUNCTION

Description **CDC::SetPolyFillMode** sets the polygon filling mode for the current **CDC** object's output DC. The two polygon filling modes, ALTERNATE and WINDING, determine the way in which Windows fills polygonal shapes. ALTERNATE is the default. The two fill methods differ in the algorithms they use to compute where fills should be drawn, and in some cases there could be a performance advantage to one or the other.

Prototype

```
//Function Prototype
//int SetPolyFillMode( int nPolyFillMode );
if ( pDC->GetPolyFillMode() == ALTERNATE )
  {
    pDC->SetPolyFillMode( WINDING );
    //Reset the fill mode...
  }
```

SetROP2 — FUNCTION

Description **CDC::SetROP2** sets the raster operation code for the current **CDC** object's output DC. **ROP2** codes determine how the bits of the pen and the bits of the background will be combined in drawing. **ROP2** codes comprise all possible outcomes if the bits of the pen and the background are combined using a combination of AND, OR, XOR and NOT bitwise operations. The possible codes are assigned mnemonic names, such as **R2_COPYPEN**, the default setting. As the name implies, this **ROP2** code draws the pixels traversed by the pen with only the pen's color.

Prototype

```
//Function Prototype
//int SetROP2 ( int nDrawMode );
//Function Prototype
if ( pDC->GetROP2() == R2_XORPEN )
  {
    pDC->.SetROP2(R2_WHITE);
        //Change the ROP2 code to make the pen
        //draw only white lines.
  }
```

SetStretchBltMode — FUNCTION

Description **CDC::SetStretchBltMode** sets the bitmap stretching mode for the current **CDC** object's output DC. Bitmap stretching is done when GDI fits a bitmap into available display real estate by resizing it. There are three ways this can be done if the bitmap is being downsized: It can do a bitwise AND on adjacent rows or a bitwise OR on adjacent rows, or drop rows out altogether. The first two methods work best for black-and-white bitmaps because they tend to preserve detail, but the third method is preferred for color bitmaps because combining adjacent rows of color pixels can produce a garish effect.

For the best results in sizing color bitmaps, use the parameter STRETCH_DELETESCANS. For black-and-white bitmaps, either STRETCH_ANDSCANS or STRETCH_ORSCANS will probably give the best results.

Prototype
```
//Function Prototype
//int SetStretchBltMode( int nStretchMode );
if( DisplayDC.GetStretchBltMode( int iStretchingMethod ) ==
STRETCH_ANDSCANS )
  {
    DisplayDC.SetStretchBltMode(STRETCH_DELETESCANS);
    //Reset stretching mode to suit a color bitmap....
  }
```

SetTextAlign   FUNCTION

Description   **CDC::SetTextAlign** establishes the text alignment settings for the current **CDC** object's *output* DC. Text alignment determines how a text string will be positioned in relation to the point passed to text output functions such as **CDC::TextOut**.

There are three basic groups of flags that have to do with text positioning. The ones that control horizontal placement within a bounding rectangle are **TA_LEFT**, **TA_CENTER** and **TA_RIGHT**. Vertical placement within a bounding rectangle is controlled by **TA_TOP**, **TA_BOTTOM** and **TA_BASELINE**. **TA_BASELINE** aligns the baseline of the font to the bottom of the bounding rectangle. (An *o* sits on the baseline, but a *y* descends below it.) Whether or not text output functions use the DC's current position when performing output operations is flagged by **TA_UPDATECP** or **TA_NOUPDATECP**, respectively.

Prototype
```
//Function Prototype
//UINT SetTextAlign( UINT nFlags);
    //Assume that we have a valid pointer to a DC
    //because most drawing is done from
    //the OnDraw member function of the view....
pDC->SetTextAlign(TA_LEFT );
    //Text will be drawn so that the left edge
    //of the leading character cell
    //will be aligned with the y coordinate
    //passed to CDC::TextOut
```

SetTextCharacterExtra
FUNCTION

Description **CDC::SetTextCharacterExtra** sets the value for additional intercharacter white space for the currently selected font in the **CDC** object's output DC. The application can specify an amount of white space that should be inserted between characters as text is written out. This capability can be useful in making small fonts more legible on blueprint-type drawings or maps. It can also be of use if text is being output one character at a time, to conform to an unusual shape, such as a stream or winding road. The extra white space value must be stated in logical units.

Prototype
```
//Function Prototype
//int SetTextCharacterExtra( int nCharExtra);
    //Assume that we have a valid pointer to a DC
    //because most drawing is done from
    //the OnDraw member function of the view....
pDC->SetTextCharExtra( iSpreadChars );
    //Set intercharacter spacing....
```

SetTextColor
FUNCTION

Description **CDC::SetTextColor** sets the text color for the current **CDC** object's output DC. The **CDC** member functions **SetBkColor** and **SetBkMode** can also influence the appearance of text drawn in the client area. The background mode determines whether the text background is erased before the text is drawn, and the background color is used to fill in the undrawn pixels of the character cell.

Like all color requests in Windows, this one is subject to the availability of a system palette entry that matches the color requested and, of course, the capabilities of the display device.

Prototype
```
//Function Prototype
// virtual COLORREF SetTextColor( COLORREF crColor );
pDC->SetTextColor( crNewTextColor );
        //Text drawing will be done with a
        //color matching crNewColor
        //as closely as the device
        //and current system palette
        //mappings permit....
```

SetTextJustification — FUNCTION

Description **CDC::SetTextJustification** specifies the total extra white space to be distributed across a line of text, to create application-specific text-justification effects. This changes the width of the font's break character. That's almost *always* white space, but it can (at the font designer's option) be anything.

This function allows the application to do full text justification (left and right edges of text are flush) by setting the amount of extra white space to be distributed over each output line, in logical units. This capability is useful for column printing or in making text flow around graphics inserted in text.

Unlike the simple output functions, such as **CDC::DrawText** and **CDC::TextOut**, this function allows the justification of text with multiple fonts in a single line. Writing a line in more than a single font requires that the application create and select the fonts as needed, output text, and do text-positioning housekeeping. As multifont text is justified, there is a likelihood that round-off errors will occur as the justification routine recomputes the white-space distribution across the text written in different fonts.

CDC::SetTextJustification keeps a running error term to adjust spacing on a line, automatically compensating for this effect. At the end of an output line, the application should clear this error term by calling **CDC::SetTextJustification** with the extra break space parameter set to 0. This function expects the break space in logical units. If the current mapping mode is other than MM_TEXT, these units must be converted to device units, with the possibility of some round-off error. No conversion takes place if the mapping mode is MM_TEXT.

Prototype
```
//Function Prototype
//int SetTextJustification( int nBreakExtra, int nBreakCount);
    //Assume that we have a valid pointer to a DC
    //because most drawing is done from
    //the OnDraw member function of the view....
pDC->SetTextJustification
( rClientArea.right - pDC->GetTextExtent(lpszTestString, iCount ),
        iSpaceCount );
    //Take the difference between the width
    //of the client area and the string extent
    //and distribute it as white space over iSpaceCount spaces
```

SetViewportExt   FUNCTION

Description   **CDC::SetViewportExt** sets the viewport extents, which are x and y measurements of the bounding rectangle in which an image can be drawn on the presentation surface. The extents of a viewport determine how much presentation real estate is devoted to drawing an image and also play a role in how the x and y axes are oriented when image coordinates are mapped from the application's logical coordinate space window to the display surface.

The extents, that is, x and y dimensions, of the area in which drawing is confined are useful for fitting images to available display space. The signs of the viewport extents are compared with the signs of the window bounding the logical coordinate space. The direction of the viewport extent is specified starting at the viewport origin and traveling in a positive direction *as specified by the current mapping mode* to the end of the desired extent.

You can use **CDC::SetViewportExt** to change the orientation of the x or y axes by setting values for either extent that differ in sign from those used for the extents of the logical coordinate system window. **CDC::SetViewportExt** returns the value of the previous viewport extents.

Unintentionally changing the direction in which axes increase can be alarming; the image may disappear from the viewport altogether when this happens or else some part of it may be displayed in an unexpected orientation. It is a good idea to check for differences in the signs of the windows and viewport extents as a defensive measure before resetting them. You might do this in the following way:

```
inline int HelperGetSign(int n)
{
    return (n > 0) ? 1 : -1;
}
CSize size = pDC->GetViewportExt(); //Get x and y extents for
                                    //the viewport
int nXSign = HelperGetSign(size.cx);  //Are they positive?
int nYSign = HelperGetSign(size.cy);
// ... more code
pDC->SetViewportExt(newX * nXSign, newY * nYSign);
                          //Adjust sign of new
                          //settings to match old ones
```

This function is used with other **CDC** member mapping functions, such as **SetMapMode**, **GetWindowOrg**, **GetViewportOrg**, **SetWindowOrg** and **SetViewportOrg**.

Prototype

```
//Function Prototype
//virtual CSize SetViewportExt ( int cx, int cy );
//virtual CSize SetViewportExt (SIZE size);
CSize sizeViewport = DisplayDC.GetViewportExt( );
    //Get the absolute dimensions
    //and the signs of the viewport extents
SetViewportExt ( sizeViewport.cx * -1, sizeViewport.cy * -1 );
    //Leave the dimensions of the viewport the same, but
    //change the orientation of the axes
```

SetViewportOrg · FUNCTION

Description

The *viewport* is the rectangular region of the display surface that establishes the bounds of graphic output in an application window's *client area*. To translate an image from the application's logical coordinate system to the presentation surface, the Windows mapping algorithm considers the origin and x-y extents of both the viewport and the bounding window on the logical coordinate space. Depending on the sense of the application's logical coordinate system window axes and those of the viewport, the origin can be at any of the four corners of the viewport's rectangle.

Several factors influence which part of an image is displayed on a presentation surface and what its orientation will be. The viewport origin and x-y extents constrain the area on the screen or printed surface in which the image can be drawn. The bounding window of the logical coordinate space constrains the actual drawing of an image. For example, if the window origin is at 0,0 and has extents of 100 units in each direction, a rectangle whose upper left corner is at 150,150 wouldn't appear inside the application's logical window.

The orientation of an image is governed by the signs of the axes in both the logical and viewport coordinate systems. If the signs differ, the sense of the viewport axis is reversed. This means that the viewport axis increases going up the screen.

For example, in the default mapping mode MM_TEXT, the viewport's y axis increases going downward. If the y extent of the logical coordinate system window is specified as *-100*, the viewport's y axis increases going upward, which is convenient for drawing graphs and charts.

389

This function is used with other **CDC** member mapping functions, such as **SetMapMode**, **GetWindowOrg**, **GetViewportOrg**, **SetWindowOrg** and **SetViewportOrg**. *See SetMapMode for more infomation about Windows coordinate systems and their settings.*

Prototype

```
//Function Prototype
//CPoint SetViewportOrg( POINT point );
//virtual CPoint SetViewportOrg( int x, y );
pDC->SetViewportOrg( rClientArea.left, rClientArea.top );
    //Set the origin of the viewport to the
    //top left corner of the application's client area
```

SetWindowExt   FUNCTION

Description   **CDC::SetWindowExt** sets the extents, or dimensions, of the bounding window on the application's logical coordinate space. The units in which the window's dimensions are returned is dependent on the current mapping mode. The window can be no more than 32k on a side, and the units must be integers, but they may be negative.

The origin and extents of the window on the application's logical coordinate space are the most important factors in how output graphics look to a user. The size of the extents should match closely the range the coordinates of an application's image uses. If, for example, an application sets the extents to their maximum possible value of 32k with an origin at 0,0, and then draws an object whose *x* and *y* coordinate maximums are 100, the rendered image will probably occupy only a couple of pixels on the viewport. See **DPtoLP** and **LPtoDP** for information on how to convert points between logical and device coordinates.

The signs of the window extents are used in determining the orientation of the axes used for drawing an image. If the signs of the viewport and logical coordinate system window extents differ, the default sense of the axes for a particular mapping mode are reversed. An unintentional change in the sense of an axis can result in an improperly oriented image or one that doesn't appear in the viewport at all. It is a good idea for applications to check to make sure that changing window extents won't affect the orientation of the axes. To do this, use **CDC::GetWindowExt** to retrieve current dimensions and signs for the logical window.

Prototype
```
//Function Prototype
//virtual CSize SetWindowExt( int cx, int cy );
//virtual CSize SetWindowExt(CSize size);
pDC->SetWindowtExt ( 1000, 1000 );
    //Set a window of 1,000 by 1,000 units
    //(Units are dependent on the current mapping mode)
```

SetWindowOrg   FUNCTION

Description   **CDC::SetWindowOrg** sets the logical coordinate system window origin. The point set as the logical window origin is aligned with the viewport origin when images are translated between the two coordinate systems. The logical coordinate system is the one defined by the application, and the viewport coordinate system covers the area of the display device in which an application can present its graphic output. The window origin may be defined anywhere within the logical coordinate system, but the overall dimensions of the system may not exceed 32k units in either the *x* or *y* direction.

The location of the window origin determines in part which region of the logical coordinate space is mapped to the output display. When an image is translated from the logical coordinate space, the origins of the logical coordinate space window and the viewport are aligned. Moving the window origin is a handy way to pan across an image in the logical coordinate space that is too large to display inside the viewport. The function returns previous settings of the window origin.

This function is used with other **CDC** member mapping functions, such as **SetMapMode**, **GetWindowOrg**, **GetViewportOrg**, **SetWindowOrg** and **SetViewportOrg**. *See SetMapMode for more information about Windows coordinate systems and their settings. See* **DPtoLP** *and* **LPtoDP** *for information on how to convert points between logical and device coordinates.*

Prototype
```
//Function Prototype
//CPoint SetWindowOrg( int x, int y );
//CPoint SetWindowOrg( POINT point );
pDC->SetWindowOrg( 0,0 );
    //Set the origin of the window to the point x=0, y=0 in the
    //application's logical coordinate space
```

StartDoc   FUNCTION

Description   **CDC::StartDoc** replaces the Windows SDK **STARTDOC** printer escape under Windows 3.1, and is the preferred method of starting a print job for Win32s and Windows NT. **CDC::StartDoc** signals the device driver that a print job is being initiated, and that all output pages signaled by **CDC::StartPage** and **CDC::EndPage** should be spooled into this document until **CDC::EndDoc** closes the document. The **CDC::StartDoc** / **CDC::EndDoc** pair bracket the pages of a multipage document as it spools, to protect it from being interspersed among pages of concurrently printing documents. This function should not be called from inside a metafile.

Prototype
```
//Function Prototype
//int StartDoc( LPDOCINFO lpDocInfo );
if (PrinterDC.StartDoc(&DocInfoStruct) == SP_ERROR)
  {
    //If StartDoc returns a spooling error, issue a warning....
  }
```

StartPage   FUNCTION

Description   **CDC::StartPage** signals the device driver that a new page is being drawn. The **CDC::StartPage/CDC::EndPage** pair bracket the output to each page of a document as it spools. This function replaces the **NEWFRAME** and **BANDINFO** printer escapes. Windows disables the **CDC::ResetDC** member function between each **CDC::StartPage/CDC::EndPage** pair.

Prototype
```
//Function Prototype
//int StartPage( );
PrinterDC.StartPage( );
    //Do page drawing ...
PrinterDC.EndPage( );
```

StretchBlt   FUNCTION

Description   **CDC::StretchBlt** transfers a bitmap from a source DC to a destination DC by doing a bitwise combination of the **CDC** object's currently selected brush, the source bitmap and the bits already on the screen at the target location. The raster operation code defines way in which the three are combined by bitwise AND, NOT, OR and XOR operations.

CDC::StretchBlt is the tool used to transfer bitmapped images to the display surface and accommodate a difference in size between source and destination bitmaps. Recall that the **CDC** object's output DC has a default bitmap object selected into it that represents either the display or the printer presentation area. (In fact, there is really not a bitmap that represents the output device. In the case of the display, output is written to display memory by Windows, and in the case of the printer, it is written to a metafile.) Each DC can have only a single bitmap selected at a time, so outputting a bitmap to either of these presentation surfaces can't be as simple as selecting a pen or brush because the transfer involves a combination of the source and the destination with the brush.

To use either of the bitmap block transfer functions, we must first create a memory DC, select into it the bitmap we want to output to the screen, and transfer our bitmap from the memory DC to the output DC. Creating the DC is accomplished by a call to **CDC::CreateDC**. We can select the bitmap into this DC by using **CDC::SelectObject**.

At this point, we are ready to transfer the bitmap with a call to **CDC::StretchBlt**.

There are 256 raster operation codes that can be used to control the result of the transfer, referred to as *ternary* ROP codes because they take into account a source bitmap, the current brush and a destination bitmap. The ROP codes combine the three by using a combination of bitwise AND, OR, XOR and NOT operations, but the most commonly used ones have descriptively named constants.

CDC::StretchBlt compresses or inflates a source bitmap if it does not match the dimensions of the destination. It can also change the orientation of the bitmap if the signs of the heights or widths of the source and destination differ.

The bitmap functions are very useful in animation and painting programs because the many ways in which bitmaps can be transferred to the screen make it easy to manicure images as they move, erasing shadows of previous images.

Not all output devices support bitmapped block transfers (plotters, for example), so it is advisable to use **CDC::GetDeviceCaps** with the RC_BITBLT argument to check a device's capability before using any of the bitmap functions. Also, ordinary bitmap files are very highly device dependent. In terms of proportion, resolution and color, bitmaps may vary considerably between output devices. If the bitmaps of the source and destination have different color encoding, **CDC:: StretchBlt** converts the source and the pattern (brush) bitmaps' color information to match the destination in the following way:

○ If the source bitmap is monochrome and the destination is in color, white source pixels are assigned the default background color of the destination DC, and black source pixels are assigned the default foreground color.

○ If the source bitmap is in color and the display monochrome, all the pixels in it that match the destination background color are set to white, and all other pixels are set to black.

At best, this sort of translation will look shoddy. About all that can be said for it is that it prevents a program from crashing if incompatible bitmap formats are sent to the output DC. If it is necessary to transfer bitmaps among devices, it is a good idea to use the Windows device-independent bitmap format, which provides information about color content, resolution and aspect ratio of a bitmap. This precaution allows an application to gracefully make its own conversions. The stretch (compression, expansion or mirroring) of the bitmap is done in memory before combining the bitmap with the destination. This process can be somewhat memory-intensive, so *always* test the error return from this function. Note that the way stretching is done is determined by using **CDC::SetStretchBltMode**.

Prototype

```
//Function Prototype
//BOOL StretchBlt( int x, int y, int nWidth, int nHeight,
        CDC* pSrcDC, int xSrc, int ySrc,
        int nSrcWidth, int nSrcHeight, DWORD dwRop);


CDC MemoryDC;
    //Create a new DC
MemoryDC.CreateCompatibleDC(NULL);
    //The NULL pointer to a DC tells the
    //function to create a DC compatible with
    //the screen....
MemoryDC.SelectObject( pBitmap);
    //Assume that we have a valid pointer to a
    //bitmap object and select it into the DC
pDC->StretchBlt( iULXDest, iULYDest, iWidth, iHeight,
        &MemoryDC, 0, 0, iSrcWidth, iSrcHeight, SRCCOPY);
    //Assume that pDC points to the current output DC;
    //Transfer the bitmap
    //to the screen with its corner aligned
    //to the point iULXDest, iULYDest.
    //The output bitmap will be stretched
```

//or compressed based on the ratio
//between source and destination bitmap dimensions.
//SRCCOPY make the bitmap overdraw the destination pixels

TabbedTextOut   FUNCTION

Description   **CDC::TabbedTextOut** takes a string that includes embedded tabs and expands them by using values for tab spacing passed to the function in an array. If the tab stop array includes only one member, all tabs are expanded by that amount. If more than one element is in the array, tabbing positions are set according to their values, to a maximum specified by an argument giving the number of tab stops. The last argument to the function gives the x coordinate on the line of text that is considered the base point from which tabs are expanded.

   CDC::TabbedTextOut is useful for creating multicolumn tables of left-justified text. It also can provide the convenience of doing the housekeeping related to text placement. A call to **CDC::TabbedTextOut** can be paired with **CDC::SetTextAlign**, to set a flag instructing Windows that **CDC::TabbedTextOut** will update the current position when it draws a string. The current position is then used to position the next output string. If you supply an argument of zero for nTabPositions and NULL for lpTabStopPositions, tabs are expanded to eight spaces, computed by taking the average character width for the current font and multiplying by eight.

   If nTabPositions is 1, lpTabStopPositions is taken to be a pointer to an int that specifies the distance between a set of regular tab stops.

   Use nTabOrigin if your application needs to make multiple calls to **TabbedTextOut** for a given line. This is the location from which tabs are expanded.

Prototype
```
//Function Prototype
//virtual BOOL TabbedTextOut ( int x, int y, LPCSTR lpszString,
//              int nCount, int nTabPositions,
//              LPINT lpTabStopPositions
//              int nTabOrigin);
   //Assume that we have a valid pointer to a DC
   //because most drawing is done from
   //the OnDraw member function of the view....
```

```
pDC->TabbedTextOut(rClientArea.left, rClientArea.top,
        lpszTableText,
        strlen( lpszTableText ),
        iNumberTabStops, lpiArrayTabs,
        rClientArea.left );
    //Draw the table of text starting in the upper
    //left corner of the client area,
    //and use the array of tab stops,
    //using the left client area boundary as the base
    //for tab expansion....
```

TextOut   FUNCTION

Description **CDC::TextOut** is the simplest text output function. It may be used whenever the application needs to draw text in its client area. **TextOut** uses the currently selected font.

This function does not change the **CDC** object's current position. If more than one line of text is to be displayed, the application must retrieve information about the current font metrics by using **CDC::GetTextMetrics** to help position the text. Also, most Windows fonts are proportionally spaced. If an application needs to know the exact dimensions of the area used to draw the text, it can use the **CDC** member functions **GetTextExtent** or **GetOutputTextExtent**.

Prototype
```
//Function Prototype
//virtual BOOL TextOut ( int x, int y, LPCSTR lpszString, int nCount);
//virtual BOOL TextOut ( int x, int y, const CString& str);
    //Assume that we have a valid pointer to a DC
    //because most drawing is done from
    //the OnDraw member function of the view....
pDC->TextOut( rClientArea.left, rClientArea.top,
    "Hello World ! ", strlen("Hello World !"));
    //Draw the string in the upper left corner
    //of the client area....
```

UpdateColors   FUNCTION

Description **CDC::UpdateColors** updates the colors of a window's client area pixel by pixel, if the application has a realized custom (logical) palette, in response to changes in the system palette. It is useful for updating inactive windows because it is faster than redrawing the window. This is not an automatic process—it does not happen in response to the palette's changing. It is a low-cost way to match to a new palette (as compared to updating the entire window).

Color-intensive applications that monitor the WM_PALETTECHANGED, WM_PALETTEISCHANGING and WM_QUERYPALETTE messages use **CDC::UpdateColors** as a quick way to respond when an application that has the input focus changes the system palette, removing some color entries that were used to paint its window. **CDC::UpdateColors** replaces one pixel at a time in the application's client area, matching the new and old colors as closely as possible, based on the new composition of the palette. There is no grand logic to this process, so after it is done there may be some degradation, particularly for dithered colors. Successive calls tend to accumulate color degradation.

Prototype

```
//Function Prototype
//void UpdateColors( );
        //We get a message telling us that the
        //system palette has been modified....
pDC->UpdateColors( );
```

Dialog

CLASS

Derivation

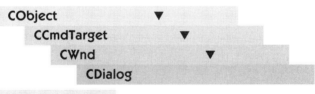

Derived Classes
CFileDialog
CColorDialog
CFontDialog
CPrintDialog
CFindReplaceDialog

Description **CDialog** is the common base class for modal and modeless dialog boxes. (Modal dialog boxes demand that users close them before an application can continue, and modeless dialog can move around the screen and allow the user access to other tools while the dialog is displayed.) This allows interaction with other parts of the UI without dismissing the dialog box. It is handy if both the facilities of the menus/client area and those provided by the dialog box are required simultaneously. A good example is a modeless search box, where the user can continue editing, then click a button and resume the search operation.

The normal way the modeless dialog box communicates with the client application is by either posting or sending messages. This is a convoluted process of finding the window, then using the returned object to invoke PostMessage.

Warning: ClassWizard supplies a default call to the base class implementation **CDialog::OnOk** and **CDialog::OnCancel**, for the Ok and Cancel handlers. You *must* remove these from the handlers of modeless dialogs if you want them to work correctly.

CDialog objects are specialized **CWnd** objects, in that the dialog object must be associated with a template defining its visible appearance. The **CDialog** object gets the dialog template from the application's resource file. A **CDialog**-derived class usually includes member variables for data from each control. After the application's dialog member variables are declared, **ClassWizard** sets up a data exchange map that allows the framework to automatically initialize controls. The DDX/DDV mechanism collects data from them at various times during the dialog's life, and after the dialog box closes, assigns the data to the appropriate member variables, validating the data according to range and type criteria set by the application. ClassWizard creates an override of the **CWnd::DoDataExchange** function and adds it to the application's dialog class to do the data exchange and validation.

Modeless dialogs have to override the **OnCancel** member function to ensure that the **CDialog** object will be completely removed when the dialog box closes. Modeless dialogs can't use the base class **OnCancel** function because it destroys the dialog window without destroying the dialog object. The override has to call **CWnd::DestroyWindow** to destroy the object in addition to the window and override **PostNcDestroy** to invoke the **delete** operator to dispose of the object identified by the **this** pointer.

The point of all of this is that you have to call **DestroyWindow** to dump the dialog box. This destroys the dialog window *and all child windows*. This last part is important because you can reasonably expect every contained control to be destroyed when you destroy the dialog window. Destroying the window does not, however, remove the abstraction used to refer to it. That's why we delete the object in response to the **PostNcDestroy** message.

CDialog is a base class for several framework classes as well as being the base class for user-derived dialog classes. Many of the base class functions are used by the framework to implement basic dialog behavior, but would not likely be called by applications. In these cases, code examples are omitted for member functions.

CDialog has three constructors. The first two are used to create modal dialogs. One uses a string containing the dialog template name, and the other uses the resource ID of the dialog template to load information about the layout of the dialog from the resource file. The second parameter identifies the parent **CWnd** of the dialog. If this parameter is omitted or **NULL**, the parent is set to the application's frame window.

The constructor for the modeless dialog is a protected member function that takes no parameters because you have to derive a class from **CDialog** to implement one. Construction of the modeless dialog is done in two steps. First the object is created with the constructor, and then either **Create** or **CreateIndirect** is called to initialize the object and optionally show the dialog.

Prototype

```
//Function Prototypes
//CDialog(LPCTSTR lpszTemplateName, CWnd* pParentWnd);
//CDialog(UINT nIDTemplate, CWnd* pParentWnd);
//CDialog( );
    //Creating a modal dialog, initializing it by loading
    //the template with ID "OURDIALOG" and launching it
CDialog("OURDIALOG").DoModal( );
```

This last line of code is interesting inasmuch as it presents a dialog box that retains no state. It may have side effects, but you can't do any DDX/DDV. As most dialog boxes are presented to solicit information and communicate it back to the application, this is not a common way to invoke a dialog. In most cases you derive a dialog object from the base class, incorporating whatever data members you need to store and exchange information passed between the user and the dialog.

Overrides

Overridable Function Name	Override to
OnInitDialog	Specialized dialog initialization.
OnSetFont	Change the default font used by the dialog box.
OnOK	Do OK button processing in a modal dialog. Do not use this function in a modeless dialog box.
OnCancel	Do Cancel or Escape processing in a modal dialog. Do not use this function in a modeless dialog box.

Member Functions

Create   FUNCTION

Description   Calling the **Create** member function is the second step in the creation of a modeless dialog box function. **Create** uses the dialog box template stored in the application's resource file to paint the dialog in the client area. Two forms of the **Create** function are supplied: one that loads the template by name and the other that loads it by resource ID. If the template includes the Windows style **WS_VISIBLE**, the dialog is displayed when **Create** returns. Otherwise, the application must call **CWnd::ShowWindow** to make the dialog appear.

Prototype
```
//Function Prototypes
//BOOL Create(LPCTSTR lpszTemplateName, CWnd* pParentWnd);
//BOOL Create(UINT nIDTemplate, CWnd* pParentWnd);
    //Construct a new CDialog-derived object on the heap
COurDialog* pOurDialog = new COurDialog( );
    //Initialize the dialog by using a template
    //with the ID OUR_MODELESS_DLG
pOurDialog->Create(OUR_MODELESS_DLG);
```

Given the fact that the resource editors in Visual C++ assign ordinals to resources by default, a more typical example uses the integral constant.

CreateIndirect   FUNCTION

Description   **CreateIndirect** can be used in place of **Create** for the second stage in modeless dialog box creation if the dialog template is already in memory. **lpDialogTemplate** is a pointer to a **DLGTEMPLATE**, which specifies the overall dimensions and attributes of the dialog box. It is normally followed by three variable-length arrays that specify the menu, class and style of the dialog box. If you specify 0x0000 for the first element, then it is assumed that none of the arrays contain values. If, however, this element is set to 0xFFFF, then the array has an additional element that is taken as the ID of a menu resource.

If the **DS_SETFONT** style is set, a 16-bit WORD follows the three arrays, which contains the point size, followed by a variable-length array that contains the face name.

Finally, there are a variable number of **DLGITEMTEMPLATE** structures, the number depending on the value of the **cdit** member of the **DLGTEMPLATE** part.

Prototype
```
//Function Prototype
//BOOL CreateIndirect(const void FAR* lpDialogTemplate,
//CWnd* pParentWnd);
```

DoModal   FUNCTION

Description   **DoModal** is called immediately after creation of a modal dialog box. It handles all painting and updating for standard control types in the dialog, and when the user clicks **OK** or **Cancel**, calls the **OnOK** or **OnCancel** message handler. *See **CDialog** for a usage example.*

Prototype
```
//Function Prototype
//virtual int DoModal( );
```

EndDialog   FUNCTION

Description   **EndDialog** sets a flag that closes a modal dialog box as soon as the most recently called message handler returns. Its parameter supplies the return value for the function **DoModal**, which initiates a modal dialog.

Prototype
```
//Function Prototype
//void EndDialog( int nResult );
    //This is the OnOK handler for a CDialog-derived object
    //named CCustListDlg
void CCustListDlg::OnOK( )
{
    //This function gets a signed value
    //from the control identified by nID
    //and saves it in a class member
    //variable named m_dlgIntValue
  m_dlgIntValue = GetDlgItemInt(nID, &bOk);
    //Then we close the dialog
  EndDialog(IDOK);
}
```

GetDefID   FUNCTION

Description   **GetDefID** retrieves the ID of the default control of the dialog box. The default is usually associated with the OK button.

Prototype
```
//Function Prototype
//DWORD GetDefID( ) const;
```

GotoDlgCtrl   FUNCTION

Description   **GotoDlgCtrl** moves the input focus to the dialog box control identified by the **CWnd** pointer. This function is used by the framework to transfer the input focus when the user presses the mouse button over a control. This function is used by Windows. The framework encapsulates the WM_NEXTDLGCTL message in this function. (It uses different parameters than the **NextDlgCtrl** function.)

Prototype
```
//Function Prototype
//void GotoDlgCtrl(CWnd* pwndControl );
```

InitModalIndirect   FUNCTION

Description   **InitModalIndirect** is used to create a modal dialog from a memory-resident dialog template. To do this, the application must call the **CDialog** constructor without any arguments, allocate a chunk of global memory, write the dialog template to it, and call **InitModalIndirect** to initialize the **CDialog**. The dialog box does not become visible until the application calls **DoModal**.

Prototype
```
//Function Prototype
//BOOL InitModalIndirect(HGLOBAL hDialogTemplate);
```

IsDialogMessage   FUNCTION

Description   **IsDialogMessage** tests whether a particular message is for this modeless dialog box and processes the message if it is a message for the dialog that did the test. **IsDialogMessage** returns TRUE if it processes the message, and FALSE if it does not. This function is used by the framework in determining how to handle message pre-translation for dialog box controls. This function is only neccessary if (1) You are doing **PreTranslateMessage** overrides that do not call the base class implementation; and (2) You have a modeless dialog box. The reason is that modal dialog boxes have their own message pumps, and therefore their own **GetMessage/ TranslateMessage/DispatchMessage** loops. Modeless dialog boxes use the application's message pump, so the distinction between messages intended for the app and those intended for the dialog box are important.

Prototype

```
//Function Prototype
//BOOL IsDialogMessage( LPMSG lpMessage );
```

MapDialogRect   FUNCTION

Description **MapDialogRect** converts the dimensions in the **RECT** data structure from dialog units to screen units. A dialog unit is one-fourth the average character height or width for the font being used by the dialog.

Prototype

```
//Function Prototype
//void MapDialogRect( LPRECT lpRect);
```

NextDlgCtrl   FUNCTION

Description **NextDlgCtrl** moves the input focus to the next dialog box control. This function is used by the framework to transfer the input focus when the user presses the Tab key. This function is used by Windows. The framework encapsulates the WM_NEXTDLGCTL message in this function.

Prototype

```
//Function Prototype
//void NextDlgCtrl( ) const;
```

PrevDlgCtrl   FUNCTION

Description **PrevDlgCtrl** moves the input focus to the previous dialog box control. This function is used by the framework to transfer the input focus when the user presses the Shift and Tab keys together. This function is used by Windows. The framework encapsulates the WM_NEXTDLGCTL message in this function.

Prototype

```
//Function Prototype
//void PrevDlgCtrl( ) const;
```

SetDefID · FUNCTION

Description   **SetDefID** sets the ID of the default control of the dialog box. It also changes the appearance both of the previous default control and the new default control.

Prototype
```
//Function Prototype
//void SetDefID( UINT nID );
```

SetHelpID · FUNCTION

Description   **SetHelpID** sets the context-sensitive help ID.

Prototype
```
//Function Prototype
//void SetHelpID( UINT nID );
```

DialogBar · CLASS

Derivation

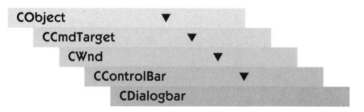

CObject
CCmdTarget
CWnd
CControlBar
CDialogbar

Description   The **CDialogBar** class implements a type of Windows control bar that behaves as a modeless dialog box that exists in a control bar. A dialog bar is an alternative to the form view. A dialog template defines its appearance and child controls. Templates used to create dialog bars specify the WS_CHILD style only. The **CDialogBar** class constructor creates the **CDialogBar** object, which is initialized and attached to a dialog window by the member function **Create**. The application must provide handler code for the dialog box controls.

Member Functions

CDialogBar	FUNCTION

Description   **CDialogBar** constructs a dialog bar object, but doesn't create or show the dialog bar window.

```
//Example
    //Construct a Dialog bar object
CDialogBar    m_OurDialogBar;
    //We create it in the parent frame window's implementation,
    //load the template by name, align the dialog box with the
//left side of the frame
    //window, and set dialog bar's control ID
m_OurDialogBar.Create(this, lspzTemplateName, CBRS_LEFT,
    ID_DIALOGBAR) ;
```

Create	FUNCTION

Description   **Create** creates the dialog window based on the application's dialog template and connects it to the **CDialogBar** object. Version 3.0 of MFC includes some new features for the **CDialogBar** class. Dockable or floating control bars are implemented in **CControlBar**, but deserve mention here. To make a dialog bar dockable, write the following code in your mainframe **OnCreate** function:

```
m_cbar.EnableDocking(CBRS_ALIGN_ANY);
EnableDocking(CBRS_ALIGN_ANY);
DockControlBar(&m_cbar);
```

Tool-Tips. These are enabled in a multi-stage process. First, in the **Create** function *or* in the CBRS_TOOLTIPS constant. Second, edit your string table, and for each ID on the dialog bar, add a string with the same ID that consists of two parts: "part to be displayed on the status bar\ntool-tip". These too are implemented in **CControlBar**.

*See **CDialogBar** for a usage example.*

Prototype
```
//Function Prototype
//BOOL Create(CWnd* pParentWnd, LPCTSTR lpszTemplateName,
//    UINT nStyle, UINT nID);
```

Document

Derivation

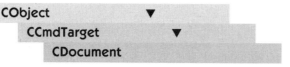

CObject
    CCmdTarget
        CDocument

Description

CDocument provides a base class for derivation of user-defined documents. A document encapsulates the data source a user accesses, generally by using the File Open and File Save commands. The **CDocument** class provides basic operations, such as opening or creating a document, but the application-derived document class members and overrides do the real work of manipulating the document.

Even though this class is provided by the framework to model a data source, there is no hard and fast tie between how the data is accessed and a **CDocument** object. For example, perhaps the user will have a CGolfCourseDoc for a golf game—this kind of document might be preopened by the application (or if not, it would be accessed by using something such as Game.Load New Course, but not File.Open).

User documents are created by deriving a class for each type of document the application will handle and adding member variables to each class to store document data. Member functions must be written to read and update the document in ways specific to the application. Many of these functions are called by the view in response to input from the user. The base class functions for serializing and deserializing (saving and loading) the document must be overridden by the application so that it can move its data to and from disk.

The data in the document is rendered by an associated **CView** object. The view and the document are connected by a document template, which specifies their relationship, usually in the application's **InitInstance** member function. However, there is no law stating that the binding between a document and a view occurs in **InitInstance**, and in at least one case it's desirable to perform this binding later: when you are switching views in place (that is, the old one disappears and is replaced by the new one).

A document may have more than one view attached to it. For example, a spreadsheet might render its data as rows and columns of figures, as a bar chart, or as both. The document receives commands from its active view and either handles them or passes them on to the document template to which it belongs. When a document changes its data, it communicates with its views by means of its **UpdateAllViews** function. This function tells all the views that they need to repaint themselves.

Overrides

Overridable Function	Triggering Event
CanCloseFrame	A frame window viewing this document is about to close.
DeleteContents	Emptying the document.
OnChangedViewList	A view is added to or removed from the document.
OnCloseDocument	The document is closing.
OnNewDocument	A document is being created.
OnOpenDocument	An existing document is being opened.
OnSaveDocument	A document is being saved to disk.
ReportSaveLoadException	An open or save to disk failed.
SaveModified	Prompting the user for a decision on whether to save a changed document.

Member Functions

AddView   FUNCTION

Description   **AddView** is not often called by application code, but can be extremely useful if you have an SDI app with multiple views of the same data. You can, in response to some menu command, **RemoveView** the old view and then **AddView** the new view. It is used by the framework to attach an existing view object to the view list for a document. File New, File Open, New Window and a split of a splitter window trigger a framework call to **AddView**.

Prototype
```
//Function Prototype
//void AddView(CView* pView);
pView = new CMyView; // Default ctor must be public
AddView(pView);
```

GetDocTemplate   FUNCTION

Description   **GetDocTemplate** retrieves a pointer to the document template that associates this document type with a view and a frame window.

Prototype
```
//Function Prototype
//CDocTemplate* GetDocTemplate( );
    //We want a pointer to the document template
CDocTemplate* pTemplate = GetDocTemplate( );
    //so that we can get information about default document
    //attributes; In this case, we are retrieving the
    //default root filename for a new document
    //of this type
pTemplate->GetDocString(rString, CDocTemplate::docName);
```

GetFirstViewPosition   FUNCTION

Description   **GetFirstViewPosition** retrieves a **POSITION** value for the first view in the list of views attached to this document. This sounds a bit obtuse because the first view obviously also has the first position, but the **POSITION** value is necessary to navigate the view list by using list member functions.

Prototype
```
//Function Prototype
//POSITION GetFirstViewPosition( ) const;
BOOL bVisible = FALSE;
    //Get the head of the view list
POSITION pos = GetFirstViewPosition( );
while (pos != NULL)
{
    //While the position is valid, iterate the list
  CView* pView = GetNextView(pos);
    //Get a pointer to the parent frame window
  CFrameWnd* pFrameWnd = pView->GetParentFrame( );
    //If the parent is visible, set a flag and break
  if (pFrameWnd->GetStyle( ) & WS_VISIBLE)
    {
      bVisible = TRUE;
        break;
    }
}
```

GetNextView   FUNCTION

Description   **GetNextView** is a companion function to **GetFirstViewPosition**. Its parameter is the **POSITION** returned by either **GetFirstViewPosition** or a previous call to **GetNextView**. *See **GetFirstViewPosition** for a usage example.*

Prototype
```
//Function Prototype
//CView* GetNextView(POSITION& rPosition) const;
```

GetPathName   FUNCTION

Description   **GetPathName** retrieves the fully qualified pathname for the document's disk file.

Prototype
```
//Function Prototype
//const CString& GetPathName( )const;
    //Get the fully qualified pathname for a document file and
    //compare it to a stored path
if (lstrcmpi(pDoc->GetPathName( ), pszPathName) == 0)
{
    //If they are identical, this document is already open
  return DOC_IS_OPEN;
}
```

GetTitle   FUNCTION

Description   **GetTitle** retrieves the document's title, which usually bears a strong resemblance to the document's file name. One difference is that a document can have a title even if it is not represented on disk. The pathname specifies the location of documents that are physically present on disk.

Prototype
```
//Function Prototype
//const CString& GetTitle( )const;
    //Copy the document title to a local buffer
lstrcpy(szDocTitle, pDocument->GetTitle( ));
```

IsModified — FUNCTION

Description   **IsModified** tests whether the document's data has changed since the last save.

Prototype
```
//Function Prototype
//BOOL IsModified( );
    //Say we have a paint program and get an Edit Clear All
    //command....We check to see whether the user has done any
    //drawing on this document
if (IsModified( ))
    //If so, we delete the contents of the document
  DeleteContents( );
    //And set the modified flag to false pending the first new
    //drawing operation
SetModifiedFlag(FALSE);
```

RemoveView — FUNCTION

Description   **RemoveView** is the companion function to **AddView**. It removes but does not delete a view from a document's view list. This task is automatically handled by the framework and is usually triggered by the closing of an MDI child window, a frame window or a splitter window pane.

Prototype
```
//Function Prototype
//void RemoveView( CView* pView );
RemoveView(pOldView);
delete pOldView;
```

SetModifiedFlag — FUNCTION

Description   **SetModifiedFlag** flags the document as changed. When the flag is set, the framework automatically asks the user whether the document should be saved before it is closed. *See **IsModified** for a usage example.*

Prototype
```
//Function Prototype
//BOOL SetModifiedFlag( BOOL bModified = TRUE);
```

SetPathName
FUNCTION

Description **SetPathName** sets the pathname for a document's disk file. Applications call this function in functions that override the framework's default File Open and File Save behavior.

Prototype
```
//Function Prototype
//void SetPathName(LPCTSTR lpszPathName, BOOL bAddToMRU);
    //Set the new pathname and add this filename to the most
    //recently used list
pSaveDoc->SetPathName(strFileName, TRUE);
```

SetTitle
FUNCTION

Description **SetTitle** sets the text string displayed in the caption bar of the frame window that contains the document's view. If the document is displayed in more than one window, this function updates all the caption bars.

Prototype
```
//Function Prototype
//void SetTitle(LPCTSTR pszTitle);
    //We have a pointer to the document, and we want to set the
    //caption bar text for all the windows in which it
    //is displayed....
pDocument->SetTitle(stringDocumentName);
```

UpdateAllViews
FUNCTION

Description **UpdateAllViews** tells all of the document's views that the document's data has changed and that the views should render the new data. This function is usually called in conjunction with SetModifiedFlag, from the view class. Because documents don't often change themselves, this function is most often called from a CView-derived class. Note that the first argument, pSender, is a pointer to the view that requests the global update. It's assumed that the sending view will have already handled its own updating, so it is skipped when OnUpdate is called for all the views. To *really* update all views, pass NULL for this parameter. The next two arguments are hints that can allow the views to do smarter repainting.

Prototype
```
//Function Prototype
//void UpdateAllViews(CView* pSender, LPARAM lHint,
//CObject* pHint)
    //In the view class, we get a
    //pointer to the document associated with the view
    //and tell all the other views that the
    //user has changed the data in the document
    //interacting with our view
GetDocument->UpdateAllViews( this );
```

C DumpContext

● ●

Description   A **CDumpContext** object mediates dumping of object contents at runtime, providing an important diagnostic tool to the programmer. Because diagnostics in general are debugging features, the **CDumpContext** is intended for use with the debugging version of the framework libraries.

The **CDumpContext** object is connected to a **CFile** object that receives the dump output. Any object derived from **CObject** inherits the base class **Dump** member function, which uses **afxDump** to dump the base class members. To dump its own objects, the application should override **CObject::Dump.** The override function calls the base class function and then dumps the member variables of the application's derived class using the **CDumpContext** insertion operator. In most cases, an application can use the predefined **CDumpContext** object **afxDump** to dump the contents of its objects.

Example
```
//Override the base class Dump function — note that we only
    //include the diagnostic code in debug builds
#ifdef _DEBUG
void OurObject::Dump( CDumpContext &dcDumpContext )
{
    //First call the base class Dump function
CObject::Dump( dcDumpContext );
```

```
    //Then dump the member vars of our object using
    //the dump context insertion operator
dcDumpContext << "First Member:" <<m_OurFirstMem << "\n"<<
"and so on...";
}
#endif
#ifdef _DEBUG
    //Later we use the prebuilt afxDump object to dump our
    //object's members
pOurObject->Dump( afxDump );
#endif
```

Member Functions

CDumpContext	FUNCTION

Description   **CDumpContext** constructs an object of the class, but does not connect it to an output file. If an application constructs its own **CDumpContext object,** it must explicitly construct a **CFile** object first and pass a pointer to the open file to the **CDumpContext** constructor. For any object derived from **CObject**, the prebuilt **afxDump** object is available, so it is not necessary to use the **CDumpContext** constructor, unless you want to direct dump output to a file. **afxDump** is sort of a standard stream, much like cerr in the iostream library. It's available to any object at any time. Dump, however, is implemented as a virtual function in CObject, and it is most likely to take advantage of **afxDump**. **afxDump<<** is an alternative to TRACE.

Prototype

```
//Function Prototype
//CDumpContext(CFile* pFile);
    //First create a CFile object and open its file
CFile fileDumpDestination;
fileDumpDestination.open( "diagfile.dmp", CFile::modeCreate |
CFile::modeWrite );
    //The call the CDumpContext constructor,
    //passing the output file
CDumpContext dcOurDumpContext( &fileDumpDestination );
    //Get the dump depth setting — if this is
    //a shallow dump, make it deep —
    //which is to say, follow CObject pointers
    //embedded in this object and dump
    //their data recursively
```

413

```
if(dcOurDumpContext.GetDepth( ) == 0)
  dcOurDumpContext.SetDepth( 1 );
    //Send a hex-formatted dump to our output file
  dcOurDumpContext.HexDump( "Flag bytes are:", pbFlagBuffer,
iFourBytesPerLine );
    //Flush the dump context buffers
  dcOurDumpContext.Flush( );
    //Close the file
  fileDumpDestination.Close( );
```

Flush   FUNCTION

Description   **Flush** flushes buffered dump output to the dump file destination. *See **CDumpContext** for a usage example.*

Prototype
```
//Function Prototype
//void Flush( )
```

GetDepth   FUNCTION

Description   **GetDepth** returns the dump depth setting of the **CDumpContext** object. It is the companion function to **SetDepth**. The depth of a dump specifies the degree to which dumping will follow object pointers embedded in the object being dumped. The concept of "deep" dumping (and deep copying) has to do with the fact that a class in C++ is often derived from other classes. Each of these classes contributes state information and is therefore responsible for dumping its own contribution. A shallow dump dumps the contribution only for the object on which it is invoked, and a deep dump effectively dumps the state of the entire object.

A depth of 0 just dumps the data of the object for which it is called. A depth greater than zero follows **CObject** pointers and dumps data recursively. *See **CDumpContext** for a usage example.*

Prototype
```
//Function Prototype
//int GetDepth( )const;
```

HexDump   FUNCTION

Description   **HexDump** labels a dump output line with the string identified by pszLabelText and follows it with a hexadecimal dump of the buffer identified by pBytesToDump. *See **CDumpContext** for a usage example.*

Prototype
```
//Function Prototype
//void HexDump(LPCTSTR pszLine, BYTE* pby, int nBytes,
//          int nWidth);
```

The text specified in the first argument appears at the beginning of each line. If the dump spans multiple lines, the text appears more than once. It can therefore be useful to do something like this:

```
afxDump << "Memory area:\n";
afxDump.HexDump("", pThing, sizeof Thing, 16);
```

operator <<   OPERATOR

Description The insertion operator writes data to the dump file. It is overloaded to handle all fundamental data types, strings, and **CObject** pointers. *See the Introduction for a usage example.*

SetDepth   FUNCTION

Description **SetDepth** sets the dump depth of the **CDumpContext** object. *See **CDumpContext** for a usage example.*

Prototype
```
//Function Prototype
//void SetDepth( int DumpDepth );
```

C DWordArray   CLASS

See **CObArray**.

CEdit

CLASS

Derivation

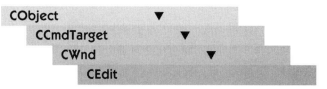

```
CObject        ▼
   CCmdTarget      ▼
      CWnd            ▼
         CEdit
```

Description The **CEdit** class encapsulates the Windows edit control. Edit controls are simplified word-processing tools that have the flavor of the Windows Notepad utility. They handle multiple lines of text, basic Clipboard operations, and Undo operations. Edit controls can be displayed in an application's client area by constructing a **CEdit** object and calling the **Create** member function to build and attach an edit window.

If an application creates edit controls independently of a dialog box, form view or dialog bar, steps must be taken to ensure that the object associated with the control is properly destroyed. Stack-based **CEdit** objects are always destroyed when the window containing them closes, but in practice they are seldom used, as they never "live" long enough to be displayed. **CEdit** objects created on the heap with **new** should be deleted with **delete**.

Member Functions

CanUndo **FUNCTION**

Description **CanUndo** returns non-zero if the last edit operation can be undone with the Undo member function.

Prototype
```
//Function Prototype
//BOOL CanUndo( )const;
    //If we can undo the last edit
if( edOurEditControl.CanUndo( ) )
    //Then undo it
    edOurEditControl.Undo( );
```

CEdit   FUNCTION

Description **CEdit** constructs a **CEdit** object, but does not create, attach, or initialize its accompanying edit control window.

Prototype
```
//Function Prototype
//void CMyView::OnInitialUpdate();
```

Clear   FUNCTION

Description **Clear** removes a selection highlight from the edit control text, but does not place the text on the clipboard. Use **Cut** to remove both text to the clipboard.

Prototype
```
//Function Prototype
//void Clear( );
    //Get the character index for the first character of the line with
    // the caret
int iCharIndex = pOurEditControl->LineIndex( -1 );
    //Get the length of the line with the caret in it
int iLineLen = pOurEditControl->LineLength( -1 );
    //Set the entire line as the current selection
int iLineLen = pOurEditControl->SetSel( iCharIndex , iCharIndex +
iLineLen );
    //Do a "Cut" in two steps
    //Copy selection to the Clipboard
pOurEdit->Copy( );
    //Remove the selected text
pOurEdit->Clear( );
```

Copy   FUNCTION

Description **Copy** copies the selected text from an edit control and places it in the Windows Clipboard in CF_TEXT format. *See **Clear** for a usage example.*

Prototype
```
//Function Prototype
//void Copy( );
```

Create
FUNCTION

Description   **Create** creates a Windows edit control, attaches it to the **CEdit** object, and shows it. Edit control properties are determined by style constants, which may be combined with one another using the bitwise OR (|). They are listed in the following table.

Edit Control Style	Meaning
ES_LEFT	Flush text left.
ES_CENTER	Center the text.
ES_RIGHT	Flush text right.
ES_MULTILINE	Word wrap at edge of control if the ES_AUTOVSCROLL style is set; use hard carriage returns to start new lines if ES_AUTOHSCROLL style is set.
ES_UPPERCASE	All text is uppercase.
ES_LOWERCASE	All text is lowercase.
ES_PASSWORD	Displays all characters input to the edit control as "*".
ES_AUTOVSCROLL	Scrolls up one page when the user presses Enter at the last line.
ES_AUTOHSCROLL	Scrolls right ten characters when input hits right edge of frame; new line on Enter.
ES_NOHIDESEL	Prevents control from hiding selection when it loses the input focus.
ES_OEMCONVERT	Does ANSI/OEM character conversion.
ES_READONLY	Doesn't allow the user to modify the text.
ES_WANTRETURN	Inserts hard carriage returns in text where user enters them. Without ES_WANTRETURN, when the user presses Enter, the keystroke is propagated to the parent (which, if it is a dialog, causes the default button to be pushed).

Prototype
```
//Function Prototype
//BOOL Create(DWORD dwStyle, const RECT& rect,
//CWnd* pParentWnd, UINT nID);
```

Cut
FUNCTION

Description   **Cut** removes the selected text from an edit control and places it in the Windows Clipboard in CF_TEXT format.

Prototype
```
//Function Prototype
//void Cut( );
    //Get the character index for the first character of the line
    //with the caret
int iCharIndex = pOurEditControl->LineIndex( -1 );
    //Get the length of the line with the caret in it
int iLineLen = pOurEditControl->LineLength( -1 );
    //Set the entire line as the current selection
int iLineLen = pOurEditControl->SetSel( iCharIndex ,
        iCharIndex + iLineLen );
    //Do a "Cut" in just one step
pOurEdit->Cut( );
    //Paste the string right back
pOurEdit->Paste( );
```

EmptyUndoBuffer — FUNCTION

Description   **EmptyUndoBuffer** clears the Undo flag of the edit control buffer. This prevents undoing of the last edit operation. *See **GetModify** for a usage example.*

Prototype
```
//Function Prototype
//void EmptyUndoBuffer( );
```

FmtLines — FUNCTION

Description   **FmtLines** toggles the insertion of soft carriage returns for word wrapping in multiline edit controls. It makes no visible difference in the way the text is displayed in the control. If text is retrieved from the control by using a handle or in response to the Windows message **WM_GETTEXT**, end of line is marked by a pair of carriage returns if **FmtLines** set the insertion flag to **TRUE**.

Prototype
```
//Function Prototype
//BOOL FmtLines( BOOL bAddEOL )const;
    //Set soft carriage returns in text
pOurEdit->FmtLines( TRUE );
```

GetHandle   FUNCTION

Description   **GetHandle** returns a handle to the memory buffer containing the text. If the edit control is part of a dialog box, the box must have set the DS_LOCALEDIT style or the handle can't be used to access the memory buffer.

Prototype
```
//Function Prototype
//HLOCAL GetHandle( )const;
    //Get the offset in the buffer of the first character of the line
    //where the caret is
int iThisLine =  pOurEdit->LineIndex( -1 );
    //NT uses unicode, so we multiply by 8 to get the byte offset
    //into the buffer
iThisLine =  * sizeof(TCHAR)/8;
    //Get a handle to the memory used to hold the text
HLOCAL hEditText = pOurEdit->GetHandle( );
```

GetLine   FUNCTION

Description   **GetLine** gets a line specified by a zero-based index from an edit control. The function returns the number of bytes copied, or if the nIndex argument is 0, the value returned is the index of the first line. The returned line is not NULL terminated.

Prototype
```
//Function Prototype
//int GetLine( int nIndex, LPSTR lpszBuffer )const;
//int GetLine( int nIndex, LPSTR lpszBuffer, int nMaxLen )const;
    //Find the zero-based index of the line the caret is on
int iCurrentLine = pOurEditControl->LineFromChar( -1 );
    //Retrieve the text in the current line of the
    //edit control
int iFirstVisible = pOurEditControl->GetLine( iCurrentLine , lpszBuffer
);
```

GetLineCount   FUNCTION

Description   **GetLineCount** returns a count of lines in a multiline edit control. *See CEdit for a usage example.*

Prototype
```
//Function Prototype
//int GetLineCount( )const;
```

GetModify — FUNCTION

Description   **GetModify** tests whether the edit buffer has been modified. The flag can be cleared by using **SetModify.**

Prototype

```
//Function Prototype
//BOOL GetModify( )const;
    //Has the control text been modified?
if (pOurEditControl->GetModify( ))
{
    //If so, clear the buffer
    pOurEditControl->Clear( );
    //Set modified flag to false
    pOurEditControl->SetModify(FALSE);
    //And now make the control read-only
    pOurEditControl->SetReadOnly(TRUE);
    //And clear the EditUndo flag
    pOurEditControl->EmptyUndoBuffer( );
}
```

GetRect — FUNCTION

Description   **GetRect** gets the current clipping rectangle in which the edit control can draw text. The clipping rectangle can be set using either **SetRect** or **SetRectNP**.

Prototype

```
//Function Prototype
//void GetRect( LPRECT lpRect );
```

GetSel — FUNCTION

Description   **GetSel** reports the zero-based starting and ending character positions of text selected in the edit control. The ending position is the first *unselected* character after the selected string.

Prototype

```
//Function Prototype
//DWORD GetSel( )const;
// void GetSel(int& nStartChar, int& nEndChar) const;
    //If there is no selected text in the edit control
if (pOurEditControl->GetSel( ) == NULL)
    //Select the whole string
    pOurEditControl->SetSel( 0, -1);
```

LimitText   FUNCTION

Description **LimitText** limits the number of characters a user can enter from the keyboard. It doesn't constrain the amount of text that can be copied to the control by using the **CWnd::SetWindowText** member function or changing the amount of text already in the control. The user can edit any existing text in the control, even if its length is greater than the limit set by **LimitText**.

Prototype
```
//Function Prototype
//void LimitText( int nChars=0 );
```

LineFromChar   FUNCTION

Description **LineFromChar** returns the zero-based line index of the line in which the character with the specified index occurs. Specify a character index of -1 to get the index for the line that contains the caret. *See **GetLine** for a usage example.*

Prototype
```
//Function Prototype
//int LineFromChar( int iLineIndex = -1)const;
```

LineIndex   FUNCTION

Description **LineIndex** returns the zero-based character index for the beginning of the line with the specified index. Specify a line index of -1 to get the index for the first character of the line that contains the caret. Portable code translates this into a byte offset by using the formula: nByteOffset = LineFromChar() * sizeof TCHAR. This is a Win32-specific feature and only applies to buffers obtained using GetHandle.

Prototype
```
//Function Prototype
//int LineIndex( int nLine = -1)const;
    //Get the character index for the first character of the line with
    //the caret
int iCharIndex = pOurEditControl->LineIndex( -1 );
    //Get the length of the line with the caret in it
int iLineLen = pOurEditControl->LineLength( -1 );
    //Set the entire line as the current selection
int iLineLen = pOurEditControl->SetSel( iCharIndex , iCharIndex +
    iLineLen );
    //Replace the current selection
pOurEditControl->ReplaceSel( "Replacement text" );
```

LineScroll   FUNCTION

Description **LineScroll** scrolls an edit control vertically and (optionally) horizontally. If the vertical scrolling parameter would scroll the last line out of view, the function would scroll only the last line to the top of the edit control window. Scrolling horizontally beyond the end of a line is permitted.

Prototype
```
//Function Prototype
//int LineScroll( int nLines, int nChars = 0);
    //Scroll vertically 5 lines, horizontally 10 chars
pOurEditControl->LineScroll( 5,10);
```

Paste   FUNCTION

Description **Paste** copies the selected text from the Windows Clipboard into an edit control at the current insertion point. *See **Cut** for a usage example.*

Prototype
```
//Function Prototype
//void Paste( );
```

PrototypeLineLength   FUNCTION

Description **LineLength** retrieves the line length for the line in which the character with the specified index occurs. Specify a line index of -1 to get the length for the first character of the line that contains the caret. *See **LineIndex** for a usage example.*

Prototype
```
//Function Prototype
//int LineLength( int nLine = -1)const;
```

ReplaceSel   FUNCTION

Description **ReplaceSel** replaces the selected text with the string identified by the parameter. *See **LineIndex** for a usage example.*

Prototype
```
//Function Prototype
//void ReplaceSel( LPCSTR lpszNewText );
```

SetHandle   FUNCTION

Description   **SetHandle** is the companion function to **GetHandle.** It sets a handle to the memory buffer to be used for the edit control text. Before setting a new handle, the application must get and free the current handle. Free it with the Windows **LocalFree** function. Setting a new buffer handle clears the Undo buffer.

Prototype
```
//Function Prototype
//void SetHandle( HLOCAL hMemoryBuffer );
    //Get a handle to the memory being used to hold the text
HLOCAL hEditText = pOurEdit->GetHandle( );
    //Free the handle, before we replace it
::LocalFree( hEditText );
    //Set a new buffer handle
pOurEdit->SetHandle( hDifferentBuffer);
    //Note that the call to Invalidate is not necessary here, as
    //the EM_SETHANDLE also signals a repaint.
```

SetModify   FUNCTION

Description   **SetModify** is the companion function to **GetModify**. It sets a flag that tracks whether the edit buffer has been modified. Windows maintains an internal flag that does this for you, so explicitly marking an edit control dirty is seldom necessary. *See **GetModify** for a usage example.*

Prototype
```
//Function Prototype
//SetModify( BOOL  bModified = TRUE );
```

SetReadOnly   FUNCTION

Description   **SetReadOnly** sets the read/write permission for an edit control. To find the current setting, call **CWnd::GetStyle** and test for the **ES_READONLY** flag. *See **GetModify** for a usage example.*

Prototype
```
//Function Prototype
//SetReadOnly( BOOL  bReadOnly = TRUE );
```

SetRect   FUNCTION

Description   **SetRect** sets a limiting rectangle inside the edit control for text entry.

Prototype
```
//Function Prototype
//void SetRect( LPCRECT lpRect )
```

SetRectNP   FUNCTION

Description   **SetRectNP** sets a limiting rectangle inside the edit control for text entry and does not repaint the edit control.

Prototype
```
//Function Prototype
//void SetRectNP( LPCRECT lpRect )
```

SetSel   FUNCTION

Description   **SetSel** sets the zero-based starting and ending character positions of text selected in the edit control. The ending position is the first *unselected* character after the selected string. To remove the selection highlight, pass -1 as the starting position. To select the whole string, pass 0 as the starting position and -1 as the ending position. *See **GetSel** for a usage example.*

Prototype
```
//Function Prototype
//void SetSel( DWORD dwSelection, BOOL bNoScroll = FALSE );
//void SetSel( int nStartChar, int nEndChar, BOOL bNoScroll =
//FALSE );
```

SetTabStops   FUNCTION

Description   **SetTabStops** sets the tab stop width for the view. Tab stops are measured in dialog units, where one unit equals one-fourth the average character width of the selected font. **CEdit** objects handle tab stops differently, so this is one case where the application must not use **CEdit** member functions to directly manipulate the text in the edit control.

Prototype
```
//Function Prototypes
//void SetTabStops(int& cxEachStop);
//void SetTabStops(int nTabStops, LPINT rgTabStops);
pOurEditControl->SetTabStops( iIndent );
```

 EditView   **CLASS**

Derivation

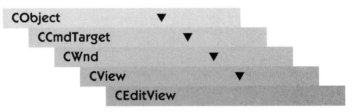

CObject
    CCmdTarget
        CWnd
            CView
                CEditView

Description   **CEditView** provides the functionality of the **CEdit** control class and the **CView** class, with the additional advantages of being attached to a document and a document template and the printing/print preview facilities. **CEditView** handles the following commands:

ID_EDIT_CUT
ID_EDIT_CLEAR
ID_EDIT_PASTE
ID_EDIT_UNDO
ID_EDIT_FIND
ID_EDIT_REPEAT
ID_EDIT_COPY
ID_EDIT_CLEAR
ID_EDIT_SELECT_ALL
ID_EDIT_REPLACE
ID_EDIT_UNDO
ID_FILE_PRINT

Classes may be derived from **CEditView** to change or extend this functionality or to declare classes that can be added to a document template by **CWinApp::AddDocTemplate**.

Overrides

Overridable Function	Triggering Event
OnFindNext	User requests a string search.
OnReplaceAll	User requests global string substitution.
OnReplaceSel	User requests replacement of selected text.
OnTextNotFound	Search text was not found.

Public Data Members

dwStyleDefault   MEMBER

Description   An application that derives a class from the edit view class must call the **CWnd::Create** function after constructing the view. **CWnd::Create** requires a parameter specifying the style of the window being created. This data member is used for the parameter.

Member Functions

CEditView   FUNCTION

Description   **CEditView** constructs an edit view, but the **CWnd** member function **Create** must be called before using the edit view. The call to **Create** is done automatically when a **CEditView** is created dynamically via a document template.

FindText   FUNCTION

Description   **FindText** does a string search either forward or backward through the edit view's text, optionally considering case. If the search text is found, the current selection is set to the text and the function returns TRUE. If you are using a **CEditView**, **FindText** is the underpinning of what ID_EDIT_FIND does, so it is crucial. Note that the added value if you use the framework-supplied stuff is that MFC presents the user with the common find dialog, gets the info, and then does the find. Should you want to "roll your own" find, this is how you do it.

Prototype
```
//Function Prototype
//BOOL FindText( LPCSTR lpszFind, BOOL bNext = TRUE,
//       BOOL bCase = TRUE );
```

GetEditCtrl   FUNCTION

Description   **GetEditCtrl** retrieves a reference to the edit control used by the edit view. The reference can be used to access the view's underlying edit control by using **CEdit** member functions. Be careful when using this function because **CEditView** caches the state of tab settings. You must use the **CEditView** function **SetTabStops** for setting tab stops.

Note: This function, unlike many other MFC functions of the same genre, returns a *reference* to the edit control instead of a pointer. You must, therefore, use object instead of pointer syntax for member-selection.

Prototype
```
//Function Prototypes
//CEdit& GetEditCtrl() const;
    //From a CEditView member, call CEdit functions this way
GetEditCtrl( ).LimitText( MAX_SIZE );
```

GetPrinterFont   FUNCTION

Description **GetPrinterFont** retrieves a pointer to a **CFont** object that defines the selected printer font.

Prototype
```
//Function Prototypes
//CFont* GetPrinterFont() const;

LOGFONT lf;
    //Get the currently set printer font, if there is one
CFont* pFont = GetPrinterFont( );
    //If a pointer to a font object was returned
if (pFont != NULL)
{
    //use the CFont's information to populate a LOGFONT structure
  pFont->GetObject(sizeof(LOGFONT), &lf);
}
```

GetSelectedText   FUNCTION

Description **GetSelectedText** copies into the **CString** reference the current text selection up to the last character of the selection or to the first carriage return.

Prototype
```
//Function Prototypes
//void GetSelectedText(CString& strResult) const;
    //Get the current text selection and test to see whether the
```

```
                        //returned string is empty
                    CString strFind;
                    GetSelectedText(strFind);
                    if (strFind.IsEmpty( ))
                        return NOTHING_SELECTED;
```

PrintInsideRect   FUNCTION

Description   **PrintInsideRect** prints text between specified starting and ending offsets within the text buffer inside a rectangle. This is useful for an implementation of "print selection." The text is wrapped if the view did not specify the ES_AUTOSCROLL style, but it is clipped if this automatic scroll style applies. The function returns the index of the next character to be printed.

Prototype
```
                    //Function Prototypes
                    //UINT PrintInsideRect(CDC* pDC, RECT& rectLayout,
                    //  UINT nIndexStart, UINT nIndexStop);
                        //We call this function in the OnPrint handler to
                        //print as much as possible in the area defined by rectClipping.
                    nStartIndex = PrintInsideRect(pDC, rectClipping, nStartIndex,
                        0xFFFF);
```

SerializeRaw   FUNCTION

Description   **SerializeRaw** moves only the text portion of a **CEditView** object to and from disk, without data describing the object. You can use it to read and write text files from and to disk.

Prototype
```
                    //Function Prototypes
                    //void SerializeRaw(CArchive& ar);
                        //Using a pointer to the view, get or store the text in the edit
                        //view
                        //Called if the application overrides Serialize
                    pView->SerializeRaw(ar);
```

SetPrinterFont   FUNCTION

Description **SetPrinterFont** is called from the **OnPreparePrinting** handler to set the application's font choice. A **CEditView** object can display text in only one font at a time. *See **SetTabStops** for a usage example.*

Prototype
```
//Function Prototypes
//void SetPrinterFont(CFont* pFont);
```

SetTabStops   FUNCTION

Description **SetTabStops** sets the tab stop width for the view. As with fonts, an edit view can have only one tab stop value at a time. Tab stops are measured in dialog units, where one unit equals one-fourth the average character width of the selected font. **CEdit** objects handle tab stops differently, so this is one case in which the application must not use **CEdit** member functions to directly manipulate the text in the edit control.

Prototype
```
//Function Prototypes
//void SetTabStops(int nTabStops);
BOOL CMyView::OnPreparePrinting(CPrintInfo* pInfo)
{
    //Set the tab stops and printer font in the OnPreparePrinting
    //handler,
    //before any painting is done

SetPrinterFont( m_pSelectedFont);
//some calculation of appropriate indent width...
SetPrinterFont( m_pSelectedFont);
//some calculation of appropriate indent width...
//usually set the tab stops relative to the currently
//selected font. Select it first or the settings can be bogus.

SetTabStops( iIndent );
```

C Exception

CLASS

Derivation

Description The **CException** class is the base class for all framework exceptions. Exceptions are powerful error-handling mechanisms that provide for destruction of stack-based objects as the stack frame is unwound to a handler for a specific exception. C++ exception handlers are *type safe*, which means that a specific handler for an exception deals with an *type* of exception that occurred while handling data of a particular type instead of requiring you to check error codes. This makes it possible for an application to supply handlers for exceptions that arise during the use of user-defined objects. It also allows for the throw site (where the problem occurred) to provide a richer context than is normally available when simply returning an error code. The code that throws the exception need not rely on the caller checking a return value; the exception can be caught several callers back in the call tree, depending on what code has the best context for handling the exception.

In versions of Visual C++ prior to 2.0, the stack is unwound, but frame-based objects are not destroyed because MFC macros are an emulation of true C++ exception handling. These same macros in version 2.0 compile to the C++ try and catch keywords, providing for true object destruction on exceptions with a recompile.

Do not confuse exceptions with errors. Errors are logical problems and normally cause ASSERTs in the framework code. This stops you in your tracks early and points you to the error in your logic. Exceptions indicate that an exceptional condition existed when executing a section of code. An example of such a condition is when the user is out of disk space or when the memory suballocator fails. The differentiation is important because you guard against logical errors by coding preconditions, or ASSERTs/ VERIFYs, into your code. These catch fundamental errors early in the development process. By contrast, an exception can happen to perfect code (if there were such a thing), and by handling the exception, the programmer can take some graceful remedial action.

431

It's useful to continue to use the macros because all macros in MFC are thrown as pointers to a CException, therefore the exception object must explicitly be deleted once you've handled the exception. The macros do this automatically, but using the C++ syntax you have to do this work yourself. For example:

```
//MFC way...
TRY {
    CFile aFile("file.txt", CFile::modeRead | CFile::shareDenyNone);
} CATCH(CFileException *e) {
    AfxMessageBox("Problem opening file.", MB_OK);
} END_CATCH
//C++ way
try{
    CFile aFile("file.txt", CFile::modeRead | CFile::shareDenyNone);
} catch(CFileException *e) {
    AfxMessageBox("Problem opening file.", MB_OK);
    delete e;
}
```

CException is never used on its own; rather, the framework's derived classes or a user-defined class is used to handle a specific type of exception. Note also that the **throw** keyword, available in Visual C++ 2.0, is not the MFC way to do things. Consider this:

```
//For the purpose of this example, we'll ignore the
//IO system error parameter to CFileException.
//MFC way
if(bOutOfDisk)
    AfxThrowFileException(CFileException::diskFull);
//C++ way
if(bOutOfDisk)
{
    throw new CFileException(CFileException::diskFull);
}
```

Derived Classes

CMemoryException
CDBException (Visual C++ 1.5 and later)
CNotSupportedException
CArchiveException
CFileException
CResourceException
COleException (Visual C++ 1.5 and later)
COleDispatchException (Visual C++ 1.5 and later)

CFieldExchange

Description The **CFieldExchange** is a stand-alone support class that assists in the record field-exchange (RFX) and -validation services of the application framework for recordsets. These services are built into **CRecordView**-derived forms, but they can be overridden by applications that need specialized record field exchange. The **CFieldExchange** object does the recordkeeping needed to support **RFX** functions that are carried out by the function **DoDataExchange**. **DoDataExchange** is overridden by Class Wizard in the course of building a **CRecordView**-based display of recordset contents. The application's version of **DoDataExchange** includes a map that ties dialog controls to specific data fields and optionally specifies acceptable ranges for their values. Most applications don't need to extend this class.

Data Members

m_nOperation   MEMBER

Description This member defines the type of data exchange that is about to take place. It can have the following values:

```
CFieldExchange::outputColumn for field data members.
CFieldExchange::param for parameter data members.
```

m_prs   MEMBER

Description This member is a pointer to the recordset that is exchanging or validating its data.

Member Functions

IsFieldType   FUNCTION

Description **IsFieldType** is used to test the data type of the field to determine whether a particular operation can be performed on it. It is used only by applications that override the framework's record field exchange service functions.

433

Prototype

```
//Function Prototype
//BOOL IsFieldType(UINT* pnField);
```

SetFieldType   FUNCTION

Description **SetFieldType** is used by the framework in building an application's field exchange map. One call is made for each record field and establishes which transfer operations are performed when the record set and the record view update one another.

Prototype

```
//Function Prototype
//void SetFieldType( UINT nFieldType);
```

 File   CLASS

. . . .

Derivation

CObject	▼
CFile	

Description The **CFile** class is the base class for the framework file-management classes. It provides unbuffered, raw file I/O. The derived classes **CStdioFile** and **CMemFile** provide specific support for disk- and memory-based files. **CFile** and derived objects open a file on construction and close it upon destruction, but static member functions can retrieve status information for files that have not been opened.

The related class **CArchive** is often used with objects of the **CFile** class to implement serialization of binary or special format objects. Applications that use the **CArchive** class to serialize objects don't have to create or manipulate **CFile** objects directly, because archival services are handled transparently by the framework. The application's **Serialize** function loads data into the archive object, and the **CArchive** object buffers the data as it is being transferred to the **CFile** object. The application framework handles the connection between the application's **Serialize** function, the **CArchive** object, and the **CFile** object, which is responsible for storing the data.

The **CFile** class is used on its own only when it is necessary to do unbuffered, unformatted disk I/O. This situation might arise for a user-derived class that does not use the framework's **CObject** as its base class, because derivation from **CObject** is necessary to the support of the framework's serialization services. (The derived **CStdioFile** class encapsulates the C runtime buffered file I/O capabilities.)

Derived Classes

CStdioFile
CMemFile

Public Data Members

m_hFile   MEMBER

Description   The meaning of **m_hFile** depends on which of the **CFile** constructors was called to create the object. If the parameterless **CFile** constructor is used to create the object, this data member is set to NULL because no file is opened. If either of the other two constructors is called, this member holds the handle to the opened file, if the open succeeds. Because it is not generally possible to tell how the object was constructed, assuming that **m_hFile** holds a valid handle is somewhat risky.

Member Functions

CFile   FUNCTION

Description   The **CFile** constructor is overloaded, which is to say that it constructs the **CFile** object in response to the three different sets of parameters it can accept. The first constructor takes no arguments and constructs the object without attempting to open a file. The file is then opened explicitly using the **Open** member function. The **CFile** constructor that takes an integer file handle as a parameter wraps the handle with the **CFile** class member functions. The constructor that takes a pathname and a set of file-open flags tries to open the file as requested and throws an exception if it fails.
  Warning! The exception-specification syntax is not supported in Microsoft Visual C++ 1.5. This is only used as a documentation aid. This is the subject of hot debate in the X3J16 committee right now, and anyone who uses this syntax is likely to have his/her code broken by a later committee decision.

Prototype
```
//Function Prototype
//CFile( );
//CFile(int hFile);
//CFile(LPCTSTR pszFileName, UINT nOpenFlags)
// throw( CFileException );
```

Example
```
    //Construct the object, but don't open the file
TRY{
    CFile fileRawData;
    //Try to open the file wavedata.smp for reading and writing
    //Note that a r/w mode and a share mode must be specified.
    if( fileRawData.Open( " wavedata.smp", CFile::modeReadWrite |
CFile::modeShareDenyWrite ) )
    {
    //If we succeed, get its length and compare it to the max we
    //can handle
    if ( (DWORD dFileLength = fileRawData.GetLength( ) ) <=
MAXLEN )
      {
    //Read the file into the memory buffer
        fileRawData.Read( lpFileBuffer, dFileLength );
      }
    //Close the file
     fileRawData.Close( );
    }
    }CATCH(CFileException e)
{
    //Process file exception
}END_CATCH
```

Close   FUNCTION

Description   **Close** is used to close a file associated with a **CFile** object before the object is destroyed. After the file is closed, the **m_hFile** is set to NULL, but you can still retrieve status information from the file and manipulate its directory entry by using the static member functions **Remove**, **Rename**, **GetStatus** and **SetStatus**. The **CFile** destructor automatically closes a file associated with an object, so it is not necessary to do this explicitly. *See CFile for usage example.*

Warning! The exception-specification syntax is not supported in Microsoft Visual C++ 1.5. This is only used as a documentation aid. This is the subject of hot debate in the X3J16 committee right now, and anyone who uses this syntax is likely to have his/her code broken by a later committee decision.

Prototype
```
//Function Prototype
//void Close( )
// throw(CFileException);
```

Duplicate   FUNCTION

Description **Duplicate** makes a new copy of an existing **CFile** object. This function is like the C **run-time _dup** function. It allows you to get a completely new file handle (create a completely new **CFile** object) to an already open file.

Warning! The exception-specification syntax is not supported in Microsoft Visual C++ 1.5. This is only used as a documentation aid. This is the subject of hot debate in the X3J16 committee right now, and anyone who uses this syntax is likely to have his/her code broken by a later committee decision.

Prototype
```
//Function Prototype
//CFile* Duplicate( ) const
// throw(CFileException);
    //We have a pointer to a CFile object,
    //and from it we create a new CFile object
CFile *pfileNew = pfileRawData->Duplicate( );
    //Now we can manipulate the physical file
    //encapsulated by the object with either
    //pfileNew or pfileRaw
    //Write out the string 123 using pfileNew
pfileNew->Write("123", strlen("123" ));
    //Write out the string 456 using pfileRaw
pfileRaw->Write("456", strlen("456" ));
```

Flush   FUNCTION

Description **Flush** moves buffered data to storage for a **CFile** object, but does not necessarily flush data for a **CFile** object that was created by the framework and coupled to a **CArchive** object. **CArchive** objects are responsible for buffering data between an application's **Serialize** function and the **CFile** object that performs the physical storage. To move data that is transferring from a serialization process, the **CArchive** object has to be flushed as well as the **CFile** object. **CArchive** includes a **Flush** member function for this purpose.

To put it more directly, **Flush** works on **CFile** objects, but don't use constructs such as this:

```
CArchive ar;
// ...
ar.GetFile->Flush();
in preference to:
ar.Flush();
```

Class **CArchive** introduces intermediate buffering and flushing the **CFile** component of a **CArchive** object does not ensure that the entire object is flushed to disk.

Warning! The exception-specification syntax is not supported in Microsoft Visual C++ 1.5. This is only used as a documentation aid. This is the subject of hot debate in the X3J16 committee right now, and anyone who uses this syntax is likely to have his/her code broken by a later committee decision.

```
// ...
ar.GetFile->Flush();
in preference to:
ar.Flush();
```

Prototype

```
//Function Prototype
//void Flush( )
//  throw(CFileException);
    //We have pointer to a CFile object,
    //and we want to make sure that all
    //updates have been written out to it
pfileRaw->Flush( );
    //Then we get the current file position
DWORD dwEndPos = pfileRaw->GetPosition( );
    //Seek to the beginning of the file, and store that position
DWORD dwEndPos = pfileRaw->SeekToBegin( );
DWORD dwBeginPos = pfileRaw->GetPosition( );
    //and lock the range up to the end of the write done by Flush
pfileRaw->LockRange( dwBeginPos, dwEndPos );
    //Write out our update while we have
    //exclusive access to the range
pfileRaw->Write( lpFileBuffer, dFileLength );
```

```
        //Reset the position to EOF
    pfileRaw->SeekToEnd( );
        //Unlock the range
    pfileRaw->UnlockRange( dwBeginPos, dwEndPos );
```

GetLength   FUNCTION

Description   **GetLength** retrieves the current logical length of the file in bytes. *See **Flush** for a usage example.*

*   **Warning!** The exception-specification syntax is *not supported in Microsoft Visual C++ 1.5*. This is only used as a documentation aid. This is the subject of hot debate in the X3J16 committee right now, and anyone who uses this syntax is likely to have his/her code broken by a later committee decision.

Prototype
```
//Function Prototype
//DWORD GetLength( ) const
// throw(CFileException);
```

GetPosition   FUNCTION

Description   **GetPosition** retrieves the current file position. The file position returned can be used as an argument to **Seek**. *See **Duplicate** for a usage example.*

*   **Warning!** *The exception-specification syntax is not supported in Microsoft Visual C++ 1.5*. This is only used as a documentation aid. This is the subject of hot debate in the X3J16 committee right now, and anyone who uses this syntax is likely to have his/her code broken by a later committee decision.

Prototype
```
//Function Prototype
//DWORD GetPosition( ) const
// throw(CFileException);
```

GetStatus   FUNCTION

Description   **GetStatus** fills in a **CFileStatus** structure. This function can be called for open or closed files. The static version of the function references directory entries to report status information on closed files.

Warning! The exception-specification syntax is not supported in Microsoft Visual C++ 1.5. This is only used as a documentation aid. This is the subject of hot debate in the X3J16 committee right now, and anyone who uses this syntax is likely to have his/her code broken by a later committee decision.

The CFileStatus structure contains the following information:

CFileStatus Member	Meaning
m_ctime	Creation date and time of file
m_mtime	Last modification date and time of file
m_atime	Last access date and time of file
m_size	Logical size of file in bytes
m_attribute	Logical OR of CFile::Attribute enum values
m_padding	Pad the structure to a WORD
m_szFullName	Absolute pathname

Prototype

```
//Function Prototype
//BOOL GetStatus(CFileStatus& rStatus) const;
//static BOOL PASCAL GetStatus(LPCTSTR pszFileName,
CFileStatus& rStatus)
//  throw(CFileException);
    //The operations below work for open or closed files
    //Get the status information for this file
CFileStatus statFile;
pfileRawData->GetStatus( statFile );
    //Reset file attributes so that the file will be archived during
next backup cycle
statFile.m_attribute | Attribute.archive;
pfileRawData->SetStatus( statFile.m_szFullName,&statFile);
    //Rename the file
pfileRawData->Rename( statFile.m_szFullName, "renamed.fil" );
```

LockRange   FUNCTION

Description **LockRange** locks a range of bytes in a file, temporarily providing exclusive access to that range to the process that made the lock. The first parameter specifies the beginning of the lock range, and the second gives the offset. If any of the range is locked at the time of the call, **LockRange** throws an exception. **LockRange** is always balanced by an **UnlockRange** call, which must unlock exactly the range locked by the first call. *See **Flush** for a usage example.*

Warning! The exception-specification syntax is not supported in Microsoft Visual C++ 1.5. This is only used as a documentation aid. This is the subject of hot debate in the X3J16 committee right now, and anyone who uses this syntax is likely to have his/her code broken by a later committee decision.

Prototype

```
//Function Prototype
//void LockRange(DWORD dwPos, DWORD dwCount)
// throw(CFileException);
```

Example An interesting wrinkle on this is that you can write code such as:

```
class FileLock
{
public:
    FileLock(CFile *f, DWORD dwPos, dwCount){
        CFile *m_f = f; m_dwPos = dwPos; m_dwCount = dwCount;
        f->LockRange(dwPos, dwCount);
    }
    ~FileLock(){
        m_f->UnlockRange(dwPos, dwCount);
    }
};
// ...
TRY{
    FileLock f(myfile, 0, 0xffff);
    //... do some writing
}    //f out of scope, file unlocked
CATCH(CFileException e)
{
    //handle case where lock can't be obtained
}END_CATCH
```

Open   FUNCTION

Description **Open** is used to open a file for a **CFile** object that was constructed using the parameterless **CFile** constructor. The other constructors automatically open files, so this function is not used with objects constructed by either of them. You have to use a minimum of a read/write open mode and a share mode when calling this function. *See **CFile** for a usage example.*

441

| Prototype | ```
//Function Prototype
//BOOL Open(LPCTSTR pszFileName, UINT nOpenFlags,
    CFileException* pError = NULL );
``` |

Read   FUNCTION

| Description | **Read** does a read of file data into the buffer specified by the first parameter and returns the number of bytes read. *See **CFile** for a usage example.*

 ***Warning!** The exception-specification syntax is not supported in Microsoft Visual C++ 1.5. This is only used as a documentation aid. This is the subject of hot debate in the X3J16 committee right now, and anyone who uses this syntax is likely to have his/her code broken by a later committee decision.* |

| Prototype | ```
//Function Prototype
//UINT Read(void FAR* lpBuf, UINT nCount)
//  throw(CFileException);
``` |

Remove   FUNCTION

| Description | **Remove** deletes a closed file only. It cannot delete an open file or a directory. Exceptions are always thrown on failure (e.g., when the file is open or in use by another process).

 ***Warning!** The exception-specification syntax is not supported in Microsoft Visual C++ 1.5. This is only used as a documentation aid. This is the subject of hot debate in the X3J16 committee right now, and anyone who uses this syntax is likely to have his/her code broken by a later committee decision.* |

| Prototype | ```
//Function Prototype
//void PASCAL Remove(LPCTSTR pszFileName)
//  throw(CFileException);
    //First close the file
pfileRawData->Close( );
    //Then we can delete the file by name
pfileRawData->Remove( "renamed.fil" );
``` |
```

Rename · FUNCTION

Description   **Rename** changes the name of a file, but can't rename a directory. *See **GetStatus** for a usage example.*

     Warning! *The exception-specification syntax is not supported in Microsoft Visual C++ 1.5.* This is only used as a documentation aid. This is the subject of hot debate in the X3J16 committee right now, and anyone who uses this syntax is likely to have his/her code broken by a later committee decision.

Prototype

```
//Function Prototype
//void PASCAL Rename(LPCTSTR pszOldName,
//LPCTSTR pszNewName)
// throw(CFileException);
```

Seek · FUNCTION

Description   **Seek** establishes the current position inside a file, relative to the beginning, end, or current file position. The first position specifies the offset, and the second parameter is the position to which the offset is applied. The possible position values are **CFile::begin**, **CFile::current**, and **Cfile::end**.

     Warning! *The exception-specification syntax is not supported in Microsoft Visual C++ 1.5.* This is only used as a documentation aid. This is the subject of hot debate in the X3J16 committee right now, and anyone who uses this syntax is likely to have his/her code broken by a later committee decision.

Prototype

```
//Function Prototype
//LONG Seek(LONG lOff, UINT nFrom)
// throw(CFileException);
    //Seek to the beginning of the file
pfileRaw->Seek( 0, CFile::begin );
    //Truncate the file
pfileRaw->SetLength( 0 );
```

SeekToBegin · FUNCTION

Description   **SeekToBegin** sets the current file position to the beginning of the file. *See **Flush** for a usage example.*

Warning! The exception-specification syntax is not supported in Microsoft Visual C++ 1.5. This is only used as a documentation aid. This is the subject of hot debate in the X3J16 committee right now, and anyone who uses this syntax is likely to have his/her code broken by a later committee decision.

Prototype
```
//Function Prototype
//void SeekToBegin( )
//  throw( CFileException );
```

SeekToEnd   FUNCTION

Description   **SeekToEnd** sets the current file position to the end of the file. *See Flush for a usage example.*

Warning! The exception-specification syntax is not supported in Microsoft Visual C++ 1.5. This is only used as a documentation aid. This is the subject of hot debate in the X3J16 committee right now, and anyone who uses this syntax is likely to have his/her code broken by a later committee decision.

Prototype
```
//Function Prototype
//void SeekToEnd( )
//  throw( CFileException );
```

SetLength   FUNCTION

Description   **SetLength** sets the current length of the file in bytes. The file will grow or be truncated as necessary to satisfy the request. *See Seek for a usage example.*

Warning! The exception-specification syntax is not supported in Microsoft Visual C++ 1.5. This is only used as a documentation aid. This is the subject of hot debate in the X3J16 committee right now, and anyone who uses this syntax is likely to have his/her code broken by a later committee decision.

Prototype
```
//Function Prototype
//void SetLength(DWORD dwNewLen)
//  throw(CFileException);
```

SetStatus   FUNCTION

Description   **SetStatus** can alter a file's directory entry information. Its parameters are a file name and a reference to an application-supplied **CFileStatus** object. *See **GetStatus** for a usage example and a listing of the **CFileStatus** structures members.*
*   **Warning**! The exception-specification syntax is not supported in Microsoft Visual C++ 1.5. This is only used as a documentation aid. This is the subject of hot debate in the X3J16 committee right now, and anyone who uses this syntax is likely to have his/her code broken by a later committee decision.*

Prototype
```
//Function Prototype
//void PASCAL SetStatus(LPCTSTR pszFileName, const CFileStatus&
//status)
//   throw(CFileException);
```

UnlockRange   FUNCTION

Description   **UnlockRange** unlocks the range of bytes locked by the **LockRange** function. *See **Flush** for a usage example.*
*   **Warning**! The exception-specification syntax is not supported in Microsoft Visual C++ 1.5. This is only used as a documentation aid. This is the subject of hot debate in the X3J16 committee right now, and anyone who uses this syntax is likely to have his/her code broken by a later committee decision.*

Prototype
```
//Function Prototype
//void UnlockRange(DWORD dwPos, DWORD dwCount)
//   throw(CFileException);
```

Write   FUNCTION

Description   **Write** does a write of file data to disk. It throws an exception if it is unable to complete the write request. *See **Duplicate** for a usage example.*

Prototype
```
//Function Prototype
//void Write(const void FAR* lpBuf, UINT nCount)
//   throw(CFileException);
```

CFileDialog

Derivation

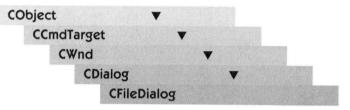

CObject
 CCmdTarget
  CWnd
   CDialog
    CFileDialog

Description The **CFileDialog** class encapsulates the common Windows file dialog box. It provides fairly complete services for picking files to open or save, as well as handling the interface elements, so it is often directly used by applications (as opposed to being used as a base class for an application-specific version). Its public member variable **m_ofn** is an **OPENFILENAME** structure used by the framework to initialize the dialog and return information to the application about the user's file selections. Setting **m_ofn.Flags** to **OFN_ALLOWMULTISELECT** before initiating the **CFileDialog** with **DoModal** allows the user to select more than one file at a time. Applications have to provide extended storage for multiple file names by placing a pointer to an application-supplied buffer in **m_ofn.lpstrFile**.

    CFileDialog objects are the commdlg dialogs. They have several protected member callback functions to allow application-specific processing of these events, but this is rarely necessary.

Public Data Members

m_ofn
MEMBER

Description **m_ofn** is a Windows **OPENFILENAME** structure, used to pass information between the application and the **CFileDialog** implementation. You do not have to fill in all the fields of the **OPENFILE** struct. The constructor does most of the work; you can then do a bit of customization.

Fields   The fields are described in this table:

Field Name	Field Type	Meaning
lStructSize	DWORD	Size of the structure in bytes.
hwndOwner	HWND	Handle of the window that owns the dialog.
hInstance	HINSTANCE	Handle to memory containing the dialog template used with OFN_ENABLETEMPLATE flag.
lpstrFilter	LPCSTR	Pointer to buffer containing filter string pairs.
lpstrCustomFilter	LPSTR	NULL unless the dialog saves to user-defined filter string pairs.
nMaxCustFilter	DWORD	Size in bytes of the application-supplied buffer for saving user-defined filter strings.
nFilterIndex	DWORD	Index into the buffer of user-defined filter strings.
lpstrFile	LPSTR	Buffer with initialization string for filename edit control.
nMaxFile	DWORD	Size in bytes of filename initialization buffer.
lpstrFileTitle	LPSTR	Title of selected file.
nMaxFileTitle	DWORD	Size in bytes of file title buffer.
lpstrInitialDir	LPCSTR	Buffer containing initial directory.
lpstrTitle	LPCSTR	Title for dialog.
Flags	DWORD	Dialog box creation attributes. (See the table of possible flag values below.)
nFileOffset	WORD	Offset in bytes from the beginning of the pathname to the filename.
nFileExtension	WORD	Offset in bytes from the beginning of the pathname to the file extension.
lpstrDefExt	LPCSTR	Buffer containing default file extension.
lCustData	DWORD	Buffer of application-specific data that is passed by the operating system to the lpfnHook function.
lpfnHook	LPOFNHOOKPROC	Pointer to a function that hooks the dialog message stream requires the OFN_ENABLEHOOK flag.
lpTemplateName;	LPCSTR	Name of an application-supplied dialog template; requires the OFN_ENABLETEMPLATE flag.

Flags   These flags are used to specify the type of file access.

Flag Name	Meaning
OFN_READONLY	Files are opened and saved with the read-only attribute.
OFN_OVERWRITEPROMPT	Prompt user before overwriting an existing file.
OFN_HIDEREADONLY	Don't show read-only files in list box.
OFN_NOCHANGEDIR	Upon closing, return a user to the directory he or she was in when the dialog opened.
OFN_SHOWHELP	Show the Help button in the dialog.
OFN_ENABLEHOOK	Enables the message stream hook function specified by lpfnHook.
OFN_ENABLETEMPLATE	Allow the application to build the dialog based on a dialog template identified by lPTemplateName.
OFN_ENABLETEMPLATEHANDLE	Allow the application to build the dialog based on a memory-resident dialog template identified by hInstance.
OFN_NOVALIDATE	Force the dialog to allow invalid characters in the filename; used by functions that hook the dialog message stream to do their own filtering.
OFN_ALLOWMULTISELECT	Allow the user to select multiple files.
OFN_EXTENSIONDIFFERENT	User entered a filename that had a different extension from the default.
OFN_PATHMUSTEXIST	Require users to specify the name of an existing file.
OFN_FILEMUSTEXIST	Require users to specify the name of an existing file.
OFN_CREATEPROMPT	Prompt the user when creating a new file.
OFN_SHAREAWARE	Used by hook functions to handle network sharing violations.
OFN_NOREADONLYRETURN	Specified file was not write-protected.
OFN_NOTESTFILECREATE	Supports file creation on write-once network nodes.
OFN_NONETWORKBUTTON	Prevents Network button from being displayed.

Overrides The following table lists the overridable callback functions for custom event handling. These are the functions that are only useful in derived classes.

Overridable Function Name	Triggering Event
OnShareViolation	Share violation has occurred.
OnFileNameOK	Filename needs to be validated.
OnLBSelChangedNotify	The listbox selection changed.

Member Functions

CFileDialog   FUNCTION

Description **CFileDialog** creates a standard Windows File dialog, initializing it with the values passed in the constructor arguments. The dialog is launched and run by **DoModal**.

Prototype

```
//Function Prototype
//CFileDialog::CFileDialog(BOOL bOpenFileDialog,
    //Default file extension
LPCTSTR lpszDefExt = NULL ,
    //Initial file name edit control string
LPCTSTR lpszFileName = NULL ,
    //Hide read-only files, prompt for overwrite on save
DWORD dwFlags = OFN_HIDEREADONLY |
OFN_OVERWRITEPROMPT ,
    //Filter string pairs
LPCTSTR lpszFilter = NULL ,
    //Parent of this dialog
CWnd* pParentWnd = NULL );

    //Create a standard file dialog
CFileDialog dlgFile(bOpenFileDialog);
    //Any flags in the OPENFILENAME struct
    //must be set before we call DoModal
    //This one makes the dialog prompt the user
    //before creating a new file
m_ofn.Flags = OFN_CREATEPROMPT;
    //Let it do all default open and save processing
    //If DoModal returns IDCANCEL
    //or there is an error, return FALSE
BOOL bRet = dlgFile.DoModal() == IDOK ? TRUE : FALSE;
return bRet;
```

DoModal
FUNCTION

Description **DoModal** displays the standard **CFileDialog,** returning **IDOK** or **IDCANCEL** if the dialog was displayed or NULL if there was an error. Applications rarely override this versatile and convenient workhorse, but those that do make use of the other member functions in this class to perform some of its tasks. *See* ***CFileDialog*** *for a usage example.*

Prototype
```
//Function Prototype
//virtual int DoModal( );
```

GetFileExt
FUNCTION

Description **GetFileExt** is used by applications that that use **CFileDialog** as is. It omits the path and root filename parts of a fully qualified filename.

Prototype
```
//Function Prototype
//CString CFileDialog::GetFileExt( ) const;
```

GetFileName
FUNCTION

Description **GetFileName** is used by applications that use **CFileDialog** as is. It omits the path and file-extension parts of a fully qualified filename.

Prototype
```
//Function Prototype
//CString CFileDialog::GetFileName( ) const;
```

GetFileTitle
FUNCTION

Description **GetFileTitle** is used by applications that that use **CFileDialog** as is. It omits the path parts of a fully qualified filename.

Prototype
```
//Function Prototype
//CString CFileDialog::GetFileTitle( ) const;
```

GetPathName
FUNCTION

Description **GetPathName** is used by applications that use **CFileDialog** as is.

Prototype
```
//Function Prototype
//CString CFileDialog::GetFileName( ) const;
```

GetReadOnlyPref FUNCTION

Description **GetReadOnlyPref** is used by applications that use **CFileDialog** as is, to test whether the Read Only check box has been checked by the user in a **FileOpen** or **FileSaveAs** dialog.

Prototype
```
//Function Prototype
//BOOL CFileDialog::GetReadOnlyPref( ) const;
```

 FileException CLASS

- -

Derivation

```
CObject                      ▼
    CException                   ▼
        CFileException
```

Description The **CFileException** class provides objects that signal file I/O-related snafus. Its public data members record both a generic, and therefore portable exception descriptor code and a platform-specific error number. The **CFileException** group of conditions is thrown from **CFile** class member functions. The constructor for this class is never called directly. Instead, the global function **AfxThrowFileException** is used. The **CFileException** object is accessible from within the handler that catches it.

Public Data Members

m_cause MEMBER

Description **m_cause** is the portable cause code for the exception. The following table lists the correspondence between specific error messages and the possible values of the **CFileException** enumeration for portable error identification.

Reported File Error	Portable CFileException Enumeration
NO_ERROR	CFileException::none;
ERROR_FILE_NOT_FOUND	CFileException::fileNotFound;
ERROR_PATH_NOT_FOUND	CFileException::badPath;
ERROR_TOO_MANY_OPEN_FILES	CFileException::tooManyOpenFiles;
ERROR_ACCESS_DENIED	CFileException::accessDenied;
ERROR_INVALID_HANDLE	CFileException::fileNotFound;
ERROR_BAD_FORMAT	CFileException::invalidFile;
ERROR_INVALID_ACCESS	CFileException::accessDenied;
ERROR_INVALID_DRIVE	CFileException::badPath;
ERROR_CURRENT_DIRECTORY	CFileException::removeCurrentDir;
ERROR_NOT_SAME_DEVICE	CFileException::badPath;
ERROR_NO_MORE_FILES	CFileException::fileNotFound;
ERROR_WRITE_PROTECT	CFileException::accessDenied;
ERROR_BAD_UNIT	CFileException::hardIO;
ERROR_BAD_COMMAND	CFileException::hardIO;
ERROR_CRC	CFileException::hardIO;
ERROR_BAD_LENGTH	CFileException::badSeek;
ERROR_SEEK	CFileException::badSeek;
ERROR_NOT_DOS_DISK	CFileException::invalidFile;
ERROR_SECTOR_NOT_FOUND	CFileException::badSeek;
ERROR_WRITE_FAULT	CFileException::accessDenied;
ERROR_READ_FAULT	CFileException::badSeek;
ERROR_SHARING_VIOLATION	CFileException::sharingViolation;
ERROR_LOCK_VIOLATION	CFileException::lockViolation;
ERROR_WRONG_DISK	CFileException::badPath;
ERROR_SHARING_BUFFER_EXCEEDED	CFileException::tooManyOpenFiles;
ERROR_HANDLE_EOF	CFileException::endOfFile;
ERROR_HANDLE_DISK_FULL	CFileException::diskFull;
ERROR_DUP_NAME	CFileException::badPath;
ERROR_BAD_NETPATH	CFileException::badPath;
ERROR_NETWORK_BUSY	CFileException::accessDenied;
ERROR_DEV_NOT_EXIST	CFileException::badPath;
ERROR_ADAP_HDW_ERR	CFileException::hardIO;
ERROR_BAD_NET_RESP	CFileException::accessDenied;
ERROR_UNEXP_NET_ERR	CFileException::hardIO;
ERROR_BAD_REM_ADAP	CFileException::invalidFile;
ERROR_NO_SPOOL_SPACE	CFileException::directoryFull;
ERROR_NETNAME_DELETED	CFileException::accessDenied;
ERROR_NETWORK_ACCESS_DENIED	CFileException::accessDenied;
ERROR_BAD_DEV_TYPE	CFileException::invalidFile;
ERROR_BAD_NET_NAME	CFileException::badPath;
ERROR_TOO_MANY_NAMES	CFileException::tooManyOpenFiles;
ERROR_SHARING_PAUSED	CFileException::badPath;
ERROR_REQ_NOT_ACCEP	CFileException::accessDenied;
ERROR_FILE_EXISTS	CFileException::accessDenied;

Reported File Error	Portable CFileException Enumeration
ERROR_CANNOT_MAKE	CFileException::accessDenied;
ERROR_ALREADY_ASSIGNED	CFileException::badPath;
ERROR_INVALID_PASSWORD	CFileException::accessDenied;
ERROR_NET_WRITE_FAULT	CFileException::hardIO;
ERROR_DISK_CHANGE	CFileException::fileNotFound;
ERROR_DRIVE_LOCKED	CFileException::lockViolation;
ERROR_BUFFER_OVERFLOW	CFileException::badPath;
ERROR_DISK_FULL	CFileException::diskFull;
ERROR_NO_MORE_SEARCH_HANDLES	CFileException::tooManyOpenFiles;
ERROR_INVALID_TARGET_HANDLE	CFileException::invalidFile;
ERROR_INVALID_CATEGORY	CFileException::hardIO;
ERROR_INVALID_NAME	CFileException::badPath;
ERROR_INVALID_LEVEL	CFileException::badPath;
ERROR_NO_VOLUME_LABEL	CFileException::badPath;
ERROR_NEGATIVE_SEEK	CFileException::badSeek;
ERROR_SEEK_ON_DEVICE	CFileException::badSeek;
ERROR_DIR_NOT_ROOT	CFileException::badPath;
ERROR_DIR_NOT_EMPTY	CFileException::removeCurrentDir;
ERROR_LABEL_TOO_LONG	CFileException::badPath;
ERROR_BAD_PATHNAME	CFileException::badPath;
ERROR_LOCK_FAILED	CFileException::lockViolation;
ERROR_BUSY	CFileException::accessDenied;
ERROR_INVALID_ORDINAL	CFileException::invalidFile;
ERROR_ALREADY_EXISTS	CFileException::accessDenied;
ERROR_INVALID_EXE_SIGNATURE	CFileException::invalidFile;
ERROR_BAD_EXE_FORMAT	CFileException::invalidFile;
ERROR_FILENAME_EXCED_RANGE	CFileException::badPath;
ERROR_META_EXPANSION_TOO_LONG	CFileException::badPath;
ERROR_DIRECTORY	CFileException::badPath;
ERROR_OPERATION_ABORTED	CFileException::hardIO;
ERROR_IO_INCOMPLETE	CFileException::hardIO;
ERROR_IO_PENDING	CFileException::hardIO;
ERROR_SWAPERROR	CFileException::accessDenied;

m_lOsError   MEMBER

Description   **m_lOsError** is the system-dependent error number for the exception.

Member Functions

CFileException FUNCTION

Description **CFileException** constructs an object of this type and stores the portable cause code and system error number for the exception in its member variables. This function is never called directly. Instead, the global function **AfxThrowFileException** is used.

Prototype
```
//Function Prototype
//If we get an error on file I/O operations,
//use the global function to
//raise the exception
if (nErrno != 0)
AfxThrowFileException(CFileException::ErrnoToException(nErrno),
_doserrno);
```

ErrnoToException FUNCTION

Description **ErrnoToException** translates a C runtime library file I/O error number to a portable enumerated exception value. These values are defined in errno.h, and are accessed using the global errno variable.

Prototype
```
//Function Prototype
//int PASCAL CFileException::ErrnoToException(int nErrno);
    //Raise an exception based on a C
    //runtime file I/O error number
if (errno != 0)
AfxThrowFileException(CFileException::ErrnoToException(errno),
errno );
```

OsErrorToException FUNCTION

Description **OsErrorToException** translates a platform-specific error number to an exception, reporting an enum that can assume one of the values listed under **m_cause.** This function returns generic if no mapping is available.

Prototype

```
//Function Prototype
//int PASCAL CFileException::OsErrorToException(LONG lOsErr);
    //Use this function if your application
    //detects a platform-specific
    //error code and then raises an exception.
if (nOsError!= 0)
AfxThrowFileException(CFileException::OsErrorToException
    (nOsError),_doserrno);
```

ThrowErrno   FUNCTION

Description **ThrowErrno** constructs a **CFileException** object using the specified runtime file I/O error and then throws the exception.

Prototype

```
//Function Prototype
//void PASCAL CFileException::ThrowErrno(int nErrno);
    //we use ferror to check the status of runtime file I/O call
    //If there was a failure, throw an exception
    //based on the value of the global
    //variable that stores runtime file error codes, errno
if (ferror ( stream ))
    CFileException::ThrowErrno(errno));
```

ThrowOsError   FUNCTION

Description **ThrowOsError** constructs a **CFileException** object by using the specified OS error and then throws the exception.

Prototype

```
//Function Prototype
//void PASCAL CFileException::ThrowOsError(LONG lOsError);
    //If the call to set file attributes fails,
    //throw a file exception based on the error
    //the call returned
if (!SetFileAttributes(pszFileName, FILE_ATTRIBUTE_SYSTEM )
    CFileException::ThrowOsError((LONG)GetLastError());
```

Note: The above code works only on Win32.

CFindReplaceDialog

Derivation

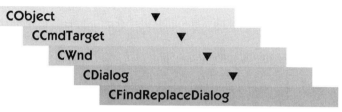

CObject
CCmdTarget
CWnd
CDialog
CFindReplaceDialog

Description The **CFindReplace** class implements the modeless Windows Find and FindReplace dialog boxes. It provides services for collecting data about string search and string search-and-replace. **CFindReplaceDialog** handles display and management of the dialog box, and the application uses the information retrieved from the user to implement specific find-and-replace operations on the document and the view.

    Because **CFindReplace** dialogs are modeless, the application handles them a little differently from other dialog classes derived from **CDialog**. First, **CFindReplace** dialogs should be constructed on the heap, using the **new** operator. Because they do not search the document for the string or replace it if it is found, they must interact with their parent window when strings are to be found and replaced. Communication between the parent and the FindReplace dialog is accomplished by registering messages by using the SDK function ::**RegisterMessage**, which returns a message number guaranteed to be unique within the instance of the application. In the application's message map, use the **ON_REGISTERED_MESSAGE** macro to associate the handler function and the unique message number. The application defines a callback function that implements the desired behavior. The callback function can directly use any of the **CFindReplace** member functions.

Example
```
class AppFrameWnd : public CFrameWnd
{
protected:
   afx_msg LONG LRESULT OnFindReplace( WPARAM wParam,
LPARAM lParam );
   DECLARE_MESSAGE_MAP( )
};
```

```
//FINDMSGSTRING is #defined "commdlg_FindReplace"
static UINT NEAR WM_FIND_REPLACE =
    ::RegisterWindowMessage( FINDMSGSTRING );
BEGIN_MESSAGE_MAP( AppFrameWnd, CFrameWnd )
    //All the usual message mapping supplied by class wizard
    //would precede
    //this next line, which associates
    //the unique message and the application's
    //callback function that
    //implements Find/Replace
    ON_REGISTERED_MESSAGE ( WM_FIND_REPLACE,
OnFindReplace );
```

The public member variable **m_fr** is a **FINDREPLACE** structure used to pass information between the application and the framework to initialize the dialog and modify its behavior.

Public Data Members

m_fr		MEMBER

Description   **m_fr** is a **FINDREPLACE** structure used to pass information between the application and the dialog.

Fields   Below is a description of the **FINDREPLACE** structure and its members.

Field Name	Type	Meaning
lStructSize	DWORD	Size of structure in bytes.
hwndOwner	HWND	Caller's window handle.
hInstance	HINSTANCE	Instance handle of .EXE that contains custom dialog template.
Flags	DWORD	Flags that modify display and behavior of dialog.
lpstrFindWhat	LPSTR	Pointer to search string.
lpstrReplaceWith	LPSTR	Pointer to replace string.
lCustData	LPARAM	Buffer of application-specific data passed by the operating system to the lpfnHook function.
lpfnHook	LPHOOKPROC	Pointer to a function that hooks the dialog message stream; requires the FR_ENABLEHOOK flag.
lpTemplateName	LPCSTR	Custom FindReplace dialog template name.

457

Flags	Flag Name	Meaning
	FR_DOWN	User clicked search-down radio button.
	FR_WHOLEWORD	Match whole word only.
	FR_MATCHCASE	Match case of search string exactly.
	FR_FINDNEXT	Find next occurrence of search string.
	FR_REPLACE	Replace the current text selection.
	FR_REPLACEALL	Replace all occurrences of search string.
	FR_DIALOGTERM	Signals that the dialog box is closing.
	FR_SHOWHELP	Shows the Help button.
	FR_ENABLEHOOK	Enables the message stream hook function specified by lpfnPrintHook.
	FR_ENABLETEMPLATE	Allows the application to build the dialog based on a dialog template identified by m_fr.lpTemplateName.
	FR_ENABLETEMPLATEHANDLE	Allows the application to build the dialog based on a memory-resident dialog template identified by m_fr.hTemplate.
	FR_HIDEUPDOWN	Hides the up-down search control.
	FR_HIDEMATCHCASE	Hides the match-case control.
	FR_HIDEWHOLEWORD	Hides the match-whole-word control.
	FR_NOUPDOWN	Disables the up-down search control.
	FR_NOMATCHCASE	Disables the match case control.
	FR_NOWHOLEWORD	Disables the match-whole-word control.

Member Functions

CFindReplace `FUNCTION`

Description **CFindReplace** constructs a dialog object, but does not display it. Find and Find Replace dialogs should be constructed on the heap because they are modeless and have the potential to exist over long periods of time. *See **Create** for a usage example.*

Create `FUNCTION`

Description **Create** initializes and displays a Find or Find Replace dialog, using information passed in the **m_fr** data member. If the first parameter is set to TRUE, the Windows Find dialog is displayed. If it is FALSE, the FindReplace dialog is displayed. The remaining parameters give the search string, the default replace string, flags that modify the search method, and a pointer to the parent window of the dialog.

Prototype
```
//Function Prototype
//BOOL CFindReplaceDialog::Create(BOOL bFindDialogOnly,
//     LPCTSTR lpszFindWhat,
//     LPCTSTR lpszReplaceWith  = NULL ,
//     DWORD dwFlags  = FR_DOWN ,
//     CWnd* pParentWnd  = NULL )
   //First construct the FindReplace object
CFindReplaceDialog FindReplaceDlg;
CString strFind = "FindIt";
CString strReplace = "ReplaceIt";
   //We'll search for the string "FindIt" and
   //replace it with the string
   //"ReplaceIt", accept the default downward search,
   //and default the main app
   //window as the parent
FindReplaceDlg.Create(bFindOnly, strFind,strReplace);
```

FindNext   FUNCTION

Description   **FindNext** tests whether the user wants to find the next occurrence of the search string. Because the application is responsible for implementing search-and-replace operations for the document and the view, **FindNext** and all the other member functions are used in the callback function, which does the search-and-replace operations.

Prototype
```
//Function Prototype
//BOOL FindNext( ) const;
   //This is the override function that our app uses
   //to do find and replace operations
LRESULT OurApp::OnFindReplace(WPARAM, LPARAM lParam)
{
BOOL bStatus;
   //Get a pointer to the dialog
CFindReplaceDialog* pDialog =
CFindReplaceDialog::GetNotifier(lParam);
if (  pDialog->IsTerminating( ) )
 {
    //If the user bailed out of the dialog,
    //destroy this window and delete the object
    pDialog->DestroyWindow( );
    delete pDialog;
 }
```

```
                    //Test for a FindNext request
                else if (pDialog->FindNext( ))
                {
                    //We call our application's search
                    //function, passing the string to search for,
                    //the search direction, a case-matching BOOL,
                    //and a whole-word-matching BOOL
                    bStatus =OnFindNext(pDialog->GetFindString( ),
                            pDialog->SearchDown( ),
                        pDialog->MatchCase( ), pDialog->MatchWholeWord( ));
                }
                    //Test for a ReplaceCurrent request
                else if (pDialog->ReplaceCurrent( ))
                {
                    //We call our application's replace current
                    //selection function,
                    //passing the replace string
                    bStatus =OnReplaceSel( pDialog->GetReplaceString( ));
                }
                    //Test for a ReplaceAll request
                else if (pDialog->ReplaceAll( ))
                {
                    //We call our application's ReplaceAll function,
                    //passing the string to search for,
                    //the search direction, a case-matching BOOL,
                    //and a whole-word-matching BOOL
                    bStatus =OnReplaceAll(pDialog->GetFindString(),
                            pDialog->GetReplaceString(),
                            pDialog->MatchCase( ),
                            pDialog->MatchWholeWord( ));
                }
                if ( bStatus )
                 return SUCCESS;
                else
                 return FAIL;
                }
```

GetFindString   FUNCTION

Description   **GetFindString** returns the search string. *See **FindNext** for a usage example.*

Prototype
```
//Function Prototype
//CString GetFindString( ) const;
```

GetNotifier   FUNCTION

Description   **GetNotifier** is called from the application's Find/Replace callback function to get a pointer to the FindReplace modeless dialog box. Using the pointer, the application can access **CFindReplace** member functions and the **m_fr** data member. *See **FindNext** for a usage example.*

Prototype
```
//Function Prototype
//static FindNextDialog* PASCAL GetNotifier( LPARAM lParam );
```

GetReplaceString   FUNCTION

Description   **GetReplaceString** returns the string that should replace found occurrences of the search string. *See **FindNext** for a usage example.*

Prototype
```
//Function Prototype
//CString GetReplaceString( ) const;
```

IsTerminating   FUNCTION

Description   **IsTerminating** returns a non-zero value if the user canceled the dialog. *See **FindNext** for a usage example.*

Prototype
```
//Function Prototype
//BOOL IsTerminating( ) const;
```

MatchCase   FUNCTION

Description   **MatchCase** returns a non-zero value if the user checked the "Match Case" control in the dialog. *See **FindNext** for a usage example.*

Prototype
```
//Function Prototype
//BOOL MatchCase( ) const;
```

461

MatchWholeWord   FUNCTION

Description   **MatchWholeWord** returns a non-zero value if the user checked the "Match Whole Word" control in the dialog. *See **FindNext** for a usage example.*

Prototype
```
//Function Prototype
//BOOL MatchWholeWord( ) const;
```

ReplaceAll   FUNCTION

Description   **ReplaceAll** returns a non-zero value if the user clicked the "Replace All" control in the dialog. *See **CFindReplace** for a usage example.*

Prototype
```
//Function Prototype
//BOOL ReplaceAll( ) const;
```

ReplaceCurrent   FUNCTION

Description   **ReplaceCurrent** returns a non-zero value if the user clicked the "Replace" control in the dialog. *See **CFindReplace** for a usage example.*

Prototype
```
//Function Prototype
//BOOL ReplaceCurrent( ) const;
```

SearchDown   FUNCTION

Description   **SearchDown** returns a non-zero value if the user clicked the "Search Down" radio control in the dialog. *See **CFindReplace** for a usage example.*

Prototype
```
//Function Prototype
//BOOL SearchDown( ) const;
```

CFont

CLASS

Derivation

CObject ▼
    CGdiObject ▼
        CFont

Description **CFont** encapsulates the Windows GDI Font. Used with **CDC** member functions for text output.

Member Functions

CFont   FUNCTION

This constructor creates an uninitialized **CFont** object.

Prototype
```
//Function Prototype
//CFont( );
CFont  theFontObject;
//creates a font object, but it is not initialized with a font
```

CreateFont   FUNCTION

Description **CreateFont** initializes a font object with a font described by its arguments. Used with the **CFont** constructor and **CDC** member functions for drawing. Font requests are subject to font matching with available fonts for the output device. The parameters that describe the font are given different weights by the font-mapping algorithm. The two most important are the height and the face name.

Prototype
```
//Function Prototype
//BOOL CreateFont

CFont theFontObject;
//creates a font object, but it is not initialized with a font
theFontObject.CreateFont( int nHeight,
            int nWidth,
            int nEscapement,
            int nOrientation,
            int nWeight,
            BYTE bItalic,
            YTE bUnderline,
            BYTE bStrikeout,
            BYTE nCharSet,
            BYTE nOutPrecision,
            BYTE nClipPrecision,
            BYTE nQuality,
            BYTE nPitchAndFamily,
            LPCSTR lpszFaceName );
//specify font description information,
        //which will tell the font mapper how to map
        //your logical font to available device fonts
```

CreateFontIndirect   FUNCTION

Description   **CreateFontIndirect** initializes a font object with a font described by a logical font structure. This function is more convenient than **CreateFont** because it has only one parameter. Font requests are subject to font matching with available fonts for the output device. The parameters that describe the font are given different weights by the font-mapping algorithm. The two most important are the height and the face name. The **LOGFONT** structure passed to it need not be completely filled in with values, but it should be zero initialized to prevent the font mapper from trying to incorporate garbage from uninitialized structure members in font-mapping logic.

Prototype
```
//Function Prototype
//BOOL CreateFontIndirect
    //assume our function was passed a
    //far pointer to a LOGFONT
CFont theFontObject;
```

```
//creates a font object, but it
//is not initialized with a font

theFontObject.CreateFontIndirect( lpLogicalFontStruct);
    //pretty easy to specify the font, and lots of the
    //LOGFONT info can be retrieved with
    //CDC::GetTextMetrics....
    //You can get a complete LOGFONT using
    //GetObject on the currently-selected font.
```

FromHandle   FUNCTION

Description

CFont::FromHandle returns a pointer to a temporary **CFont** object. The handle of the font is attached to the **CFont** object. Internally, tracking of most Windows GDI objects is done using a table of handles. MFC provides classes to wrap the handles in objects, making the member functions of the class available to act on the object identified by the handle. The **FromHandle** family provides a quick and convenient way to package the handle temporarily in an object. An object pointer returned by any of the **FromHandle** family has a life cycle of approximately one Windows message-passing cycle, so when a function that uses this call exits, the object goes out of scope and is destroyed. It is therefore not necessary for an application to destroy an object returned by **FromHandle**. This is taken care of during the idle-time processing of **CWinApp**. The object identified by the handle is not deleted along with the temporary object. The lifetime of the object referenced by the pointer is very brief, so don't store the pointer for later use. It will be invalid.

Prototype

```
//Function Prototype
//static CFont* PASCAL FromHandle( HFONThFont);
CFont* pThePreviousCFont;
    //Save the pointer to the object we are selecting
    //out of the DC; assume we have a valid pointer
    //to a CDC object called pDC
pThePreviousCFont =
    pDC->SelectObject(CFont::FromHandle(m_hObject));
    //Select a new font that is identified by the handle
    //in the public member variable of the CGdiObject
    //base class
```

FontDialog

Derivation

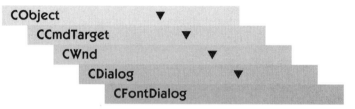

Description The **CFontDialog** class encapsulates the Windows font-selection dialog box. It provides services for setting font characteristics like typeface, weight and italics. **CFontDialog** handles display and management of the dialog box, including collecting data when the dialog closes. Its public member variable **m_cf** is a **CHOOSEFONT** structure used to pass information between the application and the framework to initialize the dialog. The information supplied to the system is used by the Windows font-mapping algorithm to create the new font.

Public Data Members

m_cf

MEMBER

Description **m_cf** is a Windows **CHOOSEFONT** structure, used to pass information between the application and the **CFontDialog** implementation. The fields and their flags are described in the following tables:

Fields

Field Name	Type	Meaning
lStructSize	DWORD	Size of the structure in bytes.
hwndOwner	HWND	Caller's window handle.
hDC	HDC	Printer DC/IC or NULL.
lpLogFont	LPLOGFONT	Pointer to a LOGFONT struct.
iPointSize	INT	Ten times size in points of selected font.
Flags	DWORD	Flags that modify display and behavior of dialog.
rgbColors	COLORREF	Returned text color.
lCustData	LPARAM	Buffer of application-specific data that is passed by the operating system to the lpfnHook function.

Field Name	Type	Meaning
pfnHook	LPCFHOOKPROCl	Pointer to a function that hooks the dialog message stream; requires the OFN_ENABLEHOOK flag.
lpTemplateName	LPCWSTR	Custom template name.
hInstance	HINSTANCE	Instance handle of .EXE that contains custom dialog template.
lpszStyle	LPWSTR	Style field returned here; must be LF_FACESIZE or bigger.
nFontType	WORD	Same value reported to the EnumFonts call back with the extra FONTTYPE bits added.
nSizeMin	INT	Minimum point size allowed.
nSizeMax	INT	Maximum point size allowed if CF_LIMITSIZE is set.

Flags

Flag Name	Meaning
CF_SCREENFONTS	List only screen fonts in the dialog box.
CF_PRINTERFONTS	List only printer fonts in the dialog box.
CF_BOTH	List both screen and printer fonts in the dialog box.
CF_SHOWHELP	Show the Help button. Note: The dialog must have an owner, supplied either by constructing with pParentWnd set to a valid window or by explicitly setting the hwndOwner member of the m_cf structure.
CF_ENABLEHOOK	Enable the message stream hook function specified by lpfnHook.
CF_ENABLETEMPLATE	Allow the application to build the dialog based on a dialog template identified by lpTemplateName.
CF_ENABLETEMPLATEHANDLE	Allow the application to build the dialog based on a memory-resident dialog template identified by hInstance.
CF_INITTOLOGFONTSTRUCT	Initialize the dialog by using values passed to the constructor in the LOGFONT struct.
CF_USESTYLE	Use LOGFONT style data to initialize the dialog.
CF_EFFECTS	Allow strikeout, underline and color effects.
CF_APPLY	Enable the Apply button.
CF_ANSIONLY	Restrict font selection to the ANSI character set.
CF_NOVECTORFONTS	Don't allow vector font selections.
CF_NOOEMFONTS	Don't allow OEM font selections.

Flag Name	Meaning
CF_NOSIMULATIONS	Don't allow simulated font selections.
CF_LIMITSIZE	Restrict font selections to the minimum and maximum sizes specified in the CHOOSEFONT struct.
CF_FIXEDPITCHONLY	Restrict font selection to fixed-pitch fonts.
CF_WYSIWYG	Restrict font selection to WYSIWYG fonts; requires CF_SCALABLEONLY and CF_BOTH.
CF_FORCEFONTEXIST	Report error if user selects a font that doesn't exist.
CF_SCALABLEONLY	Restrict font selection to scalable fonts.
CF_TTONLY	Restrict font selection to TrueType fonts.
CF_NOFACESEL	Don't allow face selections.
CF_NOSTYLESEL	Don't allow style selections.
CF_NOSIZESEL	Don't allow size selections.

Member Functions

CFontDialog   FUNCTION

Description **CFontDialog** constructs a **CFontDialog** object, setting initial font-selection parameters according to the data in the **LOGFONT** passed to it; sets flags controlling dialog behavior and appearance; specifies a printer DC to be used for printer font selection; and identifies its parent window.

Prototype
```
//Function Prototype
//CFontDialog(LPLOGFONT lplfInitData = NULL ,
//    DWORD dwFlags = CF_EFFECTS | CF_SCREENFONTS ,
//    CDC* pdcPrinter = NULL ,
//    CWnd* pParentWnd = NULL );
    //Create a standard font-selection dialog
CFontDialog dlgFont( );
    //Any flags in the CHOOSEFONT struct must
    //be set before we call DoModal
    //This one makes the dialog list only available screen fonts
m_cf.Flags = CF_SCREENFONTS;
    //DoModal shows the dialog and manages data exchange
dlgFont.DoModal( );
```

```
//When DoModal returns,
   //we can use the member functions to get font info....
CString cstrFaceName = dlgFont.GetFaceName( );
CString cstrStyleName = dlgFont.GetStyleName( );
int iPointSize = dlgFont.GetSize( );
int iWeight = dlgFont.GetWeight( );
BOOL bBold = dlgFont.IsBold( );
BOOL bIsItalic = dlgFont.IsItalic( );
COLORREF crFontColor = dlgFont.GetColor( );
LOGFONT lfUserFont;
dlgFont.GetCurrentFont( &lfUserFont );
```

DoModal   FUNCTION

Description   **DoModal** displays the Windows common font dialog box, returning **IDOK** or **IDCANCEL** if the dialog was displayed or NULL if there was an error. *See **CFontDialog** for a usage example.*

Prototype
```
//Function Prototype
//virtual int DoModal( );
```

GetColor   FUNCTION

Description   **GetColor** retrieves the color of the selected font. *See **CFontDialog** for a usage example.*

Prototype
```
//Function Prototype
//COLORREF GetColor( )const;
```

GetCurrentFont   FUNCTION

Description   **GetCurrentFont** copies the attributes of the selected font to the **LOGFONT** structure identified by the parameter. *See **CFontDialog** for a usage example.* Use **CFont::CreateFontIndirect** to create a **CFont** object from this **LOGFONT** structure.

Prototype
```
//Function Prototype
//void GetCurrentFont( LPLOGFONT lfLogFontStruct );
```

GetFaceName   FUNCTION

Description   **GetFaceName** retrieves the face name of the selected font. *See **CFontDialog** for a usage example.*

469

Prototype

```
//Function Prototype
//CString GetFaceName( )const;
```

GetSize   FUNCTION

Description **GetSize** retrieves the size in points of the selected font. *See CFontDialog for a usage example.*

Prototype

```
//Function Prototype
//int GetSize( )const;
```

GetStyleName   FUNCTION

Description **GetStyleName** retrieves the style name of the selected font. *See CFontDialog for a usage example.*

Prototype

```
//Function Prototype
//CString GetStyleName( )const;
```

GetWeight   FUNCTION

Description **GetWeight** retrieves the weight of the selected font. *See CFontDialog for a usage example.*

Prototype

```
//Function Prototype
//int GetWeight( )const;
```

IsBold   FUNCTION

Description **IsBold** returns TRUE if a font has the bold attribute. *See CFontDialog for a usage example.*

Prototype

```
//Function Prototype
//BOOL IsBold( )const;
```

IsItalic   FUNCTION

Description **IsItalic** returns TRUE if a font has the italic attribute. *See CFontDialog for a usage example.*

Prototype

```
//Function Prototype
//BOOL IsItalic( )const;
```

IsStrikeOut

Description **IsStrikeOut** returns TRUE if a font has the strikeout attribute. *See **CFontDialog** for a usage example.*

Prototype
```
//Function Prototype
//BOOL IsStrikeOut( )const;
```

IsUnderline

Description **IsUnderline** returns TRUE if a font has the underline attribute. *See **CFontDialog** for a usage example.*

Prototype
```
//Function Prototype
//BOOL IsUnderline( )const;
```

CFormView

Derivation

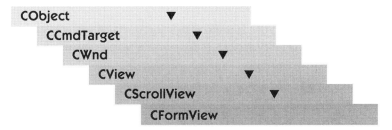

CObject
  CCmdTarget
    CWnd
      CView
        CScrollView
          CFormView

Description **CFormView** is a base class for user-derived form classes. It provides the capability of developing a dialog resource-based view that takes advantage of **CScrollView**'s automatic scrolling capabilities. Almost anything you can do in a **CDialog** you can do in a **CFormView**. Note that as of VC++ 2.0, you will have the option of creating a dialog-based application using the AppWizard, so if you had anticipated an SDI **CFormView** application, the dialog-based app is an alternative. (You always had this alternative by writing a few lines of code—for instance, the TRACER applet provided in the MFC example code.)

A user-derived class supplies its own constructor to initialize dialog control values and so forth, but it must also call the **CFormView** class constructor.

The advantage of **CFormView** over **CDialog** views is that if the containing frame window is too small to display the entire dialog, **CFormView** automatically puts up scroll bars and handles scrolling. (The only supported mapping mode for a form view is **MM_TEXT**.)

Scrolling is just one advantage. A **CFormView** is a real view, complete with all the things views have: Print preview, printing, UI enabling/disabling (including toolbars and menus), etc. A dialog is simply that and nothing more.

VC++ 2.0 removes the extra **CFormView** creation steps required in earlier versions. You simply specify that your view is derived from **CFormView** and move blithely ahead.

Note also that the dialog template you use for a form view must be special:

```
WS_VISIBLE off
WS_CHILD on
WS_BORDER off
WS_CAPTION off
```

If you don't recite this incantation exactly, your **CFormView** will not work correctly.

Overrides　　Finally, the overridable functions most useful to **CFormView** based applications are as follows:

```
CView::OnUpdate
CView::OnInitialUpdate
CView::OnPrint
```

Prototype
```
//Function Prototypes
//CFormView ( LPCSTR lpszTemplateName );
//CFormView ( UINT nIDTemplate );
    //We call the base class constructor and then do application-
    //specific construction tasks, like initializing data members
    //IDD is the ID of the dialog template that defines the
    //appearance of the form view
CThisFormView::CThisFormView( ) :
CFormView(CThisFormView::IDD)
```

```
{
    //Class wizard creates and maintains
    //this sequence of statements

    //It is the dialog data exchange member
    //variable initialization.
    //{{AFX_DATA_INIT(CThisFormView)
    m_strDate = "";
    m_strTime = "";
    m_strName = "";
    //}}AFX_DATA_INIT
```

CFrameWnd

Derivation

Description   **CFrameWnd** is the base class of frame windows. It organizes and orchestrates the activities of all of an application's visual objects. In most cases, the creation of a frame window occurs as an automatic part of startup processing, with the code to do this generated by the Visual Workbench tools. An application's derived frame window class contains the message map, which defines the relationship between messages received by the frame and the message handler functions to which they are dispatched. In the case of a frame window that contains MDI child windows, the frame tracks which of the MDI children contains the active view and dispatches command messages to it.

All the housekeeping related to the non-client areas of the frame is carried out by **CFrameWnd** in collaboration with **CCmdTarget**. For example, it updates menu items by checking and unchecking them, positions and manages the toolbar and status bar, and can translate accelerator key sequences.

The frame window is responsible for implementing drag-and-drop. It opens files dropped on the frame if the application has enabled itself as a drop target and responds to the DDE open

473

request if the user launches the application by double-clicking on a document in the File Manager.

At application close-down time, the frame window prompts the user to save modified documents and shuts down the help engine if it has been activated. Because the frame window participates in so many relationships with other application objects, it must always be destroyed by the function **CWnd::DestroyWindow** rather than by the C++ **delete** operator to ensure proper sequencing of close-down events and cleanup of objects.

Derived Classes

CMDIChildWnd
CMDIFrameWnd

Overrides

Overridable Member Function	Handles
OnSetPreviewMode	Toggling in and out of print preview mode.
OnCreateClient	Creation of controls in the main client area of the frame window; overridden in conjunction with CCreateContext objects.
RecalcLayout	Repositioning of control bars after changing the layout of the frame window.

Public Data Members

m_bAutoEnable   MEMBER

Description When **m_bAutoEnable** is TRUE, it disables menu items that don't have an ON_UPDATE_COMMAND_UI or ON_COMMAND handler. It enables an item that has an ON_COMMAND handler only. It provides a simple method of dealing with commands that are optionally enabled, depending on what the user, the view, and the document are doing. The default value of this data member is TRUE. This is best set in the constructor or **PreCreateWindow**.

rectDefault   MEMBER

Description **rectDefault** gives the frame window's initial size and position. This is best set in the constructor or **PreCreateWindow**.

Member Functions

ActivateFrame FUNCTION

Description   **ActivateFrame** activates a frame window, which makes it visible and gives it the input focus, allowing the user to interact with it. Frame windows are prompted to activate in this way when they are launched by an OLE or DDE event, as opposed to a user moving the input focus with mouse or keyboard input.

Prototype
```
//Function Prototype
//void CFrameWnd::ActivateFrame(int nCmdShow);
void CMyOleClientItem::OnShowItem()
{
    //Get the document that holds the data for this OLE item
CDocument* pDoc = GetDocument();
    //Get the position in the view list
    //of the first view of this document
POSITION pos = pDoc->GetFirstViewPosition();
    //Use the position to get a pointer to the first view
CView* pView = pDoc->GetNextView(pos));
    //Use the pointer to the view to get a
    //pointer to the frame window
CFrameWnd* pFrameWnd = pView->GetParentFrame();
    //Activate the frame window
pFrameWnd->ActivateFrame();
    //Update its title bar
pFrameWnd->OnUpdateFrameTitle(TRUE);
}
```

CFrameWnd FUNCTION

Description   **CFrameWnd** constructs a frame window, without initializing it or making it visible.

Prototype
```
//Function Prototype
//Create a CFrameWnd derived object
CMainFrame* pMainFrame = new CMainFrame;
    //Initialize the frame and make it visible by calling Create;
    //The window class is "SpecialClass",
    //and the caption is "Picture Frame".
    //Its WS_CHILDWINDOW style, size,
    //and location are given by rectOurChild
```

```
//We have a pointer to the parent window,
//no menu, no extended styles,
//and don't use a create context
pMainFrame->Create("SpecialClass",
        "PictureFrame",WS_CHILDWINDOW,
        rectOurChild, pParentWnd, NULL, 0, NULL);
//Load this window's accelerator table
pMainFrame->LoadAccelTable( IDR_PICTUREFRAME );
```

Create   FUNCTION

Description   **Create** initializes a frame window object that an application created explicitly using the **CFrameWnd** constructor. It builds a
Windows frame window and sets its Windows window class name,
style, parent and menu. It does not attach a document or a view to
the **CFrameWnd** object. Notice that **Create** does not attach a
document or a view to the frame window. See the remarks at the
beginning of this section on alternatives for creating frame windows, and **CFrameWnd** for a usage example.

Prototype
```
//Function Prototype
//BOOL CFrameWnd::Create(LPCTSTR lpszClassName,
//LPCSTR lpszWindowName,
//window style:
//DWORD dwStyle = WS_OVERLAPPEDWINDOW,
//size and position:  const RECT& rect = rectDefault,
//parent of this frame:      CWnd* pParentWnd = NULL,
//name of menu resource    LPCTSTR lpszMenuName = NULL,
//extended style attributes   DWORD dwExStyle = 0,
//ptr to CCreateContext structure
//CCreateContext* pContext = NULL);
```

GetActiveDocument   FUNCTION

Description   **GetActiveDocument** retrieves a pointer to the active document of
the **CFrameWnd** object. Frame windows created by the applica-
tion framework are attached automatically to both documents and
views. Objects constructed and initialized explicitly by an application must attach documents and views explicitly or use a document
template to create and initialize the frame window.

Prototype

```
//Function Prototype
//CDocument* CFrameWnd::GetActiveDocument();
    //Get a pointer to the active document
    //somewhere in the implementation code
    //for the frame window object
CDocument* pDocument = GetActiveDocument( );
if (!pDocument->CanCloseFrame(this))
{
    //If the document says that it can't close right now,
    //return BUSY status to the caller
  return (BUSY) ;
}
```

GetActiveView   FUNCTION

Description **GetActiveView** retrieves a pointer to the active view of the **CFrameWnd** object. Frame windows created by the application framework are attached automatically to both documents and views. Objects constructed and initialized explicitly by an application must attach documents and views explicitly or use a document template to create and initialize the frame window.

Prototype

```
//Function Prototype
//CView* CFrameWnd::GetActiveView( ) const;
    //Create a pointer to a view object
CView* pView = NULL;
    //Test for an active view
if (pFrame->GetActiveView( ) == NULL)
{
    //If there isn't one, retrieve a pointer
    //to the child whose view we want to activate
CWnd* pWnd =
pFrame->GetDescendantWindow(ID_PICTURE_CHILD, TRUE);
    //Cast the returned CWnd pointer to a CView
pView = (CView*)pWnd;
    //Make the ID_PICTURE_CHILD window's view active
pFrame->SetActiveView(pView, FALSE);
}
```

477

LoadAccelTable | FUNCTION

Description **LoadAccelTable** loads a resource file table of accelerator key-strokes that serve as alternative ways the user can issue menu commands. A frame window created by a document template is automatically initialized with its accelerator table in place, and **LoadFrame** also automatically provides this service if the accelerator table shares an ID with the other resources specified to **LoadFrame**. In other words, if the resource ID of the accelerator table == the resource ID of the frame's (for example) menu, that accelerator table is loaded without any user interaction.
*See **CFrameWnd** for a usage example.*

Prototype
```
//Function Prototype
//BOOL CFrameWnd::LoadAccelTable(LPCSTR lpszResourceName);
```

LoadFrame | FUNCTION

Description **LoadFrame** offers an alternative to the **Create** function for initializing a frame window object. **LoadFrame** gets most of the information supplied in the **Create** parameter list from the application's resource file. All the frame window attributes loaded from the resource file must share the same ID, which is specified by the first argument to **LoadFrame**. Note that **LoadFrame** does not attach a document or a view to the frame window. See the beginning of this section for alternatives for creating frame windows.

Prototype
```
//Function Prototype
//BOOL CFrameWnd::LoadFrame(UINT nIDResource,
//DWORD dwDefaultStyle,
//    CWnd* pParentWnd, CCreateContext* pContext);
    //Assume we have a pointer to a CFrameWnd object;
    //Call LoadFrame to initialize it with
    //attribute information stored in the resource
    //file — all resources used by LoadFrame share
    //the ID m_nIDResource
if (!pFrame->LoadFrame(m_nIDResource,
            WS_OVERLAPPEDWINDOW, NULL, &context))
{
    //If LoadFrame fails, return NULL to the
    //calling function
  return NULL;
}
```

SetActiveView   FUNCTION

Description   **SetActiveView** changes the input focus to a specified view. When the user shifts the input focus through keyboard or mouse input, the active view is automatically updated by the framework. *See GetActiveView for a usage example.*

Prototype
```
//Function Prototype
//void CFrameWnd::SetActiveView(CView* pViewNew,
//BOOL bNotify);
```

GdiObject

Derivation

CObject ▼
CGdiObject

Description   **CGdiObject** is exclusively a base class. Objects of this type are never created by applications directly, and its member functions are exclusively called from derived classes. The derived classes encapsulate all the Windows GDI tools, such as bitmaps, pens, brushes and fonts. When a GDI tool is needed, an object is created using one of these. The base class provides member functions which are common across all of the types of GDI objects. These include members for converting temporary pointers to GDI objects into handles, functions for attaching and detaching GDI objects from the base class object, and for retrieving stock objects.

Derived Classes

CPen
CBrush
CFont
CBitmap
CPalette
CRgn

Public Data Member

m_hObject   MEMBER

Description   This is a handle identifying the GDI tool attached to the object.

Member Functions

Attach   FUNCTION

Description   **CGdiObject::Attach** attaches a handle containing a GDI tool to an object of class **CGdiObject**. This function is not normally called by application code for this purpose. The derived classes call it in the constructors for the various GDI objects.

CGdiObject
FUNCTION

Description **CGdiObject::CGdiObject** is the constructor for the base class only. It is never called by application code to create objects of derived classes.

CreateStockObject
FUNCTION

Description **CGdiObject::CreateStockObject** is designed to retrieve a GDI object such as a pen or brush from the pool of stock objects maintained by Windows. This function is always called from one of the derived classes. It is used with the constructors for **CPen**, **CFont**, **CPalette** and **CBrush** objects, which take no arguments, initializing them with the appropriate object. The advantage of using **CGdiObject::CreateStockObject** to construct derived GDI objects is that it is always successful. (The GDI object constructors that take arguments can throw exceptions.) It retrieves a handle to the GDI object, attaches it to the **CGdiObject**, returning the usable combination to the application. There is no pool of stock bitmaps or regions from which to return **CBitmap** or **CRgn** objects. **CGdiObject::CreateStockObject** does not support these types.

DeleteObject
FUNCTION

Description **CGdiObject::DeleteObject** detaches the GDI object attached to the **CGdiObject** and then deletes the GDI object from memory, returning the storage held by it. Call this function against objects of the **CGdiObject** derived classes, after the pen, brush, etc., is no longer selected in any device context. This function should not be called against objects that were not created by the application (for example, those retrieved with **CDC::GetStockObject**). If the application creates a pattern brush, **CGdiObject::DeleteObject** does not free the storage allocated for the bitmap that defines the pattern. The bitmap must be deleted explicitly.

DeleteTempMap
FUNCTION

Description **CGdiObject::DeleteTempMap** is part of the Windows class housecleaning mechanism. It is called by the idle-time processing members of **CWinApp** and deletes the temporary **CGdiObject** objects, which typically have a lifetime of only one message-processing cycle, first detaching the handle of the associated GDI object. This function is not meant to be used by application code. It is used by the framework to manage objects of derived classes.

Detach   FUNCTION

Description   **CGdiObject::Detach** detaches a handle containing a GDI tool from an object of class **CGdiObject**. This function is used to separate the handle from the **CGdiObject** when an application or the framework wants to prevent the **CGdiObject** destructor from destroying the GDI object along with the object to which it was attached. **CGdiObject::Detach** returns the handle of the GDI object it is detaching. GDI objects should not be detached from their **CGdiObjects** while they are selected in a device context.

FromHandle   FUNCTION

Description   **CGdiObject::FromHandle** returns a pointer to a **CGdiObject** to which the GDI object identified by the handle passed to the function is attached. If the **CGdiObject** doesn't exist, a temporary one is created. This is a quick method of creating an object from a handle to a GDI object, but the object has a very short lifetime. It is typically good for only one message-processing cycle. Because the object returned by **CGdiObject::FromHandle** has a very short life span, the pointer to it can't be stored for later use. If the object is needed again, the handle to it must be preserved. An object pointer can be converted to a handle using **CGdiObject::GetSafeHandle**.

GetObject   FUNCTION

Description   **CGdiObject::GetObject** is an information function that is always called for one of the derived GDI object classes. It fills a structure specific to the type of object with descriptive information.

Type of Object	Information Returned
CPen	LOGPEN
CBrush	LOGBRUSH
CFont	LOGFONT
CBitmap	BITMAP: Only width, height and color information fields are returned. The bitmap bits must be retrieved with CBitmap::GetBitmapBits.
CPalette	Number of entries in the palette. Does not return the LOGPALETTE structure. Get palette entries by calling CPalette::GetPaletteEntries.
CRgn	Regions are not supported by this function.

GetSafeHandle   FUNCTION

Description   **CGdiObject::GetSafeHandle** returns a Windows handle for a GDI object attached to a **CGdiObject**. If a **CGdiObject** is temporary and due to be destroyed in idle-time processing, saving its attached GDI object as a handle preserves the pen, brush, etc., for later use.

UnrealizeObject   FUNCTION

Description   **CGdiObject::UnrealizeObject** is used to reset the origin of a brush or to remap a logical palette. When you're contemplating the family of functions that change the alignment of the brush, it is helpful to remember that a "brush" is nothing more than a small bitmap combined in a way the application directs with the bits in the area it will be painting. In Windows 3.*x,* the origin of the brush bitmap is the upper left corner of the display surface. As application windows move and are resized, it is possible for this bitmap to become misaligned and produce a striping effect when the window is repainted using a patterned brush.

   CGdiObject::UnrealizeObject realigns the origin of the **CBrush** object for which it is called with the origin of the window.

   CGdiObject::UnrealizeObject is also used for resetting the contents of an application's color palette. Many display devices are capable of displaying a huge range of colors, but the total number of colors that can be displayed at any given time may be limited. The subset of colors that can be displayed simultaneously is maintained in the *system palette.* Windows reserves some palette entries for its own use and then adds palette entries to the system palette as applications realize their logical palettes. Logical palettes are specific to a given application and provide a means by which applications can define their color requirements, taking full advantage of the capability of the display device but without having an undesirable effect on other application uses of color. An application specifies its palette by using member functions of the derived class **CPalette** and then makes its choices effective by calling **CDC::RealizePalette**.

   CGdiObject::UnrealizeObject causes Windows to remap an application's color palette from scratch, just as though it were being realized for the first time. The reason for doing this is usually connected with very intensive or precise color use by an application that wants to ensure that changes in the system palette don't adversely affect its color use. Neither a palette nor a brush should be unrealized while it is selected in a device context. (A palette can be selected into more than one device context at a time, as long as both contexts refer to the same output device.)

483

CHEdit

CLASS

Derivation

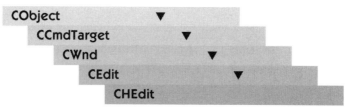

```
CObject              ▼
    CCmdTarget           ▼
        CWnd                 ▼
            CEdit                ▼
                CHEdit
```

Description   The **CHEdit** class implements the Windows handwriting-recognition edit control, used by the Windows pen interface. The **CHEdit** control inherits all the functionality of the edit control, which is essentially a simplified word-processing tool with the flavor of the Windows Notepad utility. Edit controls are implemented by the class **CEdit**. Framework application startup code automatically detects pen-equipped systems and enables any **CEdit** class controls for pen input. The **CHEdit** class basically exists to provide a way for applications to supply additional information to the handwriting-recognition engine if it can reasonably anticipate characteristics of the handwriting data. The additional information is supplied to the control in the form of alphabet codes (**ALC**) values that define what sort of characters are expected. The **ALC** codes have the following values and meanings and may be combined with the bitwise OR:

Alphabet Code Value	Meaning
1	Lowercase only
2	Uppercase only
3	Either upper- or lowercase
4	Numeric
8	Punctuation
16	Mathematical symbols
32	Monetary symbols
64	Other symbols

MFC does not emphasize handwriting recognition or the pen interface particularly, and at this point, most pen applications are being written in C rather than in C++. For this reason, code examples are omitted for the functions in this section.

Member Functions

Description   **CHEdit** constructs a **CHEdit** object, but does not create, attach or initialize its accompanying edit control window.

Prototype
```
//Function Prototype
    //we have a member variable that points to the
    //edit control

pcheOurHEdit = new CHEdit;
    //Then specify its style, location, parent, and control ID
pOurHEdit.Create( WS_CHILD | WS_VISIBLE | ES_AUTOVSCROLL |
        ES_MULTILINE, rect, this, ID_OURLIST);
```

Description   **Create** creates a Windows handwriting edit control, attaches it to the **CHEdit** object, and shows it. Like edit controls, handwriting edit control properties are determined by style constants, which may be combined with one another. They are listed in the **Create** member function entry of the **CEdit** class. *See **CHEdit** for a usage example.*

Description   **GetInflate** returns the amounts that have been added to the client area rectangle dimensions to define the area that is considered by the handwriting-recognition engine. In practice, users are not meticulous about keeping written input within the boundaries of the edit control client area. Inflating the area considered by the recognition engine usually serves to improve recognition performance. The structure that is passed to this function contains values that are added to the client area rectangle coordinates to increase (or reduce) the recognition area.

Prototype
```
//Function Prototype
//BOOL GetInflate( LPRECTOFS lpRectOfs );
```

GetInkHandle — FUNCTION

Description **GetInkHandle** returns a handle to the "ink" recorded by the edit control. *Ink* is simply a bitmap record of the user's pen input before it has been submitted for recognition processing. The handle becomes invalid after the control is destroyed. The function returns NULL if the control was not in ink mode when it was called.

Prototype
```
//Function Prototype
//HPENDATA GetInkHandle( );
```

GetRC — FUNCTION

Description **GetRC** fills in a recognition context structure.

Prototype
```
//Function Prototype
//BOOL GetRC( LPRC lpRC );
```

GetUnderline — FUNCTION

Description **GetUnderline** returns TRUE if underline mode is set.

Prototype
```
//Function Prototype
//BOOL GetUnderline( );
```

SetInflate — FUNCTION

Description **SetInflate** is the companion function to GetInflate. It sets the inflation values that are applied to the client area of the edit control by the handwriting-recognition engine.

Prototype
```
//Function Prototype
//BOOL SetInflate( LPRECTOFS lpRectOfs );
```

SetInkMode — FUNCTION

Description **SetInkMode** tells the control to collect input as "ink," or in essence, to record a bitmap picture of the pen input.

Prototype
```
//Function Prototype
//BOOL SetInkMode( HPENDATA hPenDataInitial = NULL );
```

SetRC   FUNCTION

Description   **SetRC** changes the recognition context for the handwriting-recognition engine by limiting the number of characters it is asked to recognize.

Prototype
```
//Function Prototype
//BOOL SetRC( LPRC lpRC  );
```

SetUnderline   FUNCTION

Description   **SetUnderline** toggles the underline mode of the handwriting edit control. To set underline on the edit control, the control must have been created without a border.

Prototype
```
//Function Prototype
//BOOL SetUnderline( BOOL bUnderline = TRUE );
```

StopInkMode   FUNCTION

Description   **StopInkMode** tells the control to stop collecting ink and optionally to begin handwriting recognition. Parameters have the following meaning:

Recognition Flag	Meaning
HEP_RECOG	Gets the ink and does recognition.
HEP_NORECOG	Deletes the ink from the control without doing recognition.
HEP_WAITFORTAP	Does recognition on next pen tap.

Prototype
```
//Function Prototype
//BOOL StopInkMode( UINT uiRecgnitionFlag );
```

487

ListBox   **CLASS**

Derivation

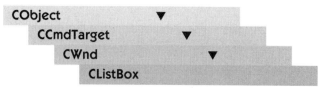

CObject
    CCmdTarget
        CWnd
            CListBox

Description
The **CListBox** class encapsulates single- and multiple-selection Windows listboxes. Listboxes can be constructed in an application's client area by constructing a listbox object (either as static data element, class member, or on the heap) and calling the **Create** member function to build and attach a listbox window. Dialogs construct listbox controls based on their template.

If an application creates listbox controls independently of a dialog box, form view or dialog bar, steps must be taken to ensure that the object associated with the control is properly destroyed. Stack-based window-type objects normally don't have sufficient duration to survive more than one Windows message. As a result, they cannot be created, seen and used.

CListBox objects created on the heap with **new** should be deleted with **delete**.

Overrides

Overridable Function Name	Triggering Event
DrawItem	An OWNERDRAW listbox needs to be repainted.
MeasureItem	Owner draw listbox is being drawn; the application must fill in a MEASUREITEM struct to define how list items are drawn.
CompareItem	A sorted OWNERDRAW listbox is inserting an item.
DeleteItem	An OWNERDRAW listbox is deleting an item.

Member Functions

AddString — FUNCTION

Description   **AddString** adds a string to listbox. If the listbox has set the **LBS_SORT** style, the new string is inserted in the list at its alphabetical rank. If it is unsorted, the string is appended to the list. To explicitly control the insertion point, use the **InsertString** member function. *See CListBox for a usage example.*

Prototype
```
//Function Prototype
//int AddString( LPCSTR lpszListItem );
```

CListBox — FUNCTION

Description   **CListBox** constructs a **CListBox** object, but does not create, attach or initialize its accompanying Windows listbox control window. **CListBox** abstracts the functionality, but much of that functionality is *implemented* in the control itself. That the control is a different object than the **CListBox** object is an implementation detail, but it does explain the two-phase construction.

Prototype
```
//Function Prototype
    //Construct a listbox in the frame
    //window's client area
//(at file scope so its lifetime is sufficient)
CListBox lbOurList;
//... intervening code, then in a function...
    //Then specify its style, location, parent, and control ID
lbOurList.Create( LBS_STANDARD, rect, this, ID_OURLIST);
    //After the listbox is created, initialize it with list items
lbOurList.AddString("First Choice");
lbOurList.AddString("Next Choice");
    //The return from the GetCount Call is 2
int iNumberListItems = lbOurList.GetCount( );
```

Create — FUNCTION

Description   **Create** creates a windows listbox, attaches it to the **CListBox** object, and shows it. Listbox properties are determined by style constants, which may be combined with one another. They are listed in the following table. *See CListBox for a usage example.*

Listbox Style	Meaning
LBS_NOTIFY	Parent window is notified for mouse clicks over items.
LBS_SORT	Strings are sorted alphabetically.
LBS_NOREDRAW	Prevent updates; can be reset by sending WM_SETREDRAW.
LBS_MULTIPLESEL	Allow multiple item selection.
LBS_OWNERDRAWFIXED	Application paints the listbox items, and items are all the same height.
LBS_OWNERDRAWVARIABLE	Application paints the listbox items, and items are variable height.
LBS_HASSTRINGS	Listbox items are strings.
LBS_USETABSTOPS	Expand tab stops in listbox strings.
LBS_NOINTEGRALHEIGHT	Don't adjust listbox size to be a multiple of item height.
LBS_MULTICOLUMN	Display list in columns.
LBS_WANTKEYBOARDINPUT	Allow user to manage listbox with keyboard input.
LBS_EXTENDEDSEL	Use Shift key with the mouse to let user select contiguous items.
LBS_STANDARD	LBS_NOTIFY | LBS_SORT | WS_VSCROLL | WS_BORDER.
LBS_DISABLENOSCROLL	When the listbox has an insufficient number of items to require a scrollbar, the scrollbar is still shown, but it is disabled. Without this style, the scrollbar is hidden in such a case.

Prototype

```
//Function Prototype
//BOOL Create(DWORD dwStyle, const RECT& rect,
//        CWnd* pParentWnd, UINT nID);
```

DeleteString   FUNCTION

Description   **DeleteString** removes the string at the zero-based index from the listbox.

Prototype

```
//Function Prototype
//int DeleteString(UINT nIndex );
    //Delete the currently selected string
lbOurList.DeleteString( lbOurList.GetCurSel( ) );
```

Dir · FUNCTION

Description **Dir** adds a list of file and directory names to the listbox, filtering by file attribute and a wildcard string. Possible file attribute flags are listed in the following table. *See **ResetContent** for a usage example.*

Attribute Flag	Meaning
0x0000	Read-write
0x0001	Read-only
0x0002	Hidden
0x0004	System file
0x0010	Directory
0x0020	Archive
0x4000	Scan all drives that match the wildcard string.
0x8000	The "exclusive" flag. In its absence, any other attributes are considered additive to the normal attribute. With this flag, you have to explicitly specify which files you want to see.

Prototype
```
//Function Prototype
//int Dir( UINT attr , LPCSTR lpszWildCard );
```

FindString · FUNCTION

Description **FindString** does a case-insensitive substring search and returns the index of the first string containing a match of its initial characters and the substring, or **LB_ERR** if no match is found. It starts the search after the item identified by the first parameter, continuing through the list and wrapping to the top. If the starting index is -1, the list is searched inclusively from top to bottom.

Prototype
```
//Function Prototype
//int FindString( int nStartAfter , LPCSTR lpszItem  );
    //Search the entire listbox for strings
    //starting with "Old", "old", "oLD", etc.
lbOurList.FindString(-1, "old" );
```

FindStringExact · FUNCTION

Description **FindStringExact** searches for a string in a listbox, but unlike **FindString**, it won't look for the string inside a word. The search is case insensitive. If the listbox is an owner-draw listbox, but does not have the style **LBS_HASSTRINGS**, then **FindStringExact** tries to match the doubleword value in the second parameter. *See* *CListBox for a usage example.*

Prototype
```
//Function Prototype
//int FindStringExact( int iStartAfterIndex,
//              LPCSTR lpszSearchString );
    //Search the entire listbox for the string "old".
lbOurList.FindString(-1, "old" );
```

GetCount   FUNCTION

Description   **GetCount** returns a value one greater than the index of the last item in the listbox. *See CListBox for a usage example.*

Prototype
```
//Function Prototype
//int GetCount( )const;
```

GetCurSel   FUNCTION

Description   **GetCurSel** retrieves the zero-based index of the current selection in a single-selection listbox. The function returns **LB_ERR** if there is no current selection or if the listbox is multiple-selection.

Prototype
```
//Function Prototype
//int GetCurSel( )const;
    //If there is no current selection
if ( LB_ERR == lbOurList.GetCurSel( ) )
    //Select the topmost visible item
    lbOurList.SetCurSel( lbOurList.GetTopIndex( ) );
```

GetHorizontalExtent   FUNCTION

Description   **GetHorizontalExtent** returns the distance in pixels a listbox with horizontal scroll bars can move.

Prototype
```
//Function Prototype
//int GetHorizontalExtent( )const;
    //Find out how far the listbox can scroll
    // — we assume that it was
    //created with the WS_HSCROLL style
int iScrollWidth = lbOurList.GetHorizontalExtent( );
```

492

```
//Test to see whether the list was scrollable
//in the x direction; if the TextExtent of a
//given list item on the current device is greater
//than the client area of the listbox,
//GetHorizontalExtent returns nonzero.

if( iScrollWidth )
    //Prevent it from scrolling and hide the scroll bar
    lbOurList.SetHorizontalExtent( 0 );
```

GetItemData   FUNCTION

Description **GetItemData** is the companion function to **SetItemData**.
SetItemData associates an application-supplied, 32-bit **DWORD**
with a given listbox item. **GetItemData** retrieves the value. *See
GetTopIndex for a usage example.*

Prototype
```
//Function Prototype
//DWORD GetItemData(int iItemIndex );
```

GetItemDataPtr   FUNCTION

Description **GetItemDataPtr** is the companion function to **SetItemDataPtr**.
SetItemDataPtr associates an application-supplied, 32-bit **void** *
with a given listbox item. **GetItemDataPtr** retrieves the pointer.
See GetTopIndex for a usage example.

Prototype
```
//Function Prototype
//void* GetItemDataPtr(int iItemIndex );
```

GetItemRect   FUNCTION

Description **GetItemRect** fills in a **RECT** structure with the dimensions of a
bounding rectangle for a listbox item, given the index of the item.
Applications that take over the drawing of their own listbox items
by setting the **LBS_OWNERDRAW** style receive this and other
drawing information in a **DRAWITEMSTRUCT** structure that is
passed to the **DrawItem** member function. However for applications that just want to implement some crude drag-and-drop or hit
testing, this works just fine.

Prototype

```
//Function Prototype
//int GetItemRect( int iItemIndex, LPRECT lprBoundingRect );
    //Get the index of the first visible listbox item
int iTopItem =  lbOurList.GetTopIndex( );
    //Get the dimensions of the bounding rectangle for the item
RECT rBoundingRect ;
int iTopItem = lbOurList.GetItemRect( iTopItem, &rBoundingRect );
    //We stored the length in pixels of the
    //longest listbox string
    //Test to see whether the string is wider than the listbox
if ( m_LengthLongestString > rBoundingRect.right )
    //If so, set a new horizontal scrolling range
    //for the listbox
lbOurList.SetHorizontalExtent( m_LengthLongestString );
```

GetSel   FUNCTION

Description **GetSel** returns a positive number if the list item identified by the zero-based index is selected, and 0 if it is not.

Prototype

```
//Function Prototype
//int GetSel ( int nIndex ) const;
    //Find out whether an item is selected
BOOL bIsSelected  = lbOurList.GetSel( iItemIndex );
    //If it is, get the length of the string
if( bIsSelected )
{
   int iLength = lbOurList.GetTextLen( iItemIndex);
    //Copy the listbox item text
CString stringlListItem;
lbOurList.GetText( iItemIndex, stringListItem);
}
```

GetSelCount   FUNCTION

Description **GetSelCount** retrieves the number of selected items in a listbox that has set the **LBS_MULTIPLESEL** style. *See **CListBox** for a usage example.*

Prototype
```
//Function Prototype
//int GetSelCount( )const;
    //Get Number of items selected
int iHowManySels = lbOurList.GetSelCount( );
    //We copy the indices of selected items
    //to the array at lpiArrayItemIndices
lbOurList.GetSelItems( iHowManySels, lpiArrayItemIndices );
```

GetSelItems   FUNCTION

Description   **GetSelItems** fills an array with the indices of selected items in a listbox that has set the **LBS_MULTIPLESEL** style. The return specifies the number of indices copied to the array. *See* ***GetSelCount*** *for a usage example.*

Prototype
```
//Function Prototype
//int GetSelItems( int nMaxItems , LPINT rgIndex   );
```

GetText   FUNCTION

Description   **GetText** retrieves the text string associated with a listbox index, optionally writing it to a buffer or a **CString** object. If it is written to a character buffer, the buffer must be long enough for the string and a terminating NULL. The return is the length in *bytes* of the string, excluding the terminal NULL. *See* ***GetSel*** *for a usage example.*

Prototype
```
//Function Prototype
//int GetText( int nIndex , LPSTR lpszBuffer);
//int GetText( int nIndex, CString& rString   );
```

GetTextLen   FUNCTION

Description   **GetTextLen** returns the length in characters of the text string associated with a listbox index. *See* ***GetSel*** *for a usage example.*

Prototype
```
//Function Prototype
//int GetTextLen( int nIndex);
```

GetTopIndex `FUNCTION`

Description   **GetTopIndex** returns the zero-based index of the first visible listbox item. This value can be non-zero, depending on how far the user has scrolled in the list.

Prototype
```
//Function Prototype
//int GetTopIndex( )const;
    //Get the index of the first visible listbox item
int iTopItem = lbOurList.GetTopIndex( );
    //Get the item data associated with it
DWORD dwTopItemData = lbOurList.GetItemData( iTopItem );
    //Test to see whether the datum is NULL
if(dwTopItemData != NULL )
    //If not, set item data to NULL
lbOurList.SetItemData( iTopItem, NULL );
    //Get the pointer associated with the next list item
void* pTopItemData = lbOurList.GetItemData( iTopItem + 1 );
    //Set the next item's pointer to the one we retrieved
lbOurList.SetItemDataPtr( iTopItem + 3, pTopItemData );
```

InsertString `FUNCTION`

Description   **InsertString** inserts the given string at the zero-based index. *See CListBox for a usage example.*

Prototype
```
//Function Prototype
//int InsertString( int nIndex , LPCSTR lpszItem );
    //Get the index of the first visible listbox item
int iTopItem = lbOurList.GetTopIndex( );
    //Insert a string at the first visible position
lbOurList.InsertString( iTopItem, lpszListItem );
```

ResetContent `FUNCTION`

Description   **ResetContent** removes all listbox items.

Prototype
```
//Function Prototype
//void ResetContent( );
    //Clear the listbox
lbOurList.ResetContent( );
    //Fill the listbox with .exe filenames
lbOurList.Dir( 0x8000, "*.exe");
```

SelectString   FUNCTION

Description   **SelectString** behaves like **FindString**, except that it selects the first matching string, scrolling the list to bring it into view if necessary. **SelectString** does not work for listboxes that have set the **LBS_MULTIPLESEL** style.

Prototype
```
//Function Prototype
//int SelectString( int nStartAfter , LPCSTR lpszItem  );
    //Search the entire listbox for strings starting with "old",
    //and select the item.
int iNewSelIndex = lbOurList.SelectString(-1, "old" );
```

SelItemRange   FUNCTION

Description   **SelItemRange** selects or unselects a contiguous range of items in a listbox that has set the **LBS_MULTIPLESEL** style. The first parameter is set to **TRUE** to select the range. *See **CListBox** for a usage example.*

Prototype
```
//Function Prototype
//int SelItemRange( BOOL bSelect, int nFirstItem , int nLastItem );
    //Get the index of the first visible listbox item and select
    //items at START_RANGE through END_RANGE
int iTopItem =  lbOurList.GetTopIndex( );
  lbOurList.SelItemRange( TRUE, START_ITEM , END_ITEM  );
```

SetColumnWidth   FUNCTION

Description   **SetColumnWidth** sets the column width in pixels for a listbox that has set the **LBS_MULTICOLUMN** style. *See **GetItemRect** for a usage example.*

Prototype
```
//Function Prototype
//void SetColumnWidth( int cxWidth );
```

SetCurSel   FUNCTION

Description   **SetCurSel** selects the item identified by the zero-based index in a single-selection listbox. *See **GetCurSel** for a usage example.* An argument of -1 clears any selection.

Prototype

```
//Function Prototype
//int SetCurSel(int nSelect);
```

SetHorizontalExtent   FUNCTION

Description   **SetHorizontalExtent** sets the distance in pixels a listbox with horizontal scroll bars can move. If the new extent is equal to or greater than the *x* dimension of the listbox, the scroll bar is shown, and the list is scrolled across the window. If the new dimension is smaller than the listbox width, the horizontal scroll bar is hidden.

The horizontal extent is recalculated each time you add an item to a listbox. For owner-draw listboxes, the value is supplied by the **OnMeasureItem** function. To test assumptions on this, simply create an owner-draw listbox and watch when the **OnMeasureItem** function is called. The point is that setting the extent to 0 only persists until the contents change. *See GetHorizontalExtent for a usage example.*

Prototype

```
//Function Prototype
//void SetHorizontalExtent(int iScrollableWidth );
```

SetItemData   FUNCTION

Description   **SetItemData** associates an application-supplied, 32-bit **DWORD** with a given listbox item. It returns **LB_ERR** if the operation fails. *See GetTopIndex for a usage example.*

Prototype

```
//Function Prototype
//int SetItemData(int iItemIndex, DWORD dwAppData );
```

SetItemDataPtr   FUNCTION

Description   **SetItemDataPtr** associates an application-supplied, 32-bit **void*** with a given listbox item. It returns **LB_ERR** if the operation fails. *See GetTopIndex for a usage example.*

Prototype

```
//Function Prototype
//int SetItemDataPtr(int iItemIndex, void* pAppData );
```

SetSel   FUNCTION

Description   **SetSel** selects or unselects an item in a listbox that has set the **LBS_MULTIPLESEL** style. If the first argument is -1, then the selection action is applied to all strings in the listbox.

Prototype
```
//Function Prototype
//int SetSel(int nIndex , BOOL bSelect );
    //Get the index of the first visible listbox
    //item and select it
int iTopItem =  lbOurList.GetTopIndex( );
  lbOurList.SetSel( iTopItem, TRUE );
```

SetTabStops   FUNCTION

Description   **SetTabStops** establishes the value for tab stops in the dialog. A listbox must have set the **LBS_USETABSTOPS** style to use this function. Tab stop settings are used to expand tabs when you're drawing the listbox text. The tab stop values are expressed in dialog base units, which are one-fourth the current system font width and one-eighth the current system font height. The parameterless version of the function sets the tab stops at 32 units, the next version sets all tabs equal to the passed value, and the last uses a count of tab stops and an array of values to set. This is about the trickiest of the **CListBox** functions to use. You first must *unset* the tabstops by calling **SetTabStops(0)**; You may then set new tabstops by using any of the three overloads shown below.
    *See **CListBox** for a usage example.*

Prototype
```
//Function Prototype
//void SetTabStops( );
//BOOL SetTabStops( const int& cxEachStop);
//BOOL SetTabStops( int nTabStops, LPINT rgTabStops);
    //Set default value for expanding tabs
    //embedded in listbox strings
lbOurList.SetTabStops( );
```

 LongBinary

Derivation	CObject ▼
	CLongBinary

Description The class **CLongBinary** provides support for storing large binary objects (also known as BLOBs), such as bitmaps or sound in an ODBC database. It is a wrapper for the global handle to the block allocated on the heap in which the binary data is stored. An application manipulates the data by using the handle stored in the data member **m_hData**.

The record field exchange mechanism moves data between a **CRecordSet** object that includes a **CLongBinary** object as one of its fields by storing the global handle in **m_hData** and the length in bytes of the **CLongBinary** object. When a **CRecordset** object that has a **CLongBinary** field is destroyed, the handle and the memory used for the **CLongBinary** object are freed.

Public Data Members

m_dwDataLength   MEMBER

Description **m_dwDataLength** is the size in bytes of the data object whose handle is specified by **m_hData**.

m_hData   MEMBER

Description **m_hData** is the Windows global handle to the memory containing the binary data.

Member Functions

CLongBinary	FUNCTION

Description   **CLongBinary** constructs a **CLongBinary** object.

Prototype
```
//Function Prototype
    //Construct the CLongBinary object
CLongBinary longbinPicture;
    //Set a global handle to some memory
    //containing a BLOB into the CLongBinary
    //data member
longbinPicture.m_hData = hPictureMem;
    //Set its length in bytes into the CLongBinary
    //data member
longbinPicture.m_dwDataLength = dwPictureSize;
```

C MapPtrToPtr

Description   **CMapPtrToPtr** is one of a collection of map classes that are derived from the common MFC base class **CObject** and encapsulate the behavior of keyed access data structures (often called "hash tables"). Strings, 16-bit words, and pointers can be transformed to unique keys to provide very fast access to associated values. Various combinations of key types and value types are provided in the map classes, with values allowed to be non-unique. Like the other groups of collections classes, the map classes have certain idiosyncrasies related to the data types they incorporate. When element pairs are removed from maps, objects to which they point are not deleted unless they are of **CString** type. The actual objects referenced by void pointers or **CObject** pointers contained in maps must therefore be deleted separately and explicitly from the map entries.

Map classes that associate values of type **CObject** with 16-bit **WORD** or **CString** keys are provided with the idea that they may be used as base classes for the derivation of user-defined maps. Typically, the value associated with a key in a user-derived map class will itself be a derivation from the **CObject** base class. Maps that include void pointers as keys or values may not be serialized, but maps including other data types may be. **CString**, **CObject** and **CObject** derived objects can serialize as either keys or values. All the constructors for maps allow the programmer to set the granularity of memory allocation when maps are originally built or when they are expanded. The default allocation block is ten map entries.

The map classes are used extensively in the application framework to manage handles and do other heavy-duty, runtime housekeeping chores. Their chief benefit is that they can provide very fast access to large dynamic data structures that depend on relationships between items. The downside is that they provide less high-level functionality than does a full-blown database toolkit and may prove somewhat difficult to adapt to application-specific needs, because a key can associate only a single value rather than a more complicated record structure.

The strength of a map is that it is lightning fast—usually O(1) if designed correctly. The problems are that you have to make a guesstimate at design time about the size of the map and do some other voodoo to optimize its behavior. If two keys translate to the same value (or if you allow duplicates), the algorithm degrades to have similar performance to a list *when collisions occur.* Growth must be managed very carefully because it can be the most expensive operation you perform on a map.

Note that there is (as of version 2.0) a templated version:

```
template <class T> class CMap(T, T&);
```

Map Collection Classes

CMapPtrToPtr   CLASS

Description This class maps void pointer keys to void pointer values. Objects of type **CMapPtrToPtr** cannot be serialized.

CMapPtrToWord   CLASS

Description This class maps void pointer keys to 16-bit **WORD** values. Objects of type **CMapPtrToWord** cannot be serialized.

CMapStringToOb   CLASS

Description This class maps **CString** keys to **CObject** pointers. Objects of type **CMapStringToOb** can be serialized.

CMapStringToPtr   CLASS

Description This class maps **CString** keys to void pointer values. Objects of type **CMapStringToPtr** cannot be serialized.

CMapStringToString   CLASS

Description This class maps **CString** keys to **CString** values. Objects of type **CMapStringToString** can be serialized.

CMapWordToOb   CLASS

Description This class maps 16-bit **WORD** keys to **CObject** pointers. Objects of type **CMapWordToOb** can be serialized.

CMapWordToPtr   CLASS

Description This class maps 16-bit **WORD** keys to void pointer values. Objects of type **CMapWordToPtr** cannot be serialized.

General Prototypes for Map Member Functions

To use the general prototypes for the map class member functions to make the prototypes for a specific map class, make the following substitutions:

For This Placeholder	Substitute This Type
KEY_TYPE	Data type of the map's key.
KEY_TYPE_PTR	Pointer to data type of the map's key.
VAL_TYPE	Data type of the map's value.
VAL_TYPE_PTR	Pointer to data type of the map's value.

Example

```
CMap***To***( int nBlockSize = 10 );
int GetCount( )const;
void GetNextAssoc( POSITION & rNextPosition,
        KEY_TYPE & rKey, VAL_TYPE & rValue );
POSITION GetStartPosition( )const;
BOOL IsEmpty( )const;
BOOL Lookup( KEY_TYPE_PTR key, VAL_TYPE_PTR & rValue );
void RemoveAll( );
BOOL RemoveKey( const KEY_TYPE_PTR key );
void SetAt( const KEY_TYPE_PTR key, VAL_TYPE_PTR newValue )
    throw( CMemoryException );
VAL_TYPE_PTR & operator[ ] ( const KEY_TYPE_PTR key );
```

Common Member Functions for Map Collection Classes

GetCount   FUNCTION

Description **GetCount** returns the number of entries in the map.

Prototype
```
//Function Prototype
int iCount = mapStringToMyOb.GetCount( );
```

GetNextAssoc — FUNCTION

Description **GetNextAssoc** retrieves the key/value pair at the position specified by the position parameter and then updates the position reference to identify the next map entry. It is used to traverse a map by position. *See **RemoveAll** for a usage example.*

GetStartPosition — FUNCTION

Description Like lists, maps may be navigated by position. **GetStartPosition** retrieves the position of the beginning of a map and is used to set up iteration. A NULL position is returned if there are no entries. See **RemoveAll** for an example of usage. No sorting or ranking is implied by the start position. In other words, the key is not lexically less than all other keys.

IsEmpty — FUNCTION

Description **IsEmpty** tests for an empty map and returns TRUE if the map has no entries.

Little-known fact: In the headers, you'll find a section marked *//advanced features for derived classes*. The two functions of particular interest are as follows:

```
UINT GetHashTableSize() const;
void InitHashTable(UINT hashSize, BOOL bAllocNow = TRUE);
```

If you accept the default provided at construction, the hash table is 17 entries long. While this is great for short dictionaries, consider a map of error numbers to messages where you have 4000 messages! You quickly fill the map, then your algorithm becomes far more like a linear search than a key transform algorithm. By calling InitHashTable(4001), you get a good-sized table and the results are astounding. Give it a try.

Prototype
```
//Function Prototype
if( ! mapStringToMyOb.IsEmpty( ) )
    {
    //do something if the map has entries....
    }
```

Lookup

Description   **Lookup** uses a hashing algorithm to find a key and writes the associated value to the address passed as the second parameter to the function. The Boolean return value signifies success or failure of the lookup.

Prototype

```
//Function Prototype
CMapStringToString stringMap;
    //If the key "sunday" is in the map...
if( stringMap.Lookup( "sunday", pHoliday ))
{
    //Lookup copies a pointer to the CString value
    //associated with the key "sunday" to pHoliday
if ( pHoliday->Compare( "DayOff" ) == 0 )
    //The CString member function Compare returns 0 if
    //the object is lexically equal to the parameter...
}
```

operator []

Description   **operator []** is a shorthand alternative to **SetAt**, but it may be used as an lvalue (one that appears on the left side of an assignment statement) *only*. If the specified key exists, the associated value is replaced. If not, a new key/value pair is inserted.

   The only parameter to the operator is the key, so if it were the source of an assignment for a key that did not exist, there would not be enough information available to construct a key/value pair. If the replaced value is a pointer, the object to which it refers persists until it is explicitly deleted.

Prototype

```
//Function Prototype
CMapStringToString mapAthletes;
    //Add two key/value pairs
mapAthletes["harding"] = new CString ( "Skaters" );
mapAthletes["kerrigan"] = new CString ( "Skaters" );
```

RemoveAll

Description   **RemoveAll** clears the map and deletes **CString** objects that were keys. The objects to which void pointers, **CObject** pointers, and pointers to user-derived objects based on **CObject** refer exist unless they are deleted explicitly. If you do a **RemoveAll**, you will wind up with a memory leak unless you first explicitly iterate the list, deleting all contained pointers.

Prototype

```
//Function Prototype
    //Assume that we have a map of string keys and user-defined
    //objects....
POSITION pos = mapStringToMyOb.GetStartPosition( );
    //Iterate through the map and delete all the objects
    //to which map values point....
while( pos != NULL )
{
    //pKey is a a CString object, and pMyObject is a pointer to
    //a user-derived object based on CObject; pos is updated to
    //identify the next map entry...
 mapStringToMyOb.GetNextAssociation( pos, cstringKey,
pMyObject );
 delete pMyObject;
}
    //Then clear the map itself...
mapStringToMyOb.RemoveAll( );
```

RemoveKey   FUNCTION

Description **RemoveKey** deletes a key/value pair from a map. If either of the replaced values is a pointer, the objects to which the pointer refers persist until explicitly deleted.

Prototype

```
//Function Prototype
CMapStringToPtr mapPictureTiles;
    //This map associates names with a group of bitmaps
    //we have in memory...
mapPictureTiles.Lookup( "leaves", pAspenLeaves )
    //Look up the key before we remove the pair from the map
    //so that we can use the pointer we are replacing to delete the
unneeded object....
 mapPictureTiles.RemoveKey( "leaves");
 delete pAspenLeaves;
```

SetAt

Description   **SetAt** replaces the value associated with a key or inserts a key/value pair if the key does not currently exist. Except for **CString** values, the replaced object is not deleted, so pointer values must be captured before the call to **SetAt** and used to explicitly delete the objects to which they refer in order to avoid memory leaks.

Note that unlike the SetAt function in other collections, this version takes a key instead of an integer to identify the element.

Prototype
```
//Function Prototype
CMapStringToPtr mapPictureTiles;
    //This map associates names with a group of bitmaps
    //we have in memory....
if ( ! mapPictureTiles.Lookup( "leaves", pAspenLeaves )
    //If the key doesn't exist, then insert the new key/value pair
 mapPictureTiles.SetAt( "leaves", pOakLeaves );
else
 {
    //The value did exist, so we need to insert the new value and
    //delete
    //the bitmap identified by the pointer value we are replacing
    mapPictureTiles.SetAt( "leaves", pOakLeaves );
    delete pAspenLeaves;
 }
```

C MapPtrToWord

. . . .

See **CMapPtrToPtr**.

C MapStringToOb

. . . .

See **CMapPtrToPtr**.

CMapStringToPtr
CLASS

See **CMapPtrToPtr**.

CMapStringToString
CLASS

See **CMapPtrToPtr**.

CMapWordToOb
CLASS

See **CMapPtrToPtr**.

CMapWordToPtr
CLASS

See **CMapPtrToPtr**.

MDIChildWnd

CLASS

Derivation

CObject

CCmdTarget

CWnd

CFrameWnd

CMDIChildWnd

Description   The **CMDIChildWnd** class is the companion class to
CMDIFrameWnd for managing multiple document interface
applications. A tightly spun web of relationships synchronize an
MDI frame window, the child windows it contains, and the views
and documents attached to the children. Most of an MDI
application's work is done in the document and view classes. The
application framework assumes most of the responsibility for
supervision, arbitration and housekeeping when it comes to rout-
ing messages to children, updating the frame window's menu, and
passing the input focus among the child windows in its implementation of MDI frame and child windows. It would be unusual for the
application to directly involve itself in the management of the MDI
child windows, so no code examples are shown for the member
functions listed in this section. With the exception of
GetMDIFrame, all the member functions of this class duplicate
services the framework automatically provides to MDI child windows.

An **CMDIChildWnd** exhibits much of the same behavior as the
CFrameWnd class, but with a few additional features. When a
child window gains the input focus, the menu of the frame window
is automatically replaced with the child's commands and settings. If
more than one child window displays a view of a single document
type, menu resources are shared by the children rather than being
duplicated for each child. On activation of the child, its caption is
appended to the caption in the MDI frame window's title bar.

Child windows are associated with only one document, though
multiple child windows can be used to display differing views of
the document inside the enclosing MDI frame window. Documents
and views are created and attached to the child windows by the
CDocTemplate object at application startup. For more information
on the connections between documents, views and windows, see
CDocTemplate.

Member Functions

CMDIChildWnd   FUNCTION

Description   **CMDIChildWnd** constructs an MDI child window object, but does not initialize it or make it visible. The **Create** function makes the window visible.

GetMDIFrame   FUNCTION

Description   **GetMDIFrame** returns a pointer to the enclosing MDI frame window for this child. It is used by the framework in updating the menu bar of the MDI frame window with menu items belonging to an activating MDI child.

Prototype
```
//Function Prototype
//CMDIFrameWnd* GetMDIFrame( );
```

MDIActivate   FUNCTION

Description   **MDIActivate** activates an MDI child window, by passing the MDI frame window. It does not change the activation status of other active windows.

Prototype
```
//Function Prototype
//void MDIActivate( );
```

MDIDestroy   FUNCTION

Description   **MDIDestroy** deactivates and destroys an MDI child window, removing its menu items from the frame window menu and erasing the text it added to the caption bar.

Prototype
```
//Function Prototype
//void MDIDestroy( );
```

MDIMaximize   FUNCTION

Description   **MDIMaximize** resizes an MDI child window to fill the entire client area of the MDI frame window and adds the child's control menu to the frame's menu bar.

Prototype
```
//Function Prototype
//void MDIMaximize( );
```

511

MDIRestore FUNCTION

Description   **MDIRestore** restores an MDI child window to the size and position in the MDI frame window's client area it had before the last maximize or minimize operation.

Prototype
```
//Function Prototype
//void MDIRestore( );
```

MDIFrameWnd CLASS

Derivation

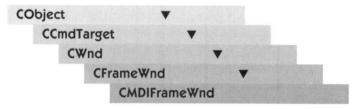

Description   **CMDIFrameWnd** is a derived class of **CFrameWnd** that extends the behavior of that class in support of frame windows that manage a multiple document interface (MDI). They handle the complex interactions and housekeeping details necessary to stage multiple views and documents. They are rarely built directly by applications because the code to implement them and create all the necessary connections to other objects is provided by AppWizard. For this reason, the member function listings include no code examples.

The **CMDIFrameWnd** window manages both an **MDICLIENT** window and any control bars. The **MDICLIENT** window is the parent of the MDI child windows that present the views of the application's documents. A special messaging relationship exists between the **CMDIFrameWnd** and the **CMDIChildWnd**. Command messages are dispatched directly to the active MDI child, which can either choose to handle them or pass them on to the frame window. When an MDI child is active, its menu is substituted for that of the frame window. When there are no active MDI children, the frame window displays a default menu of its own. The **CMDIFrameWnd** has default handlers for the Windows menu commands that change the size and position of child windows. It can tile children horizontally and vertically, cascade them, or arrange them to exactly fill the client area.

Like its parent, an MDI frame window must be destroyed by the **CWnd::Destroy** function so that the many objects to which it is related can be processed as necessary when it ceases to exist.

Overrides

Overridable Function Name	Handles
CreateClient	Creation of an MDICLIENT for the CMDIFrameWnd.
GetPopupWindowMenu	Returning a handle to the standard window menu.

Member Functions

CMDIFrameWnd   FUNCTION

Description **CMDIFrameWnd** constructs an MDI frame window, but does not initialize it or make it visible.

MDIActivate   FUNCTION

Description **MDIActivate** activates a new MDI child window of this frame. It sends a **WM_MDIACTIVATE** message to both the window that is relinquishing activation and the window that is gaining it. This same sequence of events takes place if the user changes the input focus among MDI child windows by means of mouse or keyboard input.

Prototype
```
//Function Prototype
//void MDIActivate( CWnd* pWndActivate );
```

MDICascade   FUNCTION

Description **MDICascade** arranges some or all MDI child windows in a cascade. The function can be called without parameters, and all MDI children, including currently disabled child windows, are cascaded. Passing **MDICascade** the parameter **MDITILE_SKIPDISABLED** causes it to omit disabled windows from the cascade.

Prototype
```
//Function Prototype
//void MDICascade(int nType)
```

MDIGetActive   FUNCTION

Description **MDIGetActive** retrieves a pointer to the currently active MDI child window. It returns TRUE if the active child window is maximized.

Prototype
```
//Function Prototype
//CMDIChildWnd* MDIGetActive( BOOL* pbMaximized = NULL );
```

MDIIconArrange   FUNCTION

Description **MDIIconArrange** arranges all minimized MDI child windows as rows of icons. This function has no effect on windows that are not minimized.

Prototype
```
//Function Prototype
//void MDIIconArrange( );
```

MDIMaximize   FUNCTION

Description **MDIMaximize** resizes an MDI child window to entirely fill the client area of its parent. The main frame that contains the child includes a control menu that can command the child to close, split (if appropriate), or restore itself. The name of the document in the maximized child is appended to the caption in the main frame's title bar.

Prototype
```
//Function Prototype
//void MDIMaximize( CWnd* pWnd );
```

MDINext   FUNCTION

Description **MDINext** activates the next child window in the z-order, and sends the active child to the bottom of the z-order.

Prototype
```
//Function Prototype
//void MDINext( );
```

MDIRestore   FUNCTION

Description **MDIRestore** restores an MDI child window to the last size and position it had before it was maximized or minimized.

Prototype
```
//Function Prototype
//void MDIMaximize( CWnd* pWnd );
```

MDISetMenu   FUNCTION

Description **MDISetMenu** can replace either or both menus of the MDI frame window and the window pop-up menu. If the argument specifying the menu is NULL, it is not replaced.

Prototype
```
//Function Prototype
//CMenu* MDISetMenu( CMenu* pFrameMenu, CMenu*
pWindowMenu );
```

MDITile   FUNCTION

Description **MDITile** tiles MDI child windows over the frame's entire client area. Calling the version of the function that takes no parameters tiles the windows vertically. The tiling flags have the following meaning for the version of **MDITile** that expects a parameter:

Flag Name	Action
MDITILE_HORIZONTAL	Creates a horizontal row of child windows, with upper borders all at the top of the client area.
MDITILE_VERTICAL	Creates a vertical column of child windows, with left borders all at the left of the client area.
MDITILE_SKIPDISABLED	Keeps disabled windows from tiling.

Prototype
```
//Function Prototype
//void MDITile( );
//void MDITile(int nType);
```

MemFile   CLASS

Derivation

CObject	▼	
	CFile	▼
		CMemFile

Description The **CMemFile** class implements memory-based files, essentially setting up a RAM disk facility. All the **CFile** base class functions are supported for **CMemFile** objects except **Duplicate**, **LockRange** and **UnlockRange**. Calling these objects from a **CMemFile** object results in a **CNotSupportedException** being thrown.

515

Member Functions

CMemFile	FUNCTION

Description There is only one **CMemFile** constructor, and it requires no arguments, but optionally takes a parameter that specifies the increment by which the file should grow when it needs to be enlarged. After the **CMemFile** object is constructed, the file is considered "open" and is ready to use. If the open fails, a **CFileException** and a **CMemoryException** are thrown.

Prototype
```
//Function Prototype
//CMemFile( UINT uiGrowIncrement = 1024);
//  throw( CFileException, CMemoryException );
```

Example
```
    //Construct the object and "open" the file
CMemFile fileRamFile;
    //Write to the file by using the CFile base class member function
fileRamFile.Write("123", strlen("123" );
    //Destroy the file explicitly when it is no longer needed
fileRamFile.~CMemFile( );
```

CMemoryException
CLASS
· ·

Derivation

CObject ▼
CException ▼
CMemoryException

Description The **CMemoryException** class provides an object that signals an out-of-memory condition. At first blush, this may seem a bit druid; after all, if the system is out of memory, how can it be possible to construct a new object, even if its purpose is to signal the failure? The fact is that the constructor for this class is never called directly. Instead, the global function **AfxThrowMemoryException** is used, and it allocates the new object in memory previously set aside for that purpose. The **CMemoryException** type of exceptions are thrown automatically by any failed call to **new**, but memory allocated in other ways (for example, **malloc**) does not raise this exception if the allocation request fails. In these cases, the application must detect the condition and throw an exception of its own.

CMemoryState

Description A **CMemoryState** is a diagnostic tool that helps to detect memory leaks due to failure to **delete** objects created with **new**. Since diagnostics in general are debugging features, the **CMemoryState** class only works with the debug version of the framework libraries.

The **CMemoryState** object is most useful as a means of early detection of memory leaks. *Use it early, use it often,* to paraphrase the late Mayor Daly of Chicago. The procedure for finding a leak is as follows. First, create a **CMemoryState** object, and call its **Checkpoint** member to take a snapshot of current allocation status. Run through the suspicious code, create a second **CMemoryState** object, and call **Checkpoint** again, preserving a new snapshot of memory. Create a third **CMemoryState** object and call its **Difference** function against the two previously constructed objects. **Difference** will return TRUE if it detects a difference between the two **Checkpoint** snapshots. Assuming you intended the memory state to be the same at both points, this process has narrowed your search to a small section of code. The **DumpStatistics** member function uses the information built by the **Difference** member to print statistics including how many heap bytes are allocated to objects created using **new**.

If you don't have enough information to locate the offending allocation simply by detecting an imbalance, the **CMemoryState** object member **DumpAllObjectsSince** will dump all **CObject** derived objects since the last **Checkpoint** call. This, of course, is not a technique to be used indiscriminately, because of its potential to overwhelm you with data that may not be related to the problem. Using the **DEBUG_NEW** operator will provide file and line number tracking of allocations to the **DumpAllObjectsSince** member. This is, of course, the best way to do the job. Poring through the dump is *always* rewarded with the offending allocation that is not paired with a deallocation. All other techniques are sloppy science.

The **CMemoryState** class cannot be used to detect leaks created by C runtime memory allocation functions or Windows SDK memory allocation functions.

Note: The dump is always made to the predefined stream **afxDump**. You must have trace flags enabled ("Enable Tracing" in the TRACER application) for the **CMemoryState** dumps to be sent

517

to **afxDump**. Where *is* **afxDump**? It depends on where your application is running. If it's a Windows application, then it is usually the debugger's output window. If it's a console application (DOS or Win32), it is usually stderr.

Example

```
//Example:
    //Construct the first CMemoryState object and take a snapshot
    //of the heap
CMemoryState memBegin;
memBegin.Checkpoint( );
    //In here is the code you suspect creates an object on the heap
    //with "new" that is not deallocated by a call to "delete"

    //After the suspicious code section, take a new snapshot
CMemoryState memEnd;
memEnd.Checkpoint( );
    //Compare the two memory state snapshots
CMemoryState memCompare;
if( memCompare.Difference( memBegin, memEnd ))
{
    //If we detect a difference, print our statistics to afxDump, the
    //default CDumpContext object
memCompare.DumpStatistics( );
}
```

Member Functions

Checkpoint   FUNCTION

Description **Checkpoint** takes a snapshot of memory and records it in the **CMemoryState** object.

Prototype
```
//Function Prototype
//void Checkpoint( );
```

CMemoryState   FUNCTION

Description **CMemoryState** constructs an uninitialized object which is then filled in by either the **Checkpoint** or **Difference** member function.

Prototype
```
//Function Prototype
//CMemoryState();
```

Difference — FUNCTION

Description   **Difference** compares two memory state objects initialized by the **Checkpoint** member function and records the difference between them in a third memory state object.

Prototype

```
//Function Prototype
//void Difference( );
```

DumpAllObjectsSince — FUNCTION

Description   **DumpAllObjectsSince** prints the name order, file and line number of all objects allocated since the last call to **Checkpoint**, or optionally all allocated objects if the **CMemoryState** object has not yet been initialized.

Prototype

```
//Function Prototype
//void DumpStatistics( );
    //Construct the first CMemoryState object and take a snapshot
    //of the heap
CMemoryState memBegin;
memBegin.Checkpoint( );
    //In here is the code you suspect creates an object on the heap
    //with "new" that is not deallocated by a call to "delete"

    //After the suspicious code section, print a list of all allocations
    //since Checkpoint
memBegin.DumpAllObjectsSince( );
```

DumpStatistics — FUNCTION

Description   **DumpStatistics** prints the results of a **Difference** operation to **axfDump**, the prebuilt **CDumpContext** object supplied to all **CObject**-derived classes by the framework. It prints the number of heap blocks currently allocated to objects constructed using **new**, the number of heap blocks allocated to non-object data such as arrays and structures, maximum memory used by the program, and current memory use.

Prototype

```
//Function Prototype
//void DumpStatistics( );
```

C Menu

Derivation

Description   The **CMenu** class is the framework's abstraction of the Windows menu handle (HMENU) operations. Menus are created in a couple of steps. The application constructs a local **CMenu** object, creates or loads a menu that is then attached to the object, and then sets the menu into the containing window with the **CWnd::SetMenu** function. The **CWnd** (or **CWnd**-derived) object then takes over management of the menu's graphical and messaging behavior. When the **CWnd** object takes over these functions, the **CMenu** object is no longer necessary. Because the **CMenu** object is usually constructed on the stack in an initialization function, it is important to detach it from the handle to the menu after the menu is set into the parent window. The **CMenu** member function **Detach** disconnects the menu handle from the object, ensuring that when the function in which it was constructed exits and destroys its stack-based objects, the handle to the menu that now "belongs" to the parent is not also destroyed.

Functions that manipulate menu items refer to the individual items by either menu position or resource ID, using the flag MF_BYPOSITION or MF_COMMAND, respectively.

Overrides

Overridable Function Name	Triggering Event
DrawItem	An MF_OWNERDRAW menu needs to be repainted by the application.
MeasureItem	An MF_OWNERDRAW menu item is being created, and the application is being asked to fill in a MEASUREITEMSTRUCT.

Public Data Member

m_hMenu

Description   **m_hMenu** is the Windows handle to the menu attached to the **CMenu** object.

Member Functions

AppendMenu

Description   **AppendMenu** adds an item to the bottom of a menu. The item can be either a text string or a bitmap. *See **CreateMenu** for a usage example.*

Append Menu Flag	Meaning
MF_BYCOMMAND	The first parameter is the item's ID.
MF_BYPOSITION	The first parameter is the item's position in the list of menu items.
MF_CHECKED	Check the item.
MF_UNCHECKED	Remove the check from the item.
MF_POPUP	The menu is a popup.
MF_OWNERDRAW	The item will be drawn by the application—it can't be used with bitmap menu items.
MF_STRING	The item is a string.
MF_MENUBARBREAK	Starts a new column of menu items in popup menus.
MF_DISABLED	Item is not selectable, but is not grayed.
MF_GRAYED	Grays and disables the menu item.
MF_ENABLED	Menu item is selectable and optionally ungrayed if necessary.
MF_SEPARATOR	The menu item is a horizontal separator bar.

Prototype
```
//Function Prototype
//BOOL AppendMenu( UINT uiPosFlags, UINT uiIDNewItem = 0,
//        LPCSTR lpszMenuItemString );
//BOOL AppendMenu( UINT uiPosFlags, UINT uiIDNewItem,
//        const CBitmap* pBitmap);
```

Attach

Description   **Attach** is one of the family of functions implemented in several classes of the MFC application framework that attach Windows handles to MFC objects. **CMenu::Attach** "attaches" a Windows handle to a **CMenu** object. This makes it possible to use **CMenu** class member functions to create, define or modify a menu, which is set into the parent **CWnd** object. The menu itself is likely to have a much longer lifetime than the **CMenu** object. A **CMenu** object may be created for the purpose of making specific changes to a menu and then be detached from the menu handle and destroyed. If more changes to the menu are needed at a later point, a new object can be constructed and reattached to a saved handle.

Prototype

```
//Function Prototype
//BOOL Attach(HMENU hMenu);
    //Assume that our function is passed a handle to a menu—
    //we create an object
CMenu OurMenu
    //We attach the handle to the object
OurMenu.Attach( m_hMenuSaved );
    //And then we can use CMenu functions to manipulate
    //the menu
OurMenu.CheckMenuItem( IDM_FILEOPEN, MF_BYCOMMAND );
OurMenu.DeleteMenu( IDM_FILESLOCKED, MF_BYCOMMAND );
```

CheckMenuItem   FUNCTION

Description   **CheckMenuItem** toggles a check mark by a menu item. The first parameter gives either the ID or the list position of the menu item to be checked, and the second parameter is composed of flags that specify how to interpret the first parameter and how to treat the menu item. The flags have the following names and meanings (*see* **Attach** *for a usage example*):

Check Menu Item Flag	Meaning
MF_BYCOMMAND	The first parameter is the item's ID.
MF_BYPOSITION	The first parameter is the item's position in the list of menu items.
MF_CHECKED	Check the item.
MF_UNCHECKED	Remove the check from the item.

Prototype

```
//Function Prototype
//BOOL CheckMenuItem( UINT uiCheckItem, UINT uiFlags );
```

CMenu — FUNCTION

Description   **CMenu** constructs a **CMenu** object, but does not create, attach or define its accompanying menu. Either the **CreateMenu**, **CreatePopupMenu**, **LoadMenu** or **LoadMenuIndirect** member functions are used to create and attach the menu to the object.

Prototype

```
//Function Prototype
    //Create a stack-based menu object
CMenu OurMenuObject;
    //Create and attach an empty menu
OurMenuObject.CreateMenu( );
    //Append a string menu item, at position 0, using the given text
OurMenuObject.AppendMenu( MF_STRING | MF_BYPOSITION, 0,
lpszMenuString );
    //Then insert an item above it
OurMenuObject.InsertMenu( 0, MF_STRING | MF_BYPOSITION, 0,
lpszMenuString );
    //Tell the menu to use a dot instead of a check mark to show
    //that a menu item is selected
OurMenuObject.SetMenuItemBitmaps( 0, MF_BYPOSITION, NULL,
hbmMenuDot);
OurMenuObject.SetMenuItemBitmaps( 1, MF_BYPOSITION, NULL,
hbmMenuDot);
    //Set the menu into the CWnd-derived main window
CMainFrame::SetMenu( &OurMenuObject );
    //Detach the menu handle from the object — the object is
    //destroyed when this function exits, but the menu lasts for the
    //lifetime of the app session;
    //here we return the detached menu handle to the caller
return OurMenuObject.Detach( );
```

CreateMenu — FUNCTION

Description   **CreateMenu** creates an empty menu and attaches it to the **CMenu** object. To add menu items, use the **AppendMenu** or **InsertMenu** member functions. *See **CMenu** for a usage example.*

Prototype

```
//Function Prototype
//BOOL CreateMenu( );
```

CreatePopupMenu   FUNCTION

Description   **CreatePopupMenu** creates a floating popup menu and attaches it to a **CMenu** object. The menu is initially empty and must be initialized using **AppendMenu** or **InsertMenu**. The popup is automatically destroyed when the window or menu to which it is connected is destroyed.

The reason you want your menu destroyed (as a general rule) on exit from the function is that the frame takes over its ownership and thus its destruction. How about in a popup? Nobody owns a popup. So who is responsible for its destruction and maintenance? The answer is dazzlingly simple: You always create a popup in a message handler created exactly for that purpose—normally **OnRButtonDown**. You create, track and destroy it in one normal message-passing cycle, allowing the resultant selection to be placed in the application's message queue for soonest processing.

Prototype
```
//Function Prototype
//BOOL CreatePopupMenu( );
    //Create a stack-based menu object
CMenu OurMenuObject;
    //Create and attach an empty popup menu
OurMenuObject.CreatePopupMenu( );
    //Append a string menu item, at position 0, using the given text
OurMenuObject.AppendMenu( MF_STRING, 0, lpszMenuString );
    //Gray the menu item we just added
OurMenuObject.EnableMenu( IDM_SOUNDTEST, MF_GRAYED );
```

DeleteMenu   FUNCTION

Description   **DeleteMenu** deletes a menu item by either ID or zero-based position in the list of menu items. If the first parameter is MF_BYCOMMAND, the second parameter gives the ID of the item to delete. If the first parameter is MF_BYPOSITION, the second parameter gives the zero-based position of the item to delete. *See Attach for a usage example.*

Prototype
```
//Function Prototype
//BOOL DeleteMenu( UINT uiDeletePosOrID, UINT uiFlags );
```

DeleteTempMap

Description **DeleteTempMap** is frequently called during the idle-time processing of **CWinApp**. **DeleteTempMap** scans for temporary objects created by calls to **FromHandle** and disposes of them. This system housekeeping function should not be called by application code.

Prototype
```
//Function Prototype
//void PASCAL DeleteTempMap( );
```

DestroyMenu   FUNCTION

Description **DestroyMenu** frees the system resources that are automatically allocated when **LoadMenu** or **LoadMenuIndirect** are used to initialize a **CMenu** object. It must be called before the application exits to prevent memory leaks. *See **LoadMenu** for a usage example.*

Prototype
```
//Function Prototype
//BOOL DestroyMenu( );
```

Detach   FUNCTION

Description **Detach** severs the association between a menu handle and a **CMenu** object associated with it. Detaching the handle allows the object to be destroyed without affecting the menu itself, which is important if the menu is set into a frame window by using **CWnd::SetMenu**. This is also useful when a **CMenu** object is constructed on the fly by a call to **CMenu::FromHandle**. **CMenu::FromHandle** returns a pointer to an object of type **CMenu**, creating the **CMenu** object automatically. Objects created in this way have a very short lifetime and must be quickly used, detached from the handle used to create them, and then allowed to be destroyed by **CWinApp** housekeeping processes. *See **CreateMenu** for a usage example.*

Prototype
```
//Function Prototype
//HMENU Detach( );
```

EnableMenuItem   FUNCTION

Description **EnableMenuItem** toggles the state of a menu item, optionally graying it if it is being disabled. The following flags apply:

Enable Menu Item Flag	Meaning
MF_BYCOMMAND	The first parameter is the item's ID.
MF_BYPOSITION	The first parameter is the item's position in the list of menu items.
MF_DISABLED	Item is not selectable, but is not grayed.
MF_GRAYED	Grays and disables the menu item.
MF_ENABLED	Menu item is selectable and optionally ungrayed if necessary.

See ***CreatePopupMenu*** *for a usage example.*

Prototype
```
//Function Prototype
//BOOL EnableMenuItem( UINT uiEnableItem, UINT uiFlags );
```

FromHandle FUNCTION

Description **FromHandle** is one of a family of functions in several application framework classes that create a temporary object and attach it to a handle. In its **CMenu** implementation, it provides a pointer to an initialized **CMenu** object, given a handle to a menu. This makes it possible to take a saved handle and wrap it with an object that provides access to **CMenu** member functions. The temporary object has a lifespan of one Windows message-processing cycle, so the application receiving the pointer must use it before the function in which **FromHandle** is called returns.

Prototype
```
//Function Prototype
//CMenu* PASCAL FromHandle(HMENU hMenu);
    //Get a pointer to a menu object by using a saved handle
CMenu* pMenu = CMenu::FromHandle( m_SavedMenu );
    //Find out how many items are in the menu
int iMenuItemCount = pMenu->GetMenuItemCount( );
```

GetMenuItemCount FUNCTION

Description **GetMenuItemCount** returns the number of items in the menu. See **FromHandle** for a usage example.

Prototype
```
//Function Prototype
//UINT GetCount( )const;
```

GetMenuItemId   FUNCTION

Description   **GetMenuItemId** returns the ID associated with a menu item. The item must be specified by **MF_BYPOSITION**. *See **GetMenuString** for a usage example.*

Prototype
```
//Function Prototype
//UINT GetMenuItemId ( UINT uiPos) const;
```

GetMenuState   FUNCTION

Description   **GetMenuState** returns the flags associated with a menu item, or a -1 if the item does not exist. For ordinary menus, the flags are ORed in the returned UINT. If the menu is a popup, the high-order byte is a count of menu items, and the low-order byte holds the flags. *See **GetMenuString** for a usage example.*

Prototype
```
//Function Prototype
//int GetMenuString( UINT uiPosFlags, UINT uiFlags );
```

GetMenuString   FUNCTION

Description   **GetMenuString** returns the string associated with a menu item. The item can be specified by either **MF_BYPOSITION** or **MF_BYCOMMAND**.

Prototype
```
//Function Prototype
//int GetMenuString( UINT uiPos, LPCSTR lpszMenuItemString,
//        int MenuStrlen,UINT uiFlags );
    //Retrieve the string associated with the item at the third zero-
    //based position in the menu item list and copy it to szString
char szString[256];
pMenuBar->GetMenuString( 3, szString, sizeof(szString),
MF_BYPOSITION);
    //Now get the ID associated with the item
UINT uiMenuItemId = pMenuBar->GetMenuItemId( 3 );
    //Get its check state
UINT uiMenuItemId = pMenuBar->GetMenuState( 3,
MF_BYPOSITION );
    // See if it has a popup menu
CMenu* pPopupMenu = pOurMenu->GetSubMenu( 3);
```

```
            if( pPopupMenu != -1 )
            {
                //If there is a popup, replace it with a new popup —
                //note that the new menu handle MUST be detached from a
                //CMenu object
                pMenuBar->ModifyMenu( 3, MF_POPUP, hDetachedMenuHandle);
            }
```

GetSafeHmenu   FUNCTION

Description   **GetSafeHmenu** is a **CMenu** information function that returns the handle of the menu wrapped by the **CMenu** object.

Prototype
```
//Function Prototype
//HMENU GetSafeHmenu( ) const;
    //If you have a pointer to a CMenu object, you can get a
    //menu handle like this
HMENU hWindowMenu = pWindowMenu->GetSafeHmenu( );
```

GetSubMenu   FUNCTION

Description   **GetSubMenu** returns a temporary pointer to the submenu associated with an item in a main menu at the given position. This function uses the **CMenu** member variable **m_hMenu** to identify the main menu to search. *See **GetMenuString** for a usage example.*

Prototype
```
//Function Prototype
//CMenu* GetSubMenu( UINT uiPosition );
```

InsertMenu   FUNCTION

Description   **InsertMenu** inserts a menu item at a specified position in a menu, adjusting other items downward. After the menu item is inserted, call **CWnd::DrawMenuBar** to show the change. **InsertMenu** can insert an entire popup menu as well as individual menu items, by using the **MF_POPUP** flag and passing the handle to the popup in **uiIDNewItem**. Make sure that the new menu handle is detached from the **CMenu** object used to create and define it. Use the **MF_BYCOMMAND** flag to insert a popup menu in the proper location. *See **CreateMenu** for a usage example.*

Prototype
```
//Function Prototype
//BOOL InsertMenu( UINT uiPosFlags, UINT uiPosition,
        //UINT uiIDNewItem = 0,
//        LPCSTR lpszMenuItemString );
//BOOL InsertMenu( UINT uiPosFlags, UINT uiPosition,
//            UINT uiIDNewItem, const CBitmap* pBitmap);
```

LoadMenu   FUNCTION

Description **LoadMenu** offers an alternative to using **CreateMenu** along with the append and insert functions. **LoadMenu** retrieves menu-description information from the application's resource file and automatically builds the menu. Menus created in this way must free the system resources that were automatically allocated for them by calling **DestroyMenu** before the application exits. This is the way menus are commonly created

Prototype
```
//Function Prototype
//BOOL LoadMenu(UINT nIDResource );
//BOOL LoadMenu(LPCSTR lpszMenuResourceName );
    //Create a stack-based menu object
CMenu OurMenuObject;
    //Initialize it using the menu template defined in the
    //application's resource file
OurMenuObject.LoadMenu( lpszMenuResourceName );
    //Later, before the app exits, use the saved handle of the menu
    //to attach it to a temporary object and free its resources
CMenu* pTempMenu = CMenu::FromHandle( m_SavedMenuHandle
);
pTempMenu->DestroyMenu( );
```

LoadMenuIndirect   FUNCTION

Description **LoadMenuIndirect** loads a memory-resident menu template and attaches it to a **CMenu** object. Menus created in this way must free the system resources that were automatically allocated for them by calling **DestroyMenu** before the application exits.

Prototype
```
//BOOL LoadMenu( const void FAR* lpMenuTemplate );
    //Create a stack based menu object
CMenu OurMenuObject;
    //Initialize it using a memory-resident menu template
OurMenuObject.LoadMenuIndirect( lpMenuTemplate );
```

ModifyMenu
FUNCTION

Description   **ModifyMenu** can be used to change the flags set for a particular menu item, but it is usually used for replacing popup menus. It is used like **InsertMenu**, but it automatically cleans up the resource allocations associated with the popup menu that is getting replaced. Make sure that the new menu handle is detached from the **CMenu** object used to create and define it. *See **GetMenuString** for a usage example.*

Prototype
```
//Function Prototype
//BOOL ModifyMenu( UINT uiPosFlags, UINT uiPosition, UINT
//      uiIDNewItem = 0, LPCSTR lpszMenuItemString );
//BOOL ModifyMenu( UINT uiPosFlags, UINT uiPosition, UINT
//          uiIDNewItem, const CBitmap* pBitmap);
```

RemoveMenu
FUNCTION

Description   **RemoveMenu** deletes an item from a popup menu.

Prototype
```
//Function Prototype
//BOOL RemoveMenu( UINT uiPosition, UINT uiFlags);
    //Get a pointer to the popup menu at zero-based position 3
    //in the menu pointed to by pOurMenu
CMenu* pPopupMenu = pOurMenu->GetSubMenu( 3);
    //From the popup, remove the item with the ID
IDM_BALANCESHEET
pPopupMenu->RemoveMenu( IDM_BALANCESHEET,
MF_BYCOMMAND );
```

SetMenuItemBitmaps
FUNCTION

Description   **SetMenuItemBitmaps** sets new bitmaps to signify checked and unchecked states for menu items. One or the other of the bitmaps may be NULL, but if both are NULL, Windows uses the standard check marks to denote check status. To get the dimensions of item bitmaps, use the SDK function **GetMenuCheckMarkDimensions**. The bitmaps used in the menu are not destroyed along with the menu, so the application must explicitly do this when the menu is no longer in use. *See **CMenu** for a usage example.*

Prototype

```
//Function Prototype
//BOOL SetMenuItemBitmaps( UINT uiPosition, UINT uiFlags,
//const CBitmap* pCheckedBmp const CBitmap*
//pUncheckedBmp);
```

TrackPopupMenu   FUNCTION

Description   **TrackPopupMenu** shows a floating popup menu at the specified location and routes the menu's command messages to the window identified by **pWnd**. The position of the menu and the mouse actions it tracks are set by flags given in the function's first parameter.

Screen Position Flag	Meaning
TPM_LEFTBUTTON	The menu tracks the left mouse button.
TPM_RIGHTBUTTON	The menu tracks the right mouse button.
TPM_LEFTALIGN	Centers the menu horizontally using the ixLocation parameter.
TPM_CENTERALIGN	Left-aligns the menu using the ixLocation parameter.
TPM_RIGHTALIGN	Right-aligns the menu using the ixLocation parameter.

Prototype

```
//Function Prototype
//BOOL TrackPopupMenu( UINT uiPositionFlags, int ixLocation, int
//iyLocation,
//            CWnd* pWnd, LPRECT lpRect = 0 );
```

C MetafileDC   CLASS

Derivation

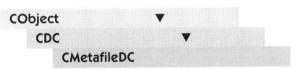

```
CObject                          ▼
    CDC                              ▼
        CMetafileDC
```

Description   The **CMetafileDC** class takes many of its characteristics from the **CDC** base class. Its basic function is to prepare a DC for recording metafile commands. A **CMetafileDC** object is typically used only in creating the metafile, and **CDC::PlayMetafile** is used to replay it. Several **SDK** functions provide for manipulation of existing metafiles as well. After a metafile is closed and a handle to it has been returned, it should be deleted, using the Windows **::DeleteMetafile** function.

Data Members

A **CMetafileDC** object has no data members of its own, but uses the **m_hDC** and **m_hAttribDC** members of the **CDC** base class from which it is derived. By default, the attribute DC member is set to NULL. A **CMetafileDC** object may make attribute calls, provided **m_hAttribDC** is set to point to a valid device context for the output destination.

Member Functions

Close   FUNCTION

Description This member function closes the metafile device context and returns a Windows metafile handle. The handle can be used by **CDC::PlayMetafile** to play the metafile, and it can also be used with **SDK** functions such as **::CopyMetafile**, which writes a metafile to disk.

Prototype

```
//Function Prototypes
// BOOL Create( LPCSTR lpszFilename  = NULL )
// HMETAFILE Close( );
//Create the Metafile DC object
CMetaFileDC MetaFileDC;
//Attach a metafile to the object
if (!MetaFileDC.Create( ))
    return CREATE_FAILED;
MetaFileDC.TextOut(0, 0, "Just a little text...");
            //Send a bit of text to the metafile
HMETAFILE hMF = MetaFileDC.Close( );
            //Close the metafile and
            //save the handle
            //so that it can be played back...
```

CMetafileDC   FUNCTION

Description **CMetafileDC::CMetafileDC** constructs a **CMetafileDC** object, but does not create the metafile. This must be done by calling the **Create** member function.

Create FUNCTION

Description This member function creates the metafile and attaches it to the **CMetafileDC** object. After **Create** is called, the metafile can record output commands.

MultiDocTemplate CLASS

Derivation

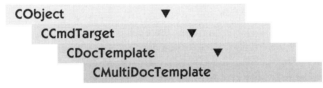

CObject ▼
 CCmdTarget ▼
  CDocTemplate ▼
   CMultiDocTemplate

Description **CMultiDocTemplate** is derived from **CDocTemplate**, which provides the organizing metaphor for application architecture in MFC. (See the **CDocTemplate** entry for an explanation of the conceptual role of a document template.) An object of the **CMultiDocTemplate** class establishes the relationship between an application's data source, the view of that data, and the frame window that manages both the data and the view, for applications that have more than one open document at any given time. The code that implements a multiple document template is always provided by the AppWizard workbench tool. One template is generated for each distinct type of document with which an application deals. For example, if the application can handle spreadsheets and text files, a document template would be created for each of these. Each of an application's types of document templates is listed in the File New dialog. When the user selects a type of document with which he or she plans to work, the document, view and MDI child window are created, and the template is used to connect them to one another. All of this occurs in the application's **InitInstance** member function, where the **CMultiDocTemplate** constructor is called.

Member Functions

CMultiDocTemplate · FUNCTION

Description **CMultiDocTemplate** constructs an MDI application's document template.

Prototype
```
//Function Prototype
//CMultiDocTemplate(UINT nIDResource, CRuntimeClass*
//pDocClass,
//CRuntimeClass* pFrameClass, CRuntimeClass* pViewClass);
    //AppWizard generates this code to create a multiple
    //document template. It is called once for each document type...
AddDocTemplate( new CMultiDocTemplate( IDR_MAINFRAME,
    RUNTIME_CLASS( CMyDoc ),
    RUNTIME_CLASS( CMainFrame ),
    RUNTIME_CLASS( CMyView ) ) );
```

NotSupportedException

Derivation

CObject	▼
CException	▼
CNotSupportedException	

Description The **CNotSupportedException** class provides an object that signals a request for an unsupported feature. It has no function or public data members and does not provide the user or the programmer with many meaningful opportunities to recover.

Member Functions

CNotSupportedException · FUNCTION

Description **CNotSupportedException** constructs an object of this type. This function is never called directly. Instead, the global function **AfxThrowNotSupportedException** is used.

Prototype
```
//Function Prototype
//This is the Nancy Reagan exception — just say No....
//raise the exception
AfxThrowNotSupportedException( );
```

C ObArray

Description **CObArray** is one of a group of array collection classes that provide dynamically sizeable (or "growable") arrays for various types of data, and as potential base classes for user-defined array types. The array object itself is not defined with a size, nor is it initialized with element values at construction. This initialization must be done explicitly using the appropriate member functions. Like C language arrays, the base index of the array classes is always zero, but upper bounds may be either fixed or dynamically expandable, subject to control by the application. Memory is allocated in one contiguous chunk, even if an array size is set that leaves elements unused.

Array elements plus overhead (approximately 100 bytes) must fit in a single 64k segment. For arrays of pointers, the maximum number of elements is influenced by the memory model, because compact and large models produce far pointers to data items.

All the array classes are derived from **CObject**. With the exception of the **CPtrArray** and the **CUIntArray** classes, the array classes provide an override of the **CObject::Serialize** function. Array elements and indices are serialized together. In the case of the **CObArray** and **CString** classes, the object identified by the pointer is serialized as well.

For the **CObArray** class, the array elements are pointers to objects of type **CObject**. **CObArray** is useful as a base class for the derivation of user-defined types. Elements in a **CObArray** are disjoint from the objects they identify. That is to say, the elements of the array are *contained* by it rather than *owned* by it. As a result, when an object is removed from the array, the array no longer tracks its existence, but it is physically still allocated in the computer store until programmatically deleted. In the "owner" model, removal of an object might also imply deletion of the object. Note the distinction I've drawn between "removing" and "deleting." Removing an array element does not delete the **CObject** object to which it pointed. Likewise, the deletion of the object does not affect the value or existence of the array element. When arrays of this type are serialized, the objects to which they point are serialized as well.

The array collection of classes includes the following:

CByteArray CLASS

Description The array elements are BYTEs and may be serialized.

CDWordArray CLASS

Description The array elements are 32-bit DWORDs and may be serialized.

CPtrArray CLASS

Description The array elements are void pointers whose size depends on the memory model. While pointer arrays don't have built-in support for one-step serialization, you can iterate through them and serialize each member. Like elements in a **CObArray,** those of a **CPtrArray** are disjoint from the objects they identify. Removing an array element does not delete the object to which it pointed. Likewise, the deletion of the object does not affect the value or existence of the array element. **CPtrArray** objects may not be serialized.

CStringArray CLASS

Description The array elements are objects of type **CString** and may be serialized. When array elements are removed, **CString** objects are deleted as well, and the memory they occupy is freed, just as for the numeric array types. Note that this is an exception: **CStringArrays** own their members.

CUIntArray CLASS

Description The array elements are unsigned integers whose physical size depends on the target operating environment. UINTs are equivalent to WORDs under Windows 3.1 and are equivalent to DWORDs under NT. While you can reliably serialize and deserialize a **CUIntArray** on the same platform, you may not be able to deserialize a **CUIntArray** that was serialized on a different platform. Because MFC was designed to be portable, no serialization methods are included in this class.

CWordArray CLASS

Description The array elements are 16-bit WORDs and may bc serialized.

Common Member Functions for Array Collection Classes

Use the following table to create function prototypes for all the array-related collection classes, making the following substitutions for the placeholder *OBJECT*:

For This Class	Replace OBJECT With
CByteArray	BYTE
CWordArray	WORD
CDWordArray	DWORD
CPtrArray	void *
CObArray	CObject *
CStringArray	For return values, substitute CString; for parameters, substitute const char *
CUintArray	UINT

Prototype

```
//Function Prototype
int GetSize( ) const;
int GetUpperBound ( ) const;
void SetSize( int iNewSize, int nGrowBy = -1)
    throw( CMemoryException);
```

The second argument specifies the granularity of array growth. You can specify zero for this, in which case, the array is exactly the size you specify, or alternatively, you can specify a larger value. This value affects future allocations. Consider the following code:

```
#include <afx.h>
#include <afxcoll.h>

void main()
{
    CByteArray b;
    b.SetSize(2, 10);  // Allocate 2 bytes
    b.SetSize(3);              // Allocate 12 bytes
}
```

The reason the second **SetSize** call allocates 12 bytes is because the granularity is set to 10. The first 3 bytes are presumably going to be used by something, and the next 7 are free for succeeding allocations.

```
void FreeExtra( );
void RemoveAll( );
OBJECT GetAt( int nIndex) const;
```

The argument is indexes array elements, and some classes declare more than one. **CObArray** and **CPtrArray** both declare both const pointer and pointer-reference returns.

```
void SetAt( int nIndex, OBJECT newElement);
OBJECT & ElementAt( int nIndex)
```

In the case of **CPtrArray**, the return type is void *&. This may not seem important, but it simply won't work if it isn't a reference to a pointer.

```
void SetAtGrow( int nIndex, OBJECT newElement)
    throw( CMemoryException);
int Add( OBJECT newElement) throw( CMemoryException);
void InsertAt( int nIndex, OBJECT newElement, int nCount = 1)
    throw( CMemoryException);void InsertAt( int nStartIndex,
OBJECT_Array* pNewArray)
    throw( CMemoryException);

void RemoveAt(int nIndex, int nCount = 1);
OBJECT &operator [](  int nIndex );
OBJECT operator [](  int nIndex ) const;
```

Add   FUNCTION

Description Adds one new element to the end of the array, allocating memory as necessary and returning the index of the added element. The **SetSize** member function can set a flag that causes the array to grow by multiple entries when an element is added.

Prototype
```
//Function Prototype
    //Add one element to the top of our array,
    //returning the increased upper bound....
nTopElement = uiArrayInts.Add( nInvoiceNumber );
```

ElementAt   FUNCTION

Description Used to implement specialized array operators, particularly the assignment operator. (Don't believe everything you read in the Microsoft documentation. There's no such thing as the left-side assignment operator. There's just the assignment operator.) Returns a *temporary* reference to a pointer to the type of object for which the function was called.

FreeExtra

Description
Frees unused memory but does not change the size or upper bound of the array.

Prototype
```
//Function Prototype
//Create an array big enough to hold the maximum number of
    //elements that could be necessary....
CUIntArray uiBigIntArray;
uiBigIntArray.SetSize( DAYS_IN_YEAR );
for( i = 0; i < uiWorkDays.GetSize( ); i++ )
  {
    //Copy only workdays into uiBigIntArray....
    uiBigIntArray[i] = uiWorkDays[i];
  }
    //Free memory allocated for the elements we didn't use....
uiBigIntArray.FreeExtra( );
```

GetAt

Description
Retrieves the array element specified by *nIndex* and returns a pointer to the type of object for which the function was called. (Or, in the case of built-in types, such as UINT or DWORD, returns the value of the element.)

Prototype
```
//Function Prototype
//This function call is equivalent to the statement
// dwOurNumber = dwBigNumberArray[3];
DWORD dwOurNumber = dwBigNumberArray. GetAt(3);
```

GetSize

Description
Returns the *number of array elements* or the highest index +1.

Prototype
```
//Function Prototype
//Loop over the members of an array....
for( int i = 0; i < uiArray.GetSize( ); i++ )
  {
    //Handle array members
    uiArray[i] += PI;
  }
```

GetUpperBound — FUNCTION

Description   Returns the *highest index* in the array, or -1 if the array is empty.

Prototype

```
//Function Prototype
    //Loop over the members of an array....
for( int i = 0; i <= uiArray.GetUpperBound( ); i++ )
  {
    //Handle array members
    uiArray[i] += PI;
  }
```

InsertAt — FUNCTION

Description   This function can insert a single entry multiple times or an array of entries, depending on the arguments passed to it. The first version inserts *nCount* copies of *newElement* at *nIndex*. The second version inserts the array of objects *pNewArray* at *nStartIndex*. Both implementations displace existing entries into higher array locations and throw an exception if the insertion fails. The default argument of *nCount* defaults to 1.

Prototype

```
//Function Prototype
    //We have an array of bytes representing
    // a sentence, and we want to
    // insert blanks for a missing word that
    //will be filled in by the user....
bytesSentence.InsertAt(bBeginBlanks, '_', MAX_WORD);
    //Later, we have collected the word from
    // the user, and we want to
    //fill in the sentence....
bytesSentence.InsertAt(bBeginBlanks, szMissingWord);
    //We still need to trim away those blanks we inserted,
    //so look at the example for RemoveAt
```

operator [] — OPERATOR

Description   The array subscript operators replace the member functions **SetAt** and **GetAt**. Return or update the value of the element at *nIndex*. *The second version is for const arrays and may not be used to update array element values.* Note that because operator [] is implemented as a convenient shortcut for **SetAt** and **ElementAt** (the const version), you do not get automatic array growth as you would using **SetAtGrow**. Also, the const version allows you to use these operators in const objects.

Prototype
```
//Function Prototype
//The array index operators replace the SetAt
//and GetAt member functions.
uiArray[i] = 1;
nTestCase = uiArray[i];
```

RemoveAll   FUNCTION

Description Clears the array and frees memory used by *array elements.* In the case of **CObArray** and **CPtrArray**, the objects to which array elements point exist until they are deleted.

Prototype
```
//Function Prototype
if( ! FIRST_STUDENT )
    {
        //We have a reusable array that we clear and reinitialize....
        cTestAnswers.RemoveAll( );
```

RemoveAt   FUNCTION

Description Prunes the *nCount* element(s) at *nIndex* from the array, shifting higher elements to lower indices. In the case of **CObArray** and **CPtrArray** elements, the pointers to the objects are removed from the array, but the objects themselves exist until they are deleted.

Prototype
```
//Function Prototype
        //We have an array of bytes representing
        //a sentence, and we want to
        //insert blanks for a missing word that
        //will be filled in by the user....
bytesSentence.InsertAt(bBeginBlanks, '_', MAX_WORD );
        //Later, we have collected the word from
        //the user, and we want to
        //fill in the sentence, but first we should
        //trim out the blanks....
bytesSentence.RemoveAt(bBeginBlanks, strlen( szMissingWord ) );
bytesSentence.InsertAt(bBeginBlanks, szMissingWord);
```

SetAt — FUNCTION

Description Replaces the array element at *nIndex* with the pointer to *newElement*. Note that **SetAt** does *not* cause the array to grow.

Prototype
```
//Function Prototype
//void SetAt( int nIndex, OBJECT newElement );
    //This function call is equivalent to the statement
    //dwBigNumberArray[3] = AVOGADRO;
dwBigNumberArray.SetAt( 3, AVOGADRO);
```

SetAtGrow — FUNCTION

Description Replaces the array element at *nIndex* with the pointer to *newElement,* allocating memory if necessary.

Prototype
```
//Function Prototype
    //We want to add space for five new
    //elements to our array and set the highest
    //one to the character 'M'....
bByteArray.SetAtGrow( bByteArray.GetUpperBound( ) + 5, 'M' );
```

The preceding example is a bit dramatic, but it makes the point. More realistically, you would iterate through a loop, using **SetAtGrow** like this:

```
for(int i=0; i<_CHAR_MAX; i++)
    bMyArray.SetAtGrow(i, 'A' + i);
```

SetSize — FUNCTION

Description Sets the size of an array by allocating memory (if necessary) for an increase, or truncating and freeing memory for a decrease. Arrays are allocated to granularity n, where n is set using the **SetSize** function. As a result, allocations don't occur every time.

If new memory can't be allocated, the function will throw an exception.

Prototype
```
//Function Prototype
//Reduce the size of an existing array by half and relinquish any
    //elements above the new upper bound
uiArray.SetSize(uiArray.GetSize() / 2, 0);
```

Alternatively, you could do this:

```
uiArray.SetSize(uiArray.GetSize() / 2);
uiArray.FreeExtra();
```

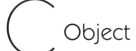Object

Description   **CObject** is the common base class for the MFC library and special-ized user-derived classes. It provides member functions for serializa-tion (object persistence, or the ability to stream an object to stor-age medium and then recreate a new one in the same state from that storage), run-time class information (similar to C++ run-time type information), diagnostics, and support for collections of user-derived objects. **CObject** has limited support for multiple inherit-ance: user-derived classes can have only one **CObject** base class, which must be at the leftmost side of the hierarchy. Structures and non-**CObject**-derived classes may occupy the rightmost branches of the hierarchy of user-derived classes that have multiple inheritance. **CObject**-derived classes can benefit from the use of several op-tional macros to dynamically create, identify and serialize objects:

Macro Name	Use
DECLARE_DYNAMIC	Allows the application to retrieve object-type information at run-time. Must be used with the IMPLEMENT_DYNAMIC macro. Always appears in the class declaration.
IMPLEMENT_DYNAMIC	Generates the C++ code necessary to provide the behavior defined by the DECLARE_DYNAMIC macro. Always appears in the implementation—that is, outside the class declaration, but also outside any function bodies.
DECLARE_DYNCREATE	Allows the application to create objects at run-time. Must be used with the IMPLEMENT_DYNCREATE macro. Always appears in the class declaration, and is often used when (1) an object is being created as a result of being deserialized; or (2) an object is being created as a result of a document template.

IMPLEMENT_DYNCREATE	Generates the C++ code necessary to provide the behavior defined by the DECLARE_DYNCREATE macro. Always appears in the implementation—that is, outside the class declaration, but also outside any function bodies.
DECLARE_SERIAL	Allows the application to serialize objects to and from archives. Must be used with the IMPLEMENT_SERIAL macro. Always appears in the class declaration.
IMPLEMENT_SERIAL	Generates the C++ code necessary to provide the behavior defined by the DECLARE_SERIAL macro. Always appears in the implementation— that is, outside the class declaration, but also outside any function bodies.

Microsoft Visual C++ tools such as AppWizard and ClassWizard automatically generate code, including the macros, when you create new classes. User-defined classes must explicitly call these macros as needed. **CObject** is intentionally limited in capability so as not to unduly burden derived classes with functionality that is not used (this is often referred to as a "light-weight class"). It has no public data, associates no visual interface elements, and has no useful specialized behavior by itself. Applications never interact with objects of this type directly, but instead with its derived classes. Almost all of the functionality of the framework is in classes derived from **CObject**. For this reason, many **CObject** member functions do not include code examples. Most of them are shown in examples relating to derived framework classes.

Derived Classes More than 80 percent of the framework classes are derived from **CObject**.

Member Functions

AssertValid FUNCTION

Description **AssertValid** checks the internal consistency of an object. Like **operator =**, such a check has no meaning in the absence of data members. Most classes derived from **CObject** override **AssertValid** because it is a useful diagnostic function. If its stability checks fail, it terminates the program with an error message and a line number. Override functions usually call the **AssertValid** function of their base classes.

This function is rarely, if ever, called from application code. Instead, the ASSERT_VALID macro is used.

You have a choice of doing a "shallow" or "deep" consistency check. This is a decision you should make before you begin your project, as it will impact how you write your **AssertValid** functions. Following are three examples of how you can implement consistency-checking policy for **CObject**-derived classes. Assume the following class declaration (where **CSomeObject** is either directly or indirectly derived from **CObject**):

```
class CMyClass : public CSomeObject
{
public:
    // Member functions, etc.
#ifdef _DEBUG
    void AssertValid() const;
#endif

private:
    CListBox *plistSomething;
    CWnd    *pwndSomething;
    UINT    nSomething;
};
#ifdef _DEBUG
// Very shallow consistency check
#ifdef VERY_SHALLOW
void CMyClass::AssertValid() const
{
    // Test any member objects
    ASSERT(nSomething < 32767);
    // Pointers and base classes ignored
}
#elif SHALLOW
void CMyClass::AssertValid() const
{
// Test base classes
    CSomeObject::AssertValid();
// Test any member objects
    ASSERT(nSomething < 32767);
// Test pointers for validity only
    ASSERT(::AfxIsValidAddress(plistSomething, sizeof(CListBox)));
    ASSERT(::AfxIsValidAddress(pwndSomething, sizeof(CWnd)));
}
```

```
#elif DEEP
void CMyClass::AssertValid() const
{
// Test base classes
    CSomeObject::AssertValid();
// Test any member objects
    ASSERT(nSomething < 32767);
// Test pointers for complete consistency
    plistSomething->AssertValid();
    pwndSomething->AssertValid();
}
#endif
#endif
```

AssertValid does you no good if you don't sprinkle ASSERT_VALID macros liberally about in your code. The reason for the macro instead of the function call is that the macro can be compiled out of release versions of your project.

Prototype

```
//Function Prototype
//virtual void AssertValid( ) const;
    //Class CTire overrides the CObject AssertValid member
void CTire::AssertValid( ) const
{
    //CTire was derived from CObject, so we want to do state
    //checking for the underlying class....
  CObject::AssertValid( );
    //Check the state of our class-specific data members —
    //don't allow negative tire pressure
ASSERT( m_inflation >= 0 );
}
```

CObject   FUNCTION

Description The **CObject** constructor optionally creates an uninitialized **CObject** or creates a copy of an existing object. **CObject** class objects are seldom constructed for their own sake because the primary role of the class is to serve as a base class.

Dump `FUNCTION`

Description   **Dump** copies the contents of an object to a **CDumpContext** object (such as **afxDump**, the predefined diagnostic stream). Derived classes override this function, and like **AssertValid**, the overrides call the **Dump** function of their base class. **Dump** overrides should not output a new line at the end of their dumping operations.

Prototype
```
//Function Prototype
//virtual void Dump(CDumpContext& dc) const;
```

GetRuntimeClass `FUNCTION`

IsKindOf `FUNCTION`

Description   **GetRuntimeClass** and **IsKindOf** are used to dynamically retrieve information about a class's type and descendancy. To use either of them, the serialization and dynamic object-creation macros listed in the preceding table must have been included in the class implementation. These functions have limited applicability for user code because they overlap the role of virtual functions, which are the preferred method of implementing polymorphism. Framework archiving functions use run-time class information in moving objects between disk and memory.
To test a class, use this line:
```
if(pGenericObject->IsKindOf(RUNTIME_CLASS("CEdit")))
    // do something...
```
The macro is a great way of staying current with C++ as the language evolves.

Prototype
```
//Function Prototype
//virtual CRuntimeClass* GetRuntimeClass( ) const;
//BOOL IsKindOf(const CRuntimeClass* pClass) const;
```

IsSerializable `FUNCTION`

Description   **IsSerializable** tests whether an object can be moved between memory and disk. Many **CObject**-derived items cannot be serialized; for example, objects of classes implementing collections can't be serialized if they contain pointers (unless the pointer points to another DYNCREATE class, in which case the object can be deserialized in the process of deserializing the current object).

Prototype

```
//Function Prototype
//BOOL IsSerializable() const;
```

operator =   OPERATOR

Description **operator** = performs a member-by-member assignment. Because **CObject** has no public data members, functions derived from **CObject** must provide an override for **operator** =.

operator delete   OPERATOR

Description **operator delete**, like **operator new**, has a release mode and debug mode of operation. In release mode, it simply frees memory allocated by **new**. In debug mode, it is involved in recordkeeping on allocations.

This debug and release modality is controlled by two factors: presence of the manifest constant _DEBUG; and linking with the debugging version of the MFC libraries.

operator new   OPERATOR

Description **operator new** has a release mode and debug mode of operation. In release mode, it simply allocates a new object. In debug mode, it is part of a mechanism that monitors allocations to help detect memory leaks. To trigger the debug behavior, include the following lines after the last include file and ahead of any implementation code in your .CPP files:

```
#define new DEBUG_NEW
#ifdef _DEBUG
#undef THIS_FILE
static char BASED_CODE THIS_FILE[] = __FILE__;
#endif
```

The framework records object and line number information for each allocation. The **CMemoryState** function **DumpAllObjectsSince** provides a listing of the allocation information. Also, by default, this information is dumped to the **afxDump** stream at the end of program execution. If you typically run under the debugger, you'll see the results in the output window of Visual C++. Any memory leak is a signal that you should go back to the allocation and find out why there isn't a deallocation of the object, as leaking memory can signal an application whose performance will degrade over time until it will no longer run.

Serialize FUNCTION

Description   **Serialize** moves a **CObject** between memory and disk. This function must be overridden to be useful to derived classes. It interacts with the **CArchive** class, which provides storage services and serialization status information.

Prototype

```
//Function Prototype
//virtual void Serialize(CArchive& ar)
// throw( CMemoryException, CArchiveException, CFileException
// );
```

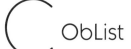

ObList CLASS

Description   **CObList** is one of the list collection classes, which encapsulate the behavior of doubly linked lists. Lists are permitted to have duplicate entries, which may be accessed by index or by position. Many list-navigation member functions return position values, and accessing list elements by using positions is very fast. Lists can be treated like arrays in some contexts, and elements can be referenced by index, but this method of access is considerably slower than position reference.

Like the other collection classes, lists are derived from **CObject** and, except for pointer lists, may be serialized. When **CObList** elements are serialized, their associated objects accompany them to the archive.

The characteristics of the various collections are as follows:

Array	Uniform access to any element. Not as easy to grow or shrink List. One of the easiest collections to iterate. Random access to a given data member varies proportionate to the size of the list. Particularly suitable for a dynamic collection where insertions and deletions are required on a reasonably frequent basis (i.e., requires an expensive allocation/deallocation).
Map	Extremely fast access to members where collisions don't take place. Suited more to static collections of data than to collections that are constantly changing. Access time to a given member cannot be computed, but can be averaged.

I also made reference to the "ownership" versus "collaborative container" relationship in an earlier GP class file. It's important to understand that the collection does not own the data, does not manage the destruction of the data objects, and hence can be deleted without deleting the associated objects (often causing memory leaks).

VC++ 2.0 introduces templated collection classes. These are the same ones, except they are templated implementations. So, for example, you can now have a declaration of the following form:

```
#include <afxtempl.h>
CList<CWnd, CWnd&> awndList;
```

This addresses the type-safety concern mentioned in **CObList**. However, templates don't solve all problems. By the nature of the way the the general purpose collections were implemented originally, we were able to support some features you have to give up in the templated version; i.e., there is an *almost* but not *exact* 1:1 mapping of functionality.

The classes in the list collection of classes include the following:

CObList CLASS

Description **CObList** elements are pointers to objects of **CObject** type. **CObList** is valuable mostly as a base class from which user-defined lists can be derived. The typical user-derived list contains pointers to objects that are also user derived, based on the **CObject** class. New lists created in this fashion are not entirely type-safe because a pointer to *any* **CObject** or derived class can be inserted in the resulting list. As with pointer lists, deletion of a list element does not cause the deletion or destruction of the object to which it points.

CPtrList CLASS

Description **CPtrList** elements are void pointers, which may *not* be serialized. Deletion of a list element does not cause the deletion or destruction of the object to which it points.

CStringList CLASS

Description **CStringList** elements are members of the **CString** class. Unlike the other two types of lists provided by the framework's collection classes, when elements are deleted from a **CStringList**, the associated **CString** object also is deleted. Comparison operation on list elements consider the actual contents of the string as opposed to its address.

This distinction is extremely important, and if you look at the way you use a **CStringList**, it makes a ton of sense that it should "own" the contents. The previous two lists contained only pointers. **CStringList**, by contrast, contains the actual **CStrings**. Arguments to the class member functions are of type **CString&** or **CString**. This makes for more Basic-like functionality.

```
CStringList myList;
myList.InsertTail("Hello");
myList.InsertTail("World");
```

Note that the code above in Basic would have looked like this:

```
Dim myList (5) as String 'Or something like that...
myList(1) = "Hello"
myList(2) = "World"
```

The point is, in neither case do you have to worry about the duration of the objects you add to the list, nor do you have to worry about the disposition of them when you are done.

Common Member Functions for List Collection Classes

Use the following table to create function prototypes for all the list collection classes by making the following substitutions for the placeholder *OBJECT:*

For This Class	Replace OBJECT With
CPtrList	void *
CObList	CObject *
CStringList	For return values, substitute CString; for parameters, CString; for parameters, substitute const char *

Find   FUNCTION

Description   **Find** performs a forward search for an *object pointer* (not a position or an index) in a list, optionally starting the search at a given position. For **CStringLists**, comparisons are done by value rather than by address, and this function returns a **CString** rather than a pointer. It returns the position at which the object pointer is found, or NULL for a failure.

Prototype

```
//Function Prototype
    //We want to know if the CString object
    //pcstringKeyWord is in the list....
if( KeyWordList.Find( pcstringKeyWord, NULL ) == NULL )
    //If not found, add the new keyword to the list....
    KeyWordList.AddHead( pcstringKeyWord );
```

FindIndex   FUNCTION

Description **FindIndex** finds an element in a list by using a zero-based index and returns its position. It is an O(n) algorithm, where n is the index supplied. Doing a FindIndex(100) costs O(100). While there is an opportunity to remember where element 100 is, thereby potentially reducing the cost of a FindIndex(101), that's not what happens. The tradeoff is one of base-class baggage (the cached state of the last **FindIndex**) and performance in this case. It is considered that this method of traversing a list will be less frequently used, and therefore the cost of carrying that baggage is unacceptable. After having said this, I should point out that while FindIndex(100); FindIndex(101) might be O(100+101), p=FindIndex(100); FindNext(p); is far more efficient.

Prototype

```
//Function Prototype
    //We want to know the position of the fifth element....
posFifthKeyWord = KeyWordList.FindIndex( FIFTH );
```

GetAt   FUNCTION

Description **GetAt** retrieves a pointer to the element at the position specified by the parameter and can optionally replace the element. Remember, this does not apply to **CStringArray**, because it doesn't use pointers. Also, you should clarify that the position variable is not an array index, but rather part of the collection's iterator. You can't, therefore, set it to 4 and get the 4th element in the list.

Prototype

```
//Function Prototype
    //Use GetAt to get a pointer to the
    //object at a given position;
CString* pAnElement = NameList.GetAt( posCurrentElement );
```

GetCount   FUNCTION

Description   **GetCount** returns the number of elements in the list. Following is
an example:

Example
```
//Loop over the members of an List....
for( i = ObjList.GetCount( ); i <= 0; i—)
{
    //Handle List members
}
```

GetHead   FUNCTION

Description   **GetHead** returns a pointer to the first element in the list, but it
should not be called for empty lists.

Prototype
```
//Function Prototype
    //Make sure that the list isn't empty....
if( ! NameStringList.IsEmpty( ) )
{
    //Get a reference  to the first
    //CString object in NameStringList....
 CString strFirstNameInList;
strFirstNameInList = NameStringList.GetHead();

}
```

GetHeadPosition   FUNCTION

Description   List navigation may be done by position. Use **GetHeadPosition** to
retrieve the position of the top of the list to begin a forward traversal.

Prototype
```
//Function Prototype
//Note that this code only works if you are using a CPtrList to //
store CStrings. You get CString& return types if it's a //CStringArray.
    //Get the position of the first list element....
POSITION posNextElement = NameList.GetHeadPosition( );
while( NULL != posElement )
{
    //Traverse the list from beginning to end;
    //GetNext retrieves pointers to the elements and
    //updates the position posNextElement to
```

```
//that of the next element....
CString* CurrentName = NameList.GetNext( posNextElement );
//Do something with this list element....
}
```

GetNext   FUNCTION

Description **GetNext** retrieves a pointer to the element at the position specified by the parameter, and then updates the position reference to identify the next list element. If the position variable is NULL, you have reached the end of the list. *See **GetHeadPosition** for a usage example.*

GetPrev   FUNCTION

Description **GetPrev** retrieves a pointer to the element at the position specified by the parameter and then updates the position reference to identify the previous list element. If the position variable is NULL, you've iterated past the head of the list. *See **GetTailPosition** for a usage example.*

GetTail   FUNCTION

Description **GetTail** returns a pointer to the last element in the list, but it should not be called for empty lists.

Prototype
```
//Function Prototype
    //Make sure that the list isn't empty....
if( ! NameStringList.IsEmpty( ) )
  {
    //Get a pointer to the last CString
    //object in NameStringList....
  CString strFirstNameInList;
  strFirstNameInList = NameStringList.GetHead();
```

GetTailPosition   FUNCTION

Description **GetTailPosition** retrieves the position of the last element of the list to begin a backward traversal.

```
//Note that this code only works if you are using a CPtrList to
//store CStrings. You get CString& return types if it's a
//CStringArray.
```

555

```
//Get the position of the last list element....
POSITION posPrevElement = NameList.GetTailPosition( );
while( NULL != posElement )
  {
    //Traverse the list from the end to the beginning;
    //GetPrev retrieves pointers to the elements and
    //backs the position through the list....
    CString* CurrentName = NameList.GetPrev( posPrevElement );
    //Do something with this list element....
  }
```

InsertAfter   FUNCTION

Description   **InsertAfter** inserts an entry into a list after the specified position.

Prototype
```
//Function Prototype
    //The position of the element in a
    //list of CStrings we want to insert before is at
    //posBookTitle
    //and pcstringNewTitle is a pointer to the
    //CString being inserted....
cstringsBestSellers.InsertAfter( posBookTitle, pcstringNewTitle );
```

InsertBefore   FUNCTION

Description   **InsertBefore** inserts an entry into a list before the specified position.

Prototype
```
//Function Prototype
    //The position of the element in a
    //list of CStrings we want to insert after is at posBookTitle,
    //and pcstringNewTitle is a pointer to the
    //CString being inserted....
cstringsBestSellers.InsertAfter( posBookTitle, pcstringNewTitle );
```

IsEmpty   FUNCTION

Description   **IsEmpty** tests for an empty list, returning TRUE or FALSE. Many list access member functions are not to be called against an empty list, so this function provides a convenient way to "guard against" inappropriate access calls.

Prototype
```
//Function Prototype
POSITION posTopOfList;
    //Attempt to get the head position
    //only if the list has some elements....
if( ! cstringList.IsEmpty( ) )
  posTopOfList = cstringListGetHeadPosition( );
```

RemoveAt   FUNCTION

Description   **RemoveAt** trims an element from a list and splices the list together again. If you are traversing the list by using **GetPrev** or **GetNext**, keep in mind that the removed element's position is invalidated when it is trimmed.

Prototype
```
//Function Prototype
POSITION posPrev, posCurrent;
    //Set up a loop that starts at the head of the list, continues
    //to the end of the list, and removes each entry in turn....
for( posCurrent = StringPtrList.GetHeadPosition( );
    posCurrent != NULL;
    pMemPtrEntry = StringPtrList.GetNext( posCurrent ) )
  { //Set posPrev equal posCurrent so that we will have a way
    //to maintain a record of our position if we remove a link
    //in the list....
    posPrev = posCurrent;
    if((*(CString*)StringPtrList.GetAt( posCurrent ) == "Unused" )
  {
    //If we do this removal, we invalidate posCurrent for use as
    //a loop control, so we need to be able to back up to a
    //valid position that we save in posPrev....
        pPrevString = StringPtrList.GetPrev( posPrev );
        StringPtrList.RemoveAt( posCurrent );
    //Reset posCurrent to the position of a list
    //element that still exists....
        posCurrent = posPrev;
    }
```

RemoveHead   FUNCTION

Description   **RemoveHead** removes the first element from a list and returns a pointer to the removed object so that it can be separately and explicitly deleted. It should not be called for an empty list.

Prototype

```
//Function Prototype
    //Make sure that the list isn't empty....
if( ! NameStringList.IsEmpty( ) )
    {
    //Get a pointer to the first CString
    //object in NameStringList....
    pFirstNameInList = NameStringList.RemoveHead( );
    //Delete the object to which the pointer refers,
    //to avoid memory leakage....
    delete pFirstNameInList;
    }
```

RemoveTail   FUNCTION

Description   **RemoveTail** removes the last element from a list and returns a pointer to the removed object so that it can be separately and explicitly deleted. It should not be called for an empty list.

Prototype

```
//Function Prototype
    //Make sure that the list isn't empty....
if( ! NameStringList.IsEmpty( ) )
    {
    //Get a reference  to the last
    //CString object in NameStringList....
    CString strFirstNameInList;
    strFirstNameInList = NameStringList.GetHead();

    //Delete the object to which the pointer refers,
    //to avoid memory leakage....
    delete pFirstNameInList;
    }
RemoveAll
```

Clears the list and frees memory used by *list elements and CString objects to which the list elements point.* In the case of **CObList** and **CPtrList**, the objects to which list elements point exist until they are deleted explicitly. What this means is that if you do a **RemoveAll** *before* you delete the objects pointed to, you'll never have a way to delete them (memory leak). With **CStringList**, however, this is not an issue, as the elements are removed and the memory freed at the same time.

Prototype
```
//Function Prototype
while(!myList.IsEmpty())
{
    //First delete all the objects to which
    //list elements point....

    delete myList.GetHead();
    //Then free memory associated with the list itself....
    myList.RemoveHead();
}
```

SetAt   FUNCTION

Description **SetAt** replaces a list element at the specified position with a pointer to a new object. Except for **CStringLists**, the old object is not deleted when replacement occurs, so they must be explicitly deleted to avoid memory leaks.

Prototype
```
//Function Prototype
    //Assume that pMemoryBlock is a void
    //pointer to a chunk of memory
    //we no longer need, and posCurrent
    //is its position in the list....
pMemoryBlock = MemoryPoolPtrList.GetAt( posCurrent );
    //Replace the pointer to pMemoryBlock
    //with a pointer to a
    //different block, using the same
    //slot in the list....
MemoryPoolPtrList.SetAt( posCurrent, pUpdatedBlock);
    //Delete the replaced block explicitly to
    //avoid memory leakage....
delete pMemoryBlock;
```

COleBusyDialog CLASS

Derivation

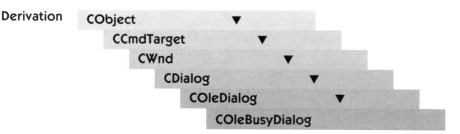

Description When a server is unable to handle a request, you can have the Server Busy dialog box displayed for the viewer. For more information about busy servers and how they respond to requests, look at the **COleMessageFilter** class.

Member Functions

COleBusyDialog FUNCTION

Description This function constructs a **COleBusyDialog** object; the dialog box itself is displayed when the **DoModal** function is called. The busy server is pointed to by the *htaskBusy*. If the server is not responding at all, as opposed to merely making the caller wait before retrying, the *bNotResponding* parameter gets set to true, and you should call the Not Responding dialog box instead of the Busy dialog box. The *dwFlags* parameter combines any of the following values using the bitwise-or operator:

BZ_DISABLECANCELBUTTON	Disables the Cancel button in the dialog box.
BZ_DISABLESWITCHTOBUTTON	Disables the Switch To button in the dialog box.
BZ_DISABLERETRYBUTTON	Disables the Retry button in the dialog box.

The last parameter, *pParentWnd*, is a pointer to the window that owns the dialog box. NULL indicates that the owner is the main application window.

Prototype	//Function Prototype
	COleBusyDialog(HTASK htaskBusy, BOOL bNotResponding = FALSE, DWORD dwFlags = 0, CWnd* pParentWnd = NULL);

DoModal   FUNCTION

Description This function is called to display the OLE Busy dialog box and is called after the object is constructed. If you want to initialize controls by setting members of the **m_bz** data member, do so before calling **DoModal**. This function returns **IDOK** if the dialog box is displayed correctly, it returns **IDCANCEL** if the user cancels the box, and returns **IDABORT** is there is an error. If the last return occurs, the **GetLastError** function from the **COleDialog** class can be used to retrieve the error code.

Prototype	//Function Prototype
	virtual int DoModal();

GetSelectionType   FUNCTION

Description When called, this function returns the selection made by the user in the Busy dialog box. It will be one of the following values:

COleBusyDialog::switchto	Switch To button was pressed.
COleBusyDialog::retry	Retry button was pressed.
COleBusyDialog::callUnblocked	The call to activate the server is no longer blocked.

Prototype	//Function Prototype
	UINT GetSelectionType();

Data Member

m_bz   MEMBER

Description This is an **OLEUIBUSY** structure that gives you the chance to control some of the properties of the Busy dialog box. Its members are as follows:

DWORD	cbStruct	Size of the structure.
DWORD	dwFlags	See list for dwFlags in the description of the COleChangeIconDialog constructor function.

HWND		hWndOwner	Handle to the owning window.
LPCTSTR		lpszCaption	Pointer to the string that is the caption of the dialog box.
LPFNOLEUIHOOK		lpfnHook	Pointer to the optional hook callback function, which you must build yourself.
LPARAM		lCustData	Optional custom data to pass to hook.
HINSTANCE		hInstance	Instance for the customized template name of the object to be inserted.
LPCTSTR		lpszTemplate:	Customized template name of the object to be inserted.
HRSRC		hResource:	Customized template handle.
HTASK		hTask	Handle to the task that is blocking the request.
HWND	FAR*	lphWndDialog	Handle to the Busy dialog box window.

C OleChangeIconDialog  **CLASS**

Derivation

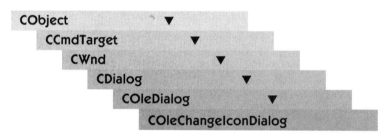

CObject ▼
  CCmdTarget ▼
    CWnd ▼
      CDialog ▼
        COleDialog ▼
          COleChangeIconDialog

Description This class creates and manages the Change Icon dialog box. The class members are straightforward. When you want to create a Change Icon dialog box, call **COleChangeIconDialog**. Use the **m_ci** data member to to initialize the values and control states for the dialog box. Call **DoModal** to display the box. Use **DoChangeIcon** to perform the change specified in the dialog box.

Member Functions

COleChangeIconDialog | FUNCTION

Description   This function creates an object, but does not actually display the box. That is done by **DoModal**. The *pItem* parameter points to the icon to be changed. Use the *pParentWnd* to point to the parent or owner window to which you wish the dialog object to belong. A NULL value here indicates that *nParentWnd* points to the application window object.

    The creation flag, *dwFlags*, can have any number of the following values:

CIF_SHOWHELP	Display the help button.
CIF_SELECTCURRENT	The Current radio button will be selected when box opens.
CIF_SELECTDEFAULT	The Default radio button will be selected when box opens.
CIF_SELECTFROMFILE	The From File radio button will be selected when box opens.
CIF_USEICONEXE	The icon will be selected from the executable file given by szIconExe field of m_ci.

Prototype
```
//Function Prototype
COleChangeIconDialog(COleClientItem* pItem, DWORD dwFlags =
CIF_SELECTCURRENT, CWnd* pParentWnd = NULL);
```

DoChangeIcon | FUNCTION

Description   You create the dialog box object with **COleChangeIconDialog**. Then you display the box with **DoModal**. If the box is successfully displayed, **DoModal** returns **IDOK**. At that point you can call **DoChangeIcon** to change the icon for the item from the one currently displayed to the one selected in the dialog box. The single parameter, *pItem*, points to the item whose icon is to be changed. The function returns TRUE if the change is successful, FALSE if not.

Prototype
```
//Function Prototype
BOOL DoChangeIcon(COleClientItem* pItem);
```

DoModal   FUNCTION

Description   Call this function to display the Change Icon dialog box. This should occur after the construction of the dialog box object, and after setting the values for **m_ci** to initialize the controls in the dialog box. The function returns one of three possibilities:

IDOK	The dialog box was displayed successfully.
IDCANCEL	The user canceled the dialog box.
IDABORT	There was an error. You can call COleDialog::GetLastError if you need more information about the error.

Prototype

```
//Function Prototype
virtual int DoModal();
```

GetIconMetafile   FUNCTION

Description   When called, this function returns the handle to the iconic aspect of the selected item. It is the new icon if the dialog box was closed by selecting OK, as opposed to Cancel. It is the old icon if the dialog box was canceled.

Prototype

```
//Function Prototype
HGLOBAL GetIconicMetafile() const;
```

Data Member

m_ci   MEMBER

Description   This structure contains specifications for the controls and properties of the dialog box. It is type **OLEUICHANGEICON**.

DWORD	cbStruct	Size of the structure.
DWORD	dwFlags	See list for dwFlags in the description of the COleChangeIconDialog constructor function.
HWND	hWndOwner	Handle to the owning window.
LPCTSTR	lpszCatption	Pointer to the string that is the caption of the dialog box.
LPFNOLEUIHOOK	lpfnHook	Pointer to the optional hook callback function, which you must build yourself.

LPARAM	lCustData	Optional custom data to pass to hook.
HINSTANCE	hInstance	Instance for the customized template name of the object to be inserted.
LPCTSTR	lpszTemplate:	Customized template name of the object to be inserted.
HRSRC	hResource:	Customized template handle.
HGLOBAL	hMetaPict	Handle to the metafile with the iconic aspect of the selected item.
CLSID	clsid	Class ID of the class used to get the default icon.
TCHAR	szIconExe [OLEUI_CCHPATHMAX]	This is a unicode string that gives the name of an executable file from which to extract the new icon.
int	cchIconExe	

COleClientItem

Derivation

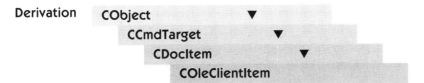

Description The **COleClientItem** class defines the container interface to OLE items that are placed into container documents to make compound documents. Now these OLE items can be embedded, neat little packages of data that are stored as a part of the compound document itself, or they can be linked data that is stored as a separate file but presented to the user as though it were a part of the document. One file can be linked to several documents.

Obviously, an embedded or linked OLE item must still be editable by the user. A number of this class's member functions are overridable functions that let the container application know about editing changes made to the OLE item, or to retrieve information needed during editing.

You use the **COleClientItem** class by deriving your own class from it, then using the **OnChange** member function to define how

565

the container will respond to changes made to that item. The **COleClientItem** class can be used with **COleDocument**, **COleLinkingDoc** or **COleServerDoc** classes. In-place activation is supported by overriding the **OnGetItemPosition** function.

Member Functions

Activate   FUNCTION

Description   This function executes the verb specified by the parameter *nVerb*. Normally **Activate** gets called by the function **DoVerb**, and then if an exception is thrown, the function **DoVerb** deals with it. By calling **Activate** directly, you can intercept the exceptions and handle them your own way. The parameter *nVerb* has several possible values:

OLEIVERB_PRIMARY	This is the response to a double-click on the item. What actually happens, the primary verb, is defined by the object, but for objects that support in-place activation, the action is usually to activate the object in place.
-1	This is the value for the secondary verb for an object. It has no symbol associated with it. What actually happens depends on how the object defines it, but the default handling is to treat it to be the same as OLEIVERB_OPEN.
OLEIVERB_SHOW	Shows the object to the user.
OLEIVERB_OPEN	If the object supports open editing, this causes the object to be open edited in a separate window. If open editing is not supported, it reverts to OLEIVERB_SHOW.
OLEIVERB_HIDE	The object removes its user interface from view.
OLEIVERB_UIACTIVATE	Activates the object in place and shows the interface tools.
OLEIVERB_INPLACEACTIVATE	Runs the object and installs its window, but doesn't install the user interface tools.
OLEIVERB_DISCARDUNDOSTATE	Discards the undo state, but doesn't deactivate the object.

If the primary verb of the item is Edit and the OLEIVERB_PRIMARY value is in *nVerb*, the server application is launched so editing can take place. If in-place activation is supported, editing occurs in place. Otherwise the server is launched in a separate window for editing. If the item only supports one verb, then no matter what the value of *nVerb* is, that is the action that will be taken.

The parameter *pView* is a pointer to the container view window that contains the OLE item. Its value is NULL if the container does not support in-place activation. The parameter *lpMsg* is a pointer to the message that caused the item to be activated.

Server applications written with the MFC library will generate a call from this function to the corresponding **COleServerItem** object's **OnDoVerb** function.

Prototype

```
//Function Prototype
void Activate(LONG nVerb, CVIEW* pView, LPMSG lpMsg = NULL);
```

ActivateAs   FUNCTION

Description   This function is called by **COleConvertDialog::DoConvert**. It activates the item as though it were of the type class referred to by *clsidNew*. If the item is a link, *clsidOld* is the class ID of the class the link refers to. If it is not a link, *clsidOld* should refer to the class ID of the actual object. The parameter *lpszUserType* is a pointer to a string that represents the target user type. An example would be "Word Document." This function returns TRUE if it is successful, FALSE if not.

Prototype

```
//Function Prototype
BOOL ActivateAs(LPCTSTR lpszUserType, REFCLSID clsidOld,
REFCLSID clsidNew);
```

AttachDataObject   FUNCTION

Description   Use the *rDataObject* parameter to send a reference to a **COleDataObject** object to initialize it. This allows access to the data in the OLE item.

Prototype

```
//Function Prototype
void AttachDataObject(ColeDataObject& rDataObject) const;
```

CanCreateFromData   FUNCTION

Description   This function checks the data object pointed to by the parameter *pDataObject* to see if the application can create an embedded object from it. If it can, it returns TRUE. The function was designed to be used for enabling or disabling the Paste and Paste Special commands.

Prototype
```
//Function Prototype
static BOOL PASCAL CanCreateFromData(const COleDataObject*
pDataObject);
```

CanCreateLinkFromData   FUNCTION

Description   This function checks the data object pointed to by the parameter *pDataObject* to see if the application can create a linked object from it. If it can, it returns TRUE. The function was designed to be used by containers for enabling or disabling the Edit Paste Special and Edit Paste Link commands.

Prototype
```
//Function Prototype
static BOOL PASCAL CanCreateLinkFromData(const
COleDataObject* pDataObject);
```

CanPaste   FUNCTION

Description   This function returns TRUE if the embedded OLE item can be pasted from the Clipboard, FALSE if not.

Prototype
```
//Function Prototype
static BOOL PASCAL CanPaste();
```

CanPasteLink   FUNCTION

Description   This function returns TRUE if the linked OLE item can be pasted from the Clipboard, FALSE if not.

Prototype
```
//Function Prototype
static BOOL PASCAL CanPasteLink();
```

Close   FUNCTION

Description   This function downshifts the item from a running state to simply a loaded state. This state has the item loaded with its handler in memory, but the server is not running. (**GetItemState** has more information on the different states of an item.) The single parameter, *dwCloseOption*, is a flag with one of three options:

OLECLOSE_SAVEIFDIRTY	Save the OLE item if any changes have been made since the last save.
OLECLOSE_NOSAVE	Don't save the OLE item.
OLECLOSE_PROMPTSAVE	Ask the user if you should save the OLE item.

Prototype
```
//Function Prototype
void Close(OLECLOSE dwCloseOption = OLECLOSE_SAVEIFDIRTY);
```

COIeClientItem   FUNCTION

Description   This function constructs a **COIeClientItem** object and adds it to the item collection in the container document printed to by the parameter *pContainerDoc*. If this parameter is NULL, the item is created but not put with any document and must be explicity added with **COIeDocument::AddItem**.

The function does not perform any OLE initialization. You must call one of the following functions before using the item:

CreateFromClipboard	CreateFromData
CreateFromFile	CreateStaticFromClipboard
CreateStaticFromData	CreateLinkFromClipboard
CreateLinkFromData	CreateLinkFromFile
CreateNewItem	CreateCloneFrom

Prototype
```
//Function Prototype
COIeClientItem(COIeDocument* pContainerDoc = NULL);
```

ConvertTo   FUNCTION

Description   This function is called automatically by **ConvertDialog**. It takes the item and converts it to the type given in the parameter *clsidNew*, which is a class ID. The function returns TRUE if it is successful, FALSE if not.

Prototype
```
//Function Prototype
BOOL ConvertTo(REFCLSID clsidNew);
```

CopyToClipboard
FUNCTION

Description This function copies the OLE item to the Clipboard, usually by message handlers that take care of the Copy or Cut commands. It presupposes that your application container handles item slection. The single parameter, *bIncludeLink*, should be TRUE if you want link information copied too. Otherwise it should be FALSE.

Prototype
```
//Function Prototype
void CopyToClipboard(BOOL bIncludeLink = FALSE);
```

CreateCloneFrom
FUNCTION

Description The function creates an identical copy of the item pointed to by the parameter *pSrcItem*. It is used to support undo operations. It returns TRUE if the creation is successful, FALSE if not.

Prototype
```
//Function Prototype
BOOL CreateCloneFrom(const COleClientItem* pSrcItem);
```

CreateFromClipboard
FUNCTION

Description This function creates an embedded item from the contents of the Clipboard. You should call it from the message handler for the Paste command, which would be enabled by the framework when **CanPaste** returns TRUE. The parameter *render* specifies how the server will render the OLE item. It is an enumerated data type with the following possible values:

OLERENDER_NONE	The container is not requesting any locally cached drawing or data retrieval capabilities. pFormatEtc is ignored if this value is selected.
OLERENDER_DRAW	The container will draw the object to the screen using IViewObject::Draw. The object determines the data formats that need to be cached. Only the ptd and dwAspect members of pFormatEtc are significant. If pFormatEtc is NULL, the object assumes the display target device and the DVASPECT_CONTENT aspect.
OLERENDER_FORMAT	The container will get one format from the object using IDataObject::GetData. The format of the data to be cached is passed in pFormatEtc, which can be NULL.

OLERENDER_ASIS	The container is not requesting any locally cached drawing or data retrieval capabilities. pFormatEtc is ignored if this value is selected. This is the same as OLERENDER_NONE except how it is handled in OleCreateFromData and OleCreateLinkFromData.

The parameter *cfCached* gives the Clipboard data format to be cached, and the parameter *lpFormatEtc* is a pointer to a **FORMATETC** structure with additonal format information for use when *render* is set to **OLERENDER_FORMAT** or **OLERENDER_DRAW**. The function returns TRUE if the creation of the object is successful, FALSE if not.

Prototype

```
//Function Prototype
BOOL CreateFromClipboard(OLERENDER render =
OLERENDER_DRAW, CLIPFORMAT cfFormat = 0, LPFORMATETC
lpFormatEtc = NULL);
```

CreateFromData   FUNCTION

Description   This function creates an embedded item from a **COleDataObject** object pointed to by the parameter *pDataObject*. This object is usually provided by a paste operation from the Clipboard or a drag-and-drop operation. It is usually used when you override **CView::OnDrop**. The parameter *render* specifies how the server will render the OLE item. It is an enumerated data type whose four possible values are explained in the **CreateFromClipboard** function. The parameter *cfFormat* gives the Clipboard format to be cached when the OLE item is created. Finally, the parameter *lpFormatEtc* is a pointer to a **FORMATETC** with additional format information for use when *render* is set to **OLERENDER_FORMAT** or **OLERENDER_DRAW**. The function returns TRUE if the creation of the object is successful, FALSE if not.

Prototype

```
//Function Prototype
BOOL CreateFromData(COleDataObject* pDataObject, OLERENDER
render = OLERENDER_DRAW, CLIPFORMAT cfFormat = 0,
LPFORMATETC lpFormatEtc = NULL);
```

CreateFromFile · FUNCTION

Description   This function creates an embedded OLE item from the file pointed to by *lpszFileName*. If the user has clicked the Create From File button in the Insert Object dialog box, then when the box is closed by clicking OK, the **CreateFromFile** function is called by the framework. The parameter *render* specifies how the server will render the OLE item. It is an enumerated data type whose four possible values are explained in the **CreateFromClipboard** function. The parameter *cfFormat* gives the Clipboard format to be cached when the OLE item is created. The parameter *lpFormatEtc* is a pointer to a **FORMATETC** structure with additional format information for use when *render* is set to **OLERENDER_FORMAT** or **OLERENDER_DRAW**. *clsid* has no purpose, but is a parameter reserved for future use. The function returns TRUE if the creation of the object is successful, FALSE if not.

Prototype
```
//Function Prototype
BOOL CreateFromFile(LPCTSTR lpszFileName, REFCLSID clsid =
CLSID_NULL, OLERENDER render = OLERENDER_DRAW,
CLIPFORMAT cfFormat = 0, LPFORMATETC lpFormatEtc = NULL);
```

CreateLinkFromClipboard · FUNCTION

Description   This function creates a linked item from the contents of the Clipboard. You should call it from the message handler for the Paste Link command, which would be enabled by the default implementation of **COleDocument** if the Clipboard has an OLE item that is linkable. The parameter *render* specifies how the server will render the OLE item. It is an enumerated data type type whose four possible values are explained in the **CreateFromClipboard** function. The parameter *cfCached* gives the Clipboard data format to be cached, and the parameter *lpFormatEtc* is a pointer to a **FORMATETC** structure with additional format information for use when *render* is set to **OLERENDER_FORMAT** or **OLERENDER_DRAW**. The function returns TRUE if the creation of the object is successful, FALSE if not.

Prototype
```
//Function Prototype
BOOL CreateLinkFromClipboard(OLERENDER render =
OLERENDER_DRAW, CLIPFORMAT cfFormat = 0, LPFORMATETC
lpFormatEtc = NULL);
```

CreateLinkFromData
FUNCTION

Description   This function creates a linked item from a **COleDataObject** object pointed to by the parameter *pDataObject*. The function is called during a drop operation if the user has requested a link. It can also handle the Edit Paste command. The framework calls this function from **COleClientItem::CreateLinkFromClipboard** and from **COlePasteSpecialDialog::CreateItem**, if the Link radio button has been clicked. The parameter *render* specifies how the server will render the OLE item. It is an enumerated data type whose four possible values are explained in the **CreateFromClipboard** function. The parameter *cfFormat* gives the Clipboard format to be cached when the OLE item is created. Finally, the parameter *lpFormatEtc* is a pointer to a **FORMATETC** structure with additional format information for use when *render* is set to **OLERENDER_FORMAT** or **OLERENDER_DRAW**. The function returns TRUE if the creation of the object is successful, FALSE if not.

Prototype
```
//Function Prototype
BOOL CreateLinkFromData(COleDataObject* pDataObject,
OLERENDER render = OLERENDER_DRAW, CLIPFORMAT cfFormat =
0, LPFORMATETC lpFormatEtc = NULL);
```

CreateLinkFromFile
FUNCTION

Description   This function creates a linked OLE item from the file pointed to by *lpszFileName*, if the user has clicked the Create From File button in the Insert Object dialog box and has the Link check box selected when the dialog box is closed. The **CreateLinkFromFile** function is called from **COleInsertDialog::CreateItem**. The parameter *render* specifies how the server will render the OLE item. It is an enumerated data type whose four possible values are explained in the **CreateFromClipboard** function. The parameter *cfFormat* gives the Clipboard format to be cached when the OLE item is created. The parameter *lpFormatEtc* is a pointer to a **FORMATETC** structure with additional format information for use when *render* is set to **OLERENDER_FORMAT** or **OLERENDER_DRAW**. The function returns TRUE if the creation of the object is successful, FALSE if not.

Prototype
```
//Function Prototype
BOOL CreateLinkFromFile(LPCTSTR lpszFileName, OLERENDER
render = OLERENDER_DRAW, CLIPFORMAT cfFormat = 0,
LPFORMATETC lpFormatEtc = NULL);
```

CreateNewItem — FUNCTION

Description When you need to create a new embedded item, call this function to launch the server application that can create the OLE item. It is called by the framework when the user has selected the Create New button in the Insert Object dialog box and has clicked the OK button as well. The new embedded object is given the ID provided by the parameter *clsid*. The parameter *render* specifies how the server will render the OLE item. It is an enumerated data type whose four possible values are listed and explained in the **CreateFromClipboard** function. The parameter *cfFormat* gives the Clipboard format to be cached when the OLE item is created. The parameter *lpFormatEtc* is a pointer to a **FORMATETC** structure with additional format information for use when *render* is set to **OLERENDER_FORMAT** or **OLERENDER_DRAW**. The function returns TRUE if the creation of the object is successful, FALSE if not.

Prototype
```
//Function Prototype
BOOL CreateNewItem(REFCLSID clsid, OLERENDER render =
OLERENDER_DRAW, CLIPFORMAT cfFormat = 0, LPFORMATETC
lpFormatEtc = NULL);
```

CreateStaticFromClipboard — FUNCTION

Description This function creates a static item from the Clipboard contents. A static item has the presentation data, but not the native data, and so can not be edited. This function is for use when the **CreateFromClipboard** function fails. The parameter *render* specifies how the server will render the OLE item. It is an enumerated data type whose four possible values are listed and explained in the **CreateFromClipboard** function. The parameter *cfFormat* gives the Clipboard format to be cached when the OLE item is created. Finally, the parameter *lpFormatEtc* is a pointer to a **FORMATETC** structure with additional format information for use when *render* is set to **OLERENDER_FORMAT** or **OLERENDER_DRAW**. The function returns TRUE if the creation of the object is successful, FALSE if not.

Prototype
```
//Function Prototype
BOOL CreateStaticFromClipboard(OLERENDER render =
OLERENDER_DRAW, CLIPFORMAT cfFormat = 0, LPFORMATETC
lpFormatEtc = NULL);
```

CreateStaticFromData — FUNCTION

Description   This function creates a static item from the **COleDataObject** object pointed to by *pDataObject*. A static item has the presentation data, but not the native data, and so cannot be edited. This function is designed to be used by **COlePasteSpecialDialog::CreateItem** when Static is selected. The parameter *render* specifies how the server will render the OLE item. It is an enumerated data type whose four possible values are listed and explained in the **CreateFromClipboard** function. The parameter *cfFormat* gives the Clipboard format to be cached when the OLE item is created. Finally, the parameter *lpFormatEtc* is a pointer to a **FORMATETC** structure with additional format information for use when *render* is set to **OLERENDER_FORMAT** or **OLERENDER_DRAW**. The function returns TRUE if the creation of the object is successful, FALSE if not.

Prototype
```
//Function Prototype
BOOL CreateStaticFromData(COleDataObject* pDataObject,
OLERENDER render = OLERENDER_DRAW, CLIPFORMAT cfFormat =
0, LPFORMATETC lpFormatEtc = NULL);
```

Deactivate — FUNCTION

Description   A call to this function deactivates the OLE item and frees up all associated resources. It is usually called when the mouse gets clicked outside the item but still within the client area. The undo state of the OLE item will be discarded when **Deactivate** is called, so **ReactivateAndUndo** cannot be called. If your application supports undo, call **DeactivateUI** instead of this function.

Prototype
```
//Function Prototype
void Deactivate();
```

DeactivateUI — FUNCTION

Description   This function returns the user interface of the container application to the state it was in before the item was in-place activated. But the undo state information is preserved, which means that **ReactivateAndUndo** can be called in case the user changes his or her mind and chooses the Undo command.

Prototype
```
//Function Prototype
void DeactivateUI();
```

Delete   FUNCTION

Description This function deletes the OLE item from the container document. To do so it calls the **Release** function described earlier. For embedded OLE items, the native data is deleted and the running server is closed. If the item is an open link, **Delete** closes it. The parameter *bAutoDelete*, when TRUE, specifies that the item be removed from the document.

Prototype
```
//Function Prototype
void Delete(BOOL bAutoDelete = TRUE);
```

DoDragDrop   FUNCTION

Description This function performs the drag-and-drop operation. To do this, it needs the following information in the function parameters:

pItemRect	This is a pointer to a CRect object or a RECT structure that has the item's rectangle coordinates, in pixels.
ptOffset	This gives the offset from the lpItemRect location to the cursor.
bIncludeLink	This should be TRUE if the link data can be copied to the Clipboard. It should be FALSE if your server application doesn't support links.
dwEffects	It can have any number of the following values:
	DROPEFFECT_COPY — Copying permitted.
	DROPEFFECT_MOVE — Moving permitted.
	DROPEFFECT_LINK — Linking permitted.
	DROPEFFECT_SCROLL — Indicates a drag scroll operation could occur.
lpRectStartDrag	This is a pointer to the rectangle that defines when a drag starts. That means the mouse must leave the rectangle before the drag actually begins. If it is set to NULL, the drag begins after the mouse moves one pixel.

Prototype
```
//Function Prototype
DROPEFFECT DodragDrop(LPCRECT lpItemRect, CPoint, ptOffset,
BOOL bIncludeLink = FALSE, DWORD dwEffects =
DROPEFFECT_COPY|DROPEFFECT_MOVE, LPCRECT lpRectStartDrag
= NULL);
```

| DoVerb | FUNCTION |

Description   This function executes the verb specified by the parameter *nVerb*, which it does by calling the function **Activate**. If an exception is thrown, **DoVerb** catches it and displays a message box to the user. The parameter *nVerb* has several possible values:

OLEIVERB_PRIMARY	This is the response to a double-click on the item. What actually happens, the primary verb, is defined by the object, but for objects that support in-place activation, the action is usually to activate the object in place.
-1	This is the value for the secondary verb for an object. It has no symbol associated with it. What actually happens depends on how the object defines it, but the default handling is to treat it to be the same as OLEIVERB_OPEN.
OLEIVERB_SHOW	Shows the object to the user.
OLEIVERB_OPEN	If the object supports open editing, this causes the object to be open edited in a separate window. If open editing is not supported, it reverts to OLEIVERB_SHOW.
OLEIVERB_HIDE	The object removes its user interface from view.
OLEIVERB_UIACTIVATE	Activates the object in place and shows the interface tools.
OLEIVERB_INPLACEACTIVATE	Runs the object and installs its window, but doesn't install the user interface tools.
OLEIVERB_DISCARDUNDOSTATE	Discards the undo state, but doesn't deactivate the object.

If the primary verb of the item is Edit and the **OLEIVERB_PRIMARY** value is in *nVerb*, the server application is launched so editing can take place. If in-place activation is supported, editing occurs in place. Otherwise the server is launched in a separate window for editing. If the item only supports one verb, than no matter what the value of *nVerb* is, that is the action that will be taken.

The parameter *pView* is a pointer to the container view window that contains the OLE item. Its value is NULL if the container does not support in-place activation. The parameter *lpMsg* is a pointer to the message that caused the item to be activated.

Prototype

```
//Function Prototype
virtual BOOL DoVerb(LONG nVerb, CView* pView, LPMSG lpMsg =
NULL);
```

Draw   FUNCTION

Description   **Draw** is usually used for screen display and draws the OLE item
inside the boundaries designated by *lpBounds*, a pointer to a RECT
structure or a **CRect** object. Rendering may require the picture to
be scaled to fit, and can be used by container applications to force a
view that scales between the screen display view and the final
printed image. *pDC* passes the device context in the form of a CDC
object.

The last parameter, *nDrawAspect*, determines how the item will
be drawn. It isn't neccessary if **Draw** is just for a screen display. If
nDrawAspect is set to equal -1 then the last aspect set by
SetDrawAspect is used. The type DVASPECT has the following
values:

DVASPECT_CONTENT	The item is represented in a way that lets it be displayed as an embedded object inside a container.
DVASPECT_THUMBNAIL	The item is displayed as a "thumbnail" rendering that permits its display inside a browsing tool.
DVASPECT_ICON	The item is displayed as an icon.
DVASPECT_DOCPRINT	The item is displayed as if it were printed.

Prototype

```
//Function Prototype
BOOL Draw(CDC* pDC, LPCRECT lpBounds, DVASPECT
nDrawAspect =
(DVASPECT)-1);
```

GetActiveView   FUNCTION

Description   This function returns a pointer to the view on which the item is in-
place activated. If it is not in-place activated, the function returns
NULL.

Prototype

```
//Function Prototype
CView* GetActiveView() const;
```

GetClassID   FUNCTION

Description   This function parameter, *pClassID*, retrieves the class ID, a 128-bit number that uniquely identifies the application that edits the item.

Prototype
```
//Function Prototype
void GetClassID(CLSID* pClassID) const;
```

GetClipboardData   FUNCTION

Description   This function gets the data for the Clipboard in the form of a **COleDataSource** object, pointed to by the parameter *pDataSource*. This function can be overridden, but should not be unless you want to offer data formats in addition to those offered by **CopyToClipboard**. If you are doing so, be sure to put those formats in the **COleDataSource** before or after calling **CopyToClipboard**, then pass the **COleDataSource** object to the **COleDataSource::SetClipboard** function.

   The remaining parameters of this function are as follows: *bIncludeLink* indicates whether or not link data is to be included. If so set it to TRUE. *lpOffset* is a pointer to the mouse cursor's offset from the object's origin, measured in pixels. *lpSize* is a pointer to the object's size, measured in pixels.

Prototype
```
//Function Prototype
void GetClipboardData(COleDataSource* pDataSource, BOOL
bIncludeLink = FALSE, LPPOINT lpOffset = NULL, LPSIZE lpSize =
NULL);
```

GetDocument   FUNCTION

Description   The function returns the pointer to the document that contains the OLE item. If the item is not part of a document, the function returns NULL.

Prototype
```
//Function Prototype
COleDocument* GetDocument() const;
```

GetDrawAspect   FUNCTION

Description   This function returns the current way the item is to be rendered, one of the following values:

DVASPECT_CONTENT	The item is represented in a way that lets it be displayed as an embedded object inside a container.
DVASPECT_THUMBNAIL	The item is displayed as a "thumbnail" rendering that permits its display inside a browsing tool.
DVASPECT_ICON	The item is displayed as an icon.
DVASPECT_DOCPRINT	The item is displayed as if it were printed.

Prototype
```
//Function Prototype
DVASPECT GetDrawAspect() const;
```

GetExtent   FUNCTION

Description   This function gets the size of the item and puts it in the *lpSize* parameter. The dimensions are in **HIMETRIC** units; that is, logical units are converted to 0.01 mm, positive x goes to the right, and positive y goes up. The *nDrawAspect* indicates what aspect of the item the size refers to. It can have the following values:

DVASPECT_CONTENT	The item is represented in a way that lets it be displayed as an embedded object inside a container.
DVASPECT_THUMBNAIL	The item is displayed as a "thumbnail" rendering that permits its display inside a browsing tool.
DVASPECT_ICON	The item is displayed as an icon.
DVASPECT_DOCPRINT	The item is displayed as if it were printed.

In applications written with the MFC library, this function generates a call to **COleServerItem::OnGetExtent**. One last thing: the size retrieved is not always going to be the same as the size last set by the **SetExtent** function, since that value is only treated as a suggestion, not a requirement.

Prototype
```
//Function Prototype
BOOL GetExtent(LPSIZE lpSize, DVASPECT nDrawAspect =
(DVASPECT)-1);
```

GetIconicMetafile   FUNCTION

Description   Usually this function is not called directly, but by the MFC/OLE dialog boxes. It returns a handle to the metafile used for drawing the item's icon. If there isn't one, a default icon is used. The metafile is cached via a call to **SetIconicMetafile** for later use. If this function is unsuccessful, it returns NULL.

Prototype
```
//Function Prototype
HGLOBAL GetIconiMetafile();
```

GetInPlaceWindow   FUNCTION

Description   Use this function to get the pointer to the window in which the item has been opened. It should only be called for an item that is in-place active.

Prototype
```
//Function Prototype
CWnd* GetInPlaceWindow();
```

GetItemState   FUNCTION

Description   This function returns the current state of the item, which will be one of the following values:

emptyState	Memory has been allocated, but the item has not been initialized.
loadedState	The item is fully created and associated with a COleClientItem-derived object.
openState	Open in the server's window as opposed to just open in place in the container document.
activeState	A brief state between simply open and UI active. It lacks user-interface components.
activeUIState	The item is active and all menus, toolbars and any other user-interface components are merged with those of the container.

Prototype
```
//Function Prototype
UINT GetItemState() const;
```

GetLastStatus   FUNCTION

Description   **GetLastStatus** returns the status code of the last OLE operation. It is a way of getting more information when another member function failed, meaning a FALSE or NULL was returned.

Prototype
```
//Function Prototype
SCODE GetLastStatus() const;
```

GetLinkUpdateOptions   FUNCTION

Description   The function returns the current link-update option for the OLE item, which can be one of two values:

OLEUPDATE_ALWAYS	The linked item gets updated whenever possible. This is the option that provides support for the Automatic link-update radio button in the Links dialog box.
OLEUPDATE_ONCALL	The linked item gets updated only when the container application requests it—that is, when the UpdateLink function is called. This is the option that provides support for the Manual link-update radio button in the Links dialog box.

This function gets called automatically by the **COleLinks** dialog class.

Prototype
```
//Function Prototype
OLEUPDATE GetLinkUpdateOptions();
```

GetType   FUNCTION

Description   This function returns the type of the OLE item, which can be one of the following:

OT_LINK	The item is a link.
OT_EMBEDDED	The item is embedded.
OT_STATIC	The item is static, meaning it is presentation data only.

Prototype
```
//Function Prototype
OLE_OBJTYPE GetType() const;
```

GetUserType `FUNCTION`

Description   This function retrieves the string that describes the OLE item type for display to the user. It first looks in the system registration database for the full type name. If that isn't present, it uses the short name. If that is not there, it looks for the user type currently stored in the OLE item. If that is an empty string, it uses the string "Unknown Object." The string is retrieved in the parameter *rString*. The parameter *nUserClassType* indicates the variant of the string describing the OLE item's type that is wanted. It has three possible values:

USERCLASSTYPE_FULL	The full type name displayed to the user.
USERCLASSTYPE_SHORT	This is a short name (up to 5 characters) for use in pop-up meus and the Edit Link dialog box.
USERCLASSTYPE_APPNAME	This is the name of the application servicing the class.

Prototype
```
//Function Prototype
void GetUserType(USERCLASSTYPE nUserClassType,
CString& rString);
```

IsInPlaceActivated `FUNCTION`

Description   "Is the item in-place active?" The function returns TRUE if it is. This is equivalent to being in the **activeState** or the **activeUIState**. *See **GetItemState** for an explanation of item states.*

Prototype
```
//Function Prototype
BOOL IsInPlaceActive() const;
```

IsLinkUpToDate `FUNCTION`

Description   This function checks to see if the OLE item is up to date. In other words, has the source document for a linked item been updated. An embedded item that contains links can be out of date the same way, and it is checked recursively. Checking whether or not an item is updated can take as long as actually updating. The function returns TRUE if the item is up to date, FALSE if it isn't.

Prototype
```
//Function Prototype
BOOL IsLinkUpToDate() const;
```

IsModified   FUNCTION

Description This function tells you whether the item has been modified since the last time it was saved. It returns TRUE if it has been modified, FALSE if not.

Prototype
```
//Function Prototype
BOOL IsModified() const;
```

IsOpen   FUNCTION

Description This function returns TRUE if the item is open in an instance of the server application running in a separated window. If it is open, it should be overlaid with a hatch pattern, using **CRectTracker**.

Prototype
```
//Function Prototype
BOOL IsOpen() const;
```

IsRunning   FUNCTION

Description **IsRunning** answers the question, "Is the item loaded and running in the server application?" It returns TRUE if it is, FALSE if it isn't.

Prototype
```
//Function Prototype
BOOL IsRunning() const;
```

ReactivateAndUndo   FUNCTION

Description As the name suggests, this function reactivates the OLE item and undoes the last editing operation of the user. You can call this function immediately after deactivation, if your application has undo support. In server applications written with the MFC library, **ReactivateAndUndo** generates a call from the server to **COleServerDoc::OnReactivateAndUndo**.

Prototype
```
//Function Prototype
BOOL ReactivateAndUndo();
```

Release   FUNCTION

Description This function is called by the **COleClientItem** destructor to clean up resources. It is also called by the **Delete** function. **Release** deletes the C++ object for the item. The single parameter, *dwCloseOption*, is a flag with one of three options:

OLECLOSE_SAVEIFDIRTY	Save the OLE item if any changes have been made since the last save.
OLECLOSE_NOSAVE	Don't save the OLE item.
OLECLOSE_PROMPTSAVE	Ask the user if you should save the OLE item.

Prototype

```
//Function Prototype
virtual void Release(OLECLOSE dwCloseOption =
OLECLOSE_NOSAVE);
```

Reload   FUNCTION

Description   This function closes then reloads the item. If the item is to be activated as a new type of class after a call to **ActivateAs**, use **Reload**. It returns TRUE if it is successful, FALSE if not.

Prototype

```
//Function Prototype
BOOL Reload();
```

Run   FUNCTION

Description   **Run** launches the application associated with the item, and should be called before activating the item. This is usually handled automatically by **ActivateAndDoVerb**. If you need to run a server in order to set an item attribute, use this function.

Prototype

```
//Function Prototype
void Run();
```

SetDrawAspect   FUNCTION

Description   This function sets the view of the item—in other words, how it is to be rendered by **COleClientItem::Draw**. It is automatically called by the Change Icon dialog box to enable iconic display. Here are the possible values for the parameter *nDrawAspect*:

DVASPECT_CONTENT	The item is represented in a way that lets it be displayed as an embedded object inside a container.
DVASPECT_THUMBNAIL	The item is displayed as a "thumbnail" rendering that permits its display inside a browsing tool.
DVASPECT_ICON	The item is displayed as an icon.
DVASPECT_DOCPRINT	The item is displayed as if it were printed.

Prototype

//Function Prototype
void SetDrawAspect(DVASPECT nDrawAspect);

SetExtent   FUNCTION

Description   This function sets the amount of space available for the OLE item, specified by the parameter *size*, and given in **HIMETRIC** units; that is, logical units are converted to 0.01 mm, positive x goes to the right, positive y goes up. The second parameter, *nDrawnAspect*, specifies the aspect, which can be any one of the following:

DVASPECT_CONTENT	The item is represented in a way that lets it be displayed as an embedded object inside a container.
DVASPECT_THUMBNAIL	The item is displayed as a "thumbnail" rendering that permits its display inside a browsing tool.
DVASPECT_ICON	The item is displayed as an icon.
DVASPECT_DOCPRINT	The item is displayed as if it were printed.

If the server application was written with the MFC library, then a call to **SetExtent** generates a call to the corresponding **COleServerItem** object's member function, **OnSetExtent**. This allows for the proper adjustment of the display.

Prototype

//Function Prototype
void SetExtent(const CSize& size, DVASPECT nDrawnAspect = DVASPECT_CONTENT);

SetHostNames   FUNCTION

Description   This function sets the user-visible name of the container application, pointed to by the *lpszHost* parameter, and it sets the identifying string of the container that holds the OLE item, pointed to by *lpszHostObj*. The strings are used in window titles for the OLE item being edited. It would be unusual to have to call this function directly, since it is automatically called for all OLE items in a container document when that document gets loaded. It does not need to be called each time an embedded object is activated for editing. The function is also called automatically with the application name and the document name when an object is loaded or when a file is saved with a different name.

SetHostNames calls the **OnSetHostNames** of the **COleServerDoc** document that contains the OLE item, if the server application was written with the MFC library.

Prototype
```
//Function Prototype
void SetHostNames(LPCTSTR lpszHost, LPCTSTR lpszHostObj);
```

SetIconicMetafile   FUNCTION

Description After **GetIconicMetafile** retrieves an item's icon metafile, that function calls this one to cache the metafile for future use. The parameter *hMetaPict* is a handle to the metafile which gets copied into the item. Since it is copied into the item, *hMetaPict* must be freed by the caller.

Prototype
```
//Function Prototype
BOOL SetIconicMetafile(HGLOBAL hMetaPict);
```

SetItemRects   FUNCTION

Description This function sets two rectangles: the rectangle that bounds the OLE item, pointed to by *lpPosRect*, and the visible rectangle of the item, pointed to by *lpClipRect*. Both positions are relative to the parent window, in client coordinates. Whenever the position or visible portion of the OLE item has changed, you need to call this function, usually via your view's member functions, **OnSize** and **OnScrollBy**. **SetItemRects** is also called by the default implementation of **OnChangeItemPosition**.

Prototype
```
//Function Prototype
BOOL SetItemRects(LPCRECT lpPosRect = NULL, LPCRECT lpClipRect
= NULL);
```

SetLinkUpdateOptions   FUNCTION

Description You can use this function to set the link-update option for the linked item. Generally, however, you should go with the option selected by the user in the Links dialog box. The parameter *dwUpdateOpt* can have one of the two following values:

OLEUPDATE_ALWAYS	The linked item gets updated whenever possible. This is the option that provides support for the Automatic link-update radio button in the Links dialog box.
OLEUPDATE_ONCALL	The linked item gets updated only when the container application requests it—that is, when the UpdateLink function is called. This is the option that provides support for the Manual link-update radio button in the Links dialog box.

587

Prototype

```
//Function Prototype
void SetLinkUpdateOptions(OLEUPDATE dwUpdateOpt);
```

SetPrintDevice   FUNCTION

Description This function is used to change the print-target device. It updates the device without refreshing the presentation cache; you need to use **COleclientItem::UpdateLink** for that. As you can see there are two prototypes. In the first, *ptd* points to a **DVTARGETDEVICE** structure that describes the target device. In the second, *ppd* points to a **PRINTDLG** structure that has information used to initialize the Print dialog box and to hold user selection information that comes from the Print dialog box.

Prototype

```
//Function Prototype
BOOL SetPrintDevice(const DVTARGETDEVICE* ptd);
BOOL SetPrintDevice(const PRINTDLG* ppd);
```

UpdateLink   FUNCTION

Description A call to this function updates the presentation of the OLE item. To update linked items, the function finds the link source, and may have to run one or more server applications. This can be slow. To update embedded items, the function recursively checks whether the item has links that are out of date, and if so updates them.

Prototype

```
//Function Prototype
BOOL UpdateLink();
```

Overridable Functions

CanActivate   FUNCTION

Description If the user tries to activate an OLE item in place, the framework calls this function to see if it is allowed. It is allowed, in the default implementation, if the container has a valid window. The function returns TRUE if in-place activation is allowed, FALSE if not.

Prototype

```
//Function Prototype
virtual BOOL CanActivate();
```

OnActivate — FUNCTION

Description This function is called to let the item know that it has been activated in place. That means only that the server is running, not that the user interface has been installed. It has not. There are no menus or toolbars for it. When the user interface is installed, then **OnActivateUI** gets called. The default implementation of **OnActivate** calls **OnChange** with **OLE_CHANGED_STATE** in the *nCode* parameter.

Prototype
```
//Function Prototype
virtual void OnActivate();
```

OnActivateUI — FUNCTION

Description When the user interface for the in-place activated item gets installed, which means that the toolbars and menus are installed, then the framework calls this function. The default implementation stores the server's **HWND** for later **GetServerWindow** calls.

Prototype
```
//Function Prototype
virtual void OnActivateUI();
```

OnChange — FUNCTION

Description Whenever the OLE item gets changed, saved or closed, the framework calls this function. The function also gets called by server applications written with the MFC library by the **Notify** member function of **COleServerDoc** or **COleServerItem**. The first parameter, *nCode*, can have one of the following values:

OLE_CHANGED	The item's appearance has changed.
OLE_SAVED	The item has been saved.
OLE_CLOSED	The item has been closed.
OLE_CHANGED_STATE	The item's state has changed.

If it is **OLE_CHANGED** or **OLE_SAVED**, the container document gets marked as modified. The second parameter, *dwParam*, is different depending on the value on *nCode*. If *nCode* is **OLE_SAVE** or **OLE_CLOSED**, *dwParam* is not used. If *nCode* is **OLE_CHANGED**, then *dwParam* tells what aspect has changed. It can have the following values:

589

DVASPECT_CONTENT	The item is represented in a way that lets it be displayed as an embedded object inside a container.
DVASPECT_THUMBNAIL	The item is displayed as a "thumbnail" rendering that permits its display inside a browsing tool.
DVASPECT_ICON	The item is displayed as an icon.
DVASPECT_DOCPRINT	The item is displayed as if it were printed.

If *nCode* is **OLE_CHANGED_STATE**, *dwParam* can have one of the following values:

emptyState	Memory has been allocated, but the item has not been initialized.
loadedState	The item is fully created and associated with a COleClientItem-derived object.
openState	Open in the server's window as opposed to just open in place in the container document.
activeState	A brief state between simply open and UI active. It lacks user-interface components.
activeUIState	The item is active and all menus, toolbars and any other user-interface components are merged with those of the container.

Prototype

```
//Function Prototype
Protected
virtual void OnChange(OLE_NOTIFICATION nCode, DWORD
dwParam);
END Protected
```

OnChangeItemPosition   FUNCTION

Description   The framework uses this function to let the OLE item's container know the item's extent has changed. In the default implementation, the new visible rectangle is determined and sent with a call to **SetItemRects** as well as to the server. If your application is written with the MFC library, **OnChangeItemPosition** calls **COleServerDoc::RequestPositionChange**.

The single parameter, *rectPos*, contains the new position, and the function returns TRUE if the position is successfully changed.

Prototype

```
//Function Prototype
virtual BOOL OnChangeItemPosition(const CRect& rectPos);
```

OnDeactivate   FUNCTION

Description This function gets called by the framework when the OLE item goes from the in-place active state to the loaded state. In this state it is deactivated. This is not an indication that the user interface is gone; when that happens, the framework calls **OnDeactivateUI**. The default implementation of **OnDeactivate** calls **OnChange** with **OLE_CHANGED_STATE** in the *nCode* parameter.

Prototype
```
//Function Prototype
virtual void OnDeactivate();
```

OnDeactivateAndUndo   FUNCTION

Description If the user has in-place activated the OLE item and then calls the *Undo* command, the framework calls this function. In the default implementation, it in turn calls the function **DeactivateUI**.

Prototype
```
//Function Prototype
Protected
vitual void OnDeactivateAndUndo();
END Protected
```

OnDeactivateUI   FUNCTION

Description This function returns the user interface of the container application to its original state—that is, before in-place activation of the item. Menus and controls that were created for the in-place activation are hidden. If the parameter *bUndoable* is TRUE, then the undo state of the container is available for **ReactivateAndUndo**. If it is FALSE, the undo state is, in effect, discarded.

Prototype
```
//Function Prototype
Protected
vitual void OnDeactivateUI(BOOL bUndoable);
END Protected
```

OnDiscardUndoState   FUNCTION

Description If the user does something while editing the item that discards the undo state, the framework calls this function. The default implementation does nothing.

Prototype

```
//Function Prototype
virtual void OnDiscardUndoState();
```

OnGetClipboardData   FUNCTION

Description The framework calls this function in response to the **CopyToClipboard** or **DoDragDrop** functions. When called, the function gets a **COleDataSource** object with the data to be placed on the Clipboard. Its default implementation is to call **GetClipboardData**. The *bIncludeLink* parameter, if set to TRUE, indicates that link data should be copied as well. It should be FALSE if your application does not support links. *lpOffset* is a pointer to the mouse cursor's offset from the object's origin, measured in pixels. *lpSize* is a pointer to the object's size, measured in pixels. Finally, the function returns a pointer to a **COleDataSource** object containing the Clipboard data.

Prototype

```
//Function Prototype
virtual COleDataSource* OnGetClipboardData(BOOL bIncludeLink,
LPPOINT lpOffset, LPSIZE lpSize);
```

OnGetClipRect   FUNCTION

Description This function gets called by the framework to get the clipping-rectangle coordinates of the item. The coordinates are retrieved in the *rClipRect* parameter, and are given in pixels relative to the container application's client area. The default implementation retrieves the client rectangle of the view on which the item is in-place active.

Prototype

```
//Function Prototype
virtual void OnGetClipRect(CRect& rClipRect);
```

OnGetItemPosition   FUNCTION

Description This function retrieves the coordinates of the item being edited in place. The coordinates, referenced in the **CRect** object pointed to by *rPosition*, are measured in pixels relative to the container application window's client area. The default implementation of this function does not do anything. Applications that support in-place editing require its implementation.

Prototype

```
//Function Prototype
Protected
vitual void OnGetItemPosition(CRect& rPosition);
END Protected
```

OnGetWindowContext   FUNCTION

Description   When an OLE item is in-place activated, the framework calls this function to retrieve information about the item's parent window. That information breaks down as follows:

For MDI applications *ppMainFrame* returns a pointer to a **CMDIFrameWnd** object and *ppDocFrame* returns a pointer to the active **CMDIChildWnd** object.

For SDI applications *ppMainFrame* returns a pointer to a **CFrameWnd** object and *ppDocFrame* returns NULL.

The members of the *lpFrameInfo* structure are filled in as follows:

UINT	cb;	Size of the OLEINPLACEFRAMEINFO structure.
BOOL	fMDIApp;	Set to TRUE if it is an MDI application, otherwise it is FALSE.
HWND	hwndFrame;	Handle to the container's frame window.
HACCEL	haccel;	Handle to the container's accelerator table.
int	cAccelEntries	Number of entries in the container's accelerator table.

Prototype

```
//Function Prototype
virtual BOOL OnGetWindowContext(CFrameWnd** ppMainFrame,
CFrameWnd** ppDocFrame, LPOLEINPLACEFRAMEINFO
lpFrameInfo);
```

OnInsertMenus   FUNCTION

Description   This function takes an empty menu, inserts the container application's menus into it, then passes it to the server which inserts its own menus. This initially empty menu is pointed to by the parameter *pMenuShared*. In the default implementation the File, Container and Window menu groups are inserted into the in-place container menu. **CDocTemplate::SetContainerInfo** is used to set this menu resource. The number of menus in File, Container and Window menu groups are placed in the appropriate array element of *lpMenuWidths*. This parameter is a pointer to a

6-element array, and each element indicates the number of menus in each of the following menu groups: File, Edit, Container, Object, Window and Help. The File, Container and Window menu groups mentioned earlier correspond to elements 0, 2 and 4 in the array.

If you override this function, also override **OnSetMenu** and **OnRemoveMenus**.

Prototype
```
//Function Prototype
virtual void OnInsertMenus(CMenu* pMenuShared,
LPOLEMENUGROUPWIDTHS lpMenuWidths);
```

OnRemoveMenus   FUNCTION

Description The framework uses this function to remove the container menus from the composite menu pointed to by the parameter *pMenuShared*. The server portion remains. Specifically, the File, Container and Window menus are removed. The submenus on *pMenuShared* may be shared by several composite menus if the server has called the function **OnInserMenus** several times. Therefore, if you override **OnRemoveMenus**, you should detach rather than delete submenus.

Prototype
```
//Function Prototype
virtual void OnRemoveMenus(CMenu* pMenuShared);
```

OnScrollBy   FUNCTION

Description The parameter *sizeExtent* tells the function how far, in pixels, to scroll in the x and y directions. It is called by the framework when a scroll request is made by the server. The default implementation doesn't do anything; you must override to get the scrolling. Also, since scrolling typically changes the visible region, you should call **SetItemRects** to update it. The function returns TRUE if the item scrolls, FALSE if it doesn't.

Prototype
```
//Function Prototype
virtual BOOL OnScrollBy(CSize sizeExtent);
```

OnSetMenu   FUNCTION

Description When in-place activation begins, the framework calls this function to install the composite menu pointed to by *pMenuShared*. This menu is composed of both container and server menus and was put together in the **OnInsertMenus** function. **OnSetMenu** is also used to remove the menu, when in-place activation ends. After an installation or removal, the default implementation of **OnSetMenu** calls the ::**OleSetMenuDescriptor** function to install or remove the dispatching code. After this installation, ::**OleSetMenuDescriptor** returns a handle to the menu descriptor in *holemenu*. For a removal, *holemenu* is set to NULL. The third parameter, *hwndActiveObject* is a handle to the OLE item editing window.

    If you override this function, also override **OnInsertMenus** and **OnRemoveMenus**.

Prototype

```
//Function Prototype
virtual void OnSetMenu(CMenu* pMenuShared, HOLEMENU
holemenu, HWND hwndActiveObject);
```

OnShowControlBars   FUNCTION

Description   The framework calls this function to hide or display the control bars in the container application. The parameter *pFrameWnd* points to the container application's frame window. If the parameter *bShow* is TRUE the control bars are shown, if it is FALSE, the control bars are hidden. The function returns TRUE if it changed the state of the control bars, and returns FALSE if the state is unchanged. For instance if *bShow* was TRUE, but the control bars were already showing, it would return FALSE. The function also returns FALSE if *pFrameWnd* does not point to the container's frame window.

Prototype

```
//Function Prototype
virtual BOOL OnShowControBars(CFrameWnd* pFrameWnd, BOOL
bShow);
```

OnShowItem   FUNCTION

Description   This function is called to make the OLE item totally visible during editing. The container application needs to support links to the embedded items, by having the document class derived from **COleLinkingDoc**. The function is called during in-place activation or when the user wants to edit an OLE item that is a link source. In the default implementation, the first view of the container document gets activated.

Prototype

```
//Function Prototype
virtual void OnShowItem();
```

OnUpdateFrameTitle   FUNCTION

Description   The framework uses this function during in-place activation to update the frame window's title bar. The title's general form is *"server app - item in docname."*

Prototype
```
//Function Prototype
virtual void OnUpdateFrameTitle();
```

C OleConvertDialog   CLASS

· ·

Derivation

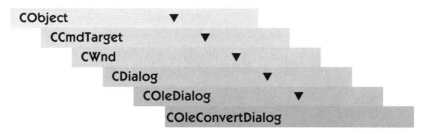

| CObject ▼ |
| CCmdTarget ▼ |
| CWnd ▼ |
| CDialog ▼ |
| COleDialog ▼ |
| COleConvertDialog |

Description   You need to create a **COleConvertDialog** object when you call an OLE Convert dialog box. The **m_cv** data member is used to initialize values and states of controls in the dialog box. The functions mediate the type conversions the user chooses in the dialog box.

Member Functions

COleConvertDialog   FUNCTION

Description   This is the constructor function for the object that supports the OLE Convert dialog box. A user can change the type of an embedded or linked item, usually for editing purposes, through this box. Typically it is called after the user chooses Item Type from the Edit menu, then selects Convert from the cascading menu. The parameter *pItem* is a pointer to the item to be converted or activated. The parameter *dwFlags* is a combination of any of the following values combined using a bitwise OR operator. These control certain presentation features of the dialog box:

CF_SHOWHELPBUTTON	Help button will be displayed when dialog box opens.
CF_SETCONVERTDEFAULT	Use the clsidConvertDefault member of the m_cv, the COleConvertDialog data member, as the default CLSID in the class list box when the Convert To radio button is selected.
CF_SETACTIVATEDEFAULT	Use the clsidConvertDefault member of the m_cv, the COleConvertDialog data member, as the default CLSID in the class list box when the Activate As radio button is selected.
CF_SELECTCONVERTTO	The Convert To radio button is already selected when the dialog box opens. This is the default.
CF_SELECTACTIVATEAS	The Activate As button will be selected when the dialog box opens.

The last two parameters are *pClassID*, which is a pointer to the class ID of the item to be converted or activated, and *pParentWnd*, which is a pointer to the window that owns the dialog box.

Prototype
```
//Function Prototype
COleConvertDialog(COleClientItem* pItem, DWORD dwFlags =
CF_SELECTCONVERTTO, CLSID FAR* pClassID = NULL, CWnd*
pParentWnd = NULL);
```

DoConvert   FUNCTION

Description This function converts or activates the **COleClientItem** pointed to by the *pItem* parameter. It should be called after **DoModal** is successful and returns **IDOK**. The function returns TRUE with a successful conversion or activation, otherwise it returns FALSE.

Prototype
```
//Function Prototype
BOOL DoConvert(COleClientItem* pItem);
```

DoModal   FUNCTION

Description This function is called to display the OLE Convert dialog box and is called after the object is constructed. If you want to initialize controls by setting members of the **m_cv** data member, do so before calling **DoModal**. This function returns **IDOK** if the dialog box is displayed correctly, it returns **IDCANCEL** if the user cancels the box, and returns **IDABORT** is there is an error. If the last return occurs, the **GetLastError** function from the **COleDialog** class can be used to retrieve the error code.

Prototype
```
//Function Prototype
virtual int DoModal();
```

GetClassID   FUNCTION

Description If **DoModal** was successful, you can use this function to get the class ID of the item selected by the user.

Prototype
```
//Function Prototype
const CLSID& GetClassID() const;
```

GetDrawAspect   FUNCTION

Description This function tells you how the user wants the selected item displayed. Call it after **DoModal** returns **IDOK**. It returns **DVASPECT_ICON** if the Display As Icon box was checked, **DVASPECT_CONTENT** if not.

Prototype
```
//Function Prototype
DVASPECT GetDrawAspect() const;
```

GetIconicMetafile   FUNCTION

Description If the Display As Icon check box was selected when the dialog box was closed, then this function will find and return the handle to the metafile that contains the iconic aspect of the selected item. If the Display As Icon box was not checked, this function will return NULL.

Prototype
```
//Function Prototype
HGLOBAL GetIconicMetafile() const;
```

GetSelectionType   FUNCTION

Description This function returns one of three possible conversion selection types:

COleConvertDialog::noConversion	The dialog box was canceled or the user selected no conversion.
COleConvertDialog::convertItem	The Convert To radio button was selected, the user chose a different item to convert to, and DoModal returned IDOK.
COleConvertDialog::activateAs	The Activate As radio button was selected, the user chose a different item to activate, and DoModal returned IDOK.

Prototype

```
//Function Prototype
UINT GetSelectionType() const;
```

Data Member

m_cv   MEMBER

Description This variable has a structure type of **OLEUICONVERT** whose members are as follows:

DWORD	cbStruct	Size of the structure.
DWORD	dwFlags	See list for dwFlags in the description of the COleChangeIconDialog constructor function.
HWND	hWndOwner	Handle to the owning window.
LPCTSTR	lpszCaption	Pointer to the string that is the caption of the dialog box.
LPFNOLEUIHOOK	lpfnHook	Pointer to the optional hook callback function, which you must build yourself.
LPARAM	lCustData	Optional custom data to pass to hook.
HINSTANCE	hInstance	Instance for the customized template name of the object to be inserted.
LPCTSTR	lpszTemplate:	Customized template name of the object to be inserted.
HRSRC	hResource:	Customized template handle.
CLSID	clsid	Class ID sent in to dialog box.
CLSID	clsidConvertDefault	Class ID to use as convert default.
CLSID	clsidActivateDefault	Class ID to use as activate default.
CLSID	clsidnew	Selected class ID.

DWORD	dvAspect	Either DVASPECT_CONTENT or DVAPSECT_ICON.
WORD	wForma	Original data format.
BOOL	fObjectsIconChanged	TRUE if Change Icon was called and not canceled.
LPSTR	lpszDefLabel	Default label for icon. If it is NULL, the short user type name will be used. If the object is a link, the caller should pass the Display name of the link source, which gets freed on exit.
UINT	cClsidExclude	Number of class IDs in lpClsidExclude.
LPCLSID	lpClsidExclude	List of class IDs to exclude from list.

OleDataObject

CLASS

· ·

Description   This class represents the destination side of a Clipboard or drag-and-drop operation. In the drag-and-drop operation, the data object is created by the framework. When the operation is a Clipboard Paste or Paste Special operation, you must create a **COleDataObject** object and use the **AttachClipboard** function to associate it with the data on the Clipboard. The functions for **COleDataObject** are concerned with attachment and detachment of data objects, with copying data, and with coordinating formats.

Member Functions

Attach

FUNCTION

Description   This function associates the **COleDataObject** with an OLE data object. The parameter *lpDataObject* is a pointer to that object, and the *bAutoRelease* parameter indicates whether the data object should be released when the **COleDatObject** instance is destroyed.

Prototype
```
//Function Prototype
void Attach(LPDATAOBJECT lpDataObject, BOOL bAutoRelease =
TRUE);
```

AttachClipboard `FUNCTION`

Description This function attaches the data object on the Clipboard to the **COleDataObject** object. If it succeeds, it returns TRUE, otherwise it returns FALSE.

Prototype
```
//Function Prototype
BOOL AttachClipboard();
```

BeginEnumFormats `FUNCTION`

Description This function sets up the formats supported by **GetData**, **GetFileData** and **GetGlobalData** for retrieval by successive calls to the function **GetNextFormat**. The first such format gets stored and then **GetNextFormat** can just run throught the list.

Prototype
```
//Function Prototype
void BeginEnumFormats();
```

COleDataObject `FUNCTION`

Description This is the constructor, and creates an instance of the class **COleDataObject**.

Prototype
```
//Function Prototype
COleDataObject();
```

Detach `FUNCTION`

Description This function detaches the OLE data object from the **COleDataObject** object. The data object is detached, but not released. For that you need to use the **Release** function.

Prototype
```
//Function Prototype
LPDATAOBJECT Detach();
```

GetData FUNCTION

Description This function retrieves the data in the format specified by the parameters *cfFormat* and *lpFormatEtc*. The first of these parameters points to a **CLIPFORMAT** structure, which describes a predefined Clipboard format. The second points to a **LPFORMATETC** structure, which can contain additional formatting information. The NULL value for this parameter in the prototype means that default values are used for the fields of the **FORMATETC** structure. The final parameter, *lpStgMedium*, is a pointer to a **STGMEDIUM** structure that is to receive the data.

Prototype
```
//Function Prototype
BOOL GetData(CLIPFORMAT cfFormat, LPSTGMEDIUM
lpStgMedium, LPFORMATETC lpFormatEtc = NULL);
```

GetFileData FUNCTION

Description This function creates a **CFile** object, or one derived from **CFile**, then retrieves the data in a format specified by the *cfFormat* and *lpFormatEtc* parameters, and returns a pointer to the **CFile** object. The *cfFormat* parameter is a predefined Clipboard format, which may be acquired by calling the **RegisterClipboardFormat** function. The *lpFormatEtc* points to a **LPFORMATETC** structure which can hold additional formating information. The NULL value for this parameter in the prototype means that default values are used for the fields of the **FORMATETC** structure. Finally the returned pointer may be an object of the **CFile**, **CSharedFile** or **COleStreamFile** class.

Prototype
```
//Function Prototype
CFile* GetFileData(CLIPFORMAT cfFormat, LPFORMATETC
lpFormatEtc = NULL);
```

GetGlobalData FUNCTION

Description This function allocates a global memory block and retrieves the data in the format specified by the *cfFormat* and *lpStgMedium* parameters. Then it returns a handle to the memory block if the allocation is successful, or it returns NULL if not. The *cfFormat* parameter is a predefined Clipboard format, which may be acquired by calling the **RegisterClipboardFormat** function. The *lpFormatEtc* points to a **LPFORMATETC** structure, which can contain additional formatting information. The NULL value for this parameter in the prototype means that default values are used for the other fields of the **FORMATETC** structure.

Prototype

```
//Function Prototype
HGLOBAL GetGlobalData(CLIPFORMAT cfFormat, LPFORMATETC
lpFormatEtc = NULL);
```

GetNextFormat   FUNCTION

Description   You call this function after you have called the **BeginEnumFormats** function, which stores the first of the **GetData**, **GetFileData** and **GetGlobalData** supported formats. Once that is done, you can call **GetNextFormat**, which retrieves that stored format. You can continue to call **GetNextFormat** to work your way through the entire list. The parameter, *lpFormatEtc*, provides a pointer to an **LPFORMATETC** structure which can hold the format information. If **GetNextFormat** has not reached the end of the list and there are more formats that can be retrieved, it returns TRUE, if there are no more formats, it returns FALSE.

Prototype

```
//Function Prototype
BOOL GetNextFormat(LPFORMATETC lpFormatEtc);
```

IsDataAvailable   FUNCTION

Description   Instead of using the combination **BeginEnumFormats** and **GetNextFormat** functions, which step you through all the available formats as you look for the one you want, just call **IsDataAvailable** with the format you are looking for specified in the two parameters, *cfFormat* and *lpFormatEtc*. The *cfFormat* parameter is a predefined Clipboard format, which may be acquired by calling the **RegisterClipboardFormat** function. The *lpFormatEtc* points to a **LPFORMATETC** structure, which can contain additional formatting information. The NULL value for this parameter in the prototype means that default values are used for the other fields of the **FORMATETC** structure. If the format is available, the function returns TRUE, if not it returns FALSE.

Prototype

```
//Function Prototype
BOOL IsDataAvailable(CLIPFORMAT cfFormat, LPFORMATETC
lpFormatEtc = NULL);
```

Release   FUNCTION

Description   This function will release ownership of the **IDataObject** object. If the parameter *bAutoRelease* in the **Attach** function had been set to FALSE when the data object was attached, then this **Release** function won't work. The caller must use its own **Release** method.

Prototype
```
//Function Prototype
void Release();
```

OleDataSource   CLASS

Derivation
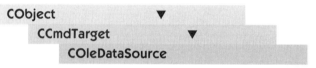

```
CObject                      ▼
    CCmdTarget                   ▼
        COleDataSource
```

Description   The **COleDataSource** class acts as a temporary storage location for data that is to be transferred, usually via the Clipboard or drag-and-drop. The sequence of events that leads to the creation of **COleDataSource** goes like this:

1. **COleClientItem** or **COleServerItem** (or a derivative class) creates an OLE data object.
2. The user cuts or copies his selection, either through the Edit menu or by drag-and-drop.
3. The application, in reponse to the user, calls a function from the data object which calls, in turn, **OnGetCliboardData**.
4. **OnGetClipboardData** then creates a **COleDataSource** class object containing the data.

Member Functions

CacheData   FUNCTION

Description   The data source calls this function to specify the format of the data to transfer for immediate rendering. You will want the data transferred using a **STGMEDIUM** structure, and once called, the pointer to the data is no longer under the control of the caller. This is the appropriate function to call for the transfer of a large amount of data, or if a structured storage medium is required. The parameters are as follows: *cfFormat* identifies the Clipboard format of the data, *psStgMedium* is a pointer to the data that is being offered, and *lpFormatEtc* is a pointer to a **FORMATETC** structure that provides additional formatting information, if needed, beyond what's in *cfFormat*.

Prototype
```
//Function Prototype
void CacheData(CLIPFORMAT cfFormat, LPSTGMEDIUM
lpStgMedium, LPFORMATETC lpFormatEtc = NULL);
```

CacheGlobalData — FUNCTION

Description If you are providing a relatively small amount of data, you can use this function to make the transfer. You must supply the data at the time of the call for immediate rendering. The parameters are similar to those of the **CacheData** function: *cfFormat* identifies the Clipboard format of the data, *hGlobal* is the handle to a memory block of data to be transferred, and *lpFormatEtc* is a pointer to a **FORMATETC** structure that provides additional formatting information, if needed, beyond what is in *cfFormat*.

Prototype
```
//Function Prototype
void CacheGlobalData(CLIPFORMAT cfFormat, HGLOBAL hGlobaL,
LPFORMATETC lpFormatEtc = NULL);
```

COleDataSource — FUNCTION

Description This constructs a **COleDataSource** class object.

Prototype
```
//Function Prototype
COleDataSource();
```

DelayRenderData — FUNCTION

Description As you may have already guessed, this function provides formatting information when there is delayed rendering. The actual transfer of data occurs when the **OnRenderData** or **OnRenderGlobalData** overridable functions are called. This function is appropriate for a data object that is *not* a **Cfile** object. For **Cfile** objects use the **DelayRenderFileData** function.

The parameters are as follows: *cfFormat* is the Clipboard format the data will be offered in, and *cfFormatEtc* is a pointer to a **FORMATETC** structure, which further describes the format of the offered data. Use this when you want to specify more information than is in *cfFormat*.

Prototype

```
//Function Prototype
void DelayRenderData(CLIPFORMAT cfFormat, LPFORMATETC
lpFormatEtc = NULL);
```

DelayRenderFileData   FUNCTION

Description   If the data to be transferred is in a **CFile** object, this is the function to use for specifying its format. Since this is for data that is delay rendered, the actual transfer of data occurs when the **OnRenderFileData** function is called.

The parameters are as follows: *cfFormat* identifies the Clipboard format of the data, and *lpFormatEtc* is a pointer to a **FORMATETC** structure that provides additional formatting information, if needed, beyond what's in *cfFormat*.

Prototype

```
//Function Prototype
void DelayRenderFileData(CLIPFORMAT cfFormat, LPFORMATETC
lpFormatEtc = NULL);
```

DelaySetData   FUNCTION

Description   The need for this function originates with a **COleServer::GetDataSource** call. A pointer to the **COleDataSource** object is returned. The framework will then call **OnSetData** to change the contents of the data object, but **DelaySetData** must be called first, with the appropriate Clipboard format in *cfFormat* and any additional formatting information in the **FORMATETC** structure of *lpFormatEtc*, otherwise the **OnSetData** function will never be called. This call to **DelaySetData** must be repeated for every Clipboard and **FORMATETC** format you support.

Prototype

```
//Function Prototype
void DelaySetData(CLIPFORMAT cfFormat, LPFORMATETC
lpFormatEtc = NULL) const;
```

DoDragDrop   FUNCTION

Description   This function should be called when

❍ A drag-and-drop operation begins for this data source.

❍ The user starts to drag a selection, usually when you get the **WM_LBUTTONDOWN** message.

The parameter *dwEffects* contains a list of drag-and-drop operations permitted on the data source. It can have any number of the following values:

DROPEFFECT_COPY	Copying permitted.
DROPEFFECT_MOVE	Moving permitted.
DROPEFFECT_LINK	Linking permitted.
DROPEFFECT_SCROLL	Indicates a drag scroll operation could occur.

A drag-and-drop operation doesn't actually start until the cursor leaves the rectangle pointed to by the parameter *lpRectStartDrag*. A NULL value represents an empty rectangle. The parameter *pDropSource* is a pointer to the drop source. A NULL value results in a default implementation of **COleDropSource.**

The function returns the drop effect produced by the drag-and-drop operation. The operation may terminate before it actually starts if the user releases the mouse button before moving the cursor out of the rectangle pointed to by *lpRectStartDrag*, in which case **DROPEFFECT_NONE** is returned.

Prototype
```
//Function Prototype
DROPEFFECT DoDragDrop(DWORD dwEffects =
DROPEFFECT_COPYΩDROPEFFECT_MOVEΩDROPEFFECT_LINK,
LPCRECT lpRectStartDrag = NULL, COleDropSource* pDropSource =
NULL);
```

Empty()   FUNCTION

Description   This function empties the data from the **COleDataSource** object, both cached and delay render formats.

Prototype
```
//Function Prototype
void Empty();
```

FlushClipboard   FUNCTION

Description   This function removes any data left in the Clipboard for immediate rendering. By doing so, OLE will not have to require the data source to perform Clipboard rendering. It also can be used to clear data from the Clipboard placed there by a previous call to **SetClipboard**.

Prototype

```
//Function Prototype
static void FlushClipboard();
```

GetClipboardOwner   FUNCTION

Description

Use this function if you need to know if the data on the Clipboard has changed since the last call to **SetClipboard**. If it has changed, the current owner is identified. The function returns the data source on the Clipboard, unless there is nothing on the Clipboard, or the current owner is the calling application. In these cases, it returns NULL.

Prototype

```
//Function Prototype
static COleDataSource* GetClipBoardOwner();
```

SetClipboard   FUNCTION

Description

Call this function to put the data from the **COleDataSource** object onto the Clipboard. This would be done after calling one of the these functions: **CacheData**, **CacheGlobalData**, **DelayRenderData**, **DelayRenderFileData**.

Prototype

```
//Function Prototype
void SetClipboard();
```

Overridable Functions

OnRenderData   FUNCTION

Description

This function is called to get data in the format pointed to by the *lpFormatEtc* parameter. This format information was put into the **COleDatasource** by either **DelayRenderData** or **DelayRenderFileData** and this function will call **OnRenderFileData** or **OnRenderGlobalData**. If the proper formats are not supplied, nothing happens. The parameter *lpStgMedium* is a pointer to a **STGMEDIUM** structure, which will hold the data to be returned.

The function returns TRUE if the retrievel is successful and FALSE if the retrieval is not successful.

Prototype
```
//Function Prototype
virtual BOOL OnRenderData(LPFORMATETC lpFormatEtc,
LPSTGMEDIUM, lpStgMedium);
```

OnRenderFileData   FUNCTION

Description   When the data must be retrieved from a file, the framework calls
this function. The format, pointed to by *lpFormatEtc*, was placed
in **COleDataSource** by **DelayRenderData**. The data will be
rendered into the **CFile** object pointed to by the *pFile* parameter.
The function returns TRUE if successful, FALSE if not successful.

Prototype
```
//Function Prototype
virtual BOOL OnRenderFileData(LPFORMATETC lpFormatEtc, CFile*
pFile);
```

OnRenderGlobalData   FUNCTION

Description   This function retrieves the data when it is in global memory. The
format is taken from the **COleDataSource** object where it was
placed by **DelayRenderData**. The allocated memory block must
be big enough for the data, and once allocated, memory cannot be
increased. If no memory at all has been allocated, then **HGLOBAL**
can, and should, be allocated and returned to *phGlobal*. The other
parameter, *lpFormatEtc*, is a pointer to a **FORMATETC** structure,
which contains the format specifications for the requested information. The function returns TRUE with a successful retrieval and
FALSE if not successful.

Prototype
```
//Function Prototype
virtual BOOL OnRenderGlobalData(LPFORMATETC lpFormatEtc,
HGLOBAL* phGlobal);
```

OnSetData   FUNCTION

Description   This function is called by the framework to set or replace the data
in the **COleDataSource** object. Once successful, the data source
takes possesion and calls the function **ReleaseStgMedium** to
release the storage medium.
   The parameter *lpFormatEtc* is a pointer to a **FORMATETC**
structure, which contains the format specifications for the requested information. The parameter *lpStgMedium* is a pointer to a
STGMEDIUM structure. It holds the data that will replace the data
already in **COleDataSource**. Finally, *bRelease* is a Boolean that

609

determines who takes ownership of the storage medium after this function is called. If TRUE, the caller takes responsibility for releasing resources. FALSE indicates that ownership goes to the data source and it must release the resources.

The function returns TRUE if successful and FALSE if not.

Prototype

```
//Function Prototype
virtual BOOL OnSetData(LPFORMATETC lpFormatEtc,
LPSTGMEDIUM lpstgMedium, BOOL bRelease);
```

COleDialog

CLASS

Derivation

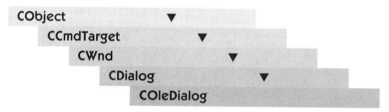

CObject	▼			
CCmdTarget		▼		
CWnd			▼	
CDialog				▼
COleDialog				

Description   This object has a single function, which retrieves error code if there is a problem with a dialog box. It works like this. The **DoModal** function from the **COleBusyDialog** class can return one of three values: **IDOK**, which means the dialog box was successfully displayed, **IDCANCEL**, which means that the user canceled the dialog box, or **IDABORT**, which means an error occurred. If you want more information about that error, you call the **GetLastError** function from the **COleDialog** class and it returns the error code.

Member Functions

GetLastError   FUNCTION

Description   As discussed just above, this function is called after the **DoModal** function from the **COleBusyDialog** class returns a value of **IDABORT**. **GetLastError** then returns the error code so you can find out more about what went wrong.

Prototype

```
//Function Prototype
UINT GetLastError() const;
```

COleDispatchDriver

CLASS

Description This class handles the client side of OLE automation. As you may recall, automation provides acces to another application's object functions. This connection to another application is mediated through the **IDispatch** dispatch interface. The **COleDispatchDriver** class has the functions to attach, detach, create and release the dispatch connection. The **InvokeHelper** function is used to simplify calling **IDispatch::Invoke**. **COleDispatchDriver** is not usually used by the programmer directly, but is used by ClassWizard when you import a type library. ClassWizard derives the new classes from **COleDispatchDriver**.

Member Functions

AttachDispatch
FUNCTION

Description The parameter *lpDispatch* provides a pointer to an **IDispatch** object, and the function attaches that pointer to the **COleDispatchDriver** object. If there was already an **IDispatch** pointer attached, it is released. When set to TRUE, the *bAutoRelease* parameter specifies that the dispatch is released when the object goes out of scope.

Prototype
```
//Function Prototype
void AttachDispatch(LPDISPATCH lpDispatch, BOOL bAutoRelease
= TRUE);
```

COleDispatchDriver
FUNCTION

Description This is the **COleDispatchDriver** object constructor. After you have created one, don't use it until you have connected it to an **IDispatch** interface with **OleDispatchDriver::CreateDispatch** or **OleDispatchDriver::AttachDispatch**.

Prototype
```
//Function Prototype
COleDispatchDriver();
```

CreateDispatch
FUNCTION

Description This function will create the **IDispatch** object to connect to the **COleDispatchDriver**. You supply the function with the class ID of the **IDispatch** connection object using the *clsid* parameter as you see in the first prototype below. Or you send a pointer to a verbal identifier, for example "Excel.document.3," using the *lpsxProgID* parameter as shown in the second prototype. The parameter *pError* is a pointer to an OLE exception object. This holds the status code from the creation. When *pError* is NULL, this function throws an exception.

If the creation is successful, the function returns TRUE, if not, it returns FALSE.

Prototype
```
//Function Prototype
BOOL CreateDispatch(REFCLSID clsid, COleException* pError =
NULL);
BOOL CreateDispatch(LPCTSTR lpsxProgID, ColeException* pError =
NULL);
```

DetachDispatch
FUNCTION

Description This function detaches the **IDispatch** pointer from **COleDispatchDriver** without releasing **IDispatch**, and the pointer is returned to the caller.

Prototype
```
//Function Prototype
LPDISPATCH DetachDispatch();
```

GetProperty
FUNCTION

Description This function retrieves the object property specified by the *dwDispID* parameter. The value type is given by the *vtProp* parameter. Possible values for *vtProp* are listed below in the description of the **InvokeHelper** parameter *vtRet*. The last parameter, *pvProp*, gives the address to which the property value will be returned.

Prototype
```
//Function Prototype
void GetProperty(DISPID dwDispID, VARTYPE vtProp, void*
pvProp) const;
```

InvokeHelper

Description **Invoke** is a function of **IDispatch**, an interface object that provides the means to access and retrieve information about an object's methods and properties. **Invoke** is the function that actually makes the connection to that object. **InvokeHelper**, as its name suggests, is a function that provides some of the essential information needed by **Invoke**. The parameter *dwDispID*, a value usually supplied by ClassWizard, identifies the method or property to be invoked.

The other function parameters are as follows:

◯ The context of the call is provided by the parameter *wFlags*.

◯ The types of the parameters to pass are provided by *pbPramInfo*.

◯ The parameters themselves are represented in the prototype by the ellipses (...).

◯ The type of return value expected is provided by *vtRe.*

◯ The address of the variable that will receive the return value or property value is provided by *pvRet*.

Let's examine some of the parameters a little more closely. The *wFlags* parameter contains flags that describe the context of the call to **IDispatch::Invoke**. It can have any number of the following values:

IOF_SHOWHELP	The Help button will be displayed when the dialog box opens.
IOF_SELECTCREATENEW	The Create New radio button will be selected when the dialog is opened. This value and the next value, IOF_SELECTCREATEFROMFILE, are mutually exclusive.
IOF_SELECTCREATEFROMFILE	The Create From File radio button will be selected when the dialog box opens. This value and the previous value, IOF_SELECTCREATENEW, are mutually exclusive.
IOF_CHECKLINK	The Link check box will be selected when the dialog box opens.
IOF_CHECKDISPLAYASICON	The Display As Icon box will be selected when the box opens. The current icon will be displayed, and the Change Icon button will be enabled.
IOF_DISABLELINK	The Link check box will be disabled.
IOF_VERIFYSERVERSEXIST	The dialog box will validate the classes it adds to the list box. This is to make sure that the servers in the registration database exist before the dialog box opens. This option may reduce performance.

The *vtRet* parameter provides the return value that is expected. It can have one of the following values:

VT_EMPTY	void
VT_I2	short
VT_I4	long
VT_R4	float
VT_R8	double
VT_CY	CY (currency value)
VT_DATE	DATE
VT_BSTR	BSTR (counted, zero terminated, binary string)
VT_DISPATCH	LPDISPATCH (pointer to an IDispatch object)
VT_ERROR	SCODE (status code)
VT_BOOL	BOOL
VT_VARIANT	VARIANT (4-byte indicater followed by the corresponding value; used in conjunction with VT_VECTOR)
VT_UNKNOWN	LPUNKNOWN (pointer to an IUnknown object)

You provide the list of *pbParamInfo* parameters as space separated values with any number of the following:

VTS_I2	short
VTS_I4	long
VTS_R4	float
VTS_R8	double
VTS_CY	const CY*
VTS_DATE	DATE
VTS_BSTR	const char* (counted, zero terminated, binary string)
VTS_DISPATCH	LPDISPATCH (pointer to an IDispatch object)
VTS_SCODE	SCODE (status code)
VTS_BOOL	BOOL
VTS_VARIANT	const VARIANT* (4-byte indicater followed by the corresponding value; used in conjunction with VT_VECTOR)
VTS_UNKNOWN	LPUNKNOWN (pointer to an IUnknown object)
VTS_PI2	short*
VTS_PI4	long*
VTS_PR4	float*
VTS_PR8	double*
VTS_PCY	CY*
VTS_PDATE	DATE*
VTS_PBSTR	BSTR*
VTS_PDISPATCH	LPDISPATCH*
VTS_PSCODE	SCODE*
VTS_PBOOL	BOOL*
VTS_PVARIANT	VARIANT*
VTS_PUNKNOWN	LPUNKNOWN*

Prototype
```
//Prototype Function
void InvokeHelper(DISPID dwDispID, WORD wFlags, VARTYPE vtRet,
void* pvRet, const BYTE FAR* pbParamInfo, ...);
```

ReleaseDispatch — FUNCTION

Description The previous function detached **IDispatch** without releasing it. This function releases it.

Prototype
```
//Function Prototype
void ReleaseDispatch();
```

SetProperty — FUNCTION

Description Use this function to set the OLE object property given by the *dwDispID* parameter. This value is usually set by ClassWizard. The parameter *vtProp* specifies the type to be set for that single property. For a list of the possible values for *vtProp*, see the list for *vtRet* in the **InvokeHelper** function.

Prototype
```
//Function Prototype
void SetProperty(DISPID dwDispID, VARTYPE vtProp, ...);
```

OleDispatchException — CLASS

Derivation

```
CObject            ▼
  CCmdTarget           ▼
    CException             ▼
      COleException            ▼
        COleDispatchException
```

Description The OLE dispatch interface is a key part of OLE automation, and exceptions specific to it are handled by the **COleDispatchException** class. It is intended to be used with the following macros: **THROW**, **THROW_LAST**, **TRY**, **CATCH**, **AND_CATCH** and **END_CATCH**.

Data Members

m_dwHelpContext   MEMBER

Description   DWORD **m_dwHelpContext**: When an expection is thrown,
AfxThrowOleDispatchException sets this member to identify
the help context in your application's help file.

m_strDescription   MEMBER

Description   CString **m_strDescription**: **AfxThrowOleDispatchException**
sets this when an exception is thrown. It contains a verbal description of the error.

m_strHelpFile   MEMBER

Description   CString **m_strHelpFile**: This holds the name of the application's
help file, put there by the framework.

m_strSource   MEMBER

Description   CString **m_strSource**: This holds the name of the application that
generated the exception, put there by the framework.

m_wCode   MEMBER

Description   WORD **m_wCode**: This holds an application-specific error code
from your application. It is put there by
AfxThrowOleDispatchException.

OleDocument

Derivation

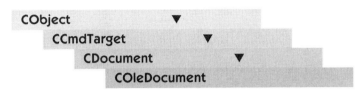

CObject ▼
  CCmdTarget ▼
    CDocument ▼
      COleDocument

Description **COleDocument** provides a base class for documents that support OLE in-place activation. It inherits the functionality of the framework's **CDocument** class, which allows your application to take advantage of the Document/View architecture in your OLE application. User documents are created by deriving a class for each type of document the application will handle and adding member variables to each class to store document data. Member functions must be written to read and update the document in ways specific to the application.

The **COleDocument** is closely related to the **CDocItem** class and its derived classes **COleClientItem** and **COleServerItem**. The components of the **COleDocument** are maintained in objects of these types. Applications can use **COleDocument** directly to create simpe OLE container documents. More complex applications make use of the derived classes **COleServerDoc** and **COleLinkingDoc** to implement their documents. **COleServerDoc** is used by applications whose documents are either OLE servers or server/container combinations. **COleLinkingDoc** objects are used in applications whose documents allow other applications to link to data embedded in these documents.

Member Functions

AddItem FUNCTION

Description Use this function when you want to add an item, pointed to by the parameter *pItem*, to a document. When this function is called by the **COleClientItem** or **COleServerItem** constructors that accept a pointer to the document, you don't need to call it explicity.

Prototype
```
//Function Prototype
virtual void AddItem(CDocItem* pItem);
```

617

ApplyPrintDevice   FUNCTION

Description When you want to change the print-target device for the **COleClientItem** items embedded in your container document, you call this function. If you want the presentation cache refreshed as well, you must also call **COleClientItem::UpdateLink**. Information for initializing the Print dialog box is in the **PRINTDLG** structure, which is the **m_pd** member of the **CPrintDialog** object. In the first prototype, you provide information on the target device driver, name and port, and specs on the device itself, with the parameter *ptd*, a pointer to a **DVTARGETDEVICE** structure. In the second prototype, *ppd* is a pointer to a **PRINTDLG** structure that is used to initialize a system-defined Print dialog box. It is also where user selections from the dialog box are stored. This function returns TRUE if the change is successful, and FALSE if not.

Prototype
```
//Function Prototype
BOOL ApplyPrintDevice(const DVTARGETDEVICE FAR* ptd);
BOOL ApplyPrintDevice(const PRINTDLG* ppd);
```

COleDocument   FUNCTION

Description **COleDocument** constructs but does not initialize a **COleDocument** object.

Prototype
```
//Function Prototype
COleDocument();
```

EnableCompoundFile   FUNCTION

Description If you want to store your document in the compound-document structured file format, you need to call this function to enable the file support. Ususally you will do this from the constructor of your **COleDocument** derived class. Without this file support, documents are stored in a nonstructured file format. So set *bEnable* to TRUE for the structured format or FALSE for the unstructured format.

Prototype
```
//Function Prototype
void EnableCompoundFile(BOOL bEnable = TRUE);
```

GetInPlaceActiveItem   FUNCTION

Description Pass *pWnd*, a pointer to the window displaying the container document, and the function returns a pointer to the currently active in-place OLE item.

Prototype
```
//Function Prototype
COleClientItem* GetInPlaceActiveItem(CWnd* pWnd);
```

GetNextClientItem   FUNCTION

Description This is really a follow-up function to the **GetStartPosition** function. The two work together to sequentially access all the client items in your document. **GetStartPosition** finds the first item and passes this to **GetNextClientItem** with the *pos* parameter. Then repeated calls to **GetNextClientItem** will move you through the document's client items. Each call returns a pointer to the next client item in your document, or returns NULL if there are no client items left.

Prototype
```
//Function Prototype
COleClientItem* GetNextClientItem(POSITION& pos) const;
```

GetNextItem   FUNCTION

Description This is another follow-up function to the **GetStartPosition** function. The two work together to sequentially access all the items in your document. **GetStartPosition** finds the first item and passes this to **GetNextItem** with the *pos* parameter. Repeated calls to **GetNextItem** will now move you through the document's items. Each call returns a pointer to the next item, or returns NULL if there are no items left.

Prototype
```
//Function Prototype
virtual CDocItem* GetNextItem(POSITION& pos) const;
```

GetNextServerItem   FUNCTION

Description Again, you use this function with the **GetStartPosition** function. The two work together to sequentially access all the server items in your document. **GetStartPosition** finds the first item and passes this to **GetNextServerItem** with the *pos* parameter. Repeated calls to **GetNextServerItem** will now move you through the document's client items. Be warned, however, that even though *pos* is

619

set for the next item after each call, it may or may not be a server item. The function returns a pointer to the next server item in your document, or returns NULL if there are no server items left.

Prototype
```
//Function Prototype
COleServerItem* GetNextServerItem(POSITION& pos) const;
```

GetStartPosition — FUNCTION

Description   This function is used to find the first item in a document, which is the return value, for the functions **GetNextItem**, **GetNextClientItem** and **GetNextServerItem**. These three are used to sequentially access items in a document. If there are no items, the function returns NULL.

Prototype
```
//Function Prototype
virtual POSITION GetStartPosition() const;
```

HasBlankItems — FUNCTION

Description   This function is called to see if a document has any blank items—that is, items whose rectangles are empty. It returns TRUE if there are blank items, FALSE if there are not.

Prototype
```
//Function Prototype
BOOLHasBlankItems() const;
```

RemoveItem — FUNCTION

Description   This function is called to remove an item, pointed to by *pItem*, from a document, and is typically called by the destructors for **COleClientItem** and **COleServerItem**.

Prototype
```
//Function Prototype
virtual void RemoveItem(CDocItem* pItem);
```

UpdateModifiedFlag — FUNCTION

Description   If any OLE item has been modified, call this function to mark it as modified, so that the framework will prompt the user to save it before closing.

Prototype
```
//Function Prototype
void UpdateModifiedFlag();
```

Overridable Functions

GetPrimarySelectedItem · FUNCTION

Description This function takes the parameter *pView*, a pointer to the active view object that is displaying a document, and searches that document's item list for the currently selected item. If there is only one, it returns the pointer to it. If there is more than one, or none, it returns NULL. **CView::IsSelected** must be overridden to use **GetPrimarySelectedItem**. And **GetPrimarySelectedItem** itself must be overridden if you use your own method of storing contained OLE items.

Prototype
```
//Function Prototype
virtual COleClientItem* GetPrimarySelectedItem(CView* pView);
```

OnShowViews · FUNCTION

Description If your document's visibility state changes, the framework calls this function with the Boolean parameter *bVisible*, which is TRUE if the document has become visible, FALSE if it has become invisible. But the default for this function doesn't do anything. You must override the function if your application does any special processing when the visibility of the document changes.

Prototype
```
//Function Prototype
Virtual void OnShowViews(BOOL bVisible);
```

OleDropSource

Derivation

| CObject | ▼ |
| CCmdTarget | ▼ |
| COleDropSource |

Description This class is a bit like the guy at the construction site who directs the crane as it hauls a beam into place. During a drag-and-drop the **COleDropSource** object keeps track of when the drag begins, how it's going and when it ends.

Member Functions

COleDropSource
FUNCTION

Description This is the object constructor.

Prototype
```
//Function Prototype
COleDropSource();
```

GiveFeedback
FUNCTION

Description This function provides feedback during dragging and returns one of two possible values: **DRAGDROP_S_USEDDEFAULTCURSORS** (dragging is occurring) or **NOERROR** (dragging is not occurring). If you want to provide more detailed feedback you need to override this function, which is called by the framework, by calling **IDropTarget::DragOver** or **IDropTarget::DragEnter**. (These functions return the same five possible values as listed below for **CView::OnDragEnter** and **CView::OnDragOver**.)

The parameter *dropEffect* can have one of five values. Each value indicates what would happen if a drop occurred. They are meant to provide feedback to the user interface. You can get the value by calling **CView::OnDragEnter** or **CView::OnDragOver**. The values and their meanings are as follows:

DROPEFFECT_NONE	No drop allowed.
DROPEFFECT_COPY	Copy operation would be done.
DROPEFFECT_MOVE	Move operation would be done.
DROPEFFECT_LINK	Dropped data would be linked to source data.
DROPEFFECT_SCROLL	A drag-scroll operation is happening, or is about to happen in the target.

Prototype
```
//Function Prototype
virtual SCODE GiveFeedback (DROPEFFECT dropEffect);
```

OnBeginDrag   FUNCTION

Description If an event occurs that could start a drag, usually the press of the left mouse button, this function is called by the framework. Normally, the mouse will stay in drag mode until the left or right mouse button is clicked or Esc is pressed. If you want to start a drag differently you need to override this function.

The parameter *pWnd* is a pointer to the window containing the selected data. This function returns TRUE when dragging is allowed, FALSE when dragging is not allowed.

Prototype
```
//Function Prototype
virtual BOOL OnBeginDrag(CWind* pWnd);
```

QueryContinueDrag   FUNCTION

Description Once a drag has begun, the framework waits anxiously for a drop to occur and keeps calling this function to check on things until the operation is complete or canceled. The usual implementation is to cancel the operation if **DRAGDROP_S_CANCEL** is returned, to complete the operation if **DRAGDROP_S_DROP** is returned, and to keep waiting if **S_OK** is returned. The first parameter, *bEscapePressed*, is a Boolean that indicates whether the Esc key has been pressed since the last call to this function. The second is *dwKeyState*, which indicates the state of the modifier keys. It can be any combination of the following:

```
MK_CONTROL
MK_SHIFT
MK_ALT
MK_LBUTTON
MK_MBUTTON
MK_RBUTTON
```

The function returns **DRAGDROP_S_CANCEL** if dragging has not started and if the Esc key is pressed, if the right mouse button is pressed, or if the left mouse button is raised. It returns **DRAGDROP_S_DROP** if a drop should occur—that is, if the left mouse button is raised after the drag has commenced. **S_OK** is returned in all other situations.

Prototype

```
//Function Prototype
virtual SCODE QueryContiueDrag (BOOL bEscapePressed, DWORD dwKeyState);
```

OleDropTarget   CLASS

Derivation

```
CObject                    ▼
    CCmdTarget                 ▼
        COleDropTarget
```

Description   This object is the communications link between your window and the OLE 2 libraries that make it possible for the window to accept data from the drag-and-drop mechanism. You need to create a **COleDropTarget** object then call its **Register** function with a pointer to the **CWnd** object.

Member Functions

COleDropTarget   FUNCTION

Description   Constructor. This function creates an instance of **COleDropTarget**.

Prototype

```
//Function Prototype
COleDropTarget();
```

Register   FUNCTION

Description   If your drop operation is to be accepted, you must have previously used this function to register your window as a drop target with the OLE 2 DLLs. The parameter *pWnd* is a pointer to the window that is the drop target. The function returns TRUE if the window is successfully registered, FALSE if the registration is unsuccessful.

Prototype

```
//Function Prototype
BOOL Register(Cwnd* pWnd);
```

Revoke   FUNCTION

Description This is the opposite of the **Register** function just described; **Revoke** removes the drop target window from the list of drop targets, and must be called before destroying a window. Usually it is done for you by **CWnd::OnDestroy** of the registered window, so you don't have to worry about it.

Prototype

```
//Function Prototype
virtual void Revoke();
```

Overridable Functons

OnDragEnter   FUNCTION

Description The framework calls this function when the cursor first enters the window, and it must be overridden if a drop is to occur; otherwise it just calls **CView::OnDragEnter**, which defaults to a return of **DROPEFFECT_NONE**. The parameter *pWnd* points to the window the cursor enters, the parameter *pDataObect* points to the data object that is to be dropped, the parameter *dwKeystate* is the state of the modifier keys, and *point* gives the location of the cursor in client coordinates.

dwKeystate can have any number of the following values:

```
MK_CONTROL
MK_SHIFT
MK_ALT
MK_LBUTTON
MK_MBUTTON
MK_RBUTTON
```

The function returns one of the following values:

DROPEFFECT_NONE	Drop would not be allowed.
DROPEFFECT_COPY	Copy operation would be performed.
DROPEFFECT_MOVE	Move operation would be performed.
DROPEFFECT_LINK	Link operation would be performed.
DROPEFFECT_SCROLL	A scroll effect is happening or about to happen.

625

Prototype

```
//Function Prototype
virtual DROPEFFECT OnDragEnter(CWnd* pWnd, COleDataObject*
pDataObject, DWORD dwKeyState, CPoint point);
```

OnDragLeave   FUNCTION

Description   This function is called by the framework when the cursor leaves
the window pointed to by *pWnd*. The default is for the function to
call **CView::OnDragLeave**, which returns DROPEFFECT_NONE. If
you want something to happen you will have to override this.

Prototype

```
//Function Prototype
virtual void OnDragLeave(CWnd* pWnd);
```

OnDragOver   FUNCTION

Description   The framework calls this function when the cursor is dragged over
a window, but by default it calls **CView::OnDragOver**, which
returns the value **DROPEFFECT_NONE**. Override this function to
allow drops. Also, since the function is called a lot, it is worth
optimizing. The parameters are as follows: *pWnd* points to the
window the cursor is dragging over, *pDataObject* is the data object
to be dropped, *dwKeyState* is the state of the modifier keys (a list is
given in the earlier overridable function, **OnDragEnter**), and *point*
is the cursor location in client coordinates.

The function returns one value of the DROPEFFECT type:

DROPEFFECT_NONE	Drop would not be allowed.
DROPEFFECT_COPY	Copy operation would be performed.
DROPEFFECT_MOVE	Move operation would be performed.
DROPEFFECT_LINK	Link operation would be performed.
DROPEFFECT_SCROLL	A scroll effect is happening or about to happen.

Prototype

```
//Function Prototype
virtual DROPEFFECT OnDragOver(CWnd* pWnd, COleDataObject*
pDataObject,
    DWORD dwKeyStat, CPoint point);
```

OnDragScroll   FUNCTION

Description   The framework calls this function to see if the cursor is in the
scrolling region of the window it is over, given by the parameter
pWnd. It is called before **OnDragEnter** or **OnDragOver**. The

function returns TRUE if the window supports scrolling and it is appropriate to do so. Otherwise, it returns FALSE. The other two parameters are *point*, which is the location of the cursor in client coordinates, and *dwKeyState*, which is the state of the modifier keys (see list in the earlier overridable function, **OnDragEnter**).

Prototype

```
//Function Prototype
virtual BOOL OnDragScroll(CWnd* pWnd, DWORD dwKeyState,
CPoint point);
```

OnDrop   FUNCTION

Description   By default, this function calls **CView::OnDrop**, whose default return is FALSE. So, you need to override this function to have a drop actually occur. The parameter *pWnd* points to the window the cusor is over, *pDataObject* is the data object to be dropped, *dropEffect* is the effect that the user wants and is one of the following values:

DROPEFFECT_NONE	Drop would not be allowed.
DROPEFFECT_COPY	Copy operation would be performed.
DROPEFFECT_MOVE	Move operation would be performed.
DROPEFFECT_LINK	Link operation would be performed.
DROPEFFECT_SCROLL	A scroll effect is happening or about to happen.

The function returns TRUE if the drop is successful, and FALSE if it isn't.

Prototype

```
//Function Prototype
virtual BOOL OnDrop(CWnd* pWnd, COleDataObject*
pDataObject, DROPEFFECT   dropEffect, CPoint point);
```

OleException

Derivation

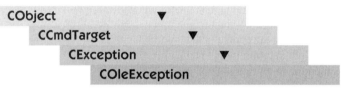

CObject ▼
CCmdTarget ▼
CException ▼
COleException

Description This object is rarely created directly, but more usually through a call to **AfxThrowOleException**. Once created, it represents an exception condition related to an OLE operation. The reason for the exception is contained in the public data member **m_sc**, which holds the status code.

Member Functions

COleException

FUNCTION

Description This is the object constructor.

Prototype
```
//Function Prototype
COleException();
```

Process

FUNCTION

Description This function is called to translate an exception, pointed to by *pAnyException*, into an OLE status code, which is returned.

Prototype
```
//Function Prototype
static SCODE PASCAL Process(const CException* pAnyException);
```

Data Member

m_sc

MEMBER

Description SCODE **m_sc**: This variable holds the OLE 2 status code indicating the reason for the exception. The value is set by the constructor.

COleInsertDialog

Derivation

CObject ▼

    CCmdTarget ▼

        CWnd ▼

            CDialog ▼

                COleDialog ▼

                    COleInsertDialog

Description   When you want to use the Insert Object dialog box, you should create a **COleInsertDialog** object. Functions in this class display the box, get the class ID of the item to be inserted, display the insertion item as an icon, if that is your desire, get the object type of the selected item, and get the path to a file that is to be inserted. Furthermore, the **m_io** data member controls the behavior of the dialog box.

Member Functions

COleInsertDialog

Description   This is the object constructor. It is not actually responsible for displaying the box; that is done by the **DoModal** function. The parameter *pParentWnd* is a pointer to the parent window, and when set to NULL indicates that the parent is the main application window. The other parameter, *dwFlags*, controls several features of the dialog box. You may include any number of the following values for *dwFlags*:

IOF_SHOWHELP	The Help button will be displayed when the dialog box opens.
IOF_SELECTCREATENEW	The Create New radio button will be selected when the dialog is opened. This value and the next value, IOF_SELECTCREATEFROMFILE, are mutually exclusive.

IOF_SELECTCREATEFROMFILE	The Create From File radio button will be selected when the dialog box opens. This value and the previous value, IOF_SELECTCREATENEW, are mutually exclusive.
IOF_CHECKLINK	The Link check box will be selected when the dialog box opens.
IOF_CHECKDISPLAYASICON	The Display As Icon box will be selected when the box opens. The current icon will be displayed, and the Change Icon button will be enabled.
IOF_DISABLELINK	The Link check box will be disabled.
IOF_VERIFYSERVERSEXIST	The dialog box will validate the classes it adds to the list box. This is to make sure that the servers in the registration database exist before the dialog box opens. This option may reduce performance.

Prototype

```
//Function Prototype
COleInsertDialog (DWORD dwFlags = IOF_SELECTCREATENEW,
CSnd* pParentWnd = NULL);
```

CreateItem   FUNCTION

Description   You can use this function to create a **COleClientItem** object. This class defines the container interface for OLE items. Be sure that the **COleClientItem** object has already been allocated before calling **CreateItem,** and provide the pointer to the function with the *pItem* parameter. And don't call **CreateItem** unless **DoModal** returns **IDOK**. The function returns TRUE if the creation was successful, FALSE, if not.

Prototype

```
//Function Prototype
BOOL CreateItem(COleClientItem* pItem);
```

DoModal   FUNCTION

Description   This function is called to display the OLE Insert Object dialog box and is called after the object is constructed. If you want to initialize controls by setting members of the **m_io** data member, do so before calling **DoModal**. This function returns **IDOK** if the dialog box is displayed correctly, it returns **IDCANCEL** if the user cancels the box, and returns **IDABORT** is there is an error. If the

IDABORT return occurs, the **GetLastError** function from the **COleDialog** class can be used to retrieve the error code.

Prototype

```
//Function Prototype
virtual int DoModal();
```

GetClassID — FUNCTION

Description This function returns the class ID for the selected item. You can use if **DoModal** returns **IDOK** and if the selection type is **COleInsertDialog::CreateNewItem**.

Prototype

```
//Function Prototype
const CLSID& GetClassID() const;
```

GetIconicMetafile — FUNCTION

Description This function first checks to see if the Display As Icon check box was selected when the dialog box was closed. If so, the function will find and return the handle to the metafile that contains the iconic aspect of the selected item. If the Display As Icon box was not checked, this function will return NULL.

Prototype

```
//Function Prototype
HGLOBAL GetIconicMetafile() const;
```

GetPathName — FUNCTION

Description This function returns the full path of the selected file, but only if **DoModal** returns **IDOK**. Also, it won't work if the selection type is **CreateNewItem**, since then there is really no file to find.

Prototype

```
//Function Prototype
CString GetPathName() const;
```

GetSelectionType — FUNCTION

Description This function returns the selection type at the time the Insert dialog box was closed. The return value indicates one of three possibilities:

○ **COleInsertDialog::createNewItem**: The Create New button was selected.

○ **COleInsertDialog::insertFromFile**: The Create From File button was selected and the Link check box was not.

○ **COleInsertDialog::linkToFile**: Both the Create From File button and the Link check box were selected.

Prototype

```
//Function Prototype
UINT GetSelectionType();
```

Data Member

m_io   MEMBER

Description   Members in this OLEUIINSERTOBJECT type structure control the behavior of the Insert Object dialog box. These members can be changed directly or through various member functions.

DWORD	cbStruct	Size of this OLEIINSERTIBJECT structure.	
DWORD	dwFlags	Any number of the following values can be included:	
		IOF_SHOWHELP	The Help button will be displayed when the dialog box opens.
		IOF_SELECTCREATENEW	The Create New radio button will be selected when the dialog is opened. This value and the next value, IOF_SELECT-CREATEFROMFILE, are mutually exclusive.
		IOF_SELECTCREATEFROMFILE	The Create From File radio button will be selected when the dialog box opens. This value and the previous value, IOF_SELECTCREATENEW, are mutually exclusive.
		IOF_CHECKLINK	The Link check box will be selected when the dialog box opens.

		IOF_CHECKDISPLAYASICON	The Display As Icon box will be selected when the box opens. The current icon will be displayed, and the Change Icon button will be enabled.
		IOF_DISABLELINK	The Link check box will be disabled.
		IOF_VERIFYSERVERSEXIST	The dialog box will validate the classes it adds to the list box. This is to make sure that the servers in the registration database exist before the dialog box opens. This option may reduce performance.
HWND	hWndOwner		Handle to the window that owns the dialog box.
LPCTSTR	lpszCaption		Pointer to the string that will be the dialog caption.
LPFNOLEUIHOOK	lpfnHook		Pointer to an optional hook callback function. You must build the function yourself.
LPARAM	lCustData		Optional custom data you want to pass to your optional hook.
HINSTANCE	hInstance		Instance for the customized template name of the object to be inserted.
LPCTSTR	lpszTemplate		Customized template name of the object to be inserted.
HRSRC	hResource		Customized template handle.
CLSID	clsid		Return space for class ID of the object being inserted.
LPTSTR	lpszFile		Pointer to the filename for inserts or links.
UINT	cchFile		Size of buffer for the file in lpszFile OLEUI_CCHPATHMAX.
UINT	cClsidExclud		CLSIDs in lpClsidExclude.
LPCLSID	lpClsidExclude		List of CLSIDs to exclude from listing of acceptable objects for insertion.
IID	iid		Requested interface on creation.
DWORD	oleRender		Rendering option.
LPFORMATETC	lpFormatEtc		Desired format.
LPOLECLIENTSITE	lplOleClientSite		Site to be used for the object.
LPSTORAGE	lplStorage		Storage used for the object.
LPVOID FAR	*ppvObj		Where the object is returned.
SCODE	sc		Result of creation calls.
HGLOBAL	hMetaPict		METAFILEPICT containing iconic aspect.

COIePFrameWnd

Derivation

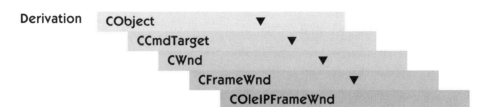

CObject ▼
    CCmdTarget ▼
        CWnd ▼
            CFrameWnd ▼
                COIePFrameWnd

Description   This class provides a base class for in-place editing window of an embedded object. It creates and places control bars in the container's document window, and handles notifications from the **COleResizeBar** object when the in-place editing window is resized.

Member Functions

COIePFrameWnd

Description   This is the object constructor.

Prototype
```
//Function Prototype
COIePFrameWnd();
```

Overridable Functions

OnCreateControlBars

Description   When an object is activated for in-place editing, the framework calls this function with pointers to the container application's frame window, *pWndFrame*, and to the container's document level window, *pWndDoc*. If you want to create your own toolbars, you must override this function. By default, this function doesn't do anything. You override when you need special processing when control bars are created. The function returns TRUE if that processing was successful, FALSE if not.

Prototype
```
//Function Prototype
virtual BOOL OnCreateControlBars(CWnd* pWndFrame, CWnd*
pWndDoc);
```

RepositionFrame — FUNCTION

Description This function is called by the framework to lay out the in-place editing window and control bars so that all are visible to the user. The parameters are two pointers to **RECT** structures or **CRect** objects. The first, *lpPosRect*, points to the frame window's current pixel coordinates, measured relative to the client area. The second, *lpClipRect*, points to the clipping-rectangle window's current pixel coordinates, also measured relative to the client area. There is a difference in the approach in laying out an OLE frame window, done by this function, and laying out a non-OLE window, done by **CFrameWnd::RecalcLayout**. The latter starts by positioning toolbars and other objects first, and the client area is whatever area is left. This **COleIPFrameWnd** function, however, starts with the client area, then positions toolbars and objects accordingly.

Prototype
```
//Function Prototype
virtual void RepositionFrame(LPCRECT lpPosRect, LPCRESECT lpClipRect);
```

OleLinkingDoc — CLASS

Derivation

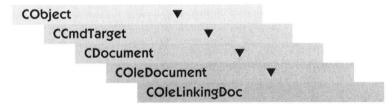

Description If you want your application to be a "link container"—that is, an OLE container that supports linking to its embedded items—then you need to derive your document class from **COleLinkingDoc** instead of **COleDocument**. The document must be designed for storing embedded or linked items, in addition to storing native data.

A link container must be able to be launched by another container application, because it may be the source for a linked item in another document. When a user decides to edit that item, the source needs to be loaded automatically. This ability to be launched programmatically is accomplished by using the **COleTemplateServer**. Here is how it works.

Declare a **COleTemplateServer** object in your application's **CWinApp**-derived class:

```
class COleClientApp : public CwinApp
{
//...
protected:
    COleTemplateServer m_server;
//...
};
```

Next you need to create a document template specifying your **COleLinkingDoc**-derived class as the document class. This is done in the **InitInstance** function of the **CWinApp**-derived class.

```
//CMainDoc is derived from COleLinkingDoc
CMultiDocTemplate* pDocTemplate = new
CMultiDocTemplate(IDR_OCLIENTTYPE,
    RUNTIME_CLASS(CMainDoc),
    RUNTIME_CLASS(CSplitFrame),
    RUNTIME_CLASS(CMainView));
pDocTemplate->SetContainerInfo(IDR_OCLIENTTYPE_CNTR_IP);
AddDocTemplate(pDocTemplate);
```

Finally, use **ConnectTemplate** to connect the **COleTemplateServer** object to your document templates and use **COleTemplateServer::RegisterAll** to register all class objects with the OLE system.

```
m_server.ConnectTemplate(clsid, pDocTemplate, FALSE);
COleTemplateServer::RegisterALL();
```

Member Functions

COleLinkingDoc · FUNCTION

Description   This constructs an object of the **COleLinkingDoc** class.

Prototype
```
//Function Prototype
COleLinkingDoc();
```

Register · FUNCTION

Description   This function lets the OLE system DLLs know that the document pointed to by the parameter *pFactory* is open. You don't need to use it if the document represents an embedded item; you do if you are creating or opening a named file. The parameter *lpszPathName* is a fully qualified path to the container document. This function is called for you if you use **COleTemplateServer**. In that case it gets called by the **COleLinkingDoc**'s use of **OnNewDocument**, **OnOpenDocument** and **OnSaveDocument**. The function returns TRUE if registration is successful, FALSE if not.

Prototype
```
//Function Prototype
BOOL Register(COleObjectFactory* pFactory, LPCTSTR
lpszpathName);
```

Revoke · FUNCTION

Description This function revokes your container document's registration with the OLE system DLLs. The function needs to be called when closing the file, but is done for you by **COleLinkingDoc**'s implementation of **OnCloseDocument**, **OnOpenDocument** and **OnSaveDocument**.

Prototype
```
//Function Prototype
void Revoke();
```

Overridable Functions

OnFindEmbeddedItem · FUNCTION

Description The framework calls this function with a pointer to the name of an embedded OLE item, and the function searches the list of items embedded in the document to see if it is there. The search is case-sensitive, and if successful returns a pointer to the **COleClientItem** object; otherwise it returns NULL. You would override if you have your own way of storing or naming embedded OLE items.

Prototype
```
//Function Prototype
virtual COleClientItem* OnFindEmbeddedItem(LPCTSTR
lpszItemName);
```

OnGetLinkedItem · FUNCTION

Description The framework calls this function to look for the name of the server item pointed to by *lpszItemName*. The default implementation is always to return NULL, but the function is overridden in the derived class **COleServerDoc**, and the list of OLE server items is searched for the item name in question. You will want to override this function if you have your own way of storing and retrieving linked server items.

Prototype

```
//Function Prototype
virtual COleServerItem* OnGetLinkedItem(PCTSTR lpszItemName);
```

OleLinksDialog   **CLASS**

Derivation

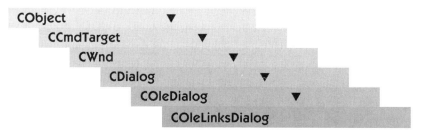

Description The Edit Links dialog box lets the user change information about the source of a linked object. The **COleLinksDialog** class of objects provides the support for this dialog box. The object is created with the **COleLinksDialog** function, the box is displayed with the **DoModal** function, and the **m_el** data member provides the programmer control over the properties of the dialog box.

Member Functions

COleLinksDialog	FUNCTION

Description This is the constructor function that creates a **COleLinksDialog** object. The actual display of the dialog box is done by the **DoModal** function. The parameter *pDoc* is a pointer to the OLE document that contains the link to be edited, while *pView* points to the current view of that document. The parameter *dwFlags* has only two possible values: **ELF_SHOWHELP**, which puts the Help button into the dialog box, or 0, in which case there is no button. The last parameter *pParentWnd* is a pointer to the window that owns the dialog box. If it is set to NULL, then the main application window is the owner.

Prototype

```
//Function Prototype
COleLinksDialog(COleDocument* pDoc, CView* pView, DWORD
dwFlags = 0, CWnd* pParentWnd = NULL);
```

DoModal   FUNCTION

Description This function is called to display the OLE Edit Links dialog box and is called after the object is constructed. If you want to initialize controls by setting members of the **m_el** data member, do so before calling **DoModal**. This function returns **IDOK** if the dialog box is displayed correctly, it returns **IDCANCEL** if the user cancels the box, and returns **IDABORT** is there is an error. If the last return occurs, the **GetLastError** function from the **COleDialog** class can be used to retrieve the error code.

Prototype

```
//Function Prototype
virtual int DoModal();
```

Data Member

m_el   MEMBER

DWORD	cbStruct	Size of the structure.
DWORD	dwFlags	See list for dwFlags in the description of the COleChangeIconDialog constructor function.
HWND	hWndOwner	Handle to the owning window.
LPCTSTR	lpszCatption	Pointer to the string that is the caption of the dialog box.
LPFNOLEUIHOOK	lpfnHook	Pointer to the optional hook callback function, which you must build yourself.
LPARAM	lCustData	Optional custom data to pass to hook.
HINSTANCE	hInstance	Instance for the customized template name of the object to be inserted.

LPCTSTR	lpszTemplate:	Customized template name of the object to be inserted.
HRSRC	hResource:	Customized template handle.
LPOLEUILINKCONTAINER	lpOleUILinkContainer	The interface for manipulating links in the container.

OleMessageFilter

CLASS

· ·

Derivation

CObject ▼
  CCmdTarget ▼
    COleMessageFilter

Description With OLE client-server calls going back and forth, an application needs a way to control access to itself. When it would be dangerous for an application's OLE accessible data or objects to accept a call, the **COleMessageFilter** class can act as the receptionist handling incoming calls: informing callers that the application is busy and not accepting calls, please try again later, or that the application is not accepting any calls. It also enables and disables feedback to the user via the "busy" dialog box and the "not responding" dialog box.

Member Functions

BeginBusyState **FUNCTION**

Description You call this function to begin a busy state. A counter keeps track of the number of times that **BeginBusyState** is called, and **EndBusyState** must be called the same number of times before the busy state is terminated. Idle processing brings about a call to the busy state by the framework. During a busy state the application can send a reply, which is determined by the **COleMessageFilter::SetBusyReply** function.

Prototype
```
//Function Prototype
virtual void BeginBusyState();
```

COleMessageFilter   FUNCTION

Description   This is the object constructor function.

Prototype
```
//Function Prototype
COleMessageFilter();
```

EnableBusyDialog   FUNCTION

Description   As explained in the description of the **SetMessagePendingDelay**
function, if an OLE call keeps calling a busy application, and has to
wait beyond the limits set by **SetMessagePendingDelay**, the
"busy" dialog box will appear, giving the user the opportunity to
bail out. If you don't want the dialog box to appear, simply set the
parameter *bEnableBusy* to FALSE.

Prototype
```
//Function Prototype
void EnableBusyDialog(BOOL bEnableBusy = TRUE);
```

EnableNotRespondingDialog   FUNCTION

Description   This is very similar to **EnableBusyDialog**. The difference is that
EnableNotRespondingDialog enables or disables the "not re-
sponding" dialog box for a keyboard or mouse message that is kept
waiting beyond the limits set by **SetMessagePendingDelay**, while
EnableBusyDialog enables and disables the "busy" dialog box
when the wait is for an OLE call. Set *bEnableNotResponding* to
TRUE to enable, FALSE to disable.

Prototype
```
//Function Prototype
void EnableNotRespondingDialog(BOOL bEnableNotReponding =
TRUE);
```

Overridable Functions

OnMessagePending   FUNCTION

Description   When a call is waiting, the framework calls this function with a
pointer to the message, *pMsg*, so messages can still be processed.
The default is for the framework to keep the window updated by
sending **WM_PAINT** messages. The function returns TRUE if
successful, FALSE if not.

Prototype
```
//Function Prototype
virtual BOOL OnMessagePending(const MSG* pMsg);
```

EndBusyState   FUNCTION

Description **EndBusyState** must be called the same number of times that **BeginBusyState** was called before the busy state can end.

Prototype
```
//Function Prototype
virtual void EndBusyState();
```

Register   FUNCTION

Description The ability to filter messages–the whole purpose of the object **COleMessageFilter**–doesn't exist until the object is registered with the OLE DLLs. This is usually done from the application's initialization code, and the default message filter is automatically registered by the framework. This registration needs to be revoked by the **Revoke** function before the application terminates. The function returns TRUE with a successful registration, FALSE if unsuccessful.

Prototype
```
//Function Prototype
BOOL Register();None
```

Revoke   FUNCTION

Description Before your application terminates, its registration with the OLE DLLs must be revoked. Default message filters are automatically revoked by the framework before an application terminates.

Prototype
```
//Function Prototype
void Revoke();
```

SetBusyReply   FUNCTION

Description When an application is put into the busy state by the function **BeginBusyState**, it will respond to calls with a reply, which will give the caller a basis for deciding what to do next. Use the parameter *nBusyReply* to set your desired response. It can be one of the following:

SEVERCALL_ISHANDLED	The application is accepting calls, but may not actually be able to process them.
SEVERCALL_REJECTED	The application will probably never be able to process a call.
SEVERCALL_RETRYLATER	The application is only temporarily unable to process a call. This is the default, and causes the calling application to retry as soon as possible.

Prototype

```
//Function Prototype
void SetBusyReply(SERVERCALL nBusyReply);
```

SetMessagePendingDelay   FUNCTION

Description The framework continually retries calling a busy application until it makes a successful call, or until the time set by **SetMessagePendingDelay** runs out. This time, in milliseconds, is in the praramter *nTimeout*. If the time does run out, the OLE "busy" dialog box is displayed and the user can decide to try again or cancel. This dialog box can be enabled or disabled with the **EnableBusyDialog** function. When a keyboard or mouse message has been kept waiting beyond the delay, the "not responding" dialog box is displayed. This box can be enabled and disabled with the **EnableNotRespondingDialog** function.

Prototype

```
//Function Prototype
void SetMessagePendingDelay(DWORD nTimeout = 5000);
```

SetRetryReply   FUNCTION

Description When an application comes calling, and the called application is busy, the message to the caller about when to try again is set by this function. If *nRetryReply* is set to 0, the message is to retry immediately; -1 signals to cancel; a positive integer indicates how long to wait, in milliseconds, before trying again. How long the caller actually waits is determined by both the **SetRetryReply** and the **SetMessagePendingDelay** functions. The framework continues to call again and again, waiting *nRetryReply* milliseconds between each attempt, until it is successful, or until the time determined by the **SetMessagePendingDelay** has run out.

Prototype

```
//Function Prototype
void SetRetryReply(DWORD nRetryReply = 0);
```

643

OleObjectFactory

Derivation

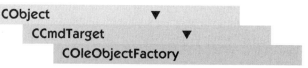

CObject ▼
CCmdTarget ▼
COleObjectFactory

Description   The OLE class factory is implemented by this class. In addition to creating the OLE objects, this class has functions for registering objects and for updating the OLE system register, as well as handling run-time registration that tells OLE that objects are running and ready to get messages.

Member Functions

COleObjectFactory   FUNCTION

Description   This function creates and initializes a **COleObjectFactory** object, and adds it to the list of factories. But it does not register it, which must be done before it can be used. The parameters are as follows: *clsid* is a reference to the OLE class ID that will be represented by this object factory, *pRuntimeClass* is a pointer to the run-time class of C++ objects that can be created by this object factory, and *bMultiInstance* indicates whether or not the application supports multiple instantiation (in other words, if it is set to TRUE, multiple instances of the application get launched with each request for one). The final parameter, *lpszProgID*, points to the string that is the verbal program identifier.

Prototype
```
//Function Prototype
COleObjectFactory(REFCLSID clsid, CRuntimeClass* pRuntimeClass,
BOOL bMultiInstance, LPCTSTR lpszProgID);
```

GetClassID · FUNCTION

Description This function returns a reference to the OLE class ID represented by this factory.

Prototype
```
//Function Prototype
REFCLSID GetClassID() const;
```

IsRegistered · FUNCTION

Description If you need to find out if the object factory is registered with the OLE system DLLs, call this function. It returns TRUE if it is registered, FALSE if it is not.

Prototype
```
//Function Prototype
BOOL IsRegistered() const;
```

Register · FUNCTION

Description Most of the time this function will be called by **CWinApp::InitInstance** when an application gets launched. When called, it registers this object factory with the OLE system DLLs. It returns TRUE if the registration is successful, FALSE if not.

Prototype
```
//Function Prototype
BOOL Register();
```

RegisterAll · FUNCTION

Description This function, like the previous function, is usually called by **CWinApp::InitInstance** when an application gets launched. When called it registers all of the object factories from that application with the OLE system DLLs. It returns TRUE if the registrations are successful, FALSE if not.

Prototype
```
//Function Prototype
static BOOL PASCAL RegisterAll();
```

Revoke · FUNCTION

Description When an application terminates, this function is automatically called to remove this factory's registration from the OLE system DLLs. It can also be called by **CWinApp::ExitInstance**, if that function is overridden.

| Prototype | //Function Prototype
void Revoke(); |

RevokeAll · FUNCTION

Description When an application terminates, this function is automatically called to remove all that application's factory registrations from the OLE system DLLs. It can also be called by **CWinApp::ExitInstance**, if that function is overridden.

Prototype
```
//Function Prototype
static void PASCAL RevokeAll();
```

UpdateRegistry · FUNCTION

Description This function, like **Register**, is usually called by **CWinApp::InitInstance** when an appliation is launched. It registers the string pointed to by the parameter *lpszProgID* with the OLE system registry. This string is a program identifier, for example, "Excel.Document.2."

Prototype
```
//Function Prototype
void UpdateRegistry(LPCTSTR lpszProgID = NULL);
```

UpdateRegistryAll · FUNCTION

Description This function registers all of an application's factories with the OLE system registry. Usually it is called by **CWinApp::InitInstance** when the application gets launched.

Prototype
```
//Function Prototype
static void PASCAL UpdateRegistry();
```

Overridable Function

OnCreateObject · FUNCTION

Description This function is called by the framework to create a new object from the **CRunTimeClass** passed to the constructor. If you intend to create the object from something else, override this function. The function returns a pointer to the new object, or returns a memory exception if the creation is unsuccessful.

Prototype   //Function Prototype
virtual CCmdTarget* OnCreateObject();

COlePasteSpecialDialog   **CLASS**

Derivation
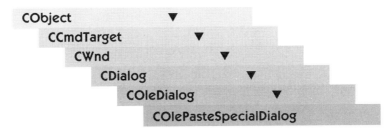

Description   This class of object supports the Paste Special dialog box. When
you wish to call this dialog box, create a **COlePasteSpecialDialog**
object, and use the data member **m_ps** to initialize its values.
Member functions allow you to add custom formats that your
application can paste, to add standard formats, to create the pasted
item in the container, to display the item as an icon, and to retrieve
information from the dialog box entered by the user.

Member Functions

AddFormat   **FUNCTION**

Description   You can add more formats to the list supported by your application
by using this function. The first prototype adds custom formats
registered with the OLE system by your application. The second
prototype adds standard formats. Let's examine each.
     The custom format parameters are as follows: *fmt* references the
data type you are adding in a **FORMATETC** structure, *lpstrFormat*
is a pointer to a string that describes the format for the user,
lpstrResult is a pointer to a string that describes the results of this
particular format, and *flags* is a bitwise combination of linking and
embedding options. Here is a list of them:

647

OLEUIPASTE_ENABLEICON	In not set, Display As Icon button is disabled.
OLEUIPASTE_PASTEONLY	Format is available for pasting only.
OLEUIPASTE_PASTE	Format is available for pasting, but not to the exclusion of linking.
OLEUIPASTE_LINKANYTYPE	All link types supported.
OLEUIPASTE_LINKTYPE1	Programmer defined link type.
OLEUIPASTE_LINKTYPE2	Programmer defined link type.
OLEUIPASTE_LINKTYPE3	Programmer defined link type.
OLEUIPASTE_LINKTYPE4	Programmer defined link type.
OLEUIPASTE_LINKTYPE5	Programmer defined link type.
OLEUIPASTE_LINKTYPE6	Programmer defined link type.
OLEUIPASTE_LINKTYPE7	Programmer defined link type.
OLEUIPASTE_LINKTYPE8	Programmer defined link type.

The standard Clipboard format parameters are as follows: *cf* identifies the Clipboard format; *tymed* is a bitwise combination of the media available in the type identified by *cf*:

D_HGLOBALTYME	Pass the data in a handle to Global memory.
TYMED_FILE	Pass the data in a file on disk.
TYMED_ISTREAM	Pass the data using an IStream interface.
TYMED_ISTORAGE	Pass the data using an IStorage interface.
TYMED_GDI	Pass the data as a Graphics Device Interface object (bitmap).
TYMED_MFPICT	Pass the data as a CF_METAFILEPICT.
TYMED_ENHMF	Pass the data as an Enhanced Format Metafile.
TYMED_NULL	No data to be transferred.

The *nFormatID* parameter is the identifier for a string that describes the format and the result of choosing the format specified by *cf*. It is, in effect, two strings seperated by \n. The first half describes the format to the user, and the second half describes the result the user will get with this format. The *bEnableIcon* parameter is a Boolean that when set to TRUE activates the Display As Icon check box when this format is selected by the user. *bLink* is another Boolean that activates the Paste Link radio button when this format is chosen.

Prototype

```
//Function Prototype
void AddFormat(const FORMATETC& fmt, LPTSTR lpstrFormat,
LPTSTR lpstrResult, DWORD flags);
    void AddFormat(UINT cf, DWORD tymed, UINT nFormatID,
    BOOL bEnableIcon, BOOL bLink);
```

AddStandardFormats   FUNCTION

Description This function adds the following formats to the list supported by your application:

CF_BITMAP	Bitmap
CF_DIB	Device independent bitmap
CF_METAFILEPICT	Metafile

If you set *bEnablelink* to TRUE, the default, the function also adds the following:

CF_LINKSOURCE	Linked object

Prototype

```
//Function Prototype
void COlePasteSpecialDialog(BOOL bEnableLink = TRUE);
```

COlePasteSpecialDialog   FUNCTION

Description This is the constructor function for **COlePasteSpecialDialog** objects. The parameters are as follows: *pDataObject* is a pointer to the **COleDataObject** on the Clipboard that is to be pasted, *pParentWnd* is a pointer to the window that own this **COleSpecialDialog** object, and *dwFlags* is a creation flag that can contain any number of the following values combined using the bitwise OR operator:

PSF_SHOWHELP	The Help button is displayed.
PSF_SELECTPASTE	The Paste radio button is checked when the dialog box is called. This flag and the next, PSF_SELECTPASTELINK, are mutually exclusive.
PSF_SELECTPASTELINK	The Paste Link radio button is checked when the dialog box is called. This flag and the previous flag, PSF_SELECTPASTE, are mutually exclusive.
PSF_CHECKDISPLAYASICON	The Display as Icon box is checked when the dialog box is called.

Prototype

```
//Function Prototype
COlePasteSpecialDialog(DWORD dwFlags = PSF_SELECTPASTE,
COleDataObject* pDataObject = NULL, CWnd* pParentWnd =
NULL);
```

649

CreateItem   FUNCTION

Description   This function creates the new item that was chosen in the Paste Special dialog box. Don't call it until **DoModal** returns **IDOK**. The parameter *pnewItem* is a pointer to the **COleClientItem** object. If the object is successfully created, the function returns TRUE, otherwise it returns FALSE.

Prototype
```
//Function Prototype
BOOL CreateItem(COleClientItem* pNewItem);
```

DoModal   FUNCTION

Description   This function is called to display the OLE Paste Special dialog box and is called after the object is constructed. If you want to initialize controls by setting members of the **m_ps** data member, do so before calling **DoModal**. This function returns **IDOK** if the dialog box is displayed correctly, it returns **IDCANCEL** if the user cancels the box, and returns **IDABORT** is there is an error. If the last return occurs, the **GetLastError** function from the **COleDialog** class can be used to retrieve the error code.

Prototype
```
//Function Prototype
virtual int DoModal();
```

GetDrawAspect   FUNCTION

Description   This function tells you how the user wants the selected item displayed. Call it after **DoModal** returns **IDOK**. It returns **DVASPECT_ICON** if the Display As Icon box was checked, **DVASPECT_CONTENT** if not.

Prototype
```
//Function Prototype
DVASPECT GetDrawAspect() const;
```

GetIconicMetafile   FUNCTION

Description   Call this function to get the handle to the metafile containing the iconic aspect of the selected item. The user must have selected the Display As Icon box in the Paste Special dialog box and **DoModal** must have returned **IDOK**. Otherwise, **GetIconicMetafile** just returns NULL.

Prototype

//Function Prototype
HGLOBAL GetIconicMetafile() const;

GetPasteIndex   FUNCTION

Description This function returns the index into the array of the
OLEUIPASTEENTRY structure that was selected by the user. This
gives you the proper format for pasting.

Prototype

//Function Prototype
int GetPasteIndex() const;

GetSelectionType   FUNCTION

Description This function returns the type of the selection made by the user. It
will be one of the following:

COlePasteSpecialDialog::pasteLink	The Paste Link Radio button was checked and the format was not a metafile.
COlePasteSpecialDialog::pasteNormal	The Paste radio button was checked and the format was not a metafile.
COlePasteSpecialDialog::pasteOther	Not a standard OLE format.
COlePasteSpecialDialog::pasteStatic	Chosen format was a metafile.

Prototype

//Function Prototype
intGetPasteIndex();

Data Member

m_ps   MEMBER

Description This is a data member of the type **OLEUIPASTESPECIAL**. It has the
following members.

DWORD	cbStruct	Size of the structure.
DWORD	dwFlags	See list for dwFlags in the description of the COleChangeIconDialog constructor function.
HWND	hWndOwner	Handle to the owning window.
LPCTSTR	lpszCaption	Pointer to the string that is the caption of the dialog box.

651

LPFNOLEUIHOOK	lpfnHook	Pointer to the optional hook callback function, which you must build yourself.
LPARAM	lCustData	Optional custom data to pass to hook.
HINSTANCE	hInstance	Instance for the customized template name of the object to be inserted.
LPCTSTR	lpszTemplate:	Customized template name of the object to be inserted.
HRSRC	hResource:	Customized template handle.
LPDATAOBJECT	lpSrcDataObj	Pointer to an OLE data object (IDataObject) that is one the Clipboard ready to paste.
LPOLEUIPASTEENTRY	arrPasteEntries	OLEUIPASTEENTRY array that specifies acceptable formats.
int	cPasteEntries	Number of OLEUIPASTEENTRY array entries.
UINT FAR*	arrLinkTypes	List of link types that are acceptable.
int	cLinkTypes	Number of link types.
UINT	cClsidExclude	Number of class IDs in lpClsidExclude (next member).
LPCLSID	lpClsidExclude	List of class IDs to exclude from list.
int	nSelectedIndex	Index of arrPasteEntries[] that the user selected.
BOOL	fLink	Indicates if Paste or Paste Link was selected.
HGLOBAL	hMetaPict	Handle to metafile containing icon and icon title selected by the user.
SIZEL	sizel	Size of the object/link in its source.

OleResizeBar **CLASS**

Derivation

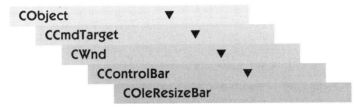

CObject ▼
 CCmdTarget ▼
  CWnd ▼
   CControlBar ▼
    COleResizeBar

Description A **COleResizeBar** object is a type of control bar that handles the resizing of in-place OLE items. It appears as a **CRectTracker** with a hatched border and outer resize handles. There are only two functions: the constructor **COleResizeBar**, and **Create**.

Member Functions

COleResizeBar FUNCTION

Description This is the constructor for the **COleResizeBar** object. The actual resize bar object is created by **Create**.

Prototype
```
//Function Prototype
ColeResizeBar();
```

Create FUNCTION

Description This function creates a child window and associates it with the **COleResizeBar** object. The *pParentWnd* is a pointer to the parent window of the resize bar and *nID* is the resize bar's child window ID. The *dwStyles* parameter specifies the window style attributes. Possible style attributes are as follows:

```
WS_OVERLAPPED
WS_POPUP
WS_CHILD
WS_MINIMIZE
WS_VISIBLE
WS_DISABLED
WS_CLIPSIBLINGS
WS_CLIPCHILDREN
```

653

WS_MAXIMIZE
WS_CAPTION
WS_BORDER
WS_DLGFRAME
WS_VSCROLL
WS_HSCROLL
WS_SYSMENU
WS_THICKFRAME
WS_GROUP
WS_TABSTOP
WS_MINIMIZEBOX
WS_MAXIMIZEBOX

Prototype

```
//Function Prototype
BOOL Create(CWnd* pParentWnd, DWORD dwStyle =
WS_CHILD|WS_VISIBLE, UINT nID = AFX_IDW_RESIZE_BAR);
```

COleServerDoc

Derivation

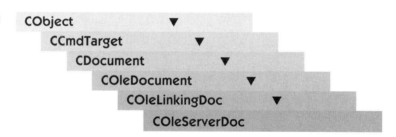

CObject ▼
CCmdTarget ▼
CDocument ▼
COleDocument ▼
COleLinkingDoc ▼
COleServerDoc

Description   An OLE server document is one based on the **COleServerDoc**
class, and it contains **COleServerItem** objects, which are the
server interface for embedded or linked items. You need to construct a **COleServerDoc**-derived class for each type of server
document your application supports. If your application supports
embedded objects but not links, then a server document will
always only have one server item. When a user wants to edit an
embedded object, the container that holds that object launches the
server application, and that embedded object gets loaded as a
server document, which is one **COleServerItem** object and is
contained in the **COleServerDoc** object.

A linked item is a little different. In that case, an existing document gets loaded, and the portion that represents the linked item is

highlighted. Also, your server application needs to create a server item each time a single selection is copied to the Clipboard.

After you have derived a class from **COleServerDoc**, you need to implement **OnGetEmbeddedItem** so your server can support embedded items. Implement these items with a **COleServerItem** - derived class and return this class of objects from **OnGetEmbeddedItem**.

The **COleServerDoc** objects can contain **COleClientItems** too, for your container-server applications. The functions for storing **COleClientItem** items and servicing **COleServerItem** objects are in the framework.

Member Functions

ActivateInPlace   FUNCTION

Description   To achieve in-place activation, this function does all of the following:

❍ Creates an in-place frame window, activates it, and sizes it to the item.

❍ Sets up shared menus and controls.

❍ Scrolls the item into view.

❍ Sets the focus to the in-place frame window.

The default implementation of **COleServerItem::OnShow** calls this function, but if you have another verb in your application for in-place activation, you need to call it yourself. If the function is successful, it returns TRUE, otherwise it returns FALSE.

Prototype
```
//Function Prototype
BOOL ActivateInPlace();
```

COleServerDoc   FUNCTION

Description   This is the object constructor. The **COleServerDoc** object is created, but is not connected to the OLE system DLLs until you call the **COleLinkingDoc::Register** function. However, if your application is using **COleTemplateServer**, that function is called for you by **COleLinkingDoc**'s implementation of **OnNewDocument**, **OnOpenDocument** and **OnSaveDocument**.

Prototype
```
//Function Prototype
COleServerDoc();
```

DeactivateAndUndo   FUNCTION

Description   If the user has activated an item, but changes his mind and selects Undo before doing any actual editing, call this function. In an application written with MFC libraries, the server's user interface also gets deactivated, because calling this function also generates a call to **COleClientItem::OnDeactivateAndUndo**. **DeactivateAndUndo** returns TRUE if it is successful, FALSE if not.

Prototype   //Function Prototype
BOOL DeactivateAndUndo();

DiscardUndoState   FUNCTION

Description   Some edits cannot be undone. In this case the resources holding the undo-state information are tied up. To flush these resources and discard the information, call this function. **DiscardUndoState** returns TRUE if successful, FALSE if not.

Prototype   //Function Prototype
BOOL DiscardUndoState();

GetEmbeddedItem   FUNCTION

Description   This function returns a pointer to an item that represents the entire document, or NULL if the operation is not successful. It calls **COleServerDoc::OnGetEmbeddedItem**, a virtual function with no default implementation.

Prototype   //Function Prototype
COleServerItem* GetEmbeddedItem();

GetItemClipRect   FUNCTION

Description   When an item is being edited in place, the user may scroll outside the visible part of the document. To find out, you can use this document to get the clipping-rectangle coordinates for the item, which will be placed in the parameter *lpClipRect*, a pointer to a **RECT** structure or a **CRect** object. The coordinates are in pixels, relative to the container application window's client area.
If the user has moved outside the visible part of the document, scroll the container by a call to **ScrollContainerBy**.

Prototype

//Function Prototype
void GetItemClipRect(LPRECT lpClipRect) const;

GetItemPosition — FUNCTION

Description This function enters the coordinates of the item being edited in place into the parameter *lpPosRect*, a pointer to a **RECT** structure or **CRect** object. The coordinates are in pixels, relative to the container window's client area, and would typically be called to compare these coordinates to the current clipping rectangle to see how much of the item is visible on the monitor.

Prototype

//Function Prototype
void GetItemPosition(LPRECT lpPosRect) const;

GetZoomFactor — FUNCTION

Description If you have an item's size, in pixels, and divide it by the item's current extent, you get the zoom factor—in other words, its apparent magnification. Call this function to have the current extent, the denominator, placed in the parameter *lpSizeDenom*, and the size, the numerator, placed in the parameter *lpSizeNum*. The third parameter, *lpPosRect*, is a pointer to the **CRect** object that has the item's new position. A NULL value makes the function use the item's current position.

The function will return FALSE if one of two conditions holds: the item is not being edited in place, or the zoom factor is 1:1. Otherwise, it returns TRUE.

Prototype

//Function Prototype
BOOL GetZoomFactor(LPSIZE lpSizeNum = NULL, LPSIZE
lpSizeDenom = NULL, LPCRECT lpPosRect = NULL) const;

IsEmbedded — FUNCTION

Description This function answers the question, "Is the document an embedded object in the container?" It returns TRUE if it is, FALSE if it is not.

Prototype

//Function Prototype
BOOL IsEmbedded() const;

IsInPlaceActive

Description   This function answers the question, "Is the item in the in-place active state?" If it is, the function returns TRUE, if not, it returns FALSE.

Prototype
```
//Function Prototype
BOOL IsInPlaceActive() const;
```

NotifyChanged

Description   After a user has changed some global attribute of a server document, this function needs to be called to notify all the items that are linked to that document. OLE items with automatic links get updated, and in MFC container applications, the **COleClientItem::OnChange** is called.

Prototype
```
//Function Prototype
void NotifyChanged();
```

NotifyClosed

Description   This function gets called when the user closes a server document. When the user chooses Close from the File menu, the function is called for you by the **COleServerDoc** implementation of **OnCloseDocument**. The OLE system DLLs then get notified, and they notify the containers. If the containers were written with MFC library, the **COleClientItem::OnChange** gets called.

Prototype
```
//Function Prototype
void NotifyClosed();
```

NotifyRename

Description   This function gets called when the user renames a server document, with the new name pointed to by the parameter *lpszNewName*. When the user chooses Save As from the File menu, the function is called for you by the **COleServerDoc** implementation of **OnSaveDocument**. The OLE system DLLs then get notified, and they notify the containers. If the containers were written with MFC library, the **COleClientItem::OnRename** gets called.

Prototype
```
//Function Prototype
void NotifyRename(LPCTSTR lpszNewName);
```

NotifySaved   FUNCTION

Description   This function gets called when the user saves a server document. When the user chooses Save from the File menu, the function is called for you by the **COleServerDoc** implementation of **OnSaveDocument**. The OLE system DLLs then get notified, and they notify the containers. If the containers were written with MFC library, the **COleClientItem::OnChange** gets called.

Prototype
```
//Function Prototype
void NotifySaved();
```

RequestPositionChange   FUNCTION

Description   After the data in an in-place active item has changed, call this function as well as **UpdateAllItems**. The request is to change the in-place editing frame and it may not occur. It it does, it is handled by the container's call to **OnSetItemRects**, but it may not be the change requested. The single parameter, *lpPosRect*, is a pointer to the **RECT** structure, or the **CRect** object that has the item's new position.

Prototype
```
//Function Prototype
void RequestPositionChange(LPCRECT lpPosRect);
```

SaveEmbedding   FUNCTION

Description   Call this function to have the container application save the embedded object. It is automatically called from **OnUpdateDocument** and the item gets updated on disk.

Prototype
```
//Function Prototype
void SaveEmbedding();
```

ScrollContainerBy   FUNCTION

Description   If you need to scroll the container document, you can use this function. Simply send the number of pixels you wish to scroll by in the parameter *sizeScroll*. A positive number scrolls down and to the right, a negative number scrolls up and to the left. A successful scroll results in a return of TRUE, otherwise the function returns FALSE.

Prototype   //Function Prototype
BOOL ScrollContainerby(CSize sizeScroll);

UpdateAllItems   FUNCTION

Description   When a document changes, linked items connected to it need to be notified. So after a user makes such a change, call this function. The first parameter is *pSender*, a pointer to the item that changed the document. A NULL value here causes all items to be updated. The parameter *lHint* can be used to provide encode information, and the parameter *pHint* point to a **CObject**-derived object with information about the modifications. The last parameter, *nDrawAspect*, determines how the item will be drawn, and can have one of the following values:

DVASPECT_CONTENT	The item is represented in a way that lets it be displayed as an embedded object inside a container.
DVASPECT_THUMBNAIL	The item is displayed as a "thumbnail" rendering that permits its display inside a browsing tool.
DVASPECT_ICON	The item is displayed as an icon.
DVASPECT_DOCPRINT	The item is displayed as if it were printed.

This function will call the **OnUpdate** function of all the document's items, with the exception of the item that called it. If an OLE item has an automatic link, it gets updated. In container applications written with MFC libraries, **COleClientItem::Onchange** gets called.

Prototype   //Function Prototype
void UpdateAllItems(ColeServerItem* pSender, LPARAM lHint = 0L,
CObject* pHint = NULL, DVASPECT nDrawAspect =
DVASPECT_CONTENT);

Overridable Functions

CreateInPlaceFrame   FUNCTION

Description   The framework calls this function to create a frame window that will be used for in-place editing. It uses the view that was the first one created for the document, and uses information from the document template to create the frame. The view gets momentarily detached from the original frame and attached to the frame that has just been created. The single parameter is *pParentWnd*, the container application's parent window. The function returns a pointer to the new in-place frame window unless the creation fails, in which case it returns NULL.

Prototype
```
//Function Prototype
Protected
virtual COleIPFrameWnd* CreateInPlaceFrame(CWnd* pParentWnd);
END Protected
```

DestroyInPlaceFrame   FUNCTION

Description The framework uses this function to destroy the in-place frame window pointed to by the parameter *bFrame*. The server application returns to the state it had before the in-place activation occurred.

Prototype
```
//Function Prototype
Protected
virtual void DestroyInPlaceFrame(COleIPFrameWnd* bFrame);
END Protected
```

OnDeactivate   FUNCTION

Description When the user deactivates the embedded or linked item, the framework calls this function. The function then returns things to "normal"—that is, the way they were before activation. Any menu or controls created by the in-place activation are destroyed, and the container application's user interface is returned to its original state. Any undo state information should be unconditionally released.

Prototype
```
//Function Prototype
Protected
virtual void OnDeactivate();
END Protected
```

OnDeactivateUI   FUNCTION

Description This function is a lot like **OnDeactivate**. When the user deactivates the embedded or lined item, the framework calls this function. The function then returns things to "normal"—that is, the way they were before activation; any menu or controls created by the in-place activation are destroyed, and the container application's user interface is returned to its original state.

OnDeactivateUI differs from **OnDeactivate** in the handling of undo information. The parameter *bUndoable* is always set to FALSE by the framework, which means editing changes cannot be undone. On the other hand, if the server supports undo, and there is something to be undone, you can call with *bUndoable* set to TRUE.

Prototype

```
//Function Prototype
Protected
virtual void OnDeactivateUI(BOOL bUndoable);
END Protected
```

OnDocWindowActivate   FUNCTION

Description This is the function called by the framework when the document window for in-place editing needs to activated or deactivated. Which one is indicated by the parameter *bActivate*: TRUE for activate, FALSE for deactivate. Once called, the function removes or adds, depending on *bActivate*, the frame-level user interface elements.

Prototype

```
//Function Prototype
Protected
virtual void OnDocWindowActivate(BOOL bActivate);
END Protected
```

OnFrameWindowActivate   FUNCTION

Description The framework calls this function if the container application's frame window is activated, or if it is deactivated. In the first case, it sends TRUE in the parameter *bActivate*, in the latter, it sends FALSE. The default implementation is for the function to cancel any help modes the frame window is in.

Prototype

```
//Function Prototype
Protected
virtual void OnFrameWindowActivate(BOOL bActivate);
END Protected
```

OnGetEmbeddedItem   FUNCTION

Description When a container calls a server to create or edit an embedded item, the framework calls this function, which has no default implementation. You override it when you want to return an item that represents a entire document, which should be a **COleServerItem**-derived class object.

Prototype
```
//Function Prototype
protected
virtual COleServerItem* OnGetEmbeddedItem() = 0;
END Protected
OnClose
```

When a container tries to close a server document, the framework calls this function with the parameter *dwCloseOption*, which can have one of the following values:

OLECLOSE_SAVEIFDIRTY	The file is saved if it has been modified.
OLECLOSE_NOSAVE	The file is closed but not saved.
OLECLOSE_PROMPTSAVE	If the file has been modified, the user is prompted to see if it should be saved.

The default implementation of this function calls **CDocument::OnCloseDocument**.

Prototype
```
//Function Prototype
Protected
virtual void OnClose(OLECLOSE dwCloseOption);
END Protected
```

OnReactivateAndUndo   FUNCTION

Description If an item has been activated in-place, then edited, then deactivated, a user may still try to undo the changes. Normally this can't be done. If it is attempted, the framework calls **OnReactivateAndUndo** and its default implementation returns FALSE, indicating that the attempt failed.

If you want to support reactivate and undo, you need to override the function. The usual way to do this is to undo the editing, then call **ActivateInPlace**. You can do this with a call to **COleClientItem::ReactivateAndUndo** if your application is written with the MFC libraries.

Prototype
```
//Function Prototype
Protected
virtual BOOL OnReactivateAndUndo();
END Protected
```

OnResizeBorder   FUNCTION

Description When an application's frame window is resized, toolbars and other user-interface elements need to be readjusted to fit the new win-

663

dow properly. The framework calls this function to accomplish this. The parameter *lpRectBorder* is a pointer to a **RECT** structure or a **CRect** object that has the window's border coordinates. The parameter *lpUIWindow* is a pointer to a **IOleInPlaceUIWindow** object that is the owner of the current in-place editing session. The last parameter, *bFrame*, is set to TRUE if *lpUIWindow* is a pointer to the container application's top-level frame window, and FALSE if it is to that application's document-level frame window.

Prototype

```
//Function Prototype
Protected
virtual void OnResizeborder(LPCRECT lpRectBorder,
LPOLEINPLACEUIWINDOW lpUIWindow, BOOL bFrame);
END Protected
```

OnSetHostNames   FUNCTION

Description When the container sets, or changes, the host names for a document, the framework calls this function with a pointer to the name of the container application, *lpszHost*, and a pointer to the name of container document, *lpszHostObj*, so that the document title of all the views that refer to the document can be changed.

Prototype

```
//Function Prototype
Protected
virtual void OnSetHostNames(LPCTSTR lpszHost, LPCTSTR
lpszHostObj);
END Protected
```

OnSetItemRects   FUNCTION

Description This function is usually called when a call to **RequestPositionChanges** has been made, but can be called anytime by the container to reposition an in-place item's frame window relative to the container application's frame window. The parameter *lpPosRect*, a pointer to a **RECT** structure or a **CRect** object, has the in-place frame window's position. The postion is relative to the container application's client area. The second parameter, *lpClipRect*, gives the in-place frame window's clipping rectangle. Again, this is relative to the container application's client area.

Prototype

```
//Function Prototype
Protected
virtual void OnSetItemRects(LPCRECT lpPosRect, LPCRECT
```

lpClipRect);
END Protected

OnShowControlBars — FUNCTION

Description This function enumerates, then hides or shows, the server application's control bars. If the parameter *bShow* is TRUE, it shows them, if it is FALSE it hides them. The parameter *bFrameWnd* is a pointer to the frame window whose control bars are to be hidden or shown.

Prototype
```
//Function Prototype
Protected
virtual void OnShowControlBars(CFrameWnd* bFrameWnd, BOOL
bShow);
END Protected
```

OnShowDocument — FUNCTION

Description If the server document needs to be hidden or shown, the framework calls this function. If *bShow*, the parameter, is TRUE, then the server application is activated if it isn't already. Then the container application scrolls until the item is visible. If *bShow* is FALSE, **OnDeactivate** gets called. Any frame windows created for the document are destroyed or hidden, with the exception of the first frame window. If there are no documents visible, then the server application also gets hidden.

Prototype
```
//Function Prototype
Protected
virtual void OnShowDocument(BOOL bShow);
END Protected
```

OnUpdateDocument — FUNCTION

Description When an embedded document is saved, the framework will call this function, whose default implementation leads to the call of **COleServerDoc::NotifySaved** and of **COleServerDoc::SaveEmbedding**. Then the document is marked clean.

Prototype
```
//Function Prototype
virtual BOOL OnUpdateDocument();
```

OleServerItem

CLASS

Derivation

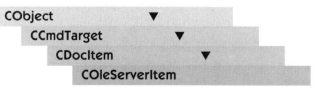

CObject ▼
    CCmdTarget ▼
        CDocItem ▼
            COleServerItem

Description Objects from the **COleServerItem** provide the server interface for linked or embedded OLE items. An embedded item always represents the whole server document. But a linked item can be just a part of a server document, as well as being an entire document. The functions of this class provide the means for handling the display of the item, executing its verbs, and retrieving its data. Usually all this is done in response to requests from the container application, especially through the fairly extensive collection of overridable functions.

Use this class by first deriving a class, then implementing the **OnDraw** function, which provides a metafile representation of the item so it can be displayed by the container application. Next use the **CObject::Serialize** function to provide a native representation. This will permit the transfer of embedded objects between server and container applications.

Member Functions

AddOtherClipboardData
FUNCTION

Description This function places presentation and conversion fomats into the **COleDataSource** object pointed to by *pDataSource*. Providing a presentation format, a metafile picture, requires that the **OnDraw** member function has been implemented. Other conversion formats can be supported by registering them with the **COleDataSource** object returned by **GetDataSource** and by overriding **OnRenderData**.

Prototype
```
//Function Prototype
void AddOtherClipboardData(COleDataSource* pDataSource);
```

GetLinkSourceData   FUNCTION

Description   This function retrieves the **CF_LINKSOURCE** data in the
STGMEDIUM structure pointed to by *lpStgMedium*. This
CF_LINKSOURCE contains the class ID of the OLE item type, and
the location information of the document that contains the item.
The function returns TRUE if the retrieval is successful, FALSE if
not.

Prototype
```
//Function Prototype
BOOL GetLinkSourceData(LPSTGMEDIUM lpStgMedium);
```

COleServerItem   FUNCTION

Description   This is the object constructor. The first parameter, *pServerDoc*, is a
pointer to the document that contains the item. The second param-
eter, *bAutoDelete*, indicates whether the item should be automatically deleted when the link to the item is released.

Prototype
```
//Function Prototype
Protected
COleserverItem(COleServerDoc* pServerDoc, BOOL bAutoDelete);
END Protected
```

CopyToClipboard   FUNCTION

Description   This function copies the OLE item to the Clipboard. It does so by
calling **OnGetClipboardData** and creating a **COleDataSource**
object that contains the item's native data, as well as its representation in **CF_METAFILEPICT**, and any data in supported conversion
formats. The object then gets copied to the Clipboard using
COleDataSource::SetClipboard. The single parameter,
bIncludeLink, indicates whether or not to copy link data to the
Clipboard as well; TRUE will include, FALSE will not.
    This function only works if **Serialize** and **OnDraw** have been
implemented.

Prototype
```
//Function Prototype
void CopyToClipboard(BOOL bIncludeLink = FALSE);
```

DoDragDrop   FUNCTION

Description   This function performs the drag-and-drop operation. To do this, it
needs the following information in the function parameters:

lpItemRect	This is a pointer to CRect object or a RECT structure that has the item's rectangle coordinates, in pixels.
ptOffset	This gives the offset from the lpItemRect location to the mouse cursor.
bIncludeLink	This should be TRUE if the link data can be copied to the Clipboard. It should be FALSE if your server application doesn't support links.
dwEffects	It can any number of the following values:
	DROPEFFECT_COPY Copying permitted.
	DROPEFFECT_MOVE Moving permitted.
	DROPEFFECT_LINK Linking permitted.
	DROPEFFECT_SCROLL Indicates a drag scroll operation could occur.
lpRectStartDrag	This is a pointer to the rectangle that defines when a drag starts. That means the mouse must leave the rectangle before the drag actually begins. If it is set to NULL, the drag begins after the mouse moves one pixel.

Prototype

```
//Function Prototype
DROPEFFECT DodragDrop(LPCRECT lpItemRect, CPoint ptOffset,
BOOL bIncludeLink = FALSE, DWORD dwEffects =
DROPEFFECT_COPY|DROPEFFECT_MOVE, LPCRECT lpRectStartDrag
= NULL);
```

GetClipboardData   FUNCTION

Description This function puts the data for the Clipboard into the form of a **COleDataSource** object, pointed to by the parameter *pDataSource*. It does this by calling **GetEmbedSourceData** to load the native data, and by calling **AddOtherClipboardData** to load the presentation format and supported conversion formats. This function can be overriden, but should not be unless you want to offer data formats in addition to those offered by **CopyToClipboard**. If you are doing so, be sure to put those formats in the **COleDataSource** before or after calling **CopyToClipboard**, then pass the **COleDataSource** object to the **COleDataSource::SetClipboard** function.

The remaining parameters of this function are as follows: *bIncludeLink* indicates whether or not link data is to be included. If set to TRUE, it does so by calling **GetLinkSourceData**. *lpOffset* is a pointer to the mouse cursor's offset from the object's origin, measured in pixels. *lpSize* is a pointer to the object's size, measured in pixels.

Prototype
//Function Prototype
void GetClipboardData(COleDataSource* pDataSource, BOOL blncludeLink = FALSE, LPPOINT lpOffset = NULL, LPSIZE lpSize = NULL);

GetDataSource   FUNCTION

Description
This function returns a pointer to the **COleDataSource** object that has the conversion formats the server application supports. Once retrieved, you can register the formats in which your server application will offer data.

Prototype
//Function Prototype
COleDataSource* GetDataSource();

GetDocument   FUNCTION

Description
This function returns a pointer to the server document that contains the item. This is the same document that was passed to the constructor. If the item is not part of a document, the function returns NULL.

Prototype
//Function Prototype
COleServerDoc* GetDocument();

GetEmbedSourceData   FUNCTION

Description
This function gets the **CF_EMBEDSOURCE** data for the item, which is received by the **STGMEDIUM** structure pointed to by *lpStgMedium*. This then gets added to the data source by a call to **COleDataSource::CacheData**, which gets called automatically if **GetEmbedSourceData** was called originally by **OnGetClipboard**.

Prototype
//Function Prototype
void GetEmbedSourceData(LPSTGMEDIUM lpStgMedium);

GetItemName   FUNCTION

Description
Use this function for linked items to get the linked item's name.

Prototype
//Function Prototype
const CString& GetItemName() const;

GetObjectDescriptorData   FUNCTION

Description This function gets the **CF_OBJECTDESCRIPTOR** data for the OLE item, retrieved in the **STGMEDIUM** structure pointed to by *lpStgMedium*. This includes information needed for the Paste Special dialog. The parameter *lpOffset* is a pointer to the offset between the position of the mouse click and the upper-left corner of the item. NULL is an acceptable value. The parameter *lpSize* is a pointer to the size of the item. It also can be NULL.

Prototype
```
//Function Prototype
void GetObjectDescriptorData(LPPOINT* lpOffset, LPSIZE* lpSize,
LPSTGMEDIUM lpStgMedium);
```

IsConnected   FUNCTION

Description This function returns TRUE if the OLE item is connected. It is considered connected if it is referenced by any containers, as indicated by the item's reference count being greater than zero. Embedded items are always considered connected.

Prototype
```
//Function Prototype
BOOL IsConnected() const;
```

IsLinkedItem   FUNCTION

Description This function determines whether an item is linked. It determines if the item is valid, and if so it examines the list of embedded items. If the item is not on the list, then it is considered linked. Just because an item is linked does not mean it is also connected. Even if your linked and embedded items are derived from the same class, **IsLinkedItem** gives you the means to handle them differently.

Prototype
```
//Function Prototype
BOOL IsLinkedItem() const;
```

NotifyChanged   FUNCTION

Description This function is called after the linked item is changed. Container items with automatic links get updated. Container applications written with the MFC library have **COleClientItem::OnChange** called. The parameter, *nDrawAspect*, determines how the item will be drawn, and can have one of the following values:

DVASPECT_CONTENT	The item is represented in a way that lets it be displayed as an embedded object inside a container.
DVASPECT_THUMBNAIL	The item is displayed as a "thumbnail" rendering that permits its display inside a browsing tool.
DVASPECT_ICON	The item is displayed as an icon.
DVASPECT_DOCPRINT	The item is displayed as if it were printed.

Prototype
```
//Function Prototype
void NotifyChanged(DVASPECT nDrawAspect =
DVASPECT_CONTENT);
```

SetItemName   FUNCTION

Description This function is used to set the name for a linked item, pointed to by *lpszItemName*, which must be unique within the document. When a linked item is to be edited in a container, the container application calls the server application. It in turn locates the item using this unique name. Embedded items don't use this function.

Prototype
```
//Function Prototype
void SetItemName(LPCTSTR lpszItemName);
```

Overridable Functions

OnDoVerb   FUNCTION

Description This function is called by the framework to execute the verb indicated by the parameter *iVerb*, which can have the following values:

OLEIVERB_PRIMARY	This is the response to a double-click on the item. What actually happens, the primary verb, is defined by the object, but for objects that support in-place activation, the action is usually to activate the object in place.
-1	This is the value for the secondary verb for an object. It has no symbol associated with it. What actually happens depends on how the object defines it, but the default handling is to treat it to be the same as OLEIVERB_OPEN.

OLEIVERB_SHOW	Shows the object to the user.
OLEIVERB_OPEN	If the object supports open editing, this causes the object to be open edited in a separate window. If open editing is not supported, it reverts to OLEIVERB_SHOW.
OLEIVERB_HIDE	The object removes its user interface from view.
OLEIVERB_UIACTIVATE	Activates the object in place and shows the interface tools.
OLEIVERB_INPLACEACTIVATE	Runs the object and installs its window, but doesn't install the user interface tools.
OLEIVERB_DISCARDUNDOSTATE	Discards the undo state, but doesn't deactivate the object.

This function is called in response to the **Activate** function of the corresponding **COleClientItem** object, if the container application is written with the MFC library. In the default implementation, if *iVerb* is **OLEIVERB_SHOW** or **OLEIVERB_PRIMARY**, the function **OnShow** gets called. If it is **OLEIVERB_HIDE**, **OnHide** gets called. If it is **OLEIVERB_OPEN** or has a value of 1, then **OnOpen** is called. Finally, if *iVerb* is any of the values other than the first five listed above, **OnShow** is called.

Prototype
```
//Function Prototype
virtual void OnDoVerb(LONG Verb);
```

OnDraw   FUNCTION

Description The framework calls this function to render the OLE item into a metafile whose representation is used to display the item in the container application. The parameter *pDC* points to the **CDC** object that gives the device context for drawing, and *rSize* references the size of the item in **HIMETRIC** units, which are 0.01 mm each (positive x goes to the right and positive y goes up). If your application is written with the MFC library, the metafile is used by the corresponding **COleClientItem** object's **Draw** function. This function returns TRUE if the item is drawn successfully, FALSE if not.

This function has no default implementation and must be overridden to draw the item into the device context given by *pDC*.

Prototype
```
//Function Prototype
virtual BOOL OnDraw(CDC* pDC, CSize& rSize) = 0;
```

OnDrawEx   FUNCTION

Description   This function gets called by the framework whenever there is drawing to be done. In the default implementation, if *nDrawAspect* is set to **DVASPECT_CONTENT**, this function calls **OnDraw** and the drawing should take place. Any other value for *nDrawAspect* requires that you override the function, otherwise it will fail. Possible values for *nDrawAspect* are as follows:

DVASPECT_CONTENT	The item is represented in a way that lets it be displayed as an embedded object inside a container.
DVASPECT_THUMBNAIL	The item is displayed as a "thumbnail" rendering that permits its display inside a browsing tool.
DVASPECT_ICON	The item is displayed as an icon.
DVASPECT_DOCPRINT	The item is displayed as if it were printed.

The parameter *pDC* points to the **CDC** object that gives the device context for drawing, and *rSize* references the size of the item in **HIMETRIC** units, which are 0.01 mm each (positive x goes to the right and positive y goes up).

The function returns TRUE if drawing is successful, otherwise it returns FALSE.

Prototype
```
//Function Prototype
virtual BOOL OnDrawEx(CDC* pDC, DVASPECT nDrawAspect,
CSize& rSize);
```

OnGetClipboardData   FUNCTION

Description   The framework calls this function in response to the **CopyToClipboard** or **DoDragDrop** functions. When called, the function gets a **COleDataSource** object with the data to be placed on the Clipboard. Its default implementation is to call **GetClipboardData**. The *bIncludeLink* parameter, if set to TRUE, indicates that link data should be copied as well. It should be FALSE if your application does not support links. *lpOffset* is a pointer to the amount of the mouse cursor's offset from the object's origin, measured in pixels. *lpSize* is a pointer to the object's size, measured in pixels. Finally, the function returns a pointer to a **COleDataSource** object containing the Clipboard data.

Prototype
```
//Function Prototype
virtual COleDataSource* OnGetClipboardData(BOOL bIncludeLink,
LPPOINT lpOffset, LPSIZE lpSize);
```

OnGetExtent — FUNCTION

Description This function, called by **COleClientItem::GetExtent** in applications written with the MFC library, retrieves the size of the item. The particular aspect whose size is requested is defined by *nDrawAspect*, which can have one of the following values:

DVASPECT_CONTENT	The item is represented in a way that lets it be displayed as an embedded object inside a container.
DVASPECT_THUMBNAIL	The item is displayed as a "thumbnail" rendering that permits its display inside a browsing tool.
DVASPECT_ICON	The item is displayed as an icon.
DVASPECT_DOCPRINT	The item is displayed as if it were printed.

The size itself is retrieved in the parameter *rSize* and is in **HIMETRIC** units, which are 0.01 mm each. The function returns TRUE if it is successful, FALSE if not.

Again, the default implementation does nothing. This function must be overridden to handle the request for a size.

Prototype
```
//Function Prototype
virtual BOOL OnGetExtent(DVASPECT nDrawAspect, CSize& rSize);
```

OnHide — FUNCTION

Description The framework calls this function to hide the OLE item. The default implementation then calls **OnShowDocument**(FALSE) to notify the container.

Prototype
```
//Function Prototype
Protected
virtual void OnHide();
END Protected
```

OnInitFromData — FUNCTION

Description This function is called to insert an object, or to replace an existing inserted object, depending on the value of *bCreation*. If *bCreation* is TRUE, the function is responding to an Insert New Object command. The OLE item is then initialized based on the contents of the **COleDataObject** object pointed to by *pDataObject*, which contains the various formats used for initialization. In the case where *bCreation* is FALSE, the function is being used to replace an existing OLE item. The function returns TRUE if successful, FALSE if not.

The default implementation actually doesn't do anything, and must be overridden to choose a proper format for initialization from *pDataObject*.

Prototype
```
//Function Prototype
virtual BOOL OnInitFromData(COleDataObject* pDataObject,
BOOL bCreation);
```

OnOpen — FUNCTION

Description This is called by the framework to display the item in a separate window instead of in place. This will be the first frame window that displays the item. If the application is a mini-server, the main window is shown. The function notifies the container once the item is open.

Prototype
```
//Function Prototype
Protected
virtual void OnShow();
END Protected
```

OnQueryUpdateItems — FUNCTION

Description The framework calls this function to find out if any linked items in the server document need updating—that is, if the source document has been changed but the linked items have not been updated. The function returns TRUE if the items need updating, FALSE if not.

Prototype
```
//Function Prototype
virtual BOOL OnQueryUpdateItems();
```

OnRenderData — FUNCTION

Description The framework uses this function to get data in the format specified by the **FORMATETC** structure pointed to by *lpFormatEtc*, and return it in the **STGMEDIUM** structure pointed to by *lpStgMedium*. The formatting data comes from a **COleDataSource** object, where it was placed by the **DelayRenderData** function or by the **DelayRenderFileData** function. By default, if the storage medium specified is a file, **OnRenderFileData** gets called. If the storage medium is memory, than **OnRenderGlobalData** gets called. If it is neither of these formats, then the default does nothing and returns zero.

If lpStgMedium->tymed is **TYMED_NULL**, use the specification in *lpForamtEtc->tymed* to allocate and fill the **STGMEDIUM** structure. If it isn't, then fill the **STGMEDIUM** structure with in-place data.

Prototype

```
//Function Prototype
virtual BOOL OnRenderData(LPFORMATETC lpFormatEtc,
LPSTGMEDIUM lpStgMedium);
```

OnRenderFileData   FUNCTION

Description When the framework needs to retrieve data within a file format, it calls this function. The format for the data is specified in the **FORMATETC** structure pointed to by *lpFormatEtc*. This formatting data comes from a **COleDataSource** object, where it was placed by the **DelayRenderData** function. The parameter *pFile* points to a **CFile** object in which the data is to be rendered. This function returns TRUE if successful, FALSE if not.

Prototype

```
//Function Prototype
virtual BOOL OnRenderFileData(LPFORMATETC lpFormatEtc, CFile*
pFile);
```

OnRenderGlobalData   FUNCTION

Description When the framework needs to retrieve data and store it in the form of global memory, it calls this function. The format for the data is specified in the **FORMATETC** structure pointed to by *lpFormatEtc*. This formatting data comes from a **COleDataSource** object, where it was placed by the **DelayRenderData** function. The parameter *phGlobal* points to a handle to global memory, if that memory has already been allocated to receive the data. The parameter may be NULL, in which case the memory must be allocated before the call is made. Be sure there is enough memory, because it cannot be reallocated to a larger size. This function returns TRUE if successful, FALSE if not.

Prototype

```
//Function Prototype
virtual BOOL OnRenderGlobalData( LPFORMATETC lpFormatEtc,
HGLOBAL* phGlobal);
```

OnSetColorScheme   FUNCTION

Description   For applications written with the MFC library, when
IOleObject::SetColorScheme gets called from the corresponding
COleClientItem object, then **OnSetColorScheme** gets called to
specify a color palette–the one pointed to by *lpLogPalette*. The
function returns TRUE if the color palette is used, FALSE if not.

Prototype
```
//Function Prototype
Protected
virtual BOOL OnSetColorScheme(const LOGPALETTE FAR*
lpLogPalette);
END Protected
```

OnSetData   FUNCTION

Description   The framework calls this function to replace the OLE item data
with the data pointed to by *pStgMedium*. The server does not take
possession of the data if the function returns FALSE. That would
mean that the data has not been successfully obtained. If the
function returns TRUE, then the data source takes ownership, and
::ReleaseStgMedium is called to free the storage medium. The
pFormateEtc parameter points to the **FORMATETC** structure that
specifies the data format. The last parameter, *bRelease*, controls
ownership of the storage medium. This determines who is responsible for releasing resources. If *bRelease* is TRUE, then the server
item takes ownership, if FALSE, then the caller keeps ownership.

    This is another function whose default implementation does
nothing, so actually replacing the OLE item's data calls for an
override.

Prototype
```
//Function Prototype
virtual BOOL OnSetData(LPFORMATETC pFormateEtc,
LPSTGMEDIUM pStgMedium, BOOL bRelease);
```

OnSetExtent   FUNCTION

Description   The default implementation sets the **m_sizeExtent** data member of
the object, setting it with the amount of space available to the item
in the container document. In applications created with the MFC
library, the function gets called by the **SetExtent** function of the
corresponding **COleClientItem** object. The aspect for which the

extent is being set is specified in *nDrawAspect*. Its possible values are set out in the previous function, **OnGetExtent**. The size itself is specified in the **CSize** structure pointed to by the parameter *size*. This function returns TRUE if successful, and FALSE if not.

Prototype

```
//Function Prototype
virtual BOOL OnSetExtent(DVASPECT nDrawAspect, const CSize&
size);
```

OnShow   FUNCTION

Description This is called by the framework to have the server application show the OLE item in place. In the default implementation, the first attempt is to open the item in place. Failing that, the function calls **OnOpen** to display the item in a separate window.

Prototype

```
//Function Prototype
Protected
virtual void OnShow();
END Protected
```

OnUpdate   FUNCTION

Description This function is called by the framework whenever the OLE item is modified. The item that modified the document is pointed to by *pSender*, which can be NULL. The parameter *lHint* can be used to provide encoded information, and the parameter *pHint* points to a **CObject**-derived object with information about the modifications. The last parameter, *nDrawAspect*, determines how the item will be drawn, and can have one of the following values:

DVASPECT_CONTENT	The item is represented in a way that lets it be displayed as an embedded object inside a container.
DVASPECT_THUMBNAIL	The item is displayed as a "thumbnail" rendering that permits its display inside a browsing tool.
DVASPECT_ICON	The item is displayed as an icon.
DVASPECT_DOCPRINT	The item is displayed as if it were printed.

Prototype

```
//Function Prototype
virtual void COleServerItem::OnUpdate(COleServerItem* pSender,
LPARAM lHint, CObject* pHint, DVASPECT nDrawAspect);
```

OnUpdateItems

FUNCTION

Description This function updates all the items in the server document. It updates all the **COleClientItem** objects with a call to **UpdateLink**.

Prototype
```
//Function Prototype
virtual void OnUpdateItems();
```

Data Member

m_sizeExtent

MEMBER

Description This is a **CSize** variable that tells the server how much of the item can be visible in the container document. The actual value is set by the **OnSetExtent** member function.

(OleStreamFile

CLASS

• •

Derivation

CObject	▼
CFile	▼
COleStreamFile	

Description An object of this class represents a data stream, as represented in an **IStream** interface. You can think of a stream like you do a file. It is a single data unit with access rights and a single seek pointer, and a **COleStreamFile** object can be manipulated just like a **CFile** object. Before you open or create a stream you must have an **IStorage** interface object, with one exception, which is if you have a memory stream. If you think of a stream as like a file, you can think of a storage object as like a directory.

Member Functions

Attach

FUNCTION

Description If you created your **COleStreamFile** object without an associated stream, you can use this function to make one. The parameter, *lpStream*, is a pointer to the stream you wish to associate with the

679

object. It cannot be NULL. Also, if the object already has a stream associated with it, you cannot use this function.

Prototype
```
//Function Prototype
void Attach(LPSTREAM lpStream);
```

COleStreamFile   FUNCTION

Description This is the constructor function, and it creates an instance of the **COleStreamFile** class. The *lpStream* parameter is a pointer to the OLE stream that you want associated with the object you are creating. If *lpStream* is NULL, then the object is not associated with a stream.

Prototype
```
//Function Prototype
COleStreamFile(LPSTREAM lpStream = NULL);
```

CreateMemoryStream   FUNCTION

Description This function safely creates a new stream out of global, shared memory even though a failure is a normal, expected condition. If you want to monitor for exceptions, than you provide a pointer to a **CFileException** object with the *pError* parameter. If the stream was created successfully, then the function returns TRUE; if not, it returns FALSE.

Prototype
```
//Function Prototype
BOOL CreateMemoryStream(CFileException* pError = NULL);
```

CreateStream   FUNCTION

Description This function creates a stream, named in the parameter *lpszName*, in a storage object supplied by the parameter *lpStrorage*, where a failure is normal and expected. *lpStorage* should never be NULL. The parameter *nOpenFiles* sets the access mode to use when opening the stream. The prototype listed below has the default values. Here is a list of all the possible values:

modeCreate	Create a new file.
modeRead	Open the file for reading only.
modeReadWrite	Open the file for reading and writing.
modeWrite	Open the file for writing only.
modeNoInherit	File cannot be inherited by child processes.
shareDenyNone	Open the file and do not deny access to reading or writing by other processes.

shareDenyRead	Open the file and deny reading access to it by other processes.
shareDenyWrite	Open the file and deny writing access to it by other processes.
shareExclusive	Open the file and deny reading and writing access to it by other processes.
shareCompat	Open the file with the compatibility mode, which allows any process on a given machine to open the file any number of times.
typeText	Set the text mode with special processing for carriage return-linefeed pairs; to be used in derived classes only.
typeBinary	Set the binary mode; to be used in derived classes only.

Finally, the parameter *pError* is a pointer to a **CFileException** object if you want to monitor exceptions, or is NULL if you don't. If the function successfully creates the stream it returns TRUE, if not it returns FALSE.

Prototype
```
//Function Prototype
BOOL CreateStream(LPSTORAGE lpStorage, LPCTSTR lpszName,
DWORD nOpenFlags =
modeReadWrite|shareExclusive|modeCreate, CFileException*
pError = NULL);
```

Detach   FUNCTION

Description Use this function to detach a stream from its associated **COleStreamFile** object. Remember that just because it is detached does not mean it is closed. It isn't, and it must be closed before the program ends. This function returns a pointer to the stream.

Prototype
```
//Function Prototype
LPSTREAM Detach();
```

OpenStream   FUNCTION

Description This function is almost the same as **CreateStream**, except it opens an existing stream instead of creating it from whole cloth, as it were. The parameter *lpStorage* points to the storage object that contains the stream you want to open. *lpszName* gives the name of the stream, and should never be NULL. The parameter *nOpenFiles* sets the access mode to use when opening the stream. The prototype listed below has the default values, and a list of all the possible values is in the description of the **CreateStream** function just above. As always, if you want to monitor exceptions, provide a pointer to a **CFileException** object for the parameter *pError*. If you are not interested in exceptions, set *pError* equal to NULL. If the function successfully opens the stream, it returns TRUE; if not, it returns FALSE.

Prototype
```
//Function Prototype
BOOL OpenStream(LPSTORAGE lpStorage, LPCTSTR lpszName,
DWORD nOpenFlags = modeReadWrite|shareExclusive,
CFileException* pError = NULL);
```

C OleTemplateServer   CLASS

Derivation

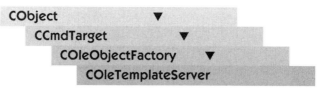

Description   The **COleTemplateServer** is used to create new documents when the request comes in from an OLE container. It does so by using information from the document template. Each document type that an application supports must have its own **COleTemplateServer** object. This class is used for OLE visual editing servers, container servers and link containers, and makes use of the **CDocTemplate** to manage server documents. You should use **COleTemplateServer** when your application is a stand-alone full server. These full servers usually support the multiple document interface, but can be single document interface.

The **COleTemplateServer** overrides **COleObjectFactory::OnCreateInstance**.

Member Functions

COleTemplateServer   FUNCTION

Description   This is the class object constructor.

Prototype
```
//Function Prototype
COleTemplateServer();
```

ConnectTemplate   FUNCTION

Description   The parameter *pDocTemplate* points to a document template. And the function **ConnectTemplate** connects this template to the underlying **COleObjectFactory** object. The parameter *clsid* is a reference to the OLE class ID that the template requests, and *bMultiInstance* indicates whether or not the application supports multiple instances.

Prototype
```
//Function Prototype
void connectTemplate(REFCLSID clsid, CDocTemplate*
pDocTemplate, BOOL bMultiInstance);
```

UpdateRegistry   FUNCTION

Description   This function takes file-type information from the document-template string and puts it in the OLE system registry. The information comes by way of a call to **CDocTemplate::GetDocString**, which retrieves three of seven substrings that are stored in the document template. These three substrings loaded are regFileTypeID, which is the document type identifier, regFileTypeName, which is the document type name, and fileNewName, which is the default name for a new document. The parameter *nAppType* identifies the type of application and can have one of the following values:

OAT_INPLACE_SERVER	This is a server with the full server interface.
OAT_SERVER	This is a server that only supports embedding.
OAT_CONTAINER	This is a container that supports links to embedded objects.
OAT_DISPATCH_OBJECT	This is an IDispatch-capable object.

The last two parameters are usually set to NULL, but they are available to register information via the **AfxOleRegisterServerClass** function. *rglpzaRegister* is an array of string pointers. These strings represent the keys and values that are added to the OLE system registry if there are no values already for those keys. *rglpszOverwrite* is similar. It is an array of pointers to strings that are keys and values to be added to the OLE system registry. The difference is that they are added if there are already values for the given keys in the registry.

This function fails if the regFileTypeID substring is empty, or if **GetDocString** fails.

Prototype

```
//Function Prototype
void UpdateRegistry(OLE_APPTYPE nAppType =
OAT_INPLACE_SERVER, LPCSTR* rglpszRegister = NULL, LPCSTR
FAR* rglpszOverwrite = NULL);
```

(OleUpdateDialog   CLASS

Derivation

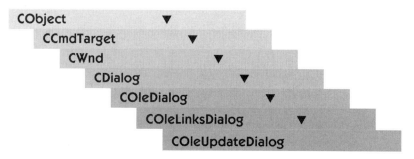

CObject
   CCmdTarget
      CWnd
         CDialog
            COleDialog
               COleLinksDialog
                  COleUpdateDialog

Description There is a special case when you need to call the Edit Links dialog box, but all the user really needs to do is update existing or embedded objects in a document. In this case, you would use the **COleUpdateDialog** class instead of the **COleLinksDialog** class. It is simpler, with only two functions: a constructor, the **COleUpdateDialog** function, and the **DoModal**, which displays the dialog box.

Member Functions

COleUpdateDialog   FUNCTION

Description This function constructs a **COleUpdateDialog** object. The parameter *pDoc* is a pointer to the document containing the links. The parameter *bUpdateLinks* is a Boolean. When set to TRUE, linked objects will be updated. Another Boolean, *bUpdateEmbeddings*, if set to TRUE determines that embedded objects will be updated. Finally, *pParentWnd* points to the window that owns the dialog box. If it is NULL, then the owner is the main application window. Remember that to actually display the dialog box, you must first construct it, then call **DoModal**.

Prototype
```
//Function Prototype
COleUpdateDialog(COleDocument* pDoc, BOOL bUpdateLinks =
TRUE, BOOL bUpdateEmbeddings = FALSE, CWnd* pParentWnd =
NULL);
```

DoModal   FUNCTION

Description This function is called to display the OLE Edit Links dialog box and is called after the object is constructed. This function returns **IDOK** if the dialog box is displayed correctly, it returns **IDCANCEL** if the user cancels the box, and returns **IDABORT** is there is an error. If the last return occurs, the **GetLastError** function from the **COleDialog** class can be used to retrieve the error code.

Prototype
```
//Function Prototype
virtual int DoModal();
```

PaintDC

Derivation

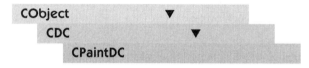

Description   The **CPaintDC** class takes most of its characteristics from the **CDC** base class. Its basic function is to prepare a DC for painting in response to a **WM_PAINT** message by calling the SDK functions **CWnd::BeginPaint** in its constructor and **CWnd::EndPaint** in its destructor. A **CPaintDC** object is typically used only in an application's **OnPaint** message-handler function, in contrast to **CClientDC** and **CWindowDC** objects, which can be used to access the window DC from other functions.

Note: You will almost never have to use a **CPaintDC** in an AppWizard-generated MFC application. You do your drawing in the **OnDraw** instead of the **OnPaint** function. Therefore, the paint DC has already been obtained and is passed as an argument to your **OnDraw** function. **CPaintDC** is for responding directly to WM_PAINT messages. As with most of the classes derived from **CDC**, it differs mainly in constructor and destructor functions.

Protected Data Members

m_hWnd   MEMBER

Description   Identifies the window for which this **CPaintDC** object is valid.

Public Data Members

m_ps   MEMBER

Description   Identifies a structure of type **PAINTSTRUCT,** which is filled in by Windows in the **CWnd::BeginPaint** of the constructor.

Member Functions

CPaintDC   FUNCTION

Description   **CPaintDC::CPaintDC** constructs a **CPaintDC** object for the application's **CWnd** object by calling **CWnd::BeginPaint**. This DC is used to access the window's client area. It encapsulates preparation for painting in the application's **OnPaint** message handler. This function is used by applications that override the **OnPaint** function of the view. The constructor throws an exception if the **::GetDC** call fails.

Prototype   Here we construct a **CPaintDC** object on the stack inside an application's **OnPaint** message handler. **OnPrepareDC** sets the mapping mode to **MM_TEXT**, which we draw a little of, and then we call the view's **OnDraw** handler, where the application's drawing is typically done. Because the DC we construct is a local object, its destructor is automatically called when it goes out of scope.

```
//Function Prototype
// CPaintDC( CWnd* pWnd )
//This is a contrived example. Its not likely you'd actually do
//drawing of this nature in the OnPaint handler
//and other drawing in the OnDraw function.
CPoint CVentanaView::OnPaint( )
{
 CPaintDC dc(this);
    //Create a CPaintDC object
 OnPrepareDC( &dc );
    //Adjust settings of the DC
 dc.TextOut(0, 0, "Just a little text...");
    //Write the string to the upper left
    //corner of the client area
 OnDraw( &dc );
    //Call the OnDraw member function for this view
}
```

~CPaintDC   FUNCTION

Description   **CPaintDC::~CPaintDC** destroys a **CPaintDC** object for the application's **CWnd** object by calling **CWnd::EndPaint,** which in turn calls **::ReleaseDC**.

Palette

Derivation

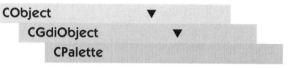

Description **CPalette** encapsulates the Windows GDI color palette. Palettes intermediate between an application and a color output device in a way designed to give the application maximum flexibility in its use of color and with a minimum effect on other applications. The Windows color-matching scheme allows each application to define a *palette,* or selection of colors, it will use in drawing. Output devices are constrained to various degrees in their capabilities to represent colors. Some can display only 16 colors, and others can display millions of colors, but even the most sophisticated devices are usually limited to a subset at any given time. Color-intensive or precise applications can therefore generate requests for colors that cannot be satisfied, so a predictable means of compromise is necessary. When Windows attempts to satisfy color requests, the greatest weight is given to the active, or *foreground,* window.

An application's logical palette is mapped to the system palette maintained by Windows in the following way: Requests for colors that are already available in the system palette are matched, and requests for new colors the device is capable of representing are added as long as space is available. When space is no longer available or the device is incapable of providing the color, the closest available system palette entry is matched to the color requested in the application's logical palette.

Member Functions

AnimatePalette   FUNCTION

Description **CPalette::AnimatePalette** provides a one-step method of updating an application's palette. The range of palette entries is copied to the logical palette attached to the **CPalette** object and is immediately mapped to the system palette. This function acts only on palette entries that have the **PC_RESERVED** flag set.

Prototype

```
//Function Prototype
//void AnimatePalette( UINT nStartIndex, UINT nNumEntries,
//        LPPALETTEENTRY lpPaletteColors );
CPalette* pNewPalette =
CPalette::FromHandle(myPalette.m_hObject));
        //We get a handle to a palette, perhaps from the Clipboard
pNewPalette->AnimatePalette( iBeginningEntry, iNumEntries,
lpPalEntries );
        //We use this quick method to replace a few colors in
        //an active palette
        //Note no call to CDC::RealizePalette required
```

CPalette   FUNCTION

Description This constructor creates an uninitialized **CPalette** object that must be initialized by the member functions of this class.

Prototype

```
//Function Prototype
//CPalette( );
CPalette thePaletteObject;
        //creates a Palette object, but it is not initialized with
        //a Palette
```

CreatePalette   FUNCTION

Description **CPalette::CreatePalette** initializes a **CPalette** object with a Windows color palette described by a **LOGPALETTE** structure. It is used with the **CPalette** constructor and **CDC** member functions that manipulate palettes. Palette entries listed in the **LOGPALETTE** structure are mapped to available system colors as closely as possible by Windows.

Prototype

```
//Function Prototype
// BOOL CreatePalette( LPLOGPALETTE lpLogPalette);

CPalette thePaletteObject;
        //creates a Palette object, but it is not initialized with
        //a Palette
thePaletteObject.CreatePalette( lpLogicalPaletteStruct );
            // initialize the Palette: the LOGPALETTE
            // *******
```

FromHandle   FUNCTION

Description   **CPalette::FromHandle** returns a pointer to a temporary **CPalette** object. The palette identified by the handle is attached to the **CPalette** object. Internally, tracking of most Windows GDI objects is done using a table of handles. The **FromHandle** family provides a quick and convenient way to package the handle temporarily in an object. MFC provides classes to wrap the handles in objects, making the member functions of the class available to act on the object identified by the handle. An object pointer returned by any of the **FromHandle** family has a life cycle of one Windows message-passing cycle. When a function that uses this call exits, the object goes out of scope and is destroyed, so don't store the pointer for later use. It will be invalid. It is not necessary for an application to destroy an object returned by **FromHandle**. This process is handled during the idle-time processing of **CWinApp**. The GDI object identified by the handle is not deleted along with the temporary object.

Prototype
```
//Function Prototype
// static CPalette* PASCAL FromHandle( HPALETTE hThePalette );
CPalette* pThePreviousCPalette;        //Save the pointer to the
                //object we are selecting
                //out of the DC; assume that we have a valid pointer
                //to a CDC object called pDC
pThePreviousCPalette = pDC->SelectObject
(CPalette::FromHandle(myPalette.m_hObject));
                //Select a new Palette that is identified by the handle
                //in the public member variable of the CGdiObject
                //base class
```

GetNearestPaletteIndex   FUNCTION

Description   **CPalette::GetNearestPaletteIndex** returns the index of the color in the current palette that most closely matches the specified color.

Prototype
```
//Function Prototype
//UINT GetNearestPaletteIndex( COLORREF crColor )const;
CPalette* pNewPalette =
CPalette::FromHandle(myPalette.m_hObject));
                //We get a handle to a palette, perhaps from the Clipboard
pNewPalette->GetNearestPaletteIndex( crTestColor);
                //Find the color in the current palette that
                //most nearly matches crTestColor
```

GetPaletteEntries · FUNCTION

Description   **CPalette::GetPaletteEntries** retrieves entries from an application's logical palette, starting at a given entry and continuing for a given range. The entries are retrieved in **PALETTEENTRY** structures, which contain values for red, green and blue color components as well as a flag that indicates how the application wants color matching to be performed.

Prototype

```
//Function Prototype
//UINT GetPaletteEntries( UINT nIndex, UINT nNumEntries,
//            LPPALETTEENTRY lpLaletteColors );
CPalette* pNewPalette =
CPalette::FromHandle(myPalette.m_hObject));
        //We get a handle to a palette, perhaps from the Clipboard
pNewPalette->GetPaletteEntries( iBeginningEntry, iNumEntries,
lpPalEntries );
        //We retrieve its entries to see whether we like the colors
        //before using them
```

ResizePalette · FUNCTION

Description   **CPalette::ResizePalette** is used to change the size of an application's logical palette. If the palette is being truncated, the entries that remain are unmodified. If the palette is enlarged, the **PALETTEENTRY** structure fields for the new entries are set to zero. This effectively makes all new entries to the color black, with their color-matching flags set to zero.

Prototype

```
//Function Prototype
//BOOL ResizePalette( UINT nNumEntries );
CPalette* pNewPalette =
CPalette::FromHandle(myPalette.m_hObject));
        //We get a handle to a palette, perhaps from the Clipboard
pNewPalette->ResizePalette( 4 );
        //This palette now has room for only four colors....
```

SetPaletteEntries · FUNCTION

Description   **CPalette::SetPaletteEntries** copies an array of palette entries into the application's logical palette. The entries are contiguous starting at the given palette index and supply new RGB values and color-matching flags for each requested color. If the logical palette to which the entries are being copied is currently selected into a device context, the palette must be *realized* before the color changes become effective. Realizing the palette triggers logical to system palette mapping and is done by a call to **CDC::RealizePalette.**

Prototype
```
//Function Prototype
//UINT SetPaletteEntries( UINT nStartIndex, UINT nNumEntries,
//        LPPALETTEENTRY lpPaletteColors );
CPalette* pNewPalette =
CPalette::FromHandle(myPalette.m_hObject));
    //We get a handle to a palette, perhaps from the Clipboard
pNewPalette->SetPaletteEntries( iBeginningEntry, iNumEntries,
lpPalEntries );
    //We set a range of entries that is critical to our app before
    //using the palette
pdc->RealizePalette();
//Make the palette change take effect in the current DC
```

Point   CLASS

Description   This class encapsulates the properties and functionality of a Windows **POINT** structure, containing an *x, y* pair. It can be used wherever a **POINT** or a POINT* would be used. **CPoint** is one of a group of classes known as *simple value* classes and is not intended to serve as a base class for user-derived classes.

Public Data Members

x   MEMBER

Description   Gives the X coordinate of the point.

y   MEMBER

Description   Gives the Y coordinate of the point.

Member Functions

CPoint

Description The **CPoint** constructors can create a point by using an *x, y* pair, an existing **POINT** structure, a **CSize** object, or a **DWORD** containing the X coordinate in the low-order word and the Y in the high-order word (handy for making a **CPoint** from an LPARAM). It can also construct an uninitialized object.

Prototype
```
//Function Prototype
CPoint ptNew( );              //Uninitialized point
CPoint ptOther( 1, 2 );       //Initialized explicitly
POINT ptStructPoint;
ptStructPoint.x = 5;
ptStructPoint.y = 15;
         //Initialized using a POINT structure
CPoint ptFromStruct( ptStructPoint );
```

Offset

Description **Offset** adds a pair of integers, a **CSize** object, a **POINT** structure or a **CPoint** to a point. It is interchangeable with the additive operators in the following table.

CPoint Operator	Usage
operator ==	Tests for equality of two CPoints.
operator !=	Tests for inequality of two CPoints.
operator +=	Moves a CPoint by a CSize.
operator -=	Moves a CPoint by a CSize.
operator +	Sums a CPoint and a CSize.
operator -	Difference between a CPoint and a CSize.

Prototype
```
//Function Prototype
CPoint ptOther( 1, 2 );       //Initialized explicitly
POINT ptStructPoint;
ptStructPoint.x = 5;
ptStructPoint.y = 15;
         //Add 5 to the x coordinate and 15 to the y coordinate
ptOther.Offset( ptStructPoint );
```

CPrintDialog

CLASS

Derivation

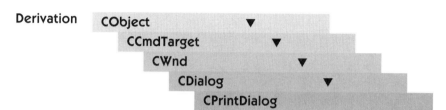

CObject
CCmdTarget
CWnd
CDialog
CPrintDialog

Description The **CPrintDialog** class encapsulates the Windows Print and Print Setup common dialog boxes. It provides services for setting print job attributes, such as number of copies and page ranges. **CPrintDialog** handles the display and management of the dialog box, including collecting data when the dialog closes. Its public member variable **m_pd** is a **PRINTDLG** structure used to pass information between the application and the framework to initialize the dialog and modify its behavior.

 m_pd includes two handles to global memory-based structures that may be used by the application. The **hDevMode** member identifies a **DEVMODE** structure, and the **hDevNames** member identifies a **DEVNAMES** structure. These handles must be freed with **GlobalFree** before the **CPrintDialog** object is destroyed, as this memory is allocated by the framework for you and failure to free it will cause a memory leak.

Public Data Members

m_pd

MEMBER

Description **m_pd** is a Windows **PRINTDLG** structure, used to pass information between the application and the **CPrintDialog** implementation. Modifying the data in **m_pd** overrides default behavior. The fields have the following names, types and meanings. The framework fills in many, if not most, of the members of this structure.

Field Name	Type	Meaning
lStructSize	DWORD	Size of the structure in bytes.
hwndOwner	HWND	Caller's window handle.
hDevMode	HGLOBAL	Global handle to a DEVMODE struct that DoModal populates.
hDevNames	HGLOBAL	Global handle to a DEVNAMES struct.
hDC	HDC	Optionally returns a handle to a device context or an information context, depending on the setting of the flags field.
Flags	DWORD	Modify display and behavior of dialog.
nFromPage	WORD	Initializes starting print page in edit control and returns starting page setting on close of dialog.
nToPage	WORD	Initializes ending print page in edit control and returns ending page setting on close of dialog.
nMinPage	WORD	Minimum starting and ending page.
nMaxPage	WORD	Maximum starting and ending page.
nCopies	WORD	Optionally used to return number of copies.
hInstance	HINSTANCE	Instance handle of .EXE that contains custom dialog template.
lCustData	LPARAM	Buffer of application-specific data passed by the operating system to the lpfnHook function.
lpfnPrintHook	LPPRINTHOOKPROC	Pointer to a function that hooks the dialog message for a Print dialog; requires the PD_ENABLEPRINTHOOK flag.
lpfnSetupHook	LPSETUPHOOKPROC	Pointer to a function that hooks the dialog message for a Print Setupdialog; requires the PD_ENABLESETUPHOOK flag.
lpPrintTemplateName	LPCSTR	Custom Print dialog template name.
lpSetupTemplateName	LPCSTR	Custom Print Setup dialog template name.
hPrintTemplate	HGLOBAL	Handle to global memory that contains custom dialog template.
hSetupTemplate	HGLOBAL	Handle to global memory that contains custom dialog template.

Following are **PRINTDLG** flags and meanings:

Flag Name	Meaning
PD_ALLPAGES	User clicked All radio button for print range.
PD_SELECTION	Set on return from DoModal if the Selection button was set.
PD_PAGENUMS	Set on return from DoModal if the Pages button was set.
PD_NOSELECTION	Disables Selection radio button.
PD_NOPAGENUMS	Disables the Pages radio button and edit control.
PD_COLLATE	User clicked Collate button.
PD_PRINTTOFILE	Print to File was selected.
PD_PRINTSETUP	Show the Print Setup dialog.
PD_NOWARNING	Prevent warning message if there is no default printer.
PD_RETURNDC	Tells the dialog to return a printer DC.
PD_RETURNIC	Tells the dialog to return a printer IC.
PD_RETURNDEFAULT	Return the DEVMODE and DEVNAME structs for the default printer without displaying the print dialog.
PD_SHOWHELP	Show the Help button.
PD_ENABLEPRINTHOOK	Enables the message stream hook function specified by lpfnPrintHook.
PD_ENABLESETUPHOOK	Enables the message stream hook function specified by lpfnSetupHook.
PD_ENABLEPRINTTEMPLATE	Allows the application to build the dialog based on a dialog template identified by m_pd.lpTemplateName.
PD_ENABLESETUPTEMPLATE	Allows the application to build the dialog based on a dialog template identified by m_pd.lpTemplateName.
PD_ENABLEPRINTTEMPLATEHANDLE	Allows the application to build the dialog based on a memory-resident dialog template identified by m_pd.hPrintTemplate.
PD_ENABLESETUPTEMPLATEHANDLE	Allows the application to build the dialog based on a memory-resident dialog template identified by m_pd.hSetupTemplate.
PD_USEDEVMODECOPIES	Uses the DEVMODE struct to set the number of copies.
PD_DISABLEPRINTTOFILE	Disables the Print to File control.
PD_HIDEPRINTTOFILE	Hides the Print to File control.
PD_NONETWORKBUTTON	Hides the Network button.

Member Functions

CPrintDialog — FUNCTION

Description   **CPrintDialog** constructs a **CPrintDialog** object, but does not show it until the **DoModal** member function is called. If the first parameter to the function is set to TRUE, only the Print Setup dialog is displayed rather than the Print dialog.

Prototype
```
//Function Prototype
//CPrintDialog(BOOL bPrintSetupOnly,
//  DWORD dwFlags =
//    PD_ALLPAGES | PD_USEDEVMODECOPIES | PD_NOPAGENUMS
//    | PD_HIDEPRINTTOFILE | PD_NOSELECTION ,
//  CWnd* pParentWnd = NULL );
    //Show the Print Dialog, not the Print Setup dialog
CPrintDialog dlgPrint(FALSE);
dlgPrint.DoModal( );
    //When DoModal returns, we can use the member functions to
    //get print info....
CString cstrDeviceName = dlgPrint.GetDeviceName( );
CString cstrPortName = dlgPrint.GetPortName( );
int iCopies = dlgPrint.GetCopies( );
int iStartPage = dlgPrint.GetFromPage( );
int iEndPage = dlgPrint.GetToPage( );
BOOL bCollate = dlgPrint.PrintCollate( );
BOOL bPrintAll = dlgPrint.PrintAll( );
```

DoModal — FUNCTION

Description   **DoModal** launches and runs a standard Print or Print Setup dialog, returning **IDOK** or **IDCANCEL** if the dialog was displayed, NULL if there was an error. *See **CPrintDialog** for a usage example.*

Prototype
```
//Function Prototype
//int CPrintDialog::DoModal();
```

GetCopies — FUNCTION

Description   **GetCopies** is called after **DoModal** returns the number of copies of the document to be printed. *See **CPrintDialog** for a usage example.*

Prototype

```
//Function Prototype
//int CPrintDialog::GetCopies() const;
```

GetDefaults   FUNCTION

Description   **GetDefaults** retrieves the default settings for the default printer without showing the dialog box. Data is copied to **m_pd**.

Prototype

```
//Function Prototype
//BOOL GetDefaults( )
    //Create the Print Dialog, not the Print Setup dialog, but don't
    //call DoModal because we don't want to show it
CPrintDialog dlgPrint(FALSE);
    //Fill in m_pd
dlgPrint.GetDefaults( );
```

GetDeviceName   FUNCTION

Description   **GetDeviceName** is called after **DoModal** returns the selected printer's name. *See **CPrintDialog** for a usage example.*

Prototype

```
//Function Prototype
//CString GetDeviceName( )const;
```

GetDevMode   FUNCTION

Description   **GetDevMode** returns a pointer to a **DEVMODE** structure, which contains information on the settings of the selected printer's device driver and environment. The returned pointer must be freed by the application with a call to **::GlobalFree**.

Prototype

```
//Function Prototype
//LPDEVMODE GetDevMode( )const;
    //Create the Print Dialog, not the Print Setup dialog
CPrintDialog dlgPrint(FALSE);
    //Fill in a DEVMODE struct for the current printer
LPDEVMODE* lpDevInfo = dlgPrint.GetDevMode( );
    //After we are done with it, free the memory it occupied, to
    //prevent a leak
::GlobalFree( (HGLOBAL) lpDevInfo );
```

Interesting random note: If you leak memory as a side effect of a GlobalAlloc, MFC's memory-leak detection diagnostics don't tell you. This is where debug Windows or Bounds Checker are great.

GetDriverName   FUNCTION

Description **GetDriverName** is called after **DoModal** returns the selected printer's device driver. *See **CPrintDialog** for a usage example.*

Prototype
```
//Function Prototype
//CString GetDriverName( )const;
```

GetFromPage   FUNCTION

Description **GetFromPage** is called after **DoModal** returns the page number of the first page in the print range. *See **CPrintDialog** for a usage example.*

Prototype
```
//Function Prototype
//int GetFromPage( )const;
```

GetPortName   FUNCTION

Description **GetPortName** is called after **DoModal** returns the name of the selected printer port. *See **CPrintDialog** for a usage example.*

Prototype
```
//Function Prototype
//CString GetPortName( )const;
```

GetPrinterDC   FUNCTION

Description **GetPrinterDC** returns a handle to the printer DC if the constructor's bPrintSetupOnly was FALSE. Use **DeleteDC** to dispose of the printer device context retrieved by this function.

Prototype
```
//Function Prototype
//HDC CPrintDialog::GetPrinterDC( ) const;
    //If we retrieve a DC for the printer like this
HDC hPrinterDC = dlgPrint.GetPrinterDC( );
if ( NULL != hPrinterDC )
{
    //Then we do something with it....
}
    //We have to delete it after we are finished
dlgPrint.DeleteDC( hPrinterDC );
```

GetToPage FUNCTION

Description **GetToPage** is called after **DoModal** returns the page number of the last page in the print range. *See **CPrintDialog** for a usage example.*

Prototype
```
//Function Prototype
//int GetToPage( )const;
```

PrintAll FUNCTION

Description **PrintAll** is called after **DoModal** returns to test whether to print all the pages in the document. *See **CPrintDialog** for a usage example.*

Prototype
```
//Function Prototype
//BOOL PrintAll( )const;
```

PrintCollate FUNCTION

Description **PrintCollate** is called after **DoModal** returns to test whether to collate copies of the document. *See **CPrintDialog** for a usage example.*

Prototype
```
//Function Prototype
//BOOL PrintCollate( )const;
```

PrintRange FUNCTION

Description **PrintRange** is called after **DoModal** returns to test whether to print a range of the pages in the document.

Prototype
```
//Function Prototype
//BOOL PrintRange( )const;
```

PrintSelection FUNCTION

Description **PrintSelection** is called after **DoModal** returns to test whether to print only the current selection of the document.

Prototype
```
//Function Prototype
//BOOL PrintSelection( )const;
```

 PrintInfo

Description **CPrintInfo** is a special-purpose class used to store information about print and print preview jobs. The **CPrintInfo** object is the vehicle of information exchange between the framework and the application view classes that do the work of printing. The framework tells the application which page to print by updating the **m_nCurPage** member variable and passing a pointer to the **CPrintInfo** object to the view's **OnPrint** handler. Your application informs the framework when the entire document has been printed by setting the **m_bContinuePrinting** member variable to FALSE.

The **CPrintInfo** object gives descriptive and status information about the print job itself, but for information about the printing environment, the application needs data stored in the **CPrintDialog** object. The **CPrintInfo** member variable **m_pPD** contains a pointer to the current job's print dialog object.

Functions That Are Passed CPrintInfo Pointers

CView::OnBeginPrinting
CView::OnEndPrinting
CView::OnEndPrintPreview
CView::OnPrepareDC
CView::OnPreparePrinting
CView::OnPrint

Public Data Members

Member Name	Meaning
m_pPD	Contains a pointer to the CPrintDialog object associated with this print job.
m_bPreview	Flag indicating whether the job is printing or previewing.
m_bContinuePrinting	Flag indicating whether the application has detected completion of the printing job; it is not necessary for the application to track completion status if the document length is set before printing starts using the SetMaxPage member function.

m_nCurPage	Page currently printing.
m_nNumPreviewPages	Tells whether we are previewing one page or two.
m_lpUserData	Pointer to a user-defined data structure.
m_rectDraw	Bounds of the printable area on a page; used by applications that override OnPrint and need page metrics to do layout.
m_strPageDesc	Format string for page number display.

Member Functions

GetFromPage   FUNCTION

Description   **GetFromPage** retrieves the page number of the first page to be printed in this job. The default value of 1 is stored in the **CPrintDialog** associated with this **CPrintInfo** object. Access the **CPrintDialog** through the pointer stored in the member variable **m_pPD**.

Prototype
```
//Function Prototypes
//UINT GetFromPage( ) const;
int iStartPage = pInfo->GetFromPage( );
```

GetMaxPage   FUNCTION

Description   **GetMaxPage** retrieves the ending page number for the document. The value is stored in the **CPrintDialog** associated with this **CPrintInfo** object. Access the **CPrintDialog** through the pointer stored in the member variable **m_pPD**. *See **SetMaxPage** for a usage example.*

Prototype
```
//Function Prototypes
//UINT GetMaxPage( ) const;
```

GetMinPage   FUNCTION

Description   **GetMinPage** retrieves the beginning page number for the document. The default value of 1 is stored in the **CPrintDialog** associated with this **CPrintInfo** object. Access the **CPrintDialog** through the pointer stored in the member variable **m_pPD**. *See **SetMaxPage** for a usage example.*

Prototype
```
//Function Prototypes
//UINT GetMinPage( ) const;
```

GetToPage   FUNCTION

Description   **GetToPage** retrieves the page number of the last page to be printed in this job. The value is stored in the **CPrintDialog** associated with this **CPrintInfo** object. Access the **CPrintDialog** through the pointer stored in the member variable **m_pPD**.

Prototype
```
//Function Prototypes
//UINT GetToPage( ) const;
int iStopPage = pInfo->GetToPage( );
```

SetMaxPage   FUNCTION

Description   **SetMaxPage** establishes the length of the document to be printed. The document length is stored in the **CPrintDialog** associated with this **CPrintInfo** object. Access the **CPrintDialog** through the pointer stored in the member variable **m_pPD**. If the length of the document can be determined in advance, call this function from the override of **OnPreparePrinting**. If you get the length from the user's entry in the print dialog, use that value stored by the print dialog, and call this function from an override of **OnBeginPrinting**. If it is not possible to determine the length of the document by either of these methods, the application must monitor the completion status of the print job and use the **m_bContinuePrinting** member datum to let the framework know when the end of the document has been reached.

Prototype
```
//Function Prototypes
//void SetMaxPage(UINT nMaxPage);
BOOL COurView::OnPreparePrinting(CPrintInfo* pInfo)
{
    //Get the page number of the document's first page
    int iFirstPage = pInfo->GetMinPage( );
    //If it is not what we expected, reset it to the constant
    if( iFirstPage != FIRST_PAGE )
    pInfo->SetMinPage( FIRST_PAGE );
    //Get the page number of the document's last page
    int iLastPage = pInfo->GetMaxPage( );
    //If it is not the same as our class member variable, reset it
    if( iLastPage != m_LastPageThisView )
    pInfo->SetMaxPage( m_LastPageThisView );
```

```
        //Set starting and ending page numbers for print job
    pInfo->SetFromPage( FIRST_PAGE );
    pInfo->SetToPage( m_LastPageThisView );
        //default preparation
    return DoPreparePrinting(pInfo);
    }
```

SetMinPage   FUNCTION

Description   **SetMinPage** establishes the first page of the document to be
included in the print job. The default value of 1 is stored in the
CPrintDialog associated with this **CPrintInfo** object. Access the
CPrintDialog through the pointer stored in the member variable
m_pPD.

Prototype   //Function Prototypes
                 //void SetMinPage(UINT nMinPage);

C PtrArray   CLASS

See **CObArray**.

C PtrList   CLASS

See **CObList**.

Recordset — **CLASS**

Derivation	**CObject** ▼
	CRecordset

Description The class **CRecordset** is used to contain and manipulate records retrieved from a **CDatabase** object. An application derives a class from **CRecordset**, then uses the **CRecordset** member functions to set access locks, select and update records, and scroll through groups of records. **CRecordset** objects can be constructed to include a "snapshot" subset of the database records or a "dynaset." A snapshot recordset queries the database one time, gathers records that meet the filtering criteria, and uses this set for all of the application's operations. A dynaset updates the copies of records held by the application whenever the user scrolls over a record that has changed. This includes changes made by other applications, as well as changes made by the application that created the recordset.

Overrides

Overridable Function Name	Triggering Event
DoFieldExchange	Data needs to be exchanged by recordset fields and data source fields.
GetDefaultConnect	A request has been made for the default connect string.
GetDefaultSQL	A request has been made for the default executable SQL string.
OnSetOptions	The options are being set on the ODBC statement.
OnWaitForDataSource	The framework is going to yield processing to asynchronous operations.

Public Data Members

m_hstmt — MEMBER

Description **m_hstmt** is a handle to the ODBC statement that defines the recordset.

m_nFields   MEMBER

Description   **m_nFields** is the number of field data members contained in the recordset.

m_nParams   MEMBER

Description   **m_nParams** is the number of parameter data members contained in the recordset.

m_strFilter   MEMBER

Description   **m_strFilter** is a string containing the SQL WHERE clause that specifies selection criteria for the recordset.

m_strSort   MEMBER

Description   **m_strSort** is a string containing the SQL ORDER BY clause that specifies how the recordset should be sorted.

Member Functions

AddNew   FUNCTION

Description   **AddNew** creates a new blank record in an opened recordset. To give value to the fields of the records, the application must explicitly assign them, then call the **Update** member function to ensure that the new record is written to the database. The new record must be written to the database before any scrolling operations or its contents will be lost. To make sure the data source can accept updates from the application, call the **CanUpdate** member function. *See **CanAppend** for a usage example.*

Prototype
```
//Function Prototype
//void AddNew( );
```

CanAppend   FUNCTION

Description   **CanAppend** tests whether the open recordset can add new records with **AddNew**.

Prototype
```
//Function Prototype
//BOOL CanAppend( )const;
    //See if the recordset allows us to add new records
```

```
if ( m_recordset.CanAppend( ) )
{
    //If so, add a new record—its fields are initially empty
m_recordset.AddNew( CRecordset::dynaset);
    //Assign values to data field members of the CRecordset object
m_NameData = "Big Bill Haywood";
    //Write the changes to the data source
m_recordset.Update( );
}
```

Cancel   FUNCTION

Description   **Cancel** halts an asynchronous operation on a data source. It is used to bail out of an operation that is waiting on an unavailable data source.

Prototype
```
//Function Prototype
//void Cancel( );
    //If the CDatabase object is waiting for an unavailable data
    //source
if( m_database.InWaitForDataSource( ) )
    //Cancel outstanding asynchronous recordset operations
 m_Recordset.Cancel( );
```

CanRestart   FUNCTION

Description   **CanRestart** tests whether or not a a recordset can restart a query using **Requery**. **Requery** refreshes a snapshot recordset after changes have been made to it. *See **Close** for a usage example.*

Prototype
```
//Function Prototype
//BOOL CanRestart( )const;
```

CanScroll   FUNCTION

Description   **CanScroll** tests whether or not a recordset can scroll its contents. *See **Close** for a usage example.*

Prototype
```
//Function Prototype
//BOOL CanScroll( )const;
```

CanTransact · FUNCTION

Description   **CanTransact** tests whether the database supports transactions. Transactions are used to guard sensitive multi-step updates so that partial completion of the steps can't corrupt the database. For example, an accounting application might wish to ensure that when a customer payment record is updated, the customer's outstanding balance record is reduced by the amount of the payment. Surrounding the receipt of the payment and the decrementing of the balance with a transaction would ensure that both steps are completed successfully before the database is updated. *See **Close** for a usage example.*

Prototype
```
//Function Prototype
//BOOL CanTransact( );
```

CanUpdate · FUNCTION

Description   **CanUpdate** tests whether the **CRecordset** object allows the application to update the data source. *See **Close** for a usage example.*

Prototype
```
//Function Prototype
//BOOL CanUpdate( )const;
```

Close · MEMBER

Description   **Close** closes a recordset and frees the memory occupied by it. If the **CRecordset** object was constructed using a NULL pointer to the **CDatabase** object, then the **CDatabase** object constructed by the framework to implement the connection to the database is destroyed at the same time.

Prototype
```
//Function Prototype
//void Close( );
    //When we are finished with the data source, close the
    //connection without destroying the CRecordset object
m_recordset.Close( );
    //Later we can reuse the CRecordset object for another
    //connection. We supply a minimum of information and let the
    //system prompt the user for details
m_recordset.Open(NULL);
    //We need to get information about the defaults for this
    //recordset...
```

```
                   //First we get the SQL string used to build the recordset
               CString stingRecsetSQL = m_recordset.GetSQL( );
                   //We get the table name if it is based on a single table
               CString stingRecsetTableName = m_recordset.GetTableName( );
                   //And we find out what services the data source supports
               BOOL bTransact = m_recordset.CanTransact( );
               BOOL bRestart= m_recordset.CanRestart( );
               BOOL bScroll = m_recordset.CanScroll( );
               BOOL bUpdate = m_recordset.CanUpdate( );
```

CRecordset   FUNCTION

Description   **CRecordset** constructs a **CRecordset** object and associates it with
a **CDatabase** object. If the **CDatabase** has not been opened, the
CRecordset constructor will attempt to open the data source. If
the pointer to the **CDatabase** is NULL, then the constructor will
create a **CDatabase** object to associate with the data source.

Prototype
```
               //Function Prototype
               //CRecordset( CDatabase* pDatabase );
                   //Construct the CRecordset object, implicitly constructing
                   //CDatabase object and opening connection to data source
               CRecordset m_recordset( NULL );
                   //Open the recordset as a dynamically updated view of the
                   //database table, accepting default access and record
                   //selection parameters
                m_recordset.Open( CRecordset::dynaset);
                   //Change the default record locking mode so that the record
                   //is locked as soon as Edit is called
               m_recordset.SetLockingMode( pessimistic );
```

Delete   FUNCTION

Description   **Delete** deletes the current record and sets its field members to
NULL. The application has to explicitly reposition with one of the
Move family of member functions after the current record is
deleted.

Prototype
```
               //Function Prototype
               //void Delete( );
                   //Move to the 10th record—record indices are zero based
               m_Recordset.Move( 9 );
                   //Delete the record
```

```
m_Recordset.Delete( );
    //Now move off the deleted record, positioning to the end of
    //the recordset
m_Recordset.MoveLast( );
```

Edit   FUNCTION

Description **Edit** is used to modify the field values of the current record, which must exist. The changes made to the record by **Edit** are not written to the database until the **Update** member function is called.

Prototype
```
//Function Prototype
//void Edit( );
    //Move to the 10th record—record indices are zero based
m_Recordset.Move( 9 );
    //Fill the CRecordset current record buffer and data field
    //members
m_Recordset.Edit( );
    //Change values of data field members
m_NameData = "Flaco Jimenez";
    //Write the changes to the data source
m_Recordset.Update( );
```

GetRecordCount   FUNCTION

Description **GetRecordCount** returns the highest numbered record the user has moved across. This means that it does not report the actual size of a recordset until it has been scrolled past its end. Also, it does not account for records added with **AddNew** or removed with **Delete**. To get an accurate count, the application has to loop over the records using one of the **Move** family of functions. **MoveLast** *does not* update the record count.

Prototype
```
//Function Prototype
//LONG GetRecordCount ( )const
    //Move to the first record
m_Recordset.MoveFirst( );
    //If the recordset has any records, we should now be
    //positioned at the first one;
    //Is BOF returns 0 on the first record
if ( ! m_Recordset.IsBOF( ) )
{
    //Now loop over all the records of the set
```

```
while( ! m_Recordset.IsEOF( ) )
{
m_Recordset.MoveNext( ):
}
    //Since we have visited all the records, we can get the count
long lNumberRecs = m_Recordset.GetRecordCount( );
```

GetSQL   FUNCTION

Description   **GetSQL** returns a constant reference to the SQL SELECT statement used to build the recordset. *See **Close** for a usage example.*

Prototype
```
//Function Prototype
//const CString& GetSQL( )const;
```

GetStatus   FUNCTION

Description   **GetStatus** fills in a **CRecordsetStatus** object. The fields and their meanings are shown in the table below.

CRecordsetStatus Field Name	Type	Meaning
m_lCurrentRecord	long	Current record index, or -1 if indeterminate.
m_bRecordCountFinal	BOOL	If the records have been navigated to EOF using MoveNext, then it contains an accurate record count.

Prototype
```
//Function Prototype
//void GetStatus( CRecordsetStatus &recStatus )const;
    //Create a CRecordsetStatus object
CRecordsetStatus recStatus;
    //See if the record count is accurate
m_Recordset.GetStatus( );
if( recStatus.m_bRecordCountFinal )
{
    //If we trust the count we can get it
 long lNumberRecs = m_Recordset.GetRecordCount( );
}
```

GetTableName — FUNCTION

Description   **GetTableName** returns the table name that was specified in the SQL string that built the recordset. The name is invalid if the query was based on joined tables. *See Close for a usage example.*

Prototype
```
//Function Prototype
//const CString& GetTableName( )const;
```

IsBOF — FUNCTION

Description   **IsBOF** tests whether or not a **CRecordset** object is currently positioned at the beginning of the recordset. At the first record it returns 0, and before or after the first record it returns non zero. *See GetRecordCount for a usage example.*

Prototype
```
//Function Prototype
//BOOL IsBOF( )const;
```

IsDeleted — FUNCTION

Description   **IsDeleted** tests whether or not the current record has been deleted. Recordset operations can't be performed on records marked as deleted.

Prototype
```
//Function Prototype
//BOOL IsDeleted( )const;
    //If the record is deleted
if( m_Recordset.IsDeleted( ) )
{
    //Then we need to explicitly move off of it—so we position to
    //mmm CRecordSet::Open the previous record
    m_Recordset.MovePrev( );
}
```

IsEOF — FUNCTION

Description   **IsEOF** tests whether or not a **CRecordset** object is currently positioned at the end of the recordset. At the last record it returns 0, and before or after the first record it returns non-zero. *See GetRecordCount for a usage example.*

Prototype
```
//Function Prototype
//BOOL IsEOF( )const;
```

IsFieldDirty — FUNCTION

Description **IsFieldDirty** tests whether the data field member specified by the pointer has changed since the recordset was built. The next call to **Update** writes out all changed fields to the database, so resetting the "dirty" flag effectively rolls back a change made to a field.

Prototype
```
//Function Prototype
//BOOL IsFieldDirty(void* pv);
    //Has the field been modified?
if( m_Recordset.IsFieldDirty( &m_NameData ) )
{
    //Reset the modified flag, which effectively rolls back
    //the changes for this one field
m_Recordset.SetFieldDirty( &m_NameData, FALSE );
}
```

IsFieldNull — FUNCTION

Description **IsFieldNull** tests whether the data field member specified by the pointer is empty.

Prototype
```
//Function Prototype
//BOOL IsFieldNull(void* pv);
    //If the name field is not null and it is allowed to be Null
if( !m_Recordset.IsFieldNull( &m_NameData ) &&
m_Recordset.IsFieldNullable( &m_NameData,))
{
    //If so, empty the field
m_Recordset.SetFieldNull( &m_NameData, FALSE );
}
```

IsFieldNullable — FUNCTION

Description **IsFieldNullable** tests whether the data field member specified by the pointer is allowed to be empty. *See **IsFieldNull** for a usage example.*

Prototype
```
//Function Prototype
//BOOL IsFieldNullable(void* pv);
```

IsOpen   FUNCTION

Description   **IsOpen** tests whether or not a **CRecordset** object is currently connected to a data source. *See **Open** for a usage example.*

Prototype
```
//Function Prototype
//BOOL IsOpen( )const;
    //If the recordset is open
if( m_Recordset.IsOpen( ) )
{
    //Refresh the view of the recordset so that it reflects any
    //changes
    m_Recordset.Requery( );
}
```

Move   FUNCTION

Description   **Move** moves the specified number of records (or rows) in the database table. To move toward the end of the file, use a positive number for **lRows**. Moving off a record that has not been **Updated** after it was added with **AddNew** or changed with **Edit** will lose the changes. **Move** will throw an exception for moves in empty recordsets, or moves that attempt to position before or after the first and last records. *See **Delete** for a usage example.*

Prototype
```
//Function Prototype
//void Move(long lRows);
```

MoveFirst   FUNCTION

Description   **MoveFirst** positions to the first record in the recordset, and throws an exception if the recordset is empty. *See **GetRecordCount** for a usage example.*

Prototype
```
//Function Prototype
//void MoveFirst( );
```

MoveLast   FUNCTION

Description   **MoveLast** positions to the last record in the recordset, and throws an exception if the recordset is empty. *See **Delete** for a usage example.*

Prototype

```
//Function Prototype
//void MoveLast( );
```

MoveNext — FUNCTION

Description   **MoveNext** positions to the next record in the recordset, and throws an exception if the recordset is empty or the current record is the last in the set. *See **GetRecordCount** for a usage example.*

Prototype

```
//Function Prototype
//void MoveNext( );
```

MovePrev — FUNCTION

Description   **MovePrev** positions to the previous record in the recordset, and throws an exception if the recordset is empty or the current record is the first in the set. *See **IsDeleted** for a usage example.*

Prototype

```
//Function Prototype
//void MovePrev( );
```

Open — FUNCTION

Description   **Open** initializes a **CRecordset** object and populates it with records. The way in which the recordset is built depends on the parameters passed to Open. A NULL parameter creates both a **CDatabase** object and a **CRecordset** object, and initializes the connection to the data source for the **CDatabase** object. A pointer to the **CDatabase** object uses the existing **CDatabase** object and opens the data source if necessary. The record set is built with the default SQL select logic. The application may specify the type of record set to be opened with one of the following **OpenType** parameters:

Open Type	Resulting Recordset
dynaset	Dynamically updated record set with bi-directional scrolling.
snapshot	A static recordset with bi-directional scrolling.
forwardonly	Read-only dynamically updated record set with bidirectional scrolling.

The application may optionally provide the SQL string that will be used to select and sort the records into the recordset. This string is passed in the **lpszSQL** parameter, but is not required. The

dwOptions parameter sets read/write options for the recordset and can have one of the following values.

Access Option	Meaning
defaultoptions	The records can be modified with Edit, Delete and AddNew.
appendonly	The records can not be modified with Edit or Delete, but they can be appended with AddNew.
readonly	Read-only access to the recordset.

*See **CRecordset** for a usage example.*

Prototype

```
//Function Prototype
BOOL Open(UINT nOpenType = snapshot ,
    LPCSTR lpszSQL = NULL , DWORD dwOptions = none );
    //We have a CRecordset object, and want to know if it is open
```

Requery   FUNCTION

Description **Requery** refreshes the record view of a static recordset, displaying changes made to the data source since the application first built the recordset. This is only necessary for "snapshot" recordsets. *See **IsOpen** for a usage example.*

Prototype

```
//Function Prototype
//BOOL Requery( );
```

SetDirtyField   FUNCTION

Description **SetDirtyField** sets the modified flag for a data field member. The next call to **Update** writes out all changed fields to the database, so resetting the "dirty" flag effectively rolls back a change made to a field. *See **IsFieldDirty** for a usage example.*

Prototype

```
//Function Prototype
//void SetFieldDirty(void* pv, BOOL bDirty);
```

SetFieldNull   FUNCTION

Description **SetFieldNull** sets the data field member specified by the pointer as empty. *See **IsFieldNull** for a usage example.*

Prototype

```
//Function Prototype
//void SetFieldNull(void* pv, BOOL bNull);
```

SetLockingMode   FUNCTION

Description   **SetLockingMode** determines when record locking will take place for updates. Use the value optimistic to set the record lock only during the call to **Update**. Use the value pessimistic to set the record lock from when Edit is called to when **Update** is called. *See CRecordset for a usage example.*

Prototype
```
//Function Prototype
//void SetLockingMode(UINT nLockMode);
```

Update   FUNCTION

Description   **Update** writes the changes to **CRecordset** data field members to the data source record. Changes made with either **AddNew** or **Edit** are not permanent until **Update** is called. *See CanAppend for a usage example.*

Prototype
```
//Function Prototype
//BOOL Update( );
```

CRecordView   CLASS

Derivation

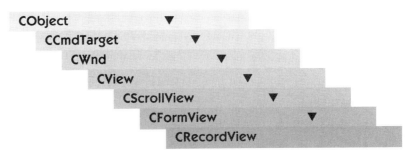

CObject ▼
CCmdTarget ▼
CWnd ▼
CView ▼
CScrollView ▼
CFormView ▼
CRecordView

Description   **CRecordView** is a base class for user-derived form classes that are attached to recordsets. It provides the capability of developing a dialog resource-based record view that takes advantage of **DDX** and **RFX** for moving data between the form and the recordset, and automatically handles field and record navigation. **CRecordView** objects can easily be developed using the Visual C++ tools and choosing ODBC support options when generating skeleton application code. It is possible to associate more than one recordset object

717

with a single **CRecordView**. For example, a list box control may be associated with a different recordset than the set of edit controls displayed by the record view form. This is almost always made easier by using the Wizards.

Overrides

Overridable Function Name	Triggering Event
OnGetRecordSet	The application is requesting a pointer to the recordset associated with the CRecordView object.
OnMove	The user is moving to a new record, and the framework is updating the current record position.

Member Functions

CRecordView   FUNCTION

Description   **CRecordView** constructs a dialog-based form view of a recordset. This function is always overridden by user applications, but it should be called in the application's record view constructor argument list. The dialog template used to construct the record view can be identified by either its resource name or resource ID.

Prototype
```
//Function Prototypes
//CRecordView ( LPCSTR lpszDialogTemplate );
//CRecordView ( UINT uiIDDialogTemplate );
    //We call the base class constructor and then do application-
    //specific construction tasks, like initializing data members
CThisRecordView::CRecordView( ) :
CRecordView(CThisRecordView::IDD)
{
    //Class Wizard creates and maintains this initialization
    //processing
    //{{AFX_DATA_INIT(CThisFormView)
    m_strDate = "";
    m_strTime = "";
    m_strName = "";
    //}}AFX_DATA_INIT
}
```

IsFirstRecord   FUNCTION

Description   **IsFirstRecord** tests whether the current record is the first record
in the recordset. The framework automatically handles record
navigation in the record view, so this function is used only when
applications customize movement across records.

Prototype
```
//Function Prototype
//BOOL CRecordView::IsFirstRecord( );
```

IsLastRecord   FUNCTION

Description   **IsLastRecord** tests whether the current record is the last record in
the recordset. Approach this function with the knowledge that it
can behave properly only if the user has moved *beyond* the last
record in the set at least once. This is not an MFC-imposed limita-
tion. It is a side-effect of the way scrollable cursors work and, in
particular, the way ODBC supports them. The framework automatically handles record navigation in the record view, so this function
is used only when applications customize movement across
records.

Prototype
```
//Function Prototype
//BOOL CRecordView::IsLastRecord( );
```

CRect   CLASS

Description   The **CRect** class provides a substitute for the rectangle-creation,
-comparison and -manipulation functions of the Windows SDK. The
class is derived from the **RECT** structure, and objects are limited in
dimension by the 32k X and Y maximum extents of the Windows
logical coordinate space. Some **CRect** member functions are
sensitive to the orientation of coordinate system axes.
IntersectRect, **UnionRect** and **PtInRect** all expect that the upper
left corner of the rectangle will be higher in the coordinate system
than the lower right corner.

　　As a general rule, you can use a **CRect** wherever you can use a
RECT structure.

Data Members

bottom   MEMBER

Description This member gives the Y coordinate of the lower right corner of the rectangle.

left   MEMBER

Description This member gives the X coordinate of the upper left corner of the rectangle.

right   MEMBER

Description This member gives the X coordinate of the lower right corner of the rectangle.

top   MEMBER

Description This member gives the Y coordinate of the upper left corner of the rectangle.

Member Functions

BottomRight   FUNCTION

Description **BottomRight** returns a reference to the lower right corner of the **CRect.**

Prototype
```
//Function Prototype
//CPoint& BottomRight ( );
CRect rectWideAndTall( 100, 100, 350, 250 );
    //Get the coordinates of the lower right corner
CPoint ptUpperLeft = rectWideAndTall.BottomRight( );
    //Change the coordinates....
rectWideAndTall.BottomRight( ) = ptNewCoords;
```

CopyRect   FUNCTION

Description **CopyRect** copies the coordinates of a **RECT** structure or **CRect** object to another **CRect** object.

Prototype
```
//Function Prototype
//void CopyRect( LPCRECT rectToCopy )
CRect rectNew;
CRect rectOther( 100, 100, 350, 250 );
    //Copies coordinate values to rectNew
rectNew.CopyRect( rectOther);
```

CRect   FUNCTION

Description The **CRect** constructors can create an object from a **RECT** data structure, a pointer to a **RECT** structure, explicit coordinate values, an upper left corner POINT, and a SIZE offset from the point, or they can simply create an uninitialized object.

Prototype
```
//Function Prototype
    //Create an uninitialized CRect
CRect rectEmpty;
    //Create an object with coordinates for corners at 100,100 and
    //350,250
CRect rectWideAndTall( 100, 100, 350, 250 );
    //Create from an existing object
CRect rectLikeAnother( LPCRECT rectWideAndTall );
    //Create from a corner point and side length
CPoint ptUpperLeft( 10, 25 );
CSize sizeSide( 125 );
CRect rectCornerAndSide( ptUpperLeft, sizeSide );
```

EqualRect   FUNCTION

Description **EqualRect** tests whether two **CRects** have the same upper left and lower right corner coordinates.

Prototype
```
//Function Prototype
//BOOL EqualRect( LPCRECT rectCompare)const;
    //Two rectangles with identical position and size....
CRect rectFirst( 100, 100, 350, 450 );
CRect rectSecond( rectFirst );
if( rectFirst.EqualRect( rectSecond ) )
 {
    //This test evaluates TRUE because corner coordinates match
 }
```

Height   FUNCTION

Description   **Height** returns the difference between the bottom and top data members of the **CRect**. Because this function is sensitive to the mapping mode and orientation of coordinate system axes, it can return a negative value for height.

Prototype
```
//Function Prototype
//int Height ( ) const;
CRect rectWideAndTall( 100, 100, 350, 250 );
    //iHeight is 350 - 100
int iHeight = rectWideAndTall.Height( );
```

InflateRect   FUNCTION

Description   **InflateRect** adds a signed value to each of the X and Y coordinates of the **CRect** corners. Because the inflation amount is added to both sets of coordinates, the rectangle's dimensions are changed by two times the amount of the X and Y increments passed to the function.

Prototype
```
//Function Prototype
//void InflateRect( int iXChange, int iYChange );
//void InflateRect( CSize sizeChange );
CRect rectOther( 100, 100, 350, 250 );
    //New dimensions will be 260 by 180
rectNew.InflateRect( 5, 15 );
```

IntersectRect   FUNCTION

Description   **IntersectRect** returns a **CRect** that represents the common area of two **CRects**.

Prototype
```
//Function Prototype
//BOOL IntersectRect ( LPCRECT rectFirst, LPCRECT rectSecond );
CRect rectIntersection;
CRect rectFirst( 0, 0, 350, 250 );
CRect rectSecond( 0, 100, 450, 250 );
    //New corners are 0,100 and 350, 250....
rectIntersection.IntersectRect( rectFirst, rectSecond)
```

IsRectEmpty   FUNCTION

Description   **IsRectEmpty** tests to see whether height or width dimensions are zero or less, and returns TRUE if they are.

Prototype
```
//Function Prototype
//BOOL IsRectEmpty( )const;
    //Width is -50
CRect rectEmpty( 100, 100, 350, 50 );
if( rectEmpty.IsRectEmpty( ) )
{
    //This test evaluates TRUE because width is equal or less than 0
}
```

IsRectNull   FUNCTION

Description   **IsRectNull** tests to see whether both height and width dimensions are zero, and returns TRUE if they are.

Prototype
```
//Function Prototype
//BOOL IsRectEmpty( )const;
    //Width is -50
CRect rectEmpty( 100, 100, 350, 50 );
if( rectEmpty.IsRectNull( ) )
{
    //This test evaluates FALSE because width is equal to or less
    //than 0, but height is greater than 0
}
```

NormalizeRect   FUNCTION

Description   Swaps the top and bottom values and/or the left and right values of the **CRect** object when necessary to ensure that both the height and width are positive. This is known as *normalizing* the **CRect** object. Some functions, such as **IntersectRect** and **UnionRect**, accept only normalized **CRect** objects. **NormalizeRect** comes in handy when working with different mapping modes and inverted rectangles.

Prototype
```
//Function Prototype
//void NormalizeRect( );
```

OffsetRect
FUNCTION

Description **OffSetRect** moves a **CRect** by the specified amount in the X and Y direction.

Prototype
```
//Function Prototype
//void OffsetRect( int iXMove, int iYMove );
//void OffsetRect( POINT ptMove);
//void OffsetRect( CSize sizeMove );
CRect rectOther( 100, 100, 350, 250 );
    //New location is left = 200, top = 50
rectNew.OffsetRect( 100, -50 );
```

PtInRect
FUNCTION

Description **PtInRect** tests whether a point falls inside a **CRect**. By definition, a point in the interior or on either the top or left side is considered to be in the rectangle, and a point that falls on the bottom or right side is considered to be outside the rectangle.

Prototype
```
//Function Prototype
//BOOL PtInRect( POINT ptTest)const;

CRect rectPointTest( 100, 100, 350, 450 );
CPoint ptTheSpot( 225, 450 )
if( rectPointTest.PtInRect( ptTheSpot ) )
{
    //This test evaluates FALSE because the point falls on the right
    //side of the CRect
}
```

SetRect
FUNCTION

Description **SetRect** explicitly sets the dimensions of the rectangle.

Prototype
```
//Function Prototype
//void SetRect( int iLeft, int iTop, int iRight, int iBottom );
    //Create an uninitialized CRect
CRect rectNew;
    //Sets coordinates for corners at 100,100 and 350,250
rectNew.SetRect( 100, 100, 350, 250 );
```

SetRectEmpty   FUNCTION

Description **SetRectEmpty** sets all coordinates to zero, creating a NULL rectangle.

Prototype
```
//Function Prototype
//void SetRectEmpty
    //Create an uninitialized CRect
CRect rectNew;
    //Set its coordinates to zero
rectNew.SetRectEmpty( );
```

Size   FUNCTION

Description **Size** returns the difference between the height and width of the
CRect in a **CSize** object. Because this function is sensitive to the
mapping mode and orientation of coordinate system axes, it can
return negative values for height and width.

Prototype
```
//Function Prototype
//CSize Size ( ) const;
CRect rectWideAndTall( 100, 100, 350, 250 );
    //Height and Width in the returned object
CSize sizeDimensions = rectWideAndTall.Height( );
```

SubtractRect   FUNCTION

Description **SubtractRect** subtracts the area of one **CRect** from another,
subject to the following constraints. The rectangle that serves as
the subtraction template must completely overlap some portion of
the rectangle being reduced from top to bottom or from side to
side. The subtraction can't be completed unless the result will still
be a rectangle, and the return value specifies whether the attempt
was successful.

Prototype
```
//Function Prototype
//BOOL SubtractRect ( LPCRECT rectReduce, LPCRECT
//rectTakeAway );
CRect rectReduce( 0, 0, 350, 250 );
CRect rectTakeAway1( 0, 100, 450, 250 );
CRect rectTakeAway2( 125, 100, 350, 250 );
```

```
    //This subtraction fails
rectReduce.SubtractRect( rectReduce, rectTakeAway2 );
    //This subtraction takes place
rectReduce.SubtractRect( rectReduce, rectTakeAway1 );
```

TopLeft   FUNCTION

Description **TopLeft** returns a reference to the upper left corner of the **CRect**.

Prototype
```
//Function Prototype
//CPoint& TopLeft ( );
CRect rectWideAndTall( 100, 100, 350, 250 );
    //Get the coordinates of the upper left corner
CPoint ptUpperLeft = rectWideAndTall.TopLeft( );
    //Change the coordinates....
rectWideAndTall.TopLeft( ) = ptNewCoords;
```

UnionRect   FUNCTION

Description **UnionRect** returns a **CRect** that represents the smallest bounding rectangle enclosing two **CRects**.

Prototype
```
//Function Prototype
//BOOL UnionRect ( LPCRECT rectFirst, LPCRECT rectSecond );
CRect rectUnion;
CRect rectFirst( 0, 0, 350, 250 );
CRect rectSecond( 0, 100, 450, 250 );
    //New corners are 0,0 and 450, 250....
rectUnion.UnionRect( rectFirst, rectSecond )
```

Width   FUNCTION

Description **Width** returns the difference between the right and left data members of the **CRect**. Because this function is sensitive to the mapping mode and orientation of coordinate system axes, it can return a negative value for width.

Prototype
```
//Function Prototype
//int Width ( ) const;
CRect rectWideAndTall( 100, 100, 350, 250 );
    //iWidth is 250 - 100
int iWidth = rectWideAndTall.Width( );
```

Operators

CRect Operators	Usage
operator LPRECT	Casts a constant CRect to a long pointer to a RECT.
operator LPCRECT	Casts a CRect to a long pointer to a CRect.
operator =	Assigns the coordinates of a RECT or CRect to a CRect.
operator ==	Tests for equality of a CRect and a RECT or CRect.
operator !=	Tests for inequality of a CRect and a RECT or CRect.
operator +=	Moves a CRect by the amount specified by a POINT.
operator -=	Moves a CRect by the amount specified by a POINT.
operator +	Returns a CRect equal to a CRect offset by a POINT.
operator -	Returns a CRect equal to a CRect offset by a POINT.
operator &	Returns a CRect equal to the intersection of two CRects.
operator |	Returns a CRect equal to the smallest bounding rectangle enclosing two CRects.
operator &=	Intersects two CRects.
operator |=	Union of two CRects.

C ResourceException CLASS

Derivation

CObject ▼
  CException ▼
    CResourceException

Description   The **CResourceException** class provides an object that signals a request to load or use an unavailable resource. It has no function or public data members and does not provide the user or the programmer with many meaningful opportunities to recover.

It could be useful in one of those cases where you pop up a message box to notify the user of some potentially correctable situation like low memory—for example, when you try to create a **CBrush** or **CPen**, or get a DC when none are available. As Windows has only so many DCs, if another app is closed or if another window in the current app is closed, then the operation might might succeed. The same sort of thing is true with the GDI objects. If you close another app, some space is freed on the GDI heap and the operation might succeed.

CResourceException FUNCTION

Description **CResourceException** constructs an object of this type. This function is never called directly. Instead, the global function **AfxThrowResourceException** is used.

Prototype
```
// Function Prototype
//We ask to create a solid brush and if the request fails...
OurBrush = ::CreateSolidBrush(clrCtlBk);
if (OurBrush == NULL)
    //We throw a resource exception
    AfxThrowResourceException();
```

 Rgn CLASS

Derivation

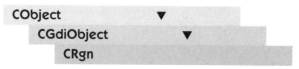

CObject ▼
   CGdiObject ▼
      CRgn

Description **CRgn** encapsulates the Windows GDI Rgn. A *region* is an area that is either an ellipse or a polygon and is used with painting and clipping member functions of the **CDC** class. Regions, like other GDI objects, are selected into the current DC for use. When the application is finished using them, they must be selected out of the DC and discarded. Regions, like bitmaps, must be explicitly defined by applications that want to use them; there is no such thing as a "default region," nor is there a pool of stock regions that can be supplied by Windows.

    The actual GDI region is limited in size and detail by the maximum dimensions of the coordinate space (32k in both x and y directions) or to 64k of data space, whichever is less.

Member Functions

CombineRgn

Description **CRgn::CombineRgn** does a Boolean combination of the areas of two regions, and the result replaces the region currently stored in the object. The two regions may be combined as shown in this table:

Region Combination Mode	Result
RGN_AND	The intersection of the two regions is preserved.
RGN_COPY	Uses only the region identified by the first parameter.
RGN_DIFF	Uses the parts of the first region that do not intersect the second region.
RGN_OR	Uses the union of the two regions.
RGN_XOR	Uses non-intersecting parts of both regions.

Prototype
```
//Function Prototype
// int CombineRgn( CRgn* pFirstRegion, CRgn* pSecondRegion, int
//COMBINATION );
CRgn BlueWater;
    //We create the regions to combine ....
CRgn* pFirstRegion = new CRgn;
CRgn* pSecondRegion = new CRgn;
    //Then initialize them with polygonal areas that will use the
    //default fill method....
pFirstRegionCreatePolygonalRegion( lpLakeOutline, iNumberPoints,
WINDING );
pSecondRegionCreatePolygonalRegion( lpIsleOutline,
iNumberPoints, WINDING );
    //Now combine them to get the region of the lake less the
    //island....
BlueWater.CombineRegion( pFirstRegion, pSecondRegion, RGN_DIFF
);
```

CopyRgn

Description **CopyRgn** copies an existing region to a **CRgn** object and replaces any previous region. Functionally, it is the same as using the **CombineRgn** function with the **RGN_COPY** combine method.

Prototype
```
//Function Prototype
// int CopyRgn( CRgn* pNewRegion );
    //We create a region object....
CRgn RegionObject;
    //and replace the region attached to it
RegionObject.CopyRegion( pReplaceRegion );
```

CreateEllipticRgn   FUNCTION

Description   **CreateEllipticRgn** creates an elliptical region bounded by a rectangle in the logical coordinate space specified by its parameters. The parameters define the upper left and lower right corners of a bounding rectangle. (A circle is a special case of an ellipse, so this function may be used to create circular regions.)

Prototype
```
//Function Prototype
//BOOL CreateEllipticRgn( int iULXCoordinate,int iULYCoordinate,
//          int iLRXCoordinate,int iLRYCoordinate);
    //Create a region object....
CRgn rgnClientEllipse;
    //Then initialize it with an ellipse bounded by the application's
    //client area....
rgnClientEllipse.CreateEllipticRgn( rClientArea.left, rClientArea.top,
                rClientArea.right, rClientArea.bottom, );
```

CreateEllipticRgnIndirect   FUNCTION

Description   **CreateEllipticRgnIndirect** creates an elliptical region bounded by a rectangle in the logical coordinate space specified by its parameter. This function is identical to **CreateEllipticRgn,** except that its parameter is a pointer to a **RECT** structure rather than a pair of coordinates for the corner of the bounding rectangle. (A circle is a special case of an ellipse, so this function may be used to create circular regions.)

Prototype
```
//Function Prototype
//BOOL CreateEllipticRgnIndirect(LPRECT lprBoundingRect);
    //Create a region object....
CRgn rgnClientEllipse;
    //Create a rect object to hold client area dimensions
CRect rClientRect;
GetClientRect(&rClientRect);
```

```
//Initialize the CRgn object with an ellipse bounded by the
//application's client area....
rgnClientEllipse.CreateEllipticRgnIndirect( &rClientRect );
```

CreatePolygonRgn — FUNCTION

Description   **CreatePolygonRgn** creates a series of polygonal regions defined by an array of **CPoint** objects that lists their vertices. If the list of vertices does not specify a closed figure (the first and last vertices in the list are identical for a closed figure), Windows closes the polygon by connecting the first and last vertices. The last parameter to the function defines the *filling mode* for the polygon. The two filling mode flags, **ALTERNATE** and **WINDING**, identify alternative methods of painting the interior of the polygon. The choice is seldom critical.

Prototype
```
//Function Prototype
//BOOL CreatePolygonRgn(LPPOINT lpPolygonVertices, int
//iNumberPoints,
//           int FILL_MODE );
    //Create a region object....
CRgn rgnPolygonRgn;
    //Initialize the CRgn object with a polygonal region defined by
    //an array of vertices....
rgnPolygonRegion.CreatePolygonRgn( lpPolygonVertices,
iNumberPoints,WINDING );
```

CreatePolyPolygonRgn — FUNCTION

Description   **CreatePolyPolygonRgn** creates a series of polygonal regions defined by an array of **CPoint** objects that lists their vertices. The vertices *must* specify closed figures. The polygons are collectively attached to the **CRgn** object and define its GDI region. The individual polygons may overlap or be entirely disjoint. The last parameter to the function defines the *filling mode* for the polygon. The two filling mode flags, **ALTERNATE** and **WINDING**, identify alternative methods of painting the interior of the polygon. The choice is seldom critical.

Prototype
```
//Function Prototype
//BOOL CreatePolyPolygonRgn(LPPOINT lpPolygonVertices,
//LPINT lpPolyCountArray,
//           int iSizePolyCountArray, int iNumberPoints,
//           int FILL_MODE );
```

731

```
//Create a region object....
CRgn rgnPolyPolygonRgn;
    //Initialize the CRgn object with multiple polygonal regions
    //all of whose vertices are stored in the array
    //lpPolygonVertices;
    //The next arg is an array of integers—each entry gives the
    //mmm CRgn::CreateEllipticRgnIndirect number of vertices
    //belonging to a particular polygon
    //The third arg gives the size of the polygon vertex count array;
    //The last arg gives the polygon fill mode....
rgnPolygonRegion.CreatePolygonRgn( pPolygonVertices,
lpPolyVertexCountArray,
            iSizePolyCountArray, iNumberPoints,WINDING );
```

CreateRectRgn   FUNCTION

Description **CreateRectRgn** creates a rectangular region defined by a rectangle in the logical coordinate space specified by its parameters. The parameters define the upper left and lower right corners of the rectangle. (A square is a special case of a rectangle, so this function may be used to create square regions.)

Prototype
```
//Function Prototype
//BOOL CreateRectRgn( int iULXCoordinate,int iULYCoordinate,
//          int iLRXCoordinate,int iLRYCoordinate);
    //Create a region object....
CRgn rgnClientRect;
    //Then initialize it with a rectangle equal to the application's
    //client area....
rgnClientRect.CreateRectRgn( rClientArea.left, rClientArea.top,
            rClientArea.right, rClientArea.bottom, );
```

CreateRectRgnIndirect   FUNCTION

Description **CreateRectRgnIndirect** creates a rectangular region defined by a rectangle in the logical coordinate space specified by its parameters. This function is identical to **CreateRectRgn,** except that its parameter is a pointer to a **RECT** structure rather than a pair of coordinates for the corners of the bounding rectangle. (A square is a special case of a rectangle, so this function may be used to create square regions.)

Prototype

```
//Function Prototype
//BOOL CreateRectRgnIndirect(LPRECT lprBoundingRect);
    //Create a region object....
CRgn rgnClientRect;
    //Create a rect object to hold client area dimensions
CRect rClientRect;
GetClientRect(&rClientRect);
    //Initialize the CRgn object with an ellipse bounded by the
    //application's client area....
rgnClientRect.CreateRectRgnIndirect( &rClientRect );
```

CreateRoundRectRgn   FUNCTION

Description   **CreateRoundRectRgn** creates a rectangular region with rounded corners. The rounded rectangular form is defined by parameters that define the upper left and lower right corners of the rectangle and the width and height of the ellipse used to draw the rounded corners.

Prototype

```
//Function Prototype
//BOOL CreateRoundRectRgn( int iULXCoordinate
//int iULYCoordinate,
//          int iLRXCoordinate,int iLRYCoordinate
//          int iCornerEllipseWidth, int iCornerEllipseHeight);
    //Create a region object....
CRgn rgnClientRect;
    //Then initialize it with a rounded rectangle in the center
    //of the client area....
rgnClientRect.CreateRoundRectRgn( rClientArea.left / 4,
rClientArea.top / 4,
        rClientArea.right / 4, rClientArea.bottom / 4,
        iCornerEllipseWidth, iCornerEllipseHeight );
```

CRgn   FUNCTION

Description   **CRgn** constructs an object of the class, but it is not initialized with the definition of an area. This step is accomplished by calling member functions of the class.

Prototype

```
//Function Prototype
    //Construct a CRgn object....
CRgn NewRgn;
```

EqualRgn — FUNCTION

Description   **EqualRgn** compares a region with the one currently attached to the CRgn object and returns whether the two regions are equal.

Prototype

```
//Function Prototype
//BOOL EqualRgn( CRgn* pCompareRegion );
if ( rgnMainRegion.EqualRgn( pCompareRegion ) )
{
    //If the regions are equal, do something....
}
```

FromHandle — FUNCTION

Description   **FromHandle** returns a pointer to a temporary **CRgn** object, given a Windows handle to a region. The handle of the region is attached to the **CRgn** object. Internally, tracking of most Windows GDI objects is done by using a table of handles. MFC provides classes to wrap the handles in objects, making the member functions of the class available to act on the object identified by the handle. The **FromHandle** family provides a quick and convenient way to package the handle temporarily in an object. An object pointer returned by any of the GDI **FromHandle** family has a life cycle of approximately one Windows message-passing cycle, so when a function that uses this call exits, the object goes out of scope and is destroyed. It is therefore not necessary for an application to destroy an object returned by **FromHandle**, because this is taken care of during the idle-time processing of **CWinApp**. The object identified by the handle is *not* deleted along with the temporary object. The lifetime of the object referenced by the pointer is very brief, so don't store the pointer for later use. It will be invalid.

Prototype

```
//Function Prototype
// static CRgn* PASCAL FromHandle( HRGN hTheRgn );
CRgn* pThePreviousCRgn;    //Save the pointer to the object we
                           //are selecting
                    //out of the DC; assume that we have a valid pointer
                    //to a CDC object called pDC
pThePreviousCRgn =
pDCSelectObject(CRgn::FromHandle(hTheRgn));
                    //Select a new Rgn that is identified by the handle
                    //in the public member variable of the CGdiObject
                    //base class
```

GetRgnBox   FUNCTION

Description   **GetRgnBox** retrieves the coordinates of the smallest bounding rectangle for the region attached to the **CRgn** object. Its return value has the following meanings:

Return Value	Meaning
COMPLEXREGION	The region has overlapping boundaries.
SIMPLEREGION	The region has no overlapping boundaries.
NULLREGION	The region is empty.
ERROR	The region handle was invalid.

Prototype
```
//Function Prototype
//int GetRgnBox( LPRECT lprRegionBoundingRect ) const;
    //Create a CRect object to hold the bounding rectangle
    //coordinates....
CRect rBoundingRect;
    //Assume that we have this CRgn object, properly initialized....
rgnMainRegion.GetRgnBox( &BoundingRect );
```

OffsetRgn   FUNCTION

Description   **OffsetRgn** translates a region in the *x* and *y* directions the number of logical units specified by the parameters. Because no region may extend beyond the boundaries of the logical coordinate space, you must ensure that the region offset operations do not result in coordinates for any point in the region larger than 32,767 or less than -32,768. The return value gives the region's type. Possible values for region type are listed in the table for **GetRgnBox.**

Prototype
```
//Function Prototype
//int OffsetRgn( int iXOffset, int iYOffset );
//int OffsetRgn( POINT ptOffset );
    //Assume that we have this CRgn object, properly initialized....
    //We add 100 logical units to every x vertex coordinate,
    //and 200 logical units to every y vertex coordinate....
rgnMainRegion.OffsetRgn( 100, 200);
```

PtInRgn   FUNCTION

Description   **PtInRgn** determines whether a given point falls within a region.

Prototype
```
//Function Prototype
//int PtInRgn( int iX, int iY );
//int PtInRgn( POINT ptOfInterest );
    //Assume that we have this CRgn object, properly initialized....
if( rgnMainRegion.PtInRgn( ptOfInterest ) )
{
    //If the point is within the region, do something....
}
```

RectInRgn   FUNCTION

Description   **RectInRgn** determines whether any portion of a given rectangle falls within a region.

Prototype
```
//Function Prototype
//int RectInRgn( LPRECT lpRectOfInterest );
    //Assume that we have this CRgn object, properly initialized....
if( rgnMainRegion.RectInRgn( &RectOfInterest ) )
{
    //If a portion of the rectangle is within the region,
    //do something....
}
```

SetRectRgn   FUNCTION

Description   **SetRectRgn** provides a means of setting up a rectangular region to *replace* one that has already been stored in a **CRgn** object. It cannot be used to initialize a brand-new region object because it is not capable of allocating memory to hold region coordinates. The advantage of this function over **CreateRectRgn** or **CreateRectRgnIndirect** is that it allows an application to avoid a call to the local memory manager.

Prototype
```
//Function Prototype
//void SetRectRgn( LPRECT lprReplacementRegion );
//void SetRectRgn( int iULXCoordinate,int iULYCoordinate,
//          int iLRXCoordinate,int iLRYCoordinate);
    //Create a region object....
CRgn rgnClientRect;
```

```
//Then initialize it with a rectangle equal to the application's
//client area....
rgnClientRect.CreateRectRgnIndirect( &rClientRect );
//Replace that region with a smaller one....
rgnClientRect.SetRectRgn( rClientArea.left / 4, rClientArea.top / 4,
rClientArea.right / 4, rClientArea.bottom /4 );
```

C RuntimeClass   CLASS

Description   **CRuntimeClass** is a structure used by all **CObject**-derived classes to dynamically provide information about the class at runtime. This enables the framework to dynamically create objects and to serialize objects that were created dynamically. The purpose of **CRuntimeClass** is to provide a kind of runtime type ID (RTTI) that's custom made for MFC, and enable dynamic creation of objects of classes derived from **CObject**. This is useful, for example, when a template calls for a view and document class to be instantiated at runtime. The concept is not unlike the "class factory" concept used in other OO environments. The IMPLEMENT_DYNAMIC, IMPLEMENT_DYNCREATE and IMPLEMENT_SERIAL macros build **CRuntimeClass** support into an object. They are automatically included in the implementation of classes built by ClassWizard. The structure has the following members:

CRuntimeClass Member	Structure Type	Used for
*m_lpszClassName	LPCSTR	Class name.
m_nObjectSize	int	Object size in bytes.
m_wSchema	WORD	Schema number for serializable classes.
void(*m_pfnConstruct)(void* p)	Pointer to function	Default constructor for classes that support dynamic creation.
m_pBaseClass	CRuntimeClass*	Pointer to the CRuntimeClass structure for the base class.

Prototype

```
//Function Prototype
    //We want to know if an object is our application's main frame
    //window, so we use the RUNTIME_CLASS macro to get a
    //pointer to its CRuntimeClass structure
CRuntimeClass* pTestFrame = RUNTIME_CLASS( *pWndObject );
    //Then compare its class name to CMainFrame
if( 0 == lstrcmp( pTestFramem_lpszClassName, "CMainFrame" )
{
    //We can take some action on the object referenced by
    //pWndObject because we know that it is of class CMainFrame
}
```

ScrollBar

Derivation

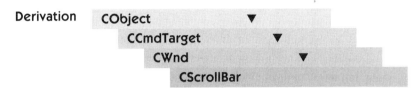

CObject ▼
CCmdTarget ▼
CWnd ▼
CScrollBar

Description   The **CScrollBar** class encapsulates the Windows scroll bar control. Scroll bar controls created using **CScrollBar** are drawn in an application's client area—the scroll bars associated with the frame window are specified in the window style and managed by Windows. (See **CWnd** for more information about frame window scrolling.) Scroll bars can be constructed in an application's client area by constructing a scroll bar object and calling the **Create** member function to build and attach a scrollbar window. Dialogs construct scroll bar controls based on their template.

If an application creates scroll bar controls independently of a dialog box, combo box, scroll view, splitter window or form view (in short, classes that provide inherent support for scrolling), steps must be taken to ensure that the object associated with the control is properly destroyed. Stack-based **CScrollBar** objects are always destroyed when the window containing them closes. **CScrollBar** objects created on the heap with **new** should be deleted with **delete**.

Member Functions

Create

Description   **Create** creates a Windows scroll bar, attaches it to the **CScrollBar** object and shows it. Scroll bar properties are determined by style constants, which may be combined with one another. They are listed in the following table. *See* ***CScrollBar*** *for a usage example.*

Scroll Bar Style	Meaning
SBS_HORZ	Horizontal scroll bar control.
SBS_VERT	Vertical scroll bar control.
SBS_TOPALIGN	Top edge aligned with top of RECT passed to Create.
SBS_LEFTALIGN	Left edge aligned with left of RECT passed to Create.
SBS_BOTTOMALIGN	Bottom edge aligned with bottom of RECT passed to Create.
SBS_RIGHTALIGN	Right edge aligned with right of RECT passed to Create.
SBS_SIZEBOXTOPLEFTALIGN	Adds a size box to a top left scroll bar.
SBS_SIZEBOXBOTTOMRIGHTALIGN	Adds a size box to a bottom right scroll bar.
SBS_SIZEBOX	Adds a sizebox to the scroll bar, and uses the RECT passed to Create to draw the scroll bar and box.

CScrollBar   FUNCTION

Description   **CScrollBar** constructs a **CScrollBar** object, but does not create, attach or initialize its accompanying scroll bar control window.

Prototype
```
//Function Prototype
    //Construct a scroll bar in the frame window's client area
CScrollBar sbOurScrollBar;
    //Then specify its style, location, parent, and control ID
sbOurScrollBar.Create( SBS_HORZ, rect, this, ID_OURSCROLLBAR);
```

EnableScrollBar   FUNCTION

Description   **EnableScrollBar** optionally enables or disables the arrows on a scroll bar control. The flags that specify the function's action are listed in the following table.

Flag Name	Meaning
ESB_ENABLE_BOTH	Enables both arrows on the scroll bar.
ESB_DISABLE_BOTH	Disables both arrows on the scroll bar.
ESB_DISABLE_RTDN	Disables right or down arrow.
ESB_DISABLE_LTUP	Disables left or up arrow.

Prototype
```
//Function Prototype
//BOOL EnableScrollBar( UINT nArrowFlags = ESB_ENABLE_BOTH );
    //Set the thumb position and scrolling range of the SBs,
    //and draw them....
sbOurHScrollBar.SetScrollPos( 0);
sbOurVScrollBar.SetScrollPos( 0);
sbOurHScrollBar.SetScrollRange(0, 100, TRUE);
sbOurVScrollBar.SetScrollRange(0, 100, TRUE);
    //Then we enable both bars.
sbOurHScrollBar.EnableScrollBar (ESB_ENABLE_BOTH);
sbOurVScrollBar.EnableScrollBar (ESB_ENABLE_BOTH);
```

GetScrollPos   FUNCTION

Description   **GetScrollPos** retrieves the current position of the scroll bar thumb. This function reports the position of the thumb for a frame window scroll bar as well as for a child window.

Prototype
```
//Function Prototype
//int GetScrollPos( ) const
    //Get the scroll range and current thumb position....
sbOurScrollBar.GetScrollRange( &iMinPos, &iMaxPos );
int iPos = sbOurScrollBar.GetScrollPos( );
```

GetScrollRange   FUNCTION

Description   **GetScrollRange** retrieves the current minimum and maximum values in the scrolling range. This function reports the scrolling range for a frame window scroll bar as well as for a child window. *See **GetScrollPos** for a usage example.*

Prototype
```
//Function Prototype
//void GetScrollRange( LPINT lpMinPos, LPINT lpMaxPos) const
```

SetScrollPos   FUNCTION

Description   **SetScrollPos** sets the position of the scroll bar thumb. This function updates the position of the thumb for a frame window scroll bar as well as for a child window. *See **EnableScrollBar** for a usage example.*

Prototype   //Function Prototype
//int SetScrollPos(int nPos, BOOL bRedraw)

SetScrollRange   FUNCTION

Description   **SetScrollRange** sets the minimum and maximum values in the scrolling range. This function updates the scrolling range for a frame window scroll bar as well as for a child window. *See **EnableScrollBar** for a usage example.*

Prototype   //Function Prototype
// void SetScrollRange(int nMinPos, int nMaxPos,
//BOOL bRedraw = TRUE);

ScrollView   CLASS

Derivation

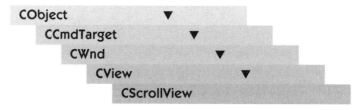

Description   **CScrollView** is a powerful and versatile derived class of **CView**. As its name implies, it incorporates scrolling capabilities, but it does much more. The most complicated aspect of drawing graphics in the Windows environment has to do with how coordinates are translated from the application's logical coordinate space to the screen. **CScrollView** manages the application's logical window, its alignment with the screen's viewport, and the mapping mode used to translate coordinates. It scrolls the screen automatically in response to scroll messages, in either "line" or "page" increments. **CScrollView** can optionally scale a document to fit in the view and display the scaled data without scroll bars.

In return for all this capability, the application is required only to set initial parameters by calling the **SetScrollSizes** member functions and to include handler code that repaints invalid areas of the screen after the window has been scrolled. An application that scales the document calls **SetScaleToFitSize**. Applications that do snazzy drawing may need to override the **CScrollView** member function **OnPrepareDC** to set pens, brushes or background colors. The override should call the base class and let it handle scaling.

CScrollView is the base class for **CFormView**, which is intended to support the display of database records.

Derived Classes   CFormView

Member Functions

CScrollView   FUNCTION

Description   **CScrollView** constructs an uninitialized scroll view object. AppWizard generates the code that makes this call.

FillOutsideRect   FUNCTION

Description   **FillOutsideRect** paints the part of the view that was not uncovered by a scrolling operation. The application calls this function in its **OnEraseBackground** message-handler function to reduce redundant erasing of areas that were actually moved during the scroll.

Prototype
```
//Function Prototype
//void FillOutsideRect(CDC* pDC, CBrush* pBrush);
```

GetDeviceScrollPosition   FUNCTION

Description   **GetDeviceScrollPosition** is a little-used function that retrieves the current location of the upper left corner of the document in *device units.* Mouse locations are reported in device (or screen) units, but drawing is done based on logical units. To get the document's current location in the logical coordinate system, use the function **GetScrollPosition**.

Prototype
```
//Function Prototype
//CPoint GetDeviceScrollPosition( ) const;
```

GetDeviceScrollSizes   FUNCTION

Description   **GetDeviceScrollSizes** is a little-used function that reports the current mapping mode, total size, and line and page sizes for the view. The sizes are reported in *device units,* which are not directly useful for drawing.

Prototype

```
//Function Prototype
//void GetDeviceScrollSizes(int& nMapMode, SIZE& sizeTotal,
//          SIZE& sizePage, SIZE& sizeLine) const;
```

GetScrollPosition   FUNCTION

Description **GetScrollPosition** retrieves the current location of the upper left corner of the document in *logical units.*

Prototype

```
//Function Prototype
//CPoint GetScrollPosition( ) const;
     //Retrieves the upper left logical coordinates of the document
CPoint pt = GetScrollPosition( );
```

GetTotalSize   FUNCTION

Description **GetTotalSize** returns the vertical and horizontal sizes of the document in logical units.

Prototype

```
//Function Prototype
//CSize GetTotalSize( ) const;
     //Get the size of the document in logical units
CSize sizeDoc = GetTotalSize( );
```

ResizeParentToFit   FUNCTION

Description **ResizeParentToFit** lets a view define the size of its parent window. There is no inherent sanity-checking on the size for which the view asks, so an application that uses this function has to make sure that the parent won't outgrow its MDI frame or even the screen. **ResizeParentToFit** should be called from an application's override of the **OnInitialUpdate** handler.

    This is a very useful function for making **CFormViews** look like dialogs (i.e., their initial size is with all fields showing). You should call **RecalcLayout** prior to calling this function.

Prototype

```
//Function Prototype
//void ResizeParentToFit(BOOL bShrinkOnly = TRUE);
void CPictureView::OnInitialUpdate()
{
    //SetScrollSizes defines the size of the document
    //in terms of the application's logical coordinate system
```

```
SetScrollSizes(MM_TWIPS, GetDocument( )->GetDocSize( ));
    //Shrink the parent window of this view to match its size
ResizeParentToFit( TRUE );
}
```

ScrollToPosition   FUNCTION

Description   **ScrollToPosition** moves the upper left corner of a document to the given position in the logical coordinate space. This function can be used only with scroll views that initialized themselves with a call to **SetScrollSizes**, and horizontal scrolling values must always be positive.

Prototype
```
//Function Prototype
//void ScrollToPosition(POINT pt);
    //Scroll to the center of the document inside a view handler
    //function....
ScrollToPosition( ptCenter );
```

SetScaleToFitSize   FUNCTION

Description   **SetScaleToFitSize** automatically scales the view of the document to fit inside a window's client area exactly. A scroll view initialized in this way displays no scroll bars. **SetScaleToFitSize** is called from within the **OnInitialUpdate** handler.

Prototype
```
//Function Prototype
//void SetScaleToFitSize(SIZE sizeTotal);
void CPictureView::OnInitialUpdate()
{
    //SetScaleToFitSize scales the document in terms
    //to fit in the frame's client area
 SetScaleToFitSize( GetDocument( )->GetDocSize( ));
}
```

SetScrollSizes   FUNCTION

Description   **SetScrollSizes** establishes the mapping mode for the view, the logical dimensions of the document, and the amount the view should scroll for each page and line. The default value for page scrolling is one-tenth the size of the view; for a line, it's one-tenth of a page. Scroll sizes are set in the **OnInitialUpdate** handler. *See ResizeParentToFit for a usage example.*

Prototype
```
//Function Prototype
//void SetScrollSizes(int nMapMode, SIZE sizeTotal,
//  const SIZE& sizePage, const SIZE& sizeLine);
```

C SingleDocTemplate

Derivation

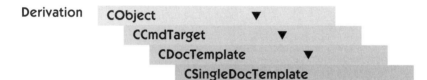

```
CObject            ▼
    CCmdTarget          ▼
        CDocTemplate        ▼
            CSingleDocTemplate
```

Description **CSingleDocTemplate** is derived from **CDocTemplate**, which provides the organizing metaphor for application architecture in MFC. (See the **CDocTemplate** entry for an explanation of the concept role of a document template.) An object of **CSingleDocTemplate** class establishes the relationship between an application's data source, the view of that data, and the frame window that manages both the data and the view, for applications that limit themselves to a single open document at any given time. The code that implements a single document template is always provided by AppWizard. The creation of the object and connection to its document, view and frame window all occur in the application's **InitInstance** member function, where the **CSingleDocTemplate** constructor is called.

Member Functions

CSingleDocTemplate	FUNCTION

Description **CSingleDocTemplate** constructs an SDI application's document template.

Prototype
```
//Function Prototype
//CSingleDocTemplate(UINT nIDResource, CRuntimeClass*
//pDocClass,
//      CRuntimeClass* pFrameClass, CRuntimeClass* pViewClass);
    //AppWizard generates this code to create
    //a single document template
    //in the InitInstance member function
```

```
AddDocTemplate( new CSingleDocTemplate( IDR_MAINFRAME,
    RUNTIME_CLASS( CMyDoc ),
    RUNTIME_CLASS( CMainFrame ),
    RUNTIME_CLASS( CMyView ) ) );
```

CSize

Description   This class captures the properties and functionality of a Windows **SIZE** structure, containing an *x, y* pair that represents a size measurement or a location. It can be used wherever a **SIZE** would be used. **CSize** is one of a group of classes known as Simple Value classes and is not intended to serve as a base class for user-derived classes.

Public Data Members

x

MEMBER

Description   Gives the X increment of the **CSize**.

y

MEMBER

Description   Gives the Y increment of the **CSize**.

Member Function

CSize

FUNCTION

Description   The **CSize** constructors can create a **CSize** by using an *x, y* pair, an existing **CSize** structure, a **CSize** object, a **POINT** or a **DWORD** containing the X coordinate in the low-order word and the Y in the high-order word. It can also construct an uninitialized object.

Prototype
```
//Function Prototype
CSize( );
CSize( int initCX, int initCY );
CSize( SIZE initSize );
CSize( POINT initPt );
```

```
CSize( DWORD dwSize );
CSize sizeNew( );              //Uninitialized CSize
CSize sizeOther( 1, 2 );       //Initialized explicitly
CPoint ptStructCSize;
ptStructCSize.x = 5;
ptStructCSize.y = 15;
              //Initialized using a CPoint structure
CSize sizeFromStruct( ptStructCSize );
```

Operators

CSize Operator	Usage
operator ==	Test for equality of two CSizes.
operator !=	Test for inequality of two CSizes.
operator +=	Add a CSize to a CSize.
operator -=	Subtract a CSize from a CSize.
operator +	Sum of two CSizes.
operator -	Difference of two CSizes.

C SplitterWnd   CLASS

Derivation

CObject ▼
CCmdTarget ▼
CWnd ▼
CSplitterWnd

Description The **CSplitterWnd** class implements the splitter window, a multiple pane window usually displayed inside a frame window or MDI child window. Typically, the panes show alternative views of data contained in an application's document. Two kinds of splitter windows can be attached to **CSplitterWnd** objects: static splitters and dynamic splitters. The panes of dynamic splitter windows are created and sized by the framework, in response to control input from the user. I like to think of this as the splitter windows being sized by the user, with the semantics provided by the framework. The application is responsible for setting minimum sizes for the panes and handling the views attached to the panes. All the panes of a dynamic splitter must be of the same class. Static splitters require more management on the part of the application, but are more flexible in some ways. For example, the panes of a static splitter may be of different classes. The individual panes of a static splitter must be created before the containing parent window is shown. The panes can be resized, but they can't be closed or reordered.

Member Functions

Create
FUNCTION

Description **Create** creates a dynamic splitter window, attaches it to the **CSplitterWnd** object, and shows it. *See **CSplitterWnd** for a usage example.*

Prototype
```
BOOL Create( CWnd* pParentWnd, int nMaxRows, int nMaxCols,
SIZE sizeMin, CCreateContext* pContext, DWORD dwStyle =
WS_CHILD | WS_VISIBLE
|WS_HSCROLL | WS_VSCROLL | SPLS_DYNAMIC_SPLIT, UINT nID =
AFX_IDW_PANE_FIRST );
```

CreateStatic
FUNCTION

Description **CreateStatic** creates a static splitter window, attaches it to the **CSplitterWnd** object and shows it. **CreateStatic** can create panes that are of different classes.

Prototype
```
//Function Prototype
//BOOL CreateStatic(CWnd* pParentWnd, int nRows, int nCols,
// DWORD dwStyle = WS_CHILD | WS_VISIBLE ,
// UINT nID = AFX_IDW_PANE_FIRST );
    //To construct a static splitter window, first declare a member
    //variable in the app's frame window class like this:
protected:
    CSplitterWnd m_wndSplitter;

    //Then create a dynamic splitter window to attach
    //to the object by overriding
    //the OnCreateClient function of the parent frame
BOOL CSplitterFrame::OnCreateClient(LPCREATESTRUCT lpcr,
                    CCreateContext* pContext)
```

```
{
    //Create a splitter with 1 row, 2 columns
m_wndSplitter.CreateStatic(this, 1, 2);
        //Create the splitter panes; static panes all must be created
        //before function exits.
        //Give the row & column the CRuntimeClass of the view, the
        //initial size of the view, and the create context
        //passed to this function
m_wndSplitter.CreateView(0, 0, pContext->m_pNewViewClass,
            CSize(130, 50), pContext))
m_wndSplitter.CreateView(0, 1,RUNTIME_CLASS(CInputView),
            CSize(0, 0), pContext))
        //Make the pane at row 0, column 1 the active view
SetActiveView((CView*)m_wndSplitter.GetPane(0,1));
}
```

CreateView   FUNCTION

Description **CreateView** creates the views for static splitter window panes. It establishes the size and location of the panes as well as the runtime class of the views for the individual panes. *See **CreateStatic** for a usage example.*

Prototype
```
//Function Prototype
//BOOL CreateView(int row, int col,
    CRuntimeClass* pViewClass, SIZE sizeInit, CCreateContext*
    pContext);
```

CSplitterWnd   FUNCTION

Description **CSplitterWnd** constructs a **CSplitterWnd** object, but does not create, attach or define its accompanying window. Either the **Create** or **CreateStatic** member function is used to create, attach and show the splitter window associated with the object. These latter two functions are best called in an override of **OnCreateClient**.

Prototype
```
//Function Prototype
    //To construct a dynamic splitter window, first declare a
    //member variable in the app's frame window class like this:
protected:
    CSplitterWnd m_wndSplitter;
```

```
//Then create a dynamic splitter window to attach to the object
//by overriding
//the OnCreateClient function of the parent frame
BOOL CParentFrame::OnCreateClient(LPCREATESTRUCT lpcs,
            CCreateContext* pContext)
{
    //We make the frame window the splitter's parent, ask for 2
    //rows and cols of panes, set the minimum size for a pane,
    //and pass the create context that was passed to
    //OnCreateClient
 return m_wndSplitter.Create(this, 2, 2, CSize(10, 10), pContext);
}
```

GetColumnCount   FUNCTION

Description **GetColumnCount** returns the number of columns displayed in a dynamic splitter window; or for a static splitter, the maximum number of columns. *See **GetRowCount** for a usage example.*

Prototype
```
//Function Prototype
//int GetColumnCount( ) const;
```

GetColumnInfo   FUNCTION

Description **GetColumnInfo** reports the current width and the minimum permitted width in pixels of the column of panes specified by the first parameter. *See **GetRowInfo** for a usage example.*

Prototype
```
//Function Prototype
//void GetColumnInfo(int col, int& cxCur, int& cxMin) const;
```

GetPane   FUNCTION

Description **GetPane** returns a **CWnd** pointer to the pane with the specified row and column position. The pointer usually identifies a **CView**-derived object associated with the pane. *See **CreateStatic** for a usage example.*

Prototype
```
//Function Prototype
//CWnd* GetPane(int row, int col) const;
```

GetRowCount   FUNCTION

Description   **GetRowCount** returns the number of rows displayed in a dynamic splitter window; or for a static splitter, the maximum number of rows.

Prototype
```
//Function Prototype
//int GetRowCount( ) const;
    //Find out how many rows and columns of split panes we have
int iRowCount = m_wndSplitter.GetRowCount( );
int iColCount = m_wndSplitter.GetColumnCount( );
    //Make an array to hold splitter pane IDs
CWordArray arrayPaneIds;
arrayPaneIds.SetSize( iRowCount * iColCount );
    //Now get IDs for all the panes
while( iRowCount —>= 0 )
{
 while( iColCount—>= 0 )
 {
 arrayPaneIds[iRowCount] [iColCount ] =
 m_wndSplitter.IdFromRowCol( iRowCount * iColCount);
 }
}
```

GetRowInfo   FUNCTION

Description   **GetRowInfo** reports the current height and the minimum permitted height in pixels of the row of panes specified by the first parameter.

Prototype
```
//Function Prototype
//void GetRowInfo(int row, int& cyCur, int& cyMin) const;
int iRowHeight, iRowMinHeight;
int iColWidth, iColMinWidth;
    //Find the current height and minimum height for pane 0,0
m_wndSplitter.GetRowInfo( 0, & iRowHeight, &iRowMinHeight );
    //Find the current width and minimum width for pane 0,0
m_wndSplitter.GetColInfo( 0, &iColWidth, &iColMinWidth );
    //Now set the ideal height and width
    //to the current minimum values
m_wndSplitter.SetRowInfo( 0, iRowMinHeight, iRowMinHeight );
m_wndSplitter.SetColInfo( 0, iColMinWidth, iColMinWidth );
    //Make sure that the changes are displayed
m_wndSplitter.RecalcLayout( );
```

IdFromRowCol   FUNCTION

Description **IdFromRowCol** returns the child ID of a splitter pane given its row and column. *See **GetRowCount** for a usage example.*

Prototype
```
//Function Prototype
//int IdFromRowCol(int row, int col) const;
```

IsChildPane   FUNCTION

Description **IsChildPane** tests a pointer to a **CWnd** object to see whether it is a child pane of the splitter. If it is, it fills in the row and column numbers by using the references passed.

Prototype
```
//Function Prototype
//BOOL IsChildPane(CWnd* pWnd, int& row, int& col);
    //We want to find the row and column of the active pane
int iRow, iCol;
    //Using a pointer to the active view
IsChildPane(pActiveView, iRow, iCol);
```

RecalcLayout   FUNCTION

Description **RecalcLayout** repaints the splitter after ideal and minimum sizes for pane width and height have been reset with **SetRowInfo** and **SetColumnInfo**. *See **GetRowInfo** for a usage example.*

Prototype
```
//Function Prototype
//void RecalcLayout( );
```

SetColumnInfo   FUNCTION

Description **SetColumnInfo** sets the current width and the minimum permitted width in pixels of the column of panes specified by the first parameter. *See **GetRowInfo** for a usage example.*

Prototype
```
//Function Prototype
//void SetColumnInfo(int col, int cxIdeal, int cxMin);
```

SetRowInfo   FUNCTION

Description **SetRowInfo** sets the current height and the minimum permitted height in pixels of the row of panes specified by the first parameter. *See **GetRowInfo** for a usage example.*

753

Prototype   //Function Prototype
//void SetRowInfo(int row, int cyIdeal, int cyMin);

Static

Derivation

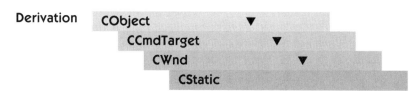

Description   The **CStatic** class implements a static text control. Static controls simply act as labels for other controls or visual elements. They generate no messages, and the user cannot interact with them. Dialog boxes create and destroy static controls defined in their templates. If an application creates static controls independent of a dialog box, form view or dialog bar, steps must be taken to ensure that the object associated with the control is properly destroyed. Stack-based **CStatic** objects are always destroyed when the window containing them closes. **CStatic** objects created on the heap with **new** should be deleted with **delete**.

Member Functions

Create

Description   **Create** builds and initializes a window, connects it to the **CStatic** object, and then shows the control. **Create** initializes a static text control with the string passed as its first parameter. If the parameter is NULL, it shows no text. The **Create** call does not set an icon for a static control created with the **SS_ICON** style. This must be done by calling **SetIcon**. Possible styles for static controls are listed in the following table.

Static Control Style Constants	Meaning
SS_LEFT	Align left.
SS_CENTER	Align center.
SS_RIGHT	Align right.
SS_ICON	Control displays an icon.
SS_BLACKRECT	Control is a solid black rectangle.
SS_GRAYRECT	Control is a solid gray rectangle.
SS_WHITERECT	Control is a solid white rectangle.
SS_BLACKFRAME	Control is a black rectangular outline.
SS_GRAYFRAME	Control is a gray rectangular outline.
SS_WHITEFRAME	Control is a white rectangular outline.
SS_SIMPLE	Display a single line of left-aligned text.
SS_LEFTNOWORDWRAP	Prevent word wrapping of control text.
SS_NOPREFIX	Don't do "&" character translation.

Prototype
```
//Function Prototype
//BOOL Create(LPCTSTR lpszText, DWORD dwStyle,
//    const RECT& rect, CWnd* pParentWnd, UINT nID);
    //Create an initially visible static control, left-aligned,
    //to display the string "Text Label"
CStatic m_OurStaticControl;
m_OurStaticControl.Create("Text Label :", WS_VISIBLE | WS_CHILD |
    SS_LEFT,
    CRect(whereLabel, sizeLabel), this, -1);
```

CStatic   FUNCTION

Description   **CStatic** constructs a static object, but does not initialize it or display it.

GetIcon   FUNCTION

Description   **GetIcon** gets an icon handle associated with a static control. This function is used only for static controls that were created with the SS_ICON style.

Prototype
```
//Function Prototype
//HICON GetIcon( )const;
    //Get the icon handle from the control
HICON hIconHandle = m_OurStaticControl.GetIcon( )
```

SetIcon

Description **SetIcon** connects an icon with a static control and returns the handle of its previous icon or NULL. This function is used only for static controls created with the SS_ICON style.

Prototype
```
//Function Prototype
//HICON SetIcon( HICON hStaticControlIcon );
CStatic m_OurStaticControl;
    //Set the icon associated with the control
HICON hiOldIconHandle = m_OurStaticControl.SetIcon( hiNewIcon
    )
    //Create an initially visible static control
    //to display a bitmap icon
m_OurStaticControl.Create(NULL, WS_VISIBLE | WS_CHILD |
SS_ICON,
        CRect(whereLabel, sizeLabel), this, -1);
```

StatusBar

Derivation

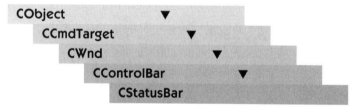

Description The **CStatusBar** class implements a type of Windows control bar that consists of a horizontal row of text panes, usually aligned with the bottom of the screen, called *indicators*. The indicators display information, such as the current page and line number of a document or a help message that briefly describes selected menu items.

The status bar panes are sized to entirely fill the width of the frame window's client area. The first pane stretches to use whatever space is left after the other indicators are built. The member function **SetIndicators** is used to assign both a control ID and a string to each of the panes. The ID is used by the application to manipulate the pane.

Member Functions

CommandToIndex   FUNCTION

Description   **CommandToIndex** returns the zero-based index of the first pane in the status bar with the specified ID.

Prototype
```
//Function Prototype
//int CommandToIndex(UINT nIDFind) const;
    //Find which pane displays the ID_PAGENUM indicator
int iIndexPageNumPane = OurAppStatusbar.CommandToIndex(
ID_PAGENUM );
```

Create   FUNCTION

Description   **Create** creates the window that contains the status bar panes, sets its default font and height, sets its location, and connects it to the **CStatusBar** object. *See CStatusBar for a usage example.*

Prototype
```
//Function Prototype
//BOOL Create(CWnd* pParentWnd,
//  DWORD dwStyle = WS_CHILD | WS_VISIBLE | CBRS_BOTTOM,
//  UINT nID = AFX_IDW_STATUSBAR );
```

CStatusBar   FUNCTION

Description   **CStatusBar** constructs a status bar object, but doesn't initialize the panes with indicator strings or show the status bar.

Prototype
```
//Function Prototype
    //Construct a status bar object
CStatusBar m_OurStatusBar;
    //We create it in the parent frame window's implementation
m_OurStatusBar.Create(this) ;
    //We call SetIndicators, which sets ID of each pane
    //and loads it with the string resource associated
    //with each of the IDs
m_OurStatusBar.SetIndicators( lpArrayPaneIDs, NUMBER_PANES);
    //We want to use the default pane width, so retrieve it here
m_OurStatusBar.GetPaneInfo( 0, nID, nStyle, cxWidth);
    //Then set the text for leftmost pane, locating it by index;
    //force repaint
m_OurStatusBar.SetPaneInfo(0, lpszDatabaseName,TRUE);
```

GetItemId `FUNCTION`

Description **GetItemId** retrieves the ID associated with a status pane, given the zero-based index of the pane.

Prototype
```
//Function Prototype
//UINT GetItemID(int nIndex) const;
    //Find the ID associated with the leftmost pane
UINT uildFirstPane = OurAppStatusbar.GetItemID( 0 );
```

GetItemRect `FUNCTION`

Description **GetItemRect** fills in a **RECT** structure with the coordinates of the enclosing rectangle for the pane specified by the zero-based index. Coordinates are in pixels, relative to the upper left corner of the status bar.

Prototype
```
//Function Prototype
//void GetItemRect(int nIndex, LPRECT lpRect) const;
```

GetPaneInfo `FUNCTION`

Description **GetPaneInfo** uses the zero-based index of the pane to retrieve its ID, style and width in pixels on the status bar. *See **CStatusBar** for a usage example.*

Prototype
```
//Function Prototype
//void GetPaneInfo(int nIndex, UINT& nID, UINT& nStyle, int& ?
//cxWidth) const;
```

GetPaneText `FUNCTION`

Description **GetPaneText** uses the index of the pane to retrieve its current text on the status bar.

Prototype
```
//Function Prototype
//void GetPaneText(int nIndex, CString& s) const;
    //Get text of pane that appears first on the status bar
 CString strTextNewPen;
 m_wndStatusBar.GetPaneText(0, strTextNewPen);
```

SetIndicators
FUNCTION

Description   **SetIndicators** associates an array of IDs with the panes on a status bar. IDs correspond to string resources that are loaded to initialize the indicator panes. *See **CStatusBar** for a usage example.*

Prototype
```
//Function Prototype
//BOOL SetIndicators(const UINT FAR* lpIDArray, int nIDCount);
```

SetPaneInfo
FUNCTION

Description   **SetPaneInfo** uses the index of the pane to set a new ID, style and width for the pane on the status bar. *See **CStatusBar** for a usage example.*

Prototype
```
//Function Prototype
//void SetPaneInfo(int nIndex, UINT nID, UINT nStyle, int cxWidth);
```

SetPaneText
FUNCTION

Description   **SetPaneText** uses the zero-based index of the pane to set a new indicator text string.

Prototype
```
//Function Prototype
//BOOL SetPaneText(int nIndex, LPCTSTR lpszNewText, BOOL
//bUpdate);
    //Get text of pane that appears first on the status bar
GetPaneText(0, nID, nStyle, iImage);
    //We have a handler to update the status bar
    //when the pen changes
void CMainFrame::OnChangePen( )
{
 CString strTextNewPen = "You have selected the " + m_strNewPen +
    " tool."
 m_wndStatusBar.SetPaneText(0, strTextNewPen);
}
```

StdioFile

Derivation	CObject ▼
	CFile ▼
	CStdioFile

Description The **CStdioFile** class encapsulates the C runtime buffered file I/O capabilities. It provides the familiar stream-handling facilities and allows a stream to be opened in text or binary mode. Text mode streams translate carriage return and line-feed pairs (0x0A, 0x0D) to the single character newline (0x0A) when a file is read into memory and reverse the translation when it is read to disk. Binary mode streams read bytes in and out exactly as they occur in a file.

    CStdioFile does not support the **CFile** member functions **Duplicate**, **LockRange** and **UnlockRange**. Calling these functions from a **CStdioFile** object results in a **CNotSupportedException** being thrown.

Public Data Members

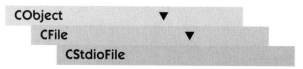

m_pStream   **MEMBER**

Description The meaning of **m_pStream** depends on which of the **CStdioFile** constructors was called to create the object. If the parameterless **CStdioFile** constructor is used to create the object, this data member is set to NULL because no file is opened. If either of the other two constructors is called, this member holds the pointer to the file returned by a call to **fopen**, if the open succeeds. Because it is not generally possible to tell how the object was constructed, assuming that **m_pStream** holds a valid pointer is somewhat risky. But even if you use the default constructor, the **m_pStream** member variable is filled in once the file is opened.

Member Functions

CStdioFile | FUNCTION

Description The **CStdioFile** constructor is overloaded, which is to say that it constructs the **CStdioFile** object in response to the three different sets of parameters it can accept. The first constructor takes no arguments and constructs the object without attempting to open a file. The file is then opened explicitly using the **Open** member function. The **CStdioFile** constructor, which takes a **FILE** pointer as a parameter, wraps the pointer with the **CStdioFile** class member functions. The **FILE** pointer can be the **stdin**, **stdout** and **stderr** streams as well as a file opened or created by the application. The constructor that takes a pathname and a set of file-open flags attempts to open the file as requested and throws an exception if it fails.

Prototype
```
//Function Prototype
//CStdioFile( );
//CStdioFile(FILE* pOpenFile);
//CStdioFile(const char* pszFileName, UINT nOpenFlags)
// throw( CFileException );
```

Example
```
    //Construct the object, but don't open the file
CStdioFile fileTextMode;
    //Try to open the text for reading and writing
if( fileTextMode.Open( "story.txt", CFile::modeReadWrite |
CFile::typeText )
{
    //If we succeed, read from the file up to
    //the first newline character
fileTextMode.ReadString( szFileBuffer, sizeof(szFileBuffer));
    //Seek to the end of the file by using
    //the CFile base class member function
fileTextMode.SeekToEnd( );
    //Write out the string at the end of the file
fileTextMode.WriteString( "The End", strlen("The End"));
}
    //Close the file by using the CFile base class member function
fileTextMode.Close( );
}
```

ReadString — FUNCTION

Description   **ReadString** reads from the file up to the number of bytes given in the second parameter or the first newline, whichever comes first. It returns a pointer to the buffer or NULL if end-of-file is reached. *See CStdioFile for a usage example.*

Prototype
```
//Function Prototype
//char FAR * ReadString(char FAR* lpsz, UINT nMax)
// throw(CFileException);
```

WriteString — FUNCTION

Description   **WriteString** copies a NULL terminated string to a file, omitting the NULL. It throws an exception if it is unable to complete the write request. *See CStdioFile for a usage example.*

Prototype
```
//Function Prototype
//void WriteString(const void FAR* lpsz)
// throw(CStdioFileException);
```

C String — CLASS

. . . .

Description   The **CString** class is one of a family known as the Simple Value classes—we often call them *general purpose classes*—which include the **CTime**, **CTimeSpan**, **CRect**, **CPoint** and **CSize** classes. In fact, about all that this divergent group has in common is that they encapsulate data items and that they are themselves base classes, as opposed to most framework classes, which are derived from **CObject**. With respect to the **CString** class, the Simple Value moniker is deceptive. This powerful and versatile formulation replaces a large amount of the functionality of the C language string-handling runtimes and improves on it by leaps and bounds in several areas.

The key concept when it comes to **CString** objects is that each one is a uniquely stored set of characters. The data in the object is a set of characters and is never a pointer to characters stored elsewhere. When **CStrings** are copied to one another, therefore, two sets of characters exist, and changes made to one object do not affect the other object. One of the greatest and obvious advantages of **CString** objects over C language character arrays is that they grow transparently. If you initialize a **CString** with "hello" and later append "world," space is automatically allocated for the new characters.

The **CString** class includes member functions for easy conversion to and from C language character pointers, so it is permissible to use them as parameters to functions that expect const pointers to **char**.

Member Functions

AnsiToOem   FUNCTION

Description Several character sets are available to a Windows programmer, but for Western language programmers, the ANSI set used by GDI and window-management subsystems is sufficient. Occasionally it is necessary to work back and forth between the ANSI set and the OEM set. **AnsiToOem** converts the characters in a string from the ANSI character set to the OEM character set. OEM character sets are single-byte sets whose exact content is specified by a *code page* identifier. In general, they share a range of printing characters for Western languages with the ANSI set, but may contain language-specific characters or graphics characters outside the usual alphabetic range. For console applications under NT, or DOS box applications under Windows 3.1, the conversions from ANSI to OEM character sets are sometimes necessary to handle characters outside the range of printing characters common to the two sets (for example, line-drawing characters used by DOS-style applications).

Prototype
```
//Function Prototype
//void AnsiToOem ( );
```

Collate   FUNCTION

Description **Collate** compares a string given by its argument and returns an integer representing the relationship between the **CString** object and the argument's rank in the *locale-specific* collating sequence. Locales are used to customize the display of dates, time and money values, as well as to set alphabetic collating order. Locales are set by using the C language API **setlocale**. Other than the fact that the locale setting is taken into account, **Collate** is used in the same way as **Compare**.

Compare

Description **Compare** compares a string given by its argument to the value of the **CString** object and returns an integer representing the relationship between the argument's and the object's rank in the ASCII collating sequence. The comparison is case sensitive, and the returns have the following meaning:

Return Value	Meaning
0	The strings have equal rank in the collating sequence.
1	The CString object for which the function was called has greater rank.
-1	The CString object for which the function was called has lesser rank.

Prototype
```
//Function Prototype
//int Compare( const char* psz );
CString stringHigh( "ABC" );
if ( stringHigh.Compare( "ABC" )
{
    //We never reach the inside of the if because the strings are
    //equal and the function returns 0....
}
```

CompareNoCase

Description **CompareNoCase** compares the string given by its argument to the value of the **CString** object and returns an integer representing the relationship between the argument's and the object's rank in the ASCII collating sequence. The comparison is case insensitive.

Prototype
```
//Function Prototype
//int CompareNoCase( const char* psz );
CString stringHigh( "ABC" );
if ( stringHigh.CompareNoCase( "abc" )
{
    //We never reach the inside of the if because the strings are
    //equal when compared without respect to case and the
    //function returns 0....
}
```

CString   FUNCTION

Description   **CString** constructs a **CString** object. **CString** constructors can perform an impressive variety of jobs.

Example

```
    //Construct an uninitialized object like this:
CString string Empty;
    //Construct an initialized string....
CString stringName("Mary" );
    //Initialize the string with the character "$" repeated ten times....
CString stringDollars('$', 10 );
        //Copy from an existing CString; stringNewName takes the value
        //"Mary"
CString stringNewName = stringName;
    //Use expressions to create the value of the string....
CString stringManyParts( " " + stringName + "Smith" );
```

Empty   FUNCTION

Description   **Empty** removes the characters in a **CString** and releases the memory they formerly occupied.

Prototype

```
    //Function Prototype
    //void Empty( );
        //Initialize the Name Field data item for a data-entry form that
        //will be reused.
    stringNameField.Empty( );
```

Find   FUNCTION

Description   **Find** searches forward through a string for a character or a string, depending on its argument, and returns the index of the first match it encounters.

Prototype

```
    //Function Prototype
    //int Find( char ch) const;
    //int Find( const char* pszSub );

    CString stringSearchIt = "The lazy brown dog, etc, etc..."
    int iIndex;
        //Return the zero-based index of the first occurrence
        //of the character 'z'....
    iIndex = stringSearchIt.Find( 'z' );
```

```
//Return the zero-based index of the first occurrence
//of the string "lazy"....
iIndex = stringSearchIt.Find( "lazy" );
```

FindOneOf   FUNCTION

Description   **FindOneOf** searches forward through a string for any of a given set of characters and returns the index of the first match it encounters.

Prototype
```
//Function Prototype
//int Find( const char* pszCharSet );

CString stringSearchIt = "The lazy brown dog, etc, etc..."
int iIndex;
    //Return the zero-based index of the first occurrence of
    //any of the characters "abcd"....
iIndex = stringSearchIt.FindOneOf( "abcd" );
    //Return the zero-based index of the first occurrence
    //of the string "lazy"....
iIndex = stringSearchIt.Find( "lazy" );
```

GetAt   FUNCTION

Description   **GetAt** returns the character located at the position in the character array specified by the parameter. The **operator [ ]** can be used in the same fashion.

Prototype
```
//Function Prototype
//char GetAt( int nIndex ) const;
CString stringCountingNumbers( "123456789" );
    //Arrays are based at 0, so this call returns the character"5"....
char cNumber = stringCountingNumbers.GetAt( 4 );
```

GetBuffer   FUNCTION

Description   **GetBuffer** returns a pointer to the internal character buffer of a **CString** object. This is useful for occasions on which it is necessary for a routine to modify the characters in the string directly; for example, in calls to the C runtime function **strtok**, which inserts NULLS after tokens in a string as it parses. The returned pointer is temporary, so it should not be stored for later use. A call to **GetBuffer** is always paired with a call to **ReleaseBuffer**, and no

CString member functions may be called in the code bracketed by the two.

Prototype

```
//Function Prototype
//char* GetBuffer( int nMinBufferLength )
// throw( CMemoryException );
CString FileName;
char *pszFileName;
char *pszExtension;
    //Get a pointer to a buffer containing
    //the fully qualified filename....
pszFileName = FileName.GetBuffer(PATH_LENGTH);
    //Find the "." in the filename and insert a NULL after it....
strtok( pszFileName, "." );
    //Return the modified buffer to the character string,
    //and let the function set the length of the string....
FileName.ReleaseBuffer(-1);
```

GetBufferSetLength   FUNCTION

Description **GetBufferSetLength** returns a pointer to the internal character buffer of a **CString** object and grows or truncates the buffer, based on the length specified in the argument. In every other respect, it performs in the same way as the **CString** member function **GetBuffer.**

Prototype

```
//Function Prototype
//char* GetBufferSetLength( int nNewLength )
// throw( CMemoryException );
CString FileName;
char *pszShortFileName;
    //Get a pointer to just the name portion,
    //and truncate the extension....
pszShortFileName = FileName.GetBufferSetLength(9);
    //After making changes to the buffer, release it....
FileName.ReleaseBuffer(-1);
```

GetLength   FUNCTION

Description **GetLength** returns the numbers of characters in the string, not including the NULL terminator.

Prototype

```
//Function Prototype
//int GetLength( ) const;
if ( stringProgramTitle.GetLength( ) > TITLE_SPACE )
{   //If the string we want to write on the title bar won't fit,
    //make an adjustment....
}
```

IsEmpty   FUNCTION

Description   **IsEmpty** returns a Boolean value indicating whether characters are stored in the string.

Prototype

```
//Function Prototype
//BOOL IsEmpty( ) const;
if ( stringGetPassword.IsEmpty( ) )
    //Issue a warning and prompt for the password again....
```

Left   FUNCTION

Description   **Left** copies the specified number of characters from one **CString** to another, starting at the beginning of the string. **Left** returns a **CString**, so it can throw an exception if there is insufficient memory available to create the new object.

Prototype

```
//Function Prototype
//CString Left( int nCount ) const
//  throw( CMemoryException );
CString stringAlphabet( "abcdefghijklmnopqrstuvwxyz" );
    //Copy the first 10 characters....
CString stringFirstTen = stringAlphabet.Left( 10 );
```

LoadString   FUNCTION

Description   **LoadString** loads a Windows string resource into a **CString** object. The resource is identified by ID, and a Boolean return signals success or failure of the call.

Prototype

```
//Function Prototype
//BOOL LoadString( UINT iResourceID );
CString stringTitle;
    //Load a new Window Titlebar String
    //which is defined in the resource file string table....
stringTitle.LoadString( IDS_MAPWINDOWTITLE );
```

MakeLower   FUNCTION

Description   **MakeLower** converts a string to lowercase.

Prototype
```
//Function Prototype
//void MakeLower( );
CString stringAllBig = "ABCDEFG";
    //After this call, the string contains "abcdefg"
stringAllSmall.MakeUpper( );
```

MakeReverse   FUNCTION

Description   **MakeReverse** reverses the order of characters in a string.

Prototype
```
//Function Prototype
//void MakeLower( );
CString stringAllSmall = "abcdefg";
    //After this call, the string contains "gfedcba"
stringAllSmall.MakeReverse( );
```

MakeUpper   FUNCTION

Description   **MakeUpper** converts a string to uppercase.

Prototype
```
//Function Prototype
//void MakeUpper( );
CString stringAllSmall = "abcdefg";
    //After this call, the string contains "ABCDEFG"
stringAllSmall.MakeUpper( );
```

Mid   FUNCTION

Description   **Mid** copies a substring from an existing **CString** into a new **CString**. It copies beginning at the zero-based index specified by the parameter either up to the range specified by the second parameter or to the end of the string if no character count is supplied. **Mid** returns a **CString**, so it can throw an exception if there is insufficient memory available to create the new object.

Prototype
```
//Function Prototype
//CString Mid( int nFirst ) const
// throw( CMemoryException );
//CString Mid( int nFirst, int nCount ) const
```

```
// throw( CMemoryException );
CString stringAlphabet( "abcdefghijklmnopqrstuvwxyz" );
    //Starting at the third zero-based array position,
    //copy eight chars to the target....
CString stringDthruK = stringAlphabet.Mid( 3, 8);
```

OemToAnsi   FUNCTION

Description   **OemToAnsi** converts the characters in a string from the OEM character set to the ANSI character set. *See the description of* **AnsiToOem** *for information on the reasons for using this function.*

Prototype
```
//Function Prototype
//void OemToAnsi ( );
```

operator +   OPERATOR

Description   **operator +** is the **CString** concatenation operator. Like the assignment operator, it can join two **CStrings**, a **CString** and a character array, or a **CString** and a single character. Memory is dynamically allocated as needed.

Prototype
```
CString stringExample = "a few words...";
CString stringTwo = "a different string";
char cArray[] = "More Chars...";
char* pszArray = cArray;
    //The concatenation and append operators
    //work on all these types....
stringExample += stringTwo + pszArray + " Versatile, huh?" + "!";
```

operator +=   OPERATOR

Description   **operator +=** appends characters to a **CString** and allocates new memory as necessary. *See* **operator +** *for a usage example.*

operator =   OPERATOR

Description   **operator =** assigns a value to a **CString** from another **CString**, an ordinary C language character array, a constant, or a single character. If the target of the assignment is not big enough to hold the source data, the target is dynamically expanded.

Prototype
```
CString stringExample
CString stringTwo = "a different string";
char cArray[] = "More Chars..."
char* pszArray = cArray;
    //Space is allocated as needed for the character array....
stringExample = "This is a test..."
    //stringTwo is copied to stringExample, and extra space is
    //automatically allocated
stringExample = stringTwo;
    //cArray is copied to stringExample
stringExample = pszArray;
```

operator [ ]   OPERATOR

Description **operator [ ]** returns the character located at the position in the character array specified by the parameter, but *cannot* be used to set a character at a given position. The **GetAt** member function can be used in the same fashion.

Prototype
```
//Function Prototype
//char operator [ ] ( int nIndex ) const;
CString stringCountingNumbers( "123456789" );
    //Arrays are based at 0, so this call returns the character"5"....
char cNumber = stringCountingNumbers[ 4 ];
```

operator ==   OPERATORS

```
operator !=
operator >=
operator <=
operator >
operator <
```

Description Comparison operators do a lexical comparison, using **CStrings** or **const char*** as operands. They return a Boolean result.

Prototype
```
CString stringEnt = "ABC";
CString stringTwo = "ABC";
char scary[] = "xyz";
char* pszString;
pszString = scAry;
    //Promote stringEnt to uppercase if stringTwo is greater....
if ( stringEnt < stringTwo )
```

```
stringOne.MakeUpper( );
//You can treat strings exactly like simple types by using the
//CString comparison and assignment operators....
stringEnt = ( stringTwo > pszArray ) ? pszArray : stringTwo;
```

operator <<   OPERATOR

Description   The **operator <<** for user-defined objects is useful in writing serialization functions. The use of the archive operator to dump context information is supported for only the debug versions of the MFC library, however.

Prototype
```
//We have a user-defined class called CColorScheme
//with just one data member
//we want to be able to serialize....
void CColorScheme::Serialize( CArchive& arColorScheme )
{
if( arColorScheme.IsStoring( ) )
{
   //Store the string member variable....
ar << (CString ) m_MainColor;
}
else
{
   //Retrieve the member variable....
(CString) m_PrimaryColor << ar ;
}
}
```

operator >>   OPERATOR

Description   The archive **operator >>** provides a quick means of doing a diagnostic dump or storing a string to an archive.

operator const char* ( )   OPERATOR

Description   **const char* ( )** casts a **CString** object to a pointer to **char**, which makes it possible to use **CStrings** with any C runtime function expecting that type as a parameter, for which automatic conversion might not take place properly. In particular, this comes up in connection with functions of the **printf** family or other functions that accept variable-length parameter lists. An explicit cast from **CString** to **const char*** is necessary.

Prototype
```
        //We declare a CString....
CString stringGreeting = "Hello World!";
        //but printf needs a const pointer to char.
        //Because its function prototype doesn't fully specify the
        //possible arguments, explicit casting is required....
printf( "%s\n", (const char*) stringGreeting );
```

ReleaseBuffer   FUNCTION

Description **ReleaseBuffer** frees memory allocated by **GetBuffer** or **GetBufferSetLength** and invalidates the pointer returned by these functions. The modified character string is copied back to the object. The released buffer can optionally be set to an exact length. This setting is required if the string in the buffer is not terminated by a NULL. If the string is NULL terminated, the length argument may be omitted, and the release function will establish the correct length for the updated buffer. *For an example of usage, see* **GetBuffer**.

Prototype
```
//Function Prototype
//void ReleaseBuffer( int BufferLength = -1);
```

ReverseFind   FUNCTION

Description **ReverseFind** searches backward through a string for a single character and returns the index of the first match it encounters.

Prototype
```
//int ReverseFind( char ch ) const;

CString stringSearchIt = "The lazy brown dog, etc, etc..."
int iIndex;
        //Return the zero-based index of the 't'
        //nearest the end of the string....
iIndex = stringSearchIt.Find( 't' );
```

Right   FUNCTION

Description **Right** copies the specified number of characters from one **CString** to another, starting at the end of the string and working toward the beginning. **Right** returns a **CString**, so it can throw an exception if there is insufficient memory available to create the new object.

Prototype
```
//Function Prototype
//CString Right( int nCount ) const
// throw( CMemoryException );
CString stringAlphabet( "abcdefghijklmnopqrstuvwxyz" );
    //Copy the first ten characters....
CString stringLastTen = stringAlphabet.Right( 10 );
```

SetAt   FUNCTION

Description   **SetAt** sets a character in the **CString** object's array to a given value, with some limitations. First, the index argument must designate a valid array position, as the array exists when the function is called. **SetAt** cannot expand the array to set the new value.

Prototype
```
//Function Prototype
//void SetAt( int nIndex, char ch );
CString stringLetters = "abcd"
    //Change "a" to "z"
stringLetters.SetAt( 0, 'z' );
```

SpanExcluding   FUNCTION

Description   **SpanExcluding** finds the largest substring in a **CString** that does not contain the characters in a given subset. **SpanExcluding** returns a **CString**, so it can throw an exception if there is insufficient memory available to create the new object.

Prototype
```
//Function Prototype
//CString SpanExcluding( const char * pszCharSet ) const
// throw( CMemoryException );
CString stringState( "Mississippi" );
    //Copy the "pp" out of "Mississsippi."
CString stringSpan = stringState.SpanExcluding( "is");
```

SpanIncluding   FUNCTION

Description   **SpanIncluding** finds the largest substring in a **CString** that contains only the characters in a given subset. **SpanIncluding** returns a **CString**, so it can throw an exception if there is insufficient memory available to create the new object.

Prototype

```
//Function Prototype
//CString SpanIncluding( const char * pszCharSet ) const
//   throw( CMemoryException );
CString stringState( "Mississippi" );
    //Copy the "ississi" out of the middle of "Mississsippi"...
CString stringSpan = stringState.Including( "is");
```

C StringArray   CLASS

· ·

See **CObArray**.

C StringList   CLASS

· ·

See **CObList**.

775

Time

CLASS

Description   The **CTime** class is one of a family known as the Simple Value classes, which includes the **CString**, **CTime**, **CTimeSpan**, **CRect**, **CPoint** and **CSize** classes. In fact, about all that this divergent group has in common is that they encapsulate data items and that they are themselves base classes, as opposed to most framework classes, which are derived from **CObject**. **CTime** encapsulates the ANSI **time_t** data type and the associated time-manipulation functions. Conversions are provided to and from Gregorian dates and 24-hour times, using Greenwich Mean Time as a reference. Local time is established by the setting of the **TZ** environment variable. **CTime** is closely related to **CTimeSpan**, which encapsulates the difference between two **CTimes** to represent elapsed time.

There are some restrictions on the use of **CTime** and **CTimeSpan**. The **CTime** function may *not* be used in Windows DLLs. It is not intended to be a base class for user-derived classes.

Member Functions

CTime

FUNCTION

Description   **CTime** constructors create objects from a great variety of data formats. A **CTime** object may be created by copying an existing object from an ANSI **time_t** value; from DOS date and time; or from explicit specification of year, month, day, hour, minute and second; or they may simply be constructed as an uninitialized object. Uninitialized **CTime** objects contain the invalid time 0. When **CTime** objects are created from user-specified data, it is the programmer's responsibility to ensure that the supplied values are within valid ranges. (Year values are constrained to 1970–2038.)

Prototype
```
//Function Prototype
    //Creates a CTime object initialized with the invalid time "0"
CTime timeStart;
    //Creates a CTime object with tTicks, an existing time_t value
CTime timeStop( tTicks );
    //Creates a CTime object with the value 11:00a.m. August 5, 1986
CTime timeNewOne(1986, 8, 5, 11, 0, 0 );
```

Format

Description **Format** converts from Greenwich Mean Time to local time and then uses a **printf**-like format string to copy **CTime** data to a **CString** object. The list of format directives is taken from the C language runtime function **strftime**.

Format Character	Meaning
%A	Full weekday name.
%a	Abbreviated weekday name.
%B	Full month name.
%b	Abbreviated month name.
%c	Locale-specific date and time format.
%d	Day of month as a decimal number.
%H	Hours in 24-hour format.
%I	Hours in 12-hour format.
%j	Day of year as decimal number.
%m	Month as decimal number.
%M	Minute as decimal number.
%p	AM/PM appended to 12-hour time format.
%S	Seconds as decimal number.
%U	Week of the year as a decimal number (0 through 51) with Sunday as first day of the week.
%w	Weekday as decimal number (0 = Sunday, 6 = Saturday).
%W	Week of the year as a decimal number (0 through 51) with Monday as first day of the week.
%x	Date representation for current locale.
%X	Time representation for current locale.
%y	Year without century as a decimal number.
%Y	Year with century as a decimal number.
%z, %Z	Time-zone name or abbreviation.

Prototype

```
//Function Prototype
//CString Format( const char* pFormat );
    //Creates a CTime object with the value 10:15:01 PM. February
    //23, 1985
CTime timeNewOne(1985, 2, 23, 22, 15, 01 );
    //CString will hold "10:15 PM Saturday, February
    //23, 1985"
CString stringSpecialDay = timeNewOne.Format ( %X%p %A, %B
%d, %Y );
```

777

FormatGmt — FUNCTION

Description **FormatGmt** works in exactly the same way as **Format**, except that it does not convert from Greenwich Mean Time to local time. It uses a **printf**-like format string to copy **CTime** data to a **CString** object in GMT. The list of format directives is taken from the C language runtime function **strftime**. *See Format for a list of format strings and a usage example.*

GetCurrentTime — FUNCTION

Description **GetCurrentTime** returns a **CTime** object representing the current time based on the system clock. **GetCurrentTime** is a static member function of the **CTime** class, which means that all occurrences of **CTime** objects share a single occurrence of this function. For this reason, it is necessary to call it by using the class name and scope resolution operator.

Prototype
```
//Function Prototype
//static CTime PASCAL GetCurrentTime( );
    //Initialize the CTime object with the current time....
CTime timeNow = CTime::GetCurrentTime( );
```

GetDay — FUNCTION

```
GetMonth
GetYear
GetHour
GetMinute
GetSecond
GetDayOfWeek
```

Description These functions return the time and date components implied by their names. It is the application's responsibility to ensure that **CTime** objects are initialized with values in the appropriate ranges for time measurement before the objects are queried by these member functions. The arbitrary range for valid years is 1970 through 2038, and hours are reported in 24-hour local time. The local time zone is established by the **TZ** environment variable. In all other cases, the normal constraints apply.

Prototype
```
//Function Prototypes
//int GetYear( ) const;
//int GetMonth( ) const;
```

```
//int GetDay( ) const;
//int GetHour( ) const;
//int GetMinute( ) const;
//int GetSecond( ) const;
//int GetDayOfWeek( ) const;
    //Creates a CTime object with the value 10:15:01 PM. February
    //23, 1985
CTime timeNewOne(1985, 2, 23, 22, 15, 01 );
    //Returns 1985
int iYear = timeNewOne.GetYear( ) ;
    //Returns 2 ( February )
int iMonth = timeNewOne.GetMonth( );
    //Returns 23
int iDay = timeNewOne.GetDay( ) ;
    //Returns 22 ( 22:00, or 10:00 p.m.)
int iHour = timeNewOne.GetHour( );
    //Returns 15
int iMinute = timeNewOne.GetMinute( );
    //Returns 1
int iSecond = timeNewOne.GetSecond( );
    //Returns 7 ( Saturday )
int iDayOfWeek = timeNewOne.GetDayOfWeek( );
```

GetDayOfWeek · FUNCTION

See **CTime::GetDay**.

GetGmtTm · FUNCTION

Description **GetGmtTm** returns the Greenwich Mean Time value for the time contained by a **CTime** object. The data is copied to a **tm** structure with the following members:

tm Structure Member	Meaning
tm_sec	Seconds
tm_minutes	Minutes
tm_hour	Hour (24-hour format)
tm_mday	Day of month (1 through 31)
tm_mon	Month (0 through 11)
tm_year	Actual year: 1900
tm_wday	Day of week (1 = Sunday, 7 = Saturday)
tm_yday	Day of year (0 through 365)
tm_isdst	Always 0

If the application supplies a reference to a **tm** structure, the data is copied to it, but if not, an internal statically allocated **tm** structure is filled in and a pointer to it is returned. The pointer may be used to access the structure members, but the data in that structure is overwritten by later calls to the function.

Prototype

```
//Function Prototype
//struct tm* GetGmtTm( struct tm* ptmTimeStruct = NULL ) const;
    //Creates a CTime object with the value 10:15:01 PM. February
    //23, 1985
CTime timeNewOne(1985, 2, 23, 22, 15, 01 );
    //Convert CTime to GMT and return pointer to internal tm
    //buffer....
struct tm* ptmGmtNewOne = timeNewOne.GetGmtTm;
    //Reference time data immediately — other calls will overwrite
    //data
    //Gmt hours are reported by this function....
int iYear = ptmGmtNewOne->tm_hour;
```

GetHour   FUNCTION

See **CTime::GetDay**.

GetLocalTime   FUNCTION

Description   **GetLocalTime** provides the same time information as **GetGmtTime**, except that the time reported is based on the local time zone as established by the environment variable **TZ**. The information is copied to a **tm** structure, which is described in the entry for **GetGmtTime**, and the same constraints apply. *See GetGmtTime for a usage example.*

Prototype

```
//Function Prototype
//struct tm* GetLocalTm( struct tm* ptm = NULL ) const;
```

GetMinute   FUNCTION

See **CTime::GetDay**.

GetMonth   FUNCTION

See **CTime::GetDay**.

GetSecond — FUNCTION

See **CTime::GetDay**.

GetTime — FUNCTION

Description **GetTime** returns the value of the **CTime** object as an ANSI **time_t** value.

Prototype
```
//Function Prototype
//time_t GetTime( )const;
//static CTime PASCAL GetCurrentTime( );
    //Initialize the CTime object with the current time....
CTime timeNow = CTime::GetCurrentTime( );
    //Retrieve an ANSI time_t value from the object....
time_t ttAnsiTime = timeNow.GetTime();
```

GetYear — FUNCTION

See **CTime::GetDay**.

operator +, -, +=, -= — OPERATORS

Description **CTime** is closely related to the class **CTime Span**. **CTime** objects are instantaneous times, and **CTimeSpan** objects are periods of time. Making this distinction is helpful in understanding the ways in which the additive operators for the **CTime** class can be used. Adding two instantaneous times together makes no sense, but subtracting one instantaneous time from another does make sense. The result is a time span. Adding or subtracting a time interval to or from an instantaneous time makes sense, again because it identifies a point in time. Using these operators, you can add or subtract a **CTimeSpan** object from a **CTime** or subtract one **CTime** from another.

Prototype
```
    //Two CTimes, with values one year apart
CTime timeOne(1994, 2, 23, 22, 15, 01 );
CTime timeTwo(1993, 2, 23, 22, 15, 01 );
    //Subtraction gives a time span
CTimeSpan timespanTS = timeOne - timeTwo;
    //Adding the time span to the timeTwo gives us the same date
    //in 1995 ....
timeTwo = timeOne + CTimeSpan timespanTS;
```

operator =

Description

operator = assigns a value to a **CTime** from another **CTime** or from a C language **time_t** value.

Prototype

```
        //Creates an uninitialized CTime object
CTime timeBirthDay;
        //Creates a CTime object with the value 10:15:01 PM. February
        //23, 1985
CTime timeNewOne(1985, 2, 23, 22, 15, 01 );
        //Copy from a CTime
timeBirthDay = timeNewOne;
```

operator ==, <, >, >=, <=, !=

Description

Comparison operators compare two instantaneous times and return the Boolean evaluation of the comparison.

Prototype

```
        //Create and initialize two CTime objects with the same value
CTime timeOne(1985, 2, 23, 22, 15, 01 );
CTime timeTwo = timeOne;
if ( timeOne < timeTwo )
{
    //Never enter this code section because comparison evaluates
    //to FALSE
}
```

operator >>, <<

Description

The archive **operator >>** provides a quick means of doing a diagnostic dump or storing a **CTime** object to an archive. The **operator <<** retrieves the object from the archive. The use of the archive operator to dump context information is supported only for the debug versions of the MFC library, however.

Prototype

```
        //Create a CArchive and a CTime
CArchive arTime;
CTime timeStart(1994, 2, 23, 22, 15, 01 );
        //If the archive is storing, write out the CTime object
if( arTimes.IsStoring( ) )
{
ar >> timeStart;
}
```

```
else
    //If the archive is loading, read in the Ctime object
    {
    timeStart << ar ;
    }
}
```

C TimeSpan

Description   A **CTimeSpan** object stores time internally in seconds and provides member functions that convert the internal value to years, months, days or hours. **CTimeSpan** objects are signed four-byte values, limiting them to the representation of no more than a 68-year range. The **CTimeSpan** class is one of a family known as the Simple Value classes, which includes the **CString**, **CTime**, **CTimeSpan**, **CRect**, **CPoint** and **CSize** classes. In fact, about all that this divergent group has in common is that they encapsulate data items and that they are themselves base classes, as opposed to most framework classes, which are derived from other classes. There are some restrictions on the use of **CTime** and **CTimeSpan**. The **CTime** and **CTimeSpan** functions may *not* be used in Windows DLLs. **CTimeSpan** is not intended to be used as a base class for user-derived classes.

Member Functions

CTimeSpan

Description   **CTimeSpan** constructors, like those of **CTime**, create objects from a variety of data formats. A **CTimeSpan** object may be created by copying an existing object from an ANSI **time_t** value or from explicit specification of days, hours, minutes and seconds, or may simply be constructed as an uninitialized object. When **CTimeSpan** objects are created from user-specified data, it is the programmer's responsibility to ensure that the supplied values are within valid ranges. The precision of a **CTimeSpan** object is limited by its representation as a four-byte signed integer. **CTimeSpan** values, like **time_t** values, are stored as seconds, which translates to a range of plus or minus 68 years.

Prototype
```
//Creates an unitialized CTimeSpan object
CTimeSpan timespanWeek;
    //Creates a CTimeSpan object with tTicks, an existing time_t
    //value
CTimeSpan timespanDays( tTicks );
    //60 is assumed to be a time_t value
CTimeSpan timespanMinute( 60 );
    //Copy from an existing CTimeSpan
CTimeSpan timespanOneMinute = timespanMinute;
    //Creates a CTimeSpan object with 2 days, 1 hour, 15 minutes,
    //and 30 seconds....
CTimeSpan timespanElapsed(2, 1, 15, 30 );
    //Creates a CTimeSpan object with -2 days....
CTimeSpan timespanPreviousPeriod(-2, 0,0,0 );
```

Format
FUNCTION

Description **Format** converts a **CTimeSpan** to a string by using a **printf**-like format string.

Format Character	Meaning
%D	Total days in the time span
%H	Time span: hours in the current day
%M	Time span: minutes in the current hour
%S	Time span: seconds in the current minute
%%	Literal insertion of a % in the string

Prototype
```
//Function Prototype
//CString Format( const char* pszFormatString );
    //Creates a CTimeSpan object with the value 2 days, 1 hour,
    //15 minutes, and 30 seconds....
CTimeSpan timespanElapsed( 176400 );
    //CString will hold "Elapsed Time = 2 days 1 hrs 15 min 30 sec"
CString stringSpecialDay =
 timespanElapsed.Format ("Elapsed Time = %D days %H hrs %M
 min %S sec");
```

GetDays | FUNCTION

GetHours
GetMinutes
GetSeconds

Description   These functions return the number of whole days, whole hours, minutes or seconds that would be necessary to define the value of the CTimeSpan by using this formula:

CTimeSpan = days + hours + minutes + seconds. To get the total number of hours, minutes or seconds that comprise a **CTimeSpan**, use the companion functions **GetTotalHours**, **GetTotalMinutes** or **GetTotalSeconds**.

Prototype
```
//Function Prototypes
//int GetDays( ) const;
//int GetHours( ) const;
//int GetMinutes( ) const;
//int GetSeconds( ) const;
    //Creates a CTimeSpan object with 2 days, 1 hour, 15 minutes,
    //and 30 seconds....
CTimeSpan timespanElapsed(2, 1, 15, 30 );
    //Returns 2 days
int iDays = timespanElapsed.GetDays( ) ;
    //Returns 1 hour
int iHours = timespanElapsed.GetHours( );
    //Returns 15 minutes
int iMinute = timespanElapsed.GetMinutes( );
    //Returns 30 seconds
int iSecond = timespanElapsed.GetSeconds( );
```

GetHours | FUNCTION

See **CTimeSpan::GetDays**.

GetMinutes | FUNCTION

See **CTimeSpan::GetDays**.

GetSeconds | FUNCTION

See **CTimeSpan::GetDays**.

GetTotalHours ~ FUNCTION

GetTotalMinutes
GetTotalSeconds

Description Each of these functions returns the total number of whole time increments (whole days, whole hours, etc.) in the **CTimeSpan** object. Because it is possible for a **CTimeSpan** object to be negative, it is also possible for any of these functions to return a negative value, constrained to a range appropriate to the units of time measurement.

Prototype
```
//Function Prototypes
//int GetTotalHours( ) const;
//int GetTotalMinutes( ) const;
//int GetTotalSeconds( ) const;
    //Creates a CTimeSpan object with 2 days, 1 hour, 15 minutes,
    //and 30 seconds....
CTimeSpan timespanElapsed(2, 1, 15, 30 );
    //Returns 49 hours
int iHour = timespanElapsed.GetHour( );
    //Returns 2955 minutes
int iMinute = timespanElapsed.GetMinute( );
    //Returns 176430 seconds
int iSecond = timespanElapsed.GetSecond( );
```

GetTotalMinutes ~ FUNCTION

See **CTimeSpan::GetTotalHours**.

GetTotalSeconds ~ FUNCTION

See **CTimeSpan::GetTotalHours.**

operator +, -, +=, -= ~ OPERATORS

Description **CTimeSpan** objects are really nothing more than simple values that express a range of time in seconds, and they behave in typical arithmetic fashion. Note that it is perfectly valid for a time span to assume a negative value.

Prototype
```
            //Two CTimeSpans, with values one hour apart
            CTimeSpan timespanOne(0);
            CTimeSpan timespanTwo( 3600 );
                //Add the two
            timespanOne += timespanTwo;
```

operator =   OPERATOR

Description   **operator** = assigns a value to a **CTimeSpan** from another.

Prototype
```
            //Creates a CTimeSpan object with the value 2 days, 1 hour,
            //15 minutes, and 30 seconds and an uninitialized
            //CTimeSpan....
            CTimeSpan timespanElapsed( 176400 );
            CTimeSpan timespanNew;
                //Assign value to uninitialized object
            timespanNew = timespanElapsed;
```

operator ==, <, >, >=, <=, !=   OPERATORS

Description   Comparison operators compare two time spans and return the Boolean evaluation of the comparison.

Prototype
```
            //Two CTimeSpans, with values one hour apart
            CTimeSpan timespanOne(0);
            CTimeSpan timespanTwo( 3600 );
            if ( timespanOne != timespanTwo )
            {
                //Comparison evaluates to TRUE
            }
```

operator >>, <<   OPERATORS

Description   The archive **operator >>** provides a quick means of doing a diagnostic dump or storing a **CTimeSpan** object to an archive. The **operator <<** retrieves the object from the archive. When the archive operator is used to dump context information, the value is formatted to a string that displays days, hours, minutes and seconds.

Prototype

```
            //Create a CArchive and a CTimeSpan
CArchive arTime;
CTimeSpan timespanHour( 3600 )
    //If the archive is storing, write out the CTimeSpan object
if( arTimes.IsStoring( ) )
{
ar >> timespanHour;
}
else
    //If the archive is loading, read in the CTime object
{
timespanHour << ar ;
}
}
```

C ToolBar

Derivation

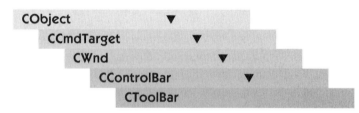

Description The **CToolBar** class implements a type of Windows control bar that consists of a horizontal row of bitmapped buttons. The individual buttons can behave as push buttons, check boxes or radio buttons. Toolbar buttons are not Windows-like dialog controls. They are rectangular regions for which hit testing is performed by the containing toolbar. Constructing and handling a toolbar is more straightforward and convenient than implementing child window controls, but the buttons are subject to a few restrictions.

The toolbar button images must be stored in a single bitmap resource, and they all must be the same size, arranged in a horizontal row. The default size of the bitmaps is 16 pixels in width by 15 pixels in height. The member function **SetButtons** is used to assign both a control ID and an image index to each of the buttons. Both the ID and the image index are used by the application to communicate with the button.

Toolbar buttons generally match frequently used pull-down menu items and may share both **OnUpdateCommandUI** and event-handling code with them.

The default behavior of a toolbar button is that of a push button. You can change the default button style to a check box by assigning it the **TTBS_CHECKBOX** style with the **SetButtons** member function. To create radio buttons, you must construct a **CCmdUI** object and create an **ON_UPDATE_COMMAND_UI** function that handles the selection state of each of the sets of radio buttons.

Member Functions

CommandToIndex FUNCTION

Description   **CommandToIndex** returns the zero-based index of the first button in the toolbar with the specified command ID.

Prototype
```
//Function Prototype
//int CommandToIndex(UINT nIDFind) const;
    //Find which button handles the ID_FILE_SAVE command
int iIdFileSaveButton = OurAppToolbar.CommandToIndex(
ID_FILE_SAVE );
```

Create FUNCTION

Description   **Create** creates the window that contains the toolbar buttons, sets its style and location, and connects it to the **CToolBar** object. *See CToolBar for a usage example.*

Prototype
```
//Function Prototype
//BOOL Create(CWnd* pParentWnd,
// DWORD dwStyle = WS_CHILD | WS_VISIBLE | CBRS_TOP,
// UINT nID = AFX_IDW_TOOLBAR );
```

CToolBar FUNCTION

Description   **CToolBar** constructs a toolbar object, but doesn't load its bitmaps or show the toolbar.

Prototype
```
//Function Prototype
    //Construct a toolbar object
CToolBar m_OurToolBar;
    //We create it in the parent frame window's implementation
m_OurToolBar.Create(this) ;
```

789

```
//Then we have to load the bitmap with the button images
m_OurToolBar.LoadBitmap(IDR_MAINFRAME);
    //Then we set the command IDs for the set of buttons
m_OurToolBar.SetButtons(NULL, 7);
    //Then set the style for each button, locating it by ID and
    //bitmap index
m_OurToolBar.SetButtonInfo(0, ID_VIEW_LONG,TBBS_BUTTON, 10);
m_OurToolBar.SetButtonInfo(1, ID_SEPARATOR,TBBS_SEPARATOR,
6);
```

GetButtonInfo   FUNCTION

Description **GetButtonInfo** uses the index of the button to retrieve its command ID, its style and the index of its image on the toolbar.

Prototype
```
//Function Prototype
//void GetButtonInfo(int nIndex, UINT& nID, UINT& nStyle, int&
iImage) const;
    //Get ID, style, and image index of the button that appears first
    //on the toolbar
GetButtonInfo(0, nID, nStyle, iImage);
```

GetItemId   FUNCTION

Description **GetItemId** retrieves the command ID for a toolbar button, given the zero-based button index.

Prototype
```
//Function Prototype
//UINT GetItemID(int nIndex) const;
    //Get the command ID for the fifth toolbar button
int iIdFileSaveButton = OurAppToolbar.GetItemID( 4 );
```

GetItemRect   FUNCTION

Description **GetItemRect** fills in a RECT structure with the coordinates of the enclosing rectangle for the button specified by the zero-based index. Coordinates are in pixels, relative to the upper left corner of the toolbar.

Prototype
```
//Function Prototype
//void GetItemRect(int nIndex, LPRECT lpRect) const;
    //This is how the framework invalidates a button to make sure
    //that it is repainted
```

```
CRect rect;
    //Get the dimensions of the entire button
GetItemRect(nIndex, &rect);
    //Exclude the borders of the bitmap button
rect.InflateRect(-CX_BORDER, -CY_BORDER);
    //Invalidate the area occupied by the bitmap
InvalidateRect(rect);
```

LoadBitmap   FUNCTION

Description **LoadBitmap** loads a single bitmap that contains images for all the buttons on the toolbar. The standard size for the bitmap images is 16 wide by 15 high, with all bitmaps the same size. If the buttons are a non-standard size, the **SetSizes** member function must be used to establish the button dimensions, and the **SetHeight** function must be used to define the height of the toolbar window. *See CToolBar for a usage example.*

Prototype
```
//Function Prototype
//BOOL LoadBitmap(LPCTSTR lpszResourceName);
//BOOL LoadBitmap(LPCTSTR nIDResource);
```

SetButtonInfo   FUNCTION

Description **SetButtonInfo** uses the index of the button to set a new command ID, style and the index of its image on the toolbar. *See CToolBar for a usage example.*

Prototype
```
//Function Prototype
//void SetButtonInfo(int nIndex, UINT nID, UINT nStyle, int iImage);
```

SetButtons   FUNCTION

Description **SetButtons** associates an array of command IDs with the buttons on a toolbar. These IDs are generally shared with corresponding pull-down menu items for which the buttons provide a shortcut. To create separators among groups of buttons, include an array element with the value ID_SEPARATOR between the groups. *See CToolBar for a usage example.*

Prototype
```
//Function Prototype
//BOOL SetButtons(const UINT FAR* lpIDArray, int nIDCount);
```

SetHeight   FUNCTION

Description   **SetHeight** is used to set the height of the overall toolbar window if the application doesn't use toolbar buttons of default sizes. *See SetSizes for a usage example.*

Prototype
```
//Function Prototype
//void SetHeight(int cyHeight);
```

SetSizes   FUNCTION

Description   **SetSizes** defines the sizes of the toolbar bitmap images, the buttons, which include a three-pixel-wide border plus the bitmap image, and the size of the containing toolbar. Normally, the application accepts the default sizes for bitmaps, buttons and the toolbar, which are established in the *Windows Application Design Guide.* Default construction and creation provides these as long as the bitmap images are sized correctly, so it is not necessary to call this member unless the toolbar is a non-standard size.

Prototype
```
//Function Prototype
//void SetSizes(SIZE sizeButton, SIZE sizeImage);
    //Assume that we have constructed and created a toolbar
    //named BigToolbar
    //We set the size of the bitmap images and set the size of the
    //button, including the image and the surrounding border
BigToolbar.SetSizes( sizeBigButtonImage, sizeBigButtonImage +
sizeButtonBorder );
    //We have to set the overall toolbar window height if we don't
    //use default sizes
BigToolbar.SetHeight( iHeightBigToolbar );
```

CUIntArray

CLASS

See **CObArray**.

CUserException

CLASS

Derivation

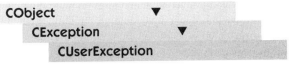

Description   The **CUserException** class provides an object that is used to halt an end-user operation. User exceptions are used by the framework to short-stop operations such as trying to load a file that is too large or warning of a failure in dialog data validation. Application code can use **CUserException objects** to handle predictable missteps also, but like other exceptions, these objects are never constructed directly. Be sure not to confuse throwing **CUserException** objects with signaling errors. Exceptions should indicate exceptional conditions in correctly functioning code. The documentation on this recommends that the application warn the user of what went wrong *before* throwing the exception. For example,

```
void GetCommData()
{
    if(bBufferOverrun)
    {
        AfxMessageBox("Buffer overrun on com1:");
        AfxThrowUserException();
    }
}
```

CUserException has no function or public data members.

CUserException
FUNCTION

Description   **CUserException** constructs an object of this type. This function is never called directly. Instead, the global function **AfxThrowUserException** is used.

Prototype

```
//Function Prototype
//Stop them before they try to load a file that is too large
if (nFileSize/sizeof(CHAR) > nMaxSize)
{
    //But first tell them what went wrong using a message box
    AfxMessageBox(AFX_IDP_FILE_TOO_LARGE);
    AfxThrowUserException();
}
```

CLASS

Derivation

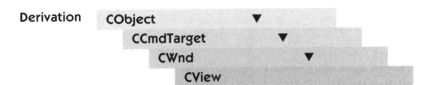

CObject	▼		
	CCmdTarget	▼	
		CWnd	▼
			CView

Description   **CView** is the base class from which user-defined views are derived. The "view" is a visual presentation of an application's document, or data. A frame window that owns and manages the view, the document, its attached view, and the frame window that owns the view are tied together by a document template that establishes their relationship as an application does its initialization processing. A document may have multiple views attached to it, but a view never belongs to more than one document. Documents with multiple views can occur in splitter windows, where a user might look at different portions of the document in the split panes. Multiple views of a document are also used in MDI applications that render data in dramatically different ways in different views. For example, a real-time MDI application might show temperature-sensor values as they are reported and a moving window graph of temperature values over a time interval.

The key distinction between documents and views is that views handle the display of data and accept user input that can modify data. Documents create and manage run-time storage as well as serialization.

In addition to defining a relationship between document, view and frame window, the document template contains information about which resources can be used to modify the document. These resources, such as menus and toolbars, define the ways in which the user can modify the document's data as displayed by the view. The commands generated by the resource-based tools are sent to the view by the frame window. The view either handles commands itself by overriding **CView** member functions or passes the command along to the document.

In addition to being the base class for user-defined views, **CView** is also the base class for several useful and powerful classes in the framework. These classes include **CScrollView**, **CFormView**,

CEditView and **CRecordView**. Before deriving your application's view class from **CView**, check these other classes to see whether the extended functionality they can provide would be useful to your application.

Derived Classes

CScrollView
CFormView
CEditView
CRecordView

Overrides

Overridable Function Name	Triggering Event
IsSelected	Test selection state of a document item (OLE function).
OnActivateView	A view is activating.
OnBeginPrinting	Print job is beginning.
OnDraw	Rendering document.
OnEndPrinting	Print job is ending.
OnEndPrintPreview	Print preview mode canceled.
OnInitialUpdate	A view has just been attached to a document.
OnPrepareDC	OnDraw or OnPrint will be called after this function.
OnPreparePrinting	A document will be printed or previewed.
OnPrint	Print or preview a page.
OnUpdate	The data in the attached document has changed.

Member Functions

CView   FUNCTION

Description **CView** is called by the framework to construct a view object. The object is not initially attached to a document.

DoPreparePrinting   FUNCTION

Description **DoPreparePrinting** invokes the standard Print dialog, gathers the dialog information, and then builds a printer DC if the application is printing. If the application is invoking print preview, it does not display the Print dialog box. To use this function, an application would have to take over its own print processing by overriding the **CView** member function **OnPreparePrinting**.

Prototype   //Function Prototype
                  //BOOL DoPreparePrinting(CPrintInfo* pInfo)

GetDocument   FUNCTION

Description   **GetDocument** retrieves a pointer to the document to which the view is attached.

Prototype   //Function Prototype
                  //CDocument* GetDocument( )const;
                      //A frame window gets a pointer to its active view
                  CView* pView = GetActiveView( );
                      //If the pointer is returned
                  if (pView != NULL)
                  return pView->GetDocument( );

CWinApp

CLASS

Derivation

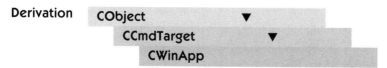

CObject ▼
    CCmdTarget ▼
        CWinApp

Description **CWinApp** is the class that encapsulates the behavior of a generic application. It starts the application, registering its window classes and creating and displaying its frame window, and then dispatches messages to the application's message-handling routines, based on the message map. AppWizard derives an application's primary class from **CWinApp**, which provides handlers for several common messages. Any of these may be overridden by the application, but only the **InitInstance** member function must be overridden. **InitInstance** determines whether copies of an application can run simultaneously. In addition, it loads standard file options from the application's .INI file, registers the application's document templates, creates a frame window for an MDI application, auto-registers the application as an OLE server (if appropriate), and processes command-line arguments. If the application needs to do specialized cleanup processing before termination, it must also override the **ExitInstance** member function.

In addition to the public member data items and functions of **CWinApp**, the foundation classes provide several global functions that are useful in interacting with application objects derived from **CWinApp**.

Overrides

Overridable Function Name	When to Override This Function
InitApplication	To perform application-specific initialization.
InitInstance	Override is mandatory to perform application-specific initialization.
Run	To perform custom message processing.
OnIdle	To perform application-specific idle-time processing.
ExitInstance	To perform application-specific termination and cleanup.
PreTranslateMessage	To filter messages before they are passed to normal translation and dispatch handlers.
SaveAllModified	To change the way the user is prompted to save modified documents.

Overridable Function Name	When to Override This Function
DoMessageBox	Replace implementation of AfxMessageBox for this application.
ProcessMessageFilter	To change the processing of messages filtered from the stream before reaching this application.
ProcessWndProcException	To catch unhandled exceptions thrown by message and command handlers.
DoWaitCursor	To modify the toggling of the wait cursor.
OnDDECommand	To take over Dynamic Data Exchange processing.
WinHelp	To call a help function other than WinHelp.

Message handlers:

Function Name	Triggering Event
OnFileNew	Called in response to ID_FILE_NEW.
OnFileOpen	Called in response to ID_FILE_OPEN.
OnFilePrintSetup	Called in response to ID_FILE_PRINT_SETUP.
OnContextHelp	User makes Shift-F1 help request.
OnHelp	User makes F1 help request.
OnHelpIndex	Handles the ID_HELP_INDEX command.
OnHelpUsing	Handles the ID_HELP_USING command.

Public Data Members

Member Datum Name	Description
m_pszAppName	Holds the name of the application.
m_hInstance	Current instance handle.
m_hPrevInstance	Previous instance handle, if any.
m_lpCmdLine	Null-terminated command line that launched the application.
m_nCmdShow	Application window's initial visibility state.
m_pMainWnd	Pointer to the application's main window.
m_bHelpMode	Asks whether the user is in Help Context mode.
m_pszExeName	Run-time module name for this application.
m_pszHelpFilePath	Path to the application's help file.
m_pszProfileName	This application's .INI filename.

Member Functions

AddDocTemplate FUNCTION

Description **AddDocTemplate** is called from an application's **InitInstance** function to establish the relationships among an application class, its document types, the view window class and the main frame window. Document templates represent each distinct data source used by an application. Document templates all must be added before the application registers them with **RegisterShellFileTypes**. Registering document templates allows the user to launch an application from File Manager by double-clicking a filename associated with a registered template.

Prototype
```
//Function Prototype
// void AddDocTemplate(CDocTemplate* pTemplate);
    //Do initial housekeeping, such as setting dialog background
    //color and loading standard INI file info,
    //like the MRU filename list
SetDialogBkColor(); // Use gray dialog background
LoadStdProfileSettings( );
    //A sound-oriented app that uses both .WAV and MIDI data
    //adds its documents....
AddDocTemplate(new CMultiDocTemplate(IDR_WAVEFORM,
        RUNTIME_CLASS(CWaveDoc), //Document Class name
        RUNTIME_CLASS(CMDIChildWave), //Frame window class
                                        //name
        RUNTIME_CLASS(CWaveView)));      //View class name
AddDocTemplate(new CMultiDocTemplate(IDR_MIDI,
        RUNTIME_CLASS(CMidiDoc),    //Document Class name
        RUNTIME_CLASS(CMDIChildMidi), //Frame window class
                                        //name
        RUNTIME_CLASS(CMidiView)));      //View class name
    //Start up the main window
CMainFrame* pMainFrame = new CMainFrame;
if (!pMainFrame->LoadFrame(IDR_MAINFRAME))
    return FALSE;
pMainFrame->ShowWindow(m_nCmdShow);
pMainFrame->UpdateWindow();
m_pMainWnd = pMainFrame;
    //Enable File Manager drag and drop
m_pMainWnd->DragAcceptFiles( );
```

```
//Set up to let the user launch by double-clicking
//a data file in File Manager
EnableShellOpen( );
RegisterShellFileTypes( );
```

AddToRecentFileList   FUNCTION

Description **AddToRecentFileList** adds a filename to the most recently used list. New filenames should be added to the list only after a call to **LoadStdProfileSettings** has retrieved the MRU list for the application. This list is updated automatically by the framework when a file is opened or the SaveAs... command saves an existing file with a new name.

Prototype
```
//Function Prototype
//virtual void AddToRecentFileList(LPCTSTR pszPathName);
```

CWinApp   FUNCTION

Description **CWinApp** is called once and only once for each application. It constructs the application's **CWinApp**-derived object.

Prototype
```
//Function Prototype
    //Derive our class from CWinApp
class COurApp : public CWinApp
```

EnableShellOpen   FUNCTION

Description **EnableShellOpen** is called in **InitInstance** and enables the application to be launched from File Manager when a user double-clicks on a data file that has been associated with one of the application's document templates. *See **AddDocTemplate** for a usage example.*

Prototype
```
//Function Prototype
//void EnableShellOpen( );
```

GetPrinterDeviceDefaults   FUNCTION

Description **GetPrinterDeviceDefaults** populates a **PRINTDLG** structure, using information stored in the Windows .INI file and the system printer configuration. The fields of the **PRINTDLG** structure correspond to the controls in the system Print dialog.

Prototype
```
//Function Prototype
//BOOL GetPrinterDeviceDefaults(PRINTDLG FAR* pPrintDlg);
    //Use the global function to get a pointer to the application
    //object and retrieve its default print settings
AfxGetApp( )->GetPrinterDeviceDefaults(pPrintDlgStruct);
```

GetProfileInt · FUNCTION

WriteProfileInt

Description These functions get and set integer values stored in an application's .INI file.

Example
```
//Function Prototype
//UINT GetProfileInt(LPCTSTR lpszSectionName, LPCTSTR
//lpszEntryName,
//      int nDefault);
//BOOL WriteProfileInt(LPCTSTR lpszSectionName, LPCTSTR
//lpszEntryName,
//      int nValue);
    //Get values in hertz for lowest and highest note
    //the app can play
nLowNoteHz = GetProfileInt(szSongster, szLowestNote,
DD_LONOTE);
nHighNoteHz = GetProfileInt(szSongster, szHighestNote,
DD_HINOTE);
```

GetProfileString · FUNCTION

WriteProfileString

Description These functions get and set string values stored in an application's .INI file.

Prototype
```
//Function Prototype
//CString GetProfileString(LPCTSTR lpszSectionName, LPCTSTR
//lpszEntryName,
//      LPCTSTR lpszDefault /*= NULL */);
//BOOL WriteProfileString(LPCTSTR lpszSectionName, LPCTSTR
//lpszEntryName,
//      LPCTSTR lpszValue);
    //Get the standard file extension from the .INI file
GetProfileString(szSongster, szFileExtension, DD_FILEEXTENSION);
```

```
        //Concatenate the name the user has given this song and the
        //file extension
    CString stringUserSongName = stringNameQuery + szFileExtension;
        //Write them back to the INI file as the value of the
        //"CurrentSong" entry
    WriteProfileString(szSongster, szCurrentFile, DD_CURRENTSONG );
```

LoadCursor — FUNCTION

LoadStandardCursor
LoadOEMCursor

Description These functions all load cursor resources for the application. **LoadStandardCursor** uses one of the manifest constants declared in windows.h beginning with the prefix **IDC_**. These constants identify system cursors. **LoadOEMCursor** loads one of the OEM cursor sets defined in windows.h. To use these, #define OEMRESOURCE before including afxwin.h. **LoadCursor** loads application-specific cursors from the application's resource file.

Prototype
```
    //Function Prototype
    //HCURSOR LoadCursor( LPCSTR lpszResourceName )const;
    //HCURSOR LoadCursor( int nIDResource )const;
    //HCURSOR LoadOEMCursor( LPCSTR lpszResourceName )const;
    //HCURSOR LoadStandardCursor( int nIDResource)const;
        //an application loads its custom cursor and saves the returned
        //cursor handle hcurLast = LoadCursor( IDC_MICROPHONE );
```

LoadIcon — FUNCTION

LoadStandardIcon
LoadOEMIcon

Description These functions all load icon resources for the application. **LoadStandardIcon** uses one of the manifest constants declared in windows.h beginning with the prefix **IDI_**. These constants identify system icons. **LoadOEMIcon** loads one of the OEM icon sets defined in windows.h. To use these, #define OEMRESOURCE before including afxwin.h. **LoadIcon** loads application-specific icons from the application's resource file.

Prototype
```
    //Function Prototype
    //HICON LoadIcon( LPCSTR lpszResourceName )const;
    //HICON LoadIcon( int nIDResource )const;
```

```
//HICON LoadOEMIcon( LPCSTR lpszResourceName )const;
//HICON LoadStandardIcon( int nIDResource )const;
    //an application loads its custom icon and saves the returned
    //icon handle HICON hIcon = LoadIcon(ID_MYICON);
```

LoadOEMCursor   FUNCTION

See CWinApp::LoadCursor.

LoadOEMIcon   FUNCTION

See CWinApp::LoadIcon.

LoadStandardCursor   FUNCTION

See CWinApp::LoadCursor.

LoadStandardIcon   FUNCTION

See CWinApp::LoadIcon.

LoadStdProfileSettings   FUNCTION

Description **LoadStdProfileSettings** is called from **InitInstance** to load the
most recently used filename list and a saved preview state. *See
AddDocTemplate for a usage example.*

Prototype
```
//Function Prototype
//void LoadStdProfileSettings( );
```

OpenDocumentFile   FUNCTION

Description **OpenDocumentFile** is called in **InitInstance** by applications that
can launch a session by opening a document named on the com-
mand line.

Prototype
```
//Function Prototype
CDocument* OpenDocumentFile(LPCTSTR lpszFileName);
    //Open an existing document, specified by the user on the
    //command line
OpenDocumentFile(m_lpCmdLine);
```

RegisterShellFileTypes   FUNCTION

Description **RegisterShellFileTypes** registers document templates. It allows
the user to launch an application from File Manager by double-
clicking a filename associated with a registered template. *See
AddDocTemplate for a usage example.*

Prototype
```
//Function Prototype
void RegisterShellFileTypes( );
```

SetDialogBkColor   FUNCTION

Description SetDialogBkColor is called in InitInstance to set the standard background color for dialog boxes. *See **AddDocTemplate** for a usage
example.*

Prototype
```
//Function Prototype
//void SetDialogBkColor(COLORREF clrCtlBk = RGB( 192,192,192 )
//        , COLORREF clrCtlText = RGB(0,0,0) );
```

WriteProfileInt   FUNCTION

See CWinApp::GetProfileInt.

WriteProfileString   FUNCTION

See GetProfileString.

WindowDC

Derivation

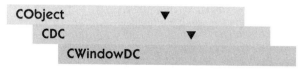

CObject

  CDC

    CWindowDC

Description   The **CWindowDC** class takes most of its characteristics from the **CDC** base class. Its basic function is to acquire a DC for the application's window area by calling the SDK functions **::GetWindowDC** in its constructor and **::ReleaseDC** in its destructor. A **CWindowDC** object can access an application's entire frame window area, in contrast to a **CClientDC** object, which can access only the client portion of the Window. It is used for painting the non-client areas of the window. As with most of the classes derived from **CDC**, it differs only in constructor and destructor functions.

Data Member

m_hWnd
MEMBER

Description   Identifies the window for which this **CWindowDC** object is valid.

Member Functions

CWindowDC
FUNCTION

Description   **CWindowDC::CWindowDC** constructs a **CWindowDC** object for the application's **CWnd** object by calling **::GetWindowDC** and then attaches it to the **CWnd** object. This DC is used to access the window's screen area (both client and non-client). The constructor throws an exception if the **::GetDC** call fails.

Example   Here we construct a **CWindowDC** object on the stack inside an application's view message handler, using a NULL pointer. This action constructs the DC without attaching it to a **CWnd** object. In this case, we only want the DC to convert a point expressed in logical coordinates to device coordinates. We set the map mode of the DC we construct so that the translation can be done using the correct logical units. Because the DC we construct is local object, its destructor is automatically called when it goes out of scope.

Prototype

```
//Function Prototype
//CWindowDC( CWnd* pWnd );
CPoint CVentanaView::ConvertPoint( CPoint ptConvert)
{
 CWindowDC dc(NULL);
    //Construct a DC for the entire app window
 dc.SetMapMode( m_CurrentMapMode );
    //Set map mode to current logical units
 dc.DPtoLP((LPPOINT)&ptConvert);
       //Convert the point from device to logical
            //coords....
 return ptConvert;
    //return the converted point....
}
```

~CWindowDC   FUNCTION

Description **CWindowDC::~CWindowDC** destroys a **CWindowDC** object for the application's **CWnd** object by calling **::ReleaseDC**.

CWnd   CLASS

Derivation

CObject	▼	
	CCmdTarget	▼
		CWnd

Description The **CWnd** class is the common base class of all windowing objects in the application framework. It encapsulates the basic elements of window behavior, much of which revolves around sending and responding to messages. One of the principal jobs of the **CWnd** class is to replace the **WndProc** of an SDK-based Windows application, by intercepting messages and dispatching them directly to handler functions. For this reason, it incorporates a very large set of message-handler member functions that are intended to be overridden by applications.

The **CWnd** object controls almost every aspect of the life cycle of a Windows program, but it does not contain the data structure that specifies the window. This makes it possible to detach the window from the **CWnd** object and deal with it independently or to acquire a handle to a window and attach it to a **CWnd** object temporarily.

Applications can create child windows by deriving them from the **CWnd** class.

Derived Classes

CFrameWnd
CControlBar
CSplitterWnd
CView
CDialog
CStatic
CButton
CListbox
CComboBox
CScrollBar
CEdit

Data Member

m_hWnd   MEMBER

Description **m_hWnd** is the handle to the Windows window attached to the **CWnd** object.

Member Functions

ArrangeIconicWindows   FUNCTION

Description **ArrangeIconicWindows** arranges icons in regularly spaced rows for the **CWnd** that calls it. To arrange icons on the desktop, use **GetDesktopWindow** to get a pointer to the Windows Desktop.

Prototype
```
//Function Prototype
//UINT ArrangeIconicWindows( );
    //Get a pointer to the desktop window
CWnd* pParent = wndTimerChild.GetParent( );
    //Arrange icons in rows
pParent.ArrangeIconicWindows( );
```

Attach   FUNCTION

Description   **Attach** attaches the window identified by a handle to a **CWnd** object. When a user creates a **CWnd** object to couple to an existing handle, usually it is done by calling the function **FromHandle**, which in turn calls **Attach**.

Prototype
```
//Function prototype
//BOOL Attach( HWND hWndNew )
```

BeginPaint   FUNCTION

Description   **BeginPaint** populates a **PAINTSTRUCT** data structure, which is necessary before any painting or GDI functions can be called for a window. Normally, an application doesn't have to call **BeginPaint** directly because the message-handler functions for the application's views are called after this and other necessary paint housekeeping and initialization have taken place. This situation is taken care of if you are using a **CPaintDC**, which is exactly what **OnDraw** does. If, however, you handle **OnPaint**, you need to either (1) call this function, or (2) create a **CPaintDC**, which is even better.

BringWindowToTop   FUNCTION

Description   **BringWindowToTop** is a quick way of bringing a particular window to the top of the z-order and causing it to activate.

Prototype
```
//Function Prototype
//void BringWindowToTop( );
    //Activate tool window and uncover any hidden portions
wndTools.BringWindowToTop( );
```

CalcWindowRect   FUNCTION

Description   **CalcWindowRect** figures the size of a window rectangle based on a size specified for the client area of a window. The dimensions of the window rectangle are written back to the **RECT** passed for the client area. If this function is called before **Create**, the resulting **RECT** can be used to construct a child window.

Prototype
```
//Function Prototype
//virtual void CalcWindowRect(LPRECT lpClientRect);
    //Assume that we initialized rectLocation with the origins and
    //dimensions we wanted the client area
    //of the edit control to occupy.
CalcWindowRect(LPRECT rectLocation);
    //Create a child edit window by using a pointer
    //to the CWnd-based parent
Create("EDIT", NULL, WS_CHILD, rectLocation, pParentWnd, nID);
```

ChangeClipboardChain   FUNCTION

Description   **ChangeClipboardChain** removes the current **CWnd** from the Clipboard viewer chain and mends the chain by using a window handle to the next viewer in line. The handle used to mend the chain was returned by the call to **SetClipboardViewer** that installed this **CWnd** in the chain. *See **GetClipboardViewer** for a usage example.*

Prototype
```
//Function Prototype
//BOOL ChangeClipboardChain( HWND hWndNextViewer );
```

CheckDlgButton   FUNCTION

Description   **CheckDlgButton** toggles the selection state of a dialog button.

Prototype
```
//Function Prototype
//void CheckDlgButton( int nIDButton, UINT nCheck );
UINT iCheckState;
    //Get the current selection state of the button and invert it
if( iCheckState = IsDlgButtonChecked( iCurrentButton ) )
  CheckDlgButton( iCurrentButton , !iCheckState );
```

CheckRadioButton   FUNCTION

Description   **CheckRadioButton** selects a radio button, which unsets the previously selected radio button in the same group. The first parameter identifies the radio button in the group with the lowest resource ID, and the second parameter identifies the radio button in the group with the greatest resource ID. IDs for the group must be consecutive between highest and lowest. *See **GetCheckedRadioButton** for a usage example.*

Prototype
```
//Function Prototype
void CheckRadioButton( int nIDFirstButton, int nIDLastButton,
    int nIDCheckButton );
```

ChildWindowFromPoint   FUNCTION

Description   **ChildWindowFromPoint** returns a pointer to the first child window found to contain a given point. If no child window contains the point but it is within the client area, a pointer to the **CWnd** for which the function was called is returned. If the point is outside the client area, the function returns NULL.

Prototype
```
//Function Prototype
//CWnd * ChildWindowFromPoint( POINT ptTestPoint ) const;
```

ClientToScreen   FUNCTION

ScreenToClient

Description   These functions convert between client area coordinates, which are always relative to the upper left corner of the client area, and screen coordinates, which are relative to the upper left corner of the entire display screen.

Prototype
```
//Function Prototype
//void ClientToScreen( LPPOINT lpPoint );
//void ClientToScreen( LPRECT lpRect );
//void ScreenToClient( LPPOINT lpPoint );
//void ScreenToClient( LPRECT lpRect );
    //lptSplit is a point at which the user has asked to display
    //another view of our document
wndDocument.ClientToScreen( lptNewViewTopLeft );
    //Get a DC for our CWnd-derived object wndDocument
CDC* pDC = wndDocument.GetDC( );
    //And find out what font was used to create the text
int iScreenHeight = pDC->GetDeviceCaps( VERTSIZE );
    //If the application acquires a DC by a call to GetDC, it must
    //release it by calling ReleaseDC....
wndDocument.ReleaseDC( pDC );
    //If the point is more than 5/6 of the way down the screen,
    //don't show the new view
if( lptNewViewTopLeft.y > 5 * (iScreenHeight / 6 ) )
  return TOO_LOW;
```

Create
FUNCTION

Description **Create** creates a child window and attaches it to a **CWnd** object. The parameters give the registered name of the window class, the title bar text, the style as defined in the WS_ section of windows.h and its size and location in the parent's client area coordinates, a pointer to the parent **CWnd** to which it will be attached, the child window's ID, and a pointer to the **Create** context of the child window, which context defaults to NULL.

Prototype
```
//Function Prototype
//virtual BOOL Create(LPCSTR lpszClassName, LPCSTR
//lpszWindowName,
//DWORD dwStyle, const RECT& rectLocation, CWnd*
//pParentWnd, UINT nID,
//CCreateContext* pContext = NULL );
    //Create a child edit window by using a pointer to the CWnd-
    //based parent
Create("EDIT", NULL, WS_CHILD, rectLocation, pParentWnd, nID);
```

CreateCaret
FUNCTION

Description **CreateCaret** makes the **CWnd** the owner of the system caret and replaces the current caret image with one defined by an application-supplied bitmap. The caret is used by a window that has the keyboard input focus to show the user the current insertion location in text. This may seem like a little thing, but systems designed for the disabled rely on the positioning of the system caret to interpret data for the hearing- or vision-impaired.

Prototype
```
//Function Prototype
//void CreateCaret( CBitmap* pBitmap );
    //A window that manages its own text editing
    //must create a caret....
pKeyboardInputView->CreateCaret( pCaretBitmap );
```

CreateGrayCaret
FUNCTION

Description **CreateGrayCaret** makes the **CWnd** owner of the system caret and replaces the current caret image with a gray rectangle or line.

Prototype

```
//Function Prototype
//void CreateGrayCaret( int n, int nHeight );
    //A window that manages its own text editing
    //creates a gray box as a caret....
pKeyboardInputView->CreateSolidCaret( CHAR_WIDTH,
    CHAR_HEIGHT );
```

CreateSolidCaret · FUNCTION

Description   **CreateSolidCaret** makes the **CWnd** the owner of the system caret and replaces the current caret image with a solid black rectangle or line.

Prototype

```
//Function Prototype
//void CreateSolidCaret( int nWidth, int nHeight );
    //A window that manages its own text editing
    //creates a black line as a caret....
pKeyboardInputView->CreateSolidCaret( 1, CHAR_HEIGHT );
```

CWnd · FUNCTION

Description   The **CWnd** constructor would not likely be called directly because this is mostly intended as a base class.

Prototype

```
//Function Prototype
// CWnd( )
```

DeleteTempMap · FUNCTION

Description   The reason temporary objects created by the **FromHandle** functions disappear after the next Windows messaging cycle is that the **CWnd** class does automatic garbage pickup during idle time. **DeleteTempMap** is the function that is responsible for this and *should not ever* be called by a user application, because this could create housekeeping havoc.

Prototype

```
//Function Prototype
//static void PASCAL DeleteTempMap( )
```

DestroyWindow · FUNCTION

Description   **DestroyWindow** disposes of all vestiges of the Windows window attached to a **CWnd** object. It detaches the window from the object, destroys child windows, destroys the menu, flushes the message queue, clears outstanding timers, relinquishes Clipboard ownership and, if the window is at the top of the Clipboard viewer chain, breaks the chain.

DestroyWindow is called by the destructors for objects derived from **CWnd**, so it is not usually necessary to call it directly.

Detach   FUNCTION

Description   **Detach** detaches a window handle from a **CWnd** object. A handle might be detached from a **CWnd** object to prevent the window from being destroyed along with the object at cleanup time. This situation usually comes up in connection with windows created using **FromHandle** and is handled automatically when the temporary **CWnd** is destroyed.

Prototype
```
//Function Prototype
//HWND Detach( )
```

DlgDirList   FUNCTION

DlgDirListComboBox

Description   **DlgDirList** and **DlgDirListComboBox** fill a list box or combo box with filenames based on a specified drive, path and wildcard specification. It optionally updates a static text control identified by the **IDStaticCntl** parameter shown in the function prototype with the current drive and path. The way files are displayed by the list is controlled by a set of flags that have the following meaning:

Flag	Meaning
DDL_READWRITE	Read-write files only
DDL_READONLY	Read-only files only
DDL_HIDDEN	Hidden files
DDL_SYSTEM	System files
DDL_DIRECTORY	Directories
DDL_ARCHIVE	Archives
DDL_POSTMSGS	LB_DIR flag, which sends DlgDirList-generated messages to the application's queue
DDL_DRIVES	Drives
DDL_EXCLUSIVE	Exclusive bit

Prototype
```
//Function Prototype
int DlgDirListComboBox( LPSTR lpPathSpec, int nIDComboBox,
int nIDStaticPath, UINT nFileType );
```

```
int DlgDirList( LPSTR lpPathSpec, int nIDListBox, int nIDStaticPath,
UINT nFileType );
    //Fill the listbox with read-write files in the path,
    //and do not update a static text
    //control with the path
DlgDirList( lpszPath, IDC_LISTBOX, NULL, DDL_READWRITE);
```

DlgDirListComboBox   FUNCTION

See **DlgDirList**.

DragAcceptFiles   FUNCTION

Description **DragAcceptFiles** is called from the **CWinApp::InitInstance** member function to signal that this window and all its children accept files dropped from the Windows File Manager.

Prototype
```
//Function Prototype
//void DragAcceptFiles( BOOL bAccept=TRUE );
    //This code is generated by AppWizard and is included in the
    //CWinApp::InitInstance function if OLE support is required
CMainFrame* pMainFrame = new CMainFrame;
if (!pMainFrame->LoadFrame(IDR_MAINFRAME))
 return FALSE;
pMainFrame->ShowWindow(m_nCmdShow);
pMainFrame->UpdateWindow();
m_pMainWnd = pMainFrame;
    //Set ourselves up to accept dropped files
m_pMainWnd->DragAcceptFiles();
```

DrawMenuBar   FUNCTION

Description **DrawMenuBar** updates the window's menu bar if changes are made after window creation. *See **SetMenu** for a usage example.*

Prototype
```
//Function Prototype
//void DrawMenuBar( );
```

EnableScrollBarCtrl   FUNCTION

Description **EnableScrollBarCtrl** optionally enables or disables a scroll bar control.

Prototype

```
//Function Prototype
//void EnableScrollBarCtrl(int nBar, BOOL bEnable=TRUE);
    //We have a pointer to a CWnd-derived object with scroll bars,
    //so we set the thumb position and scrolling range
    //of the SBs and draw them....
pwndWithScroll->SetScrollPos(SB_HORZ, 0);
pwndWithScroll->SetScrollPos(SB_VERT, 0);
pwndWithScroll->SetScrollRange(0, 100, TRUE);
pwndWithScroll->SetScrollRange(0, 100, TRUE);
    //Then we enable both bars but prevent redrawing.
pwndWithScroll->EnableScrollBarCtrl(SB_BOTH, FALSE);
```

EnableWindow   FUNCTION

Description **EnableWindow** either enables or disables a window for keyboard or mouse input. *See **IsWindowEnabled** for a usage example.*

Prototype

```
//Function Prototype
//BOOL EnableWindow(BOOL bEnable = TRUE );
```

EndPaint   FUNCTION

Description **EndPaint** is the balancing call to **BeginPaint**. It frees resources associated with the **PAINTSTRUCT**. Like its counterpart, this function is called by the framework in the normal course of behind-the-scenes paint processing and is seldom used by applications directly.

FindWindow   FUNCTION

Description Given the class name and window title bar text, **FindWindow** returns a pointer to a top-level **CWnd**. (It doesn't search for child windows, but **GetNextWindow** does.) The returned pointer should be assumed to be a pointer to a temporary **CWnd** object that will become invalid after the function returns.

Prototype

```
//Function Prototype
//static CWnd* PASCAL FindWindow( LPCSTR lpszClassName,
//              LPCSTR lpszWindowName );
    //The map-drawing window wants to know
    //whether the popup scale bar window is showing
CWnd* pMapScaleWnd = wndDrawMap.FindWindow( "ScaleBar",
"Distance in KM" );
```

```
                    //A NULL return means that the window was not found
                if( NULL == pMapScaleWnd )
                {
                    //Create the popup scale bar window
                CWnd wndScaleBar;
                wndScaleBar.Create("ScaleBar", NULL, WS_POPUP,
                        rectLocation, wndDrawMap, nID);
                }
```

FlashWindow — FUNCTION

Description   **FlashWindow** toggles a window's title bar between the appearance of an active window and an inactive window. Each call inverts the previous state if the parameter is TRUE, but the title bar is restored to an active appearance by a call with the parameter set to FALSE. *See **SetTimer** for a usage example*.

Prototype
```
//Function Prototype
//BOOL FlashWindow( BOOL bInvert );
```

FromHandle — FUNCTION

Description   **FromHandle** is used to temporarily attach a **CWnd** object to a HWND. This might come up if you got a window handle from the Clipboard and wanted to be able to treat it as a **CWnd** object. The function creates a temporary object and attaches the handle or returns a pointer to the **CWnd** to which it is currently attached. If a temporary object is created, it will have a life span of only one message-processing cycle, so the object must be used immediately, and the pointer should not be stored for later use.

Prototype
```
//Function Prototype
//CWnd* PASCAL FromHandle(HWND hWnd);
        //Assume that we got a window handle from the Clipboard —
        //pClipboardWindow gives us a way
        //to manipulate that window
        //as a CWnd, but the pointer is invalidated after the
        //function in which it is retrieved returns....
CWnd* pClipboardWindow = FromHandle(hWndClipboard);
```

FromHandlePermanent
FUNCTION

Description   **FromHandlePermanent** returns a pointer to a **CWnd** for the window handle if one is currently attached. The function returns NULL if the window handle is not attached to a **CWnd** object. Because this function does not create temporary objects, it can be used when an application wants to take care not to allocate memory or if the window handle can't exist separately from a **CWnd** object. Classes derived from **CWnd**, such as controls, fall into the last category.

Prototype
```
//Function Prototype
//CWnd* PASCAL FromHandlePermanent(HWND hWnd);
    //We have access to the window handle of a control
    //and want to access
    //it by using CWnd member functions....
CWnd* pChild = FromHandlePermanent(hWndCtrl);
```

GetActiveWindow
FUNCTION

Description   **GetActiveWindow** returns a pointer to the top-level window of the application that currently has the input focus. The pointer can reference a window owned by another application. The returned pointer should be assumed to be a pointer to a temporary **CWnd** object that will become invalid after the function returns.

Prototype
```
//Function Prototype
//static CWnd* PASCAL GetActiveWindow( );
if( wndOurApp.GetActiveWindow( ) ! = this )
{
    //Test to see whether this CWnd is the active window
    //and if not, boorishly grab the input focus
wndOurApp.SetActiveWindow( )
}
```

GetCapture
FUNCTION

Description   **GetCapture** retrieves a pointer to the **CWnd** that has captured the mouse input stream.

Prototype
```
//Function Prototype
//static CWnd* PASCAL GetCapture( );
    //Check to see whether this CWnd has the
```

```
                            //mouse input stream captured
                    if( wndChild.GetCapture( ) == this )
                        //Release the mouse stream with a call down
                        //to the SDK if we have it....
                     ::ReleaseCapture( );
                    else
                        //Get the mouse stream if we didn't have it
                    wndChild.SetCapture( );
```

GetCaretPos   FUNCTION

Description   **GetCaretPos** retrieves the current location of the caret in client
                area coordinates. *See **ShowCaret** for a usage example.*

Prototype   ```
                //Function Prototype
                //static CPoint PASCAL GetCaretPos( );
                ```

## GetCheckedRadioButton                                          FUNCTION

**Description**   **GetCheckedRadioButton** gets the ID of the currently selected
                button in a group of radio buttons.

**Prototype**      ```
                //Function Prototype
                //int GetCheckedRadioButton(int nIDFirstButton, int nIDLastButton);
                    //If the first radio button isn't checked, check it
                if( IDC_FIRSTRADIO !=
                    GetCheckedRadioButton( IDC_FIRSTRADIO, IDC_THIRDRADIO))
                 CheckRadioButton( IDC_FIRSTRADIO, IDC_THIRDRADIO,
                IDC_FIRSTRADIO);
                ```

GetClientRect   FUNCTION

Description   **GetClientRect** retrieves the coordinates of the upper left and
                lower right corners of a window's client area. Coordinates are in
                screen units relative to the upper left corner of the client area. *See
                SetWindowPos for a usage example.*

Prototype   ```
                //Function Prototype
                //void GetClientRect(LPRECT lpRect) const;
                ```
                ```

GetClipboardOwner   FUNCTION

Description   **GetClipboardOwner** retrieves a pointer to the **CWnd** that is the current owner of the Clipboard. When applications add data to the Clipboard, it is generally a very compact operation, involving opening and emptying the Clipboard, setting the new data, and closing the Clipboard. The application is only the owner between the calls to the SDK functions **EmptyClipboard** and **CloseClipboard**. The Clipboard data remains valid after the depositing application no longer owns the Clipboard. For this reason, the information provided by **GetClipboardOwner** isn't often useful.

The pointer returned by this function is to a temporary **CWnd** object and is invalidated by the return of the function in which **GetClipboardOwner** is called.

Prototype
```
//Function Prototype
//static CWnd* PASCAL GetClipboardOwner( );
    //Find out whether the Clipboard is owned
    //by another window....
if( ! CWnd* pwndOtherClipboardUser = GetClipboardOwner( ) )
{
    //If not, open the Clipboard
OpenClipboard( );
    //Use SDK functions to take ownership, insert the handle of a
    //bitmap, and close the Clipboard
::SetClipboardData( CF_BITMAP, hGlobalMem );
::EmptyClipboard( );
::CloseClipboard( );
}
```

GetClipboardViewer   FUNCTION

Description   **GetClipboardViewer** retrieves a pointer to the **CWnd** at the top of the Clipboard viewer chain. Any application that wants to monitor Clipboard messages can attach itself to the Clipboard viewer chain by calling **SetClipboardViewer**. This process is somewhat risky in that applications that are not at the top of the chain rely on the previous members to pass the messages along. A sluggish application or a break in the chain is an event outside the control of the other members of the viewer chain. The pointer to the **CWnd** returned by this function is temporary and is invalidated after the function that calls **GetClipboardViewer** returns.

Prototype

```
//Function Prototype
//static CWnd* PASCAL GetClipboardViewer( );
    //We want to join the chain
    //only if we can have the head position....
if( NULL == GetClipboardViewer )
{
    //Save the returned handle value for our call to
    //ChangeClipboardChain,
    //even though we are at the top....
 HWND hWndOldViewer = SetClipboardViewer( );
}
    //Later on, remove ourselves from the viewer chain
ChangeClipboardChain( hWndOldViewer );
```

GetDC   FUNCTION

Description **GetDC** retrieves a pointer to a device context for a **CWnd** object. A device context allows the application to call GDI functions for a window. It is generally very bad form to call any actual GDI output functions outside the paint message handlers of the view, but it can be very useful to be able to call GDI status and coordinate translation functions in other parts of a program. Any call to GetDC should be paired with a matching call to **ReleaseDC**. Failure to release a device context can be catastrophic because a pool of only five DCs services the requests of all windows for painting support.

Prototype

```
//Function Prototype
//CDC* GetDC( );
char szFontNameBuffer[32];
    //If we were going to serialize an object that contained text,
    //we might want to get the DC....
CDC* pDC = wndDocument.GetDC( );
    //And find out what font was used to create the text
pDC->GetTextFace( sizeof( szFontNameBuffer ), szFontNameBuffer
    );
    //If the application acquires a DC by a call to GetDC, it must
    //release it by calling ReleaseDC....
wndDocument.ReleaseDC( pDC );
```

GetDCEx

Description **GetDCEx** gets a DC for a **CWnd** object and provides a means of exerting control over the way clipping is handled for the window. The clipping logic provided by the framework is very sophisticated, so it is unlikely that application code would benefit from overriding it. As a result, this function is seldom used by applications.

GetDescendantWindow

Description **GetDescendantWindow** searches the **CWnd**'s tree of descendant windows to find the one associated with the specified control ID.

Prototype
```
//Function Prototype
//CWnd* GetDescendantWindow(int nID, BOOL
//bOnlyPerm=FALSE) const
    //You can get a pointer to the child CWnd if you have its ID
pChild = pWnd->GetDescendantWindow(iChildID);
```

GetDesktopWindow

Description **GetDesktopWindow** retrieves a pointer to the **CWnd** that Windows lays down as the "desktop," or in other words, the entire screen. This function can be used to find out whether a window is a top-level or popup window because, if so, its parent should be the desktop window. The returned pointer should be assumed to be a pointer to a temporary **CWnd** object that will become invalid after the function returns.

Prototype
```
//Function Prototype
//static CWnd* PASCAL GetDesktopWindow( );
    //Is it a popup or top-level window?
if (pWnd->GetParent( ) == pWnd->GetDesktopWindow( ))
    //if so, do something....
```

GetDlgCtrlID

Description **GetDlgCtrlID** retrieves the ID for a child window. In practice, this function is almost always called for a derived class, so the **CWnd** pointer it returns is usually cast to an appropriate type. The dialog control IDs are used with member functions to get and set control contents.

Prototype
```
//Function Prototype
//int GetDlgCtrlID( )const;
    //Get the control's ID
int iControlID = wndChildEdit.GetDlgCtrlID( );
    //Set the text in the control to an empty string
wndChildEdit.SetDlgItemText( iControlID, "" );
```

GetDlgItem   FUNCTION

Description **GetDlgItem** retrieves a temporary pointer to a child window
control in a dialog box. It returns NULL if the ID supplied is invalid.

Prototype
```
//Function Prototype
//CWnd* GetDlgItem( int nID )const;
    //Get a pointer to a listbox control,
    //and cast it to the appropriate type
CListBox* pList = (CListBox*)GetDlgItem(IDC_LISTBOX);
```

GetDlgItemInt   FUNCTION

Description **GetDlgItemInt** retrieves the contents of an integer dialog item. It
can optionally return a signed or unsigned value. Because zero is a
valid return from this function, the parameter **lpTrans** is used to
determine whether the retrieval succeeded.

Prototype
```
//Function Prototype
UINT GetDlgItemInt( int nID, BOOL* lpTrans = NULL,
BOOL bSigned = TRUE ) const;
    //For all the items in a listbox
for (int i = 0; bOk && i < NUMBER_LIST_ITEMS; i++)
{
    //Retrieve unsigned integer values
UnsignedValues[i] = GetDlgItemInt(IDC_LIST, &bAllOk, FALSE);
    //And reset the value to the item's rank in the list
SetDlgItemInt(IDC_LIST, i, FALSE);
}
```

GetDlgItemText   FUNCTION

Description **GetDlgItemText** retrieves the contents of a text dialog item. If the
buffer is not large enough for the item, you might get a GPF. If the
specified buffer is not large enough, the entry is is truncated. *See
SetDlgItemText for a usage example.*

Prototype
```
//Function Prototype
int GetDlgItemText( int nID, LPSTR lpStr, int nMaxCount ) const;
    //Get the text in a dialog control derived from CWnd
dlgSendFile.SetDlgItemText(IDC_SENDFILE_DOCNAME, szFilename,
 sizeof( szFilename));
```

GetExStyle — FUNCTION

Description **GetExStyle** retrieves a window's style attributes for windows created using extended styles. *See **Create** for a table of window styles.*

Prototype
```
//Function Prototype
//DWORD GetExStyle( ) const;;

if(!(pWndObject.GetExStyle() & WS_TOPMOST)) {
    //Check to see whether this CWnd will stay on top of the
    //z-order....
    }
```

GetFocus — FUNCTION

Description **GetFocus** returns a pointer to the top-level window of the application that currently has the keyboard input focus. The pointer can reference a window owned by another application. The returned pointer should be assumed to be a pointer to a temporary **CWnd** object that will become invalid after the function returns.

Prototype
```
//Function Prototype
//static CWnd* PASCAL GetFocus( );
if( wndOurApp.GetFocus( ) ! = this )
 {
    //Test to see whether this CWnd is the active window
    //and if not, boorishly grab the keyboard input focus
 wndOurApp.SetFocus( )
 }
```

GetFont — FUNCTION

Description **GetFont** retrieves a pointer to the font used to draw a window's text. The font object is temporary, so the pointer is invalidated when the function that called **GetFont** returns.

Prototype

```
//Function Prototype
//CFont* GetFont( )const;
    //We have a button with text drawn by a custom font....
CFont* fontCustomButton = pwndFirstButton.GetFont( );
    //And we want to set the font in another button to the custom
    //font and then redraw its text with the new font....
pwndSecondButton.SetFont( fontCustomButton, TRUE );
```

GetLastActivePopup — FUNCTION

Description   **GetLastActivePopup** returns a pointer to the most recently activated popup window belonging to the **CWnd**. If the **CWnd** has no popups, the window itself was the most recently activated popup or is not a top-level window, and then the function returns a pointer to the **CWnd** that called it. The returned pointer should be assumed to be a pointer to a temporary **CWnd** object that will become invalid after the function returns. This function is used by the framework during window activation to ensure that a top-level window's popups are displayed above it in the z-order.

Prototype

```
//Function Prototype
//CWnd* GetLastActivePopup( ) const
```

GetMenu — FUNCTION

Description   **GetMenu** retrieves a pointer to the **CMenu** object for the **CWnd**. Use this pointer to access and change the menu.

Prototype

```
//Function Prototype
//CMenu* GetMenu( )const;
    //Get a pointer to the menu for wndMain....
CMenu* pmenuMain = wndMain.GetMenu( );
    //Put a check mark next to the item IDM_FULLSCREEN
pmenuMain->CheckMenuItem( IDM_FULLSCREEN, MF_CHECKED );
```

GetNextDlgGroupItem — FUNCTION

Description   **GetNextDlgGroupItem** sequentially searches a group of dialog controls either forward or backward. To be found by this function, dialog items must have been specified as members of a group (have consecutive IDs and include the **WS_GROUP** flag in their definition) when they were created. The pointers returned by this function are temporary and are invalidated when the function calling **GetNextDlgGroupItem** returns.

825

Prototype
```
//Function Prototype
//CWnd* GetNextDlgGroupItem(CWnd* pwndCtl,
//           BOOL bPrevious = FALSE)const;
    //Call the function for a CWnd-derived control,
    //and cast the return value
    //Search for the second control in the group
CButton* pwndButtonControl =
(CButton*) GetNextDlgGroupItem(pwndFirstButton, FALSE);
SendMessage( BM_GETCHECK, 0, 0L);
```

GetNextDlgTabItem   FUNCTION

Description   **GetNextDlgTabItem** sequentially searches a group of dialog controls either forward or backward. To be navigated by this function, dialog items must have had a specified tab stop order (have consecutive IDs and include the **WS_TABSTOP** flag in their definition) when they were created. The pointers returned by this function are temporary and are invalidated when the function calling **GetNextDlgTabItem** returns.

Prototype
```
//Function Prototype
CWnd* GetNextDlgTabItem( CWnd* pWndCtl, BOOL bPrevious =
    FALSE ) const;
    //Get the parent of the control identified by pTabbedControl,
    //and then find the next control in the tab order,
    //and set the focus on the new control
pTabbedControl->GetParent()->
    GetNextDlgTabItem(pTabbedControl)->SetFocus( );
```

GetNextWindow   FUNCTION

Description   **GetNextWindow** walks the window manager's list of windows, returning either the next or previous window in the list. If the **CWnd** that calls the function is a top-level window, the returned pointer will be to another top-level window. If the **CWnd** that calls the function is a child, the returned pointer will be to the next child window. The returned pointer should be assumed to be a pointer to a temporary **CWnd** object that will become invalid after the function returns.

Prototype
```
//Function Prototype
//CWnd* GetNextWindow( UINT uiForwardOrBack =
GW_HWNDNEXT );
```

```
//walk through the child list
for (CWnd* pChild = GetTopWindow( ); pChild != NULL;
    pChild = pChild->GetNextWindow( ))
{
    //If we find one that is not iconic, return a flag....
 if ( ! pChild->IsIconic( ))
 return NOT_ALL_ICONS;
}
```

GetParentFrame   FUNCTION

Description **GetParentFrame** searches up the parent chain and returns the frame window object to which this **CWnd** belongs. It returns NULL if the search fails.

Prototype
```
//Function Prototype
//CFrameWnd* GetParentFrame() const;
    //Get a pointer to the frame window that owns this view
CFrameWnd* pFrame = pView->GetParentFrame();
if (pFrame != NULL)
{
    //Send the frame window a message that we are closing a file
 pFrame->PostMessage(WM_COMMAND, ID_FILE_CLOSE);
}
```

GetSafeHwnd   FUNCTION

Description **GetSafeHwnd** can be used to extract a handle to a window that may be safely stored for an extended duration, even though the **CWnd** to which it was attached may be temporary. For example, if a routine receives a pointer to a window as a parameter but has no way of knowing whether the pointer is to a permanent or temporary **CWnd**, it can extract and store a handle to a Windows window that will be valid after the **CWnd** is deleted. It can also be used to extract an hWnd value from an object when it is necessary to call an SDK function that requires an HWND parameter.

Prototype
```
//Function Prototype
//HWND GetSafeHwnd( )const;
    //Handle to a Device Context
HDC hDC;
    //We want to get a DC for a CWnd object called wndDraw
hDC =::GetDC( wndDraw.GetSafeHwnd( ))
```

GetScrollBarCtrl   FUNCTION

Description   **GetScrollBarCtrl** returns a pointer to a scroll bar control, but not to the scroll bars of a frame window that were specified as window creation parameters. Because **CWnd** objects have no scroll bar controls, in practice this function is useful only for objects derived from **CWnd**, such as **CView**.

Prototype
```
//Function Prototype
//virtual CScrollBar* GetScrollBarCtrl( int nBar )const;
void CScrollView::GetScrollInfo(CSize& sizeRange, int& Pos)
{
    //Test to see whether a horizontal scroll bar is in this view
    if ( NULL != CScrollBar* pScrollBar = GetScrollBarCtrl(SB_HORZ) )
    {
        //If so, get the scroll range and current thumb position....
    GetScrollRange( SB_HORZ, sizeRange.cx, sizeRange.cy );
    Pos = GetScrollRange( SB_HORZ );
    }
    return;
}
```

GetScrollPos   FUNCTION

Description   **GetScrollPos** retrieves the current position of the scroll bar thumb. This function reports the position of the thumb for a frame window scroll bar as well as for a child window. *See* **GetScrollBarCtrl** *for a usage example*.

Prototype
```
//Function Prototype
//int GetScrollPos(int nBar) const
```

GetScrollRange   FUNCTION

Description   **GetScrollRange** retrieves the current minimum and maximum values in the scrolling range. This function reports the scrolling range for a frame window scroll bar as well as for a child window. *See* **GetScrollBarCtrl** *for a usage example*.

Prototype
```
//Function Prototype
//void GetScrollRange(int nBar, LPINT lpMinPos, LPINT lpMaxPos)
//const
```

GetStyle   FUNCTION

Description   **GetStyle** retrieves a window's style attributes. *See **Create** for a table of window styles.*

Prototype
```
//Function Prototype
//DWORD GetStyle( ) const;

if(!(pWndObject.GetStyle() & WS_CHILD))     // WS_CHILD bit set?
{
    //Check to see whether this CWnd has WS_CHILD style ....
}
```

GetSystemMenu   FUNCTION

Description   **GetSystemMenu** returns a pointer to the system menu, which enables an application to call **CMenu** class member functions to alter it. Standard menu items have ID values greater than 0xf000, so give IDs of modified items less than this threshold value.

Prototype
```
//Function Prototype
//CMenu* GetSystemMenu( BOOL bRevert )const;
    //Get a pointer to the system menu
CMenu* pmenuSys = wndMain.GetSystemMenu( FALSE);
    //Append the string "Screen Snapshot" to the bottom
    //of the system menu, and give it an ID
    //less than 0xf000 specified by IDM_SNAPSHOT
pMenuSys->AppendMenu( MF_STRING, IDM_SNAPSHOT, "Screen
    Snapshot" );
```

GetTopWindow   FUNCTION

Description   **GetTopWindow** returns a pointer to the top-level child window of the CWnd and returns NULL if there are no children. The returned pointer should be assumed to be a pointer to a temporary **CWnd** object that will become invalid after the function returns. *See **GetNextWindow** for a usage example.*

Prototype
```
//Function Prototype
//CWnd* GetTopWindow( )const;
```

GetUpdateRect

Description   Windows does fairly elaborate bookkeeping to enable it to repaint the smallest area possible. **GetUpdateRect** retrieves the coordinates of the smallest bounding rectangle that encloses the part of the application's client area that is flagged for repainting on the next **WM_PAINT** message. Like other functions related to clipping, this one is not often useful to applications–unless, of course, you're doing something like a draw or CAD program where each vector costs computationally. This can save tremendously on the number of cycles you spend on the redraw.

GetUpdateRgn

Description   This function retrieves the region that encloses the part of the application's client area that is flagged for repainting on the next **WM_PAINT** message. It works in the same way as **GetUpdateRect,** and like other functions related to clipping, this one is not often useful to applications.

GetWindow

Description   **GetWindow** returns a temporary pointer to a **CWnd** with the following relationship to the object that called the function:

GetWindow Parameter	Relationship
GW_CHILD	The first child window.
GW_HWNDFIRST	For child windows, the first sibling; for top-level windows, the first top-level window in the window manager's list.
GW_HWNDLAST	For child windows, the last sibling; for top-level windows, the last top-level window in the window manager's list.
GW_HWNDNEXT	The next window manager list entry.
GW_HWNDPREV	The previous window manager list entry.
GW_OWNER	The owner of this CWnd.

Prototype
```
//Function Prototype
//CWnd* GetWindow( UINT nCmd );
    //A child window gets a pointer to its owner
CWnd* pOwner = wndChild.GetWindow(GW_OWNER);
//The child gets the parent's window rectangle location
//and dimensions
RECT rParent;
```

```
pOwner.GetWindowRect( rParent);
rcParent.left += rcParent.right / 2;
rcParent.top += rcParent.bottom / 2;
    //The child moves to the lower right corner
    //of the parent's window rectangle
wndChild.MoveWindow( rParentClientArea, TRUE );
```

GetWindowDC   FUNCTION

Description   **GetWindowDC** retrieves a device context for a window's entire area, including non-client areas, such as the caption bar or scroll bars. Because all non-client painting is handled by Windows, it is potentially dangerous for the application to attempt to insert itself in this process, so this function is seldom used by application code.

Prototype
```
//Function Prototype
//CDC* GetWindowDC( )
```

GetWindowRect   FUNCTION

Description   **GetWindowRect** retrieves the coordinates of the upper left and lower right corners of a window. Coordinates are in screen units. *See **SetWindowPos** for a usage example.*

Prototype
```
//Function Prototype
//void GetWindowRect( LPRECT lpRect ) const;
```

GetWindowText   FUNCTION

Description   **GetWindowText** retrieves the title on the window caption bar for frame windows, or the text in a control. The text is truncated if the parameter specifies a pointer to a character array that is too small to hold the string. If the parameter specifies a **CString** object, the object dynamically grows to accommodate the string if necessary, subject to the availability of memory. *See **SetWindowText** for a usage example*.

Prototype
```
//Function Prototype
int GetWindowText( LPSTR lpszStringBuf, int nMaxCount ) const;
void GetWindowText( CString& rString ) const;
```

GetWindowTextLength   FUNCTION

Description   **GetWindowTextLength** gives the number of characters in the window text, not including a terminating NULL. See **SetWindowText** for a usage example.

Prototype
```
//Function Prototype
//int GetWindowTextLength( ) const;
```

HideCaret   FUNCTION

Description   An application must hide the system caret by using **HideCaret** if it is going to repaint the client area without having received a **WM_PAINT** message. This situation might come up in connection with application management of keyboard input where, for example, overhead would be too great to call the paint handler every time the user backspaced. The caret is hidden automatically in the course of message-driven painting, so it isn't necessary to hide the caret in a paint message handler. Every call to **HideCaret** must be balanced by a call to **ShowCaret**. *See **ShowCaret** for a usage example*.

Prototype
```
//Function Prototype
//void HideCaret( );
```

HiliteMenuItem   FUNCTION

Description   **HiliteMenuItem** adds or removes a highlight from a menu item. The last parameter specifies whether the item should be highlighted or unhighlighted. *See **SetMenu** for a usage example*.

Prototype
```
//Function Prototype
BOOL HiliteMenuItem( CMenu* pMenu, UINT nIDHiliteItem,
UINT nHilite );
```

InvalidateRect   FUNCTION

See InvalidateRgn.

InvalidateRgn   FUNCTION

Description   An application can ensure that a portion of the client area it has changed is painted immediately by explicitly invalidating it. The functions **Invalidate**, **InvalidateRect** and **InvalidateRgn** flag portions of a window's client area for repainting on the next **WM_PAINT** message. They specify the entire client area, a rectangle or a region, respectively. They are often used in conjunction with **UpdateWindow**, which forces immediate repainting. *See **UpdateWindow** for a usage example.*

Prototype
```
//Function Prototype
//void Invalidate(BOOL bErase = TRUE );
//void InvalidateRect(LPRECT lpRect, BOOL bErase = TRUE );
//void InvalidateRgn(CRgn* pRgn,BOOL bErase = TRUE );
```

IsChild FUNCTION

Description **IsChild** tests whether a **CWnd** is the child of a window on which this function is invoked.

Prototype
```
//Function Prototype
//BOOL IsChild( const CWnd* pWnd ) const;
CWnd* pParent = wndOurApp.GetParent( );
CWnd* pDesktopWnd = wndOurApp.GetDesktopWindow( );
    //Assert whether the parent window is the desktop window
    //or whether the parent window of wndOurApp
    //is a child of the desktop window....
ASSERT(pParent == pDesktopWnd || pDesktopWnd-> IsChild
    (pParent));
```

IsDlgButtonChecked FUNCTION

Description **IsDlgButtonChecked** tests the selection state of a radio button or checkbox control. A non-zero return indicates that the control is selected. *See **CheckDlgButton** for a usage example.*

Prototype
```
//Function Prototype
//UINT IsDlgButtonChecked( int nIDButton );
```

IsIconic FUNCTION

Description **IsIconic** tests whether a **CWnd** is iconic.

Prototype
```
//Function Prototype
//BOOL IsIconic( )const;
if( wndChild.IsIconic( ) )
```

```
                    //Arrange all the icons of child windows in our client area
                    wndParent.ArrangeIconicWindows( );
```

IsWindowEnabled   FUNCTION

Description   **IsWindowEnabled** returns whether or not the **CWnd** is enabled for keyboard and mouse input. When child windows are disabled, their input stream is routed to the parent window.

Prototype
```
                    //Function Prototype
                    //BOOL IsWindowEnabled( )const;
                    if( ! wndChild.IsWindowEnabled( ) )
                    {
                        //If the child window is disabled, enable it....
                        wndChild.EnableWindow(TRUE);
                    }
```

IsWindowVisible   FUNCTION

Description   **IsWindowVisible** tells whether a window has been hidden by a call to **ShowWindow**.

Example
```
                    //Function Prototype
                    //BOOL IsWindowVisible( )const;
                        //We have a pointer to a CWnd, and we are testing to see
                        //whether the window is currently visible.
                    if (!pOurWnd->IsWindowVisible())
                        //If not, display and activate it in its previous location
                    pOurWnd->ShowWindow( SW_RESTORE );
                        //But hide all of its popup windows
                    pOurWnd->ShowOwnedPopups( FALSE );
```

IsZoomed   FUNCTION

Description   **IsZoomed** tests whether a **CWnd** is maximized.

Prototype
```
                    //Function Prototype
                    //BOOL IsZoomed( )const;
                    if( wndOurApp.IsZoomed( ) )
                        //If the window is zoomed, make it iconic.
                    wndOurApp.ShowWindow( SW_MINIMIZE );
```

KillTimer

Description **Kill Timer** deletes the timer created by **SetTimer** and discards any **WM_TIMER** messages remaining in the application's message queue for the timer specified by its parameter. The parameter to this function must be equal to the first parameter passed to **SetTimer** when the timer was created. *See **SetTimer** for a usage example.*

Prototype
```
//Function Prototype
//BOOL KillTimer( int iIDEvent );
```

MoveWindow

Description **MoveWindow** repositions and resizes windows. For top-level and popup windows, specify the new location in screen coordinates. For child windows, specify the new location in coordinates of the parent's client area.

Prototype
```
//Function Prototype
void MoveWindow( int x, int y, int nWidth, int nHeight,
    BOOL bRepaint = TRUE );
void MoveWindow( LPCRECT lpRect, BOOL bRepaint = TRUE );
RECT rParentClientArea;
    //Get a pointer to the parent CWnd
CWnd* pParent = wndChild.GetParent( );
    //Get the dimensions of the parent client area
pParent->GetClientRect( rParentClientArea );
    //Reposition the child window to cover
    //the parent's whole client area
wndChild.MoveWindow( rParentClientArea, TRUE );
```

OpenClipboard

Description **OpenClipboard** opens the Clipboard for read or write access by an application. An application can't add any data to the Clipboard without first calling the SDK function **EmptyClipboard**, however. *See **GetClipboardOwner** for a usage example.*

Prototype
```
//Function Prototype
// BOOL OpenClipboard( );
```

PostMessage FUNCTION

Description **PostMessage** posts a message to a window's message queue and returns immediately to the function from which it was called.

Prototype
```
//Function Prototype
//BOOL PostMessage(UINT message, WPARAM wParam = 0,
//LPARAM lParam = 0);
    //We want this window to close a file, but it is not necessary
    //for our application to pause and wait for that to happen....
pFrame->PostMessage(WM_COMMAND, ID_FILE_CLOSE);
```

PreCreateWindow FUNCTION

Description This function is called by the framework to do recordkeeping before a Windows window is created and attached to a **CWnd** object.

RedrawWindow FUNCTION

Description **RedrawWindow** can be used to redraw part of a window's client area without sending the window a **WM_PAINT** message. It relies on a set of region and flag parameters that have complex interactions and circumvent processing steps normally undertaken by the view's paint message handlers. It is seldom useful to application code.

Prototype
```
BOOL RedrawWindow( LPCRECT lpRectUpdate = NULL,
CRgn* prgnUpdate = NULL, UINT flags = RDW_INVALIDATE |
RDW_UPDATENOW | RDW_ERASE );GetWindowDC
```

ReleaseDC FUNCTION

Description **ReleaseDC** returns a device context that was acquired by a call to **GetDC** to the common device pool. It is very important that all device contexts explicitly acquired by an application be released because a pool of only five is used by all applications and Windows as well. In the course of normal paint message processing by an application's views, DCs are both acquired and released by the framework. Applications should not attempt to release DCs that are provided by the framework. *See **GetDC** for a usage example.*

Prototype
```
//Function Prototype
// int ReleaseDC( CDC* pDC );
```

RepositionBars   FUNCTION

Description   **RepositionBars** is called by the frame window member function **RecalcLayout** when the application adds or removes control bars. This messy and tedious business is managed entirely by the framework, so applications generally have no reason to use this function.

Prototype
```
//Function Prototype
void RepositionBars( UINT nIDFirst, UINT nIDLast, UINT nIDLeftOver,
UINT nFlag = CWnd::reposDefault, LPRECT lpRectParam = NULL,
LPCRECT
lpRectClient = NULL );
```

Valid values for nFlag are as follows:

CWnd::reposDefault	Performs the layout of the control bars. lpRectParam is not used and can be NULL.
CWnd::reposQuery	The layout of the control bars is not done; instead lpRectParam is initialized with the size of the client area, as if the layout had actually been done.
CWnd::reposExtra	Adds the values of lpRectParam to the client area of nIDLast and also performs the layout.

ScreenToClient   FUNCTION

See ClientToScreen.

ScrollWindow   FUNCTION

Description   **ScrollWindow** is useful in moving the image displayed in the client area in response to single-line scroll messages. **ScrollWindow** scrolls child windows right along with the rest of the client area unless they are specifically excluded by specifying a clipping rectangle for them. The application can identify a subset of the client area to scroll by specifying a scrolling rectangle. To prevent repainting anomalies, always call **UpdateWindow** before scrolling a window containing child windows that must be clipped.

Prototype
```
//Function Prototype
void ScrollWindow( int xAmount, int yAmount, LPCRECT lpRect =
    NULL, LPCRECT lpClipRect = NULL );
    //COurView is a class derived from CWnd
void COurView::ScrollXandY(POINT ptMove)
```

```
{
    //Use current scroll bar positions as the origin of the client area
    //for this scrolling operation
    int xOrig = SetScrollPos(SB_HORZ, ptMove.x);
    int yOrig = SetScrollPos(SB_VERT, ptMove.y);
        //Scroll the client area by the amount of ptMove.x and
        ptMove.y
    ScrollWindow(xOrig - ptMove.x, yOrig - ptMove.y);
}
```

ScrollWindowEx   FUNCTION

Description **ScrollWindowEx** is used for the same jobs as **ScrollWindow**, but
it allows an application to take control of its clipping region and
some aspects of repainting the newly invalidated area.
ScrollWindowEx can optionally report a region or rectangle that
has been invalidated by the scrolling operation and can erase the
invalid region. **ScrollWindow** and **ScrollWindowEx** are most
useful for situations in which the scrolling operation takes in the
entire client area and no clipping of child windows is necessary.

Prototype
```
//Function Prototype
int ScrollWindowEx( int dx, int dy, LPCRECT lpRectScroll, LPCRECT
lpRectClip, CRgn* prgnUpdate, LPRECT lpRectUpdate, UINT flags );
    //Assume that we have the same function shown in the
    //example for ScrollWindow. Scroll the client area by the
    //amount of ptMove.x and ptMove.y, and erase the
    //newly invalidated area....
ScrollWindow(xOrig - ptMove.x, yOrig - ptMove.y, NULL, NULL,
SW_ERASE);
```

Valid values for flags are as follows:

SW_ERASE	When specified with SW_INVALIDATE, erases the newly invalidated region by sending a WM_ERASEBKGND message to the window.
SW_INVALIDATE	Invalidates the region identified by prgnUpdate after scrolling.
SW_SCROLLCHILDREN	Scrolls all child windows that intersect the rectangle pointed to by lpRectScroll by the number of pixels specified in dx and dy.

SendDlgItemMessage   FUNCTION

Description   **SendDlgItemMessage** sends a Windows message to a dialog control and does not return until the message has been processed.

Prototype
```
//Function Prototype
//LRESULT SendDlgItemMessage(int nID, UINT message,
//             WPARAM = 0, LPARAM = 0);
    //Sending a user-defined message directly to the control
ID_MYLIST
MyDialog.SendDlgItemMessage(ID_MYLIST,
WM_USERMESSAGEBLINK, 0, 0);
```

SendMessage   FUNCTION

Description   **SendMessage** sends a message directly to this window and waits until message processing is finished before it returns.

Prototype
```
//Function Prototype
//LRESULT SendMessage( UINT message, WPARAM wParam = 0,
//             LPARAM lParam = 0 );
    //Tell the window referenced by pwnd to do initial update
    //processing, and don't return to the caller
    //until initialization is finished
pWnd->SendMessage(WM_INITIALUPDATE);
```

SendMessageToDescendants   FUNCTION

Description   This function sends a Windows message to all descendants of a **CWnd**. If the last parameter is set to FALSE, only the first level of descendants is messaged.

Prototype
```
//Function Prototype
//void SendMessageToDescendants(UINT message,WPARAM
//wParam,
//             LPARAM lParam, BOOL bDeep, BOOL
//bOnlyPerm=FALSE);
    //Tell all the child windoMessagews to do initial painting tasks
wndMainAppWindow.SendMessageToDescendants
    (WM_INITIALUPDATE, 0, 0, TRUE);
```

SetActiveWindow   FUNCTION

Description   **SetActiveWindow** unilaterally grabs the input focus. This is rarely justified because it overrides the user's keyboard and mouse control of where the input focus should be. *See **GetActiveWindow** for a usage example.*

SetCapture   FUNCTION

Description   **SetCapture** routes the mouse input stream to the **CWnd** for which it was called, returning a pointer to the previous owner of the input stream or NULL if the stream was not captured. *See **GetCapture** for a usage example.*

SetCaretPos   FUNCTION

Description   **SetCaretPos** sets a new location for the caret in client area coordinates. *See **ShowCaret** for a usage example.*

Prototype
```
//Function Prototype
//static CPoint PASCAL SetCaretPos( );
```

SetClipboardViewer   FUNCTION

Description   **SetClipboardViewer** makes the current **CWnd** a member of the Clipboard viewer chain. *See **GetClipboardViewer** for a usage example and more information on the way the chain works.*

Prototype
```
//Function Prototype
//HWND SetClipboardViewer( );
```

SetDlgItemInt   FUNCTION

Description   **SetDlgItemInt** sets the contents of an integer dialog item. It can optionally set a signed or unsigned value. *See **GetDlgItemInt** for a usage example.*

Prototype
```
//Function Prototype
void SetDlgItemInt( int nID, UINT nValue, BOOL bSigned = TRUE );
```

SetDlgItemText

Description   **SetDlgItemText** sets the contents of a text dialog item.

Prototype
```
//Function Prototype
void SetDlgItemText( int nID, LPCSTR lpszString );
    //Set the text in a dialog control derived from CWnd
dlgSendFile.SetDlgItemText(IDC_SENDFILE_DOCNAME, szFilename);
```

SetFocus

Description   **SetFocus** unilaterally grabs the input focus. This is rarely justified because it overrides the user's control of where the keyboard input focus should be. Focus changes are usually handled by the framework as window activation status changes. *See **GetFocus** for a usage example*.

Prototype
```
//Function Prototype
//CWnd* SetFocus( )
```

SetFont

Description   **SetFont** sets the font used to draw a window's text. This is mostly useful for **CWnd**-derived objects, such as listboxes or buttons. *See **GetFont** for a usage example.*

Prototype
```
//Function Prototype
//void SetFont( CFont* pFont, BOOL bRedraw=TRUE );
```

SetMenu

Description   **SetMenu** sets a new menu for a window and redraws the menu bar to reflect the change. It returns the success or failure of the attempt to change the menu.

Prototype
```
//Function Prototype
//BOOL SetMenu( CMenu* pMenu );
    //Create a menu object ....
CMenu menuNew;
    //Load a menu template from the resource file
    //and attach it to the menu object
menuNew.LoadMenu(ID_SECOND_MENU);
    //Set this as the window's new menu, highlight the first item,
```

```
//and redraw to reflect the change....
wndMain.SetMenu( menuNew );
wndMain.HiliteMenuItem( menuNew, IDM_FIRSTITEM, MF_HILITE );
wndMain.DrawMenuBar( );
```

SetParent   FUNCTION

Description **SetParent** makes a child window the descendant of the **CWnd** identified by its parameter. A temporary pointer to the previous parent is returned. If a NULL **CWnd*** is passed, the desktop window becomes the parent.

Prototype
```
//Function Prototype
//CWnd* SetParent( CWnd* pWndNewParent );
    //This sets the desktop window as the owner
    //of the CWnd identified by pOurChild
pOurChild->SetParent( NULL );
```

SetRedraw   FUNCTION

Description **SetRedraw** allows the application to suspend repainting temporarily as it does repetitive updates. For example, if it were adding or deleting several items from an **OWNERDRAW** listbox, it could set the redraw flag to false, make the changes, invalidate the entire area that needs redrawing, set redraw to true, and either force immediate update with **UpdateWindow** or wait for normal paint processing to take place. Owner drawing takes place in the listbox **DrawItem** message handler function of a derived object. Applications override this **CWnd** function.

Prototype
```
//Function Prototype
// void SetRedraw( BOOL bRedraw = TRUE );
```

SetScrollPos   FUNCTION

Description **SetScrollPos** sets the position of the scroll bar thumb. This function updates the position of the thumb for a frame window scroll bar as well as for a child window. *See **EnableScrollBar** for a usage example.*

Prototype
```
//Function Prototype
//int SetScrollPos(int nBar, int nPos, BOOL bRedraw)
```

SetScrollRange   FUNCTION

Description **SetScrollRange** sets the minimum and maximum values in the scrolling range. This function updates the scrolling range for a frame window scroll bar as well as for a child window. *See **EnableScrollBar** for a usage example*.

Prototype
```
//Function Prototype
//void SetScrollRange(int nBar, int nMinPos, int nMaxPos, BOOL
//bRedraw)
```

SetTimer   FUNCTION

Description **SetTimer** is used to establish a means by which the application can monitor elapsed time. This might be done so that an application can periodically yield some resource or to see whether a response or condition has been signaled by a device. The application can either supply the address of a callback function to process **WM_TIMER** messages or let the framework put timer messages in the message queue, where they are routed to the handler function of the **CWnd** or **CWnd**-derived class.

There is a limited pool of timers, so it is important to check the return value of **SetTimer** to make sure that it succeeded and to kill the timer by calling **KillTimer** when it is no longer needed.

Prototype
```
//Function Prototype
UINT SetTimer( UINT nIDEvent, UINT nElapse, void
(CALLBACK EXPORT* lpfnTimer)(HWND, UINT, UINT, DWORD) );
    //Set the timer to send messages every half-second to the
    //CWnd-derived handler function
wndMain.SetTimer( 1, 500, NULL);
    //In the override of the CWnd OnTimer Message handler,
    //flash the window title bar to alert the user
    //to some condition....
void OnTimer( iFlashWindow )
{
FlashWindow( TRUE );
}
    //Set the title bar to an active appearance and free the timer....
FlashWindow( FALSE );
wndMain.KillTimer( 1 );
```

SetWindowPos   FUNCTION

Description   **SetWindowPos** is used mainly to control a window's position in the z-order, but it can also modify a window's location and dimensions. A couple of rules apply to its use. Top-level and popup windows specify the new location in screen coordinates, and child windows specify the new location in coordinates of the parent's client area. When a parent window changes its z-order, all the windows it owns stay on top of it. An activating window must come to the top of the z-order. Special values are provided to identify the window behind which the **CWnd** calling this function will be placed. **wndTop** places a window at the top, **wndBottom** places a window at the bottom, **wndTopMost** permanently places a window at the top even when the window deactivates, and **wndNoTopMost** places a window behind all topmost windows.

Prototype
```
//Function Prototype
BOOL SetWindowPos( const CWnd* pWndInsertAfter, int x, int y,
    int cx, int cy, UINT nFlags );
RECT rParentClientArea;
RECT rTimerClientArea;
    //Get the parent CWnd of a child window
    //that displays elapsed time....
CWnd* pParent = wndTimerChild.GetParent( );
    //Get the dimensions of the parent and timer client areas
pParent->GetClientRect( rParentClientArea );
pParent->GetClientRect( rTimerClientArea );
    //Figure the dimensions of the entire timer window
wndTimerChild.GetWindowRect(LPRECT rTimerClientArea);
    //Force the timer window to remain on top of all other
    //windows in the lower left corner of the client area
wndTimerChild.SetWindowPos
    ( wndTopMost, rParentClientArea.bottom +
    (rTimerClientArea.bottom -rTimerClientArea.top),
    (rTimerClientArea.right -rTimerClientArea.left),
    (rTimerClientArea.bottom -rTimerClientArea.top),
    SWP_SHOWWINDOW );
```

SetWindowText   FUNCTION

Description   **SetWindowText** sets a new title on the window caption bar for frame windows or sets text in a control. This function is also used for setting control text (buttons, static, edit) as an alternative to **SetDlgItemText**.

Example
```
//Function Prototype
//void SetWindowText( LPCSTR lpszNewText );
    //We have a pointer to a CWnd-derived button control; we
    //find out whether the button's text will fit in the buffer we
    //have without truncation
if ( sizeof(szOldString) >= pButton->GetWindowTextLength( ) )
{
    //If so, we retrieve the old text
pButton->GetWindowText(szOldString, sizeof(szOldString));
    //Then we write a new string into the button....
pButton->SetWindowText("Panic Button");
}
```

ShowCaret   FUNCTION

Description   An application that has hidden the system caret by using
HideCaret to repaint the client area without having received a
WM_PAINT message must show it again after painting is complete
by calling **ShowCaret**. The caret is hidden and shown automatically in the course of message-driven painting, so it isn't necessary
to hide the caret in a paint message handler. Every call to
HideCaret must be balanced by a call to **ShowCaret**.

Prototype
```
//Function Prototype
//void ShowCaret( );
    //This example puts a character on the screen without calling
    //a paint handler to update the window....
    //Get the location of the new character
CPoint ptCaretLocation = GetCaretPosition( );
    //Hide the cursor before we paint
HideCaret( );
    //Get a DC and paint the character
CDC *pDC = GetDC( );
pDC->TextOut(ptCaretLocation.x, ptCaretLocation.y, szNewChar, 1 );
    //Update the caret position
SetCaretPosition( ptCaretLocation.x + CHAR_WIDTH,
    ptCaretLocation.y );
    //Cleanup: Show the caret after we are done,
    //and release the DC
ShowCaret( );
ReleaseDC( pDC );
```

ShowOwnedPopups   FUNCTION

Description   **ShowOwnedPopups** shows or hides all of a window's popup windows. *See **IsWindowVisible** for a usage example.*

Prototype
```
//Function Prototype
//void ShowOwnedPopups( BOOL bAllPopupsShown = TRUE );
```

ShowScrollBar   FUNCTION

Description   **ShowScrollBar** optionally shows or hides frame window and child window scroll bar controls. For frame windows, the scroll bar is identified by the constants **SB_BOTH**, **SB_VERT** or **SB_HORZ**. Scroll bar controls are identified by their resource ID.

Prototype
```
//Function Prototype
//void ShowScrollBar( UINT nBar, BOOL bShow = TRUE );
    //Assume that we have a pointer to the app's main window
    //and have figured the number of client area lines
    //it will take to show a document....
if ( iDocumentLines <= iClientAreaLines )
    //Hide the vertical scroll bar if the document fits
    //in a single window....
pFrameWindow->ShowScrollBar( SB_VERT, FALSE );
```

ShowWindow   FUNCTION

Description   **ShowWindow** is a versatile and powerful function that sets the visibility state of a window. For the application's main window, this function is called in the template code generated by AppWizard to create the application's initial appearance and behavior. To alter that, or to control the appearance and behavior of child windows, **ShowWindow** can be called with the following parameters:

ShowWindow Parameter	Meaning
SW_HIDE	Hide/deactivate the window.
SW_MINIMIZE	Make window iconic and activate top-level window in the system window manager list.
SW_RESTORE	Activate and display window with size and position it had at last activation.
SW_SHOW	Activate and display window using initial size and position.
SW_SHOWMAXIMIZED	Activate and maximize window.
SW_SHOWMINIMIZED	Activate window as icon.

ShowWindow Parameter	Meaning
SW_SHOWMINNOACTIVE	The window is inactive and iconic.
SW_SHOWNA	The window's activation state and appearance remain unchanged.
SW_SHOWNOACTIVATE	Display window with size and position it had at last activation, but don't change its activation state.
SW_SHOWNORMAL	Activate and display window using initial size and position.

Example

```
//Function Prototype
//BOOL ShowWindow( int nCmdShow );
    //We have a CWnd derived class named COurWnd; we
    //create the object....
COurWnd* pParentWnd = new COurWnd;
    //Then we create and attach a child window to the object....
pParentWnd->Create("EDIT", NULL, WS_CHILD, rectLocation,
    pParentWnd, nID);
    //Then we activate and show the child window
pParentWnd->ShowWindow(SW_SHOWNORMAL );
```

SubclassDlgItem   FUNCTION

Description   **SubclassDlgItem** replaces the default message processing for a control with that of the **CWnd** calling the function.

Prototype
```
//Function Prototype
//BOOL SubclassDlgItem(UINT nID, CWnd* pParent)
```

SubclassWindow   FUNCTION

Description   **SubclassWindow** allows the user to dynamically route the subclassed window's message stream through the message map of the **CWnd** that subclassed it. It does this by replacing the subclassed window's **WndProc** and **AfxWndProc** with its own. As an example of how it might be used, suppose that in a graphics program, the user can specify an irregular polygon that will be cut from the screen image. He or she does this by choosing a scissors tool from a tool palette and clicking the left mouse button to indicate where the vertices of the polygon are. If the user chooses a pencil icon from the tool palette, left-mouse-button-clicks establish the vertices of a drawn line. By subclassing the drawing window when the user chooses a tool from the tool palette, there can be

847

two entirely different sets of message-handler functions for the two activities, neither of which will have to do mode testing when processing left mouse button events.

The old **WndProc** address is stored at a location returned by **GetSuperWndProcAddr**, which means that you must override that function for every unique window class you want to subclass.

Prototype

```
//Function Prototype
//BOOL SubclassWindow(HWND hWnd)
```

UpdateData   FUNCTION

Description   **UpdateData** is a function called by the framework when dialog control data needs to be initialized or retrieved.

Prototype

```
BOOL UpdateData( BOOL bSaveAndValidate = TRUE );
```

UpdateDialogControls   FUNCTION

Description   **UpdateDialogControls** is a function called by the framework in the course of normal idle-time processing to repaint dialog controls as necessary.

Prototype

```
//Funtion Prototype
//void UpdateDialogControls( CCmdTarget* pTarget, BOOL
//bDisableIfNoHndler )
```

UpdateWindow   FUNCTION

Description   **UpdateWindow** forces immediate repainting of a window by sending a **WM_PAINT** message directly to the paint handler, bypassing the message queue. Before calling **UpdateWindow**, the application may want to ensure that the region it intends to update has been invalidated by calling **Invalidate**, **InvalidateRect** or **InvalidateRgn**. These functions flag portions of a window's client area for repainting on the next **WM_PAINT** message.

Prototype

```
//Function Prototype
//void UpdateWindow( );
    //First we get the client rectangle for this CWnd
RECT rClient;
wndOurApp.GetClientRect( rClient );
    //We flag the whole client area for repainting
wndOurApp.InvalidateRect(rClient);
```

```
//Then we force immediate repainting by calling
UpdateWindow
wndOurApp.UpdateWindow( );
```

ValidateRgn FUNCTION

Description   **ValidateRect** and **ValidateRgn** remove portions of a window's client area from the area designated for repainting on the next **WM_PAINT** message. They specify a rectangle or a region, respectively. Validation of the entire client area occurs automatically after the **BeginPaint** function is called, so it is not usually necessary for an application to explicitly validate repainted client areas.

WindowFromPoint FUNCTION

Description   **WindowFromPoint** returns a temporary pointer to the **CWnd** containing a point, unless its window is hidden, disabled or transparent. **ChildWindowFromPoint** tests child windows regardless of status.

Prototype
```
//Function Prototype
//static CWnd* WindowFromPoint( POINT point );
    //Get a pointer to the child window the cursor is over
CWnd* pChildHit = wndOurApp.WindowFromPoint(ptCursor);
```

Overridable Functions

CWnd is valuable mostly as a base class for objects that support windowing. Though many of its member functions are useful directly, applications interact most with the virtual functions it includes to handle messaging. The handlers are named according to a convention that prefaces the descriptive part of a Windows message name with the word "On" (for example, "OnKeyDown" handles the message **WM_KEYDOWN**). The entry in the Triggering Event column of the table is the condition that causes the handler to be invoked.

Function Name	Triggering Event
GetSuperWndProcAddress	Returns a pointer to the default WndProc for this class.
WindowProc	Dispatches messages according to the application's message map.
DefWindowProc	Calls default message processing for messages not handled by the application.

849

Function Name	Triggering Event
PostNcDestroy	Provided for application-derived classes that need to handle specialized cleanup tasks after a window is destroyed.
OnChildNotify	Exclusively intended to be overridden by applications to extend the way in which a child window responds to notification messages.
DoDataExchange	Exclusively intended to be overridden by applications to support DDX/DDV.

Initialization message handlers:

Function Name	Triggering Event
OnInitMenu	New menu is active.
OnInitMenuPopup	New popup menu is active.

System message handlers:

Function Name	Triggering Event
OnSysChar	Keystroke has been translated to system character.
OnSysCommand	User issued control menu command or pushed the Minimize or Maximize button.
OnSysDeadChar	Keystroke has been translated to system dead character.
OnSysKeyDown	Alt key pressed in tandem with another key.
OnSysKeyUp	Alt key pressed in tandem with another key, and the companion key is released.
OnCompacting	Low memory is prompting garbage collection and reallocation.
OnDevModeChange	User changed the device mode; all top-level windows are notified.
OnFontChange	Pool of font resources changed.
OnPalettelsChanging	An application is preparing to realize its logical palette.
OnPaletteChanged	Notifies windows that have realized logical palettes that the system palette has changed.
OnSysColorChange	A system color has changed; all top-level Windows are notified.
OnWindowPosChanging	The size, location or z-order of a window is about to change.
OnWindowPosChanged	The size, location or z-order of a window has changed.

Function Name	Triggering Event
OnDropFiles	The user dropped files over a window that has registered itself as a drop target.
OnSpoolerStatus	Print Manager has added or removed a job.
OnWinIniChange	WIN.INI has changed; all top-level windows are notified.
OnTimeChange	The system time changed; all top-level windows are notified.

Common message handlers:

Function Name	Triggering Event
OnCommand	User issued command.
OnActivate	CWnd is being activated or deactivated.
OnCancelMode	CWnd is canceling internal modes such as mouse capture.
OnChildActivate	Notify MDI child Windows that a CWnd is activating, deactivating, changing size or moving.
OnClose	Signal CWnd to close.
OnCreate	A step in window creation.
OnCtlColor	A child window control is about to be drawn.
OnDestroy	CWnd is being destroyed.
OnEnable	CWnd is being enabled or disabled.
OnEndSession	Session is ending.
OnEnterIdle	Main window is notified when a dialog box or menu is entering an idle state.
OnEraseBkgnd	Window background needs to be erased.
OnGetMinMaxInfo	Windows needs to know the maximum position or size of a window or the minimum or maximum tracking size.
OnIconEraseBkgnd	CWnd is iconic and the background has to be painted before the icon is drawn.
OnKillFocus	A CWnd is about to lose the input focus.
OnMDIActivate	MDI child window is activating or deactivating.
OnMenuChar	User presses a menu mnemonic that doesn't occur in the current menu.
OnMenuSelect	User selected a menu item.
OnMove	CWnd's position has changed.
OnPaint	Some portion of the window needs to be painted.
OnParentNotify	Child window was created or destroyed or received mouse click input.
OnQueryDragIcon	Iconic CWnd is about to be dragged by the user.
OnQueryEndSession	User is ending Windows session.
OnQueryNewPalette	Input focus is about to change; application may want to realize its logical palette.
OnQueryOpen	User is opening an iconic CWnd.

Function Name	Triggering Event
OnSetFocus	CWnd has gained the input focus.
OnShowWindow	CWnd is being hidden or shown.
OnSize	Window size change.

Control message handlers:

Function Name	Triggering Event
OnCharToItem	Child listbox with LBS_WANTKEYBOARDINPUT style got a WM_CHAR message.
OnCompareItem	Find the rank of a new item in a sorted list for child owner-draw list or combo boxes.
OnDeleteItem	Child owner-draw list or combo box is being destroyed or list item is being removed.
OnDrawItem	Redraw a portion of an owner-draw control.
OnGetDlgCode	Lets a control process Tab and arrow key input.
OnMeasureItem	Used by CWnd to specify dimensions of an owner-draw control to Windows.
OnVKeyToItem	A listbox owned by this CWnd received a WM_KEYDOWN message.

Input message handlers:

Function Name	Triggering Event
OnChar	Keystroke was translated to a non-system character.
OnDeadChar	Keystroke was translated to a non-system dead character (accent marks).
OnHScroll	User clicked the horizontal scroll bar.
OnKeyDown	Non-system key is pressed.
OnKeyUp	Non-system key was released.
OnLButtonDblClick	User double-clicked left mouse button.
OnLButtonDown	User pressed left mouse button.
OnLButtonUp	User released left mouse button.
OnMButtonDblClick	User double-clicked middle mouse button.
OnMButtonDown	User pressed middle mouse button.
OnMButtonUp	User released middle mouse button.
OnRButtonDblClick	User double-clicked right mouse button.
OnRButtonDown	User pressed right mouse button.
OnRButtonUp	User released right mouse button.
OnSetCursor	Mouse input is not being captured, and user moves cursor with the mouse.
OnTimer	Called periodically according to value established by SetTimer.
OnVScroll	User clicked the vertical scroll bar.

Non-client area message handlers:

Function Name	Triggering Event
OnNcActivate	Non-client area needs to be updated to reflect activation status.
OnNcCalcSize	Size and position of client area of a CWnd are needed.
OnNcCreate	Non-client areas of the window are being created.
OnNcDestroy	Non-client areas of the window are being destroyed.
OnNcHitTest	Called for every mouse move in a window that is under the cursor or has captured mouse input.
OnNcLButtonDblClick	User double-clicked left mouse button over non-client area of CWnd.
OnNcLButtonDown	User pressed left mouse button over non-client area of CWnd.
OnNcLButtonUp	User released left mouse button over non-client area of CWnd.
OnNcMButtonDblClick	User double-clicked middle mouse button over non-client area of CWnd.
OnNcMButtonDown	User pressed middle mouse button over non-client area of CWnd.
OnNcMButtonUp	User released middle mouse button over non-client area of CWnd.
OnNcRButtonDblClick	User double-clicked right mouse button over non-client area of CWnd.
OnNcRButtonDown	User pressed right mouse button over non-client area of CWnd.
OnNcRButtonUp	User released right mouse button over non-client area of CWnd.
OnNcMouseMove	Cursor moved in a non-client area of the CWnd.
OnNcPaint	Non-client area needs painting.

Clipboard message handlers:

Function Name	Triggering Event
OnAskCbFormatName	Applications override this function to get names of formats in which a Clipboard owner will render Clipboard data for them.
OnChangeCbChain	Specified window is being removed from the Clipboard viewer chain.
OnDestroyClipboard	The Windows SDK function EmptyClipboard is going to be called.
OnDrawClipboard	Contents of the Clipboard are about to change.

Function Name	Triggering Event
OnHScrollClipboard	Tell the Clipboard owner to scroll the Clipboard horizontally, repaint as necessary, and update scroll bar values.
OnPaintClipboard	Trigger repainting of Clipboard viewer client area.
OnRenderAllFormats	Application supplying data to Clipboard is closing and should render all formats it made available to Clipboard viewers.
OnRenderFormat	Clipboard owner should render a format for which it specified delayed rendering.
OnSizeClipboard	The client area of the Clipboard viewer changed.
OnVScrollClipboard	Tell the Clipboard owner to scroll the Clipboard vertically, repaint as necessary, and update scroll bar values.

CWordArray

CLASS

See **CObArray**.

INDEX to Sections I–III

Colophon

This book was created on a variety of Macintoshes, including a Quadra 650, a Quadra 700 and two Power Macs. Pages were laid out in Aldus PageMaker 5.0. The body text is set in DTC Garamond. Subheads, sidebars and segments of computer code are set in varying weights of DTC Kabel. Chapter titles are set in DTC Bernhard Fashion. Pages were imaged directly to film using a Linotronic 330.

VENTANA'S VISUAL GUIDE SERIES

The Visual Guide to Visual Basic for Windows, Third Edition
$34.95
1400 pages, illustrated
ISBN: 1-56604-192-9

This best-selling guide to the most popular Windows programming language has become the classic Visual Basic reference. Organized as a visual encyclopedia, this book clearly and thoroughly explains more than 300 commands, techniques and tools available in Visual Basic. Helps readers create applications that look as professional and perform as efficiently as any commercial software.

The Visual Guide to Visual Basic for Applications
$27.95
408 pages, illustrated
ISBN: 1-56604-147-3

This book teaches nonprogrammers how to customize Microsoft Word, Project, Access and Excel using Visual Basic for Applications. The step-by-step, illustrated examples are included in both in the book and on the companion disk.

The Visual Guide to Microsoft Access
$29.95
664 pages, illustrated
ISBN: 1-56604-070-1

The Visual Guide to Microsoft Access makes traditional text-heavy tech talk obsolete with a presentation as visually based as Windows itself. Illustrations on virtually every page highlight this handbook designed for beginning users through intermediate database developers. Learn how pictures, icons, buttons, graphics and more have transformed complex database development into a matter of simple drag-and-drop operations. Includes a companion disk crammed with file examples.

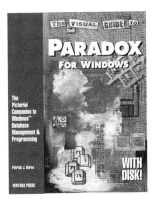

The Visual Guide to Paradox for Windows

$29.95
682 pages, illustrated
ISBN: 1-56604-150-3
Whether you're a DOS veteran or a newcomer to Paradox, this Visual Guide will help you with your Windows database management and programming. Covers all the new graphical capabilities of Windows as well as the latest features of Paradox—including the graphic Query Editor; BOCA (Borland Object Component Architecture); and ObjectPAL, Paradox's new object-oriented program language.

The Visual Guide to Visual C++

$29.95
888 pages, illustrated
ISBN: 1-56604-079-5
This graphically oriented encyclopedia is a unique visual reference guide to Microsoft's next-generation programming language. Written for new and experienced C++ programmers alike, it features a complete overview of tools and features. Ideal for day-to-day reference, this Visual Guide gives users the know-how to create efficient Windows programs with this revolutionary programming language.

The Visual Guide to dBASE for Windows

$29.95
576 pages, illustrated
ISBN: 1-56604-178-3
Using this Visual Guide, database users and programmers who want to become more productive can now get the most out of dBASE for Windows™, the powerful object-oriented development tool. With savvy advice on designing databases, The Visual Guide to dBASE for Windows takes you through a hands-on approach to learning every aspect of dBASE for Windows without writing a line of code—the perfect visually oriented tutorial for beginners or intermediate users!

RIDE THE WINDOWS™ WAVE

WITH BOOKS FROM VENTANA PRESS

Voodoo Windows

$19.95
312 pages, illustrated
ISBN:1-56604-005-1
Work Windows wizardry with productivity-enhancing tips.
Organized by subject, this book offers a wealth of Windows
techniques, shortcuts and never-before-published tricks that will
streamline your daily tasks and save time. A great reference for
beginners and experienced users alike.

The Official America Online for Windows
Membership Kit & Tour Guide, Second Edition

$27.95
460 pages, illustrated
ISBN: 1-56604-128-7
This book takes Windows users on a lively romp through the
friendly AOL cyberscape. Best-selling author Tom Lichty, a.k.a.
MajorTom, shows you how to make friends, find your way
around, and save time and money online. Complete with software
to get you started. BONUS: 20 free hours of online time for new
members.

The Windows Shareware 500

$39.95
458 pages, illustrated
ISBN: 1-56604-045-0
The best Windows shareware available, from thousands of
contenders. Includes utilities, sounds, fonts, icons, games, clip art,
multimedia and more. BONUS: Four companion disks featuring top-
rated programs, including an America Online membership disk,
along with 10 hours free online time!

The Windows Internet Tour Guide

$24.95
384 pages, illustrated
ISBN: 1-56604-081-7
Windows users can now navigate the Internet the easy way: by pointing and clicking, dragging and dropping. In easy-to-read, entertaining prose, Internet expert Michael Fraase leads you through installing and using the software enclosed in the book to send and receive e-mail, transfer files, search the Internet's vast resources and more!

SmartSuite Desktop Companion

$24.95
752 pages, illustrated
ISBN: 1-56604-184-8
The essential reference and guidebook to the most fully integrated Windows software suite. Easy-to-read sections offer dozens of tips, techniques and shortcuts to help users of all levels manage business data individually or in workgroup collaboration, including the latest versions of Lotus 1-2-3, Ami Pro, Approach, Freelance Graphics, Organizer, and Windows itself. The companion disk contains tutorials and exercises on basic commands and features of the programs.

Looking Good in Print, Third Edition

$24.95
462 pages, illustrated
ISBN: 1-56604-047-7
For use with any software or hardware, this desktop design bible has become the standard among novice and experienced desktop publishers alike. With more than 300,000 copies in print, *Looking Good in Print* is even better, with new sections on photography and scanning.

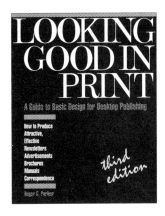

WEB
WALKING
WITH MOSAIC

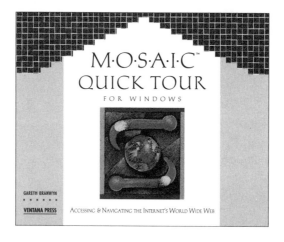

Mosaic. The Internet's **KILLER APP**. Able to leap global spaces
in a burst of electrons. Able to tie together text, graphics, sound files
and video across the **WORLD WIDE WEB**. Able to
BROWSE HYPERTEXT with the click of a mouse.

The **MOSAIC QUICK TOUR**, available for both
Mac and Windows, is the perfect guide for this revolutionary application.
Learn what the World Wide Web is all about. Learn how to use
Mosaic to read newsgroups. To transfer files. To conduct Gopher searches.
And, of course, to browse the exponentially expanding Web.
Not to mention author **GARETH BRANWYN**'s expansive tour of cool Web pages.

The price for all this valuable information? $12.00 suggested retail. Order today.

800/743-5369

See your local bookstore or software dealer for these and other bestsellers!

TO ORDER ANY VENTANA PRESS TITLE, COMPLETE THIS ORDER FORM AND MAIL IT TO US WITH PAYMENT FOR QUICK SHIPMENT.

	Quantity		Price		Total
The Visual Guide to Visual Basic for Windows, 3rd Edition	_____	x	$34.95	=	$ _____
The Visual Guide to Visual Basic for Applications	_____	x	$27.95	=	$ _____
The Visual Guide to Microsoft Access	_____	x	$29.95	=	$ _____
The Visual Guide to Paradox for Windows	_____	x	$29.95	=	$ _____
Visual Guide to Visual C++	_____	x	$29.95	=	$ _____
The Visual Guide to dBASE for Windows	_____	x	$29.95	=	$ _____
Voodoo Windows	_____	x	$19.95	=	$ _____
The Official America Online for Windows Membership Kit & Tour Guide, 2nd Edition	_____	x	$27.95	=	$ _____
The Windows Shareware 500	_____	x	$39.95	=	$ _____
The Windows Internet Tour Guide	_____	x	$24.95	=	$ _____
SmartSuite Desktop Companion	_____	x	$24.95	=	$ _____
Looking Good in Print, 3rd Edition	_____	x	$24.95	=	$ _____
Mosaic Quick Tour for Windows	_____	x	$12.00	=	$ _____
			Subtotal	=	$ _____

SHIPPING:
For all standard orders, please <u>add</u> $4.50/first book, $1.35/each additional.   = $ _____
For "two-day air," <u>add</u> $8.25/first book, $2.25/each additional.   = $ _____
For orders to Canada, <u>add</u> $6.50/book.   = $ _____
For orders sent C.O.D., <u>add</u> $4.50 to your shipping rate.   = $ _____
North Carolina residents must <u>add</u> 6% sales tax.   = $ _____
International orders require additional shipping charges.   **TOTAL** = $ _____

Name _____   Company _____

Address (No PO Box) _____

City_____   State_____ Zip _____

Daytime Telephone _____

____ Payment enclosed ____VISA ____ MC Acc't # _____   Exp. Date_____

Signature _____

Mail to: Ventana Press, PO Box 2468, Chapel Hill, NC 27515

CAN'T WAIT? CALL OR FAX TOLL-FREE
☎ 800/743-5369 FAX 800/877-7955 (U.S. only)

Check your local bookstores or software retailers for these and other best-selling Ventana titles!